Analyzing American Politics

A New Perspective

Wadsworth Series in Politics

General Editor

Bernard C. Hennessy

The Pennsylvania State University

Published

American Political Interest Groups: Readings in Theory and Research	*Betty H. Zisk* *Boston University*
The Irony of Democracy: An Uncommon Introduction to American Politics	*Thomas R. Dye and* *L. Harmon Zeigler* *The Florida State University,* *University of Oregon*
The Congressional System: Notes and Readings	*Leroy N. Rieselbach* *Indiana University*
Techniques of Political Analysis: An Introduction	*Lyman Tower Sargent and* *Thomas A. Zant* *University of Missouri at St. Louis*
Public Opinion, Second Edition	*Bernard C. Hennessy* *The Pennsylvania State University*
An Introduction to the Study of Public Policy	*Charles O. Jones* *University of Pittsburgh*
A Logic of Public Policy: Aspects of Political Economy	*L. L. Wade and Robert Curry* *University of California, Davis,* *Sacramento State College*
Political Life and Social Change: An Introduction to Political Science	*Charles Andrain* *San Diego State College*
The People, Maybe: Seeking Democracy in America	*Karl Lamb* *University of California, Santa Cruz*
Analyzing American Politics: A New Perspective	*Walter A. Rosenbaum, John W.* *Spanier, and William C. Burris* *University of Florida, University* *of Florida, Guilford College*

Forthcoming

The Black Politician: His Search for Power	*Mervyn M. Dymally, Senator,* *California State Legislature*

Analyzing American Politics

A New Perspective

William A. Rosenbaum
University of Florida

John W. Spanier
University of Florida

William Burris
Guilford College

Wadsworth Publishing Company, Inc.
Belmont, California

Photographs:

p. 2   — © 1969 Howard Harrison
p. 4   — © 1969 Howard Harrison
p. 21   — © 1968 Howard Harrison
p. 24   — © 1968 Howard Harrison
p. 64   — Elliott Erwitt, © 1964 Magnum Photos
p. 108 — Eve Arnold, Magnum Photos
p. 160 — © 1968 Howard Harrison
p. 192 — © 1969 Howard Harrison
p. 252 — © 1968 Howard Harrison
p. 308 — Dennis Brack, Black Star
p. 338 — Jon Lewis, The Photophile
p. 384 — F. W. Owen, Black Star
p. 444 — Paul Schutzer, LIFE Magazine © Time Inc.
p. 492 — © 1971 Howard Harrison
p. 494 — Bob Henriques, © 1962 Magnum Photos
p. 510 — © 1969 Howard Harrison
p. 548 — © 1970 Howard Harrison

L. C. Cat. Card No.: 74–146537

Printed in the United States of America

1 2 3 4 5 6 7 8 9 10—74 73 72 71

Preface

This is meant to be an unusual textbook—one that provides some information and perspectives on American government that are seldom, and often never, emphasized at the introductory level. While we have included some essential topics that will be found in almost all introductory texts, we have also included some subjects that are uncommon, and hopefully innovative, in introductory texts. In some respects, also, the general design and emphasis of the book is different from most books in this field.

Our primary goal was to produce a relatively short book that emphasizes ideas and concepts, elaborates on them in modest detail, and leaves the teacher free to develop the topics as he thinks best. We aimed at creating a core text that could easily be supplemented by additional material. We particularly wished to avoid creating a seed catalogue of American government—a book that dwelt upon most important aspects of American government with relentless detail that fatigues the reader. So, we have not focused upon the institutional details of American government at great length but have emphasized what seem to be the significance of the details; this is what readers remember, anyway.

Substantively, this book is devoted almost exclusively to the American national government, largely omitting state and local government. This omission is partly for brevity's sake, partly because the book would seem more useful as a core text without a discussion of state and local government; in any case, the book can be easily supplemented by state and local governmental studies of the instructor's choosing. We have particularly stressed those perspectives and ideas on the "growing edge" of the discipline. Often, it seems that these ideas are extraordinarily slow in reaching the introductory government level, even after they have become a major concern in other government courses. Sometimes, also, our emphasis is upon topics (new or old) which have become currently important to students as well as to political scientists. We have given particular attention to these topics:

1. We put considerable emphasis upon the *concepts of political analysis:* the political system, the government, legitimacy, political socialization, political culture, and many other ideas. Our objective is to provide the reader with an analytical political vocabulary as well as factual information about his political system.

2. We have considered some *comparative aspects* of American government. We introduce the student to some concepts in political comparison that will help him to appreciate which features of his political system are unique and which ones are not.

3. We emphasize the *impact of international politics* on the domestic political system. We want the reader to appreciate the pervasive influence of the international milieu upon his own political life, even when the influence is subtle.

4. Instead of a scattered discussion throughout the book, an entire chapter is devoted to the *politics of black Americans.*

5. We have given some attention to the problems of *national political unification in the United States.* At a time when problems of dissent, political legitimacy, and national unity have become important concerns in the United States, we think it appropriate to explore the conditions under which national government, in the United States and elsewhere, is possible.

6. We have emphasized some contemporary *critiques of American politics,* particularly from the new left and blacks. Many readers will already be aware of such dissent; we think this will add additional stimulus to class discussions and student thinking about our political system.

Despite our interest in these topics, we have tried not to stray from other customary, fundamental aspects of American government that must belong in any responsible discussion of the national government; we hope this book will balance traditional concerns and newer, stimulating approaches to the subject. We believe we have created a different, interesting, and relevant text for today's student.

This book has numerous collaborators; without their help, it would have been impossible to write. Bernard C. Hennessy, Pennsylvania State University, and Roger H. Davidson, University of California, Santa Barbara, read, reread and read again the entire manuscript. Their contribution to the book is enormous and merits special acknowledgment. Chapters or entire sections were reviewed by: Charles F. Cnudde, University of Wisconsin; Kenneth M. Dolbeare, University of Wisconsin; Allan Kornberg, Duke University; Richard H. Kraemer, University of Texas; Robert L. Lineberry, University of Texas; Edgar Litt, University of Connecticut; William C. Mitchell, University of Oregon; Frank J. Sorauf, University of Minnesota; and Raymond Wolfinger, Stanford University. Individually and collectively they made improvements too numerous to mention.

Our graduate assistants, Jan Taylor, Margaret Aiesi, and Joan Warren cheerfully went on mysterious missions in search of apparently exotic information at our request. Special thanks goes to our editor, Bob Gormley, whose confidence and encouragement provided constant support during both difficult and good days. In the end—alas!—the errors are our own. Some of the best features in the book are the result of our collaborators' suggestions.

Our wives know their contribution. They endured our lamentations, scuttled children from our desks, explained to others why their husbands were subject to such peculiar moods, bore other indignities while we completed the book. Even the Post Office deserves a curious tribute. Having lost one of our chapters during the hectic days when we were rushing the edited manuscript to completion, they miraculously found it again—a month late, but still in time to get the book under the deadline. The government giveth and taketh away, but this time it gave when it counted.

Contents

13 *Crises of Political Unification in the United States* *511*

14 *The Meaning of the Seventies* *549*

Analyzing American Politics

A New Perspective

Part One

1

Making Sense of Politics

"Mmmmmmmmm . . ." We hear a mother humming, then she begins to speak. "He's so adorable . . . I wonder what he'll be like when he's older. . . . What's going to happen to him. . . . I hope he won't be afraid the way we are. . . . There's so much violence now. . . . I wouldn't be so scared if I felt they understood what it's all about. . . . And they cared." While the mother continues to hum her lullaby in the background a bold, confident announcer's voice declares: "Hubert Humphrey has said that every man has the right to a decent and safe neighborhood. And on this there can be no compromise.

But for every jail that Mr. Nixon would build, Mr. Humphrey would also build a house.

For every policeman that Mr. Wallace would hire, Mr. Humphrey would also have a good teacher.

"Ahh." The baby gives one last contented sigh.[1]

---

[1] Thomas J. Fleming, "Selling the Product Named Humphrey," *The New York Times Magazine* (November 13, 1968), pp. 45–47. © 1968 by The New York Times Company. Reprinted by permission. For the selling of Richard Nixon, see Joe McGinnis, *The Selling of the President* (New York: Trident, 1969).

For Americans, there is no escape from politics. It converges upon us from different directions, speaking in many voices, casting many images, and shaping the course of our lives; the brooding omnipresence of politics is with us whether we know it or like it. During election years, politics comes uninvited into the living room, smoothly packaged by Madison Avenue; the topic is presidential elections and the commodity sold in 1968 was Hubert Humphrey, but in 1972 and 1976 other mothers will probably croon their babies to sleep with yet another candidate's name on their lips.

Politics is also muted protest uttered on the editorial page where an agitated citizen expresses his views on a great issue:

> Dear Editor: It seems inconceivable that we are engaged in a war of "controlled restraint" [in Vietnam] while at the same time being engaged at a so-called [Paris] peace table in conciliatory talks of "uncontrolled concessions." America sits at the table in the role of beggar while an arrogant assemblage of little dictators make pompous demands . . . it is sickening.

American politics is the slick-sell campaign and outraged protest from a military hard-liner, but sometimes it strikes an urgent humanitarianism that transcends national interests:

> The crisis of environment will certainly be one of the great issues of the seventies. . . . Divisions between reactionaries and radicals, conservatives and liberals, have become blurred in the struggle to save the air, water, and fertile earth necessary for human survival. Activist students participated in a conference convened by Governor Ronald Reagan of California and heard Mr. Reagan admit that California had been severely damaged . . .[2]

And some young Americans will also play their role in American politics in their own dramatic way:

> It finally happened to Harvard, too. . . . A small band of student rebels seized an administration building to protest university policies and to deliberately provoke a crisis. Police were then summoned to oust the intruders: moderate students, angered at both the fact of the "bust" and what they felt was police brutality, were radicalized into organizing a strike.[3]

American politics is not always this exciting; much that matters in American political life occurs quietly, almost unnoticed—something relegated to the

---

[2] Frank K. Kelly, "The Possibilities of Transformation," *Saturday Review* (March 7, 1970), p. 19.

[3] "Harvard and Beyond: The University under Seige," *Time* (April 18, 1969), p. 47.

second page of the morning paper: a presidential meeting with a foreign ambassador, budget reforms by the governor, or increased tax millage for local schools. Since nothing ages more quickly than yesterday's news, presidential elections, Vietnam, and the Harvard strike will yield to fresher issues. Still, irrespective of the particular issues or who becomes involved in them, the stuff of American politics matters urgently and immediately to us; even if we ignore it or are unaware of it, it will affect us. For example, many students reading this book are attending college on government loans and fellowships. Classroom buildings —and dormitories as well—may have been built with federal funds. At state-supported institutions, public taxes underwrite expenses; even private schools usually derive a large part of their income from the government.

Politics can touch us very personally. Every male college student carries a draft registration card, a constant reminder that his future, perhaps his life, hangs on decisions made in Washington, Moscow, Peking, Hanoi, or wherever peace and war are determined. When the student leaves college, his disposable income will depend upon how much of a tax bite local, state, and national governments will take from his salary. Yet social security and Medicare may relieve his young family from much of the financial burdens of supporting aging parents and paying medical costs. One can cite such examples endlessly; they all prove that none of us is free from the effects of politics. Even if we renounce the political world, to where will we escape? There are no political hermits in twentieth-century America.

Beyond the little world of private interests, politics shapes the present and future of all men. Civilization could be engulfed in the flames of a thermonuclear war if Moscow or Washington so decided; the leaders of the great nuclear powers command destructive forces men of the Middle Ages did not even credit to devils. In the United States, we face an era of social revolutions—some fully revealed, others seemingly emergent—which may challenge sharply and profoundly the capacity of traditional governmental institutions to accommodate them.

The current of social change sometimes threatens to become a riptide. After two centuries of forced inferiority, increasing numbers of black Americans are assailing all the political, social, and economic restraints that have denied them a dignified and honorable place in American life. The federal government, especially, has undertaken major programs (against enormous odds and divisive forces from within and without) to make legal and social equality a reality for American blacks; a whole new political vocabulary has been generated by the struggle—"bussing," "backlash," "the Wallace movement," "militancy," and "Black Power." A relatively small but impassioned group of young people, mostly the sons and daughters of the American middle and upper classes, has turned in anger and estrangement on many traditional American political institutions. They perceive a deep rift between the professed ideas and the actual practices of American politics. They allege that despite our official commitment to the right of national self-determination, we have militarily intervened in the civil affairs of other countries and behaved like a traditional imperialist power. They see racial discrimination and widespread poverty in the midst of great wealth even though the American system proclaims its dedication to the equality and freedom of all men. Social justice, they suggest, should not be a meaningless slogan. Because of the gap between idealism and reality, promise and performance, some young people find the system hypocritical and unworthy of their respect. They seek, therefore, to restructure it radically.

To the majority of young people committed to major reforms to improve the quality of American life, the way we are using our air, water, and soil has become a major issue. Young people, together with many other Americans, are awakening public consciousness and governmental leadership to the wholesale pollution and destruction of our physical environment that threatens to become irreversible unless quickly abated. The ferment of change dominates our era. Like most people only half aware of their place in history, we are living at a time when the political influence, military power, and economic power of the United States encircles the globe; the United States, itself in the midst of vast domestic changes, surpasses the Roman Empire at its zenith in its ability to affect the world for good or for ill. What happens in the United States, thus, has repercussions throughout the world. History may not be all politics, but politics shapes history.

No matter how directly politics influences us, a great many Americans, including the intelligent and well educated, shrink from serious political study and discussion. This is not simply because politics is emotional and contentious. Most people find politics confusing. A recent poll suggests that seven in ten Americans believe politics is too bewildering to understand much of the time.[4] It therefore seems appropriate to begin with a few comments about approaching politics intelligently. How can one make sense of politics, or at least *more* sense of it than most people do? We shall answer this question by suggesting, first, some common sources of confusion in studying political life. Then we will suggest how this book attempts to deal with these matters. In the process, we will introduce the reader to the plan of the book and illustrate how key ideas have governed the angle at which we approach this most important of subjects. Thus, this brief chapter is a prologue which seeks to give the reader a blueprint for what follows.

Obstacles to Political Analysis

Among the ways to learn intelligently about political life, some are better than others, and some are worse; some ways encourage clarity, while others can lead to avoidable confusion. Unfortunately, no method is errorless; compared to

---

[4] John P. Robinson, Jerrold G. Rusk, and Kendra B. Head (eds.), *Measures of Political Attitudes* (Ann Arbor, Mich.: Institute for Social Research, 1969), pp. 635, 637.

the ideal, clearminded, impartial observer, even the expert may often seem shortsighted or prejudiced. But there are ways to minimize errors if they are recognized.

First, politics abounds with *loaded words*. Almost all political terms are fraught with emotional overtones that trigger strongly irrational feelings and shape attitudes before subjects are even discussed; it is difficult to look at politics reasonably when the words affect the emotions rather than the intellect. Earlier we saw an excellent example of a political discussion quickly reduced to bristling argument by loaded words: a letter writer had translated the delicate negotiations on the Vietnamese War to a confrontation between "beggars" (the United States) and "an arrogant assemblage of little dictators" (representatives of North Vietnam). One can change the whole complexion of a discussion by introducing a governmental official as a "federal executive" instead of a "bureaucrat"; one feels quite differently toward the congressman who is called a "statesman" instead of a "politician." At its very minimum, intelligent political study demands constant awareness of the difference between the meaning and the feeling of a word; we shall often point out this difference as we proceed to specific matters.

Second, politics involves *ambiguous words*. Political terms are seldom fixed in common conversation; their meaning varies according to the prejudice of the speaker. Politicians themselves are among the worst offenders in using words to suit their fancy. It is not surprising that Americans find the political vocabulary sprinkled with insubstantial, cotton-candy phrases that sound clearer than they are meant to be. The English writer George Orwell complained that the political vocabulary is full of "question-begging and sheer cloudy vagueness"; he offered the following example of how to abuse the word "democracy":

> It is almost universally felt that when we call a country democratic we are praising it; consequently, the defenders of every regime claim that it is a democracy, and fear that they might have to stop using the word if it were tied to any one meaning.[5]

This confusion of meaning appears constantly in contemporary political oratory. When the Northern liberal who espouses school integration, and the Southern conservative who opposes it, both cite the Constitution and the "rights of the people" to justify their conflicting viewpoints, the political vocabulary has become intolerably elastic. A reasonable approach to politics means fixing definitions and using the same words in the same sense thoroughly a discussion. The reader will find that we have attempted to define key concepts at the outset of chapters—not to provide the universally accepted meaning, but only to suggest one meaning which will be used consistently in that chapter.

---

[5] George Orwell, "Politics and the English Language," in *A Collection of Essays* (Garden City, N.Y.: Doubleday & Co., 1954), p. 169.

Third, *selective perception* distorts our picture of political life. A student-police riot is televised: some people see dirty no-good hippies who don't know how good they have it; others see earnest students against whom the establishment is overreacting. Viewers select what they perceive on the basis of what threatens them or on what *a priori* sympathies they have. Everyone, expert and amateur alike, sees the political world incompletely. Limited vision is serious when it is unrecognized—that is, when one does not know whether one's information may be incomplete. It might be tempting, for example, to leap from a reading of a Hubert Humphrey campaign spot to the glib conclusion that presidential campaigns (or perhaps Democratic campaigns) appeal to the simple-minded. But if we had also heard Mr. Humphrey on *Meet the Press,* our judgment might be more charitable; we might have found him thoughtful and sophisticated in approaching his audience. Selective perceptions occur not only from a lack of information but from the very human tendency to see what we want to in any political situation.[6] Voting studies suggest that a passionate Republican or Democrat is strongly disposed to like his party's presidential candidate, whoever he may be.[7] Students are usually keenly aware of selective perception. In writing exams or term papers, they may be subtly guided in their attitudes by their knowledge of the professor's opinions.

Throughout the following chapters we have treated selective perception in two ways. First, we have outlined at the beginning of each major section what particular matters we have chosen to emphasize and thereby made explicit our particular view of American politics. Second, we will suggest from time to time—perhaps to the disappointment of those seeking unqualified truths—where information is inadequate and uncertain. We wish the reader to know when he had better reserve his judgment, as well as when he can seize conclusions bravely.

Finally, making sense of politics means overcoming *fragmented information.* Political information bombards us daily in no particular order; information about the president's press conference, the latest platitude delivered by a county commissioner, a new integration crisis somewhere—it comes in all forms. We can stockpile information endlessly but it becomes incoherent, like the "ditty bag

---

[6] Prejudice and preconception are difficult to disentangle from all scientific inquiry. For brief but thoughtful discussions of the role of values and prejudice in scientific inquiry, see: J. Bronowski, *The Common Sense of Science* (New York: Vintage Books), Chapters I, II; W. I. B. Beveridge, *The Art of Scientific Investigation* (New York: Vintage Books, 1959), Chapter IX; and Abraham Kaplan, *The Conduct of Inquiry* (San Francisco: Chandler Publishing Co., 1964), Chapter X. For commentary on the role of prejudice and preconception in political science research, see especially: David Easton, *The Political System* (New York: Alfred A. Knopf, 1963), Chapters I, II, VIII; Eugene J. Meehan, *Contemporary Political Thought* (Homewood, Ill.: Dorsey Press, 1967), Chapter I; and Frank J. Sorauf, *Political Science: An Informal Overview* (Columbus: Charles E. Merrill Books, 1965) especially pp. 60–74.

[7] On the impact of party identification on perceptions of candidates, see Angus Campbell et al., *The American Voter* (New York: John Wiley, 1960), Chapter 6.

of an idiot, filled with pebbles, straws, feathers, and other random hoardings."[8] Politics makes sense only when information is *organized*. Organized information is facts placed in some order, facts interpreted. Psychologists know that people can memorize numbers with greater ease when the numbers have a relationship than when they are random. Political understanding also requires grouping the facts in some pattern.

To summarize: any intelligent study of politics must begin with some attention to how information is gathered.[9] The obvious sources of misunderstanding just outlined all involve bad techniques for collecting information. Most students accept as an article of faith that writers of a political science textbook follow the proper techniques and that therefore what is written can be treated as gospel. This, alas, is not always so. Often a reader does not know how political information has been obtained; nor does he know how to discriminate between a good technique and a bad technique, or judge whether one is more reliable than another. Having suggested where problems in political interpretation arise, let us now turn to some ways to minimize these problems, especially as they occur in this book.

The Essential Steps of Political Analysis

If one wishes to remove impediments to clear political thinking, one had better respect the ancient adage that "In the kingdom of the blind, the one-eyed man rules." We cannot eliminate all errors of analysis with our present knowledge, perhaps we never can. At best, one becomes a "one-eyed" observer, more aware of where bias and preconception enter into political thinking than those who do not know where it lies. In attempting to reduce these sources of confusion, certain key steps have been followed in this book that explain its organization; in different ways these procedures are followed by most political analysts.

---

[8] Robert Lynd, quoted in Donald R. Matthews, *The Social Background of Political Decision Makers* (New York: Random House, 1967), p. 6.

[9] More formal and detailed discussions of research technique, suited to an individual beginning original research, may be found in Sorauf, *op. cit.,* Chapter 3; Thomas W. Madron, "Fundamentals of Research Design," in George S. Masannat and Thomas W. Madron (eds.), *The Political Arena* (New York: Charles Scribner's 1969); elementary ground rules for statistical approaches are suggested in Fred N. Kerlinger, *Foundations of Behavioral Research* (New York: Holt, Rinehart and Winston, 1965), Chapters 15–19. On the special problems of research in the social sciences, see: Ernest Nagel, *The Structure of Science* (New York: Harcourt Brace Jovanovich, 1961), Chapters 13 and 14; George C. Homans, *The Nature of Social Science* (New York: Harcourt Brace Jovanovich, 1967); and James C. Charlesworth (ed.), *Contemporary Political Analysis* (New York: The Free Press, 1967), pp. 1–72. More advanced students should read Samuel G. Eldersveld, "Research in Political Behavior," *American Political Science Review* (December 1952), pp. 1003–1032.

Using Explicit and
Consistent Definitions

Since political scientists have shown a hearty disinclination to use the same terms in the same way, we have defined how we understand key terms as we proceed through the various chapters. In political analysis, as Robert Dahl remarks, definitions have become "proposed treaties governing the use of terms" and the terms of the treaty change with each writer.[10] There is nothing wrong if authors use the same term differently, but this makes the task of clarification all the more important. Hence our concern with definitions.

Using Theories

It would be impossible to make sense of politics without theories. A theory, basically, is a conceptual tool for ordering and arranging what we call the facts of political life so that "isolated observable phenomena . . . are brought together and related systematically."[11] A theory, in brief, is a set of ideas that pulls bits and pieces of political life together into some pattern and assigns some meaning to it; thus, theories deal with the previously mentioned problem of fragmented information.

Theories perform several important functions in political analysis. First, they provide the means to *classify* political entities and events, to put the matters of political life into meaningful categories and groups. We often, for example, divide the world's nations into democracies or dictatorships on the basis of concepts, or theories, about what nations with each of these characteristics are like; having decided upon ideas that qualify a nation for one category or the other, we distinguish between political systems on this basis.

More importantly, theories attempt *to explain* political events. This makes what otherwise might seem like isolated events cohere into a meaningful and related pattern. Suppose we argue that urban racial violence results from racial discrimination or that a man is a Republican because he is wealthy. We have, in effect, offered two theories, or explanations, of political life that link racial discrimination to urban violence and relate a man's income to his party allegiance; we have taken a few facts—a riot and racial discrimination, a man's party choice and his paycheck—and explained one fact in terms of another in each case. Obviously, we have far too little information to be very confident

---

[10] Robert A. Dahl, *Modern Political Analysis* (Englewood Cliffs, N.J.: Prentice-Hall, 1963), p. 8.

[11] Eugene J. Meehan, *The Theory and Method of Political Analysis* (Homewood, Ill.: Dorsey Press, 1965), p. 128.

about our explanations, but this illustrates how an explanatory theory ties the facts together.

Finally, theories are used *to predict*. A great many interpretations of political life are based on this use of theories. In Chapters 4 and 5, we have predicted that the poor and the black—two of the least educated American social groups—will probably participate more actively in political life as their educational levels advance. This prediction is based on our knowledge of the past relationship between rising income and political participation. Of course, we do not know that the relationship will hold true in this case.

It should be clear that we all theorize about politics; none of us looks at the political world as merely a set of unrelated happenings, even if we do not think we are theorizing.[12] This gives the lie to a distinction often erroneously made between two kinds of political observers: the hard-headed, no-nonsense type who gets the facts and the kind who theorizes (the theorist is supposed to be less reliable because he has no practical experience, no eye for facts). But even the political practitioner does not really rely on hunches that emerged from an intellectual vacuum; rather, his hunches derive from theories in the back of his mind. If we say that punitive peace treaties ought to be imposed upon our enemies at the end of a war, we are deducing this from a theory which holds that states will repeat their aggression unless severely punished. If, on the other hand, we advocate a generous peace treaty, we are drawing a conclusion from a theory which suggests that hostile states may change their behavior if the victors hold out a hand of reconciliation. Thus the distinction between theorist and practitioner is unreal. The real distinction is between those who make their theories *explicit* and *recognize that they are theorizing* and those who leave them implicit and deny their existence.

Furthermore, some theories are quite reliable; others are flimsy. If, again, we theorize that heads of state are preoccupied with national security and survival we would be fairly accurate; if we suggest all governments are naturally imperialist we would be offering a clumsy cliché. Thus, the particularly crucial reason for emphasizing the impact of theory on political analysis is that every book on American politics is an *interpretation* and, usually, one of several possible interpretations. No study of American politics contains simply the facts. We invite the reader to view our book in this light and to question, when it seems appropriate, our specific interpretations of American politics.

---

[12] Literature on the place of theory in political research has reached voluminous proportions in the last ten years. For the beginner, the following are interesting and lucid: Heinz Eulau, *The Behavioral Persuasion* (New York: Random House, 1963), Chapter 1; Arthur S. Goldberg, "Political Science as Science," in Robert A. Dahl and Deane E. Neubauer (eds.), *Readings in Modern Political Analysis* (Englewood Cliffs, N.J.: Prentice-Hall, 1968), pp. 15–30; and Don R. Bowen, *Political Behavior of the American Public* (Columbus, Ohio: Charles E. Merrill Books, 1968), Chapter 2. For a lively account of the hazards that beset even the disciplined investigator, see Melville Dalton, "Preconcepts and Methods in 'Men Who Manage,'" in Phillip E. Hammond (ed.), *Sociologists at Work* (New York: Basic Books, 1964), pp. 50–95.

Being Selective Observers

A moment ago we noted that one reason we do not comprehend politics better is that we observe selectively. Yet we *must* be selective. We cannot describe every aspect of American politics; we cannot proceed like a fanatic, collecting all available facts in the misplaced faith that sooner or later they will add up to something.

Anyone who proposes to describe American political life intelligently proceeds like a painter before a sweeping landscape. He cannot paint everything; no good artist would try. Rather, some objects are thrown into sharp relief, others are relegated to the background, some ignored totally. The finished canvas will be a landscape interpreted through the painter's eye, from his angle and perspective. In studying politics, the same problems of scope and emphasis occur: what shall the perspective be? In this last section, therefore, we will suggest our own selective approach to American political life and in the process describe what angle this book will take.

Three Perspectives on American Politics

Three key ideas shape all the material to follow. They are (1) the comparative approach, (2) the importance of the international environment in understanding domestic politics, and (3) the use of models to simplify political life.

Why Comparisons?

Each of the three major sections of this book opens with a chapter that explicitly compares the United States in broad terms to other political systems. In Chapter 2 we will call the United States a "western democracy" and explain how American politics resembles that of other nations, predominantly European nations. In Chapter 12 we shall call the United States a unified political system and make more comparisons. Elsewhere, limited comparisons appear: political culture in the United States and Europe; American and Soviet perceptions of the international environment; and decision making in different political systems. It is, of course, quite possible to discuss American politics without drawing conscious, explicit comparisons. Why then follow a comparative approach?[13]

Explicit comparisons, first of all, minimize culture-bound thinking—the

---

[13] A brief but thorough examination of the comparative method is found in Howard A. Scarrow, *Comparative Political Analysis* (New York: Harper & Row, Publishers, 1969). For a more extended discussion with case studies, see Richard L. Merritt and Stein Rokkan, *Comparing Nations* (New Haven: Yale University Press, 1966).

tendency to generalize from our own political system to others without adequate information. Our political vision, unless corrected, is customarily nearsighted. Often, what is familiar is assumed to be correct. Americans, accustomed to elections involving competing candidates and the right to a choice, are likely to think that the major function of an election is to choose a government. In the Soviet Union, the ballot customarily contains the name of only one candidate for office, usually chosen by the inner circles of the Communist Party; a Soviet citizen may vote for or against the candidate but almost never for someone else. The government, in effect, has already been chosen by the party committees that nominate the candidates. So dull and predictable are Soviet popular elections that fairs, festivities, and patriotic celebrations are used to enliven the day and give it significance. Thus, in the Soviet Union popular elections are not meant to choose a government but are intended as ritualistic celebrations of loyalty to the political system. Even this very modest comparison alerts us to the fact that elections have different cultural and political functions.

Comparisons also reveal that the United States political system is not unique in the sense that it is wholly unlike any other. Often the "American way" is touted as if Americans somehow invented a political system so singular that comparisons reveal only its uniqueness (and, probably, its superiority). In truth, the American political system resembles other political systems in some ways and not in others; therefore, comparisons are revealing. Almost all political systems must solve the potentially dangerous problem of transferring power. In totalitarian systems, this may be a perilous and violent process, as Stalin's rivals for power after Lenin's death discovered in their prison cells or execution chambers. In some other systems, particularly in Latin America and Africa, *coups d'état* are frequently the procedure for dislodging the incumbent regime. In the United States, Great Britain, France (at least most of the time), and other European nations, elections have become peaceful revolutions, means of displacing old rulers and replacing them with a new set; power is transferred by the ballot within the constraints of public values that sanction this method. Governments must also deal with the opposition. In some regimes, members of the opposition are outlawed, treated as traitors, viciously suppressed, harassed, or even killed. In contrast, Great Britain's government pays the salary of the Leader of the Opposition in Parliament on the assumption that there can be no government without a "loyal opposition."

Comparisons thus suggest that political systems differ according to the way they deal with many similar problems. Each society has its own political formula, its particular institutional arrangements for dealing with such common matters as transferring power, dealing with political opposition, as well as other issues. In this context, this book constitutes a discussion and analysis of the American political formula.

We constantly describe American politics in comparative terms, though perhaps unwittingly. Consider, for example, the comparison involved in calling the United States a democracy. We mean that *in relation to other nations* our country is democratic; presumably, there are some that are less democratic. Let us imagine all the world's nations arranged on an imaginary scale with those that permit absolutely no public participation in political life at one end and at the other end, nations that involve the public in almost all political decisions—their national politics would be patterned after a town meeting. A democracy would be a nation lying beyond some point on the hypothetical scale where public political participation begins. We do not, of course, customarily think of such a common political term in a comparative perspective but the comparison is implicit. Open and detailed comparisons greatly expand our political sophistication and our understanding of concepts.

The International Environment.   For most of its history, the United States isolated itself from what we today call world politics (but which, in fact, was European politics since all the great powers were European). America concentrated instead upon domestic affairs. Unfortunately, the United States can no longer ignore this external environment. In a world of over 3.2 billion people—overwhelmingly nonwhite and non-Christian—America's total of just over 200 million makes up only a small percentage of the world's population. Furthermore, some of these people, organized into nation-states, are no longer willing to leave us alone; reciprocally, we have political and economic interests abroad. Consequently, as a highly industrialized and powerful state, we have become a world power—indeed, a superpower—deeply and irrevocably involved in world affairs.

Yet many Americans still do not appreciate the full implication of our involvement. At the height of the Cold War in 1949, after four years of trouble with the Soviet Union and after a series of highly publicized actions which, in fact, constituted a "revolution of American foreign policy," Martin Kriesberg argued from opinion-polling research that approximately 30 percent of the voters were "unaware of almost any given event"; 45 percent were "aware but uninformed," remembering little information and not able to "frame intelligent arguments" about the affairs they had heard and seen discussed; only the remaining 25 percent of the electorate showed "knowledge of foreign affairs."[14] In 1961, James Rosenau, in a study of public opinion and foreign policy, argued America has a public which

> is uninformed about either specific foreign-policy issues or foreign affairs in general; [a public whose] members pay little, if any, attention to day-to-day developments in world politics. Being uninformed and without initiative, they lack structured opinions. . . . The most predominant mood of the mass

---

[14] Lester Markel (ed.), *Public Opinion and Foreign Policy* (New York: Harper & Row, Publishers, 1949), pp. 35–6.

public is . . . indifference and passivity. Except for acute peace-or-war crises (and not always then), the mass public is usually unmoved by the course of world events.[15]

More specifically, what Americans do not yet realize is, first, that international affairs permeate almost *all* levels of American political life, affecting many matters that in past years were considered to be almost entirely domestic; and second, that the American response to the international environment depends upon the peculiarities of American political institutions and American styles of political thinking. The key themes that we will emphasize, therefore, will be the impact of the international environment upon our domestic policies and politics and, conversely, the influences of various internal factors upon our conduct of foreign policy. Thus, foreign affairs do not begin south of Key West or east of Boston. Nor are the international and domestic political systems any longer neatly separable, if indeed they ever have been. By setting our study in the context of the international environment, we create a global-sized picture of American politics, free of the illusion that politics "out there" and "in here" merge only occasionally.

Models.   Each major section of this book opens with what we have called a "model." The model identifies various aspects of political life we wish to study, relates them in a preliminary way and suggests their importance; then, except for the chapter on the model of the state system, succeeding chapters of a section take up various elements of the model in detail, and elaborate and apply them specifically to the United States. Models of different sorts are a specialized, useful intellectual tool for interpreting the world and, more specifically, political affairs; indeed, most of us have at some time used a model, perhaps unwittingly. It will be helpful to explain briefly what models do and how they fit into this book.

The word "model" has several different meanings; even in political analysis (to cite another case of confused and ambiguous political terminology), a model can mean several things. Basically, all models are an intellectual shorthand, a way of simplifying the real world by selecting certain aspects for particular attention and analysis. The emphasis is usually upon the *relationship* between the various parts; in the end, a model encourages one to see the various parts as a unit of interconnected elements. Models can be used to describe reality, to attempt predictions about reality, or simply to stimulate new ways of looking at reality. In any case, they represent a particular way of theorizing about the world.

[15] James N. Rosenau, *Public Opinion and Foreign Policy* (New York: Random House, 1961), pp. 35–6.

Perhaps the simplest kind of model to understand is a physical one. Children often construct model airplanes and cars by putting together the various pieces into a unit—essentially, these models are miniatures of the actual cars and planes they imitate. These small, concrete reproductions are like reality in a rather obvious way, even though simplified and reduced in scale compared to operational cars and planes. In such models, there is a great physical resemblance between the model and reality. Yet a physical model sometimes suggests a new perspective. For example, Karl Deutsch suggests that the model of the clock influenced the founding fathers' concept of government:

> The development of clockwork, under progress ever since the thirteenth century, yielded the classic model of the mechanism—a model applied to a description of the stars in the system of Newton; to government in the writings of Machiavelli and Hobbes, to theories about the "balance of power" and "checks and balances" by . . . the founding fathers of the American constitution.[16]

Political conversation is rich in analogies between physical models and political life: we speak of governmental machinery, and of hot and cold wars. Such words subtly guide our interpretation of political life. A political machine is supposed to *act* like a machine, smoothly meshing different parts, predictably producing anticipated results, and nicely balancing the elements in it.[17] Obviously, a physical model can not only describe some aspect of reality rather closely, but can suggest unexpected perspectives on government.

Models can also be constructed from ideas, symbols, or related concepts that are applied to the real world. Perhaps the most rigorous, carefully constructed models of this kind are found in the physical, biological, and mathematical sciences; these depend heavily upon very abstract concepts and symbols. These formal models are particularly useful in generating theories to be tested.[18] A mathematical equation—a collection of related symbols—describes how nuclear fission occurs and enables scientists to understand and predict the actual process that triggers an atomic explosion. At present, a model with this predictive precision and sophistication is apparently nonexistent in political analysis, but more modest models are still useful and common.

The models appearing in this book take various concepts and theories—

---

[16] Karl W. Deutsch, *The Nerves of Government* (New York: The Free Press, 1963), pp. 26–27. This book attempts to interpret political systems in terms of a cybernetic communications model.

[17] An interesting and critical evaluation of political language and implicit imagery is found in Martin Landau, "On the Use of Metaphor in Political Science," *Social Research* (Autumn 1961), pp. 331–353.

[18] These formal models conform to two requirements usually stated by specialists in formal logic for any model: *isomorphism* between the model and the reality it purports to discuss or interpret, and *limited structural correspondence*. On the meaning of formal

without which it would be impossible to make sense of politics—and arrange them into a pattern that suggests an overall relationship and order. In this way, the models we present relate to theories and concepts in roughly the same way that a building relates to bricks. In creating a building, components (bricks) are placed in a pattern; order and shape emerge. In the same way, our models take individual concepts and theories—the bricks of analysis—and arrange them in a structure of relationship. To take a very limited example of how a model of this kind might work, let us consider voting. Earlier in the chapter, we suggested that we might assume a man votes Republican because he is wealthy—we have a theory about voting behavior. To create a model, we would want to relate a man's income to his age, his occupation, his past voting behavior, or any other important variable and evaluate the relative weight of income among these other factors to arrive at some verdict concerning why he votes as he does. In short, the model ties together several different potential influences on voting and attempts to make some statement about their mutual relationship. Thus, this model arranges different concepts and theories into some broader pattern of relationship.

The models that introduce the various sections of the book all attempt to tie many concepts and theories about politics into some orderly arrangement before we examine the elements of the model in detail. In Chapter 2, for example, we refer to the United States as a "western democracy" and briefly explain what elements in the American political system make it "western" and "democratic"; once done, in the remaining chapters of that section we will explore these various elements and relationships in greater detail. In Chapter 3, to further clarify the important elements in international politics, we utilize another, briefer model. Finally, in Chapter 12 we call the United States a "politically unified" nation and emphasize some general components and relationships found within a politically unified system before turning to detailed analysis.

The models we will present, in brief, are basically descriptions of how we believe certain key concepts in American politics are related and what we understand the concepts to mean. This is a method for creating an intellectual framework for ideas in advance of more detailed discussions of them.

A Closing Word

The essential tool of political analysis is a respect for the complexity of politics and the limitations of our own knowledge; we are still one-eyed. Students

---

models, see Abraham Kaplan, *The Conduct of Inquiry* (San Francisco: Chandler Press, 1964), Chapter 7; a brief but instructive examination of models in political science may be found in Alan C. Issak, *Scope and Methods of Political Science* (Homewood, Ill.: Dorsey Press, 1969), p. 8. The closest approach to a formal model in political analysis—still far from the logician's requirements, however—may be found in some types of game theory and simulation.

often expect a textbook to present The Truth, but as we have suggested, we can present only *a* truth. Why stress such constant caution when bold assertion would better suit the imagination?

For one thing, something new and unexpected always happens in political life. How many French experts, just finishing their current interpretation of French politics in 1969, were surprised by de Gaulle's sudden, unexpected resignation? Or how many American political experts expected Lyndon Johnson's almost unprecedented, equally sudden withdrawal from national politics in 1968? Unanticipated change haunts all political analysts; political prophecy is a notoriously precarious business. In addition, information is not always as accurate as we would like. For example, we can describe what kinds of influence sway a voter's presidential preference, but we are not confident about their relative importance.

We want you to turn to the following discussion with critical interest— "critical" because this brief prologue should suggest the limitations of our knowledge and approach; "interest" because few topics are more important to modern Americans. When he visited the United States early in the last century, the French historian Alexis de Tocqueville wrote advice that deserves repetition:

> I am informed every morning when I awake that some general and eternal law has just been discovered which I never heard mentioned before. There is not a mediocre scribbler who does not try his hand at discovering truths applicable to a great kingdom and who is not ill pleased with himself if he does not succeed in compressing the human race into the compass of an article.[19]

For anyone who wants to study politics intelligently, this serves as both a warning and a challenge.

---

[19] Alexis de Tocqueville, *Democracy in America,* Vol. II (New York: Vintage Books, 1954), p. 15.

Part Two

2

The Politics of
Western Democracies

A great many Americans who survived the Revolutionary War to witness the framing of the Constitution believed they were living at the dawn of a new era. In the first flush of nationalism, Americans increasingly began to regard themselves and their vigorous young nation as unique in their political and social life, abandoning the outworn, sterile formulas of Europe. In 1790, a Frenchman–turned–American named Michel de Crèvecoeur described the emergent American temperament: *"He* is an American, who leaving behind him all his ancient prejudices and manners, receives new ones from his new mode of life. . . . The American is a new man who acts upon new principles; he must therefore entertain new ideas and form new opinions."[1]

This theme never disappeared from American thinking; indeed, there is much to justify this national egocentrism. The Constitution is a singular document; no other government has a national executive resembling the American president, nor the peculiar three-fold division of federal government, nor the particular form of federalism found in the United States. The American government has been extraordinarily stable, the majority of its people increasingly prosperous, its technological achievements unrivaled. This, of course, is the

---

[1] Michel Guillaume Jean de Crèvecoeur, *Letters from an American Farmer* quoted in *The Making of the Nation* (New York: Simon and Schuster), p. 92.

shiny side of American history. There is also an America that has denied its abundance to the blacks, an America blighted with deteriorating cities, an America exploiting its bounty of natural resources with prodigal abandon. But most Americans chose in the past to see the good side, and it impressed them.

Yet the ideas that inspired the American political formula are not all unique to the United States. In the broadest perspective, our political system represents a solution to some social problems more or less common to all men. Moreover, even allowing for considerable variation in the way societies arrange their political affairs, our procedures closely resemble in many respects those found in other nations we call western democracies. This does not mean that the United States has never acted on purely new principles or conducted its politics on the basis of new ideas and new opinions, as de Crèvecoeur suggested. But in this chapter, we are concerned primarily with what is *not* unique to American politics. This means comparing the United States with other nations in search of similarities.

Of the many similarities between political life in the United States and other nations, none is more basic than the fact that almost all societies have a political system. At first, their apparent diversity is most impressive. There are democracies and dictatorships, governments led by presidents and premiers, while others—seemingly reluctant to abandon the forms of the past—still support kings and queens. There are nations with huge, elaborate bureaucracies and others so small and impoverished that their entire administrative apparatus seems scarcely more than a large office staff. This rich diversity, however, conceals some profound similarities. Political systems, despite their variety, grow from some common features of societies and perform many common tasks crucial to social life; to understand what political systems are and what they do, one must understand something about the nature of society itself.

Let us begin by considering a few features of social life which help explain the nature of political systems.

The Social
Setting of Political Life

Man is a creature in society and of society. He depends upon nature for material sustenance, but he depends upon other men—upon society—for the emotional, physical, intellectual, and spiritual nurture without which he would ordinarily remain an uncivilized, highly intelligent brute. Man often pays a fearful price, it is true, for being a social animal; the catalog of these evils is long and depressing. But it is equally true that man's great intellectual achievements, his moments of artistic accomplishment, and the fulfillment of his deepest needs also depend upon society. Thus, it seems, if man is to fulfill his potential, he must live in society and find ways to make society productive; many common features of societies exist in order to make social life possible and desirable.

Though societies differ in many ways, they are initially similar because men normally create many different systems for carrying on social life. These systems deal with the complexities of social living, divide human labor, and organize individuals into cooperative work. We have been speaking of the political system; this is one of many social systems, in many respects the most important one. Since a political system has many characteristics common to all social systems, it will be helpful to explain what a social system is.

Social Systems

The essential meaning of a system is rather simple. Basically, it is any set whose elements have some patterned relationship to each other, that function as a unit, that are interdependent.[2] Most of us can readily recognize a great many systems in our physical world: the wrist watch with its intricately related gears and springs; the engine of an automobile; the electrical circuitry of a building; and so forth. Clearly, all the elements in these systems have a patterned relationship to each other, act as a unit, and influence each other (as any child learns by bending a gear of a clock, thus stopping it).

Looking at a society, we observe that human beings organize their lives into different patterns of behavior in many ways analogous to a system. For example, our economic system is composed of an interlocking web of human activities— activities directed toward the production and distribution of goods and services for the society together with other activities that make this possible. There are producers and consumers of raw materials and finished products, managers of capital directing money through investment and credit into production facilities, and others who attempt to fashion public taste for the producers of goods ("Wouldn't you really rather have a Buick?"). Not only are these activities related and patterned, but they are interdependent. If an auto manufacturer, for instance, raises prices, then consumers may buy fewer cars, seek expanded credit, or buy less of some other product; if the steel industry raises prices in hope of expanded profits, unions may respond with escalating wage demands. In a similar vein, in the United States there is an educational system, a transportation system, and many other systems of human behavior to meet many human

---

[2] Oran R. Young, *Political Systems* (Englewood Cliffs, N.J.: Prentice-Hall, 1968), p. 15. This work captures the essence of the systems concept in most social theory and provides an excellent survey and summary of systems theory in political science. More elaborate definitions of a social system are customary in political literature; for example, for two interpretations of systems theory stressing the multiple variables and structural characteristics involved, see David Easton, *A Framework For Political Analysis* (Englewood Cliffs, N.J.: Prentice-Hall, 1965), especially Chapter 2; and Fred Frohock, *The Nature of Political Inquiry* (Homewood, Ill.: Dorsey Press, 1967), p. 74 ff.

needs, all consisting of many human beings whose activities fall into a related pattern.[3] In the end, therefore, "a society is not an atomic sandpile of separate individuals but a set of interconnected human beings living in a vast web of vital relationships."[4]

In less advanced and populous societies, these systems may be fewer, or less complicated, or less specialized, but such patterns in social life are almost inevitable. This is true even though a man may not think of himself as the member of some system; instead, he may believe he is simply "getting along," or living normally. Yet we live, knowingly or not, within the bounds of these systems. (Indeed, it is common to recognize this fact negatively; the system— political, economic, or whatever—is often an enemy assaulted by those who believe social life smothers individual initiative, freedom, or morality.)

Though social systems seem a very real part of society, to compare social life to a system means to create a model of human affairs, yet the analogy between any system and the behavior of actual human beings is always imperfect. Men are neither mindless automatons nor mechanical elements locked into some imperious system they cannot change. Still, thinking of society as a mix of different systems for human behavior encourages us to see the relatedness of human activities and to ask what role these systems play in social life, how they influence each other, and how the elements in them relate. Visualizing a society in these terms, we shall shortly inquire into the place of the *political* system in society.

The Problem of Order

By way of introducing a second important aspect of social life, consider that luckless, lovable nonhero of the cartoon *Peanuts,* Charlie Brown. He has bruised his ego in one of his endless collisions with his waist-high society and in a moment of exasperation he exclaims, "Sometimes I think I am living in a stacked deck!" Charlie Brown is a social philosopher of sorts; like him, man living in society lives in a "stacked deck." Social life would not be possible—nor could various social systems develop—unless man develops predictable, orderly, routine relationships, unless he learns to fit into living patterns with others. A major problem in all societies is to create and maintain this social order, to assure that men do in fact develop and maintain a great variety of predictable

---

[3] Technically, many social scientists would insist that the economic, educational, familial, and political arrangements of a society are subsystems of the larger social system. See, for instance, a brief explanation in Robert A. Dahl, *Modern Political Analysis* (Englewood Cliffs, N.J.: Prentice-Hall, 1965), pp. 9–13. A more elaborate theoretical explicaton of society considered as systems of behavior may be found in H. V. Wiseman, *Political Systems* (New York: Praeger, 1966), Chapter 1.

[4] W. Lloyd Warner, quoted in St. Clair Drake and Horace R. Clayton, *Black Metropolis* (New York: Harcourt Brace Jovanovich, 1945), p. 775.

and compatible behaviors. Powerful social forces daily press upon man to fit him into his society and its many systems; society has "stacked the deck" for every man in some manner so that, usually, he will conform reasonably well to many prevailing norms and values.[5]

The order and predictability in life may excite little surprise or notice, so normal might it seem. In the United States, for instance, drivers follow rules of the road, most parents accept roles that provide basic economic and emotional support for their children—or they try. Professors teach, and students learn; congressmen legislate, and men shake hands upon formal introduction. To live in a society is to share with others a multitude of implicit, unspoken understandings about behavior and values. Without some sharing of values and understandings about behavior, social systems would be impossible, and each man would be an atom of impulse and morality peculiar to himself, destined to collide with others propelled by their own individualistic standards. The potential for violence among men left to their own untutored understanding of acceptable behavior led the political philosopher Thomas Hobbes to liken the state in which man lived without society to "a war of all against all" and to call society itself "the conquest of violence."[6]

Yet this order must be created and recreated. How is this done? Two primary methods exist. First, individuals are taught from childhood to behave in socially acceptable ways; they grow up believing that what they are doing is what they *want* to do, and what they want to do is very often what is necessary for them to fit reasonably well into the existing social order. Such individuals have been socialized into the system. Early in life, most of us are taught rules of conduct, dress, manners, and speech that equip us to deal with others; as children, we are expected to be good citizens, to get ahead, and to respect authority; all this powerfully predisposes us to accept the status quo. We may deviate sometimes, but in *most* respects, *most of the time,* we have been socialized into our society before we know what is happening. Second, force— visible or concealed, blunt or subtle—also keeps behavior within socially acceptable limits. A respect for law is often a respect for the force that lies

---

[5] In sociological theory, a person living in society has usually been oriented toward others through shared values, premises about behavior, and some compatible life styles. Virtually every social theorist will assert, as Chalmers Johnson does, that "the possession of mutual expectations by members . . . allowing them to orient their behaviors to others" is an absolutely minimum precondition for a society. Chalmers Johnson, *Revolutionary Change* (Boston: Little, Brown and Co., 1966), p. 8. Two different, comprehensive works on the theoretical status of social systems built upon the assumption of orientations are Talcott Parsons and Edward A. Shils, *Toward a Theory of Social Action* (Cambridge: Harvard University Press, 1962); and Marion J. Levy, Jr., *The Structure of Society* (Princeton: Princeton University Press, 1952). An interpretation of Parsons' ideas in terms of political science may be found in William C. Mitchell, *Sociological Analysis and Politics* (Englewood Cliffs, N.J.: Prentice-Hall, 1967).

[6] A short, perceptive, and lively introduction to social theory for the beginner is Peter L. Berger, *Invitation to Sociology* (New York: Doubleday & Co., 1963).

behind the law. Overt force, however, is less commonly a direct influence upon our behavior than the covert social pressure applied by many institutions; the opinions of friends, family, peers, church, or other reference groups constantly orient our behavior, for the opinion of others is important, and social disapproval is customarily painful. One may be a nonconformist to some extent, but unremitting, conspicuous nonconformity usually provokes compelling punishment. And, if this fails, one may be removed from society entirely—imprisoned, banished, or killed. Thus, a multitude of social institutions combine in various ways to guide our behavior into socially correct channels and, in doing this, contribute to the preservation of a social order.

Coping with Change

Societies ordinarily survive by developing the ability to serve two seemingly incompatible masters. On the one hand, man in society needs order; on the other hand, he must simultaneously find ways to adapt himself, his institutions, and his values to change. Just as societies would not endure without some fairly stable behavior patterns that develop into social systems, so societies would also perish in most cases if their institutions, values, and life styles became so rigid that they were unalterable in the face of events demanding adaptation and change.[7]

To what kind of changes must society adjust? One prominent domestic agent of change is technology. One product—the car—has transformed American society.[8] The automobile spurred the massive development of the petroleum and automobile industries, which now constitute the majority of the ten largest corporations in the United States and the world. The car gave Americans unprecedented mobility, breeched localistic cultures and limited social vistas previously common in American life, and revolutionized courtship patterns. To spin the web of implications still further, the development of the automobile led to demands upon local, state, and national governments for the creation of highways, fostered the powerful industrial lobbies speaking for automakers and

[7] Social scientists can usually agree upon the need for adaptive capacities in social systems but not upon how this adaptation occurs nor what consequences may follow various kinds of adaptation. We have obviously avoided this prickly issue. An interesting, lucid explanation of social and political change suitable for the beginner may be found in Heinz Eulau, *The Behavioral Persuasion in Politics* (New York: Random House, 1963). More theoretical treatments may be found in H. C. Bredemeier and R. M. Stephenson, *The Analysis of Social Systems* (New York: Holt, Rinehart and Winston, 1962); for emphasis upon the impact of change and its mechanism in the political system, see Young, *op. cit.*

[8] For a brief but comprehensive examination of the impact of technological change on the economy, see James E. Anderson, *Politics and the Economy* (Boston: Little, Brown and Co., 1966), especially Chapter 1. For a more extended, detailed examination of industrialization in the United States, see Harold Underwood Faulkner, *American Economic History* (New York: Harper & Row, Publishers, 1960).

related manufacturers, and opened new tax resources to government. Finally, the automobile became a formidable polluter of the atmosphere.

Other forces and events in the external or international setting of a society may challenge existing institutions and values, throw into question the old ways, or stimulate new social patterns. Wars and invasions pose a mortal threat to established institutions and basic social structures. Germany's defeat in World War I spelled the end of its monarchy; Russia's defeats on the battlefield during that conflict so weakened Tsarism that the forces of change erupted into revolution. And after World War II, the eastern European states were not only occupied but communized. Even without the goad of a hot war, important alterations in the balance of military power and political alliances in the world may produce alterations in the social structures of many societies. Through most of its history, the United States grudgingly had supported only a very modest, meagerly financed military establishment; socially and in terms of prestige and governmental attention, the military was relegated to second-class citizenship. However, following World War II and the advent of the cold war, the military became the largest single branch of the federal government in manpower and budget, reflecting what American governmental leaders believed to be the necessity for large standing military forces to counter the threat of a hostile Soviet Union and its allies throughout the world.[9]

Regardless of how change may begin in a society, it usually means that some men will look at reality in new ways; new facts and a new perspective will emerge. Such change affects existing values and life styles. It tests their worth and adequacy, and in the process it throws the problem of adaptation among social institutions into sharp relief.[10]

To summarize, beyond the differences that rightly cause us to say each society is in some ways different from all others, at least three fundamental similarities remain: the development of social systems, the problems of order, and change. Social systems themselves could not endure without striking a crucial balance between the stability and change necessary for their continuation; in the end, all three aspects are related. With these essential facts about society in mind, we can now state with some precision what role a political system plays in social life.

---

[9] It can be argued that almost all social change in the modern world is stimulated or abetted by various external events and situations: ". . . [social] change is generally not a problem basic to separate and relatively autonomous systems but one overwhelmingly related to interactions among systems." Lucien Pye, *Aspects of Political Development* (Boston: Little, Brown and Co., 1960), p. 55. To Europeans, for instance, it is the progressive americanization of their cultures that often seems the most important social change in the last decade. Some consider this a great problem.

[10] In the view of some social scientists, change produces new values and living patterns because older life styles do not satisfy the psychological needs of individuals confronted with a new life situation. In this view, all values and life styles persist only because they are functional to man psychologically. For a statement of this argument, see Everett E. Hagen, *On the Theory of Social Change* (Homewood, Ill.: Dorsey Press, 1962), p. 7.

What Political Systems Do

Despite many definitions of a political system, most of them emphasize *a system in a society concerned with making and executing policy for a whole society.*[11] In the terms we have just discussed, the political system in a society has the most comprehensive powers for dealing with problems of stability and change in social life; to one social scientist, the political system could be distinguished from other social subsystems precisely because it deals with these matters: it is "the legitimate order-maintaining and order-transforming system within a society."[12] Stated less formally, the political system in a society makes society's decisions about order and change.

The creation of a political system is a way through which political activities —almost always found at all levels of most societies—can be organized for the broadest social purposes. In our perspective, politics involves relations of power, influence, and authority between individuals—anytime, anywhere.[13] Politics is the moving of man by man found almost always in social life. We recognize this ubiquitous meaning of politics when we refer to "office politics," "fraternity politics," or "church politics." It seems basic to human relationships that there will always be those who influence and those who are influenced, those with authority and those subject to it, the powerful and the powerless. Indeed, there is even "family politics"; within a home, adults wield power, influence, and authority over children in a miniature state.[14]

---

[11] This definition closely follows that suggested by David Easton in "An Approach to the Analysis of Political Systems," *World Politics* (April 1957); later, Easton interpreted the functions of a political system in terms of "input-output" variables more strictly compatible with systems theory. Most definitions of a political system, otherwise so varied, do include —as Lucien Pye has emphasized—the making of "society-sized" decisions. For an excellent summary of concepts related to the political system, see Wiseman, *op. cit.,* Chapters 3 and 4. Not all political scientists would accept the ideas that most or all political systems perform at least some equivalent functions. In our opinion, comparisons of this kind are possible. As Lucy Mair suggests in discussing the difference between primitive and modern government, "It is *ways of doing things* which can be described as primitive or otherwise." We will suggest that it is ways of doing things rather than differences in broad functions that distinguish political systems much of the time. Lucy Mair, *Primitive Government* (London: Penguin Books, 1962), p. 8.

[12] Gabriel Almond and James S. Coleman, *The Politics of Developing Areas* (Princeton: Princeton University Press, 1960), p. 7.

[13] Robert A. Dahl, *op. cit.,* p. 6. Dahl, however, believes this defines a political system! For our purposes, we have chosen to call this activity "politics" while keeping "political system" more restricted as above. This should demonstrate conclusively the plasticity of current political terminology—among scholars surely—and the importance of establishing definitions at the outset of discussion.

[14] For an interesting and amusing example of politics among 200 primitive people in the dark backwater jungles of Brazil, see Claude Levi-Strauss, "The Social and Psychological Aspects of Chieftainship in a Primitive Tribe: The Nambikauara of Northwestern Mato

The distinction between the politics of family, office, or fraternity and a political system is that within the political system, the power, influence, and authority of politics are aimed at policy-making for an entire society. In brief, a political system structures and organizes for the broadest social purposes the politics which is present in all social life.

We have been speaking very generally about the political system's role in "making and executing policy for a whole society." In more concrete terms, how does this system deal with problems of social stability and change? We can examine a few examples.

Maintaining Social Order

Political systems deal in the most comprehensive ways with social order. At a minimum, political systems are concerned with preserving civil peace, suppressing or inhibiting violence, and doing whatever else is considered necessary to preserve domestic tranquillity. Moreover, political systems are usually expected to deal with other matters that may endanger public health or safety. The United States government, for instance, is now expected to pass judgment on the medical and social implications of cigarette smoking and birth-control pills among a multitude of other health-related items; in the United States—as in most other industrialized nations—the government also provides a comprehensive retirement and health insurance program for its senior citizens.

If established social institutions, resources, or values are threatened, the political system—the government especially—is usually supposed to come to the rescue. Conservationists have looked to the federal government to protect America's diminishing wilderness; more than 30 million acres of this wilderness rest in federal control as a consequence. When America's small businessmen seemed threatened by mammoth corporations and retail chains, the federal government attempted to enact another kind of conservation act by creating a multitude of tax incentives and subsidies, as well as the Small Business Administration to save the Main Street merchant from extinction at the hands of corporate giants.

Most social analysts recognize that some institutions with comprehensive powers must exist in a society to create and maintain at least a minimum of civil order and to preserve important social institutions. Writing in the fifth century, St. Augustine, though concerned more with man's soul than with his political affairs, acknowledged that a political system was God's providential gift to save man from his natural impulse to selfishness, disorderliness, and pillaging. Writing thirteen centuries later, Thomas Jefferson—always vigilant against

---

Grosso," in Robert Cohen and John Middleton (eds.), *Comparative Political Systems: Studies in the Politics of Pre-Industrial Societies* (New York: Natural History Press, 1967), pp. 54–55. The entire book is an interesting examination of politics in relatively backward societies.

powerful governments that might suffocate human freedom—nonetheless recognized that government was indispensable to a healthy society. "Governments are instituted among men," asserts the Declaration of Independence, to secure "life, liberty, and the pursuit of happiness."

The problem of maintaining order and continuity in social life is especially pressing in modern societies. The many social systems found within a society often involve different rules and behaviors. In his home, a child may be expected to respect authority ("Respect your elders"), to accept the adults' life style ("Always associate with the right people"), and the adults' values ("Don't let anyone push you around"). In school, however, the same child may be encouraged to question ideas, accept different social values, and form friendships and life aspirations outside the range of family tolerance. Later, the child may learn in church to be morally sensitive, self-renouncing, and responsive to others' needs. Finally, the maturing child may enter an occupation in which success requires aggressiveness, constant competition, and respect for rules which are not necessarily moral in terms of his theological perspective. In short, a maturing individual not only encounters different social codes, but he constantly moves from one behavioral system to another as an adult. In stable societies with a great many systems, most individuals can make the transition between them relatively easily as long as the different systems are compatible. (In this respect, note that John Kennedy's 1960 election was possible in good part because he was able to convince millions of dubious voters that a conscientious Catholic could owe primary political allegiance to the Constitution rather than to his church's hierarchy).[15] But a potential conflict is always threatened. When only a few dissent from majority attitudes, the tension seldom disrupts a society. The Jehovah's Witnesses may refuse to salute the flag, or the Amish may not send their children to high school. Yet this hardly creates national turmoil. But when a major labor union refuses to renew a contract with management and strikes, paralyzing the trucking industry or the railroads, or when blacks engage in nation-wide demonstrations of civil disobedience, major economic and racial interests are so deeply involved that widespread violence, economic disruption, and civil disorder occur.

Allocating Resources

Harold Lasswell once suggested that the purpose of a political system can be stated simply: it is the business of deciding "who gets what, when, and how."[16]

---

[15] See John Kennedy's famous 1960 speech to the Houston Ministerial Association in U.S. Senate, Committee on Commerce, Subcommittee of the Subcommittee on Communications. "The Speeches, Remarks, Press Conferences, and Statements of Senator John F. Kennedy," pp. 206–211.

[16] Harold D. Lasswell, *Politics: Who Gets What, When, How?* (New York: Meridian, 1968).

David Easton has suggested that a political system should be considered a device for "the authoritative allocation of values," implying that through the political system, a society sets a collective agenda for social action and allocates resources for the task.[17] As both these definitions suggest, a major purpose of a political system is to define where the human and material resources of a society should be directed and to create the means for getting these resources channeled in the determined directions. The allocation of social resources is a major means through which a society deals with the problems of order and change. If a developing Afro-Asian nation wishes to industrialize, for example, then it must try to take from its population and its physical environment the requisites for rapid industrialization and deny these resources for other purposes.

Understandably, the allocation of resources is a contentious task in most societies; there is never enough of any particular resource to meet all the demands upon it—never enough money, manpower, food, goods, taxes, or whatever to satisfy all who want them. But, equally apparent, societies need some means through which priorities can be set for using the total resources of a people; there must be some social mechanism by which this is accomplished.

In the United States, one of the most effective means through which our political system allocates resources is the federal budget.[18] The process of deciding how the more than $200 billion in this budget will be raised and spent is, in effect, a process of social planning. Decisions must be made about the relative priorities for defense, environmental pollution, health care, aid to the cities, and numerous other matters claiming equal attention. Furthermore, the total size of the budget must be decided; this involves determining how much of the nation's spendable income should be extracted from the private sector through taxes and administratively spent by the federal government. Clearly, the federal government uses the budget to define the purposes for which public money and public officials will work.

One reason the process of resource allocation in most societies is contentious is because all these decision-making systems are loaded in such a way that some interests get more of what there is to have, some get less, and some get nothing. In this respect—to anticipate a point we shall elaborate in Chapter 8—the rules of the game through which a political system arranges the distribution of social resources are never unbiased; accidentally or intentionally, all systems will favor some interests over others by the way in which the procedures operate. In the end, even before the pie of social resources is divided in the political system, some interests can expect a larger piece and more preferential treatment; others, at the opposite extreme, need not bother coming to the table for they will not be served.

---

[17] David Easton, *The Political System* (New York: Alfred A. Knopf, 1963), p. 129.

[18] In recent years, political scientists have given increasingly detailed attention to budgeting and its intricacies as a policy-making process. Two excellent studies which emphasize how social values become enmeshed in budgeting are Ira Sharkansky, *The Politics of Taxing and Spending* (New York: Bobbs-Merrill Co., 1969); and Aaron Wildavsky, *The Politics of the Budgetary Process* (Boston: Little, Brown and Co., 1964).

Adapting to Change

A society whose culture is untroubled by currents and change is rare. Not so rare is the fact that most adaptive problems come unwanted to political leaders; but they do come and, ordinarily, political systems are expected to find the resources, programs, and strategies for making the society's adaptations to change. This is apparent enough in the face of social convulsions such as war, depression, or other emergencies. If war comes, then the enemy must be defeated and the society mobilized for victory or steeled for endurance. If depression ensues, the means to end the slump must be found. If natural disasters strike, the government is expected to alleviate the suffering and the political system must find means to prevent their repetition.

Slower change may also call for adaptive action from the political system. The immensely grave and complex problems of the contemporary American city resulted, after many years of lobbying by urban interests, in the creation of a cabinet-level Department of Urban Affairs as the federal government attempted to channel resources toward the urban problem. Not long afterward, repeated warnings by scientists and laymen about the dangers of environmental contamination led to the creation of the first Presidential Commission on Environmental Quality. Thus, when Americans are caught in urban traffic, choke on smoggy air, or perceive a variety of other major social problems looming, it is natural for them to ask what the government or the politicians expect to do about it. Even in somewhat simpler societies, perhaps happily spared the scourge of urban blight and environmental pollution, there will ordinarily arise social problems so generalized that they require some comprehensive response that can be engineered, if at all, only through the political system.

Thus, making society's decisions—dealing with society's problems of change and order and allocating resources for this—are functions which seem to belong especially to a society's political system. Therefore, these activities distinguish the political system from other social systems.[19] But like any other social system, the political one consists of interrelated parts; let us examine what these are and how they are related.

---

[19] The intended consequences of political action may not be the accomplished results—there are, as social analysts insist, unintended consequences of many political acts. Thus, when European powers colonized Africa and Asia, they sent promising native intellectuals to Europe for an education to equip them for colonial administration and the preservation of the colonial establishment. Ironically, once educated, the native intellectuals often formed the core of the anticolonial movement, and consequently, attempts to create a conservative native elite were partially counterproductive.

The Components
of a Political System

Political scientists differ about what specific components should be included in the concept of a political system. The argument is not likely to be settled soon, but fortunately at least four key elements are usually mentioned:

1. A government
2. Linking institutions between government and society
3. A political culture
4. An international environment

While this list by no means includes all the interesting and relevant aspects of a political system, it includes the elements that reveal the workings of a political system and the interrelatedness of its elements. It is in the nature of a model, in any case, to simplify reality; we have concentrated upon core elements in political life.

Government

"When we ask in the common tongue for the marketplace of 'politics,' students are happy to direct us to any old castle called 'government.' "[20] Most people would instinctively think of "government" when a political system is discussed as well, but a government is not figuratively or literally "any old castle." *A government is a specific set of institutions that makes authoritative decisions for a society regarding social order, resource allocation, and social change.* Governments are probably the most universally recognized components of a political system because they are ordinarily the most visible.

The most distinctive characteristic of a government is its power to enforce its decisions. Governments, "quite against one's will, . . . tax one, draft one into the military, make one obey its innumerable rules and regulations, if need be put one into prison, and in the last resort will kill one."[21] To make its decisions binding, government ordinarily employs "ultimate, comprehensive, and legitimate physical coercion."[22] Such a tough-minded definition emphasizes only one aspect of government. A more tender-minded view would also emphasize that

[20] Bernard Crick, *In Defense of Politics* (London: Penguin Books, 1954), p. 162.
[21] Berger, *op. cit.,* p. 74.
[22] Wiseman, *op. cit.,* p. 24.

governments reconcile social conflict, engineer necessary social changes, and meet the legitimate needs of individuals. The definition of government one chooses is a matter of selective emphasis since both aspects are true.

Americans are apt to have a particularly narrow concept of government. The United States, like most modern nations, has specific institutions whose primary role is to govern; ordinarily, government does not overlap with the church, the economic structure, or other social institutions. Furthermore, the president, Congress, and the courts—the government—do, in fact, make authoritative decisions regarding social control and resource allocation. In many societies, no attempt is made to distinguish the government from other social institutions. In primitive and pre-industrial societies, for example, the concept and word for "government" do not exist; in such societies, the function of government may be performed by religious, racial, or family leaders. In other societies, the official government is a legal fiction; the *real* government is elsewhere. The very elaborate governmental apparatus in Communist China and the Soviet Union is a facade; it is a public secret that the authoritative decisions are usually reached within party circles, then ratified and administered through the governmental apparatus. One cannot always be confident even when examining the official government of the United States that it includes all the elements in the effective government.[23]

Thus, in speaking of a government, remember that there can be a distinction between a legal government and an effective one, and that many societies without a formal government may still have a functioning one.[24] However important a government may be, whatever its form it is but one element in a political sy tem and not necessarily the most important one. This is apparent when we examine the institutions that link government with the society around it.

Linking Institutions

In most societies, a variety of different institutions bridge the gap between the government and the society in which it exists. These institutions perform a variety of functions essential to a government's effective operation.

---

[23] One gray area in defining the American government concerns political parties. The Constitution says nothing of them; many of the founding fathers, disliking parties, deliberately tried to prevent them from effectively controlling the government. But the two major parties today perform critical roles that are virtually governmental: (1) they recruit, select, and promote candidates for public office, especially the presidency; and (2) they attempt to organize legislatures and to determine national governmental policy. Do they belong to the government that makes socially binding decisions? Political scientists disagree and often resolve the problem by hedging; the parties are called "quasi-governmental." We have placed them in the political system but outside the government.

[24] The urban boss, who was the effective government of many a major American city, is another excellent example of why one should distinguish between official and effective governments. The boss often held no governmental or party position; the mayors, aldermen, and administrators who constituted the official government were often so much window dressing to conceal the source of the real government.

In general, these institutions communicate political demands and problems to the government; they establish an intelligence network through which various social problems are defined and various demands upon the government's resources and powers are fed into the governmental structure.[25] In addition, some institutions mobilize support for the government (or some of its leaders) and perhaps there are institutions to mobilize others against the government, against some of its leaders, or against some of its policies. In a sense, these institutions organize the public for political action—whether it be voting, peaceful dissent, protest, or rioting. There are other institutions through which the members of the government itself are recruited; these institutions are arrangements for selecting and designating who among society's members will govern. In a variety of different ways, therefore, the linking institutions create a constant flow and interchange of information, demands, personnel, and support opposition between society and government.

Linking institutions are most familiar to Americans in the form of political parties, interest groups, and the mass media. These institutions may perform several different functions. Political parties in the United States recruit members of the government through the process of nominations; party platforms—especially the platforms in the presidential nominating conventions—are also a means through which certain demands upon government can be defined and articulated. Once a party captures the White House, its organization continuously seeks to mobilize support for the President and his administration. Special-interest groups are involved in activating various social groups to make demands upon the government and to watch attentively the conduct of government. The mass media also are an extremely important source of information on the state of the nation and the government; through the dissemination of information, they may also help to mobilize various groups in support of or opposition to governmental policy. In these and other ways, the activities of linking institutions often overlap.

So important are these linking institutions in the United States that they have been called "the capillary structure of democracy" because "unless they are connected effectively with the primary structure of the community—family, friends, religious groups, work groups, and the like—there can be no effective flow of individual impulses [and] needs . . . into the political system."[26]

---

[25] The various functions we have aggregated under "linking institutions" are usually differentiated in various ways. In comparative literature, see Gabriel Almond and G. Bingham Powell, *Comparative Politics: A Developmental Approach* (Boston: Little, Brown and Co., 1966), especially Chapters 4, 5, and 7, for distinctions between interest group activities, political mobilization, and the communications function. David Easton, *A Systems Analysis of Political Life* (New York: John Wiley, 1965), Parts 2 and 3, makes the distinctions in terms of "inputs" and "supports" of various kinds for the government and political system. We have avoided the useful but complex distinctions between various linking institutions and their functions at this point for brevity.

[26] Gabriel Almond and Sidney Verba, *The Civic Culture* (Boston: Little, Brown and Co., 1965), p. 105.

Even in nondemocratic societies, or in those that are neither large nor modern, these linking institutions are probably essential in providing governments with the information they must have and the personnel they need to function. These linking institutions may not resemble what we call political parties or interest groups, although they perform some of the same functions. In some societies, demands upon government may flow almost entirely through the administrative apparatus of the state itself, especially when voluntary associations of the kind found in the United States are prohibited by the regime. Or, in simpler societies, family or religious groups may take the place of the political parties or other specialized institutions found in highly modernized societies. But whatever their form and wherever they are found in a society, the linking institutions are clearly a vital part of a political system, and the failure of these institutions to provide the essential information, support, or personnel needed by a government to function effectively may be a prelude to governmental impotence and deterioration.

Political Culture

Political systems also have a psychological dimension. Those who live within a society usually have a variety of attitudes, beliefs, and feelings about the political system, its various parts, and those who play major roles in political affairs. A government exists alongside public attitudes about the worth of the government and evaluations of its performance. Laws exist alongside beliefs about the rightness or wrongness of laws. Public officials must deal with public feelings about their office. And members of a society are likely to have some convictions about how they can and should participate in civic affairs. In brief, a political system lives in the minds of men; there it can assume almost infinite shadings of feeling and cognition. A political culture deals with this psychological dimension.

Lucian Pye aptly defines a political culture as "the set of attitudes, beliefs, and sentiments that give order and meaning to the political process and that provide underlying assumptions and rules that govern behavior in a political system."[27] The sum of these attitudes will orient a person toward his political system. Like light passed through a prism, this orientation can be broken into different components. Among important dimensions of a political culture are:

---

[27] Pye, *op. cit.,* p. 104. For slightly different but equally useful definitions of political culture, see Eulau, *op. cit.,* pp. 72–73; Almond and Verba, *op. cit.,* p. 13; and Richard E. Dawson and Kenneth Prewitt, *Political Socialization* (Boston: Little, Brown and Co., 1969), Chapter 1. For comparative studies, see Lucien Pye and Sydney Verba, eds., *Political Culture and Political Development* (Princeton: Princeton University Press, 1965); and Edward C. Banfield, *The Moral Basis of a Backward Society* (New York: The Free Press, 1967). The role of attitudes in structuring political life among primitive people is discussed at many points in Mair, *op. it.*

(1) the extent of public information about the officials and procedures of the political system; (2) public beliefs about the way the political system operates and evaluations of the system's performance; (3) attitudes toward public officials and their offices; (4) beliefs concerning what political rules are valid; and (5) beliefs about how one can participate in political life and related behavior. We shall deal with these specific matters later, primarily in Chapter 4; what concerns us here is their impact on the political system.

A political culture concerns the "gut feelings" of political life. Governments must depend upon predictable public support (or at least tolerance) for effective performance; otherwise, though a government might prevail at bayonet point, the officials, procedures, and symbols of the system elicit no spontaneous, sustained public loyalty that ensures continuity or survival through crisis. In any case, public attitudes toward the political system will powerfully affect the way the system operates. If, for instance, a great many people believe that the political rules of the game should be quite different from the legal ones—if a majority, say, prefers to suppress free speech rather than tolerate it—the law will probably be unenforced, regularly violated, or widely ignored. Thus, a political culture at many points determines both the effectiveness of a government and, in extreme cases, its survival.

Earlier we noted that man in society lives by a multitude of unspoken, shared understandings concerning behavior; the political culture is part of these broad understandings and, as such, affects behavior quietly but effectively. Consider, for instance, the contrast in style of doing business with public officials in the United States and India. In the United States, lobbyists generally follow a common strategy in dealing with public officials:[28] (1) be pleasant and nonoffensive; (2) convince the official that your visit is important; (3) be prepared and informed; (4) be personally convinced; (5) be succinct and direct; and (6) use the soft-sell. Getting governmental business done in India requires a different tactic:

> The system of corruption, or what is widely known in India as the payment of *bakshish,* is a highly stable one. Businessmen and agriculturalists often regard the payment of bakshish to be as much a part of an application for government service as filing a government form. The rates of payment are generally based upon the rank of the office, the character of the service being requested, and the financial means of the claimant.[29]

Indian officials are not necessarily more corrupt than their American counterparts (wining, dining, and providing small favors for public officials is standard

---

[28] Lester W. Milbrath, *The Washington Lobbyists* (Chicago: Rand, McNally & Co., 1963), pp. 220–227.

[29] Myron Weiner, "India: Two Political Cultures," in Pye and Verba, *op. cit.,* p. 222.

practice in the United States); this comparison illustrates, instead, that beliefs about the proper procedures for conducting politics—one element in political culture—alters the conduct of political life in different nations.

The International Environment

The great English writer John Donne remarked that "No man is an island, entire of itself." This applies to nations as well. National political life cannot be conducted today without considering the behavior of other nations. In the twentieth century, the world is organized into nation-states preoccupied with the balance of power; since World War II, an ideological conflict between giant coalitions of nuclear superpowers has dominated the state system. Because nations are so intensely concerned with each other's behavior, national politics untouched by the larger issues of world politics is impossible.

Yet the influence of international affairs, the behavior of the other nations occupying this globe, and the constant effects of the international system upon domestic politics often escape the appreciation of even those deeply involved in political affairs. "It is a curious fact that most people who portray their vision of an ideal political system ignore the limits imposed by the existence of other systems," writes Robert Dahl. The result is often miscalculation:

> It is easier to imagine "the good society" if one does not bother with other, and quite possibly "bad," societies that might clutter up the surrounding land- scape. Consequently, political utopias are usually portrayed without the trou- blesome limitations imposed by foreign relations, which are eliminated by either ignoring them entirely or solving them according to some simple plan.[30]

The true extent of our involvement in world affairs and its impact upon us is easily discoverable. Today nations are related economically, politically, and militarily. According to the logic of international trade, one nation becomes a consumer of another's products and also a producer of goods for the interna- tional market. Americans eat Russian caviar, Africans buy German automobiles, Europeans drink Brazilian coffee, and mainland Chinese purchase British tex- tiles. More significantly, a complex web of military defense and assistance pacts dictated by balance of power considerations ties the military security of many of the more important nations together and threatens to involve them simulta- neously in major wars should one member become involved.

---

[30] Dahl, *op. cit.*, p. 22.

Mankind has got into its hands for the first time the tools by which it can unfailingly accomplish its own extermination. . . . Death stands at attention, obedient, expectant, ready, if called on, to pulverise, without hope of repair, what is left of civilisation. He awaits only the word of command. He awaits it from a frail, bewildered being, long his victim, now—for one occasion only—his Master.[31]

These words were written by Winston Churchill after World War II; they are even more appropriate today. The atomic bombs dropped on Hiroshima and Nagasaki were each equivalent to only 20 kilotons, or 20 thousand tons, of TNT. Today, an average-sized bomb carried by a U.S. Strategic Air Command B-52 bomber is equivalent to 25 megatons, or 25 million tons, of TNT—a total of 125 times greater than the entire explosive power of all bombs dropped during World War II, including the two atomic bombs! The Soviets have tested a bomb as large as 58 megatons. Actually, bombs can be made any size one wishes. Indeed, above ten megatons, each additional ton of explosive costs only about a penny more, so they can be produced in truly economy sizes. Because instant death is a constant possibility, the United States has devoted a major portion of its national resources to safeguarding a fragile peace based upon the assumption that strong military forces would best be able to prevent the eruption of a nuclear conflagration; in 1968, almost 56 percent of the federal budget was allocated to defense expenditures alone.[32] Since World War II, this country has dispatched troops to the Dominican Republic, Lebanon, Korea, western Europe, Berlin, Thailand, and Vietnam because successive presidents have believed our national interest dictated it. Troops of the Soviet Union reoccupied Hungary in 1956 and invaded Czechoslovakia in 1968 to ensure that both countries would remain under Communist party control and within the Soviet sphere of influence established at the end of World War II. Almost any nation, however small or politically impotent itself, can become a pawn in the game of Great Power international politics, courted, threatened, assisted, allied, and manipulated by a major power. Thus, a world exists in which virtually no aspect of purely domestic politics is unaffected by the international environment; almost all nations are bound up in each other's affairs, inevitably if not willingly.

To summarize: political systems have broad similarities that make comparisons possible. A list of minimum elements would include a government, a political culture, linking institutions, and an international environment. These

---

[31] Winston Churchill, *The Second World War,* Vol. I (Boston: Houghton Mifflin Co., 1948), p. 40.

[32] This estimate is probably conservative, since it includes only expenditures *primarily* related to national defense and excludes, among other items, military assistance to other nations. See U.S. Bureau of the Census, *The U.S. Book of Facts, Statistics, and Information 1968* (Washington, D.C.: Government Printing Office, 1968), Section 9, Table 357.

can be called the common denominators of a political system, the fundamental elements. The elements are interrelated—changes in one element will produce changes in the other elements—which is why the various components are called a *system*. This will become clear as we examine the particular qualities of a western democratic system, that of the United States. We will see why our political life resembles that of several other nations.

The Social Setting of Western Politics

American politics is described as "western" because most of the nations that share the American political pattern are located in western Europe and Anglo-America. Since World War II, a few nations that are not geographically in the West have attempted to import political styles with limited success; but only the Japanese, under the sharp goad of an American occupation government, have apparently succeeded.

To understand the pattern of western politics, it is necessary to begin with an analysis of some very broad similarities in western social structures. It is impossible to understand the distinctive features of western politics without considering the more comprehensive features of western societies; for, as we have seen, the social system establishes many of the problems, resources, and institutions with which the political system must deal.

Western Nations Are Industrialized

One of the sharpest comparisons between western and nonwestern nations is economic: almost all western nations are industrialized, most nonwestern ones are not. In 1966, more than 80 percent of western nations were highly industrialized, while 90 percent of those outside the West were not.[33] In the United States and other western nations, industrialization transformed both landscape and society; because they were the first to enjoy the fruits of industrialization, the larger western nations became world powers. Further, while industrialization alone did not shape contemporary western political and social life, it profoundly

---

[33] Banks and Textor, *A Cross-Polity Survey* (Cambridge: Massachusetts Institute of Technology Press, 1963), p. 41. The following nations are listed as economically developed or already industrialized: Australia, Luxembourg, Belgium, Netherlands, Canada, New Zealand, Czechoslovakia, Norway, Denmark, Sweden, Finland, Switzerland, France, Soviet Union, Germany, United Kingdom, United States, and Italy. Japan should probably be added.

altered it to the point where world economists can speak of industrialized and pre-industrialized societies as two distinct social worlds.[34]

Industrialization created international political power because it produced sophisticated military hardware in great abundance, generated new sources of national wealth, produced the goods of modern international trade, and provided governments with the resources for ambitious international political, economic, and military initiatives. Industry also changed the occupational character of western societies by drawing the bulk of the labor force away from agriculture and into industry. In 1790, George Washington led a nation of farmers; in 1967, less than 3 percent of the American labor force was agriculturally employed, in contrast to 35 percent in industrial occupations.[35] One direct benefit of industrial muscle was mounting production of goods for internal and international commerce; the industrialized western nations today produce about 65 percent of the world's goods and services with less than one third of the world's population. High production nourished growing affluence; in most western countries industry produced not only life's necessities but the luxuries that came to be regarded as part of the good life.[36] The fruits of industry were so persuasive to the political elites in emergent African and Asian nations that they came to equate industrialization with modernization, and pressed, often too ambitiously in light of their limited resources, for rapid industrialization.

The capacity to produce goods in a quantity and variety that approaches glut has deeply impressed Americans themselves. Often Americans will argue that economic prosperity vindicates American democracy; that prosperity—or at least industrialization—is the first necessary step to democracy abroad, especially in the newly emergent nations; that technology will yield a cure to practically any social problem. (Americans can appreciate the remark attributed to Franklin Roosevelt that if he could place one American book in the hands of every Russian it would be the Sears and Roebuck catalogue.[37]) Often, as David

---

[34] In comparative studies, the industrialized nations are also called "the First World," "the developed countries," or "modernized," though these terms may be used to refer to other characteristics beside industrialization. For an examination of the differences between industrialized and nonindustrialized nations, see especially: Irving L. Horowitz, *Three Worlds of Development* (New York: Oxford University Press, 1966); Arnold M. Rose (ed.), *The Institutions of Advanced Societies* (Minneapolis: University of Minnesota Press, 1958); Eugene V. Schneider, *Industrial Sociology* (New York: McGraw-Hill Book Co., 1957); and Wiseman, *op. cit.*, especially pp. 56–58. A good discussion of the political impact of industrialization can be found in Robert E. Lane, *Political Life* (New York: The Free Press, 1965), part 4.

[35] Based on statistics in U.S. Bureau of Commerce, *The U.S. Book of Facts, Statistics, and Information* (Washington, D.C.: Government Printing Office, 1968), Table 314.

[36] It is a backhanded tribute to American affluence, for instance, that in the United States obesity is a serious medical problem. Prime television time is purchased for the sale of weight-reduction preparations. One recent advertisement suggested, for instance, that indigestion resulted from eating "too *well*"—not too much. Thus does overconsumption become virtue.

[37] David Potter, *People of Plenty* (Chicago: University of Chicago Press, 1954), p. 80.

Potter suggests, it was not our democracy but our prosperity that has most impressed others: "We supposed that our revelation was 'democracy revolutionizing the world' but in reality it was 'abundance revolutionizing the world.' "[38] Yet the material prosperity that attended industrialization, while diffused, was still uneven. In 1968, the United States—the richest of the industrialized nations—still had more than 10 percent of its population earning yearly incomes below $2,000. The abundance that benefitted most Americans widened the social chasm between them and the poor. By the 1960s, this domestic disparity had become a national preoccupation, while the chasm between the richer and poorer nations widened.

Western Nations Are Scientific

Science spawned industry. Industry accelerated the development of the scientific community and gave it the marvelous technology that fascinates Americans. In western nations, generally, science in all forms spurred the pace of social change while providing government with progressively more sophisticated and effective tools to carry out its tasks. The single most dramatic and convincing example of scientific impact on government, the atomic and hydrogen bombs—the ultimate symbol of "big power" status—has irrevocably changed the whole calculus of international politics and made the Great Powers aware of the interdependence of their fate. A more familiar example of the effects of technology on a changing society is the automobile: urbanization, rapid transportation, the huge automobile and petroleum industries are but some of these; air pollution, steeply rising taxes for highway construction, urban congestion, and the annual highway slaughter are others.

The emerging scientific communities made western nations the Eldorado of the world's scientists and technicians; the resulting brain drain caused a steady movement of scientists from nonwestern to western nations and from Europe to the United States. Between 1949 and 1961 more than 43,000 scientists and engineers migrated to the United States, most to stay. By the early 1960s, more than one fourth of the scientists and one half of the engineers in the United States worked directly or indirectly for the federal government; today, federal funds underwrite about 65 percent of all American scientific research.[39] By the

---

[38] The industrial revolution swept western nations rapidly. It began in England about 1830 and crested there in 1850. The first modern factory did not appear in the United States until 1850; it was the Civil War that converted the North into an industrial colossus. In 1860, American industry produced only $2 billion in goods. By 1870, this figure had doubled; by 1880, it had tripled; by 1890, it had quadrupled. By 1894, the U.S. was the world's industrial leader, a position it has never surrendered. Figures cited by Schneider, *op. cit.*, p. 58. See also August C. Boline, *The Development of the American Economy* (Columbus, Ohio: Charles E. Merrill Books, 1966), p. 209 ff.

[39] Figures cited are based on Warner R. Schilling, "Scientists, Foreign Policy, and Politics," *American Political Science Review* (June 1962), pp. 287–300.

mid-1960s, the rivalry between the United States and the Soviet Union had become as much a competition of technology as anything else; although the race to the moon was the most dramatic test to many Americans, the technological competition had deeper, more lethal overtones: "The crucial advantage in the issue of power is likely to be with the nation whose scientific program can produce the next revolutionary advance in military tactics. . . ."[40] Science had become a critical variable in the equation of national power and, perhaps, survival; those nations which controlled advanced technologies effectively set the terms of international power.

Western Nations Are Highly Literate

By world-wide standards, the majority of people in western nations are unusually well educated. Among all western nations, at least half of the population is literate; more than 80 percent of these nations have 90 percent literacy.[41] The average adult American in 1940 had 8.6 years of formal education, in 1950 it was 9.3 years, and in 1968 it was 12 years; the figure continues to rise.

The United States has gone farther than most other western nations to promote free, extended mass education, yet all western governments have been vitally interested in literacy and education. Without literacy, an industrialized society is impossible; it is illiteracy, as much as any other problem, that poses such a formidable obstacle to industrial development among the emergent nations. Furthermore, education has a direct political relevance to western governments. Western governments have always operated on the premise that education is closely tied to the regime's survival; education is one method through which individuals can be socialized into their political system, taught its values, instructed in its rituals, and led to allegiance to it. In democracies, an education has been considered almost essential if individuals are to discharge the responsibilities placed on them by a political system that expects them to participate regularly, actively, and intelligently in its political life.

Western Nations Are Pluralistic

Industrialized societies, founded on science and technology, rooted in industrial processes, and containing a multitude of educated individuals, are extraordinarily complex in almost all respects. It is this social complexity that

---

[40] Don K. Price, "The Scientific Revolution," in William R. Nelson (ed.), *The Politics of Science* (New York: Oxford University Press, 1968), p. 5.

[41] Banks and Textor, *op. cit.*

leads to many of the characteristic political qualities and problems in the West.

In the United States, as in other western nations, a great many occupational, religious, ethnic, and cultural groups coexist. The Bureau of the Census lists at least 200 *major* occupations, each with many subcategories. This means American society is *pluralistic:* it includes many different, competing, and conflicting social groups, social values, life styles, and interests.[42] This social diversity can be traced to the Industrial Revolution, which unrooted men from an essentially rural and agricultural life with its relatively modest range of occupational groups; in place of such a traditional society, industrialization produced the familiar modern society with its typical social divisions and interests. Paralleling this transformation was the decline of a sense of community.

> Before the industrial revolution, communities had to be somewhat isolated from each other, and their members were governed by a strong adherence to common meanings and values. In their limited circle, people were in adequate communication with each other and they had a strong sense of belonging and of loyalty to the community.[43]

Two very significant political results followed from this pluralism. First, the number and variety of demands upon government multiplied. Second, the potential for civil war in society mounted with the growth of conflicting interests. Thus, the cost of industrialization was the division and subdivision of social groups in a process of social fragmentation that still continues. Western political systems were expected to deal with the political ramifications of this cultural pluralism and in the process became the arbiter, referee, and often the guardian of such interests.

Western Political Systems

Many of the political institutions and procedures that Americans consider normal are distinctively western in origin. Today, nations that are considered modernized are usually expected to organize their political system along lines that follow the early western pattern.

---

[42] A useful distinction is often made between cultural and social pluralism. Social pluralism means many different social groups within a society; cultural pluralism refers to the existence of many different values, orientations, and life styles among a group of people. The United States is both culturally and socially pluralistic (although not nearly as culturally pluralistic as many other societies).

[43] Rose, *op. cit.,* p. 186.

Western Government
and Social Penetration

No matter what particular ideology sways the imagination of western political leaders—be it democracy, fascism, socialism, or something else—the governments of western nations have common features: they are big in manpower and resources, powerful in their ability to penetrate society, bureaucratic, and—in the case of democracies—some are constitutional. These characteristics are well illustrated by the United States government.

The federal government owns $347 billion worth of property, employs about 3 million civilians (equal to the population of Washington State) and in fiscal 1969 spent about $195 billion; the budget of the federal government exceeded the gross national product of all but four other nations. State and local governments spend an additional $100 billion annually. All levels of American government employ one eighth of the national work force and own about 20 percent of the nation's capital assets. The federal government is the largest, wealthiest, most impressive of all American institutions.

The federal government has constantly expanded since the Constitution was adopted. Partly, this expansion represents an adjustment to an increasingly large, populous nation where even the most modest governmental housekeeping functions must be organized on a broad scale. The United States is the fourth largest nation in size and population in the world; it has expanded without interruption for almost two centuries. The first census of 1791 reported in 56 thin pages that the population was 3,596,100; in 1970, this figure was 208 million.[44]

Industrialization also contributed to governmental expansion and relentlessly broadened the ambit of governmental powers. Industry, as we saw, produced pluralism. The resulting diversity of major interests soon expected government to legislate to their advantage, adjudicate their conflicts, and protect their interests. Almost every major department of the federal government memorializes the success of a major interest in converting its concerns into governmental ones: the Departments of Agriculture, Commerce, Health-Education-Welfare, Defense, Urban Affairs, Labor, Interior, and Transportation, among others. This gravitation toward government was probably inevitable but, in any case, it was irreversible. The problems that agitate major economic interests in industrialized societies are so sweeping that only governments are likely to have the authority and resources to deal with them. Big government will yield to bigger government.[45]

---

[44] The definitive source of historical statistics is U.S. Bureau of the Census, *Historical Statistics of the United States, Colonial Times to 1957* (Washington, D.C.: Government Printing Office, 1960); and the supplementary volume *Continuation to 1962 and Revisions.*

[45] Not only the *size* of government but its particular *form* was related to western culture. "Government as we are familiar with it—bureaucratically organized, responsible to a

Large governments wielding broad social powers can penetrate almost all areas of social life. A big government with such an ample reach is not predestined to survive or handle social problems effectively, but a government whose powers are constricted to the point where it has neither the authority nor the resources to handle large social problems is precarious indeed. This has, in fact, impeded the political stabilization of many nonwestern nations. Their governments have often been weak, if not entirely impotent, in the face of internal crises, civil wars, and external threats. Modern Americans are probably unaware of the extent to which the federal government alleviates potential crises and buffers them when they occur, thus preventing considerable human suffering. For instance, the 1968 federal budget included a modest $11 billion for "Health, Labor and Welfare" which touched almost all Americans in some respect. Through this appropriation the government paid insurance premiums for the aged, widows, and the physically disabled, provided retirement incomes for federal employees, contributed to state disability insurance and workman's compensation, and funded Medicare, medical research, the school health program, and the Public Health Service.

The Scope of Political Problems

Because western governments penetrate society so extensively, *practically every significant social problem becomes a political one.* Western societies have become increasingly politicized because the separation of private and public concerns constantly narrows. This convergence of public and private matters is apparent, for instance, in the United States, where the federal and state governments in recent years have been actively involved in such diverse matters as birth control, the sale of residences to blacks, and auto safety—all matters which appear frequently in contemporary newspapers, but all of which would have been considered private concerns a relatively few years ago. Western governments still do not intervene in all aspects of social life as much as totalitarian governments do. During the years when Joseph Stalin was unchallenged dictator of the Soviet Union, the government (often Stalin himself) decided the merits of music, art, and literature; works that lacked "socialist realism" (or offended Stalin personally, since it meant the same thing) were stillborn or suppressed. The internationally famous Soviet composer Dimitri Shostakovitch, for example, was forced to withdraw his "Fourth Symphony" from public performance because it was too "bourgeois." Less cooperative artists often received one-way fellowships to Siberia. Compared to totalitarian regimes,

---

people's legislature, and topped by an executive who is flanked by secretaries or ministers— belongs to Europe and America." John J. Honigmann, *Understanding Culture* (New York: Harper & Row, Publishers, 1963), p. 116.

governmental penetration in the West ordinarily leaves considerable latitude for private affairs.

Bureaucracy

Western governments are large and powerful because they also have become *bureaucratic.* Of all the institutions of government, the administrative and executive branches of western government have expanded most rapidly. Indeed, when one speaks of big government, one usually means big bureaucracy. Again, the United States federal government is an excellent example of the growth of Byzantine multi-tiered administrative bureaucracies familiar to all western citizens. In 1792, the fledgling federal administration included only 800 officials, excluding postmasters; 600 of these officials served in the Treasury. In 1801, the Department of State employed nine officers including the secretary and a messenger; as late as 1901, the whole White House staff serving the president consisted of three secretaries, six clerks, and a few doorkeepers and messengers. President McKinley frequently opened and answered his own mail, sitting on the edge of his Secretary's desk. By the late 1960s the nine-member Department of State of 1801 had grown to 44,000, the White House staff to 300, the civil service to 3 million.[46]

Western governments could not have dealt effectively with the crush of demands upon them without large bureaucracies. The modern bureaucracy is a reservoir of highly skilled, technologically oriented individuals whose talents must be brought to bear on the complicated problems of modern societies. Furthermore, effective legislation is *administered* legislation. Governmental effectiveness hangs on the ability of its executive branch to implement policy decisions. Governmental bureaucracies also introduced their own particular dynamics to the governmental process, not universally admired. Big bureaucracy was skilled, but as it matured it, too, became sluggish and prone to conservatism; departments, agencies, and bureaus developed a strong vested interest in their own survival. Once created, the bureaucracy in the United States quickly sent its own representatives to the legislative and executive branches to protect its share of the budget, control key programs, and preserve its prestige. Bureaucracy became a pressure group created by government within the government itself, an internal lobby of considerable dedication, influence, and ingenuity.

---

[46] Figures cited in W. Lloyd Warner *et al., The American Federal Executive* (New Haven: Yale University Press, 1963), pp. 7–10. Gone, too, is the desk-straddling chief executive: ". . . the president's personal mail was, and is, divided among staff assistants for reply over the president's signature. By the end of the day, a 'signing table' in President Johnson's office would be piled two to three feet high with letters, messages, and statements awaiting his signature. . . . The load on the writers was at times staggering. I was one of six or eight people who regularly wrote letters for Mr. Johnson, and my secretary once noted that in a 50-day period I had written 131 'presidentials.' " Peter Benchley, "Rose Garden Rubbish and Other Glorious Compositions," *Life* (May 23, 1969), p. 64.

Constitutionalism

Constitutions like the United States' were born in the West. They represent one of the West's major contributions to political history. A tribute to the world-wide prestige of constitutions is that virtually any nation with pretensions of being modern adopts a constitution—often, however, as a meaningless scrap of paper quite irrelevant to the real conduct of political life within the nation. In the United States, the Constitution has often been venerated as the fountainhead of the political system, a parchment on which eternal verities are inscribed with almost biblical authority. At the very least, the Constitution for many Americans is the single paramount symbol of the political system, the document which bestows legitimacy on the government itself. When the founding fathers wrote the Constitution of 1789, now the oldest written constitution in the world, they were following a revolutionary impulse which arose in the West during the eighteenth century and shaped the character of western political systems.[47]

Basically, a constitution is an attempt to define the form of a government, its powers and limitations, and its objectives. But political systems have existed without written constitutions; what is important about constitutions is less what they contain than why they exist. Written constitutions developed in the West in the eighteenth century as a radical attack on autocratic kings and, in a longer perspective, on autocratic governments in general. Constitutions imposed legal limitations on government by creating a higher, impersonal law binding upon the government itself. At their inception, constitutions had three purposes: (1) they were compacts between citizens of a nation concerning the nature of their government; (2) they restrained governmental power in order to (3) protect individual liberties—"inalienable rights," as the United States Constitution words it—from violation or suppression by government. Because constitutions were swept into the mainstream of western history on the wave of revolutionary democracy, they came to be identified especially with democracy and the protection of individuals from the state.

The United States Constitution has affected every aspect of the American political system. In addition to establishing the basic form of the American government, it defines basic liberties such as freedom of speech, religion, assembly, and petition; these freedoms are supposed to be norms that define the rules of the game for political life and the values which are to be honored. The two most important articulating institutions in the United States—political

---

[47] The material on constitutions is drawn from Herbert J. Spiro, *Government by Constitution* (New York: Random House, 1959) and Robert Rienow, *Introduction to Government* (New York: Alfred A. Knopf, 1965), Chapter 9.

parties and interest groups—grow directly from the right to vote, petition, and express one's opinion freely. Even in dealing with the international system, the president of the United States must heed such Constitutional strictures as submitting treaties to the Senate so it can "advise and consent" to them, while his powers in foreign affairs are enormously strengthened by his constitutional position as commander-in-chief of the armed forces. There is good reason, then, for Americans to look first at the Constitution to understand their political system—provided it is not assumed to describe all major aspects of American political life.

Beyond its day-to-day influence on the conduct of political life, a constitution is one method for settling one of the most essential problems in any political system, the problem of *legitimacy*. Why do individuals obey governments? Why *should* they obey government? There are several possible answers: people obey because they are forced to do so, because they have no objection to doing so, perhaps because they want to do so. Yet many people give their allegiance to government because it is "legitimate" in their eyes—it is right and proper for them and society; indeed a great many people in the United States have never questioned the legitimacy of their government since they cannot conceive of any other form of government to which allegiance would be proper. But what makes a government legitimate? In recent history, one answer has been that a constitution legitimates a government; this is so in the United States. Yet there are other solutions.

Particularly in the past, the government and political system often have been accepted because they were traditional. Where tradition forms the basis of political legitimacy, one accepts the standards of political life because that is the way things have always been done; history sanctifies. Or, a government may achieve its legitimacy by the personal stature of a great leader whose control of public loyalty so dominates political thinking that he imparts to the government and political system, which were created in his image, a legitimacy it might not otherwise enjoy. This charismatic leader may appear in the person of a Hitler, a Nasser, or a Castro. When a government's legitimacy depends upon the personality of the leader, it is inherently unstable. When the leader dies, retires, or is unable to command the imagination of his people, the political structure may collapse.

Stable governments usually survive on a mixture of all three sources of legitimacy. Even though the Constitution of 1789 legitimates our government, in its earliest days George Washington's presence conferred upon the embryonic government a stature it could not otherwise have obtained, for the Constitution was far from universally admired in the beginning. Many colonial legislatures accepted the new document because they knew George Washington would be the first president. Furthermore, after almost two centuries, the crust of tradition further legitimates the government and the Constitution. Thus, to some degree stable political systems depend upon various sources of legitimacy, but no historian would deny that constitutions are in themselves powerful legitimating documents in the West.

Two qualifications must be added: (1) constitutions do not guarantee governmental legitimacy, and (2) constitutions may not even describe how political systems operate. Western nations have endured the collapse of constitutional governments in this century. One conspicuous failure occurred between 1919 and 1932 in Germany. Germany's monarchy fell after its military defeat in World War I, and the Weimar Constitution was put into effect. At the time, it was considered the most democratic constitution in the world; the Weimar Constitution was supposed to be an antidote to the Prussian monarchs, a breath of democratic reform in a society permeated by militarism and authoritarianism. The Weimar Constitution failed dismally. The German masses never embraced it; there had been no time to make the transition from monarchy to parliamentary democracy, to undo centuries of history and tradition by slow experimentation, and to recast the fabric of a society which supported the monarchy. When Hitler's National Socialist Party (NAZI) assumed power in 1933 it was clear how shallow and inadequate this attempt at constitutional engineering had been. After only twelve years, a vicious dictatorship succeeded a model democratic constitution. A constitution without roots in public loyalty and understanding is always brittle.

Even constitutions that endure do not necessarily prevail. The Soviet Union's Constitution of 1936, written during Joseph Stalin's rule, described a political system that did not exist then nor during the rest of his lifetime in any important respect. For instance, constitutional changes which should have been approved through legislative means were often achieved by decree; the impressive powers granted to the national legislature—the Supreme Soviet—were usually exercised by the bureaucracy of the Communist party and then ratified by the Supreme Soviet. In any nation there will, of course, be some disparity between the constitutional description of government and its actual functioning. The United States Constitution may assert that no citizen may be deprived of liberty without due process of law but the Southern black who could not vote in the past would have disputed that the words were truly descriptive or operational. Still, the very great disparity between the Soviet constitution and the actual processes of government in the Soviet Union illustrates that sometimes a constitution bears very little resemblance to a nation's actual political life.

A Democratic System

The United States is politically western *and* democratic. All western nations are not democratic while some nonwestern ones—Japan and India—are struggling to become so. Fewer than twenty of the world's over 120 nations are customarily placed in the category of "western democracy" on the basis of their geographic location and political organization.[48] Democracy has been closely identified with the West because it orginated in the revolutionary ferment of the eighteenth century in the West and flourishes most vigorously there.

The Meaning of Democracy

Political discourse has confused and corrupted the meaning of "democracy" so effectively that this term, of all political terms, needs particularly careful definition. The word is used in at least two ways. First, it may stand for an idealized model of a political system incorporating all the characteristics one would expect in a democracy, however defined. In this context, it may mean what a political system *should* be, for no political system yet devised by man can meet the requirements normally stated for a "pure" democracy in anyone's vision. More commonly, the word has a second, more limited, concrete, and practical meaning: it refers to certain nations whose political affairs more closely approach a model democracy than do those of other nations. Thus, the term always has a relative meaning. To an American, for instance, West Germany is a democracy while East Germany's Democratic People's Republic is communist— and to the Soviet communist, the American democracy is capitalist exploitation while Soviet communism is actually socialist democracy. To be called a democracy is such a prestige symbol in international politics that a sort of verbal egalitarianism prevails: all systems can be considered democratic from someone's point of view.

The United States has been commonly called a democracy because it, together with many other western nations, has certain political characteristics that many political scientists believe essential to any democratic order:

1. It is based on a constitution.
2. The constitution provides for regular elections at which an electoral majority can elect leaders and change regimes.
3. Citizens are guaranteed freedom of speech, freedom to express dissent from the regime, freedom of religion, and other expressive privileges.[49]

---

[48] The number of the world's nations will continue to rise. A current estimate of this is made by Banks and Textor, *op. cit.* The rough limit of twenty for western democracies is based on combining Banks' and Textor's estimates for nations that are geographically "western" and politically "democratic." However, comparative studies frequently classify any nation "western" if it resembles most geographically western nations in economic respects. Thus, in economic terms, Japan and the Soviet Union are also "western." For more detailed explanations of such comparisons and relevant statistics see Banks and Textor, *op. cit.*, and Bruce *et al., World Handbook of Political and Social Indicators* (New Haven: Yale University Press, 1964).

[49] Definitions of democracy can be found in almost any introductory book of American government, political philosophy, and political science; they provide useful comparisons to this definition. For a few specific references, see: Robert A. Dahl, *Preface to Democratic*

4. There is widespread, voluntary participation in political life.
5. Institutions exist inside and outside the government for the free flow of political opinion and information.

Looking at this list, the first three items refer to the formal, official structures of the system. The last two items, in contrast, insist that a democratic system is not only one of formal elections and participatory rights—some of the most flagrant dictatorships, after all, have officially permitted this—but one in which these rights can be and actually are freely exercised. Only when the first three items are coupled with the last two, when actual patterns of behavior correspond reasonably well to legal forms, can a democracy be said to exist.

In recent years this scheme for defining democracy—and for characterizing the United States as a democracy—has been severely attacked. At issue is a profound argument over the nature of democracy and our own political system. The most visible critics have been the young white militants, the newly mobilized and aggressive black spokesmen, and the outspoken intellectuals. These critics have staged protest marches, "teach-ins," and other displays of dissent against the American system. Less publicly but no less vehemently or comprehensively, many scholars have turned to searching inquiries about the meaning of democracy and the appropriateness of applying this term to the United States.

Diverse in membership and spirit, divided on objectives and methods, these contemporary critics nevertheless cite some common indictments of the United States to fortify their claim that it is undemocratic.[50] One argument alleges that the United States has always emphasized *procedural* democracy at the expense of *substantive* democracy: although we may have majority elections, trial by jury, due process, and other procedures that are supposedly democratic, these do not add up to equal opportunities for life, liberty, or the pursuit of happiness for all Americans. Thus, the argument concludes, the political rules, however democratic in theory, do not produce a real democracy of opportunity and security for all Americans. Another indictment points to the American capitalist economic system. Critics argue that, whatever the faults in our political order, true democracy cannot be produced by tinkering with the political system to make it more responsive; rather, economic considerations are fundamental. The capitalist system, these critics charge, discriminates against the poor and remains antagonistic to their needs because it serves the middle and upper classes; the political system merely serves the economic order. It is the economic system

Theory (New Haven: Yale University Press, 1956); Seymour M. Lipset, *Political Man* (New York: Doubleday & Co., 1960), p. 45; and Deane E. Neubauer, "Some Conditions of Democracy," *American Political Science Review* (December 1967), pp. 1002–1009.

[50] An interesting critique of American "liberal" democracy suitable for beginning students is Robert Wolff, *The Poverty of Liberalism* (New York: Bobbs-Merrill Co., 1969); more advanced students will find Theodore Lowi, *The End of Liberalism* (New York: W. W. Norton & Co., 1970), interesting and comprehensive.

which therefore must be radically transformed if all men are to live in freedom and justice.[51]

In various ways, these arguments reject some of the traditional reasons the United States and other nations have been labelled democracies. Ultimately, arguments over the degree of democracy in the United States or elsewhere will rest— as political judgments often do—upon definitions of terms and disagreements over the facts of political life. We have attempted only to explain how the United States and other nations have traditionally been classified as democracies and to explore briefly some objections to this procedure.

The Conditions of Democracy

Compared to the thousands of societies of which we have records, democracies have never been numerous; fewer than 25 nations, by the most generous estimate, can be called democratic today by traditional standards. In recent years, the conditions that promote or inhibit democratic regimes have been pondered by social scientists and national political leaders; our whole foreign aid program in the years immediately following World War II was based, among other considerations, on a theory that political democracy was untenable without a sufficient economic foundation. Hence we launched our programs for the economic reconstruction of Europe and the development of Asia in the hope of creating conditions congenial to the rise of a democratic political order.

Still, as Hans Morgenthau has often remarked, democracy is not a piece of plumbing that can be installed in any national household. Debates continue, still quite inconclusively, over what conditions are most advantageous for a democratic order. Is it economic prosperity? A large middle class? The way in which individuals are politically socialized? We can suggest only a few of the answers to these problems, answers which are frequently stated and therefore merit consideration.

Economic Development

Many social scientists believe that democracy is strongly related to economic development. Seymour Lipset stated the matter succinctly: "The more well-to-do a nation, the greater the chances that it will sustain democracy."[52] Generally, most comparative studies indicate that economic prosperity—which means,

---

[51] See, for example, Michael Harrington, *Towards a New Democratic Left* (New York: Penguin Books, 1969).

[52] Lipset, *op. cit.*, p. 48.

essentially, industrialization—does correlate reasonably well with having a democratic system. But industrialization and prosperity are a threshold phenomenon for democracy; industrialization may be a prerequisite for the existence of democracy but other conditions are necessary as well. A modern Germany until the end of World War II and the Soviet Union amply illustrate this. Still, the fact that most democratic nations are industrialized strongly implies that the association between industrialization and democracy is not purely accidental.

Several reasons indicate why industrialization and democracy may be related. First, industrialization produces cultural pluralism. Many large, well-organized and economically potent interests form into groups to compete with government for power and influence; these countervailing power groups activate individuals, define political interests, inform individuals about political life, and otherwise energize citizens to participate actively in political life. Furthermore, such groups provide access to the political system for many individuals who might not otherwise have any direct means of influencing the government. Also, group activity is a way of manifesting cleavages and problems within a society and eliciting governmental responses.

Second, many social scientists believe that industrialization produces the individual economic security that moderates political conflict and creates a stake in the system. Robert Lane has stated this position clearly:

> . . . the economy must provide some degree of economic independence for those granted the franchise. And for the system of government based upon a broad franchise to endure, there must be a general lack of frustration or at least the possibility of achievement consequent with aspiration.[53]

A society capable of producing abundant goods and prosperous living conditions is likely to encourage bargaining and compromise; the economic pie is ample enough to be divided in ways that permits many significant segments of society to enjoy at least a portion of the goods and services to be enjoyed—and to hope for more in the future. The society, in brief, can afford to deal everyone in. In contrast, a society in which there is little give in the economy, where each confrontation between clashing economic interests can result only in one group getting almost everything and the other nothing, means a society where postponement of demands, compromise, and tolerance for competing economic interests is extremely difficult; each conflict becomes a crisis in which group survival may be the issue. Even in an industrialized society, competing groups may not necessarily divide the economic pie so that the most important interests gain a satisfactory share. But without the *possibility* of such a solution, democracy is precarious indeed.

---

[53] Lane, *op. cit.,* p. 37.

Finally, industrialization is associated with the growth of the middle class which has traditionally been the foundation of democratic politics. A middle class usually represents a stabilizing element in democratic systems. Earning well-above-marginal incomes and aspiring to the condition of the rich, the middle class is a numerical majority in most democracies. The middle class usually enjoys enough of the system's material rewards to prevent it from rejecting the status quo; furthermore, democracy was the vehicle through which the middle class initially gained its comfortable economic position in most western nations. Historically, it has been the middle class that first clamored for greater democracy in industrializing nations. With industrialization, the middle class became numerous and vocal. The factories of England, where the industrial revolution began, produced the owners and managers, the bankers and technicians whose wealth and status depended on the system. Growing prosperous and numerous, they gradually forced the king and parliament to grant them representation in government by turning the democratic ideology against the landed aristocracy of England. The terms of democratic politics were defined by the middle class in such a way that "democracy" meant primarily *middle-class* democracy: "The democratic heaven, in no matter whose vision, is a society of gentlemen, every one, and all in good broadcloth suits."[54] In other words, the ideal society would differ from England's existing one because everyone would approach the middle class ideal: one would be a gentleman (not a lord, and not a pauper); one would dress in broadcloth (not rags, not brocades).

Education

Education, too, may be related to democracy. Almost all the modern democratic nations have high literacy rates, usually in excess of 90 percent of the population. Several reasons are customarily given for the dependence of democracy upon education. Education appears to broaden an individual's understanding of his society and the world, discourages reliance on overly simple, trite explanations of life and politics. Democracy emphasizes partial solutions, delayed gratifications, the normality of domestic conflict and the necessity to tolerate it, plus the importance of respecting the political rights of others; to accept these conditions requires a sophistication not usually found among the uneducated. Education is, furthermore, associated in almost all societies with income, social status, and economic security. The better educated a man is, the more likely he is to have a decent income and the hope for advancement within his society. Such an individual is less likely to believe the political system is an oppressive mechanism whose grinding demands can be overturned only by

---

[54] Mark Roelofs, *The Language of Modern Politics* (Homewood, Ill.: Dorsey Press, 1967), p. 185.

revolution. Finally, democratic politics rests upon the assumption that men can and will inform themselves about political matters and express their judgment through the political process. Education increases a feeling of competence regarding political matters, an awareness of political issues and officials, and a belief that one can achieve important rewards through politics. Comparative studies of voting and political participation have demonstrated that education is a primary indicator of political activism; the better educated a man is, the more likely he is to become a political participant. Without high rates of political participation—even if expressed only in voting—democracy is untenable. The man who lives with rats and lice, whose ability to earn daily bread is never assured, who has neither the skills nor the knowledge to change his environment or his own condition is a poor candidate for a democratic citizen.

Finally, education can produce a sound skepticism of the "exaggerated language, the substanceless promises, and the emotion-tapping appeals of politicians who are avoiding hard realities and disciplined reasoning."[55] Education tends to encourage a mental outlook on life and politics that sees complexity, that resists oversimplification, and that holds a healthy reserve toward political promises that are part of responsible democratic citizenship.

Interest Groups and Parties

Many social scientists would add one more necessary condition for democratic politics: the existence of interest groups and competitive political parties. Among nations where a significant degree of democracy exists, at least 80 percent of them have many active, politically important interest groups. In contrast, among nondemocratic nations, less than 5 percent show evidence of such groups. There are about 100,000 voluntary associations in the United States; those representing the largest economic interests—business, labor, agriculture, and so forth—are deeply involved in the governmental process. Voluntary associations of all kinds deeply permeate American life. Arnold Rose notes, for instance, that almost two thirds of the Detroit population he studied belonged to some nonchurch groups. In Bennington, Vermont, a comparatively small town, an equally diverse associational life existed; 64 percent of the community sample studied reported membership in some voluntary associations besides a church.

Democracies also have competitive party systems in which at least two, and often more, political parties regularly promote candidates for governmental office and create sufficient support among the electorate to maintain at least some representation in government. Among the 22 western nations, 20 have a competitive party system compared to 23 among the 68 nonwestern countries.

---

55 Pye, *op. cit.*, p. 82.

Like a variety of politically effective interest groups, political parties with a continuing base in the electorate compete for members and powers and seek to involve citizens in political life. Competing parties dependent upon majorities for electoral success are constantly encouraged to mobilize the politically uninvolved, often the newly immigrated (as in the United States during the nineteenth century) or the numerous but economically or racially disadvantaged strata. In an important sense, competing political parties and interest groups constitute a noisy, often acrimonious, usually confusing, but effective counterweight to government; through their number and vigor, they are a catalyst to political involvement. While not always far-sighted and often narrowly selfish in their programs, they provide the means for large numbers of individuals to articulate their interests and define their stake in the political system.

From Models to the United States: A Transitional Note

This chapter has been a combined table of contents and a rough blueprint for the remainder of the book. We should add only a brief word about the applicability to the United States of the models we have discussed.

First, no political system, including that of the United States, will fit a model exactly. Political systems are mixed because some aspects of national political life will be somewhat different than a model might suggest they should be. For instance, in our model of a western political system we suggested that in western nations, public officials are bound in their behavior by impersonal laws rather than permitted to do as they wish according to whim or inspiration. This is true in a relative sense. Most often, the various political functions are conducted in western nations by understood legal formulas, but there are always exceptions. One relatively minor but instructive example occurs almost daily in the courts. Judges and juries are instructed to examine only the facts of a case and to conduct themselves as impartial arbiters but, in practice, judges and juries can be swayed by the personalities of lawyers and witnesses and the emotional leverage a courtroom actor might use on their thinking. Still, in western nations, legal precedents and procedures force judicial proceedings to conform to minimum standards considered to be fair and legal, and procedures exist to rectify abuse of this norm.

Second, a number of political systems may have the characteristics expected in a model but their forms, or manifestations, may be quite different. In the United States, the executive of the government represents the people because he is elected on the basis of nation-wide popular voting (allowing for the antique electoral college that still forces a technically indirect vote); his accession to office depends on his electoral strength. In parliamentary systems such as Great

Britain and France, the executive is a prime minister who is elected by the majority of the legislative body who, in turn, are directly elected by the people. Though both the president of the United States and the British prime minister are supposed to represent electoral majorities, they are placed in office by different procedures. This means that each political system within a broad category may have a somewhat different political formula—a different set of institutions and offices. However, for purposes of comparison, these systems must be viewed in terms of what is accomplished through the institutions.

Finally, models will change as information changes. All models are provisional; eventually, they yield to better insight and newer facts. Thus, our models are not The Truth nor are they satisfactory to all experts on political matters. The attempt to understand political life forces one to accept change and limited vision as inevitable, if not always welcome, companions.

3

America in World Affairs

The total estimated American nuclear stockpile in 1962 was approximately equal to 35 kilomegatons or 35 billion tons of TNT—"enough bang to provide 10 tons of explosive power for everyone in the world. In the form of TNT, this much explosive power would fill a string of freight cars stretching from the earth to the moon and back 15 times (about 240,000 miles each way)."[1] In 1968, upon leaving the White House, President Johnson disclosed that the United States had a nuclear fire power equivalent to 30,000 tons of TNT for every human being.[2] In six years, our fire power had thus multiplied 3,000 times! The Soviet Union's total stockpile at that time, while somewhat smaller, was enormous, too. The necessity to avoid a nuclear clash between the two superpowers in such a highly flammable world therefore needs little emphasis. However, we should remember that the maintenance of peace is the prerequisite for the survival of the United States and the enjoyment by most citizens of the American way of life. President Kennedy once said that in the opening hours of a nuclear war, 300 million people would die: 100 million Americans, 100 million Russians, and 100 million Europeans. A mistake in foreign policy, therefore,

---

[1] Arthur T. Hadley, *The Nation's Safety and Arms Control* (New York: Viking Press, 1961), p. 3.

[2] Lyndon B. Johnson, "In Quest of Peace," *Reader's Digest* (February 1969), p. 248.

could kill us, while a failure in domestic policy would be merely a setback.[3] He could not have stated more aptly or succinctly the reason we start our study of American politics with an examination of the external environment. The American political system is part of the larger international state system; it cannot therefore be discussed and analyzed as if it were a self-contained unit.

This system impinges on almost every phase of American life and politics. It has on occasion divided us deeply and made a mockery of the phrase "one nation, indivisible." And since the end of World War II, it has not allowed us to concentrate our attention and resources on the purposes of American society. In former President Johnson's words, "the agony and the cruelty of the American presidency in the last half of the twentieth century is that, whatever the purposes of its incumbent at home, the world will not permit the occupant of the office—nor the American people themselves—to attend the needs of this society without diversion."[4] Thus, Truman wanted a Fair Deal for the country but devoted most of his time to the reorientation of American foreign policy; Johnson sought the Great Society but was overwhelmed by the increasingly costly and unpopular war in Vietnam. By contrast, Presidents Eisenhower, Kennedy, and Nixon were primarily interested in foreign policy. That these three presidents were more concerned with foreign affairs rather than domestic matters testifies to the strength of the external pressures.

Johnson was the single exception to the post-Truman presidents in being primarily interested in domestic affairs and he became chief executive only because of an assassin's bullet. His fate shows what happens to a president whose principal orientation and experience were domestic. By concentrating his first two years in office on his domestic programs, pushing more significant social legislation through the Congress than any of his immediate predecessors, in addition to winning the 1964 presidential election, Johnson failed to grant foreign policy—and especially Vietnam, which had already become critical under Kennedy—the time it needed. Thus, he never had the opportunity to learn from his early mistakes, as Kennedy had after the abortive Bay of Pigs invasion of Cuba; foreign policy proved his undoing.

It would therefore seem only a slight exaggeration to say, as one political analyst has said, that in the post-World War II period, "foreign policy concerns tended to drive out domestic policy."[5] Perhaps it would be more accurate to say that domestic affairs were relegated to a secondary status during most of this period. Indeed, presidents tend to become so preoccupied with pressing foreign events, trying to understand them, calculating their possible effects upon United States' interests, formulating policies to deal with these urgent problems, and securing congressional and popular support for these policies whenever necessary, that even low-level external crises do not receive the attention they deserve.

---

[3] Arthur M. Schlesinger, Jr., *A Thousand Days* (New York: Fawcett World Library, 1967), p. 395.

[4] Johnson, *op. cit.,* p. 222.

[5] Aaron Wildavsky, "The Two Presidencies," *Trans*-action (December 1966), p. 8.

Consequently, they may escalate into full-fledged crises; then, and only then, do presidents give them their complete attention in order to defend the national interests and avoid a nuclear conflict.

Arthur Schlesinger, Jr., a Kennedy advisor, has called the American intervention in Vietnam an example of the triumph of the politics of inadvertence.[6] President Kennedy, he has remarked, was so busy with more pressing problems during 1961–1963 (mainly foreign problems such as Cuba, Berlin, Latin America, the preservation of our European alliance, nuclear testing, and the far more threatening Communist expansion in Laos), that the increasingly grave situation in Vietnam was never thoroughly examined and debated. Instead, American military "advisors" were committed to Vietnam on a piecemeal basis to help the South Vietnamese defeat the Vietcong; as the political and military situation continued to deteriorate, however, more advisors were sent until American power and prestige were so involved in South Vietnam by 1965 that President Johnson—whose foreign policy advisors were all Kennedy-appointed men—felt he could not allow a Vietcong victory. He began an even larger direct intervention with American forces. With this kind of competition for presidential attention, domestic problems are bound to suffer. During the summer of 1963, Secretary of the Interior Stewart Udall tried to talk to President Kennedy about conservation but remarked, "He's imprisoned by Berlin,"[7] eloquent testimony indeed to the domination of foreign policy considerations because of the great danger of war; conservation was bound to take second place to conserving the nation. "That son of a bitch [Khrushchev] won't pay any attention to words," Kennedy remarked bitterly about Berlin. "He has to see you move."[8] It was deciding which moves to make that imprisoned the president.

Domestic affairs in these circumstances intruded primarily when they, too, became critical, as they did after years of neglect and insufficient intellectual and economic resources; increasingly during the 1960s, attention was drawn to domestic problems, and their urgency was emphasized by dramatic, even violent, activity. Indeed, at times it seemed as if only violence would attract attention and perhaps bring results to them. So, 100 years after the Civil War, the lot of American blacks was brought before the nation's consciousness and conscience first by nonviolent resistance and then by rioting, burning, looting, militant demands for Black Power, and the calling out of troops to maintain law and order. The vehement opposition of many younger people, especially college students, to the war in Vietnam also symbolized the demand for less involvement abroad and more attention to such domestic issues as racial injustice and poverty and, more broadly, the creation of a society fully consistent with America's repeatedly self-professed virtues. The question is, why did it take a Vietnam and a protracted, costly, and seemingly endless conflict, plus numerous protest

---

[6] Arthur M. Schlesinger, Jr., *The Bitter Heritage* (New York: Fawcett World Library, 1967), p. 47.

[7] Schlesinger, *A Thousand Days,* p. 363.

[8] *Ibid.*

marches and seizures of college administration buildings, to raise explicitly and publicly the fundamental issue of the priorities of foreign and domestic policies? Why, indeed, had foreign policy been given such primacy for most of the post-war years? The answers will be clearer after an examination of first, a model of the state system and second, the domestic sources of foreign policy.

The State System and the Balance of Power

The cornerstone and first characteristic of the state system is the nation-state. The number of these national political units has more than doubled since 1945. When the United Nations was founded that year, it had 51 members, most of whom were from Europe or related areas, such as the white British Commonwealth countries. Twenty-five years later, there were over 120 members; whereas originally there were only 9 Asian and 3 African countries, the new ex-colonial nations now constituted a majority of the international organization's General Assembly. The number of Latin-American states has stayed nearly constant. Admittedly, there have been some countertrends to this proliferation of nation-states: the establishment of a universal organization like the United Nations, whose membership includes most existing states, tends to make nation-states act together in various blocs; regional organizations like the Arab League and Organization of African States do the same. But the United Nations remains an institution which, like the international system, is composed of individual states and, by and large, therefore reflects their conflicts and tensions. It is certainly not a supranational organization with a will and power of its own transcending those of its members. Nor is it likely to become a world government in our time. The African and Arab states' attempts to work more closely together on a regional basis have produced only limited successes; one reason for this is that cooperation has been hampered by traditional national rivalries and jealousies.

Only in western Europe has there been a serious move toward supranational organization of the continental nations. Starting with the integration of the coal and steel sections of their economies, West Germany, France, Italy, and the Benelux countries (Belgium, the Netherlands, and Luxembourg) have moved more and more toward a common market in all areas of their economies. The "spill-over" of integration from the economic to the political sphere has lagged behind, however; while supranational institutions were founded and vested with authority, the trend toward a federal government for the Inner Six slowed in the late 1950s.[9] Yet attitudinal changes within Europe, particularly on the part of

---

[9] Karl W. Deutsch *et al., France, Germany, and the Western Alliance* (New York: Charles Scribner's, 1967).

youth,[10] the continuing publicly expressed desire of all six partners for a more politically unified Europe, the desire of England to enter the Common Market after she had remained aloof from the continent for over a decade, and the abdication of French President de Gaulle, who throughout the 1960s vigorously opposed further moves toward a federal European state, are hopeful signs for the future. But at the moment, the states of Europe remain sovereign, each acting according to its specific national interest.

The second characteristic of the state system distinguishing it from western democratic political systems is the absence of both a central government which makes legitimate policy decisions and a single political culture.[11] Their absence is a primary reason why one so often hears it said that international conflicts are settled with the bullet while domestically they are resolved by the ballot. This distinction is, to be sure, oversimplified. Not all quarrels between states lead to war; most are settled without using even the threat of violence. Nor are all domestic clashes of interest resolved without force or violent disturbance, even within western political systems.

Yet, the bullet-ballot analogy is valid to a degree. A brief look at the differences between the national and international systems will tell us why. In western systems, an executive branch of government administers and enforces the law. The significant point about the executive branch is that it normally holds a preponderance, if not a monopoly, of organized violence with which it can legitimately implement the law, protect society, and discourage potential rebels. The executive controls the armed forces and national police and it disarms the citizens of the nation by regulating the ownership of arms and forbidding the existence of private or party paramilitary forces. Domestic peace is, therefore, always armed. If the executive loses this superiority of power—either because all or part of the army deserts and refuses to support it, as in pre-Hitler Germany or pre-Franco Spain, or because other political parties arise which possess their own armed forces, as the Nazis or Communist Chinese did—the government may be challenged and the nation plunged into civil war.

Western political systems also institutionalize a legislative channel through which conflicts of interest within a society, articulated by political parties and interest groups, can be channeled and resolved peacefully. The significance of the process of legislation is that law-making is essentially synonymous with the issue of domestic war and peace. The most controversial, significant, and bitter conflicts in society revolve around the question of what the law should be. Should blacks be given full equality in American society, and should discrimination in interstate travel, housing, or employment be removed? Should the law

---

[10] Ron Inglehart, "An End to European Integration?" *American Political Science Review* (March 1967), pp. 91–105. For a cautious evaluation of future integration, see Leon N. Lindbergh and Stuart A. Scheingold, *Europe's Would-Be Polity* (Englewood Cliffs, N.J.: Prentice-Hall, 1970).

[11] Stanley Hoffmann, *Contemporary Theory in International Relations* (Englewood Cliffs, N.J.: Prentice-Hall, 1960), pp. 1–4.

provide some kind of help to the unemployed, aged, sick, or hungry? Should labor be allowed to bargain collectively? These questions pose major social issues, and they arouse strong passions. Yet they are unavoidable, for in a pluralistic society, new demands are continuously being advanced which must be satisfied to some degree if violence is to be avoided. If a political system does not permit peaceful changes, it will sooner or later erupt in revolution. It must either meet important aspirations of rising and discontented new strata in society or confront violent upheaval. Then, even the executive branch's superiority of power cannot prevent the government's fall since the army and police are largely recruited from the dissatisfied sections of the population; and in the ultimate test of revolution, they are unlikely to suppress their own people.

Finally, a judiciary, together with the other institutions, helps maintain expectations of individual and social justice. Resort to violence, domestic or international, is normally a last resort. As long as hope remains that peaceful change is possible through existing political processes, rebellion will usually be avoided. But just as there is no international executive that can protect all states, or an international legislative authority that can provide for peaceful change, the state system lacks an international judiciary which, like the American judiciary and especially the Supreme Court, has the authority to help preserve this sense of justice.

The state system lacks both the effective political institutions that integrate and regulate the behavior of states as well as an international political culture which is comparable to the one existing within most western states. Individuals, especially the politically active within such countries, possess a number of common political values and attitudes, particularly toward such fundamental issues as the legitimacy of the government and the way in which major political decisions should be made. National politics is, therefore, conducted within a system whose members share, whether consciously or not, a high degree of allegiance and a socially sanctioned code of behavior which forbids certain types of actions which destroy law and order; nations conduct their public business according to widely understood rules of the game. States do not share such a common loyalty or identity with their system. Instead of broad agreement which buffers and limits areas of conflicts, the only common international values are survival and security which *maximize* division and conflict between nations. This kind of minimal international political culture can easily lead to a shredding of the whole social fabric—a Hobbesian "war of all against all." The principal systemic restraint and control is the power of other states; otherwise states are free to pursue their purposes. The basic condition of the system in these circumstances is therefore one of potential war among its members.[12]

---

[12] The domestic system in the United States assumes that people will generally obey the law voluntarily. This is clearly shown by the contrast between the limited number of policemen—the national, state, and local branches are certainly not large enough to deal with massive resistance to the law—and the number of men in the armed forces for use

This is because the third characteristic of the state system, in the absence of a common institutional structure and shared values besides survival, is its decentralized or anarchical environment. Man's highest secular loyalty being to the nation, policymakers of all states will be intensely committed to the maintenance of national security, the prerequisite for the enjoyment of the national values or way of life. If it is further correct that the external milieu is anarchical, posing a constant danger to this way of life, policy-makers responsible for protecting the nation will react fearfully against perceived threats to their country. For all states can rely only upon themselves for the protection of the national interests which their policy-makers articulate.

More specifically, we might say that states living in an environment in which none can acquire absolute security are bound to feel insecure and therefore feel compelled to reduce their sense of insecurity by enhancing their power. In Hobbes' words, in a state of nature—comparable to our state system—there is a "continual fear and danger of violent death. . . ."[13] It is the resulting mutual fear and suspicion which states harbor for one another that gives rise to the phenomenon of power politics. When a nation sees its neighbor as a potential foe, it will seek to prevent a possible attack upon itself by becoming a little stronger than its neighbor; the latter, in turn, also fearing an attack, feels that he must be stronger to ward off an attack or win if deterrence should fail. In the resulting atmosphere of "kill or be killed," states feel severely tempted to strike first lest they perish in a preventive attack. This only enhances their insecurity with the result that each feels compelled to acquire even greater power. As each subsequently watches its neighbor's power grow, however, the sense of insecurity recurs, compelling them to seek even more power. Each nation is thus trapped by the state system and its inherent security dilemma.[14] It is, in short, the nature of the system and not any alleged aggressive instinct[15] or desire for maximum power by man[16] which is therefore the cause for international conflict and war.

The final characteristic of the state system, following from the security and power problem confronted by all states, is that they pursue balance-of-power policies as the chief means of deterring potential attackers and assuring their

---

outside the United States. For an interesting analysis contrasting the willingness of governments to use force against other governments but their reluctance, if not unwillingness, to use them against their own populations, see E. E. Schattschneider, *Two Hundred Million Americans in Search of a Government* (New York: Holt, Rinehart and Winston, 1969), pp. 17–22.

[13] Thomas Hobbes, *Leviathan* (New York: E. P. Dutton & Co., 1950), p. 104; also, Stanley Hoffmann, *The State of War* (New York: Praeger, 1965).

[14] John Herz, *International Politics in the Atomic Age* (New York: Columbia University Press, 1959), p. 231.

[15] Konrad Lorenz, *On Aggression* (New York: Bantam Books, 1967).

[16] Hans Morgenthau, *Politics among Nations*, 4th ed. (New York: Alfred A. Knopf, 1967).

own independence.[17] The assumption of the balance of power, and the reason why it is employed, is the fear that if one nation were to gain a predominance of power, it might impose its will upon other states. In Arnold Wolfers' words:

> Under these conditions of anarchy the expectation of violence and even of annihilation is ever-present. To forget this and thus fail in the concern for enhanced power spells the doom of a state. This does not mean constant open warfare; expansion of power at the expense of others will not take place if there is enough counterpower to deter or to stop states from undertaking it. Although no state is interested in a mere balance of power, the efforts of all states to maximize power may lead to equilibrium. If and when that happens, there is "peace" or, more exactly, a condition of stalemate or truce. Under the conditions described here, this balancing-of-power process is the only available "peace" strategy.[18]

Power thus begets countervailing power, but note that the aim of a balance-of-power policy is to protect the security of each state, not the preservation of peace. To be sure, most states normally feel secure when they are at peace, but peace is the product of a balance acceptable to the leading powers because it assures their individual security. This is the reason that their preferences for peace are not unqualified and why, when they believe their security is endangered, they have historically sacrificed peace and fought. No major nation wants peace at any price.

The state system, in short, is a primitive political system whose primary feature is an anarchy moderated by a modicum of order imposed by the balance of power.[19] Its fundamental assumptions are: (1) that nation-states place a high value on national security in order to protect their political independence and territorial integrity; (2) that states will react fearfully against threats to their security and therefore seek to enhance their power; (3) that states are responsible only to themselves and self-help is the common and most fundamental rule of the game; and (4) that their relationship is determined by the interaction of their respective strengths. Policy-makers are aware of these assumptions, as well as the penalty the system will exact if they do not play power politics. A writer of the last century, Walter Bagehot, called these "the facts that live in the office [of policy makers]." The result, as a contemporary writer has stated it, is that

---

[17] Morton Kaplan, *Systems and Process in International Politics* (New York: John Wiley, 1964), pp. 22–36; Ernst Haas, "The Balance of Power: Prescription, Concept, or Propaganda," *World Politics* (July 1953), pp. 442–477; Inis L. Claude, *Power and International Relations* (New York: Random House, 1962), pp. 11–39.

[18] Arnold Wolfers, *Discord and Collaboration: Essays on International Politics* (Baltimore: The Johns Hopkins Press, 1962), p. 83.

[19] See Roger D. Masters, "World Politics as a Primitive System," *World Politics* (July 1964), pp. 595–619, for the suggestive analogy of a primitive stateless society.

Effective freedom in foreign affairs . . . is the capacity to choose between relatively few options. As in a card game, the government in foreign policies is dealt a hand of cards by circumstances. There is no freedom to play a card not in the hand. . . . Of the cards in the hand, there is always a card, possibly two, which is the "right card" to play in the prevailing state of the game. It is "right" in the sense that when the game is finished, all the hands known, and the entire history reconstructed, that card was the appropriate one to play in the circumstances given. . . . [the assumption is that] the player is out to win the game.[20]

The system, in other words, places constraints upon its members and presents them with only a limited number of options and, in some situations, no options at all. The degree of constraint and the foreign policy alternatives available to a state in responding to the external environment—and therefore, the available attention and resources which can be devoted to domestic purposes—depends on the particular distribution of power.

Extensive-Intensive Bipolarity and the Lack of Options

A bipolar balance, in which the major states are grouped around those two among them whose strength is so far superior that they are recognized as "superpowers," is the distribution in which national policy-makers perceive that they have the least choice.[21] Indeed, bipolarity leaves the principal adversaries feeling such a high degree of insecurity that they are virtually compelled to react against one another's external threats. The reason is that in such a distribution of power the balance is constantly at stake. Each superpower, fearing that its adversary will achieve hegemony, will be extremely sensitive to the slightest shifts of power. Neither can make what the other would consider an innocent move; each will see the other's move as a deliberate attempt to enhance its position and take counteraction. For, in this condition of what might almost be called institutionalized paranoia, a gain of power and security for one will be seen as a loss of power and security by the other. Each state's attention is therefore riveted upon its rival. When one pushes, the other feels he must push back.[22]

[20] F. S. Northedge (ed.), *The Foreign Policies of the Powers* (New York: Praeger, 1969), pp. 14–15.

[21] Kaplan, *op. cit.,* pp. 43–45; Raymond Aron, *Peace and War* (New York: Praeger, 1967), pp. 136–146.

[22] For an incisive analysis of the post-war bipolar system, see Kenneth N. Waltz, "The Stability of a Bipolar World," *Daedalus* (Summer 1964), pp. 881–909; and for a response,

The beginning of the Cold War is a case in point. The post-war American-Soviet rivalry after the disintegration of the wartime alliance against Germany was unavoidable. It was the threat of German hegemony over Europe that had brought the two nations together. The termination of this threat was bound to turn their attention to one another. The nature of the state system and the resultant security dilemma with which each nation had to cope meant—if our model is correct—that the two principal powers which emerged after Europe's collapse would wish to assure themselves a strong position for a possible future conflict. Thus Russia's actions immediately after the war were typical of a great power, irrespective of ideology: the conversion of Poland, Hungary, Bulgaria, Romania, and Albania into satellites (Yugoslavia was already under Tito's control and Czechoslovakia was living under the Red Army's shadow); the attempt to pressure first Iran, and then Turkey, into becoming satellites and sub-vert Greece by means of a guerrilla war.

Russia was bound to feel fearful in terms of the system's norms of behavior. She had, after all, been defeated by Imperial Germany during World War I and almost defeated again by Nazi Germany twenty-four years later. These twentieth century experiences had reinforced a fear of invasion and defeat which had existed even before the nineteenth century. This left Russia—a nation which, unlike the United States or Great Braitain, possessed no natural frontiers to protect her—with a double legacy: internally, the establishment of an authoritarian government which sought to centralize power for better defense and greater security; externally, a defensive expansionism to obtain security beyond her frontiers.[23]

Ironically, the nation to which Russia attributed enmity was the one major country in the state system which, as a result of its isolationism and lack of socialization in power politics, had during World War II expressed sentiments of good will and amity in great volume—and therefore taken no precautionary measures, as it should have done in terms of systemic behavior, against the possibility of a future conflict with the Soviet Union. Quite to the contrary, American thinking on foreign affairs believed that a harmony among nations, producing peace, was the normal condition of the state system, and regarded conflict and war as abnormalities; that the use of power, and especially of violence, was immoral and to be used only by authoritarian states; that democracies used force solely for the moral purpose of defeating and punishing aggressors; and that other countries who joined this nation in such a crusade were equally moral, selfless, and "peace-loving."[24] Thus the dissolution of the

---

Richard N. Rosecrance, "Bipolarity, Multipolarity, and the Future," *The Journal of Conflict Resolution* (September 1966), pp. 314–327.

[23] Louis J. Halle, *The Cold War as History* (New York: Harper & Row, Publishers, 1967), pp. 10–19. For the various ways in which Soviet foreign policy may be interpreted, see Richard F. Rosser, *An Introduction to Soviet Foreign Policy* (Englewood Cliffs, N.J.: Prentice-Hall, 1969), pp. 15–38.

[24] See below for discussion of the impact of domestic attitudes toward foreign policy, as well as some of the revisionist histories of American-Soviet relations during this period.

wartime alliance with the Soviet Union was unexpected and proved to be a shock. But it left this country no choice but to establish a new post-war balance.

The resulting bipolar confrontation confirmed the high degree to which external pressures "determined" state behavior. It was, first of all, an extensive confrontation because the Soviet challenges and American responses were global. Soviet pressure on Turkey and communist guerrillas seeking to overthrow the Greek government led to the Truman Doctrine in 1947. The imposition of Soviet control on eastern Europe, dramatized by the Czech *coup d'état* in 1948, led to the Marshall Plan for the economic reconstruction of western Europe and the formation of the North Atlantic Treaty Organization under which the United States for the first time committed itself formally in peacetime to the preservation of the European balance of power. The American plan to form a West German government led the Soviets to initiate the Berlin Blockade to drive the United States out of West Berlin and undermine the credibility of American power; in turn, this resulted in the famous airlift to sustain the western half of the city and the western powers' presence there.

The attack upon South Korea in 1950 led to the American military intervention to save the Republic of Korea. When victory over the North Korean forces tempted the United States to cross into North Korea, destroy the communist regime, and unify Korea under American auspices, Russia's new ally, Communist China, intervened to save her neighbor and protect her own security. The war thus ended where it had started—at the 38th parallel. In Indochina, now called Vietnam, the United States was at first unsympathetic to France's attempt to reimpose its prewar colonial control (which also compelled all genuine Vietnamese nationalists to join the communist-controlled Vietminh in the common fight to gain independence from France). But after the outbreak of the Korean War, Washington sent large-scale military and economic aid to the French in their losing fight. Anti-communism took priority over self-proclaimed support of anti-colonialism. As France's defeat became a certainty in 1954, we threatened intervention to prevent the loss of the "gateway" to Southeast Asia; and after the subsequent division of the country into North and South Vietnam, we extended American protection to the latter. The result of these challenges and responses, from Berlin to Cuba and Quemoy-Matsu to Vietnam, was the drawing of lines, or frontiers, between the Soviet and American-led spheres; in this manner, "hands off" or "cross at your own risk" signs were posted around the world to avoid possible miscalculations which might ignite the highly combustible post-war system.

Second, this confrontation was intensive as each superpower, fearful of the slightest change of the balance, searched for allies. The United States has often been accused of suffering from "pactomania," of indiscriminately collecting allies, whether they are strategically located or not, strong or weak, developed or underdeveloped. NATO in Europe, METO in the Middle East (with which we are clearly associated even though it is officially led by Britain), SEATO in

Southeast Asia and ANZUS (Australia and New Zealand), plus defense treaties with Nationalist China and Japan, have all been a means of drawing the Cold War frontiers, granting the United States the right to intervene unilaterally if an area is attacked, and in one case—that of NATO—to add the organization's potentially great power to our own. Russia's Warsaw Pact with eastern European countries and the Sino-Soviet Treaty, prior to its schism, suggests that the Soviet Union, too, has been concerned with finding allies. However, as a state whose primary relations with other communist countries are at the party rather than state level, the Soviet Union has not been quite as compulsive in seeking allies as the United States.

The particularly striking feature of the two superpowers' principal alliances, NATO and the Sino-Soviet alliance, was their cohesiveness during the first decade of the Cold War. Indeed, it was common to refer to them as "blocs" as if each were a single actor, a center of political decision, military organization, and diplomatic cooperation. America's European partners were exhausted from World War II and were completely dependent upon the United States for economic aid and military protection. They were therefore willing to subordinate themselves to the needs of the alliance and accept American political and military direction, even though they were not always in agreement with specific American policies. Similarly, Communist China was willing to acquiesce to Soviet leadership. The Chinese, like the Soviets, defined the United States as their principal enemy, and therefore sought only to strengthen and unify this bloc in the common struggle against American imperialism. During this period, therefore, Washington saw the communist world as a monolith. It opposed any communist extension of power anywhere in the world, even in Korea and Vietnam, for in the intensive bipolarity existing during the first decade of the Cold War such an extension would have been equivalent to an extension of Soviet power.

A third feature of this intensive bipolar confrontation was that each superpower was sensitive to any actual or attempted defections from their blocs. Each bloc was to be guarded from within; bloc loyalty was to be assured. The communists excluded all noncommunist parties from power throughout the entire Sino-Soviet bloc. The western nations excluded all communist parties from power after the Cold War began, and subsequently the United States frequently intervened in European and other elections by publicly declaring which party it favored. Where defections occurred, or threatened to occur, counteraction was taken. Thus the Central Intelligence Agency organized the overthrow of what was asserted to be a pro-communist government in Guatemala, and tried unsuccessfully to overthrow Castro in 1961 by organizing an invasion of Cuba by a refugee force. Four years later, the United States landed troops in the Dominican Republic to prevent a possible victory of what the Johnson administration called "Castro Communists." Earlier, in 1956, the CIA supported South Vietnam's refusal to participate in the country-wide election stipulated by the

1954 Geneva Agreements because it feared that Ho Chi Minh could win a popular election because of his identification with Vietnamese nationalism. Similarly, the Soviets in 1948 seized control of Czechoslovakia to "fill out" their eastern security belt, suppressed the East German revolt in 1953, threatened to intervene in Poland three years later, and did intervene in Hungary in that year and in Czechoslovakia in 1968 when the communist regimes in these countries seemed unable or unwilling to preserve their monopoly of power and stay in the Warsaw Pact. The Soviets have also refused to permit the East German population to express its opinions in a free election on the issue of reunification with West Germany; and the 1945 Yalta obligation to permit such elections in the other countries of eastern Europe has simply been ignored. Finally, the American-led attempt to eliminate the North Korean regime precipitated Communist China's intervention, just as the North Vietnamese–directed effort to take over South Vietnam led to American counteraction.[25]

The intensity of the bipolar struggle was, however, most dramatically visible in the military sphere, because the precariousness of the balance was bound to render the two superpowers sensitive to any changes in military strength. The change in nuclear technology, in fact, rendered them hypersensitive since it fundamentally changed the manner in which military strength could be employed. Historically, force has been used either to deter wars or, once wars had erupted, to win them. But in prenuclear times when no weapons were so destructive that their employment threatened their user with extinction, the crucial test of military strategy had not been the prevention of hostilities but the ability to achieve victory once they had erupted. The gains to be won outweighed the costs of fighting. War was therefore considered a rational instrument of national policy. Nuclear arms, however, threatened the very substance of life which military force was supposed to protect. Total war thus became suicidal and irrational, resulting in a shift in emphasis of military policy to deterrence. This meant threatening the enemy with virtually total destruction so he would be convinced at all times that the consequences of an attack would be wholly disproportionate to any conceivable gains. Only in this way could deterrence be made permanent; the one mistake—which would be one too many—could be avoided. The result is a paradox: military power has to be strong in order *not* to be employed. The test of strategy becomes the prevention of war; the outbreak of an all-out war would signal the failure of strategy.

Each of the two superpowers must therefore constantly concern itself with maintaining its offensive superiority since its adversary must never doubt that he can be destroyed. Because each is continuously trying to devise new defensive weapons to improve his protective capacity, the maintenance of an offensive edge demands sustained effort. In these circumstances, both powers tend to be consumed by the constant fear that a technological break-through would grant

---

[25] Douglas Pike, *Vietcong* (Cambridge: Massachusetts Institute of Technology Press, 1966), and Bernard Fall, *Vietnam Witness, 1953–66* (New York: Praeger, 1966).

its opponent a temporary advantage that could be exploited to end the conflict on his terms. Since both are highly industrialized nations with sophisticated technological knowledge, this possibility of a breakthrough is seen as a very real threat by each protagonist. And rightly so. For the marriage of such knowledge to intense mutual fear leads to a fantastically large investment of resources and skills in the development of ever newer arms, in order to keep the offensive ahead of the defense and, on the other hand, for the defense to try and catch up with the offense. Thus the proverbial arms race becomes a series of arms races as technology constantly devises new weapons. Warner Schilling has commented upon this continuous technological change as follows:

> As the United States and the Soviet Union throw one weapons system after another into the effort to maintain at least a balance of terror, neither dares fall behind in either the discovery of new physical relationships or in the application of scientific knowledge to military hardware and political-military strategy. Thus, by the end of the first decade of the Cold War, about 50 percent of the engineers in the United States and 25 percent of the scientists were employed by the federal government, either directly or on contract, and about 65 percent of the scientific research in universities and 57 percent of that in private industry was government-financed.[26]

The resulting rapidity of offensive weapons changes, for instance, has been truly remarkable. The Flying Fortress airplane of World War II fame, for example, was in production at the beginning of war; and it was still the backbone of the Army Air Force at the conclusion of that conflict. The Superfortress, which made its appearance toward the end of that war and dropped the atomic bombs on Japan, soon became obsolete and had to be replaced by the intercontinental range B-36; it, too, rather rapidly became obsolete as faster Soviet fighters came into service. Thus, pure jet bombers were required to implement deterrence; the B-47 and B-52 met this need. The former was retired after about a decade, the latter survived in ever dwindling numbers into the 1970s. But by the late 1960s, the backbone of deterrence was the intercontinental missile, which also went through several technological changes: liquid fuel to solid fuel and from a small, single warhead with a small payload—less than one megaton —to a larger payload, to multiple warheads. Each new weapon, of course, cost more than its predecessor with the result that these arms races became ever increasing financial burdens for both superpowers. Yet in the extensive and intensive bipolar system, the superpowers felt that they had little, if any, choice about what they had to do to preserve the balance of power.

---

[26] Warner R. Schilling, "Scientists, Foreign Policy, and Politics," *The American Political Science Review* (June 1962), p. 288.

Relaxed Bipolarity
and Policy Alternatives

It is difficult to pinpoint the exact moment when the extensive and intensive bipolarity of the early Cold War period began to change. It could be dated from 1957 when the Soviet Union tested the first ICBM. In any event, it was certainly clear after the Cuban Missile Crisis in 1962 that a fundamental change had occurred in the state system and that, while the Soviet Union and the United States remained the only superpowers, other nations were again more active, playing international politics as independent centers of foreign policy decisions. Some observers have called this new system multipolar or polycentric, but this is probably inaccurate since it suggests the existence of about six approximately equal powers, as before World Wars I and II. Others have somewhat more correctly called it bi-multipolar[27] or loose bipolar,[28] thereby emphasizing the continued ascendance of the two nuclear giants but not minimizing the new and increasingly complex diplomatic relationships; we have chosen to call it relaxed bipolarity. After first noting the nature of some of the principal systemic changes, we shall see why they offered policy-makers a greater choice in the foreign policies they could adopt.

Paradoxically, it was the increasing awareness of the dangers of bipolar confrontation and nuclear war which moderated the Cold War and changed the behavior of the United States and the Soviet Union. Both superpowers drew the same conclusion from their common fate of being, in Robert Oppenheimer's words, "two scorpions in a bottle." The conclusion that the principal inventor of the atom bomb drew was that both had every reason to avoid stinging one another. By 1955, President Eisenhower recognized this and proclaimed that there was "no alternative to peace": shortly thereafter, Khrushchev, the new Soviet leader, declared that Lenin's prophecy of an inevitable war between communism and capitalism had been outmoded by modern technology. The leaders of both nations, in brief, recognized the starkness of their alternatives: coexistence or nonexistence. Thus, Russia and America became increasingly cautious in their external behavior as they realized that the crucial issue was not their ability to mobilize their power but to exercise it with restraint. After their "eyeball to eyeball" confrontation over Cuba during 1962 had brought this lesson home to both of them, they transformed their new-found common awareness of the catastrophe of nuclear warfare into the realization that they had a common stake in the preservation of peace and needed to cooperate with one another for the purpose of arms control.

---

[27] Rosecrance, *op. cit.*
[28] Kaplan, *op. cit.;* also Aron, *op. cit.,* pp. 128–136.

More specifically, the two powers established a "hot line" between the White House and the Kremlin for instant communication during crises, a limited ban on testing nuclear weapons, a prohibition against orbiting nuclear weapons in space or, proliferating them to other nations. In the realm of strategy, they sought to stabilize mutual deterrence. This was not easy. Their hostility to one another and need to protect themselves continued to inspire mutual fear and grip them in an action-reaction arms cycle. If one side saw the other as offensively superior and sought increased protection and enhanced deterrence with anti-ballistic missiles, the other interpreted such an increased defensive capacity as an offensive threat because it might weaken his own deterrent capability. He therefore also sought ABMs to ensure that enough of his retaliatory force would survive an initial enemy strike, irrespective of the size of the attacking force. At the same time, the ABM build-up had the feedback result that further accumulation of missiles with multiple warheads seemed necessary; each side felt he needed more missiles to penetrate the enemy defenses to deliver his retaliatory blow.

Simultaneously, both superpowers had to confront the danger of a large-scale deployment of new offensive and defensive arms and the possibility that in the resulting atmosphere of uncertainty, miscalculation or fear by one or the other nation that the balance of power was turning against it, might result in a military clash. In addition, there was the factor of the fantastic, yet ever-mounting, costs of new weapons and an increased awareness of the need for resources for nonmilitary purposes. The United States and Soviet Union therefore decided to negotiate to see whether an agreement limiting their respective offensive and defensive arms was possible *before* embarking on their massive production and deployment. This would have been inconceivable in the days of intensive bipolarity; the mutual distrust would have been too high and the great fear each had of the other would not have allowed for a delay and time for diplomacy. By the late 1960s, however, American and Soviet leaders were far more conscious of the degree to which their common interests cut across their continuing conflicts.[29]

Nothing symbolized this new relationship more clearly than each super-power's discipline of its allies, as well as its own abstinence from actions which might jeopardize the peace. Thus, the United States restrained Nationalist Chinese forces on Formosa from attacking the mainland; it did not intervene in Hungary in 1956, or in Czechoslovakia in 1968 to help the anti-Soviet revolts; it compelled its two closest allies, Britain and France, to halt their attack upon Egypt during the Suez War; it negotiated with Moscow bilaterally over such tense issues as Berlin even when its major allies were opposed to such negotiation; and it signed the limited test ban and negotiated the antiproliferation treaty despite the open opposition of France and, in the latter case, the reluctance of

---

[29] President Nixon's speech on the ABM, *The New York Times,* March 15, 1969.

West Germany. Similarly, the Soviets refused to extend their nuclear umbrella over Chinese Communist efforts to capture Formosa; they vehemently opposed Peking's attacks upon India during the early 1960s and, to China's rage, supported India diplomatically and sent her military supplies; they did not allow the Arab-Israeli War of 1967 to turn into a direct clash with the United States, although the Arabs attempted to do so in order to avoid defeat; despite Vietnam, Moscow's accusations of Washington as a warmonger were on the whole mild and she continued to improve her bilateral relations with us; and in Latin-America, she opposed Castro's strategy of attempting to overthrow governments through guerrilla warfare.

Stabilizing the military environment, and therefore lowering the international tensions so that sparks in this highly flammable world would not ignite it, was thus part of the new pattern of Soviet-American relations. Admittedly, it was not the total pattern. The two superpowers continued to have major conflicts which could cut across their limited cooperation: arms negotiations could fail and another cycle of new weapons build-ups could occur; quarrels such as the one between Israel and Egypt, in which the Soviet Union seeks to exploit the Arab countries' nationalism and anti-American animus to dislodge western influence and substitute its own, are bound to test the new cooperation severely at times. There will undoubtedly be failures and setbacks. Yet it is this trend of cooperation, so different from the pattern of intense hostility of the first decade of the Cold War, which is significant.

This trend, in turn, started eroding America's principal alliance, NATO. Our partners had become apprehensive that the United States might have become so intimidated by the risk of war that they could no longer count on Washington to protect them at the cost of Washington's own immolation. The United States had pledged itself to Europe's security at a time when it possessed an atomic monopoly and therefore could not be attacked. The fact that Britain and France built small nuclear deterrents of their own, and that West Germany sought a greater voice in the use of the American deterrent testified to their doubts about the protection they might receive in future confrontations in Europe. Similarly, the Chinese, who had wished to preserve a united communist bloc (whose combined strength would be militantly exerted against American imperialism), saw their chief reason for Sino-Soviet unity disappear as American-Soviet tensions declined. It was only at this point that Peking charged Moscow with pursuing a "no-win" policy, thereby betraying the international communist cause through cowardice, and raising the question of Sino-Soviet boundaries of the Chinese territories seized by the Tsars and still held by the Soviet Union. In brief, the principal western allies on one hand and China on the other felt that their interests, as they defined them, had become increasingly subordinated to the strategic caution of their respective superpower.

This erosion was furthered by the determination of the allies to cast off their subordinate status. When NATO was founded, Europe was weak and exhausted;

the alliance was founded upon an unequal distribution of power. It was inevitable, therefore, that as the European states regained their economic health and political self-confidence, they would react against American domination and reject playing an inferior role within the alliance. Indeed, one of the original purposes of the movement for greater European unity and power was that it would provide an alternative to remaining subservient to the United States and without much influence in the NATO area or in the wider state system. China and the countries of eastern Europe also rebelled against their subsidiary status. As the first communist state, the Soviet Union had long controlled the international communist movement; it was used to giving directions. The rise of communist states not controlled by Moscow, such as Yugoslavia and China, undermined this capacity to command as they rejected Soviet control and determined to travel their "different roads to socialism." Even the Soviet satellite regimes began to assert a greater degree of internal autonomy and, in a number of cases, independence in foreign policy.

Thus, the days of extensive and intensive bipolarity had passed. But why does this new state system present American policy-makers with a greater choice of policies? The reason is that international tensions were generally lower and the relationships between enemies, as well as between allies, were more complex. The degree of security threat was no longer as intense and thus the policies that needed to be adopted were correspondingly less self-evident. Consequently, alternative policies were available. In the intensive bipolar system, for example, our intervention and increasing military commitment in Vietnam would not have become more of a major political issue than the Korean intervention; only how the war was being fought and the nature of the proclaimed political goals would, as in Korea, have become matters of controversy. In a system in which each alliance was still a cohesive bloc and each superpower highly sensitive to the slightest alteration of the balance, the United States would have equated a Vietcong victory with an extension of Soviet power. Whether the war in South Vietnam had started as a genuine civil war or as North Vietnamese aggression in the guise of a civil war would have been irrelevant. The basic issue would have been that a communist success would have been equated with a significant loss of American security. The loss of a client state we had helped create and to whom we had pledged our defense, however vaguely, would have been perceived as undermining the credibility of other American commitments, driving our allies into neutralism and possibly enticing the Soviets and Chinese into expansionist probes elsewhere.

But in a period of American-Soviet relaxation of tensions or detente and disintegrating alliances, policy-makers confronted a more complicated world. Was the war basically a civil war or disguised northern aggression? Would a win for the Vietcong be a gain for Russia, China, or neither one? Would a communist Vietnam with its great sense of national pride contain Peking's influence in southeast Asia or act in concert with Peking, or even alone, to extend communist influence further southward and eastward? Can guerrilla wars or "wars of national liberation," as communists call them, be "exported" to other lands or not? Would American security be diminished by a loss of South Vietnam, and by the possible loss of additional southeast Asian nations or not? If it were diminished, would the loss of security be relatively minor or sufficiently great to warrant American intervention? If so, with about how many troops and at what cost in life and money? Were conditions in South Vietnam ripe so that these forces could be successfully employed? One's answers to these and other questions depend upon one's perception of this more complex world, the origins of this war, the relationship of the Vietcong to Hanoi, Moscow, and Peking, the impact on American security, the costs to be paid for specific external gains, and the importance of domestic versus external problems. No wonder that the massive American intervention became a topic of fierce and widespread domestic debate among policy-makers and the general public; there was no obvious, single set of answers.[30]

Globalism had made sense as long as any communist expansion had meant an addition to Soviet strength. It was one thing to "fight communism" as long as there was only one communism to fight. But once communism was a many-splintered thing, was our extensive role as "world policeman" still necessary? When there were many communisms, we had to decide whether all communist states were still, in fact, our enemies or, at least, equally hostile to us. Which communism did we "fight" now? More specifically, what changes in the power distribution could we safely allow and where, if anywhere, did we still have to draw frontiers?[31] This was the crucial question. Relaxed bipolarity, it seemed, presented American policy-makers with some difficult questions to which there were alternative responses. It also presented them with the opportunity to reassess the issue of foreign and domestic priorities.

The Systemic Impact
upon Domestic Politics

Perhaps the most obvious effect of America's emergence as a world power into an intensive bipolar system was the relegation of domestic policies to a secondary status for most of the period since World War II. If American foreign policy was largely a response to a high degree of environmental threat, then the

[30] Schlesinger, *Bitter Harvest;* E. O. Reischauer, *Beyond Vietnam: The United States and Asia* (New York: Vintage Books, 1967), among many others.

[31] For further analysis of America's post-Vietnam role, see Chapter 14. Also see President Nixon's first annual foreign affairs message to Congress, entitled "United States Foreign Policy for the 1970s: A New Strategy for Peace." *The New York Times,* February 19, 1970.

priority of presidential attention and national resources which foreign policy received was hardly surprising. For the greater the perceived external security threat, the greater the disposition of a state to enhance its power. Guns, to simplify the matter somewhat, will take precedence over butter. The need for military strength and other elements which confer prestige and a reputation of power will then divert funds from domestic welfare programs. America's manned moon-landing on July 21, 1969—a dramatic example—testifies to the impact of power politics upon space exploration and the allocation of the nation's resources. Within a month of the abortive Bay of Pigs invasion of Cuba and Russia's placing Yuri Gagarin as the first man in orbit on April 12, 1961—two successive major blows to American prestige—President Kennedy declared that the United States would land a man on the moon and return him safely to earth "before this decade is out." A second-rate, second-place space effort by a nation whose prowess was in large part due to its technological capability, Kennedy felt, was hardly consistent with our historical tradition, our security, or our role as world leader. The Soviet achievement had excited universal admiration and had been acclaimed by Moscow as demonstrating the superiority of communism. The president's motivation was therefore clear: to beat the Russians, recoup the nation's—and his personal—prestige, show the world the superiority of American science and strength and, presumably, also of the American way of life. The lunar landing would demand the highest kind of national priority, including the diversion of scientific manpower and funds from other important projects. But in the context of American-Soviet rivalry, Kennedy felt the United States needed a "space program which promises dramatic results . . . (and) which we could win."[32] Eight years and $36.25 billion later—$23 billion of which went for manned space flight—the moon rocket dramatically lifted off from the John F. Kennedy Space Center in Florida.

On the other hand, when a nation no longer feels gravely threatened, it will have greater choice between the values it wishes to promote. Security will remain an important value but not necessarily the predominant one. Policy makers might choose to place greater stress on welfare by seeking to end poverty in this country or on democracy by promoting greater opportunities for racial minorities. This is why the bitter reaction to Vietnam, the more relaxed bipolarity of the 1960s, and the host of internal problems which had accumulated over a twenty year period (in good measure due to the primacy of foreign policy), could lead to demands that this priority be reexamined. Should Vietnam and more broadly, foreign policy in general, take precedence over the black revolution, war on poverty, education, health, crime, air and water pollution, and urban renewal; should these be further neglected if the quality of our life is thus lowered or if the social fabric uniting us as one people gradually disappears?

---

[32] Theodore Sorensen, *Kennedy* (New York: Bantam Books, 1966), pp. 589–596. For a detailed analysis, see John M. Logsdon, *We Should Go to the Moon: Space Policy and National Decision-Making* (Cambridge: Massachusetts Institute of Technology Press, 1970).

The contrast in spending, not only in the United States, but indeed on a global basis, between armaments and public education, for instance, was dramatically summed up by the U.S. Arms Control and Disarmament Agency in 1969: "The average annual expenditure per soldier, world-wide, is $7,800. For the estimated one billion young people in the world of school-age population (ages 5–19), public expenditures for education average $100 a year." In 1969, approximately 20 million people were in active duty in the world's military forces, 30 million were involved in military-related employment, and $185 billion was being spent on arms; only two thirds of this figure was going into public education, only one third into public health.[33] In any event, the increasing perception of domestic issues as America's number one problem was strongly underlined by the National Commission on the Causes and Prevention of Violence, also in 1969, when it insisted the major threat to the nation's security stemmed from internal causes rather than foreign aggression.

This changing mood about the nation's priorities—a mood sparked so dramatically by Vietnam on the one hand and racial and campus confrontations and violence on the other—was perhaps most dramatically expressed by the pre-convention presidential campaign of 1968 which was notable because it was the first such campaign since 1945 with little of the usual anti-communist rhetoric of politicians; instead, there was a widespread desire to end the war in Vietnam—if "honorable" terms could be negotiated—and for a concentration on our grave and divisive internal problems. Symbolically, President Johnson, who was identified with the war, announced he would not run for a second term. He withdrew after his nomination was contested by Senators Eugene McCarthy and Robert Kennedy, both of whom ran as "peace candidates" and thereby provided a rallying point for an increasingly large number of Americans disenchanted with the war. Conversely, Vice-President Humphrey, who became the Democrats' standard-bearer, was defensive about the war, both before and after his nomination; his inability as a member of the administration to disavow the war and strike his own "risk for peace" until late in the presidential campaign proved his greatest handicap. In these circumstances, former Vice-President Nixon, the leading Republican contender for the nomination and a long-time hawk, no longer found it expedient to charge the Democrats with a "no-win" policy and softened his views on the war. The menace abroad suddenly became the "moral decay" at home. In general, the candidates of both parties fell over themselves in their eagerness to abandon anti-communist slogans and the war, offering instead prescriptions for international peace and "law and order" at home.

After the election, this issue of national priorities became a primary struggle between the President and the Democratic Congress. The opposition came chiefly from liberal Democrats and moderates plus a number of similarly-minded Republicans who decided to battle President Nixon on the Safeguard ABM

---

[33] James Reston, *The New York Times,* November 19, 1969.

defense system and military spending in general. They sought sizable cuts in military appropriations and a far greater investment of resources in what was now widely recognized as a massive domestic crisis: on the one hand, they charged, we were paying farmers $3 billion a year not to plant food while seven million American children did not have enough to eat;[34] on the other hand, the nation was paying billions for an ABM system of perhaps doubtful utility and the development of a supersonic transport plane to speed very few people to London a couple of hours faster. The opposition demanded a greater shift in resources from external to internal purposes than the President had suggested in his first State of the Union message in 1970 with its emphasis on environmental problems.[35]

Although domestic policies generally took a back seat to foreign policy until the 1970s, this did not mean that they remained unaffected by the latter. Historically, of course, the United States has considered itself a democratic model for the world, a self-declared New World, and an example for all mankind. We had historically isolated ourselves lest we become tainted by the Old World's corrupt ways. We were determined to realize the American Dream in the United States for our own reasons; if others did not wish to accept our democracy, we would remain faithful to our vision of a free society which had given birth and meaning to this country. Since the 1950s, however, many of the arguments advanced for effecting social and political changes were based on reasons external to this vision. To cite the most prominent example, to grant the blacks their inalienable rights as American citizens was to strike a blow for America and against communism. Thus, Vice-President Nixon hailed the Supreme Court's 1954 desegregation decision as this country's greatest victory in the Cold War! This type of argument was considered more persuasive than one based on the necessity for justice, as defined by our own values. Justice for blacks seemed important mainly because America had to prove to the world—a majority of whose citizens are colored—that our democracy is still a meaningful and beneficial political system and one worthy of imitation.

Thus, foreign policy considerations could provide at least an extra argument, and possibly a greater urgency, for the undertaking of domestic policies which might otherwise have been left untouched or implemented only halfheartedly. If racial injustice was a poor example of our "democracy in action," how about

---

[34] Nick Kotz, *Let Them Eat Promises* (New York: Prentice-Hall, 1969). Ironically, the cutback in foreign and military spending in favor of domestic needs—vigorously advocated by many university professors—also led to a major reduction of funding for the National Defense Act. The Eisenhower administration had passed this Act in 1958 under the shock of the first Soviet Sputnik. The Act was intended to improve education in certain areas (science, mathematics, foreign languages, and regional studies). Politicians felt that Soviet supremacy in these areas accounted for their space success. This inward turn of government, public, and universities cannot help but affect the future available manpower supply for foreign affairs.

[35] William Proxmire, *Report from Wasteland* (New York: Praeger, 1970).

unemployment, ill-health, poverty, urban slums, and decaying cities? Wouldn't these, also, be blemishes on our record, especially in our competition with a nation which promised social justice and the good life for all men? Reaching the moon and landing on it first and the various other firsts in the space race were considered important national objectives because of the prestige and reputation for power their attainment would confer upon the United States. If this was true, wasn't it equally important to show the world that we, as a country which proudly proclaimed the virtues of private enterprise, could achieve a more rapid rate of economic growth than Russia with its planned economy? As President Kennedy said in his State of the Union message of 1961: "In short, the American economy is in trouble. The most resourceful industrialized country on earth ranks among the last in the rate of economic growth. . . . We must show the world what a free economy can do.[36]

Systemic pressures also altered the structure and functions of governmental institutions. These pressures have been felt most directly in the executive branch. After the beginning of the Cold War and the growing awareness that a prolonged period of international conflict lay ahead, it became quite clear that the traditional executive organization was not designed to cope with the problems of national security in the atomic age. Atomic weapons, the expansion of military services, the inevitable linkage between military policy and foreign policy, the need to retain civilian control over decision-making in the field of national security, and the obvious necessity of assuring responsibility and accountability in all aspects of defense and foreign policy planning suggested the desirability of a complete reorganization of governmental institutions connected directly with external policy-making. The result was the National Security Act of 1947 which created a new Department of Defense under a civilian secretary, placed all three military services under his authority, established a National Security Council with responsibilities in the area of formulation and control of national policy, and created a Central Intelligence Agency to centralize the collection and evaluation of intelligence related to national security.[37]

These changes in the institutional structure of the executive branch were made in direct response to conditions existing in the international environment after 1945. The impact of these new structures on the political system and on American society have been significant. The most spectacular has undoubtedly been the Department of Defense, which has since World War II expanded to mammoth proportions. It employs over a million people and spends nearly a hundred billion dollars each year. Its expenditures for military equipment represent a huge portion of annual governmental spending; its impact on the

[36] "The State of the Union: Message of President Kennedy delivered to the Congress, January 30, 1961," 87th Congress, 1st Session; Council on Foreign Relations, *Documents on American Foreign Relations, 1961* (New York: Harper & Row, Publishers, 1961), p. 16ff.

[37] Walter Millis, *Arms and the State* (New York: Twentieth Century Fund, 1958), pp. 139–186.

American economy is almost beyond measure. The Defense Department and the industrial corporations that supply its expensive and sophisticated weapon systems represent a military-industrial complex which is tantamount to a gigantic concentration of socialism in the midst of our capitalist economy. Its capacity to influence the volume of defense spending and the "hardness" of our foreign policy has undoubtedly been exaggerated. The evidence suggests that Presidents Truman and Eisenhower first decided the total volume of government spending within certain fiscal restraints, then the level of defense spending, and only at that point determined military strategy;[38] their successors have generally reversed this process and first decided national strategy and then the essential weapons needed in terms of their cost-effectiveness.[39] These decisions, moreover, were at all times made by the civilian executive leadership which never forgot the maxim that if you listened to a doctor, you were never considered healthy; if you listened to a minister, you were never without sin; if you listened to a military man, you were never secure. Therefore, although the military services were consulted, they rarely stopped grumbling about all the weapons they did *not* receive; the result was that they competed with one another for money and weapons. The Defense Department's constituents, the industrial corporations, and the political supporters of the services and corporations in Congress were, as in the case of other Departments, also involved in the policy process, but their role was primarily limited to competing with one another for contracts *after* the basic issue of funds and strategy had been decided by the president. His control over the military was, in fact, strengthened by their intense interservice and intercorporation rivalry. He ruled because they were so deeply divided. In brief, there wasn't *a* military-industrial complex, but *several* military-industrial complexes, all in competition with each other.

But if the military industrial complex was not the all-powerful monolith it has frequently been portrayed to be, particularly in its influence on foreign policy,[40] there can be little doubt that the defense industries constitute a

---

[38] Samuel Huntington, *The Common Defense* (New York: Columbia University Press, 1961).

[39] William Kaufmann, *The McNamara Story* (New York: Harper & Row, Publishers, 1964).

[40] A characteristic view of the role of the military was of "the alliance of the military with powerful economic groups to secure appropriations on the one hand for a constantly increasing military and naval establishment, and on the other hand, the constant threat of the use of that swollen military establishment in behalf of the economic interests at home and abroad of the industrialists supporting it. It meant the subjugation of the people of the various countries to the uniform, self-interested identification of patriotism with commercialism, and the removal of the military from the control of civil law." Interestingly enough, this statement, which could have been spoken by a liberal senator or a representative of the Students for a Democratic Society, is from Senator Nye's investigation of the 1930s (!) which attributed our involvement in World War I to the military-industrial complex of its time. It is from *Munitions Industry: Report on Existing Legislation,* Senate Report No. 994, Part 5, 74th Congress, 2nd Session (Washington, D.C.: Government Publications Office, 1936), pp. 8–9. Quoted in Hans Morgenthau and Kenneth Thompson (eds.), *Principles and Problems of International Politics* (New York: Alfred A. Knopf, 1950), pp. 62–63.

planned sector of the economy. Their purchase of up to one tenth of the Gross National Product has been a major means of subsidizing the rest of the economy, as well as stoking the inflation and diverting resources from civilian needs.[41] There is also little doubt that many Americans besides the soldiers and arms manufacturers profit from the spending of tens of billions in goods and services: politicians who bring home industry and jobs, workers and unions, storekeepers, real estate men, grocers, and car salesmen. The aerospace industries and states in which they are located—Washington and southern California on the West coast, Massachusetts and New York on the East coast—have, to a large degree, been subsidized by this form of "military socialism." So, clearly, have a number of private universities, such as M.I.T., Columbia, Pennsylvania, and Stanford as well as public universities such as the Universities of Michigan and California (Berkeley and Los Angeles) for scientific research and development. It is certainly true that American politics can no longer be discussed only in terms of the interactions between Big Business, Big Labor, Big Agriculture, and Big Government; the Big Military, too, must be included. Some would go further and argue, as Senator Fulbright has done, that we have become converted into a "militarized society." "More and more our economy, our government, and our universities are adapting themselves to the requirements of continuing war— total war, limited war, and cold war."[42] Ralph Lapp has called American culture the "weapons culture."[43] Whether one agrees with that characterization or not, the military-industrial complex serves as an excellent example of a government, driven by a compelling foreign and military situation, penetrating society at every level, including the scientific and educational communities, as well as every man's wallet.

Other structural changes have also occurred throughout the executive branch in response to systemic pressures. New agencies such as the Agency for International Development have been created to administer American foreign aid

---

[41] It is questionable if this division between resources needed for armaments and resources which presumably could be more usefully employed domestically (were they not diverted by the military-industrial complex) is not a bit oversimplified. "Where each state must tend to its own security as best it can, the means adopted by one state must be geared to the efforts of others. The cost of the American nuclear establishment, maintained in peaceful readiness, is functionally comparable to the costs incurred by a government in order to maintain domestic order and provide internal security. Such expenditure is not productive in the sense that spending to build roads is, but it is not unproductive either." Kenneth N. Waltz, "International Structure, National Force, and the Balance of World Power," *Journal of International Affairs,* Vol. 21, No. 2 (1967), p. 223.

[42] *The New York Times,* December 14, 1969.

[43] Ralph E. Lapp, *The Weapons Culture* (New York: W. W. Norton & Co., 1968). See appendices for disbursement of defense funds to the states, major industrial corporations, and universities. For three very critical, somewhat polemical books, see Fred J. Cook, *The Warfare State* (New York: Macmillan Co., 1964); Tristram Coffin, *The Armed Society* (Baltimore: Pelican Pub., 1964); and Richard J. Barnet, *The Economy of Death* (New York: Atheneum, 1969).

programs around the world; the United States Information Agency was designed to carry out the government's policies in the area of political propaganda; the Peace Corps was created as an instrument of assistance and good will for the nations of the world who requested its services; and the Arms Control and Disarmament Agency to serve both as a source of ideas and an instrument of negotiation in these key areas. There have also been informal structural changes. Particularly notable has been the addition to the White House staff of a national security staff which in recent years has been headed by such strong and incisive men as McGeorge Bundy (Kennedy and Johnson), Walt Rostow (Johnson) and Henry Kissinger (Nixon), who have at times seemed to be more influential than the Secretary of State. Similarly, the Office of Science and Technology is symbolic of the significant role scientists, too, play in the policy process through, for example, their technical evaluation of weapons plus their estimation of the political and psychological consequences of adopting new weapon systems.[44]

The overall effect, however, of America's contemporary global involvement—as the military-industrial complex example amply illustrates—has been less structural than political. Even before the outbreak of World War II, the president was becoming the axle around which the wheel of government revolved. As leader of his party and the one political figure in the country with anything resembling a national mandate, the president had already become chief legislator and keeper of a healthy state of the union. But while the evolution of the welfare state, the nationalization of social and economic norms, and the revolution in communications have contributed to the rise of a powerful presidency, the principle of executive supremacy in foreign affairs has been a significant factor in extending the power and personality of the president into practically every important area of domestic politics. As director of foreign policy and commander-in-chief of the armed forces, the president has moved into the center of American political life. It is he who formulates foreign and domestic programs; Congress either approves, rejects, or amends them. In foreign policy, moreover, the president has considerable discretion. By his actions, he can frequently leave Congress little choice but to support him so that the nation can confront its foes with national unity.[45]

Conversely, Congress is left chiefly to perform a reactive and legitimating function; and every once in a while it advertises its sense of frustration and helplessness by trying to restrict the president's authority in the conduct of foreign policy. In the 1950s it sought to restrain him lest he "appease" the communists and "sell-out" American interests; in the late 1960s and early 1970s, it sought to restrain him because he was too anti-communist and

---

[44] For the role of scientists in the policy process, see particularly Albert Wohlstetter, "Scientists, Seers, and Strategy," *Foreign Affairs* (April 1963), pp. 466–478; and Robert Gilpin, *American Scientists and Nuclear Weapons Policy* (Princeton: Princeton University Press, 1962).

[45] The president's vital role in the policy process is analyzed in Chapter 9.

involving the country militarily in too many near and far-away places. This pattern of executive dominance and supremacy and legislative subordination—if not debility—has, admittedly, occurred in virtually all modern political systems and it is not unique in the United States. It stems from the changing nature of modern politics and from the expanded problem solving functions of governments as a result of the electorate's demands upon government within and the state system's demands without. Nowhere, however, has this been more clearly illustrated than in the American government where the president is not merely the first among three allegedly coequal branches of government, but, as an English writer wrote about the prime minister, "He is, rather, a sun around which planets revolve."[46]

Foreign policy has not only placed the president at the center of American political life; it has also affected the recruitment of presidential candidates. The latter have increasingly come from the Senate where they presumably have been exposed to foreign affairs rather than from the rank of governors whose primary knowledge and experience is in domestic matters. Since 1960—that is, after Truman, a senator, and Eisenhower, a general—all presidential nominees have come from the Senate: Kennedy, Nixon, Johnson, Goldwater, and Humphrey. The campaign for the 1968 Republican nomination was particularly instructive in this respect. One of the candidates was Governor Romney of Michigan, a moderate Republican with a good record on domestic issues. But Vietnam proved his undoing; his handling of the war issue was so inept that even before his withdrawal from the contest it was clear that he had little chance to be selected as his party's candidate. Only Governor Rockefeller, who had fought Barry Goldwater's nomination in 1964 and belatedly contested Richard Nixon in 1968, had extensive foreign policy experience. Even the vice-presidential candidates had until 1968 come from the Senate (with the exception of Goldwater's running mate, William Miller) although these senators were not necessarily chosen for their foreign policy experience. Johnson, for example, was selected to hold the South for Kennedy. Yet some acquaintance with foreign policy issues could be assumed. Nixon broke whatever precedent existed by picking Governor Agnew of Maryland, a border state, to do what Johnson had done for Kennedy, namely to win Southern support for his nomination and Southern votes to win the election. Needless to say, this Vice-Presidential candidate's experience in foreign affairs was zero; his experience was strictly domestic.

Furthermore, whatever their prior knowledge and training, American political leaders and their principal advisors were quickly socialized by the state system once they had been elected. They learned rapidly how to respond appropriately to the external conditions which confronted them. Even though the intensive bipolarity of the early Cold War years helped this adaptive process, it is

---

[46] Ivor W. Jennings, *Cabinet Government* (Cambridge: Cambridge University Press, 1951), p. 183.

nevertheless remarkable with what speed Harry Truman could achieve such a fundamental reorientation of policies and make so many significant decisions in the short period from 1947 to 1951: the Truman Doctrine, the Marshall Plan, the Berlin Airlift, the formation of NATO, and the intervention in Korea all were organized during this time. Even more remarkable is that the basic pattern of containment, from which all other major decisions for over a decade were to follow, was decided in only fifteen weeks! On February 21, 1947, the United States was confronted with the Greek-Turkish crisis; on March 12, the President announced the Truman Doctrine in a speech to a joint session of Congress; on June 5, the Secretary of State gave his Marshall Plan speech.[47] What has been particularly impressive about this adaptation of American leaders to the external milieu has been how well they have learned the skills of deterrence.[48] In the many confrontations and crises that have occurred, they have shown both firmness and flexibility and avoided both suicide and surrender. For a nation that had been isolationist, unskilled in power politics, moralistic in outlook, and impulsive by temperament, that was no mean achievement. In a real sense, the measure of that achievement remains unrecognized because total war did *not* erupt. One need only look at how the great powers of Europe mismanaged the crises of 1914 or 1939 or how we, ourselves, blundered prior to Pearl Harbor to realize how easy it is to miscalculate badly and end up in a war. Yet for over two decades, American leaders have preserved the general peace and protected American security;[49] two decades after World War I, Europe was engaged in another war.

This socialization has included the leaders of both parties. This was not always what, in retrospect, seems an obvious and foregone conclusion. By 1952, the Republican Party—out of power since 1932—was deeply and bitterly divided over domestic *and* foreign policy issues. Admittedly, its more liberal and internationalist wing led by Senator Vandenberg (a former isolationist from Michigan), supported the Truman containment policy immediately after World War II.[50] But this bipartisan support did not survive the Republican Party's

---

[47] The exciting story of these few weeks is recounted by Joseph Jones, *The Fifteen Weeks* (New York: Viking Press, 1955).

[48] In large part, this has been due to the writings of the "civilian strategists" whose books were understandable to laymen and thereby took the mystery out of what most of them had previously regarded as a highly specialized and technical subject: Bernard Brodie, *Strategy in the Missile Age* (Princeton: Princeton University Press, 1959); Henry Kissinger, *Nuclear Weapons and Foreign Policy* (New York: Harper and Row, Publishers, 1957); Thomas C. Schelling, *The Strategy of Conflict* (Cambridge: Harvard University Press, 1960); and Herman Kahn, *On Thermonuclear War* (Princeton: Princeton University Press, 1960).

[49] Kennedy used to tell of a conversation between two German leaders after the outbreak of war in 1914 in which one asked, "How did it all happen?" and the other replied, "Ah, if only one knew." Kennedy commented that if this planet were ravaged by nuclear warfare, he did not want one of the survivors to ask how it had all happened and receive this incredible response. Sorensen, *op. cit.,* pp. 577–578.

[50] Arthur H. Vandenberg, Jr. (ed.), *The Private Papers of Senator Vandenberg* (Boston: Houghton Mifflin Co., 1952); for a balanced study of bipartisanship, see Cecil V. Crabb,

defeat in 1948, Vandenberg's death, the collapse of China, and the outbreak of the Korean War. The new leadership came from the party's stronger conservative and nationalist wing led by Senator Taft from Ohio. Taft, who was seeking the Republican presidential nomination in 1952, savagely attacked the Democratic domestic and foreign policies. The internationalists persuaded Eisenhower to run to save the party from Taft and ensure a responsible American foreign policy. The vicious battle within the party at the Republican convention settled the issue of party leadership; and Eisenhower's policies—he neither dismantled the welfare state nor reverted to isolationism, as demanded by the conservatives—ensured the continuity of American domestic and foreign policies. By consolidating and extending the social policies of his predecessors and following the broad outlines of containment, Eisenhower helped adjust the Republican Party to cope with the internal and external environments and transform the party from a basically irresponsible opposition to a responsible governing political instrument. While the internal party conflict was later reopened by Goldwater's nomination, the results of the 1964 election were not lost upon Republican leaders; while the hearts of many Republican delegates in 1968 might have been with Governor Reagan of California, their heads were with Richard Nixon, a moderate, who could gain wider public support and therefore possibly win.

One of the problems hampering the conduct of a responsible foreign policy, however, was the tendency of presidential candidates to exploit anti-communism as a means of manipulating power, either for soliciting votes to win elections or afterwards of eliciting Congressional and public support for significant foreign policies. While anti-communism was a simple, dramatic, and emotional means of arousing support, the price for employing this technique was at times rather high. Thus, at the beginning of the Cold War, when President Truman was seeking Congressional funds to help Greece, he posed the issue in terms of a universal struggle between democracy and totalitarianism, freedom and slavery—even though Greece, whatever its geopolitical importance, could hardly be called a democracy. "Totalitarian regimes imposed on free people, by direct or indirect aggression, undermine the foundations of international peace and hence the security of the United States."[51]

If this broad assertion unqualified in any way by either time, place, or circumstance was true, why did we not do more to prevent the collapse of Nationalist China, the out-party asked? If we were indeed committed to an undiscriminating policy of anti-communism in all corners of the world, irrespective of the nature or seriousness of the threat, why couldn't the in-party be accused of being poor guardians of the national interest and "softness" on

Bipartisan Foreign Policy: Myth or Reality (White Plains, N.Y.: Row, Peterson & Co., 1957).

[51] Paul Seabury, *The Rise and Decline of the Cold War* (New York: Basic Books, 1967), p. 39. This source contains an excellent critique of the Truman Doctrine and a balanced evaluation of the containment policy on pp. 39–53.

communism when there were setbacks? If communism were evil, would negotiations with Moscow or the recognition of Peking not constitute appeasement?
Thus having used anti-communism to whip up support for the containment
policy, Truman now found himself committed to tough policies with little room
for diplomatic manoeuvre. His resulting inability, for example, to recognize
Communist China diplomatically in early 1950 was to haunt him a few months
later when we became involved in the Korean War and, upon the defeat of the
communist forces in South Korea, advanced into North Korea. Since it adjoined
China, one of the risks we accepted was the possibility of Chinese intervention.
But Washington had no representatives in Peking and could not gather first-hand
information about her intentions, and it distrusted the second-hand information
from the Indian government that China would enter the conflict. Hence we
advanced toward China's frontier with Korea and precipitated the Chinese
intervention.[52]

The conduct of the Korean War also showed a number of other occasions
which were influenced by anti-communism. The Truman Administration's decision to advance into North Korea was certainly influenced by the fact that the
mid-term congressional election was coming up, and that a victory in Korea
could deflect accusations of softness on communism, and permit the Democrats
to present themselves as vigorous anti-communist crusaders and defenders of
America. But the subsequent Chinese intervention which produced a stalemate
on the 38th parallel, the line on which the war had started, led to a renewal of
these charges. The result was that the Administration could not sign an armistice
which accepted the pre-war partition of Korea, representing allegedly a peace
without victory, without risking defeat in the upcoming 1952 presidential election. Truman was thus trapped. He could not extend the war without risking
greater escalation, casualties, and costs, nor could he end the war. The continuing
and frustrating battlefield stalemate was a major factor in the Republican
victory. Only Eisenhower, who could hardly be classified as an appeaser, could
sign a peace accepting the division of Korea.[53]

In a similar fashion, when in 1960 it became popular "to stand up to
Castro," candidate Kennedy dramatized his anti-communism with vigorous
attacks on Castro and suggestions that the Cuban "freedom fighters" be allowed
to invade Cuba. When he came into office, he found that the Eisenhower Administrations had been planning precisely such an operation. Despite his own uneasy
feelings about the C.I.A.–planned and –sponsored invasion, he felt he could not
call it off. If the operation were canceled and the news were leaked by its
proponents in the government, as well as by the Cuban exiles who had been

---

[52] John W. Spanier, *The Truman-MacArthur Controversy and The Korean War* (New
York: W. W. Norton & Co., 1959), pp. 84–113; Allen S. Whiting, *China Crosses the Yalu*
(New York: Macmillan Co., 1960).

[53] For an analysis of the conduct of the war and the interrelationship between domestic
and foreign policy variables, see Spanier, *op. cit.*

trained for this invasion and would not be returning from their camps, he would stand exposed as being less anti-communist than his predecessor and as a president who lacked nerve and brought discredit on Washington. So he let the operation proceed despite misgivings which turned out to be correct.[54] It was a humiliating personal and national experience for the Administration and ironically left Kennedy vulnerable to the accusation that he was unwilling to stand up to the communists. As the situation in Vietnam, therefore, proceeded to disintegrate later in 1961, it is not surprising that the President would introduce American military "advisors"; he felt they could help defeat the Vietcong. And he was surely influenced by the desire to recoup his reputation after the Bay of Pigs, the Berlin Wall, and his agreement to a coalition government in Laos, and being bullied by Khrushchev at Vienna.[55] Far more than any of his predecessors, Kennedy sought to base his national popularity on his conduct of foreign affairs.

An additional result of this use of anti-communism by our leading political figures—and this tactic was adopted by thousands of politicians running for lesser offices—was that by the early 1950s the fear of communism had reached pathological proportions and this, in turn, had widespread domestic effects as well. "Reds" were seen not only in government but in the universities, labor unions, churches—everywhere. Communism was portrayed as an all-powerful demonic force seeking to subvert and destroy the American way of life. It had to be rooted out. In this climate of opinion (when it could even be suggested that *Robin Hood* should be banned from public libraries because, as a man who stole from the rich and gave to the poor, he was obviously a communist and a subversive influence on impressionable young minds), the Congress and state legislatures supported official investigations of private citizens, schools, and government agencies; they demanded loyalty oaths from government employees and passed laws directed at subversion and at any activities that even appeared to be unpatriotic or un-American. The passing of Speaker Ban laws by several state legislatures, for example, and the attempt to dictate the policies of state universities concerning visiting lecturers was but one of many domestic indications of the extent to which the fear of communism took precedence over common sense, academic freedom, and the spirit of the United States Constitution. Other indications were the burning of "suspected" books by the United States Information Agency; the dismissal of State Department officers who during the war had correctly predicted that the Chinese Communists would defeat the corrupt and ineffective Nationalist Chinese regime—and who were therefore thought to be procommunist; the accusation of such men as Robert Oppenheimer, the father of the atom bomb, of being a security risk;[56] and even the accusation of Secretary of

---

[54] Schlesinger, *A Thousand Days*, pp. 227–228; Sorensen, *op. cit.*, p. 331.
[55] Tom Wicker, *JFK and LBJ* (New York: William Morrow & Co., 1968), pp. 192–193.
[56] Philip M. Stern, *The Oppenheimer Case* (New York: Harper & Row, Publishers, 1969).

State Marshall as the leader of the Kremlin's American operation to "sell-out" this country. (In the late fifties, the John Birch Society went one better by accusing Republican President Eisenhower and Secretary of State Dulles of actually being communist agents.) The zealous hunt and accusations of lesser men proceeded in total disregard for any due process of law. Thus, external systemic pressures in the 1950s were the cause for widespread McCarthyism, or witch-hunting of those who were widely believed to constitute a menace to our democratic system.[57]

Domestic Sources of Foreign Policy[58]

If the distribution of power in the state system provides one key explanation of state behavior, domestic variables provide another.[59] Most of these variables —political culture, public opinion, and especially political institutions and the decision-making process—and their role in shaping American foreign policy will be analyzed in some detail later. Here we will focus only on one aspect of political culture because foreign policy is decided within the context of a national set of attitudes toward politics, including international politics. No state comes into the state system, so to speak, without a picture in its head of the external world. All states wear colored glasses because all possess a repertoire of re-sponses derived from their previous domestic and foreign experience. Thus they all perceive the state system selectively. While they share, as we saw, a number of assumptions about this system and how states operate in this environment, the manner in which they will react to external pressures is greatly influenced by

---

[57] For an illuminating interpretation of the author of McCarthyism, Senator Joseph McCarthy, see Richard Revere, *Senator Joe McCarthy* (New York: Meridian Books, 1960); an incisive indictment and analysis of McCarthyism will be found in Hans Morgenthau, *The Purpose of American Politics* (New York: Alfred A. Knopf, 1960), pp. 143–157; and the historical tendency of Americans to look for domestic conspiracies is well analyzed by Richard Hofstadter, *The Paranoid Style in American Politics* (New York: Vintage Books, 1967).

[58] Our analysis here of the American approach to foreign policy leaves for later— Chapter 14—a broad division which might be made between the policy-makers and "the people." For present purposes, we can say that on the one hand, policy-makers share many of the mass values, and, therefore, thinking on foreign affairs as other Americans; on the other hand, they are also socialized by the external system and in a sense compelled to act in terms of its norms. Yet, in a democratic political system such as that of the United States, the policy-makers cannot ignore public preferences and attitudes because the system is in a state of constant electioneering. The result tends to be the creation of tensions between the demands of the internal and external systems.

[59] For further elaboration, see James N. Rosenau (ed.), *Domestic Sources of Foreign Policy* (New York: The Free Press, 1968); and James N. Rosenau (ed.), *Linkage Politics* (New York: The Free Press, 1969), which is a systematic attempt to relate the reciprocal effects of domestic and foreign policies.

their perceptions: whom they define as an opponent, how they operate in this environment, and how they define their role in the state system are examples of judgments based on selective perceptions.

One need only look at our chief adversary to see how the ideological values of its leaders influenced their definition of adversaries. Earlier we explained the outbreak of the Cold War in terms of Soviet behavior that was characteristic of a great power anticipating a future conflict. For the Soviet leaders, this conflict was not, however, a mere possibility; because communist ideology defined the United States as an enemy—despite our war-time efforts to create mutual trust and goodwill between the two nations—that conflict was considered unavoidable.

More specifically, the Soviet Union, as a revolutionary state, saw the United States as not just another state trapped by the same security dilemma as she, but also as a capitalist state which had to be eliminated.[60] Moscow rejected the concept that national insecurity and international conflict were the result of *only* the state system. It believed that international antagonism and hostility, as well as domestic poverty, unemployment, ill-health, and ignorance were also due to the internal nature of the system's leading states. Capitalism was the cause of all social evil. Internally, the majority of men lived in destitution because a capitalist minority exploited them by paying absolute minimum wages and squeezing maximum profits out of them. Externally, international conflict and wars were fought because capitalist states clashed with one another in the search for new markets, cheap new materials, and labor in the nonwestern or colonial world. Thus capitalism with its central profit motive based upon the private ownership of property had to be completely destroyed if men were to be freed from economic exploitation, political despotism and wars. Only if the Communist party, representing the exploited majority, or proletariat, possessed control and removed industry from private ownership, would mankind finally live free from social injustice, deprivation, and war.

Thus, post-war Stalinist Russia felt obligated to "liberate" mankind and create a new international system based upon communist social and economic values. As a promise to deliver men from evil and bring them domestic justice and external peace, communism in fact constituted a secular religion of damnation and salvation which conferred upon the Soviet Union the messianic duty of converting all men to the "true faith." The Soviet Union, therefore, thought of itself as engaged in a constant and irreconcilable "holy war" with all noncommunist states. Committed to remaking the system in its own image, it sought a monopoly of power or hegemony. The potential conflict between the two superpowers arising out of their individual security dilemmas was therefore unavoidable because of a Soviet hostility which was ideological and preconceived. It was a hostility which Lenin and Stalin had felt even before they had

---

[60] Kissinger, *op. cit.,* pp. 316–361 and *American Foreign Policy* (New York: W. W. Norton & Co., 1969), pp. 11–16, 34–39. For an analysis of post-war international politics in the context of a revolutionary state system, see John W. Spanier, *World Politics in an Age of Revolution* (New York: Praeger, 1967).

seized power in Russia and before western governments had adopted any anti-Soviet policies; it was an enmity deduced from first principles and based not on what western governments *did* but on what they were alleged *to be*.[61] Western actions were almost irrelevant. All noncommunist states were defined as capitalist, and capitalist governments were ipso facto aggressive. Unfriendly actions such as the western intervention in the Russian Civil War after 1917 were used to prove the original premise of capitalist hostility; but attempts such as the American efforts from 1941 to 1945 to reassure Moscow of this nation's benevolent intentions were also seen as an indication of enmity. One of two explanations generally allowed the Soviet leaders to square American actions with their basic premise: American policy was friendly because it was designed to lure the Soviet Union into complacency for subsequent attempts to pressure it into major concessions; or, if a particular president demonstrated his personal desire to get along with the Soviet Union, his policy could not be taken at face value since he was the political leader of a capitalist system which, by its very nature, had to be hostile. The logical conclusion was the self-fulfilling prophecy. Once noncommunist states were declared hostile, and official declarations and policies were formulated upon that assumption, it was hardly astounding that western nations would at times be less than friendly, on occasion overreact, and that the Soviet leaders would reap the fruits of the policy they had sown. Communist ideology thus raised the level of mutual fear and suspicion resulting from the state system and caused Moscow to undertake both defensive expansionism—due to its enhanced apprehension of foreign attack—and offensive expansionism—due to its determination to shrink the capitalist world. Any modus vivendi except a lengthy armed truce was in the circumstances of 1945, therefore, excluded and the United States had no choice but to contain Soviet power by establishing a new post-war balance.

Our own set of attitudes toward foreign policy were not drawn from an officially held and interpreted ideology; instead, they were the product of American experience and, in the absence of sufficient international experience, this primarily meant domestic experience.[62] Indeed, the first characteristic of our

---

[61] George F. Kennan, *Russia and the West under Lenin and Stalin* (Boston: Little, Brown and Co., 1961), pp. 179–183; also see his "Sources of Soviet Conduct" in *American Diplomacy 1900–1950* (Chicago: University of Chicago Press, 1951), pp. 107–128. For an account by a diplomat present at the Allied wartime conferences at the beginning of the Cold War, see Charles E. Bohlen, *The Transformation of American Foreign Policy* (New York: W. W. Norton & Co., 1969). A brilliant attempt to reconstruct the Soviet side is found in Adam B. Ulam, *Expansion and Coexistence: The History of Soviet Foreign Policy, 1917–1967* (New York: Praeger, 1968).

[62] Kennan, *op. cit.*, analyzes what he calls the American "moral-legalistic" framework from 1900 to 1950; John W. Spanier analyzes the post-war foreign policy in *American Foreign Policy Since World War II*, 4th ed. (New York: Praeger, 1971). See also Robert E. Osgood, *Ideals and Self-Interest in America's Foreign Relations* (Chicago: University of Chicago Press, 1953); Hans J. Morgenthau, *In Defense of the National Interest* (New York: Alfred A. Knopf, 1957); and especially Gabriel Almond, *The American People and Foreign Policy* (New York: Praeger, 1960).

attitudes toward foreign policy has historically been its secondary nature. The nation concentrated on continental expansion and modernization. Foreign affairs were considered a diversion from these primary internal tasks. The United States therefore turned its attention to the external world only when provoked. The foreign threat first had to constitute so clear and present a danger that it could no longer be ignored. This point cannot be overemphasized: the United States rarely initiated policy; the stimuli which were responsible for the formation of foreign policy normally came from beyond America's frontiers. The result, historically, has been that our foreign policy was essentially both reactive and discontinuous, responding to external pressure when there was a "clear and present danger" and concentrating again upon more important domestic matters when that danger has passed. Long-range involvement, commitments, and foreign policy planning therefore tended to be difficult. Indeed, American policy even today tends to be a crisis policy in which we manage each crisis on its merits and when it is over, relax and wait for the next one.

Our attitude was also distinguished by a high degree of moralism and missionary zeal stemming from the nation's long consideration of itself as a unique and morally superior society. The United States had been born a democracy, the world's first nation to devote itself to improving the life of the common man, the forgotten man of history. In the words inscribed on the Statue of Liberty, "Give me your tired, your poor, Your huddled masses yearning to breathe free. . . ." The perfect union was to be a free and egalitarian society. The United States was a post-European society and Americans were the chosen people. The New World stood for opportunity, democracy, and peace; the Old World for poverty, exploitation, and war. The waves of emigration from Europe during the nineteenth and early twentieth centuries testified to the fact that the rejection of Europe was, after all, the nation's principal reason for existing. Lincoln phrased it briefly and aptly: America, he said, was "the last, best hope of earth." The Civil War in this context would decide not only this nation's destiny but the destiny of mankind for whom this country served as a beacon of liberty. Moralism in foreign policy thus reflected the awareness and pride of a society which considered that it was carving out a better domestic order, free of men's age-old tyrants of oppression and injustice.

Isolationism from European power politics—not isolationism from Latin America or Asia—was not, therefore, just a matter of geographic distance from Europe. Rather, it had been largely a voluntary means of guarding American morality and purity. Self-quarantine was the best way of preventing the nation from being corrupted and tainted by Europe's undemocratic domestic institutions and foreign policy behavior. Withdrawal from the world and providing it with an example to follow was the only morally correct course. On the other hand, once it became increasingly impossible to remain aloof in this century, the country went to the other extreme by launching crusades. If we were a morally and politically superior system, we could remain uncontaminated only by eradicating those who might infect us. Thus, once we had been provoked, we acted as a missionary power and sought to make the world safe for American democracy by democratizing or Americanizing other nations into peaceful replicas of ourselves. American crusading, like isolationism, thus sprang from the same source.

A third characteristic follows from those liberal democratic values upon which the nation was founded and the high degree of resulting moralism: a depreciation of power politics with its connotations of conflict, destruction, and death. Just as the use of power within the national political system was legitimated by democratic purposes—and even there politics is still widely regarded with some suspicion; the wielder of power, the politician, is frequently looked upon as a moral leper—its employment in the state system can be justified only by a moral cause. Specifically, this means that it cannot be employed without arousing all sorts of guilt feelings unless the nation confronts a morally unambiguous case of aggression. Since democracies were conceived of as peaceful states—because the people who elected their rulers and suffered the hardships of war were considered peace-loving—the outbreak of war was attributed to authoritarian states whose rulers, unrestrained by democratic public opinion, wielded power for their own personal aggrandizement. Their removal was therefore a condition for peace and the end of power politics itself.

Thus, while the exercise of power by American democracy might be sinful, salvation could be gained by the very nobility of our purpose. Paradoxically, war, the ultimate instrument of power politics, in this way becomes the means for its own extermination. In Woodrow Wilson's famous phrase about World War I, Americans fight wars to end all wars. American power was "righteous power." Ironically, therefore, our only morally justifiable and emotionally satisfying wars were total wars whose aim was total military victory.[63] Like the cowboy, we "shoot 'em dead" and emerge victorious.

The fact that we were twice victorious in this century when we applied all our power also strengthened another attitude: that the United States was omnipotent, that once engaged in a conflict she could "lick anyone in the system." This attitude that the nation was invincible tended to be reinforced by its many domestic successes. The westward movement, the massive urbanization and industrialization, the Americanization of a huge immigrant population, widespread education of its people, and victory in two world wars were all part of an almost unbroken success story until 1945. Tragedies such as defeat and conquest, experienced by virtually all other states, were unknown and therefore the illusion of omnipotence was part of our historical consciousness. All problems could be solved; it was only a matter of finding the proper techniques. The question is never whether, only how.

---

[63] This belief that a moral society can justify its high moral purpose only with total war and that all other wars (for example, limited wars which are far less destructive) are immoral was particularly noticeable during the Vietnamese war. As Paul Seabury has perceptively noted, "only huge wars, raising huge ethical problems, are worthy of moral approbation," *op. cit.,* p. 88, n. 8.

Indeed, this pragmatic attitude is another major characteristic of American foreign policy. It might more appropriately even be called the engineering approach to external problems. Robert Tucker aptly captured the spirit of this attitude when he said:

> A pragmatic or instrumental approach to world problems typifies the western policy-maker. Not theoretical conceptions enabling him to relate policy to the general trends of events, but know-how in the face of concrete problem-situations is what he typically emphasizes. He wants to "solve" the immediate, given, concrete problem that is causing "trouble," and be done with it. Accordingly, diplomatic experience—always of great importance, of course—is exalted as the supreme qualification for leadership in foreign policy. For experience is the royal road to know-how. It teaches the statesman how to negotiate with the Russians, how to coordinate policy with the allies, how to respond to emergencies, and so on.
>
> In facing foreign-policy problems it is not the western habit to attempt first of all to form a valid general picture of the world-setting events in which the problems have arisen. The tendency is rather to isolate the given problem-situation from the larger movement of history and ask: what can and should we do about it?[64]

More specifically, this means that the United States tackles each problem as it arises. In the abstract, this makes sense. After all, until a situation has occurred and the facts are in, how can one react? The trouble is that by the time sufficient facts are in, the situation may well be so far developed that it is too late to do much about it or, if one does, the difficulties just multiply. Our quest for certainty, in other words, is carried too far. Policy-making is, in essence, tackling problems early enough so that one's influence can still be usefully brought to bear; but this can usually only be done when there is still insufficient information. By the time the situation is clear, a crisis is usually already at hand and it is too late for any effective action short of applying military power and perhaps it is even too late for that. Pragmatism, in brief, reinforces the reactive and discontinuous nature of the American conduct of foreign policy, and the emphasis on the immediate and short-run to the detriment of long-run policy consideration.

These are but a few of our attitudes toward international politics; they by no means exhaust the list.[65] The question is, in what ways do they affect our external behavior? The war years provide one illustration and a contrast of

---

[64] Robert C. Tucker, *The Soviet Political Mind* (New York: Praeger, 1963), pp. 181–182.

[65] An exhaustive analysis of the American "style," applied to a number of post-war problems, may be found in Stanley J. Hoffmann, *Gullivers' Troubles, or The Setting of American Foreign Policy* (New York: McGraw-Hill Book Co., 1968), Part II, pp. 87–213.

perceptions and behavior.[66] Moscow saw the United States as only a temporary
ally because, as the strongest western power, she would be Russia's principal
enemy after Germany's defeat in the continuing struggle with capitalism. The
United States thought of World War II as a temporary dislocation of the
normally peaceful condition among "peace-loving" nations. After the conclusion
of hostilities, American policy-makers expected to live in harmony and friendship with the Soviet Union. The chief American objective in Europe from 1941 to
1945 was the strictly military goal of Germany's unconditional surrender in the
quickest possible time. The aim was total victory and the elimination of Hitler;
the post-war balance of power against Russia played no role in the formulation
of American wartime planning and strategy. Soviet policy-makers, foreseeing the
post-war conflict, remained highly suspicious of the West; they quickly consolidated the Soviet Union's hold on eastern Europe in the wake of the retreating
German armies and immediately sought to extend its power right after World
War II. The United States, on the other hand, brought most of its troops home,
demobilized them, and expected to concentrate once more on domestic affairs.

If American policy was basically reactive in the subsequent Cold War, it
meant that our identification of another nation as an enemy depended upon *his*
actions. Our attitudes affected our pattern of behavior primarily *after* we had
become engaged. Once that had occurred, our moralism, for example, became
transformed into militant anti-communism. This was hardly surprising, particularly during the period of extensive and intensive bipolarity. Policy-makers and
the public alike abhorred communism. The antithesis between American democratic values and Soviet communist values was striking; it was a clear case of
good against bad. Policy-makers, to be sure, were quickly socialized or "tamed"
by the state system from indulging in any military crusade. They aimed only at
containment, not total victory; but they still had to mobilize a public whose
orientation was internal and aroused only by crusades. Anti-communism was
therefore an obvious tool because it conveyed the meaning of the Cold War in
the traditional context of New World democracy versus Old World despotism; in
a democracy composed of people convinced of the superiority of the American
way of life, this was a simpler and easier way to elicit popular support for a
foreign policy than long, intricate explanations which would also have to be
made in terms of the abhorred power politics.

There were several results. Containment, for example, put off any negotiations of a political settlement with Russia until after communism had "mellowed," that is, changed its character; until then, negotiations were thought to be
not only useless because of the expansionist aims of the Soviet leadership, but

---

[66] Soviet behavior during the war and immediate post-war has been remarkably well
reconstructed by Ulam, *op. cit.,* pp. 314–455; the American side may be found in: Herbert
Feis, *Churchill–Roosevelt–Stalin* (Princeton: Princeton University Press, 1957); Robert E.
Sherwood, *Roosevelt and Hopkins* (New York: Bantam Books, 1950); or in such a shorter
historical analysis as John L. Snell, *Illusion and Necessity* (Boston: Houghton Mifflin Co.,
1963).

also immoral. The recognition of Communist China in this atmosphere of anti-communism became impossible; Chinese intervention in Korea only confirmed our appraisal of communist regimes as evil, even though we had ourselves precipitated this intervention by our march up to China's frontier with North Korea. Similarly, if communism per se was the enemy, then America had to oppose it everywhere, regardless of whether the system was intensively bipolar or relaxed, or whether the area to be defended was of primary or secondary interest to our security; almost equally indiscriminately, the United States must support any anti-communist regime, regardless of whether it is democratic or not—a Franco, a Chiang Kai-Shek, a Diem, or a subsequent Saigon government, to name a few among many.[67] Or, to take a final example, since communism is wicked, it will delay the recognition of differences among communist states and hamper the exploitation of these divisions; for the impact of nationalism as a divisive factor within the communist world will be played down if all communist states are considered equally immoral.

The fervor of our anti-communism did not, however, mean that the nation liked long international involvement. Indeed, our desire to concentrate once again on domestic affairs, combined with our moralistic depreciation of power politics and belief that our omnipotence could resolve all problems quickly, tended to result in a fluctuating public mood and support for foreign policy. When power is not used totally and therefore presumably for moral purposes, if it does not achieve the elimination of conflict and power politics, the guilt feelings induced by the use of power reassert themselves. Expression of such guilt feelings takes the form of revisionist literature, suggesting that the United States had no vital interest in the conflict, that the country was deluded into hostilities by propagandists, political leaders, or a military-industrial complex (or in the more colorful words of the 1930s, the "merchants of death"), and that we could and should have stayed out of the war and not have resorted to power politics.[68] Thus the mood of optimism that with our great power and missionary zeal we could improve the world is replaced by a mood of disillusionment as we realize that the wicked world beyond our borders cannot be quickly or totally

---

[67] For some recent criticisms of American "globalism" see: William J. Fulbright, *The Arrogence of Power* (New York: Vintage Books, 1967); Ronald Steel, *Pax Americana* (New York: Viking Compass, 1968); and Edmund Stillman and William Pfaff, *Power and Impotence* (New York: Vintage Books, 1967).

[68] For some of the revisionist history placing the responsibility for the beginning of the Cold War upon the United States, see, among others: D. F. Fleming, *The Cold War and Its Origins,* 2 vols. (Garden City, N.Y.: Doubleday & Co., 1961); Gar Alperovitz, *Atomic Diplomacy: Hiroshima and Potsdam* (New York: Vintage Books, 1967); William A. Williams, *The Tragedy of American Diplomacy* (Cleveland: World Publishing Co., 1959); and Gabriel Kolko, *The Politics of War; the World and United States Foreign Policy, 1943–1945* (New York: Random House, 1968). The Williams–Kolko school finds the fault in the imperialistic nature of American capitalism. A short but excellent evaluation of the Fleming–Alperovitz thesis, which directly blames Truman's anti-communism, may be found in Arthur Schlesinger, Jr., "The Origins of the Cold War," *Foreign Affairs* (October 1967), pp. 22–52.

reformed. Then, cynicism about whether this world is indeed worthy of being saved by us creates both a despair and a renewed determination to concentrate on America and the improvement of her national life so that the superiority and greater morality of the American way of life will again radiate to the world and be worthy of imitation; setting an example for the rest of the world, instead of corrupting our soul with power politics, is then said to be our task.[69] The American approach to foreign policy has been one of dichotomies: either peace or war, either noninvolvement or total commitment, either no force or maximum force, and last but not least, passionate crusading or disillusioned withdrawal. Only in America does the moralistic gladiator of today convert into the repentant sinner of tomorrow and then back again the day afterwards. But as gladiator or repentant sinner, as a defender of orthodoxy or the critic of official policy, the moralism of his political thinking remains constant; so does his expectation that this country can regenerate mankind—by force or by example.

It is, however, our "cowboy approach" to international conflict which has been perhaps the most severely tested in the post-war period. In a world in which total war was suicidal, we could no longer apply maximum violence. Instead, we suddenly confronted limited wars. These did not sit well with the public, whose emotions remained committed to the old-fashioned, red-blooded American way of handling the "bad guys." The two presidents—Truman and Johnson—who engaged in them did not even bother to run for a second term and in each case the Republican Party won the presidency from the mass frustrations which Korea and Vietnam created. As one astute observer of the television cowboy observed a few years ago:

Maybe our diplomats and political leaders could learn something. For example, would Wyatt Earp stop at some frontier equivalent of the 38th parallel when the rustlers were escaping with the herd? Ridiculous! Would Marshall Dillon refuse to allow his deputies to use shotguns for their own defense because of the terrible nature of the weapon? Ha! Would the Lone Ranger under any circumstances allow himself to be bullied and threatened by those who sought to destroy the principles by which he lives? Would "Restless Gun" or Jim Hardy of "Wells Fargo" attempt to buy friends who would not support them otherwise? Can you imagine Paladin of "Have Gun, Will Travel" standing aside while women and children were being massacred? (Dare I mention Hungary?) Can you imagine Cheyenne living in a perpetual state of jitters because he feared the next move of some gun-slinger?[70]

---

[69] See Chapter 14 for an elaboration of this theme and the probable difficulties the United States will face in conducting a foreign policy in a post-Vietnam period when American policy-makers can no longer wave the red flag of anticommunism and expect the public to shout "Charge!"

[70] David Shea Teeple, "TV Westerns Tell a Story—Our Diplomats Should Watch Them," *Human Events* (March 10, 1958).

Indeed, our addiction to military power for resolving international problems as quickly as possible, once we have been provoked, had a great deal to do with our involvement in Vietnam and then our inability to win it and end the hostilities. We had a choice whether we should intervene or not; our attitudes predisposed that choice. Neither the Kennedy nor Johnson Administrations grasped the true nature of guerrilla warfare. If they had understood the political nature of such an unconventional war better—and counterguerrilla warfare as well—they might not have intervened.[71]

A counterguerrilla war can be won only if the native government can enlist the support of its people. This it must achieve by carrying out the political and social reforms necessary to meet popular aspirations and alleviate existing grievances. If it is successful in this task and mobilizes popular support, the war will be won; if it fails, the people will continue to support the guerrillas and supply them with the information, recruits, food, and aid necessary for their victory. In the former circumstances, American forces can be usefully employed as a supplement to the government forces. The latter conditions, however, prevailed in South Vietnam. The government's arbitrary rule had by the early 1960s alienated virtually every stratum of society; government forces were ineffective and dispirited. It is because we did not really understand the political basis of guerrilla warfare that we failed to see that even large-scale military commitments on behalf of unpopular Saigon regimes could not defeat the communist forces who were identified by most of the population with nationalism and a better life.

Instead, we characteristically regarded the war as basically military: our superior fire power and helicopter mobility would enable us to completely destroy enemy forces. The political aspects of the war—above all the basic land reforms needed to capture the support of the peasantry—were largely ignored and no South Vietnamese government could therefore win popular support. We simply conducted the hostilities as if we were fighting a conventional, although limited war. Large-scale search–and–destroy operations rarely found large enemy forces to "chew up"; the Vietcong, usually knowing where we would land by the pre-landing bombardments of an area, frequently vanished leaving behind only frustrated American commanders. The further indiscriminate use of air power and artillery fire resulting in the destruction of many southern villages did little to help create the peasantry support needed to win a counterguerrilla operation. The result was that the war in South Vietnam could not be won. But again we told ourselves that the reason for this was military: the infiltration of North Vietnamese troops and weapons prevented our victory. So we started bombing the North, expecting to pound it into submission. The bombing did not, however,

---

[71] For an illuminating account of the difficulty American policy-makers had understanding the political nature of guerrilla warfare and the conflicts over Vietnam within the Kennedy Administration, see Roger Hilsman, *To Move a Nation* (New York: Doubleday & Co., 1967), pp. 413–523; the early years of the war in Vietnam and guerrilla warfare are excellently analyzed in Bernard Fall, *The Two Vietnams: A Political and Military Analysis,* 2d. rev. ed. (New York: Praeger, 1964), pp. 316–384.

decrease the volume of men and supplies flowing southward, destroy the people's morale, or pressure Hanoi into ending the war. Quite the contrary.

As the war dragged on and our casualties and impatience grew, the state system's impact on American politics resulted in two responses: those who advocated escalation in the hope of attaining clear-cut military victory and those who proposed withdrawal since victory seemed elusive. Indeed, the two sides of this typical either-or response were frequently advocated by the same persons. Thus President Johnson found himself under increasing pressure. He could escalate in order to appease this pressure and, while this could be momentarily popular, eventually it would rebound if it failed to achieve the desired result; on the other hand, he could withdraw but then he would risk being charged with appeasement. If he chose the middle course of neither expansion nor retreat, domestic opinion would further bifurcate and weaken the center even more. Whatever he therefore did, the President was trapped; his own party was so deeply divided that it could not unite behind either him or its other candidate, domestic and international liberal Hubert Humphrey, against their hated arch-rival, Richard Nixon, anathema to most Democrats for what they regarded as his tactics smearing them with charges of being "soft on communism" during the Eisenhower years.

Just as the war deeply divided the nation, the domestic disunity in turn affected the war again by prolonging the fighting. While Hanoi seemed, in any event, in no hurry to end the fighting because it expected South Vietnam's society to collapse under the strain of war, its expectation that the United States would grow increasingly tired of the war also seemed to have been a factor—the longer it waited, the greater the price the Americans would pay to be able to withdraw. As North Vietnam's chief strategist shrewdly commented about a democratic nation's capacity to fight a prolonged war: "The enemy will be caught in a dilemma. He has to drag out the war in order to win and does not possess, on the other hand, the psychological and political means to fight a long, drawn-out war."[72] He knew that a guerrilla force wins if it does not lose, while the regular army loses if it cannot win. In addition, one of the fronts—if not the main front—for fighting the war is the opponent's home front where support for the war in the field can be eroded. The reciprocal impact of foreign and domestic politics could hardly be more startlingly revealed, nor the effect of some of our national attitudes on foreign policy be more dramatically symbolized than by Vietnam.

---

[72] Quoted by Fall, *op. cit.*, p. 113.

4

What We Know, What We Believe: The Domestic Political Culture

It was a County Commissioners' election and it was dull. The county's Registrar of Voters, sensing no popular enthusiasm for the affair, predicted that a quarter of the eligible electorate might vote, and this was optimistic. In the modestly populated Southern county, the five candidates struggling to win two commissioner's seats were fighting, then, for the favor of a few thousand voters at most.

With apathy to the right of them and rivals on the left, however, two candidates gamely made what contest they could of it. One evening shortly before election day, the local newspaper offered readers the following advertisement:

Benjamin Franklin Said:

"A Penny Saved Is A Penny Earned"

JOE E. DOE

As YOUR COUNTY COMMISSIONER will save
your tax dollars by SOUND BUSINESS PRACTICES

A page later, one of Joe E. Doe's rivals counterattacked:

Elect
SAM B. ("BILL") SMITH
CIVIC AND YOUTH WORKER
13 Years a Scoutmaster
14 Years Sunday School Teacher
PTA Member and Officer
Past President of Exchange Club

The contest never became more elevated or exciting. It passed with two winners and three losers into the unremembered annals of backwater politics in the United States. At first glance, these advertisements—like the candidates and the election itself—seem unpromising material for revealing anything important about American politics. The artless advertising prompts the sophisticated to smile; there are no great issues or personalities to infuse meaning or color to the events; no one (with the exception of the candidates and friends) probably remembers the contest. Essentially, it is an unremarkable event save for one significant aspect: the candidates were clumsily paying respect to the existence of political culture and, in their unconscious way, demonstrating how deeply political culture permeates all political activity in the United States. Let us consider for a moment why Joe E. Doe and Sam B. ("Bill") Smith merit mention in understanding political culture.

What Political Culture Means

In the simplest sense, a "culture" is a set of attitudes, beliefs, values, or ways of looking at the world shared by some large group of individuals.[1] A *political* culture determines how individuals in a society are oriented toward their political system, and in almost all modern societies, this takes place in a variety of ways. Political researchers are especially interested in discovering what these patterns are and how they influence the behavior of individuals in political life.

But what has this to do with Joe E. Doe and Sam B. ("Bill") Smith? One aspect of a political culture that we will explore involves how people evaluate public officials and their offices; among other things, this includes beliefs about who is qualified to govern and how citizens should conduct themselves. In different ways, each candidate attempts to tap these beliefs for this own purpose, each gambling that he knows what these beliefs are. Joe E. Doe pitched his appeal on "sound business practices," hoping that the local electors preferred officials who, like Ben Franklin, knew the value of a penny and would conduct their office with

---

[1] This definition of culture is suggested by H. W. Wiseman, *Political Systems* (New York: Praeger, 1966), p. 21.

businesslike dispatch. Sam B. ("Bill") Smith, wrapped in the mantle of the Boy Scouts, Sunday School, and P.T.A., assumed this trinity was dear to the hearts of the electorate; against "sound business practices" he wagered the voter would prefer a candidate associated with the church, school and children. Each candidate was following the politician's impulse to seize upon widely distributed political preferences in a society and to manipulate them—no matter how crudely—to his own advantage. Though neither candidate would have understood the term, each was risking success on his understanding of the local political culture.[2]

Most of us seldom think consciously about political culture or pause to observe its operation. Rather, we express political culture in our thinking and behavior. For example, suppose we are asked to react to the words "George Washington." We probably imagine a dignified gentleman, the father of our country in the powdered wig, frock coat, and sober visage he wears in history books. We know he is an American, the military architect of the Revolution, the first president, and a symbol of the political system. But how do we react to the King of Sweden, the First Secretary of the Soviet Communist party, or the "Lion of Judah?" None of these is likely to arouse much response from an American, but a Swede, Russian, or Ethiopian would react quite differently to at least one of them, just as he would have a different idea of George Washington. Our frames of reference, which are determined by our political culture, differ. This should suggest how intimately a political culture is involved in daily political affairs and its force in guiding our perceptions of the political world and our response to it.

Because a political culture does shape public political thinking and activity so importantly, the way this culture is created and transmitted also merits attention. Of the many influences that shape a political culture, one—political socialization—deserves special attention. In this chapter we shall move from the content of American political culture to this process of political socialization— from what we know and believe about our political system to how our political information, attitudes, and perceptions have been formed.

Political Socialization

A college sophomore defined political socialization quite accurately if awkwardly: "It gives us the eyes through which we view our political system." Most

---

[2] Edwin Hargrove aptly remarks upon the relationship of politician to political culture: "Leaders, even when they are preaching, are technicians, not philosophers. They must draw moral inspiration from the political formulae." Edwin Hargrove, "Political Leadership in the Anglo-American Democracies," in Lewis J. Edinger (ed.), *Political Leadership in Industrialized Societies* (New York: John Wiley, 1967), p. 218.

political attitudes, values, and behaviors are customarily learned, most political information acquired from others. Initially, young children usually adopt the political orientation of parents and other authority figures; later, education and the opinions of peers influence perceptions and information about the political world. Adults continue to acquire political orientations through contact with friends, associates, various interest groups, and information conveyed by the media.

Political socialization deals with how political culture is learned, how it is transmitted to individuals, and by whom.[3] While it is especially important in the earliest years of an individual when he acquires basic concepts about his political system, its officials, and its procedures, it is also a process of lifelong learning. This learning occurs in a particular social environment that differs among individuals; the "eyes through which we see the political system" are directed in a certain way as we are taught what to see according to our social niche.

This occurs in all societies. It is part of a much more comprehensive socialization process. Long before an American child enters school, he has learned to use a language, to manipulate common eating utensils, to observe (sometimes) minimum rules for civil behavior, and to obey individuals who have authority over him. Human beings are not socialized into any human community at birth; they must be taught codes of behavior and belief, values and attitudes, and skills appropriate to the culture. In political terms, a child is born without political loyalties and allegiances, he is psychologically the citizen of no nation, he lacks concepts about good and bad political rules, has no ideas about what political figures he should honor, ignore, or despise. These and many other orientations will be created or powerfully molded by political socialization. Moreover, the way most individuals are socialized into a political system will affect the continuity of the political culture itself.

Political socialization can serve three purposes. It can *maintain* a political culture by teaching the young to follow modes of political thinking and behavior accepted by the adult community. Political socialization can also *create* a political culture. In the newly emergent African nations, for example, national boundaries were often drawn to include numerous tribes, geographical groups, and racial minorities which had never shared a sense of national identity nor developed a sense of community. The educational system in these states has often attempted to create this sense of national community and political consensus in the young. Finally, political socialization can *transform* a political

---

[3] Many studies of political socialization assume a somewhat narrower concept of this process. Such studies stress *early* political learning and those orientations related to a society's *basic* political structures and processes. See, for example, Richard E. Dawson and Kenneth Prewitt, *Political Socialization* (Boston: Little, Brown and Co., 1969); and Lucian W. Pye and Sydney Verba (eds.), *Political Culture and Political Development* (Princeton: Princeton University Press, 1965). We, too, have stressed early learning and attitudes toward basic institutions and procedures, but prefer to emphasize that these orientations can and do change throughout an individual's life.

culture.[4] Through the process of early education, new political values can be introduced into a society; this often is vitally necessary when new political attitudes must be developed to enable the system to adjust to changing internal and external problems.

In a political system where the government and the political structure have been stable, the impact of political socialization is essentially conservative. The young are initiated into a political orientation which stresses loyalty and acceptance toward the established political structure, its officials, and its norms.

It should be apparent why governments are vitally concerned with political socialization and why they devote considerable time, resources, and effort to manipulating the institutions which socialize the young. Every political system exists one generation away from potential collapse; it must mold future support for the system. If it fails, the political culture of the new generation may be incompatible with or hostile to the political institutions of the disappearing generation. While such a situation seldom materializes, the knowledge that it can develop motivates governments and political officials to try to preclude it by political socialization.[5]

To summarize: political socialization affects both an individual's relationship to his political system and the nature of a whole society's political culture. Political socialization is, in effect, a form of education. What individuals are taught will eventually form an important part of succeeding political cultures in a society as one generation yields to another. In many respects, therefore, if one wishes to know the shape of our political culture in the future, one needs to pay close attention to what tomorrow's Americans are learning today.

American Political Culture in Five Perspectives

The political information, beliefs, and attitudes of more than 200 million Americans includes a prodigious number of topics and issues. Earlier, in Chapter 2, we suggested five major aspects of political culture found in most societies which we shall explore in detail in the United States. These are only a few of the elements in our political culture that might be explored, but they provide an important and manageable list which has the additional virtue of being supported by a considerable amount of information from the extensive survey research of several decades.

---

[4] Dawson and Prewitt, *op. cit.,* p. 13.

[5] Some political analysts argue that incompatable and hostile political cultures are currently developing between younger Americans and older ones. How much "polarization" of values has occurred between these generations and the implications of this are still highly debatable; firm conclusions are difficult to make. See Chapter 13 for a further discussion of this matter.

First, we shall study *levels of political information* among Americans. This deals with what facts people know about their political structure, including familiarity with the individuals who hold political office, knowledge of the procedures and institutions in the governmental system, acquaintance with salient political issues, understanding of political events, and the ability to recognize the rules supposed to govern political life—the "official norms." At this point, an individual's feelings about political information or the sense (perhaps nonsense) he makes of information are unimportant. We wish to know only how much of the system's ongoing activities and processes have permeated public perceptions.

Next, we are concerned with *public beliefs about how the political system operates and how Americans evaluate these operations.* We are dealing here with what people believe, subjectively, is going on in their political system, with how they assume it operates, and how they feel about the conduct of political affairs as they understand them. Thus, unlike our first concern, this is not a matter of how much factual information an individual has about political life, such as knowledge of candidates, elections, or the content of the Constitution; rather, we are interested in what, from a personal, subjective viewpoint, is real in political affairs to Americans.[6] Often attitudes toward the political system, beliefs about its operation, and emotion combine in such a way that they are interdependent. Robert Lane describes an interview in an industrial Eastern seaboard city with a Mr. De Angelo, a factory operative who struggles to explain what he likes in the American political system:

> To me, voting is the thing, the right to put in the guy you want—that's the big thing I mean. I know that over there they don't have that and they have a lot of trouble. The kid that was born to Princess Elizabeth—he is going to be king someday. That's all there is to it. Nobody else is gonna run it, know what I mean? . . . Here, there's always a contest against each other trying to serve the people the best way they could to stay in power. And that's a good thing.[7]

Here, a belief about voting ("there's always a contest against each other trying to serve the people") combines with judgment and emotion ("that's a good thing"). De Angelo's perceptions are starkly simplified, his understanding of British politics wildly inaccurate; but he clearly demonstrates how his subjective

---

[6] Most individuals, of course, consider that what they *believe* to be true actually *is* true; they don't acknowledge that their beliefs and actual reality could be inconsistent. Such beliefs become, as Heinz Eulau remarks, "self-evident propositions that everybody knows to be true without need of further proof." Heinz Eulau, *The Behavioral Persuasion* (New York: Random House, 1963), pp. 72–73.

[7] Robert E. Lane, *Political Ideology* (New York: The Free Press, 1962), p. 166.

perceptions of political life form an emotional bond between himself and the political system.

We shall study, as well, public beliefs about *what political rules are valid.* Here we are dealing with people's values and preferences for handling political matters, their convictions about what rules of the game should be followed or ignored in civic life. Some of these beliefs can be framed in such dramatic terms as the revolutionist's "burn, baby, burn" or the silent majority's "law and order." Others can be expressed less menacingly: "a man has a right to speak," or "the majority rules." In various ways, these convictions about how political affairs should be conducted defined what is acceptable and legitimate in the eyes of Americans when it comes to political rights and obligations for oneself and others.

We are interested also in *attitudes toward public officials and offices.* How do Americans react to a man called "a politician," to the president, the governor, the city officials? What status do public offices enjoy in the public's perceptions and how does the public apportion prestige among the many official positions in the political system? In various ways, these questions all relate to how the most visible symbols of the political system impress the public and what emotions these officials elicit from it.

Finally, we are interested in *how Americans feel they can participate in political life and how they do, actually, participate.* We are concerned with how often Americans engage in various forms of political activity and what role they believe they can play individually in civic affairs. In short, we are investigating which groups express themselves in politics and how they choose to do so.

What Americans Know about Their Political System

Most Americans are exposed to several types of political information. Textbook information, encountered first in elementary school, is data about the fundamental constitutional structures and principles of the United States: the variety and powers of governmental bodies, the content of the Constitution itself including the Bill of Rights, and election procedures. There is also current affairs information—current political events, personalities, issues in the news, and information about the candidates and officeholders in the system at any given time. This information is usually transmitted through the mass media.

Public opinion surveys consistently reveal widespread public ignorance concerning "textbook facts." The majority of Americans are unable to define presumably familiar political words and concepts; most Americans appear uncertain about the structure and powers of major political institutions and offices; they are surprisingly ill-informed on contemporary political events considering the attention given to them in all the media. The questions in Table 4.1 from a variety of public opinion surveys in the last twenty years suggest this public ignorance.

Table 4.1. The presidency

	Correct	Incorrect, Don't Know
1. What is meant by the electoral college? (1955)	35%	65%
2. For how many years is a president of the United States elected—that is, how many years are there in one term of office? (1952)	93	7
3. Can you tell me what the term "veto" means to you? For example, what does it mean when the president vetoes a bill sent to him by Congress? (1947)	80	20
4. Who are the candidates for president? (1948)	90	10
5. Who is the Democratic vice-presidential candidate? (1960)	72	28

The Constitution

	Correct	Incorrect, Don't Know
6. What do you know about the Bill of Rights? Do you know anything it says? (1945)	21%	79%
7. What are the first 10 amendments in the Constitution called? (1954)	33	67
8. How many U.S. senators are there from your state? (1954)	64	36
9. Will each of the 48 states elect members of the House of Representatives this fall, or not? (1952)	37	63
10. What are the three branches of the federal government called? (1954)	19	81

Source: Hazel Gaudet Erskine, "The Polls: Textbook Knowledge," *Public Opinion Quarterly* (Spring 1963), pp. 133–141.

A limitation of polls that imply that the average American is politically illiterate is that these polls often depend on an individual's ability to recall technical information that most adults encountered years earlier in school. Younger respondents closer in time to their civics courses often score better on these matters: on the question regarding the number of senators from a state, 66 percent of those between 18 and 20 answered correctly in contrast to 47 percent of those over fifty.[8] Also, Americans are not consistently uninformed on political matters; a majority of those with a post-high school education, for instance, can answer all the preceding questions correctly.

[8] Hazel Gaudet Erskine, "The Polls: Textbook Knowledge," *Public Opinion Quarterly* (Spring 1963), p. 137.

Information about current events is another useful indicator of public interest and attention to political affairs, since these questions are asked when the matters involved are topically important and generally reported; correct answers usually require little more than an ability to remember the news. Table 4.2 contains a selection of such questions asked over the last twenty years.

Table 4.2. Elections and candidates

	Correct	Incorrect, Don't Know
1. Can you recall the names of your senators? (1954)	31%	69%
2. Do you happen to know the name of the present representative in Congress from your district? (1966)	46	54
3. Who is the Republican candidate for vice-president? (1960)	67	33
4. Can you name any candidate for president or vice-president? (1960)	94	6
5. Do you know for how many years a United States senator is elected? (1966)	20	80
6. Do you know the name of the present governor of your state? (1966)	90	10

Source: Questions 1, 3, and 4 are adopted from Erskine, *The Polls: Textbook Knowledge,* question 2 from Opinion Research Corporation, Gallup Poll *Index,* August 1966, p. 11; questions 5 and 6 from John P. Robinson, Jerrold G. Rusk, and Kendra B. Head, *Measures of Political Attitude* (Ann Arbor, Mich.: Institute for Social Research, 1968).

Americans score slightly better on current affairs than they do on questions about the structure of the political system, but this does not indicate that Americans generally understand the implications of political events nor do they appear to devote much attention to considering them.[9] Looking at these questions superficially, they suggest a disappointingly bleak image of the average American when he is compared to the ideal participant in a democracy. Such a participant, at least as political philosophers and social critics define him, is an informed, interested citizen, a sturdy yeoman of civic life, and the backbone of democracy. Often the survival of democracy is equated with such a citizen. But, as Lane and Sears emphasize, the stability of a political system, including a democracy, does not depend primarily upon the amount and quality of public political information:

Attachment to the system comes in other ways; it comes from early loyalties to the society (not to the polity) of which one is a member; from moralized references of parents, from fear of deviance or ostracism; from leading

[9] In 1968, the University of Michigan's Survey Research Center found that not more than one third of their sample of American voters paid a "good deal of attention" to national affairs—this in a presidential election year when political stimuli are most plentiful. Survey Research Center, 1968 Election Survey, Variable 432.

a more or less gratifying life, from the rewards of compliance, obedience, and conformity.[10]

As this quotation suggests, the loyalties of Americans to their political system depend on how they *feel* about political institutions, how well they *accept* its principles, and how well they derive satisfaction—or expect to in the future—from the society which the government represents. Political loyalties are not necessarily based upon the quality of political information an individual possesses; often beliefs and feelings about political life exist apart from information and often in direct contradiction to it. This is clearly apparent in the information to follow.

What Americans Believe about Their Political System

A frequently stated and casually accepted assumption about American political culture is that it is and has been a culture with considerable consensus.[11] In the United States, so the argument runs, the political system has historically been stable; there has been continuity of political institutions because most Americans agree on the basic rules and values for political life. Even if Americans are not especially well informed politically (and many don't care to be), this argument asserts that Americans are highly cohesive—or have been—when it comes to political fundamentals. In the light of survey information, however, these assumptions need severe qualification. Comparing public attitudes to the consensus theory is a case of slaying a beautiful hypothesis with ugly facts.

The American past provides ample evidence that the broad American political consensus of the past is a myth. At almost all times, there have been substantial minorities whose political values conflicted with the official norms. The American Civil War is the most arresting instance of a massive collapse in political consensus between North and South. On the eve of World War II, as another example, the German-American Bund (a native imitation of Hitler's Fascist party in program, technique, and even uniforms) could rally more than 20,000 Americans to Madison Square Garden to shout approval for the forcible suppression of Jews, Negroes, and other "non-Americans." In the 1960s and early 1970s, alienation and rejection of the political system appeared in the

[10] Robert Lane and David Sears, *Public Opinion* (Englewood Cliffs, N.J.: Prentice-Hall, 1964), p. 61.

[11] The requirements for a consensus will vary from one expert to another. Herbert McClosky suggests 75 percent agreement on a value is a consensus, others suggest 66 percent; however, as it is operationally defined, it customarily means significantly more than a bare majority. See, for instance, Herbert McClosky, "Consensus and Ideology in American Politics," *American Political Science Review* (June 1964), pp. 361–382.

rhetoric of militant blacks and student radicals. The rejection expressed itself among some blacks in demands for a black state, in the advocacy of black nationalism that implied severing native black allegiance from the political system and seeking a new homeland, in the Black Panthers' seething hostility toward the police, the court system, and most white political officials. This angry rhetoric—which appealed also to many white radicals—symbolized the militant black's mounting impatience with the pace of political change and his growing conviction that the political system was unequal to the task of meeting his grievances. Such opinions did not reflect the disposition of the majority of American blacks, but the undercurrent of dissent from our political system did—and does—exist.[12]

Though he mellowed enough to believe that a peaceful solution to the civil rights struggle was possible, Malcolm X, a symbol of black militancy until his 1965 assassination, reflected the militant Negro's limited tolerance for dominant political values:

> I don't speak against the sincere, well-meaning, good white people. I have learned that there *are* some. I have learned that not all white people are racists. I am speaking against and my fight is against the white *racist*. I firmly believe that Negroes have the right to fight against these racists, by any means that are necessary. . . . I *am* for violence if nonviolence means we continue postponing a solution to the American black man's problem.[13]

Because the United States is a comparatively open society where information on political events, public opinion, and political dissent is readily available, the divisions and conflicts over government and politics are quite visible. However, in many nations, especially in dictatorships, the evidence of disaffection and the symptoms of alienation are suppressed or hidden from outsiders and, if possible, from the domestic public as well. For example, the testimony to internal discontent in the Soviet Union comes most often to the West indirectly, through pamphlets and other political documents smuggled out by Soviet intellectuals to friends in Europe. So, all political systems must constantly reinforce and renew public loyalties to the system, and almost all face challenges of dissent from within; most cannot count upon a massive consensus.

Evidence suggests that a political consensus in any society is not likely to be massive and consistent, that varying degrees of dissent from the system and varying numbers of the alienated can be found in most nations; this is a more realistic perspective on political culture in the U.S. and elsewhere than assuming that a "great consensus" exists in any nation and that political opinions remain

---

[12] For black opinions, see Chapter 5.

[13] Alex Hadley, *The Autobiography of Malcolm X* (New York: Grove Press, 1965), p. 367.

static. The more immediate matter is how opinions are divided within the American political culture and upon what issues. A good place to begin such an investigation is with American attitudes toward the government.

Many polls suggest that public confidence in government is qualified, that considerable portions of the public—often a majority—are dubious about the virtues of their political system, that many have some dismal opinions about the behavior of those who govern them. Consider, for instance, Table 4.3, showing the results of a question that the University of Michigan's Survey Research Center has asked samples of the American public periodically since 1958 dealing with public confidence in the federal government.

Table 4.3

"How much of the time do you think we can trust the government in Washington to do what is right?"

	1958	1964	1966	1968
Always, just about always	57%	14%	17%	6.3%
Most of the time	16	63	48	46.5
Some of the time	23	22	28	31.2
None of the time, almost never	—	—	3	0.1

Source: Robinson et al., *op. cit.,* p. 643; Survey Research Center, 1968 Election Study, Variable 504.

The ten-year shift from predominantly uncritical belief that government can "always do what is right" to growing reservation may indicate an emerging public mood in the early 1970s in which the virtue of government and the competence of its officials are increasingly debated.[14] In part, this may reflect the fact that public judgments about governmental performance are highly sensitive to short-range alterations in the news. Many develop a generalized conviction that the times are "good" or "bad" and lay the responsibility at government's doorstep. Since the 1960s were punctuated with racial violence, urban riots, the Vietnamese conflict, the looming poverty problems, and pitched battles on college campuses growing from student radicalism, public perceptions of government may well reflect growing public unease with these accumulating problems.

It is still too early to determine how deeply the events of the 1960s affected basic citizen confidence in political institutions and whether the apparent shift to greater public reservation about governmental performance is long-range or

---

[14] Or, consider another question in the Survey Research Center's 1968 poll. To the statement "People have a lot to say in government," 75.3 percent of the national sample replied that they felt they "did not have much to say." Survey Research Center, 1968 Election Study, Variable 144.

not.[15] It seems clear that the public mood of the early 1970s differed from that of the early 1960s. Perhaps the Kennedy years were not, as John Kennedy had wished, "a new beginning" but the twilight of the Eisenhower years instead: a public that could still bask in the fading, generally uncompromised political confidence of the early 1960s apparently had lost this simple confidence a decade later.

Yet now, and apparently at many points in the past, considerable cynicism prevails. Almost all polls dealing with public beliefs about the conduct of government reveal that a large minority suspects the worst. For instance, in the Survey Research Center polls mentioned earlier, one question, shown in Table 4.4, suggests that a large segment of the public does not believe it carries much weight in governmental decisions.

Table 4.4

"I don't think public officials care much what people like me think."

	1966		1968
Strongly agree	9%		
Somewhat agree	26		
Not sure, depends	8	Officials care	60%
Disagree	49	Officials don't care	40
Strongly disagree	8		

Source: Robinson et al., *op. cit.,* p. 638. Survey Research Center, 1968 Election Study, Variable 490.

This table implies that between 40 to 45 percent of the public apparently entertains doubts ranging from uncertainty to positive conviction that the government ignores public opinion.[16] Other polls suggest that almost half of the public believes "big business" is the most frequently benefited interest in governmental decisions.

---

[15] Two problems are especially important when researching changes in public attitudes: (1) what indicators to use, and (2) a lack of repeated polls over a sustained period using the same questions. Regarding the indicators, for example, at the time when the 1966 question in Table 4.4 was asked, another question by different investigators suggested that the president, U.S. senators, supreme court justices, and governors ranked at the top of public prestige scales. See Walter Murphy and Joseph Tannenhaus, *1966 Election Study* (Ann Arbor, Mich.: Inter-University Consortium, 1968), p. 98. Students interested in repeated questions which might relate to public support over time should consult especially the Gallup Poll *Index,* the Lew Harris polls and John P. Robinson, Jerrold G. Rusk, and Kendra B. Head, *Measures of Political Attitude* (Ann Arbor: Institute for Social Research, 1968).

[16] Similar opinions have been revealed in other polls. The Louis Harris polls in August 1966 and April 1968 asked a sample of Americans to respond to the statement "People running the country don't really care what happens to me," and found 28 percent in 1966 and 39 percent in 1968 agreed.

On questions dealing with the integrity of public officials, the same ambivalence appears, as shown in Table 4.5.

Table 4.5

"Do you think that quite a few of the people running the government are a little crooked; not very many are, or do you think hardly any of them are crooked at all?"

	1958	1964	1968
Hardly any	26%	18%	19%
Not many	44	49	52
Quite a lot	24	29	25
Don't know	6	4	4

Source: Robinson et al., *op. cit.*, p. 646; Survey Research Center, 1968 Election Study, Variable 507.

Public conviction about official honesty is reasonably high; yet the fact that more than a quarter of the sample believes that "quite a lot" of officials are crooked is a reminder that a great many Americans believe political morals are very low.

Regardless of how his elders may feel, the very young American has few doubts about the virtue of his political system. Adult civic pride is the fruition of attitudes first implanted in the public school. Easton and Dennis concluded from their study of 12,052 Chicago grade-school children that the earliest and most intense expression of political loyalty approaches worship:

> We find that the small child sees a vision of holiness when he chances to glance in the direction of government—a sanctity and rightness of the demigoddess who dispenses the milk of human kindness. The government protects us, helps us, is good, and cares for us when we are in need, answers the child.[17]

"The most conspicuous difference between adult political orientations and those of the children" writes Fred Greenstein in another study, "was in attitudes of cynicism and distrust toward politics. Virtually *no* children entertained these widespread adult views."[18]

[17] David Easton and Jack Dennis, "The Child's Image of Government," in Roberta Sigel (ed.), *Political Socialization: Its Role in the Political Process* (Philadelphia: Annals of the American Academy of Political and Social Science, September 1965), p. 43. This applies to *most* children but there are exceptions, apparently when they live in a domestic situation where parents are alienated from the political system. See: Dean Jaros, Herbert Hirsch, and Frederic J. Fleron, Jr., "The Malevolent Leader: Political Socialization in an American Subculture," *American Political Science Review* (June 1968), pp. 564–575.

[18] Fred I. Greenstein, *Children and Politics* (New Haven: Yale University Press, 1965), p. 31.

A very young student's innocent political confidence can be attributed to the tendency of small children to trust authority implicitly and to their carefully edited textbooks that commend political leaders past and present in terms that elevate them beyond mortal frailties. Educators, like most adults, strive to protect the small, impressionable child from the more realistic but conflicted and abrasive political opinions of adults. Yet it appears that the majority of adults and schoolchildren do share a presumption of virtue about their political system which represents a residue of early emotional training. This attitude persists among maturing schoolchildren and remains undiminished through all early grades. Easton and Dennis, for instance, received the responses shown in Table 4.6 to a question dealing with trust in government.[19]

Table 4.6

"Government usually knows best."

Grade	Percent Agreeing
3	80%
4	77
5	87
6	84
7	91
8	84

Source: David Easton and Jack Dennis, "The Child's Image of Government," in Roberta Sigel (ed.), *Political Socialization* (Philadelphia: The Annals of The American Academy of Political and Social Science, 1965), page 52. Copyright 1965. Reprinted by permission of the authors.

Before long, these children will be more critical of government, yet the unanimity of opinion at this age undoubtedly carries into adulthood some continuing sense of allegiance and pride among many Americans.

Pride and Satisfaction. On the positive side, when opinion polls in the past have asked relatively uncomplicated questions about public pride or satisfaction with their government, there often seems to be "an uncommonly high degree of loyalty and satisfaction with things American," strengthening the impression of a substantial, affirmative consensus on the system's worth. Here, a striking inconsistency in American political culture seems to appear. Alongside the evidence of fairly widespread cynicism and suspicion of government, there coexist

[19] Easton and Dennis, *op. cit.*, p. 52.

other expressions of affirmation and support for the system. Why do such apparently contradictory attitudes exist within the political culture?

One answer is that cynicism and suspicion of government on one side and an affirmative, patriotic support of government on the other are both historic traditions in American political culture; undoubtedly, most Americans are exposed to both viewpoints and retain opinions derived from each one. Moreover, public opinion studies show that many Americans can compartmentalize their opinions, enabling them to hold conflicting views. Indeed, like most people, the majority of Americans do not ordinarily think through their opinions sufficiently to recognize and resolve contradictions and inconsistencies, nor are they usually forced to do so. Thus, it is quite possible—and likely—that many Americans esteem their national government highly while also remaining suspicious and cynical about it in some respects—and both attitudes can be sincere.

Another explanation involves differences in the element of the government to which an individual is reacting. For example, he may have negative feelings toward "public officials" (which he may interpret to mean bureaucrats or politicians), yet be very positively oriented toward the presidency. In general, it appears that Americans express more general support and esteem for relatively abstract, impersonal, diffuse symbols of the system such as "the government," "our constitutional principles" or "our checks-and-balances system" than they do for particular, concrete aspects of the government such as specific public officials, agencies, or policies. In short, individuals are not similarly oriented toward all aspects of the national government.

Finally, it may be that many apparent contradictions in public evaluations of government are created by the words used to stimulate and measure these opinions. For instance, a great many more people might express confidence in the government if, instead of being asked whether they "trust the government in Washington to do what is right," they were asked whether they could "trust the president (or Congress) to do what is right." It is difficult to know, at times, whether the phrasing of public opinion surveys creates an inaccurate impression of public attitudes toward the government; it is possible, at least, that the emotional charge behind various political words may create the impression of greater public confusion on political attitudes than fundamentally exist.

In any case, it seems clear that most Americans have reacted affirmatively in the past to general questions about the value of our political system. In the early 1960s, for instance, a comparative study of citizens in the United States, Great Britain, Germany, Italy, and Mexico suggested that Americans took considerably more pride in their political system than members of the other nations did; indeed, the American sample was the only one among the five to list its government and political system as the most frequent object of pride.[20] (In response to the question "Generally speaking, what are the things about this

---

[20] Gabriel Almond and Sydney Verba, *The Civic Culture* (Boston: Little, Brown and Co., 1965), p. 64.

country you are most proud of?" about 85 percent of the Americans mentioned their political institutions; in comparison, the next highest rating of a political system was found in Great Britain, where only 46 percent of the sample chose this item.)

In 1965, after the glow of the Eisenhower years vanished and those relatively untroubled times yielded to John Kennedy's assassination, a great many Americans of both races still seemed to be able to think positively about their political system in spite of mounting racial tensions, the escalation of the Vietnamese War, and other serious evidence of major political problems. In Table 4.7, public responses to several questions related directly or indirectly to the political system are shown.

Table 4.7

"I want to hand you a card with some good things that have been said about life here in America. For each, please tell me if you feel personally satisfied that you have it."

	Total	White	Negroes
Life in a free country	91%	93%	67%
Right to privacy	92	93	86
Good recreation opportunities	89	91	77
Chance to change jobs	89	92	66
Chance to move residence	89	92	69
Get children well educated	87	89	70
Chance to get ahead on job	86	89	57
High standard of living	78	80	51

Source: Harris Survey, "Living Freely Tops American Benefits List" by Louis Harris, *The Washington Post,* October 25, 1965. Reprinted by permission of Louis Harris and Associates, Inc., New York, New York.

Although Negroes in this poll seem clearly less convinced they have "some good things" supposed to be available in American life, rather substantial majorities in both groups seem to be reasonably content with basic liberties and opportunities directly traceable to the political system and its operation. On the basis of polls such as this and the preceding one, an observer might conclude that most Americans were fairly content with the way their political system operated.

Contradictory attitudes of pride in the political system and reservations about the honesty of its administration are characteristic of American culture. During the late nineteenth century when urban political bosses, political machines, and blatant corruption in the election of public officials were far more common than today, Americans seemed able to accept this without its upsetting their faith in the system itself:

Despite the vulgarities of American political life, it became apparent to most commentators that the American had an extraordinary faith in his formal political institutions. Not only was the American loath to challenge the political order; he was hardly prone to challenge even its sordidness.[21]

This coexistence of civic pride and political cynicism may be quite healthy and perhaps inevitable. Some political cynicism undoubtedly represents public learning from the often splenetic and barbed exchanges between competing candidates and parties. Competition for office is conducted by means of attack and counterattack on the character and judgment of the opposition; a certain negative residue undoubtedly remains in the public mind.[22] From the founding of the republic, American political culture has always been suffused with suspicion to the extent that even George Washington, whose place in the pantheon of national heroes was assured in his lifetime, was accused by the opposition press of aspiring to be King George. Harry Truman's characteristically tart remark, "The president . . . cannot spend his time replying to personal attacks and insinuations. If he did, his time would be fully occupied with nothing else," reveals the common lot of the politician in a society where considerable vitriol as well as praise is directed toward public officials. Moderate political cynicism is a healthy antidote to the blandishments of aspiring demagogues and a necessary corrective to public expectations of governmental performance so exaggerated that the inevitable failure to meet expectations leads to even greater disillusion. To have a public at least *somewhat* cynical of the virtues of government is a healthy trait in a democracy.

Beliefs about the Rules of the Game.   Political beliefs are often expressed in behavior. The beliefs that most directly affect political life are those dealing with concrete situations in which an individual can do something in a direct way or not do something. The conduct of politics involves the continuing, practical application of the rules of the game. The political rules are similar to the rules of any game; they define the terms under which individuals will relate to each other—who will have what privileges, what is permitted and prohibited, how one achieves success in the game. There are at least two sources for these rules and they may not be consistent. First, there are laws. The Constitution in the United States defines some basic rules to govern political affairs. These rules include

---

[21] Irving L. Horowitz, *Three Worlds of Development* (New York: Oxford University Press, 1966), p. 85.

[22] Most American historians agree that modern political campaigns are almost antiseptic compared to the often vulgar oratory of the last century. Students interested in the seamier side of nineteenth-century campaigns should read, for instance, Eugene Rosenbloom, *A History of Presidential Elections* (New York: Macmillan Co., 1957), and Marcus Cunliffe, *The American Heritage History of the Presidency* (New York: Simon and Schuster, 1968), Chapter 5.

procedures for electing public officials, for passing legislation, for the conduct of the president, the judiciary, and Congress. The first ten amendments of the Constitution (the Bill of Rights) define rules which are supposed to bind all citizens impartially, whether they be public officials or private individuals. Freedom of speech, religion, petition, peaceable assembly, and the like are definitions for public conduct.

Some rules are unwritten, nonlegal, but widely accepted agreements among individuals. These can be called the informal rules. When political machines dominated Eastern urban politics, the informal rules of the game were anything but constitutional, yet they prevailed. Bribery, illegal voting, malfeasance in office, the intimidation of minorities, and occasional violence were widely accepted. In the American South, the political rules of the game until recently were as racially differentiated as everything else: whites could vote, but Negroes could not; white politicians could be economically liberal (even radical) provided they were segregationists. Numerous other examples could be cited to illustrate how a community, a region, a social group, or a political elite can create these informal rules resting on no legal foundation but governing political conduct nonetheless.

Whether they are legal or informal, these rules of the game can be applied in practically any social situation. Should one support a candidate who advocates free speech for communists? How should one express dissent from administration policies in a university? Defining the rules of the game means defining political values. In the United States, willingness to embrace the constitutional rules in theory *and practice* is one measure of commitment to the political system. The United States Constitution, in fact, is primarily concerned with political procedures—rules for the conduct of politics. The Constitution emphasizes how decisions shall be made in government, how political opinion may be expressed, what obligations the government owes to citizens, and what legal responsibilities one citizen owes to another.

Do Americans accept the official norms—that is, the constitutional ones— for the political system? On the evidence of public opinion surveys, the answer is (1) that many Americans do not understand the rules either in theory or in practice, (2) that there is a persistent discrepancy between the public's acceptance of a rule in theory and the ability and willingness to apply it in practice, and (3) that there does not appear to be any clear, consistently discernible consensus on constitutional principles.

One revelation of American ambivalence concerning the legal norms is the public's response to questions concerning principles embodied in the Bill of Rights. Public opinion surveys almost always reveal that large numbers of Americans do not seem to understand or sympathize with the freedoms expressly protected in that document. For instance, as early as 1954, during the McCarthy days, Samuel Stouffer asked whether his respondents would permit various individuals to speak in their community; he found that while 70 percent would grant freedom of speech to a man accused of being a communist who denies it, only 58 percent would do so for someone advocating government ownership of private industry, a still smaller 37 percent would permit an opponent of churches and religion to speak, and only 27 percent would allow freedom of speech to an admitted communist.[23]

Americans customarily give overwhelming support to statements about belief in freedom of speech, but they are, as Stouffer's study suggests, considerably more selective when granting this freedom to specific individuals. This flaw in translating political principle into practice is also revealed in a later study which compared the attitude of 244 representative voters in Tallahassee, Florida, and Ann Arbor, Michigan, toward democratic principles and their application. In the study, Prothro and Griggs found that about 96 percent of the voters agreed that "every citizen should have an equal chance to influence government policy," but 51 percent also believed that in a city referendum "only people who are well informed about the problem being voted on should be allowed to vote." In another question, almost all voters agreed that people in a minority "should be free to try to win majority support for their decisions" but almost a quarter of the sample said that if a Negro were legally elected mayor of their city "the white people should not allow him to take office."[24] Many Americans believe that some people are—or should be—more equal than others before the law.

That this lack of sympathy with applying the Bill of Rights in practice is a rather persistent trait among the American public is confirmed, finally, by a CBS News poll of 1,136 Americans in April 1970, which revealed:[25]

About three fourths of those sampled would not permit extremist groups to demonstrate against the government, even if no clear danger of violence occurred.

About half of those sampled would not give everyone the right to criticize the government if the criticism were thought to damage the national interest.

Nearly three fifths of those sampled believed that if a person were found innocent of a serious crime but new evidence were uncovered after the trial he should be tried again.

About three fifths of those sampled believed the police should hold a man in jail if they suspected him of a serious crime until they can find enough evidence to charge him.

---

[23] Samuel A. Stouffer, *Communism, Conformity, and Civil Liberties* (Garden City. N.Y.: Doubleday Co., 1955), pp. 29–42.

[24] James Prothro and Charles M. Griggs, "Fundamental Principles of Democracy: Bases of Agreement and Disagreement," *Journal of Politics* (May 2, 1960), pp. 276–294. On the question dealing with a Negro mayor there was an important difference in the samples: 14.4 percent of the Ann Arbor group and 42 percent of the Tallahassee sample would oppose him. Also, as Prothro and Griggs emphasize, the better educated and the wealthier voters were much more likely to "translate" the principles correctly than were the less educated, less affluent respondents.

[25] The results of this poll were reported by James Reston in *The New York Times,* April 19, 1970. © 1970 by The New York Times Company. Reprinted by permission.

In effect, a clear majority of the public in this poll would be willing to limit freedom of speech seriously, to submit a man to double jeopardy, and to suspend the writ of *habeus corpus,* all clearly contradicting the Bill of Rights.

Besides respecting constitutional norms, Americans are constantly admonished to be "good citizens." Being a "good citizen" implies that one accepts informal rules of conduct compatible with the spirit of the Constitution—for instance, respecting "fair play" in dealing with others. In the early 1960s, Herbert McClosky asked a sample of 1,484 voters to express an opinion on statements relating to "good citizenship." A sample of the responses is presented in Table 4.8.

Table 4.8

American beliefs about the rules of the game	% Agreeing
There are times when it almost seems better for people to take the law into their own hands rather than wait for the machinery of government to act.	26.9
We might as well make up our minds that in order to make the world better a lot of innocent people will have to suffer.	41.6
I don't mind a politician's methods if he manages to get the right things done.	42.4
People ought to be allowed to vote even if they can't do so intelligently.	47.6
Very few politicians have clean records so why get excited about the mudslinging that sometimes goes on?	38.1
It is all right to get around the law if you don't actually break it.	30.2
The true American way of life is disappearing so fast that we may have to use force to save it.	34.6

Source: Herbert McClosky, "Consensus and Ideology in American Politics," *American Political Science Review* (June 1964), pp. 361–382.

McClosky concluded that the average man's ideology "is little comfort to those who wish to believe that a passion for freedom, tolerance, justice, and other democratic values springs spontaneously from the lower depths of the society."[26] McClosky's point is not that the average man is invariably an anti-democrat but that there is no nationwide democratic consensus.

The contradiction and inconsistency between the official political rules and the citizen's ideas of the rules does not imply mass alienation from the political system nor does it foretell the imminent collapse of democracy. It is quite

---

[26] McClosky, *op. cit.,* p. 375.

possible for an individual to feel strong allegiance to the political system without understanding all its legal norms or even agreeing with them. Additionally, a great many Americans who do not necessarily accept various procedural rules will tolerate them. But most important, so long as those with the responsibility for interpreting and applying the rules officially are reasonably committed to the rules in theory and practice, the political system may operate according to the prescribed formulas, however uncomprehending or indifferent the masses may be.

Opinions about Public Officials.   The stature of governmental officials and that of the government itself are related. To many Americans, the president, governor, judge, and administrator *are* the government; citizens see such officials in the perspective of their general attitudes toward government. Conversely, the status of a public official also adds to or detracts from general confidence in government. One can see this two-way relationship constantly. It is doubtful that the present Constitution would have existed had not George Washington bestowed his approval upon it by endorsement and a promise to be the first chief executive; in this instance, Washington's enormous prestige was an irreplaceable asset in nation-building. Yet the office also shapes perceptions of the man; the modern presidency is, in a sense, a mantle that cloaks its incumbent with the power to summon the public emotion and affection that he never could command privately. Opinion polls always reveal that an incumbent president will be among the nation's ten most admired men. He seldom achieves such prestige before his election.

Public images of offices and officeholders have other consequences. The more important the office in the popular mind, the more likely people are to vote in contests for it. The public's ranking of offices in terms of prestige closely follows the federal system. About 65 percent of the eligible electorate normally vote in a presidential election but less than 35 percent ordinarily turn out for off-year congressional elections; a purely local election seldom entices one quarter of the registered voters to the polls.

The public image of political office also affects the government's ability to recruit adequate personnel. Men of intelligence, achievement, and status in private life whose talents are vitally necessary to government are not likely to seek public office if such office is generally considered appropriate only for men who cannot succeed at a more honorable job. Conversely, the higher the status of office, the more coveted it becomes and, hence, the more it will attract men of superior accomplishment.

Americans regard public officials with respect and cynicism. Most Americans rate major political offices near the top of all professions. Nevertheless, a great many Americans also nourish "a contempt for things political"—the

American can admire specific politicians and offices while simultaneously distrusting the "politician." A 1966 poll asked individuals to rank a number of occupations in terms of their prestige. It deliberately confined the list to those that always rank high. The following results are quite typical of other similar studies.

1. President of the United States
2. Famous doctor
3. Bishop, other church official
4. Governor of the state
5. U.S. supreme court justice
6. U.S. senator
7. Professor in a large university
8. Atomic scientist
9. President of a large corporation
10. General, admiral
11. Well-known athlete

The president, as usual, headed the list; four of the first six rankings were given to political offices. This is especially revealing of the status an office bestows on the incumbent, considering that the prestige was in all cases attached to the offices rather than to any particular occupant.[27]

The American public is nicely discriminating in its ranking of political offices. Federal positions such as president, supreme court justice, cabinet member, diplomat, congressman, and senator usually are ranked ahead of governors and other state officials who, in turn, generally rank above local officials. Members of the executive departments are generally granted more deference than members of other branches of government are. Several reasons have been suggested for this. First, this order generally follows the adult's earliest pattern of political education.[28] Beginning with the president, whose preeminence in the constellation of national heroes is never challenged by young children, political officials past and present are cast in a guise intended to elicit respect and emulation from the young. "The great of the past are elevated into paragons who would scarcely be recognizable to their contemporaries."[29] This

[27] Murphy and Tanenhaus, *op. cit.,* p. 98. The tendency for the most visible political offices to cluster at the top of the prestige scale is quite common. This list corresponds with one developed by the Bureau of the Census in 1950 and cited in A. N. Oppenheim, *Questionnaire Design and Attitude Measurements* (New York: Basic Books, 1966), pp. 264–286.

[28] For evidence that children customarily consider the president the "most important" American official see Greenstein, *op. cit.,* p. 32 ff.

[29] V. O. Key, Jr., *Public Opinion and American Democracy* (New York: Alfred A. Knopf, 1962), p. 317.

deification creates a mythology about public officials which makes them, like all heroes, larger than life. Innumerable parks, lakes, playgrounds, schools, monuments, streets, libraries, and public buildings bear the names of political leaders, eulogized as examples to others. George Washington, "first in war, first in peace, and first in the hearts of his countrymen," must surely be first in memorials as well:

> . . . his surname [has been] appropriated for one American state, seven mountains, eight streams, ten lakes, thirty-three counties; for nine American colleges; for one hundred and twenty-one American towns and villages. His birthday has long been a national holiday. His visage is on coins and banks and postage stamps. . . . His head—sixty feet from chin to scalp—has been carved out of a mountainside in South Dakota.[30]

Beyond the importance of early education, more than eight in ten Americans depend upon television for most political news; this medium more than any other is heavily programmed toward national and international events—those events that would magnify the importance of federal officials and the executive and legislative departments generally.[31]

The men who occupy political office, of course, "borrow" the images of the office for themselves. The Survey Research Center at the University of Michigan found in 1952 that the public was likely to perceive the successful presidential candidate in more favorable terms after his election than before it. Almond and Verba found that the 970 Americans they sampled in the cross-national study generally believed they would receive decent treatment from any occupant of a political office. When asked if they would receive "equal treatment by governmental authorities," the proportion of positive answers went from a low of 80 percent among those with a primary school education or less to 88 percent among Americans with a college education.[32]

Measured by social accomplishments, political and governmental officials in the United States are a social elite. Warner and Van Riper report that 80 percent of top federal career executives were college graduates, 25 percent had earned a Master's Degree, and 10 percent had earned a Ph.D.[33] Seven in ten congress-

---

[30] Marcus Cunliffe, *George Washington: The Man and the Monument* (New York: Mentor Books, 1960), p. 16.

[31] Opinion Research Center, "The Public's View of Television and Other Media, 1959–1964," in Edward C. Dreyer and Walter A. Rosenbaum, *Political Opinion and Electoral Behavior* (Belmont, Calif.: Wadsworth, 1966), pp. 309–318.

[32] Angus Campbell et al., *The American Voter* (New York: John Wiley, 1960), pp. 42–63; Almond and Verba, *op. cit.*, p. 73; Arnold Rose, *The Power Structure* (New York: Oxford University Press, 1967), pp. 174–177.

[33] W. Lloyd Warner et al., *The American Federal Executive* (New Haven: Yale University Press, 1963), p. 11 ff.

men ordinarily have a college degree; about 60 percent are lawyers. The holders of major public office in the United States are decidedly middle and upper class, an indication that our political system recruits heavily from the better educated, more prestigious social groups. That high social status and political office are intermingled is an important source of support for the political system; the politician and public official is often able to play upon his social and intellectual accomplishments to increase the respect he hopes to receive by virtue of his political position. "A man with a fairly high social status has met the society's definition of success . . . ," observes Donald Matthews. "Thus, when the factory worker votes for the lawyer, he is voting for a man who is what he would *like* to be."[34]

Americans may admire major public officials but, as we saw earlier, politics and politicians draw slight praise. In 1944, the National Opinion Research Center asked 2,560 Americans whether they would wish their son to be a politician; they received an overwhelmingly negative response of 69 percent answering "no," 18 percent "yes," and the remainder wavering. If political life was as the majority described it, their response was understandable.

> If he is a good Christian man, politics will ruin him. I believe no man in politics remains honest.

> My father was a politician for 25 years and all he got out of it was bad luck and no friends.

> Political jobs are too unstable.[35]

Twenty-four years later, the Gallup Poll asked younger and presumably better educated Americans the same question and got virtually the same response. In the 1968 question, 28 percent of Americans between 21 and 29 years old agreed they would "like to see [my] son go into politics as a life's work" but 57 percent answered "no." The reasons for the "no" were strikingly similar to the earlier ones: "Too much corruption" (16 percent), "Thankless job" (14 percent), and "Lack of opportunity and security" (13 percent) were most often mentioned.[36]

Why is this double standard applied to the public official? Perhaps, as William Mitchell has suggested, Americans equate political office with sharply different attributes: on one side, an ability to get things done and social accomplishment but on the other side, demagoguery, the exploitation of public

---

[34] Donald B. Matthews, *The Social Background of Political Decision-Makers* (New York: Random House, 1967), p. 32.

[35] Cited in William Mitchell, "The Ambivalent Social Status of the American Politician," *Western Political Quarterly* (September 1959), p. 690.

[36] Gallup Poll *Index* (March 1968), pp. 15–16.

trust, betrayal of principles, and an itch for financial gain. Also, as Mitchell and many others have mentioned, perceptions of politics vary with the social experience of those evaluating it. In the latter 1960s, many American college students apparently equated the politician with the Vietnamese war, the draft, the civil rights controversy, and the vague but sinister institution known as the Establishment. In the early 1960s, student political perceptions were quite different. These were the Kennedy years when the college generation identified with the youthful, vigorous president; enrollments in political science classes escalated and politics temporarily became a glamorous profession. Regardless of how one explains the dubious social standing of the politician, it represents the darker side of American perceptions of political office, and it seems likely to remain true in the minds of most Americans.

Political Participation

What Americans *do* politically is as important as what they think. Voting, campaigning, contributing to campaigns, and expressing political opinions have a direct impact on the political system. Indeed, the daily political life of the nation is largely directed by the political *activity* of individuals. The politician, preoccupied with responsibilities, might be concerned with public opinion in general, but he is most sensitive to what people are doing in the political system because participation has a high impact. An individual who condemns the current administration is less effective than an individual who *votes* his convictions.

Lester Milbrath suggests that political participation runs along a continuum from "spectator" to "gladiator."[37] At the spectator end of the scale are passive, relatively costless activities like listening to political broadcasts, exchanging political opinions, and reading political information. At the other end are active, aggressive modes of participation such as running for office, soliciting political contributions, and attending political meetings. Moving from spectator to gladiator activities means a progressively greater investment of time, interest, and resources in political life.

Most Americans are political spectators whose most assertive political act is voting.[38] This is apparent in Table 4.9 which reports political activism in five recent presidential election years when the stimulus to participate is greatest. Some forms of "participation" probably do not express much political interest. More than 85 percent of Americans listen to political information, but this is almost inevitable when capsulated political news appears in all media, especially

---

[37] Lester Milbrath, *Political Participation* (Chicago: Rand, McNally & Co., 1965).

[38] According to a Survey Research Center estimate in 1964, 63 percent of all Americans engaged in no significant activity once voting was excluded; 22 percent engaged in one activity but those engaged in two activities or more was less than 10 percent. See Robinson *et al., op. cit.,* p. 574.

on television, now considered an almost indispensable appliance. A "political discussion" may be nothing but an off-hand remark sandwiched between football scores and neighborhood gossip. Even voting does not always signify much political interest; numerous Americans vote more from a sense of civic duty than from strong personal involvement in elections.[39]

Table 4.9. American Political Activities, 1952 to 1968

Percent of respondents who:	1952	1956	1960	1964	1968
Belong to a political club	2	3	3	4	4
Work for parties	3	3	6	5	6
Go to meetings	7	10	8	9	9
Give money	4	10	12	11	9
Use stickers or a button	–	16	21	16	15
Give opinions	27	28	33	31	33
Vote in an election	73	73	74	78	76

Source: Data from 1952–1964 from Robinson et al., *op. cit.,* p. 591. Copyright 1968. Reprinted by permission. 1968 data from Survey Research Center, 1968 Election Study, Variables 421–429.

Several explanations have been offered for low levels of political activism in the United States. Most Americans believe that voting is the most effective way of influencing the government; other modes of activism may seem less appealing. Many Americans find politics confusing and intimidating; they tend to withdraw from sustained political exposure. Certainly, as Table 4.10 indicates, the average American feels little comprehension or mastery of political events.

Table 4.10

"Sometimes politics and government seem so complicated that a person like me can't really understand what's going on."

	1952	1956	1960	1964	1966	1968
Agree	71%	64%	59%	67%	70%	45%
Disagree	28	36	41	32	26	55
Don't know, depends	1			1	4	

Source: Robinson et al., *op. cit.,* pp. 635, 637 for data from 1952–66. Copyright 1968. Reprinted by permission. 1968 data taken from Survey Research Center, 1968 Election Study, Variable 167.

[39] The "civic duty" motivation probably plays a particularly strong role in bringing citizens to the polls when local elections—especially undramatic ones—are involved. See William Buchanan, "An Inquiry into Purposive Voting," *Journal of Politics* (May 1956), pp. 281–296.

Some commentators emphasize that the average American home does little to motivate children to be adult participators since politics is quite peripheral to daily domestic concerns. Perhaps, also, political activism depends upon psychological factors such as aggressiveness, articulateness, and ego-strength—together with a tolerance for conflict—which relatively few Americans possess.

Activists, Marginals, Nonpoliticals: Three American Civic Types

One universally recognized fact of political life is that social position and political behaviors are related. This is why, for example, it is possible to predict with considerable accuracy the party identification of an individual when one knows his occupation, income, religion, and family background. To generalize a bit, different social positions tend to incubate different political orientations. Individuals with similar social backgrounds are not always alike, but they are predisposed to develop common attitudes. The three types of political participators we will discuss—activists, marginals, and nonpoliticals—show this relationship between political and social characteristics.

Activists

By the most generous estimate, fewer than 10 percent of Americans are "activists," or the small, conspicuous stratum of the American population that holds public office, campaigns for it, and provides government executives and bureaucrats. Activists ring doorbells and solicit money during campaigns; they are opinion leaders and partisans in most public issues. The activists are engaged in the most time-consuming, demanding, sustained forms of political involvement. While percentages vary, the majority of activists represent the American social elite, usually middle and upper class, well-educated, and professionally successful. Milbrath estimates that 95 percent of Washington lobbyists rank near the top of the American social system in prestige, income, and accomplishment. Warner and Van Riper found a similar situation among top-level federal career executives: at least 64 percent came from middle- and upper-class families. Congressmen and state legislators are almost entirely professionals and businessmen. Donald Matthews, after studying the social composition of political offices in the United States, concluded that political office was related to social stratification: "There seems to be a sort of class ranking of public offices in the

United States—the more important the office, the higher the status of its normal incumbent."[40]

Other forms of political activism are also related to social status. Contributors to political campaigns, roughly 11 percent of the American population, are almost entirely middle- to upper-class individuals. Studies of the 1956 elections reveal that 30 percent of those in the highest income categories (estimated at the time to be those with an annual income of $10,000 or more) were political contributors. Lane reports the familiar finding that business and professional men are more likely than other individuals to write to a political official.[41]

Voting turnout is also related to social status in the United States. Although many Americans at all but the lowest social levels vote at least occasionally, the higher-status occupations produce the greatest proportion of their numbers at the polls and are the most consistent voters. Even during presidential elections when this Great American Spectacle offers the maximum stimulation to public interest and electoral participation, the higher-status occupations have the highest proportional turnout, as Table 4.11 indicates.

Table 4.11. Occupational Levels and Presidential Voting, 1952–1964

| Occupation | Percent Voting | | | |
	1952	1956	1960	1964
Professional and Managerial	78%	85%	92%	80%
Other white-collar	72	79	84	79
Skilled and semi-skilled	68	72	78	69
Farmers	63	73	83	79
Unskilled	55	54	76	64

Source: Reprinted by permission of Markham Publishing Company from James David Barber *Citizen Politics: An Introduction to Political Behavior* (Chicago: Markham, 1969), p. 12.

Political activism among the socially advantaged has been explained in several ways. High social status is associated with educational attainment; since the best-educated Americans usually enter high-status occupations, they are most likely to perceive the relevance of political events to themselves and most likely to feel competent and informed on civic affairs. It has also been suggested

[40] Matthews, *op. cit.*, p. 32. See also Lester Milbrath, *The Washington Lobbyist* (Chicago: Rand, McNally & Co., 1963), p. 91; Warner, *op. cit.*, p. 29; Key, *op. cit.*, pp. 149–150. There is some evidence suggesting that purely local, small-town offices will probably be considered unrespectable by "respectable" people. See, for instance, Robert Presthus, *Men at the Top* (New York: Oxford University Press, 1964), pp. 207–284.

[41] Robert E. Lane, *Political Life* (New York: The Free Press, 1965), p. 67.

that people with higher-than-average income feel a great stake in political decisions; they bear heavy tax loads, stand to benefit or suffer most immediately from governmental decisions, and are likely to be heard and respected by political officials who share the same social background. High-status people are likely to possess skills relevant to gladiatorial politics—the ability to verbalize, organizational experience, and a sense of political competence. High-status Americans customarily have the time and money available for political participation.

Not only are political activists socially different from most Americans; their political attitudes vary as well. The activist is better informed, more concerned, and more opinionated on political matters than most Americans. The strong relationship between political information and political activism is shown in Table 4.12 where levels of political information were compared to political activism in a representative population sample in 1956.

Table 4.12.   Familiarity with Political Issues

Issue Familiarity		Level of Participation		
		Low	Medium	High
High	4	16%	30%	45%
	3	17	27	27
	2	18	19	16
Low	1	49	24	12

Source: Survey Research Center, University of Michigan. Cited in Key, *op. cit.*, p. 185.

What makes the political activist distinctive is that for him, politics is a primary value: he usually feels no social space between himself and political life. Often, indeed, the activist cannot separate personal and political values:

They say this is an angry campaign. Well, yes, I *am* angry. I made a few visits to Vietnam and I've met mothers who had their kids bombed. . . . They hold me accountable because I'm white and because I'm an American. And when I tried to talk to them about democracy, they said "That gibberish . . .[42]

I don't suppose it occurred to me in a million years that I would vote Republican. But there was a bad slum fire, and . . . it became clear that it had occurred because a building inspector had been bribed. I remember brooding

[42] Serge Lang, *The Scheer Campaign* (New York: W. A. Benjamin, 1967), p. 43.

over this and thinking, how many people have to die because I can't bear to pull the Republican lever.[43]

Stopping the Communists, and destroying their conspiracy . . . not only must occupy the front spot in all our thinking, it is the driving danger which should determine our thinking about almost everything else.[44]

Political activism also corresponds to a relatively high level of agreement with the idealized norms of American politics; as a group, political activists usually score well above other Americans in this respect. During 1957 to 1958, Herbert McClosky compared the political attitudes of 1,484 political activists with 3,020 randomly selected voters in respect to their political values.[45] Answers were arranged on scales which dealt with faith in democracy, belief in procedural rights, tolerance, and faith in freedom. McClosky found a pattern familiar in opinion surveys: the activists as a group averaged consistently higher scores in verbal agreement with basic democratic values, acceptance of procedural rights guaranteed by the Constitution, tolerance for dissent and unpopular opinions, and faith in the virtues of political freedom. Moreover, the activists seemed more consistent in applying these various principles in specific cases.

The political activist is also likely to be a social optimist. Americans of all social conditions are, to some extent, politically cynical and socially pessimistic, but the American Dream seems least blighted among the social groups supplying most of the political activists. The political participators come from the social stratum that expresses greatest satisfaction with its immediate condition, anticipates the future hopefully, and sustains a diffuse confidence in their fellow men and in their own potential. Political activists perceive a political system where a man can still fight city hall, can expect reasonably fair and impartial treatment from administrators, and can make his influence felt. Political activism expresses in a variety of ways a belief in one's capacity to affect society—and to change it.[46]

To summarize, the activists are a substantial part of the American political establishment. Not only are these the leaders of the system—in the sense that they occupy the political roles and mobilize support for the governmental structure—but they are also the mechanics and technologists of the system, the

---

[43] James Q. Wilson, *The Amateur Democrat* (Chicago: University of Chicago Press, 1966), p. 185.

[44] Robert Welch, *The Blue Book of the* [John Birch] *Society* (Belmont, Mass.: The Society, 1961), p. 171.

[45] Herbert McClosky, *op. cit.* McClosky's "influentials," whom we here have called "activists," were delegates to the major party nominating conventions in 1956.

[46] See Key, *op. cit.*, p. 129; Rose, *op. cit.*, pp. 174–177; Presthus, *op. cit.*, p. 337; Almond and Verba, *op. cit.*, p. 73.

people who make it work by repeatedly acting out the rituals and values that are part of the official norms.

Marginals

Most Americans stand midway between the busy political activist and the completely apathetic citizen in terms of political interest, involvement, and activism. The politically marginal American approaches political life and withdraws from it intermittently and irregularly. In a moment of patriotic enthusiasm we may describe a government "of the people, by the people, for the people," but a coldly realistic respect for facts would justify amending Lincoln's phrase to read "government of the people, by some of the people, and occasionally interesting to most of the people." Most Americans, in short, have bleacher seats in the great game of politics. "The game . . . is partially for entertainment . . . the spectator pattern of American mass behavior . . . is a pervasive feature of the culture.[47]

Like the political activist, a number of related political behaviors and attitudes characterize the marginal American. In terms of political participation, he lives at the "spectator" end of the scale. In terms of political attitudes, his political information, interest, and involvement lie midway between the small band of gladiators and the much larger strata of the completely uninvolved, uninterested, and uninformed people. In terms of political beliefs, the marginal American subscribes to general but vague democratic principles most of the time but often fails to translate them consistently in practical situations; he is in conflict about his impact on the political system. Marginals are the largest, most socially mixed of all the political types.

It is difficult to estimate the number of marginals with satisfactory precision, but rough estimates are available. If we begin with political participation, about 60 to 65 percent of the population would qualify because they are essentially spectators. For these Americans, casting a ballot ends political participation; yet even voting is not necessarily an indication of political involvement and interest. Many Americans vote irregularly; a 1968 Gallup Poll reported, for instance, that only 35 percent of Americans between ages 21 and 29 voted regularly; Matthews and Prothro found in a study of white Southern voters that one third of their sample could not cite a specific reason for registering to vote, while another third explained only that they had "come of age."[48]

If one measures the marginal population by concentrating on political attitudes, this group still seems as large. In Table 4.13, a variety of Americans in different social positions were compared according to their sense of "political

---

[47] Eulau, *op. cit.*, p. 65.

[48] Donald R. Matthews and James W. Prothro, *Negroes and the New Southern Politics* (New York: Harcourt Brace Jovanovich, 1966), p. 73.

efficacy"—the feeling of effectiveness in relation to what they could do politically. The marginals would be those in the middle to lower range of such a scale.

Table 4.13. Sense of Political Efficacy: By Occupation, 1956

Sense of Political Efficacy	Professional	Business	Clerical	Skilled	Unskilled	Farm
Low	10%	19%	25%	25%	40%	47%
Medium	17	22	25	31	28	25
High	73	59	50	44	32	28
N =	(99)	(217)	(65)	(302)	(233)	(660)

Source: Survey Research Center, University of Michigan. Cited in Key, *op. cit.,* p. 303.

The number of marginals increases as one moves down the social ladder and into the more populous categories. Although this table deals only with the sense of political efficacy, the pattern would be roughly similar if political interest, information, or some other indicator of political involvement would be used. The number of those in the middle range would usually increase as one moves away from high-status individuals. The fact that most Americans are only moderately involved in political life cannot be explained as being due to lack of opportunity or stimuli, as is often alleged. When Americans are given hypothetical questions in which they are asked if they would contribute money to campaigns or work for candidates of their choice, the majority give a predictable, overwhelming no.[49]

The marginal American's opinions are usually unsophisticated and unstructured. His political ideas are a sort of simple hornbook for civic life, consisting of some maxims ("I think government should help a man to help himself"), bits and pieces of opinions usually formed in impromptu response to currently important issues and some familiar if not altogether understood labels applied to oneself and others ("I'm a liberal"). Opinion polls suggest that the information supporting even intense opinions is often meager, that inconsistent opinions and values are held simultaneously by probably a majority of Americans, and that perceptions of candidates, issues, and political events often fail to correspond to reality. After studying the American electorate in 1952 and 1956, the University of Michigan's Survey Research Center concluded that less than 5 percent of the American voters had a consistent and reasonably integrated set of political values, could summon and utilize political information to justify their political opinions, and could interpret specific political events in terms of a broader frame of values, giving meaning and direction response to these events.[50]

[49] On the matter of hypothetical questions, see Murphy and Tanenhaus, *op. cit.,* p. 59; and the Gallup Poll *Index* (August 1966).

[50] Campbell, *op. cit.,* pp. 188–266.

The Survey Research Center was dealing specifically with public attitudes and information about political parties but, as we saw earlier, the generally low level of political information, acquaintance with current political events, and interest in political affairs extends to most matters of civic importance.

The inconsistency and disorganization of the marginal American's political thinking does not necessarily signify individual stupidity or political irresponsibility. This indicates, instead, that political affairs are mostly too unimportant to most Americans to merit sustained and careful reflection. Opinions become organized and coherent when they are thought through; when a person must defend his political opinions, or when he is expected to formulate a fairly consistent attitude toward public affairs, he is likely to think about them. Most Americans are not placed in roles where political attitudes must be developed and refined in order to achieve some personal or social need. This is another indication of the generalized nonpoliticism of American civic life. Another explanation for the untidy state of opinion relates to the "other-directedness" of Americans. Though they are not compulsive conformists, Americans do defer to the opinions of family, friends, occupational associates, or anyone who offers emotional support and social reward. Individuals often react with seismographic sensitivity to these "others" to the extent of changing political opinions and values when they perceive it necessary. Thus, most individuals tack and turn over time, attempting to square themselves with the changing opinion environment. The result is that many Americans hold clusters of inconsistent and fragmented opinions which reflect their social history and the short-range changes in their social environment. It is, additionally, unrealistic to expect most people to be rationally consistent and carefully logical in their political opinions since they cannot meet these standards in any other area of opinion. Political issues often incite irrationality, unthinking passion, or plain obscurity. The speeches of candidates and public officials are often masterpieces of vagary and indirection; even a well-motivated and conscientious citizen can be confused by the pronouncements of public officials.

Nonpoliticals

Psychologically, the nonpolitical American lives outside the political system; he is removed from the civic processes and issues around him. Such a person almost never votes. He takes no notice of political affairs, seldom retains sufficient information to discuss politics intelligently, and follows a life style almost completely focused on personal problems. The nonpolitical American implicitly testifies that government and its problems command no part of his important resources. That such a withdrawal exists invites disbelief and a suspicion that this group must be a small and irrelevant portion of the society.

One can better judge the size of the nonpolitical population by looking at voting. Conservative estimates suggest that between 15 and 20 percent of Americans eligible to vote will not do so in their lifetime.[51] If we add to the nonvoters those who vote once or twice in a lifetime, the number of Americans who voluntarily refrained in the past from casting a ballot might be as high as 30 percent of the adult population. Nonvoting outside the South is customarily associated with low levels of political information, interest, and activity; Americans who score lowest on these items, therefore, are not likely to cast a ballot. At a mimimum, a dependable 10 percent of Americans will always report they do not discuss politics to any significant degree; some estimates approach 25 percent.[52] Almond and Verba found that about 9 percent of their American sample believed a person's community obligations ended with participation in church work, or in being "upright in personal life;" they had nothing to do with local government. Another 11 percent reported they didn't know what community obligations an ordinary man had. In the summer of 1968, during a vigorously contested presidential election, the Gallup Poll estimated that 5 percent of the population was totally uninterested in the Great American Spectacle and another 29 percent were only slightly concerned.[53]

If a sense of political futility is what defines the nonpolitical population, it is quite large. In his 1957–1958 study of Wayne County (Detroit), Samuel Eldersveld found that (1) 26 percent of his sample agreed that "People like me don't have any say about what government does," and (2) about 19 percent did not believe that "Public officials really care about what people like me think." Using a measure of "political futility" in his 1959 study, cited earlier, McClosky recorded citizen responses to selected statements (see Table 4.14).

Table 4.14.   Measures of Political Futility, 1959

	% Agreeing
It's no use worrying my head about public affairs; I can't do anything about them anyhow.	20.5
Nothing I ever do seems to have any effect upon what happens in politics.	61.5
It seems to me that whoever you vote for, things go on pretty much the same.	51.3

Source: Samuel J. Eldersveld, *Political Parties* (Chicago: Rand-McNally, 1964), p. 498; Herbert McClosky, "Consensus and Ideology in American Politics," *American Political Science Review* (June 1964), p. 371.

[51] For estimates of nonvoting, see Walter Dean Burnham, "The Changing Shape of the American Political Universe," *American Political Science Review* (March 1965), pp. 7–28.

[52] Almond and Verba, *op. cit.;* see p. 79 for the high estimate.

[53] *Ibid.,* p. 127; Gallup Poll *Index* (March 1968), p. 14.

Other polls utilizing different measures of political cynicism, alienation, and nonparticipation all indicate, as these do, that millions of Americans qualify as nonpoliticals. A safely conservative estimate of the Americans who seldom if ever vote, who express little or no political interest, and whose sense of political competence and political information is low would be at least 10 percent of the population, or somewhere around 20 million.

In the past, this group was concentrated at the lower end of the social hierarchy: the poor, the unskilled, the marginal sharecropper, the ghetto black, the illiterate, and others with culturally marginal skills are prime candidates for nonpolitical status.[54] The life experiences and meager financial resources of such Americans do not equip them intellectually or psychologically for customary forms of political activism. Voluntary associations, which develop a sense of group-mindedness, provide experience in social cooperation, translate civic issues into group terms, and mobilize individuals to pursue political matters, are practically nonexistent or ineffective at this social level. Lower-class people often feel generalized social distrust which mitigates against civic cooperation. The nonpolitical American's attitude toward civic affairs in many ways expresses a broader, pervasive orientation toward life and society in which futility, a sense of vulnerability and powerlessness, and a gnawing conviction of grievance and alienation are dominant themes. Standing at the bottom of the social ladder, the nonpolitical often recognizes that he has not succeeded in terms of American values. He recognizes, often, that he has an economically marginal position, and that his social mobility and life options are rigidly circumscribed. From the social vantage point where most nonpoliticals stand, the political system symbolizes the larger society and summons the same emotions that arise toward other social institutions.

Of these three groups, the nonpolitical seems destined for the most dramatic change in the next decade. Massive federal voting registration supplemented with the sharp goad of the federal courts have forced states in the deep South to open the polls to blacks: between 1952 and 1962, black voter registrations increased in the South by 400,000 when the Justice Department forced a quicker pace; 750,000 additional blacks were registered between 1962 and 1964.[55] Beginning with the Kennedy Administration in the early 1960s, federal agencies concerned with welfare, school desegregation, and cultural enrichment for children of pov-

---

[54] Not *all* nonpoliticals are of low status. In Table 4.13, for example, note that ten percent of the professionals rated "low" on political efficacy, a hint that many were probably close to nonpolitical in behavior. The reason there are so many nonpoliticals is that the social groups from which nonpoliticals arise are larger than many Americans realize. The Bureau of the Census estimates that 18.5 million Americans have not finished grade school; half did not complete the fourth grade, and 2.5 million are illiterate. In 1968, about 17 percent of the American population lived in poverty. See U.S. Department of Commerce, Bureau of the Census, *U.S. Book of Facts, Statistics, and Information* (New York: Department of Commerce, 1969), especially Sections 4 and 8.

[55] Estimate in Southern Regional Council, *Politics in America* (Washington: Congressional Quarterly Service, 1965), p. 76.

erty have attempted to politicize segments of the normally nonpolitical population; the federal government encouraged the development of neighborhood civic action programs, citizen advisory councils, and other devices which would recruit lower-class political leaders and provide them with independent support within their own milieu. The results of these programs are uneven and often disappointing in light of expectations, but they have significantly increased political activism among social groups whose political potential was untapped.

If efforts to provide a decent education to the poor succeed to any significant degree, this alone will probably bring greater political activism. Rising educational levels are so generally associated with rising levels of political participation, interest, and involvement that the public expenditure of billions of dollars for the education of the underprivileged will undoubtedly increase their civic participation. A pointed example is that of young American Negroes. The new generation of youthful Negro militants who initiated the sit-ins and other forms of aggressive civic rights programs, who forced older civil rights leaders to broaden the scope and quicken the pace of their attack on racial inequality, and who have formed the core of newer, militant civil rights organizations are primarily high-school and college people whose parents, with few exceptions, were poorly educated.

The changes that are still emergent in the heavily nonpolitical strata remind us that political cultures are the product of social forces and historical experiences acting upon individuals over time. We have, to this point, concentrated primarily on how various political attitudes are distributed in the United States. Let us turn to the question of how this distribution is created—that is, let us ask what social processes produce various forms of political orientation. How do we, individually, arrive at our particular picture of the political world? What events and influences acting over our lifetime and the collective experiences of others produce activists, marginals, nonpoliticals, and many others who defy simple description? In the following section, we will describe the institutions of political socialization and their impact upon us.

Political Socialization

Earlier we observed that political socialization involves those procedures through which an individual acquires the basic political values, attitudes, and beliefs that create his orientation toward his political system. While attitudes toward his political system often alter throughout one's life, many basic orientations will be formed or heavily influenced by the family and school—not surprisingly, since these institutions figure prominently in the American child's earliest cultural experiences. Let us examine briefly what part family and school play in this political socialization and how this contribution may be changing.

The Family

"The family affects basic political orientations very strongly. It is the key agent through which the political culture is transmitted from one generation to the next."[56] The single most important political inheritance a family transmits to a child is a social position, a location in the social world called "class," "status," or "social group." A family determines where the child starts in life experience, what resources and expectations he confronts and, in general, what he will learn and observe in the critical early years of political socialization. The child's "ethnic, linguistic, religious, . . . cultural, and educational values and achievements, his occupational and economic aspirations, and his exposure to others are determined largely by family."[57] Most individuals do not reflect upon the extent to which their version of political reality is tied to social experience, in part because they seldom have contact with others far enough removed in social status to reveal the significant differences in political learning which accompanies different social loci. Numerous examples suggest the association of social position with political socialization. Middle-class and upper-class children, for example, are more likely to believe in the importance of political participation and their own capacity to influence civic life than lower-class children are. Children from lower-class families are inclined to be more apathetic toward political affairs and less likely to believe in their ability to affect government directly.[58] The Negro child (like other nonwhite children) learns the cold lesson that skin color is tied to social privilege and acceptance, to what social rights are given, and to what social duties are expected. Southern white children are more likely to believe in legal segregation than non-Southern white children; rural young people are more politically and socially conservative than urban children. The impact of social position on political socialization is pervasive and unavoidable.

Beyond defining a child's social position, the family also affects at least two specific political attitudes: (1) interest and attention to political matters and (2) party identification.[59] The common relationship between political interest of children and parents is described in Table 4.15.

[56] *Ibid.,* p. 107.

[57] *Ibid.,* pp. 109–110.

[58] See, for example, Joan E. Lawrence and Harry Scoble, "Ideology and Consensus among Children of the Metropolitan Socioeconomic Elite," *Western Political Quarterly* (March 1969), pp. 151–162 for an excellent illustration of how high socioeconomic status in parents tends to correlate with strong pro-democratic values in fairly young children at grade school levels.

[59] Some commentators would add that family also encourages a sense of either acceptance or hostility toward the political system. For some arguments for this proposition, see especially Jaros *et al., op. cit.,* and Kenneth Kenniston, *Young Radicals* (New York: Harcourt, Brace & World, 1968), Chapter 2.

Table 4.15. Political Involvement of Parents and Their Children, 1958

Respondent's involvement		Parental Political Interest		
		High	Medium	Low
High	1	36%	19%	14%
	2	25	27	12
	3	19	29	19
Low	4	20	25	55
	N =	(658)	(422)	(274)

Source: Survey Research Center, University of Michigan. Cited in Key, *op. cit.*, p. 302.

The higher the level of parental political involvement, the higher the level of political involvement usually reported by the children—though the correlation is not perfect.[60] Most American homes, however, do not produce politically involved children because a child ordinarily learns that politics is not especially important for it is not primary to one's life work. This nonpoliticism indicates an interesting separation between political perception and political reality. We noted the extent to which the American government penetrates social life. Most American parents apparently behave as if political and private affairs can be easily separated; politics is still "out there" rather than "in here."

If the ordinary American child is not predestined to political activism, neither is he taught to be a political radical—or even a critic—in most American homes. Most children are expected to conform to the dominant political institutions of the society or, sometimes, to the distinctive institutions and norms of the local community. Depending upon one's values, this can be considered a lesson in unquestioning obedience to the *status quo* or a contribution to social stability; in any case, it means that political socialization in American families is definitely conservative:

> . . . it tends to project into the future the prevailing patterns of social and occupational status with the associated political outlooks. . . . It tends to perpetuate the prevailing system of identifications with political parties and other politically relevant groups.[61]

The continuation of parental political orientations through children is also apparent in regard to party identification. Most American children can express party identification by the fifth grade; beginning at this early age and continuing

[60] The correlation between children's and parents' political involvement is especially strong when *both* parents are approximately equal in political involvement.

[61] Key, *op. cit.*, p. 313.

for most adults throughout their lives, the sense of party identification originates in the home. The transmission of party identification across generations is imperfect at times; the American family *disposes* the child toward adult party identification rather than determines it.

Beyond communicating partisan feeling and stimulating or discouraging political activism, the family's political impact on the child is quite uncertain despite assumptions that most children will be taught to "see" the political world in almost all respects in the home. Recent studies, for instance, imply that young Americans are not political carbon copies of their parents in their attitudes toward such matters as civil rights, desegregation, and prayer in public schools.[62] Apparently the parent is far less successful in shaping youthful attitudes on political *issues* than he may be in respect to partisanship and political interest. Probably a major reason for the limited impact of family political values of children is that from the age of five, the family yields its unchallenged position as a socializing agent to the public schools, and another phase of youthful political development begins.

Education

A major justification for the enormous cost of public education has been that it teaches "good citizenship." The public schools have been expected to take the major responsibility in this area. With the possible exception of the family, no other institution commands more time from the young and communicates more socially important information than the public schools during the formative years of citizens. By the early 1970s, approximately 59 million Americans will be enrolled in schools from kindergarten through college; this represents about 60 percent of the American population between the age of 5 and 34. Between ages 5 and 17, school attendance is compulsory; about 95 percent of the eligible children are in the classroom.

No other social institution including the family is charged with as much responsibility for political socialization as the schools. This socialization begins quickly. In the earliest grades, the child is taught to recognize and accept the political structure, to identify and admire political heroes, to place himself in the continuum of his national history, and to develop a political self-concept that corresponds to the official norms for good citizens. It is this earliest socialization which, if successful, will become strategic in setting the direction and intensity of his later political attitudes. In almost all political systems about which we have appropriate information, as educational levels rise within a population, so do levels of political information, interest, and activism; moreover, education

---

[62] See M. Kent Jennings and Richard G. Niemi, "The Transmission of Political Values from Parent to Child," *American Political Science Review*, March 1968, pp. 169–184.

seems to strengthen an individual's confidence that he can understand the political world and apparently enhances his ability to form organized, coherent opinions on political affairs. Indeed, education often seems the *key* social attribute in determining an individual's interest, involvement, and information concerning his political system.

Grade School.   In the earliest grades, the child learns about home, family, and community. Beginning at about the fourth grade, the content of civic education shifts toward one's state, to the basic structures and leaders of the federal government and American history. This study of American political history and structures instituted in the fourth grade continues in various forms through high school. Greenstein found in his study of New Haven school children that political perceptions were formed in a certain order. First, federal and local political leaders become familiar—among the New Haven children through the third grade, the president and the mayor were the most familiar political figures although the president easily won the popularity contest. Awareness of the president or mayor also reflects the tendency, found by a number of investigators, for younger children to be most impressed with and interested in the executive departments of government.[63]

In the first four or five grades of primary school, the political history they learn would cause few children to doubt either the worth of their society or its estimable place in history. The young child's response to government as he understands it is trust, confidence in the benevolence of public officials, and belief in the government's interest in him. Researchers found this as early as the third grade among Chicago school children. In tracing the growth of political confidence through the early grades, they report that an increasing number of students would not agree to the proposition that "What happens in government will happen no matter what people do." Also, they answered negatively to the related statement that "My family doesn't have any say about what government does."[64] This lack of political cynicism apparently prevails at least until the eighth grade; it does not appear to vary significantly among children of different racial, religious, or socioeconomic groups.

As children move through the elementary grades, their concept of government changes. In the early years, the government is personalized; the president, the mayor, or the policeman. By the eighth grade, most school children appreciate that the national government (and state government as well) is made up of three different branches; they attribute much greater importance to Congress and the law-making functions of government, and can understand in a

---

[63] Greenstein, *op. cit.*, p. 32 ff.
[64] Easton and Dennis, *op. cit.*, pp. 30–31.

rudimentary way the meaning of impersonal law; they demonstrate more confidence in their political opinions as the number of "don't know" and "no
opinion" responses to questions decline sharply. The president has fallen from
his lofty, irreproachable position. By the eighth grade, only 2 percent of the
children Greenstein tested still believed the president was "the best person in the
world." Despite the growing complexity of the child's political perceptions and
his decreasing idealization of political leaders, his trusting, optimistic orientation
toward the political system remains through all the first eight grades as a
constant, fixed point in a constellation of changing political perceptions.

High School.   Adolescence is the end of political innocence. The typical
grade school student trusts government implicitly, believes it is benevolent and
wise, and respects national heroes and public officials with little reservation; his
political system is idealized. The high school student is more reserved and
cautious. His confidence in governmental benevolence is qualified; his faith in
the government's responsiveness to his interests and in his own ability to
influence government wavers. Though he is better informed factually about the
political system, he is still ignorant of many fundamental political facts. He is
particularly contradictory concerning constitutional principles and civil liberties;
often, a hint of cynicism colors his perceptions of government. The high school
years mark the transition of most Americans from largely uncritical regard for
their political system to the complex and variable attitudes of adults.

High school students are generally better informed on "textbook facts" than
the average American but not uniformly so. Despite his greater exposure to such
information and the frequent requirement that he take classes in civics and
American history, the high school student often remains unfamiliar with basic
political facts. In a recent study, for example, fewer than one third of the 1,669
representative high school seniors interviewed were able to identify correctly
which of the two major political parties was considered more conservative;
among the rest, four in ten could not make any decision.[65] Studies over many
years have confirmed the highly variable quality of political information among
high school students.

In respect to believing in their ability to influence political decisions and
affecting the course of government, high school students are divided. In the late
1950s, researchers found from their study of 2,500 American teenagers the
familiar pattern that a large minority of students did not believe they had much
influence upon government. In their summary, for example, the authors reported

---

[65] Kenneth P. Langton and M. Kent Jennings, "Political Socialization and the High
School Civics Curriculum in the United States," *American Political Science Review*
(September 1968), p. 860.

that 41 percent of the students felt it was not worthwhile to send letters or telegrams to congressmen and 33 percent expressed a conviction that they could do nothing to help prevent a war.[66] Among the high school seniors in Langton and Jennings' study, there was no group that showed a majority with a high sense of political efficacy—a strong belief in their ability to affect governmental decisions—when seniors were compared first on the basis of the number of civics courses they had, and then alternately according to the educational background of their parents.

Regarding the Constitution and the official norms of the political system, the same unevenness of opinion appears in virtually all recent studies. Like adults, high school students customarily profess strong agreement with abstract constitutional principles but fail to apply them in practical situations. In the late 1950s, for example, 39 percent of the students would deny visiting foreigners any right to criticize the United States, and 34 percent agreed that "government should prohibit some people from making speeches."[67]

Except for their ages, however, high school students are a heterogeneous population with mixed intelligence, socioeconomic backgrounds, and life experiences; differences in political orientations sometimes correspond to these social distinctions. Students from families with high socioeconomic status in which one or both parents are college educated will score somewhat better than children from lower-class families or with relatively less-educated parents on such matters as political information, political efficacy, and agreement with democratic norms. Students with relatively high IQs also score better than students with lower intelligence scores on these matters. Yet differences between students on various levels of social and economic status are not so consistently or sufficiently great to suggest a strong, uniformly positive relationship between intelligence or socioeconomic status and political orientations. In a study of three civic-education classes in three different schools with different socioeconomic environments, for instance, Edgar Litt found no significant difference among the classes in their support for political participation and only a slight difference between students in civic-education classes and those who were not in these classes concerning their support for the democratic creed.

In recent years, growing evidence suggests that high school civics courses or "American problems" courses appear to have relatively little impact upon student political orientations; there is usually no significant difference in political attitudes between students who have had such courses and those who have not.[68] Interestingly, Jennings and Langton found that a third of the high school seniors they interviewed had never had a course in high school civics and a

---

[66] H. H. Remmers and D. H. Radler, *The American Teenager* (Indianapolis: Bobbs-Merrill Co., 1957), p. 179.

[67] *Ibid.*

[68] Edgar Litt, "Civic Education, Norms, and Political Indoctrination," in Robinson, et al., *op. cit.,* p. 476.

majority of the rest had taken only one. Nor do other forms of high school activity seem strongly related to the development of political attitudes, not even those designed to encourage a sense of political efficacy and respect for democratic norms. Almond and Verba found in their five-nation study that American adults who had an opportunity to participate in political debate and discussion during their high school years scored only slightly better in their sense of political competence than those who did not participate in such activities. In a related study, another investigator interested in the relationship between participation in extracurricular activities and positive orientations toward politics did not discover a significantly positive association.[69]

In the past, high school political socialization appears to have had mixed results, with two main orientations becoming apparent. First, the student was becoming more realistic in his political perceptions. His qualified judgment, ability to discriminate between what he is told and what he believes, and his widening range of political information reflect some appreciation of the complexities and inconsistencies of political life. In this capacity to stand back from political life, to criticize and to reject some political values while still retaining a sense of allegiance to the system, he showed a healthy independence.[70] Second, however, many of his political values also indicated a growing rejection of basic civil liberties guaranteed by the Constitution. In this respect, high school political education also resulted in increased cynicism and rejection of official political norms, though seldom in the proportions of a total negation of the system. Thus, if a major objective for high school education has been to produce attitudes consistent with the official norms of the society, the result has been quite uneven.

During the 1970s, however, it may be increasingly necessary to speak of these patterns of political socialization in the past tense. There is evidence—still fragmentary and tentative—that the oncoming generation of high school students, apparently following the cue from some college students, is becoming more politically active and sensitive, less satisfied with existing political procedures and structures, more overtly responsive to the larger social issues that affect them, and more willing to defy authorities in quest of radical political action. If this is true, then the high school of the 1970s may be more politicized than previously, and its students may be more directly caught up in the wave of political ferment already evident on college campuses.[71] The appearance of

[69] David Ziblatt, "High School Extracurricular Activities and Political Socialization," in Roberta Sigel (ed.), *Political Socialization: Its Role in the Political Process* (The Annals of the American Academy of Political and Social Science, September 1965), pp. 20–31.

[70] Very recently, some evidence shows that high school students are becoming more "radicalized" and politicized. They want a larger voice in school administration and greater attention to current social and political issues in the classroom. How durable this upsurging social alertness will be remains uncertain. See, for instance, Louis Harris, "What People Think about their High Schools," *Life* (May 16, 1969), pp. 22–33.

[71] Three studies that argue for increasing high school radicalization and offer a sampling of high school political opinion are John Birmingham (ed.), *Our Time Is Now* (New York:

underground student newspapers launching vigorous attacks on many traditional academic and political institutions and procedures, the tensions and conflicts introduced on the high school campus by racial integration, the omnipresent consciousness of the draft and other factors may signify that high school students have come a long way from the student council and elections for campus kings and queens in their understanding of political activism. Whether we are witnessing the first stirring of a revolution in high school political socialization, a transient episode of political activism soon to disappear, or something between the two is yet to be decided.

The College Years.   Until the 1950s, high school represented the last structured and controlled educational environment for most Americans and the end of educationally-related political socialization. Since the middle 1950s, the proportion of high school seniors entering college has risen steadily and will continue to do so for many years to come. The impact of college on political thinking has always been important in a nation which has recruited its political leadership primarily from the college-educated; now that a growing body of all Americans attend college, its impact on the whole political system is greater.

First, the college-educated are different from the noncollege-educated when it comes to political orientations. College education seems to develop a particular intellectual style for handling political problems.

> The college-educated have been more apt to consider particular issues or events in a broader, more general, and more abstract context, as related to other issues and principles, and to objectives or styles of public policy; they have also been more apt to perceive the practical implications of alternative policies—such as high taxes. Those who have completed only grade school, on the other hand, have tended much more to view each event of which they are aware in isolation from historical or other background factors and from long-range implications.[72]

Partly because college-educated adults are likely to see a particular issue in depth and breadth and to relate it to other values and experiences, there is a corresponding tendency to be somewhat less dogmatic in their political opinions.

Second, college-educated Americans tend to be more liberal than the general American public on most social questions. This social liberalism does not

Praeger, 1970); Diane Divoky (ed.), *How Old Will You Be in 1984?* (New York: Avon-Discus, 1970); and Marc Libarle and Tom Seligson (eds.), *The High School Revolutionaries* (New York: Random House, 1970).

[72] Robinson et al., *op. cit.,* p. 39.

necessarily mean that they are more politically liberal—the majority of college graduates, for instance are Republicans and in the context of American politics favor the more conservative of the major parties. Instead, the liberalism of the college graduate refers to a relatively more receptive attitude toward ideas, more moderation in opinions, and less resistance to change and experimentation. College education encourages "appreciation of the complexity of people and social events, openness to new experience, flexibility in thinking, compassion in judgment of people."[73] A college-educated American, for instance, is much more likely than other Americans to reject extreme punishment of social deviation such as homosexuality, outspoken political extremism, or crimes of passion; he is less likely to be dogmatic and belligerent in his attitudes toward foreign and domestic political issues.

Third, the college-educated American is more politically involved in his society. College graduates are usually (1) more interested in politics and better informed about it; (2) more perceptive about the impact of political events upon them; (3) more politically active; and (4) more consistent in applying constitutional principles in concrete instances. The difference between the college graduate and other Americans is, of course, relative. Still, the college-educated adult will normally stay ahead of other Americans in these respects. The association of college with high levels of familiarity with political issues is apparent in Table 4.16 which compares Americans in a national sample according to their education and their acquaintance with the issues of the 1952 and 1956 presidential campaigns. Though a college education will not inevitably produce a civic activist, a sophisticated political observer, or a model citizen, it is more likely to clarify political orientations and to motivate political interest than any other educational experience.

Table 4.16.   Education and Issue Familiarity,
1952, 1956

Familiarity with Issues	8 Grades or Less	Some or All High School	Some or All College
High	21%	31%	50%
Medium	37	47	44
Low	42	22	6
N =	(543)	(890)	(331)

Source: Reprinted with permission from Angus Campbell et al., *The American Voter* (New York: Wiley, 1960), p. 102.

By the early 1960s, the college student, himself, had become the national issue. The years since the middle 1960s have been called years of mounting

---

[73] Mervin B. Freedman, *The College Experience* (San Francisco: Jossey-Bass, 1967), p. 6.

student radicalism. Many commentators allege that this radicalism signals a growing collegiate alienation from the political system and established social institutions. Unlike the students of the "Eisenhower generation" a decade earlier (the argument runs), the new students are rapidly retreating from the dominant political culture. Commentators cite as evidence the militant civil rights demonstrations, vigorous and occasionally violent protests on and off campuses against the Vietnamese conflict, the military establishment, and the power structure. However the collegiate. mood was interpreted, it seemed to many thoughtful observers that the American college was breeding a new student generation with political values that might produce a political revolution, peaceful or otherwise. Given the rapidly rising college enrollment and the centrality of a college education for occupational success in contemporary America, whatever was happening on the college campus was bound to affect the future course of the political system.

The current information on student political behavior sheds enough light on the new student to permit some qualified generalizations. It reveals that the new image of the college student is part truth, part myth. Several studies reveal that the majority of students are only occasionally politically active, a great many not at all. In the presidential election year 1968, the Gallup Poll reported that only about one third of college students expressed a "great deal of interest" in politics and that 47 percent of college students eligible to vote had done so.[74]

Studies of on-campus activism suggest that a minority of the college population were actively involved. The National Student Association estimated that in the first half of 1968 about 2.6 percent of all students enrolled in college had participated in major demonstrations; the Gallup Poll, in comparison, reported the number to be one in five.[75] A number of studies conducted in 1968 and 1969 indicated that no more than 2 percent of the college enrollment belonged to "radical" organizations.

Students do not, for the most part, describe themselves in terms of political extremes though they definitely congregate at the liberal end of the political scale. An interesting comparison of student opinion appears in Table 4.17 which contrasts the result of a nationwide poll in 1961 with another in 1969; in both instances, the students were asked where they stood in the political spectrum.

Even though relatively few students directly involved themselves in campus demonstrations, a considerable—and apparently growing—number were sympathetic or tolerant. A nationwide campus poll by *Fortune* in early 1969

---

[74] Gallup Poll *Index* (May 1968), p. 40. The percentage of students expressing high political interest was well above the national average, however.

[75] *The New York Times,* August 27, 1968, June 29, 1968, and November 10, 1968. Demonstrations were not for the same reasons. The National Student Association lists many issues: Black Power (97 incidents); Student Power (50); Vietnam (26); Dow Chemical Company (14); supporting a professor or administrator (14); against armed campus police (6); poor people (2); military recruitment (2); bad food (2); the Central Intelligence Agency (1); and causes unknown (4).

Table 4.17.   Where College Students Stood Politically, 1961 and 1969

1961		1969	
Extremely conservative	3.3%	Extremely conservative	2%
Moderately conservative	29.2	Moderately conservative	19
Moderately liberal	46.8	Middle of road	24
Highly liberal	13.7	Moderately liberal	41
Socialist	2.7	Highly liberal	12
No political views	4.3	No political views	2

Source: Russell Middleton and Snell Putney, "Student Rebellion against Parental Political Beliefs," *Social Forces* (May 1963), p. 380; Gallup Poll *Index* (May 1969).

found that, while 58 percent of the students were attending college for "practical benefits of improved social and economic status," another 42 percent had less concrete objectives which included learning to change the existing social system. These were, in *Fortune*'s opinion, the "forerunners" of a new student majority dedicated to radical social change.[76] Furthermore, in almost all national student polls, fewer than one third of students interviewed expressed strong opposition to the demonstrations.

It is hazardous to generalize. Widely dispersed polls, different samples, and different questions do not lead to firm conclusions about the current college impact on American students. First, it is not clear whether changing collegiate values can be directly attributed to college itself; college may not liberalize students but, rather, more liberal students may go to college. It is also conceivable that changing student values—if they are enduring changes—may result from changes in the broader culture. Some observers suggest that student radicalism results from growing economic security and social mobility which liberates the student from occupational anxiety; others cite burgeoning campus enrollments, a growing national population, and a pervasive social impersonality. By this logic, militant students are struggling to reestablish a sense of identity and renewed personal influence in an increasingly mass society. Finally, the durability of student values has not yet been tested. It is not inevitable, but campus liberalism often dissipates when the graduate becomes occupied with family, career, and social obligation; the sense of urgency and dissent dies.

Subject to these limitations, guarded conclusions are possible. There is still no persuasive evidence of a generalized shift in campus political values among the student majority that would yet justify calling the present campus population radical; the campus is not necessarily socializing the student majority into political perspectives incompatible with the dominant culture. However, the evidence is equally clear that a growing minority of students, especially student leaders, see their role and their purposes in very different terms from their counterparts of a decade earlier. The core leadership of militant student movements ordinarily

[76] David Seligman, "A Special Kind of Rebellion," *Fortune* (January 1969), pp. 67–69.

includes intelligent, middle-class students with demonstrated academic and personal success in previous years—the kind of student colleges traditionally welcome and who seek out college; there is little prospect in the near future that radical movements will lack leaders. Finally, the college has always been a source of creative dissent and critical appraisal of American society; it is not particularly remarkable that it should occur in especially dramatic form now. The current controversy over campus radicalism reflects the essential tension between two potentially conflicting expectations for the college: on one side, that it teach the ability to be critical and allow unfettered creative thinking; on the other side, that it serve society and not disrupt the basic social structure which makes its existence possible.

American Political Culture: A Summary Appraisal

Americans do not share a broad, extensive political orientation to the extent that one can speak unqualifiedly of a "great American consensus." Most Americans are *individually* inconsistent and contradictory in political attitudes and values; often they are ill-informed about basic features of their political system. There are also sharp discontinuities *among* Americans in regard to political values, information, support for the rules of the game, and other political orientations. In addition, individual political orientations often change with time and circumstances; there is nothing necessarily static about an individual's political attitudes.

In place of massive agreement on political fundamentals, most Americans agree only on some matters: Americans do not share a democratic ideology, only isolated democratic beliefs. An "ideology" is a functionally related set of beliefs, an intellectual structure in which the various components are compatible and interdependent. The average American's political thinking falls far short of such sophistication because his political attitudes, values, and behavior show little of this intellectual order and consistency.

Americans, generally, share enough beliefs to provide a limited consensus. Most Americans apparently agree upon the legitimacy of their political system and identify at an emotional level with its symbols and procedures. This is, in effect, a broad consensus of emotion rather than extended agreement on political details. Undoubtedly, this basic shared feeling originates in school and home; childhood political socialization makes the child the father of the man, politically speaking, because youthful loyalties have great tenacity among adults. Still, the community of feeling about the political system that imparts a sort of consensus to American political thinking quickly evaporates when the details of political life—values, attitudes, and behavior—are discussed.

There is both an elite and a mass American political culture, overlapping but different. The political activists perform the major political functions: governing, recruiting political leadership, articulating interests, and other activities necessary for political life. The activists, as we have seen, are most completely socialized into the official norms and procedures of the system. They are the most socially and ideologically homogeneous political group in the United States. The tone of political life, therefore, is determined most of the time by these activists. In a system that includes regular elections, pressure groups, many modes of expressing public opinion, and a government highly sensitive to mass opinion shifts, the activists must take constant cues from the masses and attend to mass thinking. Also, the day-to-day work of the political system rests with these activists and they, more than the American masses, impart their values to civic life because they have the opportunity and resources to do so.

There are many patterns of political socialization in the United States. If we think of an individual's political orientation as the product of cumulative learning initiated in home and school and later augmented by other experiences, Americans are not learning the same collective lessons; we are, in effect, graduates of different schools of political education. This is not surprising. It would be more surprising if Americans substantially agreed on most political matters. A western nation, the United States is culturally pluralistic since it is an outgrowth of industrialization: the many different occupational, ethnic, social, and religious subpopulations that have emerged from industrialization are bound to foster differences in political interest and outlook. This would be true even if the schools and government were to proclaim a universal political gospel consistently.

Despite divergent patterns of political socialization, there is enough core of common content in most political socialization to buffer the potentially deep conflict which comes with different political outlooks. In the past, Americans have been almost completely socialized into accepting the basic forms of government—the political formula—and feeling a sense of emotive attachment to them. American politics has ordinarily been conducted within these constraining boundaries which permit conflict within some consensus.

Finally, as the late V. O. Key, Jr., observed, American political life has customarily been conducted as if we had a consensus. The public opinion survey with its coldly impersonal numbers has destroyed the illusion of a great American consensus today but it would probably have done so at most points in the American past as well. Thus, in all probability, there is nothing unique about the present inconsistencies in the pattern of American political thinking except that, unlike our ancestors, we know they exist.

Though the information currently available about American political culture may not square with older, unthinking assumptions about American society, it does correspond in some respects with information about other political cultures. No nation in which public opinion surveys have been extensively conducted has a uniform political culture, or a "great consensus." Most political cultures exhibit the American mass-elite differences. The elite cultures of most societies resemble that of the United States in many ways: the elites are customarily better educated, members of more prestigious social groups, more informed, committed, and more consistent in political affairs. Like the United States, most men in most societies—now and probably always—are half-attentive and fitful political participators.

In some societies, the mass-elite cultures may be not merely different but incompatible; there may be few shared values, little mutual trust or shared social experiences, few of the attitudes that bridge the potential separation between elite and mass. In the United States, the two cultures have been generally compatible. "The citizen is neither so deeply involved and active in politics as to destroy the ability of government to make authoritative decisions nor so inactive and indifferent as to give political elites completely free rein in making decisions."

Thus, to summarize, Americans are by no means cut from the same political mold; indeed, much of the internal political conflict and tension within the society arises because Americans are not standardized in this way. American political culture has created a milieu in which a stable political system could develop and a continuity of political procedures could emerge because there was *enough* consensus on a *limited* number of attitudes and values to permit stability; equally important, most Americans were willing to tolerate much that they did not necessarily endorse in political life.

5

Black Americans: Portrait of a Political Subculture

Certain eras are so sharply etched in memory that a fragment of music, a voice, a word, or a newspaper clipping can recall them instantly. Most Americans will recall the critical 1960s through the vocabulary of racial conflict:

Henry Thomas, a lanky Negro student, and I entered the white lunch room and sat at the counter. The restaurant owner dashed away from the counter to phone the police. Within two minutes a police officer . . . stepped over and drawled to Thomas, "Come with me, boy!"[1]

"Two, four, six, eight, we don't want to integrate."

My fellow Americans: we have endured a week such as no nation should live through; a time of violence and tragedy. For a few minutes tonight, I want to talk about that tragedy—and I want to talk about the deeper questions it raises for us all.[2]

[1] James Peck, *Freedom Ride: Washington to New Orleans* (New York: Simon and Schuster, 1962); cited in Alan Westin (ed.), *Freedom Now* (New York: Basic Books, 1965), p. 244.

[2] Lyndon B. Johnson, "Address to the Nation on Civil Disorders," July 27, 1967.

I have a dream. . . .

Black Power!

The black American was central to the history of this decade and will be strategic—perhaps decisive—in fashioning the temper of the 1970s. Belatedly, the black American has asserted himself so forcefully in almost every aspect of American political life that his condition, his opinions, and his behavior cannot be ignored or dismissed even by the most socially insensitive citizen. The growing self-consciousness of the black American and his abrasive confrontation with whites beginning in the 1960s raise in peculiarly American terms a far broader problem that few modern nations can avoid: how to deal with political subcultures.

The Meaning of a Political Subculture

In most large societies, and certainly in industrialized societies such as the United States with its enormous social complexity, there will usually be individuals whose orientation toward political life differs significantly from that of the majority. If a group is alike in sharing many political orientations that distinguishes it from the majority, it is often called a political subculture.

Essentially, members of a political subculture are those whose political thinking and activities fall outside common patterns in a political culture. Sometimes this may happen because groups of individuals choose not to adopt majority political orientations or have yet to be socialized into them. Some religious sects in the United States, like the Jehovah's Witnesses and the Amish, stubbornly maintain loyalty to religious scruples that directly conflict with dominant political attitudes; the Witnesses refuse to salute the American flag and the Amish refuse to send their children to high school voluntarily. When European immigrants reached the United States during the last century, they neither understood nor initially accepted many of its dominant political practices, although later generations usually were socialized through education and experience to accept them.

A political subculture may also be created by subjecting some individuals in a society to special rules, to various discriminatory institutions and practices, and to community pressures and attitudes that will set them apart from the majority in political terms. Such is the experience of black Americans. Through racial discrimination in all its manifold forms, the black American was forced to learn a special role in American social and political life and to adopt special behaviors. Not surprisingly, individuals subjected to discriminatory rules (like American blacks) or those who make themselves different from most of a society (like the Amish or Jehovah's Witnesses) will often find themselves developing distinctive ways of looking at political life; members of such groups will stand outside the broad pattern of a political culture in many important respects.

Even though members of a political subculture may differ from prevailing majority political orientations, this does not mean that they are necessarily hostile to the official norms of a society. In some instances, quite the contrary. As we shall see, the majority of black Americans in the past embraced the values expressed by the Bill of Rights and many other constitutional principles with a frequency equal to or surpassing that of white Americans. And many white Americans, as we repeatedly observed in the previous chapter, are far from understanding or accepting many of the constitutional norms supposed to govern American political life. Thus, it is not always true that to be a member of a subculture means to lack sympathy with a society's official political rules.

Why do political subcultures exist? What impact do they exert on political systems? People who constitute a political subculture often differ from the majority not only politically but *socially* as well. They may speak an uncommon tongue, share a peculiar historical background, follow unusual occupations or life styles, or have different religious principles. Indeed, individuals often differ politically *because* they are socially different. In modern Canada, for example, there is a persistent grudging resistance to the central government which has almost reached the point of a separatist movement in Quebec. It originates in the cultural disparity between the population of Quebec and the Canadian majority: the Quebec population is preponderantly French-speaking, Catholic, and Gallic culturally; the rest of Canada is mostly English-speaking, Protestant, and British in heritage. Quebec has fiercely resisted and resented attempts to Anglicize the local schools and customs; to a great many residents of Quebec, the fight against the central government is a battle for cultural survival.

Political subcultures often exist in a state of tension with the dominant political culture. If the subculture is large, the situation can be explosive. Often, as Claude Ake suggests, "The political subculture is 'minimally integrated.' "[3] The members of the subculture become "subjects" of the political system. They obey rulers "not out of a sense of obligation, but only because they are obliged to."[4] Force, or primarily force, often cements the subculture to the political system. Members of the subculture lack the numbers, resources, will, or perhaps the opportunity to break free of the system. Sometimes, also, passivity and inertia achieve the same end as force when political consciousness among a subculture is so weak or undeveloped that there is little dissent from or rebellion

---

[3] Claude Ake, *Political Integration* (Homewood, Ill.: Dorsey Press, 1967), p. 4.
[4] *Ibid.*

against the dominant culture. The prevalence of tension between culture and subculture is easier to understand if one remembers that open deviance from the dominant culture constitutes a social behavior which most societies at best tolerate.

Yet a subculture generates and reinforces a sense of group identity and solidarity among its members and thus tends to perpetuate itself. It always challenges the prevailing norms. Ordinarily, political subcultures survive by finding some form of accommodation with the dominant culture which falls short of awakening so much fear that it will be violently suppressed. Sometimes, however, the subculture disappears by slow absorption over several generations into the dominant culture.

Political subcultures exist in almost all modern nations. To the blacks in America and the French Canadians, one can add the Catholics of Northern Ireland, the Ibos of Nigeria, the Palestinian Arabs, and a great many other groups throughout the world who live, often unreconciled and resisting, within political systems that include them only nominally.

Many political subcultures have evolved and disappeared in the United States; the American "melting pot" efficiently fused them into the cultural mainstream. Between 1841 and 1910, more than 26 million Irish, Germans, Italians, eastern Europeans, and non-Europeans immigrated to the United States. Initially, as they huddled in ethnic ghettos amid the squalor of Eastern urban society, they were culturally displaced—in no sense "Americans." Today, many of these "hyphenated Americans" still feel a sense of cultural identity born of common origins but in most respects the grandsons and great-grandsons of the immigrants have, after three or four generations, joined the American mainstream. Yet, other subcultures have been absorbed only slightly or not at all. The American Indian—the original American—remains a distinctive subcultural group along with the majority of Puerto Ricans and many Mexican-Americans, all of whom have resisted cultural assimilation.

Black Americans are easily the largest and most conspicuous political subculture; they have lived in the United States for over two hundred years, yet they remain unassimilated. The blacks can claim to be America's permanent minority.

Black Political Orientations: The Major Themes

Since the moment more than three centuries ago when the first Negroes unwillingly arrived on the American continent, they have been different. Blacks have been compelled to learn political norms applied to them solely on the basis of color. Until 1860, most blacks were not recognized as persons before the law; until the mid-twentieth century, Southern blacks could not participate openly in political life at all. In the North, the ghetto Negro seldom enjoyed the protections from indiscriminate police harassment that most middle-class whites accept as basic. The purpose of these racially differentiated norms was to keep the blacks "in their place"; their "place" being the social cellar where they occupied a segregated niche.

Underlying this treatment was a way of perceiving the Negro that originated in colonial times. To the white colonist who imported slaves,

> it seemed clear that an immense gulf separated the early colonists from the Africans whom they had purchased. Physically and culturally, the Negro was different, and the settlers believed it would be impossible to incorporate him into their community as a free and equal member. They were convinced he was inherently inferior and that only corruption and evil would result from mixing his race and theirs.[5]

From the outset of his arrival in North America, therefore, his confrontation with the white man triggered the social forces which shaped the black's life for several centuries. He was assigned an inferior social status; an intricate web of social attitudes and institutions kept him there. By ostracizing him from white culture, the white majority assured that the black would develop the distinctive psychology of a subculture; the common experience of slavery and later of discrimination shaped a strong feeling of group identity and grievance. In the South especially, the black approached the condition of a "biological caste."[6] The black's status was created, enforced, and perpetuated by the political system which provided legal force and authority to put other restraints on his behavior.

The history of the black American since the Revolution is the unfolding story of his struggle to alter his condition. Although the Northern victory at Appomatox ended slavery and gave the majority of blacks a short-lived measure of political equality for the first time, the great changes in their political situation have come in the last three decades. It is the experience of three hundred years, however, that has shaped black consciousness and the black's understanding of his place in American society. It has molded his current mood of anger, humiliation, and despair.

---

[5] Eli Ginzberg and Alfred S. Eichner, *The Troublesome Presence* (New York: New American Library, 1966), p. 14.

[6] For an excellent statement of the psychology of inferior caste see John Dollard, *Caste and Class in a Southern Town* (Garden City, N.Y.: Doubleday & Co., 1957), p. 62 ff. For a more modern restatement of this argument in psychiatric terms, see William H. Grier and Price M. Cobbs, *Black Rage* (New York: Basic Books, 1968).

Race Consciousness and
the Conviction of Grievance

Black group consciousness surpasses that of any other large domestic political group—with the possible exception of Jewish Americans. The black's view
of all political questions is through "race-colored glasses." This perception is
hardly surprising considering that his grievances result from his historical experience, as may be seen from black responses to a question dealing with
the Negroes' role in America's past:

> I think [we] have played an important part but have received no credit for
> it. In my opinion, if a Negro has the ability, the white man will pull him
> down. A Negro would be more decent than a white man, more fair because
> he would realize that he isn't the only one who has to live.

> We have cooperated in everything, but we have benefited nothing—except
> a lot of promises. A lot of Negroes looked up to Martin Luther King. There
> are so many Negroes in Vietnam, dying, and I don't know what they're fight-
> ing for. So many of them are right on the front line.

> We've made many contributions but somehow we've been left out of the
> history books.[7]

Black Americans now, as in the past, have always disagreed about the proper
remedies to their plight; as the black sees things, however, the basic problem is
white racism: "They are keenly aware that as a separate-subordinate group, the
dice are loaded against the individual. Everybody knows that 'no matter how
high a Negro gets, he's still a Negro.' "[8] This consciousness permeates all levels
of the Negro community to such an extent that upper- and lower-class blacks,
often divided on other matters, share at least this feeling. To the lower-class
black, discrimination means unrelieved economic and cultural subordination; to
the relatively well-to-do Negro, it is also a constant impediment: Negro professionals "must compete with their white counterparts for Negro clientele, whereas
laws and customs prevent them from competing with the white professionals for
their white clientele."[9]

---

[7] Opinion Research Corporation, *White and Negro Attitudes towards Race-Related Issues
and Activities* (Princeton: Opinion Research Corporation, 1968), p. 21. This poll was
commissioned by CBS News.

[8] St. Clair Drake and Horace R. Cayton, *Black Metropolis* (New York: Harcourt Brace
Jovanovich, 1945), p. 723.

[9] Daniel C. Thompson, *The Negro Leadership Class* (Englewood Cliffs, N.J.: Prentice-
Hall, 1963), p. 81.

Many black Americans—though, surprisingly, not a majority of them—
believe they confront an unsympathetic, hostile white majority. Blacks are not by
any means unanimous about the white's implacable hostility; nevertheless, this
"cultural paranoia" means that few blacks view the white man without suspicion. In 1964, Brink and Harris asked a representative cross-section of black
Americans what they thought the attitude of "most whites" was toward the
colored man. The responses appear in Table 5.1.

Table 5.1.   Negro Evaluations of White Attitudes, 1964

Most Whites	Total Rank and File	Non-South	South
Want to keep the Negro down	42%	35%	47%
Want a better break for the Negro	25	28	23
Don't care	17	21	13
Not sure	16	16	17

Source: William Brink and Louis Harris, "The Negro Revolution in America,"
p. 126; Copyright Newsweek, Inc., 1964.

This poll indicates that among the black subgroup polled, no more than 28
percent believed the white Americans had constructive aims in dealing with
blacks.[10]

Blacks correctly perceived that a great many whites *are* antagonistic to their
race and their social objectives. In another national poll, Brink and Harris found
a rising number of whites who wanted the pace of civil rights progress to
slacken: in 1964, 34 percent of the national white sample thought civil rights
progress was too fast but in 1966 the number had risen to 85 percent.[11] The
polls which estimate the extent of white resistance to civil rights programs
produce highly variable results, but in all cases the number of white objectors is
considerable. White resistance to black political demands rests, in a good many
instances, on a sort of economic moralism. Many whites allege that the black
wants "something for nothing," that he is individually lazy and unwilling to work
steadfastly at a job or to acquire the requisite skills through training and
education which would advance him; the Puritan ethic of hard work, thrift, and
diligence is turned against the black. By this logic, the black wants an "unfair"
break:

---

[10] Later polls are little different. In the poll taken for CBS News in May-June 1968,
Negro respondents were asked if they thought "most whites in this country are sympathetic
or are not sympathetic to the problems of Negroes (blacks)?" Response: "Yes, sympathetic"
—28 percent; "No, not sympathetic"—59 percent; "No opinion"—13 percent. Opinion
Research Corporation, *op. cit.,* p. 7.

[11] William Brink and Louis Harris, *Black and White* (New York: Simon and Schuster,
1967), p. 121.

Since Lincoln freed the slaves who had a lack of education, they didn't care. Now the younger people want what the white people have. They would have it now if the older Negroes had worked for it and educated their children. If you let something go and don't fix it, you can't blame someone else for not having it.[12]

Despite the fact that many white Americans do not share these opinions, it appears from a variety of studies that a great many whites not only blame the Negro for his condition, but do not believe that he is the object of discrimination. Both these attitudes are apparent in Table 5.2. Because many white Americans hold these opinions, it is understandable, for instance, that one third of a national sample of whites in 1968 blamed urban violence entirely on criminals and "outside agitators" while giving no weight to the existence of legitimate black grievances.[13]

Table 5.2. White Attitudes toward Negroes

"In your opinion, how well do you think Negroes are being treated in this community?"

	National	East	Regions Midwest	South	West
Same as whites	70%	62%	75%	71%	73%
Not very well	17	22	14	17	16
Badly	3	6	2	3	2
Other	10	10	9	9	9

"Who do you think is *more* to blame for the present conditions in which Negroes find themselves?"

	National	East	Midwest	South	West
White people	24%	27%	22%	23%	25%
Negroes	54	47	58	56	57
No opinion	22	26	20	21	18

Source: Gallup Poll *Index* (July 1968), pp. 19, 20. Copyright 1968, The American Institute of Public Opinion.

The social location of white resistance is as important as its size. White resistance to black demands for better education, housing, and jobs becomes most pronounced at the impact points of these demands. Whites living where

[12] Other studies of white attitudes on discrimination, some suggesting less insensitivity to the black, are found in Opinion Research Corporation, *op. cit.*, p. 1, and Brink and Harris, *Black and White*, p. 125.

[13] *The New York Times,* July 7, 1968, p. 48.

open housing demonstrations occur are overwhelmingly opposed to open housing; white resistance to expanded black job opportunities is especially stiff where the largest number of blacks are employed.[14] The tolerant, approving whites are likely to be middle- or upper-class suburbanites comfortably ensconced many miles from the conflict.

In any event, there is a pervasive white tendency to blame "troublemakers" for black riots and protest. Many whites are unwilling or unable to comprehend that black violence is a protest against the conditions of Negro life—its squalid living conditions, unemployment, and especially its denial of dignity as a free and equal people; society's failure to remedy deep dissatisfactions has led to the rise of increasingly militant black groups, exemplified by the Black Panthers. The shouts for Black Power, the emphasis upon black pride, and the revolutionary cry to destroy the American social system found among such radical black groups are one kind of answer to white insensitivity.

Notwithstanding these facts, the image of blacks and whites facing each other across lines of mutual distrust in a bipolar conflict is oversimplified. Leaders of traditional Negro political organizations, better-educated blacks, and the majority of other blacks with political responsibilities still tend to be at least cautiously hopeful about the possibility of white cooperation. A great many blacks, in addition, expect the future to bring improved racial conditions; a great many rank-and-file blacks express at least some satisfaction with their present economic condition and expect improvement in the future. In short, the major thrust of black protest has been rooted in fundamental American values and seeks not the overthrow of American society but the fulfillment of its promises. Furthermore, many whites express agreement both with this aspiration and the catalogue of Negro complaints against his past history and current treatment. A poll taken for the President's Commission on Civil Disorders indicated, for instance, that one third of the whites polled agreed that urban riots were based on legitimate black grievances, while 95 percent disapproved of job discrimination.[15] The evidence, therefore, does not indicate that black and white political attitudes have yet polarized. But the vast majority of blacks and whites do not seem able to agree upon the terms of racial coexistence in the United States. It is for this reason, as we shall see later, that the mood of the black community has been shifting toward greater militancy. In this respect, it seems clear that most blacks do not believe their *fundamental* position has changed.

---

[14] See Brink and Harris, *Black and White,* pp. 20–23, 109; Donald Matthews and James Prothro, *Negroes and the New Southern Politics* (New York: Harcourt Brace Jovanovich, 1966), pp. 337–338; and the 1968 three-volume report of the U.S. Equal Employment Opportunity Commission.

[15] *The New York Times,* July 28, 1968. For mixed black opinions on the present and future, see Gallup Poll *Index* (August 1968), p. 18; (May 1969), pp. 8, 10; William Brink and Louis Harris, *The Negro Revolution in America* (New York: Simon and Schuster, 1964), p. 73.

Political Allegiance and Trust

The black American has had little historical reason to feel allegiance or loyalty to the American political system. At the conclusion of the Civil War, to be sure, it looked for the moment as if the Thirteenth, Fourteenth, and Fifteenth Amendments would confer on blacks the basic constitutional protections and privileges enjoyed by other Americans; Congressional passage of the Civil Rights Act of 1875 seemed to provide the means to protect these guarantees. All this proved to be a passing illusion. By 1877, native white governments returned to all the states of the Old Confederacy and rewrote the suffrage provisions of state constitutions to include literacy tests, "grandfather clauses," the poll tax, and the other legal devices for disenfranchising the black. Before this time, the Klu Klux Klan and other white terrorist groups had made black political participation increasingly hazardous. Between 1877 and 1900, the black was methodically squeezed out of Southern political life. In 1896, for instance, there were 130,000 registered Negro voters in Louisiana; by 1900 there were 5,320.[16] When the Supreme Court declared the constitutionality of "separate but equal" facilities in *Plessy* v. *Ferguson* (1896), the legal basis was laid for the Southern black's return to a life only slightly more elevated than his former slave status.

Northern Negroes and those who migrated there from the South fared little better. Between 1910 and 1960, more than 4.5 million Southern blacks "voted with their feet" by moving North and, to a lesser extent, West. In the North, strict housing ordinances, discriminatory employment practices, and the inferior job skills possessed by most blacks fostered the familiar black ghetto. Northern blacks could vote. On occasion, they created political machines. But the black politician dealt with the white power structure essentially as a petitioner or junior partner who had to respect the carefully limited white tolerances. Very modest political and social advances might be made, but the cost was great; the Northern black was rewarded only if he stayed "in his place."[17]

In addition to political deprivations, the black masses never enjoyed the material rewards the economy so liberally dispensed to most whites. The average Negro lived under a low economic ceiling, able to move horizontally—from janitor and unskilled worker, say, to yardman or chauffeur—but seldom vertically. In 1966, about 11.9 percent of whites but 40.6 percent of nonwhites lived below the poverty level (defined by the Social Security Administration as income less than $3,335 for a family of four); 22 percent of Negro families in

---

[16] National Advisory Commission on Civil Disorders, *Report* (New York: Bantam Books, 1968), p. 214. This document, popularly known as the Kerner Report, provides an excellent brief political history of blacks on pp. 206–235.

[17] Excellent histories of the black political situation, in addition to the others cited, are C. Vann Woodward, *The Strange Career of Jim Crow* (New York: Oxford University Press, 1957); and Gunnar Myrdal, *An American Dilemma* (New York: Harper & Row, Publishers, 1944).

1968 had incomes under $2,000 per year.[18] Looking at the Negro American, therefore, we do not find the kind of experiences and life situations that encourage citizen patriotism; one would expect the black masses to be alienated, antagonistic, or indifferent toward a political system in whose language, after all, the very word "black" is a bad word—"black day," "blacklist," and "black-mail," for instance.

In fact, the black American is considerably more complex in his political loyalties. Many American Negroes, perhaps a majority, have demonstrated considerable support for the political system. Blacks in large numbers fought in all major American wars. During the Revolution when one-half million Negro slaves resided in the thirteen colonies, the majority of those who fought in the war joined with Washington; there were 5,000 blacks in Washington's 300,000-man army. More than 186,000 blacks defended the Union during the Civil War, 350,000 fought in World War I and a million in World War II. In World War II, Korea, and Vietnam, blacks have had proportionally higher enlistment and casualty rates than whites. For many black servicemen in Vietnam, military experience threw into stark relief the contradiction which they perceived between the risks to which they were exposed defending the country and the position they once more assumed in American society upon demobilization. Among the 120,000 Negro veterans of the Vietnamese war, many felt betrayed: "The [Negro] in Vietnam closed his eyes to the prejudice he knew existed and hoped against hope that Americans would change," explained one 21-year-old veteran, "but it don't make a bit of difference."[19] The return of the black veteran to civilian life, according to most observers, will add additional impetus to the black demand for immediate and dramatic changes in black conditions. The black serviceman may fight for America, but in the future he will also want it to be his country, not just a nation in which he lives but does not fully participate.

Besides military service, blacks also express a sense of commitment to the political system in less direct ways. In 1966, for example, more than eight out of ten blacks in a national poll replied that the United States was "worth fighting for"—though many added, parenthetically, that it was a racially undiscriminated America they would be most willing to defend.[20] Among grade school children, there are seldom significant differences between black and white youngsters

---

[18] Data cited in the Kerner Report, *op. cit.,* p. 14, and U.S. Bureau of Census, *U.S. Book of Facts, Statistics and Information, 1968* (New York: U.S. Dept. of Commerce, 1969), Table 476.

[19] Enlistment figures taken from Ginzberg and Eichner, *op. cit.,* pp. 243–262. Many blacks join the armed forces for the very practical reason that it offers educational opportunities, living facilities, and economic rewards superior to civilian life. For the viewpoint of black veterans, see *The New York Times,* July 29, 1968.

[20] Brink and Harris, *The Negro Revolution,* p. 61. One curious finding in the Kerner Report is that even among black urban rioters, a surprising number will answer affirmatively to this question. Among the rioters in Detroit (1967), 55.3 percent of those polled reported the U.S. was "worth fighting for;" in another sample from Newark rioters (1968), 33 percent also answered affirmatively. Among black nonrioters in the two cities, the affirmative answers were 75 percent and 50 percent respectively. See the Kerner Report, *op. cit.,* p. 178.

regarding political allegiance. One stimulus for black support in the past was that most American Negroes believed the federal government gave them the best chance for fair employment and had on the whole been a protector of their interests. Thus, in most opinion polls, the president and federal judiciary usually topped the list of institutions cited for their help to the race. Dwaine Marvick took an equal number of black and white respondents from a 1960 national survey and mixed each group so that, as nearly as possible, the white and black subsamples contained equal proportions of individuals by income, education, residence, occupation, and other social characteristics. He then studied a series of responses to questions regarding trust in government among these two socially similar samples. The results appear in Table 5.3. Middle- and upper-class Negroes are considerably less suspicious of government and more willing to express allegiance than less successful blacks. At all social levels, however, that government which is geographically and politically closest to the people, the local one, is most often criticized.

Blacks are far more likely than the average white to be in continual and intimate contact with local government. Most whites know local government through indirect, relatively unobtrusive contacts; it provides sewage, garbage, and utility services; it periodically demands taxes and occasionally dispenses traffic tickets. Most blacks are poor and, consequently, government is

a network of agencies that affects their lives directly and often [because] they spend a large proportion of their time waiting for interviews in welfare offices or answering a caseworker's questions in their homes; when they are sick, they wait in the county clinic to see a doctor; they go to a state employment agency for jobs. Because their children frequently get into trouble at school, they are visited by truant officers. . . .[21]

Table 5.3.   White and Negro Expected Treatment from Officialdom, 1960

	Negro	White
Government officials would give equal treatment	49%	90%
Police would give equal treatment	60	85
Officials will listen and take views seriously	30	45
Police would listen and take views seriously	36	48

Source: Dwaine Marvick, "The Political Socialization of the American Negro," in Roberta Sigel (ed.), *Political Socialization* (Annals of the American Academy of Political and Social Science (September 1965), p. 119. © 1965. Reprinted by permission of the author.

21 Paul Jacobs, *Prelude to a Riot* (New York: Random House, 1966), p. 7.

The officials administering welfare are often perceived to be hostile, unsympathetic, or bureaucratically impersonal. Given this dependence upon local governments, almost all serious life problems for blacks become entangled with and complicated by governmental bureaucracy.

It is the police, however, who evoke the harshest criticism. To a great many blacks, the policeman is the enforcer of the segregation system. While most whites identify the police with law and order or the protection of life and property, many Negroes see the police as the strong arm without which racial discrimination would be unenforced—"All forms of Negro adaptation," observed one social scientist, "are ultimately based on the prospect that this force will be utilized."[22] Beyond the frequently voiced complaint of "police brutality," blacks cite a long litany of other accusations: the police are dependably rude and abrupt with blacks, take liberties, seek occasions to harass blacks doing nothing objectionable, approach all blacks with the presumption that they are criminals, and so forth.[23] There is often substance to these charges, but the real situation is more complicated. For one thing, the policeman's legitimate responsibilities are bound to bring him into direct conflict with many blacks. Illicit activities—involving bookmaking, numbers, moonshine, prostitution, and narcotics—flourish in the urban ghetto and the Southern shantytown, quite often, to be sure, with the tacit approval of white leaders and considerable white patronage. Since the nature of ghetto life denies many blacks opportunities in legitimate occupations, criminal activity is frequently the only viable substitute. In addition, young, racially militant blacks are often quite skilled at police-baiting and engineering situations where the patience and judgment of the police are fiercely challenged. Notwithstanding this, mounting evidence suggests that the police, collectively, are often equally to blame for racial incidents involving law enforcement officials.[24]

Despite this antipathy toward police and local government, studies do not suggest that black Americans are generally alienated from the political system. What distinguishes black from white attitudes are that levels of political support and confidence tend to be consistently lower among blacks and political confidence falls off abruptly below the federal level. This profile reveals the black to be "different" but still "American." Instead of confidence and pride, the black

---

[22] Dollard, *op. cit.,* p. 333.

[23] *The New York Times* reported in 1964 that 43 percent of Harlem residents questioned believed in the existence of police brutality. A 1965 Gallup Poll found 35 percent of Negro men believed in this brutality compared to 7 percent of white males. See the Kerner Report, p. 302, for a summary of these findings.

[24] See Burton Levy, "Cops in the Ghetto: A Problem of the Police System," in Louis H. Masotti and Don R. Bowen (eds.), *Riots and Rebellion: Civil Violence in the Urban Community* (Beverly Hills, Calif.: Sage Publications, Inc., 1968), pp. 347–358; Jerome Skolnick, *Justice Without Trial* (New York: John Wiley, 1966); and Arthur Niederhoffer, *Behind the Shield* (New York: Doubleday & Co., 1967). For a view of the problem from the black policeman's viewpoint, see Nicholas Alex, *Black in Blue* (New York: Appleton-Century-Crofts, 1969).

feels hope but uncertainty about his government. He still expects the political
system to produce the benefits it delivers to others; anyway, he knows no other
culture or political arrangement. The most sobering aspect of this orientation is
not the degree to which the black is withdrawn and hostile, but the extent to
which he is not.

Political Interest and Participation

From the Civil War to the middle of this century, political affairs occupied a
very thin stratum of the Negro community. In the South, voting and other forms
of overt political behavior were discouraged and dangerous; a "good nigger"
was, by definition, politically passive.[25] In the North, where political liberties
were less restricted, blacks voted in modest numbers; in some of the larger cities,
blacks created their own political organizations.[26] But the sociology of the
Northern black community worked to keep political interest and participation
below white levels. The Negro class structure reverses the white one; there is a
very small middle class and an enormously large lower class. Lower-class
Negroes, like their white counterparts, were mostly politically apathetic due to
economic circumstances and the failure of Northern black politicians to provide
practical benefits.

For the average black, survival—not politics—was the paramount value. In
their important study of Bronzeville, Chicago's westside ghetto, Drake and Cayton
described life values in 1945 to be, in this order, (1) staying alive, (2) having a
good time, (3) praising God, (4) getting ahead, and (5) advancing the race. [27]
The low priority for anything resembling political activity in the Chicago slum is
easily explained by ghetto conditions. A steady income was seldom certain; if
there was one, it kept one only marginally above subsistence level. Most blacks,
in Chicago and elsewhere, had to concentrate on obtaining the necessities for
survival and compensating for, in whatever ways possible, the crowded shabbi-
ness and deterioration of the ghetto.

The Negro political organizations that did operate in the North and South
seldom inspired most blacks. For one thing, as Kenneth Clark observed, the

---

[25] The Southern black was not, however, entirely politically passive and unconcerned. As
Matthews and Prothro point out, the Southern black had to avoid the *visible* political
activities that most threatened whites. In their interviews with Southern Negroes, Matthews
and Prothro found that their respondents talked about politics almost as often as whites did,
they contributed to political campaigns more often than whites did, and they belonged more
often to political associations such as the National Association for the Advancement of
Colored People. Matthews and Prothro, *op. cit.,* p. 40 ff.

[26] Two excellent studies of Northern Negro political machines are found in James Q.
Wilson, *Negro Politics* (New York: The Free Press, 1960); and in an older classic, Harold
Gosnell's *Negro Politicians* (Chicago: University of Chicago Press, 1935).

[27] Drake and Cayton, *op. cit.,* p. 385.

black politician—middle-class for the most part—did not confront his white counterpart as an equal. "It is difficult, if not impossible, to behave as one with power when all one's experience has indicated that one has none."[28] Black politicians found it difficult or impossible to create sustained, vigorous civic action supporting a set of community goals. As late as the early 1960s, James Wilson observed that black political leaders in Chicago's ghetto, with a population of 750,000, could not meet modest budgets to support hospitals, welfare, and other Negro charities without the help of white donors.[29] In cities such as New York, Boston, and Chicago, the black political machines often bartered votes for concessions from the white power structure but the rewards were apportioned to a select black minority who received patronage or service contracts.

This combination of Southern segregation, Northern ghetto conditions, and a politically inert lower class determined the patterns of political activism in the black community during the first half of this century. At times, the Northern black turnout exceeded white turnout in comparable social categories. Nonetheless, when total numbers are taken into account, black America did not approach the white majority in converting its potential electorate into actual votes.

Beyond voting, political activism was almost completely middle-class, but middle-class black politics differed materially from middle-class white politics. Until quite recently, only 10 percent of the Negro community could be considered middle-class; hence, there was a much smaller base for political workers and leaders in black society. In small communities, especially in the South, there often were no political leaders though the Southern black often *thought* he had leaders; in truth, such "leaders" carried no weight among whites.

The black middle class was also separated from the black masses culturally and economically. The middle-class Negro moved from the ghetto if he could, intermingled with white society, and adopted an outlook similar to the white middle class. He sought respectability, a stable family, professional advancement, and the rewards of a decent income: a good home, vacations, cars, clothes, and educational advantages for his children. He was thus isolated from the black masses; the middle class sought status and symbolic goals, the lower class demanded welfare and other tangible rewards. As Whitney Young, himself a middle-class Negro and the executive director of the Urban League, put it:

> Middle-class Americans are extremely concerned with conformity. Negroes who enter the middle class become even more rigid in their class values, more

---

[28] Kenneth B. Clark, *Dark Ghetto* (New York: Harper & Row, Publishers, 1965), p. 156.

[29] Wilson, *op. cit.*, pp. 4–5. The Chicago Urban League, for instance, raised only $10,000 of its $80,000 budget from the Negro community; the Joint Negro Appeal was struggling at the time to raise $25,000 a year.

conscious of status than do white middle-class folks. The new Negro middle class clings more desperately to the status symbols, is more careful and correct in behavior. . . . Certain middle-class Negroes are now exhibiting an unfortunate tendency to be indifferent if not actually hostile to those black Americans less fortunate and privileged.[30]

In the past, the middle-class Negro activist could not escape the consciousness that he was expected to be a "race man," upholding black pride by demonstrating his success and fighting for racial rights. Since he dealt with the white community, his power depended upon a minimum of good standing among colored masses. But he appealed primarily to other middle-class blacks.

Middle-class estrangement had its counterpart in lower-class black alienation. If the middle-class Negro often expressed his exasperation and embarrassment at lower-class blacks, they reciprocated; they considered the middle-class to be too self-interested, too accommodating to whites, too concerned with symbolic victories which produced no tangible gains for most blacks, and altogether too conservative. "The trouble is Negro against Negro," remarked a redcap to one researcher, "The Negro don't believe in the future. The educated Negro in this city comes first, the laborer, last. That's bad."[31]

The small Negro middle class was not only estranged from the core of the black community; it was quite different from the white middle class in its occupations, a difference born of the peculiar political problems, inherent in a segregated society. Like so many other aspects of Negro life, the character of Negro leadership depended upon the white social structure. Black leaders initially had to come from occupations immune to white control, specifically those which were created and maintained entirely from within black society. The Negro church provided much of the traditional leadership and still does; since the Civil War, the black church has been equally concerned with the affairs of heaven and black politics on earth. This clerical mingling in political affairs infused the language of the early leadership with Biblical imagery and Old Testament cadences. Negro political rallies had the flavor of a camp meeting: "They are," wrote an observer in the 1940s, "charged with great emotional appeal. . . . When a speaker says something which strikes a popular chord, people yell, clap, or wave programs, hats, or hands in the air."[32]

Besides ministers, an assortment of physicians, lawyers, undertakers, professors, school teachers, taxi owners, and an occasional businessman or black officeholder filled leadership positions. This pattern has for the most part persisted. In their 1966 study, Matthews and Prothro estimated the occupational distribution of black leaders in four Southern counties as in Table 5.4.

---

[30] Whitney M. Young, Jr., "Middle-Class Negroes and the Negro Masses," *Ebony* (September 1963). Reprinted in Westin, *op. cit.,* pp. 317–318.

[31] Drake and Cayton, *op. cit.,* p. 730.

[32] *Ibid.,* p. 374.

Table 5.4. Occupations of Negro Political Leaders in
Four Southern Counties, 1966

Preachers, ministers	34%	Teachers, principals	12%
Lawyers	6	College administrators	3
Doctors	3	County agents	1
College professors	1	Businessmen	11
		Other	29

Source: Donald Matthews and James Prothro, *Negroes and the New Southern Politics* (New York: Harcourt Brace Jovanovich, 1966), p. 181.

The last two decades, however, have brought important alterations in black political interest and participation. First, Negro registration and voting have swung steeply upward, due principally to massive federal registration programs in the South. In 1940, only 5 percent of the eligible Negroes voted in the states of the old Confederacy. In 1952 this figure reached 20 percent, in 1960 it was 28 percent, and in 1966 it had climbed to 46 percent. In the North, black voting turnout rose from approximately 55 percent of the potential electorate in 1950 to 62 percent in 1966.[33] In the South and North, the remaining obstacle to black voting appears to be apathy.

Second—especially in the South—political activism beyond voting is rising. Once the segregationist prohibitions on political activism are removed, black activism increases. In some areas of the contemporary South, rates of black activism probably exceed that of white activism. As early as 1964, Brink and Harris found that about half of their sample of Southern Negroes expressed willingness to march in demonstrations, engage in sit-ins, go to jail, or picket.[34]

Finally, the *forms* of black activism everywhere have changed radically. The traditional forms of Negro activity have been voting, attending political meetings, negotiating with the white community across the bargaining table, contributing time and money to campaigns. These were middle-class forms, accommodating to the white, honored by venerable traditions and—considering the full range of political action open to the black—polite. In black America, older ground rules are now so widely violated that the 1960s will undoubtedly be remembered as a period of revolution in techniques of black activism. As the Negro journalist Louis Lomax writes, "Once upon a time—and everybody didn't live happily ever after—the Negro, North and South, could be relied upon to behave in a fairly well-prescribed manner." Now, "the unpredictable Negro is on the loose; he is apt to oppose segregation anywhere, any time, in any manner."[35] Ironically, this was written in 1961 when the "Freedom Ride" was considered radical. That is, it was written before the Detroit and Watts riots, before the

[33] Figures cited in Matthews and Prothro, *op. cit.*, p. 18.

[34] Brink and Harris, *The Negro Revolution*, p. 68.

[35] Louis Lomax, "The Unpredictable Negro," *New Leader* (June 5, 1961), cited in Westin, *op. cit.*, p. 24.

Poor People's March, before the assassination of Martin Luther King, Jr., and before the days of the Black Panthers. Today, the modes of political action the black American has adopted are an open issue in black and white America. The change in the forms of black activism indicate an ongoing revolution in black rules of the game.

The Rules of the Game

The black American has always been keenly sensitive to the discrepancy between the official political norms and the norms applied to him. When it came to interpreting political norms, black spokesmen have, to say the least, been constitutional literalists. Such traditional spokesmen for the blacks as the NAACP, the Urban League, and the Sleeping Car Porters when they demanded "first-class citizenship" were speaking entirely within the framework of officially sanctioned American political values. The black leadership reminded the white elite to take its own oft-expressed norms seriously. The black leadership by the nature of its demands demonstrated the extent to which it had been socialized by constitutional values. Black leaders for the most part were framing political demands and creating political objectives in unimpeachably American terms: equal protection of the law, freedom from indiscriminate arrest, trial by a jury of peers that included blacks, the freedoms granted by the Bill of Rights and, of course, the right to vote. The majority of black leaders rejected the *actual* rules of the game applied to them because they were punitive. "At no time have Negroes accepted their subordinate social status as morally, ethically, or legally just."[36] Black leaders were using the official political norms as a weapon against the white majority. In effect, black leaders turned these norms of the society against the society, treating the Constitution as a promissory note that white America had written and must now fulfill for the Negro.

Between the Civil War and the 1950s, most forms of black activism, when it was possible, conformed to the traditional American pattern. The techniques that black leaders used in dealing with the white power structure depended upon the organization of white politics. In cases where a segregationist, white elite governed, the "Uncle Tom" spoke for blacks. The options open to the Uncle Tom were severely limited. He was "an essential but pathetic figure" who existed because some communication between black and white societies had to be maintained.[37] The Uncle Tom "never demands on the basis of the Negroes' rights, but instead begs for favors. His job, additionally, is to make his people

---

[36] Thompson, *op. cit.*, pp. 18–19.
[37] Matthews and Prothro, *op. cit.*, p. 186.

understand what the white man had done for the Negro."[38] Uncle Tom was a broker between a subordinate and dominant class; his job was to wring, if possible, concessions from the white community while keeping blacks in line. The result was that

> All too often he cannot command the respect and confidence of the white leaders and at the same time retain that of the Negro masses. His source of influence in dealing with whites is not the power of his followers . . . but the fact that . . . he has to maintain prestige among Negroes. And this requires that he demonstrate some influence among whites.[39]

For his demeaning work, Uncle Tom might produce piecemeal results: a new classroom for the Negro school, a park and some swings, a little additional welfare money, perhaps an adjustment in police treatment of blacks.

Whatever his work, the current young, militant blacks regard the Uncle Tom as a despised symbol of black passiveness and impotence, seemingly the epitome of black dependence on whites and accommodation to them. Indeed, so identified has Uncle Tom become with a lack of racial pride and agressiveness that his name becomes an insult hurled at any black leader—including even men like Martin Luther King, Jr. and Roy Wilkins of the NAACP—who is believed to lack sufficient aggressiveness and courage in dealing with whites. In truth, the Uncle Tom deserves somewhat better. Even though he was extremely accommodating to whites and usually content with a few crumbs from the white man's table, the Uncle Tom of the past usually operated in a situation where his opportunities were extremely limited, his room for maneuvering very narrow. Usually, he confronted a monolithic, segregationist, white power structure in the South or, in the North, white leaders only slightly more liberal. He represented a people with few political rights and few social resources and other advantages that carried weight with whites; he operated, moreover, in a hostile political and legal milieu. Often, therefore, he made the most of a bad situation. Whatever his many faults may be when viewed from the present, in his own time he may have served his people as best he could.

In the North and wherever the white leadership was racially moderate, black leaders adopted the role of "racial diplomat" which came to be the characteristic middle-class black political style. The racial diplomat pushed vigorously for "first-class citizenship" but his technique was moderation, pragmatism, bargaining, and negotiation. The racial diplomat preferred to work within established constitutional norms. He placed great reliance upon judicial remedies

[38] Thompson, *op. cit.,* pp. 62–63.
[39] Matthews and Prothro, *op. cit.*

when other methods failed. It was characteristic of the racial diplomat that he tried to "interpret the peculiar needs of the Negro in terms of general community well-being";[40] racial diplomacy emphasized the *common* interests of black and white, and the white liberal was the racial diplomat's ally.

The racial diplomat, leading the NAACP and Urban League, concentrated on federal legislation and Supreme Court test cases; in the process, he gained much for black America. Through his leadership, a historic set of Supreme Court decisions between 1920 and 1950 destroyed the white primary, "grandfather clauses," and other legal obstacles to Negro voting; the Court steadily constricted the right of states to bar Negroes from professional schools. Finally, in the Warren Court's most historic decision, *Brown* v. *Topeka* (1954), a unanimous court declared that "separate schools are inherently unequal," thereby destroying the legal barriers to integrated education.

The year 1954 has a special significance in the history of black politics. It brought one era to an end and was the threshold of an onrushing revolution. *Brown* v. *Topeka* was possibly the most important memorial to political action by litigation, to the primacy of politics by constitutional remedies. Though few blacks knew it at the time, the days of the racial diplomat and the middle-class political style were ending. A year later, Martin Luther King, Jr., initiated the Montgomery bus boycott and announced his "direct action" philosophy. Montgomery was a decisive break with the past, setting in motion the forces which altered black concepts of political action.

Like most revolutions, this one was fed by many sources. At the base lay the restive black masses, increasingly impatient with middle-class leaders and sullenly resentful at promises too long unfulfilled. As Richard Merelman has remarked, among the poor, loyalty to political leadership is likely to develop in proportion to the tangible rewards it can produce.[41] In the early 1950s, tangible rewards were conspicuously lacking. Nine in ten Negroes lived in economic impoverishment; 76 percent of all Negroes were semiskilled or unskilled. Though Negro wages rose between 1940 and 1950, they still averaged only two thirds of comparable white income. The majority of blacks had not graduated from grade school and lived in housing considered unfit for human habitation. Furthermore, the "revolution of rising expectations" cut deeply into black consciousness. The Negro masses were living in the most affluent nation in the world's history, one that dangled the pleasures of wealth before blacks daily, visibly, and emphatically. In a consumption-oriented society, the acquisition of goods and services is a primary value; the success ethic—the secular religion of the white middle class—is no less compelling to black Americans. The rising, widely distributed prosperity of middle-class whites, advertised widely by the mass media and especially television, underlined the disparity between white and black America. The result was anger and frustration:

---

[40] Thompson, *op. cit.,* pp. 68–70.

[41] Richard M. Merelman, "Learning and Legitimacy," *American Political Science Review* (September 1966), pp. 548–561.

No one with a mop can expect respect from a banker, or an attorney, or men who create jobs, and all you have is a mop. Whoever heard of integration between a mop and a banker?[42]

This gap between expectation and fulfillment, of which poor blacks were increasingly aware, seemed unlikely to disappear soon. The Negro's opportunity to escape the ghetto and poverty seemed far smaller than that of the European immigrants who had done so previously. There were several reasons why the black could not easily imitate the immigrant's pattern: the contemporary American economy was highly industrialized, demanding mostly skilled and educated labor in contrast to the earlier economy which was still in the process of industrializing and could absorb unskilled and uneducated manpower; there was racial discrimination in many industries that white immigrants did not face; and the many political machines which served the new arrivals to the country, straightened out their problems with the law, and eased the transition into a new society were seldom available to blacks. Nor should it be forgotten that in our time, looking back, the ease of the immigrants' escape from the ghetto has no doubt been exaggerated, particularly in the case of those from southern and eastern Europe. In short, the model of social and economic advancement held out by the immigrant simply did not fit the urban black.[43]

In addition to the grievances of the poor blacks, a younger, better-educated, more prosperous generation of blacks had matured in the 1950s, a generation hyperconscious of the Negro's lot and prepared to articulate its impatience, its racial pride, and its demands for "freedom now." Many in this generation had never been socialized, as were their parents, into the role of the "good nigger"; also, they had the resources and opportunities to protest. They were ready to respond to King's challenge: "We're through with tokenism and gradualism and see-how-far-you've-comism. . . . We can't wait any longer. Now is the time." This leadership favored direct, face-to-face, sustained confrontation with the white community over specific grievances, although nonviolently. The "legality" of their behavior, King asserted, was not the most compelling consideration:

There are *just* laws and there are *unjust* laws. I would be the first to advocate obeying just laws. One has not only a legal but a moral responsibility to obey just laws. Conversely, one has a moral responsibility to disobey unjust laws. I would agree with Saint Augustine that "an unjust law is no law at all."

All segregation statutes are unjust because segregation distorts the soul and damages the personality. . . . An unjust law is a code that a majority inflicts on a minority that is not binding on itself. This is difference made legal.[44]

---

[42] Clark, *op. cit.,* p. 2.

[43] For fuller comparisons see the Kerner Report, *op. cit.,* pp. 278–282.

[44] Martin Luther King, Jr., "Letter from Birmingham Jail," in Westin, *op. cit.,* p. 15.

Direct action and civil disobedience were the catalysts that, for the first time, drew the black masses into sustained interest and sympathy with black leaders because, among other things, their confrontations made interesting reading that attracted the black masses, dramatically focused on relevant, concrete problems, and seemed to accomplish something tangible.

This direct action would not have succeeded without the energetic commitment of Negro college students who often were the principal participators in the sit-ins, lie-ins, kneel-ins, and other forms of confrontation with whites. Among the Southern black college students Matthews and Prothro studied in 1966, one quarter had participated in a sit-in and fully 85 percent of them approved of sit-ins. Direct action, however, had a broader appeal to the entire black community. In 1964, a national survey of Negroes revealed the extent of this sympathy with direct action (see Table 5.5).

Table 5.5.   Negro Willingness To Participate in
Mass Action

Activity	Percent Who Would Participate	
	Rank-and-File	Leaders
March in a demonstration	51%	57%
Sit-in	49	57
Go to jail	47	58
Picket	46	57

Source: Brink and Harris, "The Negro Revolution in America," (New York: Simon & Schuster, 1964) p. 68.   Copyright Newsweek, Inc.

"Direct confrontation," with its priority on nonviolence, represented the moderate phase of the revolution started by Martin Luther King, Jr. In the 1960s, a more militant phase began. The "long, hot summer" of 1966, which was punctuated by racial riots in major urban areas, seemed to auger a menacing mood in black America. To a great many white Americans, it seemed that a yet younger generation of black leaders, crossing the boundary between nonviolence and violence, were espousing a philosophy of black political action that approached an incitement to civil insurrection. Those black militants who repudiated direct action were not united in a common program, but whites were troubled by the repeated emphasis on violence that seemed to permeate all the angry rhetoric:

This is a real revolution. . . . Revolutions are never based upon love-your-enemy-and-pray-for-those-who-spitefully-use-you. . . . Revolutions are

based on bloodshed. . . . Revolutions overturn systems. And there is no system on this earth which has proven itself more corrupt, more criminal, than
this system that in 1964 still colonizes 22 million African-Americans. (Malcolm X)

Black folks built America, and if America don't come around, we're going
to burn America down. (H. Rap Brown)[45]

Many whites, linking the sudden emergence of this seething outrage to the urban
racial violence of the late 1960s, feared that the mood of black America had
shifted still farther beyond the possibility of peaceful and constitutional redress
of grievance.

The new militancy was more than a simple recourse to violence; the strident
voices on both sides made it difficult to discern what was actually happening
within the black community. It seems clear that increasing militancy was a
symptom, not the *cause,* of black alienation from peaceful political procedures.
The spokesmen for the younger militants were equally estranged from the whites
and the black middle class. Basic to their complaint was the failure of what the
militants called "civil rights groups" to produce meaningful results for the black
rank-and-file; in the militant's logic, the political action of Martin Luther
King—the nonviolent protester—and the white liberal was inadequate. King and
others like him were now condemned as the new Uncle Toms. Stokely Carmichael, who began his political career as a moderate and later became a leading
proponent of Black Power, expressed the militant black's disappointment at
nonviolent techniques:

. . . up to this point there has been no national organization which could
speak to the growing militancy of the young black people in the urban ghettos and black-belt South. There has been only a "civil rights" movement,
whose tone of voice was adapted to an audience of middle-class whites.

It claimed to speak for the needs of a community, but it did not speak in
the tone of that community. None of its so-called leaders could go into a rioting community and be listened to. . . . Each time the black people in those
cities saw Dr. Martin Luther King get slapped, they became angry. When
they saw little black girls bombed to death *in a church* and civil rights workers ambushed and murdered, they were angrier. . . . We had nothing to
offer that they could see, except to go out and be beaten again.[46]

---

[45] Robert L. Scott and Wayne Brockriede, *The Rhetoric of Black Power* (New York:
Harper & Row, Publishers, 1969), pp. 131, 134. The authors emphasize that this is what
Brown is inaccurately reported to have said. This particular quote appeared in *Newsweek.*

[46] Stokely Carmichael and Charles V. Hamilton, *Black Power* (New York: Vintage
Books, 1967), p. 50.

As this quote suggests, Black Power was less a program or ideology than a mood and a style which rejected earlier methods of action. It even rejected the traditional end of black political action—an integrated society.

By the early 1970s, it seemed obvious that black leaders had been constantly involved in flanking movements, as one moved continually to the left of others, always in the direction of rejecting their predecessor's mode of political action. The leadership of the black community had become splintered and divided. But where did the majority of blacks stand? To what extent did the confusing crosscurrents of leadership philosophies reflect the black masses?

Studies of black America do not indicate that the majority of Negroes are prepared to reject peaceful political techniques for violent ones. But opinions about the rewards of violence are divided. In 1966, a poll by Brink and Harris reported black responses to a question concerning the value of urban riots; the poll is reproduced in Table 5.6. Since at least one third of all black groups in this survey agreed that the riots "helped," one may assume that violence has, from the black point of view, helped produce racial gains. A 1968 report concluded that "Riots are justified by most Negroes, but they are not recommended."[47] Nevertheless, the rank-and-file black does not prefer violence or embrace militant leaders. Black majorities consistently give the greatest approval to moderate, nonviolent leaders—the Kings, Wilkins, Abernathys—although the most militant leaders—the late Malcolm X, Stokely Carmichael, H. Rap Brown, and Eldridge Cleaver—attract strong and apparently growing minority support.[48]

Table 5.6.   How Negroes Feel about Riots, 1966

	Total Rank and File	Non-South	South	Under 35	Leadership Group
Riots helped	34%	32%	35%	38%	41%
Riots hurt	20	26	15	21	19
No difference	17	23	16	15	18
Would join riot	15	13	18	19	1
Would not join	61	62	59	57	75
Will be more riots	61	62	61	66	79
Will not be more riots	8	7	8	7	2

Source: William Brink and Louis Harris, *Black and White* (New York: Simon and Schuster, 1967), p. 67. Copyright Newsweek, Inc.

[47] Based on opinion studies of Negroes in fifteen major U.S. cities by the University of Michigan's Survey Research Center, *The New York Times,* July 7, 1968.

[48] See, for instance, polls which rate black approval of a variety of various leaders in Opinion Research Corporation, *op. cit.,* p. 12; Brink and Harris, *Black and White,* p. 54.

Thus, to summarize: the major themes in contemporary black concepts of political action are (1) a growing impatience with middle-class styles of moderation and compromise; (2) a growing acceptance of militancy—among the majority of blacks for nonviolent direct action and among the younger for more aggressive modes; (3) an apparent decline in the political status of black middle-class leaders among the black masses; and (4) a shift in the center of gravity of black opinion to preferences outside the traditional forms of political action whites understand or accept. As the President's National Advisory Commission on Civil Disorders summarized,

> Over the years the character of Negro protest has changed. Originally, it was a white liberal and a Negro upper-class movement aimed at securing the constitutional rights of Negroes through propaganda, lawsuits, and legislation. In recent years, the emphasis in tactics has shifted first to direct action and then—among the most militant—to the rhetoric of Black Power. The role of the white liberals declined as Negroes came to direct the struggle. At the same time, the Negro protest movement became more of a mass movement with increasing participation of the working class.[49]

The majority of blacks are not alienated in the sense that they reject traditional forms of political activism. Yet, the mood appears to be a mixture of uncertainty, experimentation, and division about the rules of the game. Most blacks are not *yet* beyond the scope of traditional American political rules, but the future is uncertain.

The Future of Black America

Between the dominant white culture and the black subculture, politically and in all other ways, the *status quo* is dead. The 1970s will be revolutionary times. Like all such periods, this will be creative and dangerous. Black and white leaders, caught up in the ferment of racial revolution, are like men "playing craps with destiny."

Two conclusions seem inescapable. First, the black American is abandoning in increasing numbers the older forms of political thinking and action that bound him to his subordinate status. In doing this, he is changing the traditional script for black and white politics; the previous framework is disappearing, and a stable new one is not yet written. Second, no matter how blacks and whites may feel about the matter, their futures are interdependent—inescapably. Both these

---

[49] The Kerner Report, *op. cit.*, p. 236.

facts are clearly apparent from social and political statistics. Increasingly, therefore, the paramount question in race relations in the 1970s is which direction will the revolution take—peaceful or violent, within or outside traditional political styles?

Population and Black Politics

The black American will soon constitute such a large proportion of the American population that his political behavior will set the tone of American politics in many critical areas. Negro Americans constitute about 11 percent of the United States population at present. This proportion is expected to increase; there are approximately 27 black children born for every 18 white children. This is particularly significant because it increases the probability that American urban politics and society will become increasingly black politics and society—a conclusion strengthened by other facts. There is a continuing northward and westward migration of blacks from the South and an exodus of middle-class whites from the central cities to the suburbs at a rate approaching one-half million yearly. Indeed, programs to improve ghetto life ironically will attract more blacks to the cities, intensify discontent, and move the nation as a whole nearer to an unofficial apartheid of proletarian central cities surrounded by affluent bourgeois outer suburbs.[50] Indeed, many major American cities will become predominantly black in the 1970s. Between 1960 and 1966, the Negro metropolitán population had already increased at about twice the rate of the white urban residential growth: white urban population increased at a modest 9.3 percent compared to 21.2 percent among Negroes.[51] On the basis of population projections, by 1980 more than half of the population will be Negro in Washington, D.C., Jacksonville (Fla.), Baltimore, Detroit, St. Louis, New Orleans, Nashville, Trenton, Birmingham, Atlanta, Memphis, Cleveland, Jackson (Miss.), Philadelphia, and Chicago.

In the South, where blacks were historically the most politically impotent, the politics of the old Confederacy are changing. In 1940, there were only 250,000 registered Negro voters in all these states; by 1968, over half the eligible blacks were registered. It has been axiomatic in American politics that numbers count when converted into votes. These black votes are beginning to count. In 1960, for instance, if only white Americans had voted, Richard Nixon would have won 52 to 48 percent; John Kennedy, however, was favored 78 to 22 percent among American Negroes, and this gave him the margin for victory. In

---

[50] For the statistics of Negro migration patterns and the formation of black ghettos, see the Kerner Report, *op. cit.*, pp. 236–247.

[51] *The New York Times,* February 28, 1969.

1964, Edward Brooke of Massachusetts, the first Negro senator since Reconstruction, took his place in the Senate. By 1970, Cleveland (Ohio) and Gary (Ind.), two large industrial cities, had black mayors. These were, to be sure, scattered victories, but by weight of numbers, blacks are bound to affect the nomination and election of major offices in the future.

The New Black Generation

The most militant, impatient, dissatisfied Negro is the young Negro, whether he is relatively well-educated or not, employed or not, middle-class or lower-class. Among the young, militancy cuts across the previously vast gap between the middle and lower classes. These political attitudes will weigh heavily in shaping the racial future.

There is some evidence that black Americans, generally, are becoming increasingly alienated from white society. A month before the assassination of Martin Luther King, Jr., in 1968, Louis Harris reported that "the number of Negroes feeling alienated increased from 34 percent to 56 percent."[52] Among young Negroes of all conditions, toying with ideas of violence—often acting them out—and alienation are fairly common. The National Advisory Commission on Civil Disorders (the Kerner Commission) reported in 1968 that the typical rioter was a teenager or young adult, a life-long resident of the city in which he rioted. Contrary to many assumptions, the rioter was better educated than the nonrioter. He held a job, was proud of his race, and was hostile to both whites and middle-class Negroes.[53] Young blacks are far more willing than their elders to engage in the most aggressive forms of political action, though they do not prefer violence. A great many blacks believe that what racial progress was achieved during the late 1960s was more the result of black militancy than white cooperation.

Among younger blacks, the new militancy was part of a new self-image in which "thinking black" was paramount. Militancy reflected the basic premise that America was a racist society, that Negroes could no longer depend on Whitey's or "Mr. Charley's" promises to help, that the Negro had to "think black" for his own survival. To "think black" was to be proud of one's race, to rediscover a sense of identity and dignity, and "save" oneself. To be black was to be beautiful; dashikis and natural hair styles—increasingly rejected in modernizing Africa—became the vogue among many of the young. Above all, Black Power and other militant slogans were the signal that the young intended to reject white society:

---

[52] *The New York Times,* April 16, 1968.
[53] The Kerner Report, *op. cit.,* pp. 127–135.

"The Negro now isn't the bubble-eyed, buck-toothed clown who was only good at stealing chickens and tap-dancing on a barrel by the docks the way they always showed us we were in the movies."

"You don't want me. O.K., well, let me tell you, I don't want you, your hair, your food, or nothin' to do with you."[54]

Affluence

Ironically, the undisputed success of the American economy has aggravated the racial situation in the United States. Almost all studies of black culture underscore that the black's demands and dissatisfactions result from his awareness that, in a society of greatly distributed wealth, he has little himself and is prevented by white society from the opportunity of acquiring his share.

What black America sees on television, in particular, has become an incitement to revolution. Television, with all the other mass media, has portrayed in the most concrete terms what blacks should aspire to have, what they might have, what others *do* have. In a sense, the black American "wants in" on the capitalist revolution. So long as the American economy continues to function so effectively, levels of black aspiration will continue to rise. And yet, his unemployment, low skills, and education—plus the loud promises of such political programs as Wars on Poverty (which, however, do not receive the large funds other wars do)—continue to remind him of the frustrating gap between his rising expectations and actual achievements. It is symbolic that urban rioters frequently have made their attack upon business establishments, carrying away millions of dollars in goods from shops open to them on equal terms for perhaps the first time.

White Racial Myths

The terms under which black and white America will relate to each other in the future depend ultimately upon whether racial leaders can agree on the nature of the problems in black America, whether leaders can accept a set of shared premises about the causes and consequences of black militancy. A number of white attitudes—frequently found especially among local government officials—complicate this problem.

First, many whites believe the *"riff-raff" theory of black violence*. This

---

[54] "What Must Be Done," *Newsweek* (November 20, 1967).

theory asserts that racial violence is caused principally by a small band of criminal, irresponsible, black "outside agitators" who incite otherwise civil blacks to aggression. This theory is based on an unsound premise about black behavior in two respects. It fails to measure accurately the *extent* of mass black frustration with racial conditions in the United States; in fact, it denies that there are legitimate *causes* of urban violence—segregation, white racism, and economic deprivation with all their attendant miseries—by suggesting that all would be well but for these trouble-makers.

Second, many whites tend to believe *that the ultimate solution to racial problems is economic.* It is argued, often implicitly, that the Negro would become less unhappy if he were to earn a decent income and gain some measure of economic security. While black frustrations certainly have an economic dimension, the militant black's complaint is that his economic condition is a symptom of the real racial problem, *white racism.* A great many blacks are gravely concerned because they are treated as inferior and objectionable people. To many blacks, and particularly to the young, the problem in the United States is not simply the economic condition of black America—which, after all, might be cured by structural changes in the economy—but white *thinking,* which is not so amenable to manipulation.

Many white Americans cannot easily understand the subjective experience of the Negro and cannot share with black Americans their view of the world which underlies and motivates their current political behavior:

> The white person, no matter how liberal he may be, exists in the cocoon of a white-dominated society. Living in a white residential area, sending his children to white schools, he must exert a special effort to expose himself to the actual conditions under which large numbers of Negroes live. Even when such exposure occurs, his perception is likely to be superficial and distorted. The substandard house may be overshadowed by the television aerial or the automobile outside the house. Even more important, he does not perceive the subjective inequalities inherent in the system of segregation as the Negro does.[55]

Finally, given the fact that the United States is experiencing a revolution in race relations, the most dangerous—and tempting—myth is a *belief in inevitable moderation.* American politics, in both its objectives and styles, has throughout most of our history been centrist and moderate; most Americans are accustomed to politics by bargaining and compromise. The mounting evidence that black political opinion is moving toward militancy makes the idea of inevitable

[55] Lewis Killian and Charles Grigg, *Racial Crisis in America* (Englewood Cliffs, N.J.: Prentice-Hall, 1964), p. 73. Quoted also in Carmichael and Hamilton, *op. cit.,* p. 61.

moderation in the racial problem a dangerous hypothesis. Many blacks, indeed, have nothing to lose by entirely abandoning the customary rules of the game.

> I can't loose by rioting. Done lost. Been lost. Gonna be lost some more. I'm sayin' to the Man: "You including me in this game or not?" and I know his answer, so I'm getting ready to get basic.[56]

This is not yet the majority opinion in black America, but it may become so.

---

[56] Newsweek, *op. cit.*

6

Political Linkage: The Politics of Parties, Pressure Groups, and the Street

On the ellipse south of the White House, more than 100,000 protesters had gathered below a broiling sun in the spring of 1970. They were angry about the President's decision to send American troops into Cambodia, about the death of four college students shot by Ohio National Guardsmen during a confrontation in another protest, and about much else they believed wrong with the administration and American society. "[The] audience was made up primarily of the instant army of the young, the mobile children who received basic protest training in the late '60s, who can travel fast and light for the peace movement . . ." wrote one observer.[1] Not all were young, some were only curious or sportive, a few craved violence. But the majority were sober, disturbed, convinced they were right, and intensely interested. The issues were new but the situation had become familiar.

We are concerned in this chapter with how demands are made upon government and how individuals are organized for political action—political linkage. The protest march is a dramatically visible way to achieve this. The campus, a focal point for protest marches and other forms of activity intended to link individuals with their government, is becoming increasingly politicized. Thus, at a time when students are seeking techniques and strategies to move the minds of government officials, current campus events are an important aspect of

---

[1] "At War with War," *Time* (May 18, 1970), p. 7.

political linkage, but they are only one way through which individuals may be linked to their government and only one of many purposes that such linkage may serve. To understand how the many linking institutions operate and the various functions they perform, let us examine the meaning and significance of political linkage.

What Linkage Means

If governments are to perform their fundamental social tasks effectively—making authoritative decisions regarding social order, social change, and the allocation of society's resources—a number of institutions and activities must link the governmental apparatus to the larger society.

Creating and
Organizing Public Opinion

No matter what the dominant ideology of a society may be, opinions are created, expressed, and fed into the governmental apparatus. However, the results depend on the environment of that society.[2] Nations we have previously called democracies usually permit open organization and expression of opinion from a variety of independent sources while providing many channels through which such opinion can be registered in governmental circles. But even officials in societies that reject the free airing of public views must maintain contact with public moods and attitudes. Governments, moreover, quite often attempt to create and manipulate public opinion themselves. In democracies, this usually occurs in a competitive opinion marketplace where other groups may counter governmental efforts; in totalitarian systems, governments attempt to monopolize the means for opinion formation and expression. Still, "murmurings in the tents," as a tribal chief described the opinions of his people, are discussed in all governments.[3]

---

[2] The significance of institutions for the creation, organization, and transmission of opinion within political systems has been noted by almost all analysts of political systems. In recent years, the theoretical status of these institutions has been explored, especially by specialists in comparative government, systems theory, and communications theory. Among the works suggestive in shaping our approach, see the functionalist approach in Gabriel A. Almond and James S. Coleman (eds.), *The Politics of Developing Areas* (Princeton: Princeton University Press, 1960), pp. 572–577; the systems approach is most fully explored in David Easton, *A Systems Analysis of Political Life* (New York: John Wiley, 1965), Chapters 3–21; and for communications theory, see Karl Deutsch, *The Nerves of Government* (New York: The Free Press, 1963). It will be obvious that we have greatly simplified many of the ideas offered in these volumes.

[3] There is no assurance that an accurate version of public opinion will reach government officials. The methods through which opinions are organized can distort or misrepresent the

Looking more closely at the process of opinion formation and expression, we note several steps. First, *political demands are made upon government.*[4] These demands are claims upon a society's resources and the government's powers: they are ways in which social problems and needs arc identified and conflicting issues are defined; they are attempts to determine what government should be doing and what social problems and social groups it should be serving. These political demands, the grist for the governmental mills, appear in a great variety of forms in the United States, as a sampling of any morning newspaper suggests:

> In Key Biscayne, about 200 peace demonstrators marched more than two miles under a broiling sun to the Florida White House.

> In a report prepared for the House Judiciary Committee hearings, a committee of the Association of the Bar of the City of New York calls a bill poorly drafted and hastily considered and urges its complete revision. . . .

> . . . on Tuesday a trial will open in which Curt Flood, former outfielder of the St. Louis Cardinals, will challenge baseball's reserve system and attempt to prove that baseball is a monopoly operating in restraint of trade.

In modern industrialized societies such as the United States, these demands will range over the whole economic and social spectrum, since almost all social problems are eventually dumped into the governmental lap. In the United States and in other democracies, these demands are most often articulated by political parties, autonomous interest groups, uncensored mass media, and other institutions that make public these demands and conflicts. In totalitarian societies, however, these demands are customarily channeled through the apparatus of the totalitarian political party and the governmental bureaucracy. Thus, they remain, for the most part, removed from public notice and debate.

Through the process of opinion formation and expression, *political demands are combined, compromised, and aggregated* through various institutions.[5] Perhaps the most familiar example of this activity to Americans is the fashioning

---

public mind, and conflicting opinions may make it difficult to determine which, if any, opinions dominate. Moreover, various institutions engaged in opinion expression may fail to communicate vital information to government leaders. Still, political leaders must depend on the opinion profiles available when calculating the impact of their decisions.

[4] In recent political science literature this is often called "interest articulation." A thorough examination of the literature on this topic and its significance may be found in Gabriel A. Almond and G. Bingham Powell, Jr., *Comparative Politics* (Boston: Little, Brown and Co., 1966), Chapter 4.

[5] A good review of political aggregation may be found in Almond and Powell, *op. cit.,* Chapter 5.

of a major party platform at the presidential nominating conventions, an activity that clearly involves an attempt to merge a multitude of different, often conflicting demands into a compatible program which the party ostensibly pledges its candidate to fulfill.

This process of interest aggregation, as it is usually called, is extremely important in pluralistic, industrialized, large societies. Without it, the "civil war potential" within such societies can be great since there is a multitude of different, often competing groups and interests who clash in their political demands upon and expectations from the government. Interest aggregation is a way of inhibiting many of these conflicts and reconciling many of the divisive tendencies. Even interest groups in the United States—usually considered to be single-minded and narrowly self-interested—often do some interest aggregating in order to arrive at programs acceptable to various factions within their own membership. Indeed, the process of interest aggregation might well be considered a form of political technology that helps to make effective government in a pluralistic society possible.[6]

Finally, in creating and organizing public opinion, *a great many groups and individuals succeed in "politicizing" segments of the public.* Essentially, this means alerting individuals to their stake in political issues, providing them with information upon which to form political opinions, shaping their political preferences, and defining what political issues are important to a society. In their efforts to create public opinion, organize it, and relate it to government, therefore, many different groups and individuals often make politics relevant to members of a society; this brings individuals psychologically within the ambit of the political system and stimulates involvement in political affairs. This is an especially important activity in as populous a society as the United States. The national government itself is large and complex; the issues it must resolve daily are numerous and complicated. Often, individuals have little information about these issues and do not know whether they are affected by governmental decisions. Frequently, it is governmental leaders, interest group spokesmen, or candidates for public office who, through the mass media, educate the public on political matters and thus prepare them for some sort of politically relevant response.

Consider, for example, how segments of the American public were politicized on the problem of inflation. Shortly after assuming office, President Nixon proposed a number of measures to Congress intended to curb the domestic inflationary cycle of the early 1970s. To make the problem and his legislative proposals to curb it relevant to many Americans, the President discussed his proposals during a nation-wide address and appealed for support, thus bringing the issue into millions of American homes, underscoring the political aspects of

---

[6] It is the weakness of these aggregating institutions in the face of extreme pluralism that frequently defeats attempts to create stable national governments. In fact, many scholars argue that strong aggregating institutions are a prerequisite for a stable political order. See Lucian W. Pye, *Aspects of Political Development* (Boston: Little, Brown and Co., 1966), Chapter 4, especially pp. 81–85, for a brief but lucid discussion of this problem.

the problem, and suggesting a response. Moreover, the President chose an unusual mid-afternoon presentation, apparently hoping to make a major impact on the large number of housewives who are the principal afternoon television viewers. While the President's anti-inflationary measures were before Congress, numerous interest groups, including labor unions, business associations, and consumer cooperatives were also weighing the significance of the proposals and informing their memberships on the implications. In these and other ways, numerous Americans were not only sensitized to the problem of inflation (if the cost of living had not already done this), but they were informed about how the government was attempting to solve the problem and how this might affect them.

In democracies like the United States, many governmental and nongovernmental groups and individuals attempt to educate the public about the important political issues of the day, to influence their opinions on these matters, and to shape how they will respond. As a result, there will usually be a wide range of issues brought before the public with competing interpretations about their significance and the appropriate response to them. In totalitarian societies, however, the government usually attempts to monopolize channels of political communication to insure that the public will be politicized along lines suitable to the regime. Usually, this means the regime will alert citizens only to political issues it wants publicized, will release only information conducive to the opinions it wants the public to form, and will stimulate the public only to those modes of political response it desires. To cite an extreme but interesting example of such manipulation: by the middle of 1970, the people of mainland China had not officially been told that American astronauts had landed on the moon; the Peking government suppressed the information. Apparently, the Chinese Communist leadership had concluded it was unwise for the Chinese masses to know of the American space achievements—possibly because, by implication, the masses would compare them with Chinese space achievements and draw conclusions unfavorable to the government.

Politicizing the public, obviously, is a way to make politics meaningful to members of all societies and a powerful tool in shaping public attitudes toward a political system and its rulers. However, like other activities that involve creating and organizing public opinion, it is only one of several ways through which individuals can be linked to their government. Linkage also involves mobilizing individuals; this is a way of converting opinions and demands upon the government into political action.

Political Mobilization

Political mobilization includes all those activities through which individuals are actually involved in political affairs. Although public attitudes, opinions, and values may be the source of political activity, governments are often most directly influenced by what individuals *do*. It was not student opinion alone, but a massive student strike against the French government in 1968 that forced the normally proud and aloof Charles de Gaulle to make concessions to the students and their sympathizers. When opponents of American policy in Vietnam took their convictions to the polls in the presidential primaries of 1968 and voted for such doves in the Vietnamese conflict as Eugene McCarthy, they convincingly underscored the need for a major reappraisal of American policy there. And when millions of white Southerners, no longer willing to abide the Johnson administration's pressure for massive school integration, voted for Republican Richard Nixon in hope of slowing the pace of integration, they contributed to a Republican victory that seemed to signify a slackening of federal pressure for complete school integration. In these and many other ways, political action of many kinds may directly affect the course of government.

Political leaders may not only be influenced by political activity; they must often depend upon political mobilization to accomplish their own purposes. Unless members of a polity act out the rituals and give at least modest support to the symbols of the government, its powers will soon shrink. In the United States, for instance, public officials constantly preach "democracy" and "tolerance" in private and public affairs, thus attempting to persuade citizens to act in ways compatible to the political system's official norms.

Political Recruitment

In any political system, there must be some arrangements for recruiting members of the government, or to designate who in society will be administrators and bureaucrats, military leaders, judicial officials, heads of government, representatives of the people, or whatever officials constitute the government. In modern nations, this political recruitment is complicated and, especially when leaders of the government are selected, it can be violent as the melancholy history of recent civil wars, *coups d'état,* political assassinations, and disputed elections throughout the world testifies.

Minimal requirements for recruiting leaders of government are some methods for designating who will be eligible and who among the contenders for the office will win. In the United States, as in other western democracies, political parties provide one solution to the problem of selecting leaders of government and members of legislative bodies to represent the people; by nominating candidates, arranging for their public promotion and providing the resources for their election, the parties are a major vehicle for political recruitment in the United States and other democracies. In some nonwestern societies where modern political parties are nonexistent, political leaders may be chosen by tribal leaders, family groups, religious rites, or regional interests; in totalitarian societies, it may be through a vicious power struggle within the single political party; in other societies, a civil war or military *coup* may settle the issue.

Regardless of what methods are used in a political system to recruit its governmental personnel, the various individuals, institutions, and activities involved in this process provide an important link between the masses of the society and its government. When this linkage operates effectively, it provides the necessary flow of manpower and leadership into government for its operation and utilizes the society's human resources for the task of government.

Political Linkage in the West: Parties and Interest Groups

The activities that link a government with a society may be found in any political system, but which institutions and individuals are involved in these activities will vary among nations. Not all nations, for instance, permit privately organized interest groups to mold public opinion and mobilize it for political action as they do in the United States; conversely, in some nations, official religious bodies or leaders play a much more prominent role in recruiting the nation's political leadership than they do in the United States. Sometimes, moreover, a single institution within a society may serve multiple purposes. Political parties, for instance, may attempt to shape public opinion, to mobilize individuals, and to recruit government officials simultaneously.[7] Then, too, new forms of linkage or uncommon methods may suddenly emerge. In the United States, the "politics of the street"—as some commentators call mass marches, protest rallies, and riots—has seemingly gained vitality among the young and among racial minorities. All of this, of course, is a reminder of how guarded generalizations about political life must be.

Even though political linkage always differs in some detail among nations, in western societies three institutions, in different combinations, are commonly used for political linkage: political parties, interest groups, and elections.[8] In this chapter, we shall concentrate upon political parties and interest groups as well as politics of the street; in the following chapter we will turn to elections.

---

[7] The validity of assigning a particular set of functions to any political institution is sharply debated in social analysis. We have assigned functions to parties and interest groups which are, however, almost always assumed, implicitly or explicitly, by most social commentators. For an excellent examination of the problems in such a functional approach, see the brief but excellent summary in Arnold Rose (ed.), *The Institutions of Advanced Societies* (Minneapolis: University of Minnesota Press, 1958), pp. 19–22.

[8] The mass media should undoubtedly be added to this list. Our selective emphasis limits us, however, to parties, interest groups, and elections.

A Western Invention

Both the political party and the interest group developed first among western nations but rather late in western history; neither existed in its current form before 1800.[9] The parties that first developed in America at the turn of the last century were "not only the first parties to adventure on the precarious ground of politics in an emerging nation but the first true parties in modern times, appearing well before such formations developed in England or other European countries."[10] By the 1830s, however, crude prototypes of modern parties had also appeared in Great Britain as "registration societies"; within a decade, similar groups were emerging on the continent.[11] Interest groups—or "voluntary associations" as they were often called—were active in the American colonies well before the Revolution, often in the form of guilds. By 1830, therefore, the United States was well on the way to sustaining modern political parties and interest groups that would soon appear and multiply in other western nations.

Why this emergence of parties and interest groups in the United States? A number of factors seem to be involved. Industrialization and economic development proved a powerful incentive to their formation due to the expanding social pluralism that resulted; as the number of social and economic interests increased, competition for economic and political power intensified, and the need for some form of group organization became obvious. Many groups, particularly those in business, the trades, and the professions, saw the logic and advantage of voluntary associations: such associations could be an effective tool for political action, would encourage group-mindedness and cohesion, and often could act as a "private government" to regulate the economic affairs among its members. The success of such organizations caused the appearance of counter-organizations: organized business prompted labor to organize, coal trade associations spurred lumber interests to follow the example, and so forth. Thus, the formation of

---

[9] A modern party, in contrast to earlier political factions, has a durable structure and seeks governmental power through elections. It "links leaders at the center of government to a significant popular following in the political arena and its local enclaves, and generates in-group perspectives or at least symbols of identification." William Nisbet Chambers, "Party Development and the American Mainstream," in William Nisbet Chambers and Walter Dean Burnham (eds.), *The American Party Systems* (New York: Oxford University Press, 1967), p. 5.

[10] William Nisbet Chambers, *Political Parties in a New Nation* (New York: Oxford University Press, 1963), p. 1.

[11] A brief historical sketch of western party development may be found in Joseph LaPalombara and Myron Weiner (eds.), *Political Parties and Political Development* (Princeton: Princeton University Press, 1966), pp. 3–42. A standard reference work on British parties is Robert MacKenzie, *British Political Parties* (New York: St. Martin's Press, 1955).

interest groups proceeded in waves.[12] (Nor has the process stopped. In recent years, as we shall shortly elaborate, the underprivileged, the minorities, and others historically without organization in the United States have taken the cue from the middle class and now appear to be following their example in forming interest associations. For example, the United States may well boast the only organized pressure group composed of welfare recipients.)

Aside from economic incentives, the political climate in the United States also proved congenial to the rise of political parties and interest groups. Guarantees of free speech, the right to peaceful assembly and to petition for the redress of grievances that encouraged both parties and interest groups were written into the Constitution; moreover, the need for political parties became especially acute as the states steadily expanded voting rights to thousands of Americans who needed to be organized politically. Behind these specific measures lay a particular interpretation of "democracy" that was espoused by the nation's early political leaders, an interpretation that was itself a powerful goad for both parties and interest groups to form in the new nation.

American Democracy, Parties, and Interest Groups

At least two different elements in early American democratic theory led to a climate favorable to the emergence of political parties and interest groups. First, many of the founding fathers who profoundly influenced the drafting of the Constitution and the administration of the new government assumed that societies were naturally composed of many different, competing political interests; they accepted as a first principle what we have called "social pluralism" with all its manifest conflicts, tensions, and competing values. In addition, insisting that the right to vote be broadened (at least to the middle class) meant that some institutions would develop which would organize voters and mobilize them for political action.

James Madison acknowledged that pluralism meant the existence of "factions" and "conflict" as "a central and enduring reality" and had no illusions about its source:[13]

---

[12] Many group theorists would add that emergency and crisis also stimulated the rise of interest groups in the United States. These and other explanations for the emergence of interest groups in the United States are thoroughly and usefully explored in David Truman, *The Governmental Process* (New York: Alfred A. Knopf, 1960), Part II.

[13] Many of the Founding Fathers accepted "factions," as we shall see in more detail in Chapter 13, but they regarded them as an evil to be carefully controlled. The idea of competing political parties was greeted with equal aversion. To Vice President John Adams, "the division of the republic into two great parties [was] to be feared as the greatest evil under our Constitution." Jefferson was also emphatic: "If I could not go to heaven but with a party, I would not go at all." He later changed his mind. Quoted in Marcus Cunliffe, *The American Heritage History of the Presidency* (New York: Simon and Schuster, 1968), p. 100.

> The latent causes of faction are thus sown in the nature of man; and we
> see them everywhere brought into different degrees of activity. . . . A zeal
> for different opinions concerning religion, concerning government, and many
> other points, as well of speculation as of practice; an attachment of different
> leaders, ambitiously contending for preeminence and power; or to persons of
> other description whose fortunes have been interesting to the human pas-
> sions, have, in turn, divided mankind into parties, inflamed them with mutual
> animosity, and rendered them much more disposed to vex and oppress each
> other than to cooperate for their common good.[14]

Madison and other American revolutionary leaders fully appreciated the danger
of factions and declared a major task of government to be their management.
"The regulation of these various and interfering interests," wrote Madison,
"forms the principal task of modern legislation and involves the spirit of party
and faction in the necessary and ordinary operation of the government."[15]

Democratic values ordinarily assumed that competing interests should be
permitted life and organizational expression with minimal governmental interference. Thus, the first ten amendments to the Constitution—the familiar Bill of
Rights—explicitly protect freedom of speech, assembly, religion, and petition as
much for the sake of groups as for individuals.

Permitting—indeed, encouraging—such a broad and potentially disruptive
interplay of interests in a society also required strategies for resolving political
conflict based on a half-a-loaf psychology. For democracy to prevail amid such
pluralism, it seemed necessary to have a political elite that nourished an instinct
for bargaining, compromise, pragmatism, and partial solutions to problems. In
such a system, compromise had to be a preferred strategy for dealing with
competing interests rather than a dirty word. In a sense, the importance of what
we have called "interest aggregation" was underlined: politics, as many of the
founding fathers understood it, meant the balancing of interests and, if possible,
their reconciliation. In short, while they gave ample opportunity to the free
development and interplay of organized interests in the new nation, many of the
framers of the Constitution also feared political fundamentalism—the dogmatic,
truculent determination of particular interests to have their way irrespective of
the opposition.

These beliefs implied that organized opposition to the political regime was
acceptable, whether by groups opposed to a particular policy or to the entire
current administration. In practice, the acceptance of this idea came last and
hardest as it usually does in most developing political systems.[16] Yet democratic

---

[14] James Madison, *The Federalist Papers, No. 10* (New York: New American Library, 1962), p. 79.

[15] *Ibid.*

[16] The difficulty the federalists had in accepting the emergence of an organized opposition party has been noted by most American historians. For an interpretation of this problem in the context of newer nations and their own handling of the same matter, see Seymour M. Lipset, *The First New Nation* (New York: Basic Books, 1963), Chapter 1.

theorists asserted in various ways that an opposition to a government was not only legitimate but necessary in a truly adequate political order; there must be not only a regime but a mobilized opposition that can criticize, clarify, and evaluate the regime while offering alternatives and educating the public. How far opposition to a regime should be tolerated is always a bitterly contentious issue in democracies; the founding fathers' difficulty in accepting such an opposition merely underscores its constant troublesomeness. Still, the foundations of western democracy clearly pronounce that no government has the prerogative to suppress opposition or group conflict simply because it is disturbing.

Beyond various ideas that were congenial to interest groups and political parties, various proponents of democracy in the United States created an immediate problem that also promoted the formation of political parties: there was a large, and constantly expanding, population of voters to be organized. The Constitution itself left the determination of voting rights mostly to the individual states; the pressure upon state legislatures to expand the vote was almost immediately successful. The various property requirements for voting common among the states in 1787 limited the electorate to approximately one in four white males. By contrast, property requirements were so reduced between 1820 and 1840 that almost all adult white males could vote—a 300 percent increase in the eligible electorate that was further expanded by the addition of new states to the Union.[17]

As long as the voting population had been small and composed primarily of upper-class colonists, the various state and federal office holders felt little need to create formal, elaborate campaign organizations. The job of organizing voter opinions, mobilizing the electorate, and recruiting candidates for office could be conducted rather informally among a relatively small group of individuals, many of whom moved within the same social and economic circles anyway. The expanded franchise changed this. Increasing thousands of potential voters, spread across the geographic expanse of many states, now had to be influenced and organized if various legislative groups were to stay in office. Thus, facing the practical problem of mobilizing this electorate, various candidates and governmental factions began to organize rudimentary forms of political parties. Necessity had proven the inspiration for invention in politics.

Today, the political party—or at least its form—has become so closely identified with democracy that even nondemocratic regimes seem compelled to demonstrate that they are really democratic by producing some semblance of a party organization. And political parties have become so identified with the West and political modernization that many political elites in the new Afro-Asian nations, attempting to imitate what they believe to be a norm in western nations, have engineered parties into existence through Constitutions or other procedures, thereby producing the window dressing of democracy and modernization. These parties usually function quite differently than they do in western nations; they

---

[17] Dudley O. McGovney, *The American Suffrage Medley* (Chicago: University of Chicago Press, 1949), p. 16.

are often merely an arm of the regime suitable for mass mobilization and, just as often, one party alone is permitted legal existence. It is, perhaps, a supreme tribute to the ascendency of democracy as a world-wide prestige symbol that the most viciously anti-democratic governments will claim at least the trappings of political parties and free elections.

American Political Parties: Organization and Activities

The only element common to all political parties is that they are bands of partisans who attempt to control governments.[18] Beyond this, diversity prevails. The Communist parties in the Soviet Union and eastern Europe are tightly disciplined and cohesive; others, like those in the United States, seem so loosely structured and undisciplined that they have been called, only half jestingly, "states of mind." The fascist parties of the 1930s were para-military organizations, well endowed with alley brawlers ready to use fists and guns to steal an election. Party leaders may speak with the decorum of British Members of Parliament or, as happened occasionally in French Parliament during the Fourth Republic, hurl inkwells at one another. Amid such diversity, one can discern fairly broad patterns of party behavior; the American parties fall within the "western" group.

Western Party Politics

In the United States, western Europe, Great Britain and most of her colonies, the political parties, developing out of broadly analogous circumstances, came to resemble each other, especially when compared to parties outside the West.

Mass Membership. Western parties have a mass base, in contrast to totalitarian parties which restrict membership to a highly select, carefully trained minority; the Soviet Union with a population of 231 million permits only about 4 million the privilege of being members of the Communist party. Joining western parties is not always as absurdly easy as it is in the United States where one "joins" by informing the voting registrar that one is a Republican, Demo-

---

[18] A useful summary of different concepts of party may be found in Dwight MacDonald, *The Study of Political Parties* (New York: Doubleday & Co., 1955), especially Chapters 1–3.

crat, or something else or (in a few states) by taking an unenforceable oath to support party nominees in forthcoming elections. In France, as in many other European countries, a prospective party member ordinarily fills out a membership form including information about his age, family, and occupation; he declares his intention to observe party rules; he pays a nominal subscription fee to the party annually without which he cannot participate in party affairs.[19] Despite these variations, most western parties are quite open and accessible to the public.

Permanent Organization. Americans are quite accustomed to the major American parties' continuing organizational existence despite changing leaders and dominant coalitions within them; indeed, the resiliency and durability of our two major parties has been remarkable. Among other things, this continuing organizational existence permits the development of stable voter loyalties and attachments to party symbols and spokesmen over many generations, while also providing a party officialdom and bureaucracy to supply continuing leadership.

In many nonwestern societies, political parties lack this organizational continuity and stability. Often, the political party may be an organizational adjunct to a charismatic leader—a Sukarno, Nkrumah, or Chiang Kai-shek; such parties wax and wane according to the fortunes of the leaders and quite often collapse following their demise. However, such personalist parties have appeared in the West: the German National Socialist Party (Nazi) inspired by Adolf Hitler and the French Rassemblement du Peuple Français (RPF) during the Fourth Republic (united more by dedication to Charles de Gaulle than by an ideology) are examples.[20]

Competitive Parties. Western parties are competitive. In most western nations two or usually more parties compete for the vote. Within western nations, the number of parties varies widely. At one extreme are the unusually stable two-party systems of the United States and Great Britain. Most Scandinavian countries have a stable four-party pattern. Perhaps the finest example of party competition carried to its logical conclusion has been, until recently, France; at least seven major parties have been represented in the French Parliament since 1945 and at some elections, in a display almost approaching a

[19] Maurice Duverger, *Political Parties* (New York: John Wiley, 1963), p. 71.

[20] In the United States, Theodore Roosevelt's Bullmoose party of 1912, which finished ahead of the Republicans, and the American Independent party of George Wallace in 1968 are examples of charismatic parties.

partisan anarchy, as many as fifteen or more parties have offered candidates. This thriving partisanship has permitted almost every important gradient of political opinion some expression. It might be considered admirable since it seems to register the true distribution of voter opinions with sensitivity; but it also contributed to the chronic political instability of the French Parliament where majorities shifted dangerously and erratically. Lacking any commanding majority party, cabinets were overturned with regularity—between 1947 and 1953, sixteen French premiers were elected and dismissed.

Several factors seem to account for the number of parties found in western nations. In part, party competition itself reflects the willingness of most western regimes to tolerate open political conflict and organized opposition most of the time; also, as we shall later explain, the number of parties that can effectively organize in a political system seems related to the kind of electoral system used, upon the distribution of voter opinions throughout the polity, and where the areas of agreement lie across the spectrum of issues.[21]

American Parties: The Basic Pattern

By one authoritative estimate, at least 1,403 political parties have competed in the United States for the voter's allegiance.[22] Most have been little clusters of zealots pursuing eccentric, unremembered political gospels. But at least a dozen parties—Republican, Democrat, Farmer-Laborites, Bullmoose adherents, Whigs, and others—have made important contributions in shaping American political life. While the United States has had a very robust party tradition, the major American parties assume the status of a rather unconventional relative in a fairly conventional family when compared to parties in other western nations. The direct primary, the presidential nominating convention with its pungent blend of Roman circus and pep rally, the casual American approach to party membership, and many other features common to American parties are found nowhere else. In comparison to British and European parties, those in the United States are consistently more disorderly, undisciplined, fragmented, ideologically vague, and liable to unpredictable behavior. At times, the parties do seem so disorganized that one can appreciate why a writer would introduce an essay on American parties with the assertion that they are "wholly improbable, illogical, and theoretically nonsensible."[23] Though American political parties may indeed be less disciplined and cohesive than European parties, they are still far from "improbable, illogical, and theoretically nonsensible." American parties

[21] The theoretical relationship between opinion distributions and party competition has been suggested by Anthony Downs, *An Economic Theory of Democracy* (New York: Harper & Row, Publishers, 1957), Chapter 8.

[22] Estimate by Historical Data Recovery Program, University of Michigan Survey Research Center.

[23] Jessie Bernard, "The United States," in Arnold Rose (ed.), *The Institutions of Advanced Societies* (Minneapolis: University of Minnesota Press, 1958).

have had to adapt to a unique political milieu, pursuing their goals within a framework of limitations and opportunities imposed by the American constitution, political culture, and political history. Against this background, there is nothing especially puzzling or illogical about the way they developed.

The Contradictory Milieu. A very common observation, often a complaint, is that American political parties are "weak," "disunited," internally too undisciplined, and lacking the ideological clarity and solidarity common to many party organizations elsewhere. Critics point out that leaders with drastically different political perspectives often use the same party label: Nelson Rockefeller and Barry Goldwater are both Republicans; Hubert Humphrey and George Wallace are both Democrats. One can observe breakaway factions almost constantly in either major American party, seemingly able and willing to ignore the national leadership or program with impunity. In recent years, articulate intellectuals, leaders of the young, and a multitude of minorities have further attacked the major parties on the grounds that they are too concerned with votes and not committed enough to principles, and that they are not really representative of the true majority opinions in the United States.

However, many characteristic features of American parties, especially their seeming lack of cohesion, arise in part from the structure of the American government and the Constitution. We noted earlier that political parties are part of a political *system,* bound to be influenced by other elements in the system. This point is well illustrated here. The way our parties have developed demonstrates how one element in our political system influences another; the major parties have evolved within a governmental structure that imposes contradictory demands and limitations upon them and the parties have had to make their peace with these conflicting influences.[24] Let us briefly examine how this occurs.

Even though the Constitution encourages the development of political parties, it also impedes their unity and frustrates centralized party control of government. First, unlike most other western nations, our Constitution creates a so-called "separation of powers" by dividing the legislative and executive powers between two institutions—Congress and the presidency—and adds an independent judiciary as well. The result is three coequal, semi-independent, competing governmental branches, all invested with authority to resist domination by the other two.

This separation of powers discourages strong parties in several ways.

---

[24] An excellent discussion of various environmental influences on American party development is found in Austin Ranney and Willmoore Kendall, *Democracy and the American Party System* (New York: Harcourt Brace Jovanovich, 1956), Chapters 20–22; a brief but useful summary may be found in Frank Sorauf, *Political Parties in the American System* (Boston: Little, Brown and Co., 1964), Chapters 8–9.

Dividing power within the federal government often sets one branch against another, produces rivalries and jealousies, and undercuts party unity since members of the same party may feel loyal to different branches. Further, since each branch of the federal government is semi-autonomous, a party may gain control of one—say the presidency—yet be unable to impose a program or to guide the work of another branch. In effect, no faction or coalition of factions controlling any one branch is usually able to impose its will upon other branches. Thus, the president can veto a bill but cannot prevent its passage over a veto. Congress, in turn cannot command the armed services but neither can the president as commander-in-chief carry out that duty without the money only Congress can appropriate.[25] Justices of the Supreme Court, once appointed, are under no constitutional obligation to follow the lead of either Congress or the president in interpreting the law.

Ironically, the separation of powers within the federal government also makes the existence of political parties especially important, if not essential, and powerfully encourages their emergence. Some means was necessary to bridge the gap between these institutions and to assure—or attempt to assure—smooth functioning between these branches. Parties, therefore, came into existence partially as a means for linking and coordinating these various branches within the federal government. In effect, separation of powers introduces an internal tension within the federal government: the three branches are rivals to each other, not bound to follow a common outlook or behavior, yet at the same time forced to work with each other if government is to run effectively. It is within these contradictory forces of unity and disunity at the federal level that parties have been forced to operate.

There is also a second aspect of our Constitution that undercuts party cohesion. The federalist structure of our government, with its division of power between national, state, and local governments means there is an array of semi-independent, competitive governments with their own particular interests which often undermine party unity. Within both major parties, consequently, leaders and followers may be divided by conflicting loyalties to various governmental levels. In recent decades, for instance, both major parties have struggled to reconcile conservative, Southern segregationists with the more liberal, nationally-oriented integrationists of the party usually represented by the presidential nominees and their supporters. Since 1948, the Democrats have been steadily losing support in the previously "solid South" because of this conflict. The Republicans, in turn, have been gaining Southern support but at a cost. While Richard Nixon was able to win considerable Southern backing in 1968, criticism

---

[25] Congress, it is true, is ordinarily reluctant to deny the president the funds he needs for military initiatives, even when such military action involves a major undeclared land war in Asia, as the Vietnamese conflict does. However, the *threat* to deny or diminish funds for a military action may carry considerable force with the president, and Congress still enjoys the freedom to cut off the funds if it is inclined to do so.

of the President by many of his prominent Southern supporters after the election suggests that many Southern leaders still consider the President and his administration too "liberal" on racial matters.

Federalism may divide the nation into different governmental levels frequently with competing interests, yet because the president is nationally elected, political parties must find ways to combine these various elements into a coalition broad and strong enough to win this election. Thus, while federalism often encourages division within the parties, the necessity for party units to cooperate in order to elect the president is to some extent a countervailing force, one that overcomes some of the divisive tendencies within the governmental structure.

The Two-Party Pattern. For more than a century, the Republican and Democratic parties have been the organizing centers of American party politics. No other party has elected a chief executive, controlled a session of Congress, or even effectively contested these offices. Since 1888, the durability of this dualism has been remarkable. The Republicans have captured the White House eleven times, the Democrats ten times. Though one party has controlled the presidency for long uninterrupted periods in the past century, the vote has generally been close, indicating the stability of public loyalties to the parties. In three fourths of the presidential elections between 1888 and 1964, a shift in only 10 percent of the vote would have given the opposition party a victory. Some elections were won by paper-thin pluralities: 3.4 percent of the vote in the Wilson-Hughes contest of 1916 (not until California's vote was in could the winner be known early the following morning), 4.6 percent of the vote in 1948, .2 percent in the Kennedy-Nixon 1960 struggle, and .4 percent in the 1968 Nixon-Humphrey contest. Only Warren Harding (1920), Franklin Roosevelt (1936), Dwight Eisenhower (1956), and Lyndon Johnson (1964) can claim landslide victories. Divisions of electoral strength between parties in the House have been even narrower; in election years since 1900, the average difference in votes cast for candidates of the two parties for House seats has been 6.7 percent.[26] Governorships and state legislatures have yielded infrequently and only temporarily to other parties.

Aggregate voting across the United States for the presidency and Congress clearly shows this national two-party pattern. Party divisions within the states, by comparison, are less even, with at least four patterns of party competition within the states.[27] According to one estimate of state voting between 1946 and

---

[26] Frank J. Sorauf, *Party Politics in America* (Boston: Little, Brown and Co., 1968), pp. 28–31.

[27] Austin Ranney, "Parties in State Politics," in Herbert Jacob and Kenneth Vines (eds.), *Politics in the American States* (Boston: Little, Brown and Co., 1965), pp. 63–67.

1963, in eight Southern states, the Democratic party controlled almost all important state offices and, hence, this group was called "one-party Democratic." In nine additional states, Republicans won a significant share of offices but Democrats still predominated; these were "modified one-party Democratic." The third and largest category consisted of twenty-five "two party" states where both parties shared about equally in electoral victories. Finally, eight states— mostly in the Midwest and in New England—were "modified one-party Republican" because Republicans won most of the state offices.[28] (There are no "one-party Republican" states.)

The party patterns within the States are complicated, however, by the fact that voting for state and national offices may not follow the same partisan directions. For instance, while eight Southern states—South Carolina, Georgia, Louisiana, Mississippi, Texas, Alabama, Arkansas, and Florida—were classified as "one-party Democratic" on the basis of state-wide offices, since 1948 Florida has cast its presidential electoral votes for a Republican five times and elected a Republican governor in 1966. Georgia chose Goldwater in 1964 and George Wallace's American Independent Party in 1968; Mississippi and Alabama followed the Georgia pattern. There is no "solid South" in presidential elections today, and there has not been since 1948. Nor, in fact, are state party patterns elsewhere consistently related to national voting patterns. Political analysts, therefore, speak of the "two-party pattern" in the limited sense that candidates of the two major parties are the only ones who normally contest and win state and national elections.

With due respect for these variations in party competition across the United States, the fact that the same major parties have exercised almost complete control over the electoral process for the last one hundred years is still quite exceptional by world-wide standards. Table 6.1 illustrates the results of a survey of party competition throughout the world in the early 1960s; we can see how rare a true two-party pattern is.

Why the Two-Party Pattern?   A number of explanations have been offered as to why Americans for over a century have cast their ballots almost always for one of the major parties. Why haven't third, fourth, or fifth parties successfully challenged this duality?

One explanation begins with the distribution of political opinion in the

---

[28] At the midpoint of this period, 1955, in only six states was party strength balanced to the extent that one party controlled less than 55 percent of the legislative and congressional seats. Study by Warren Miller cited in James David Barber, *The Lawmakers* (New Haven: Yale University Press, 1965), p. 3.

Table 6.1. National Patterns of Party
Competition in the World, 1962

Type of Competition	Number of Nations Where Predominant
One-party entirely	34
One-party dominant	13
One and one-half party*	3
Two-party	11
Multi-party	30
No-party	5

* A minority party occasionally wins a few electoral seats or controls the government for brief periods.
Source: Arthur S. Banks and Robert B. Textor, *A Cross-Polity Survey* (Cambridge: Massachusetts Institute of Technology Press, 1963), p. 97. Reprinted by permission of the authors.

United States.[29] At the beginning of the nation, so the argument runs, Americans divided into two opinion groups at the same time parties developed. There were federalists, strongly committed to the new constitution and a powerful national government, and anti-federalists, who wanted less federal power and more decentralization of authority in the hands of state governments. Our initial party politics, therefore, reflected this dualism of opinion. Later, so the argument continues, the nation again divided into two camps over the issue of slavery, states' rights and the preservation of the Union, encouraging yet another dualism around which two parties developed. Since the end of the Civil War, this reasoning concludes, the two-party pattern established during the Civil War tended to perpetuate itself. As individuals were socialized into the political system, they came to orient themselves to one or the other of the major national parties and these two parties, in turn, were able to move to the left or right to accommodate important new opinion groups without destroying the dualism.

Another interpretation of public opinion as a major factor in two-partyism emphasizes that Americans over the last century as a rule have not been sharply divided into mutually exclusive opinion groups on most public issues. Instead, most Americans separate into groups that are either more or less in favor of major policies. Each of the two major parties, so this reasoning goes, will take up the cause of one of these two opinion clusters. There is very little opportunity in this case for a third, fourth, or fifth party to establish a firm national following; once those who vote for the major parties are counted, the remaining Americans with more extreme positions simply are not numerous enough to support any additional national parties over a sustained period. In essence, this

[29] See Downs, *op. cit.*, Chapters 7–8. This argument is elaborated, for example, in V. O. Key, Jr., *Politics, Parties, and Pressure Groups*, fifth ed. (New York: Thomas Y. Crowell Co., 1964), pp. 228–254.

argument suggests that our two-partyism in recent decades has reflected the essential moderateness of most public opinion (or perhaps public indifference).[30]

Another explanation for American two-partyism cites the American electoral system with its winner-take-all logic, the system used in almost all American national and state elections.[31] The United States is among a small group of nations, including Canada, Great Britain and her former colonies, where the "single-member, plurality" electoral system exists. This system has two features familiar to all Americans: (1) the candidate receiving the most votes (at least a plurality) wins office in the decisive contest, while those who do not receive a plurality are awarded nothing; and (2) ordinarily, only one elective official for a given level of government is elected at any single election for a given constituency. Congressional elections illustrate these principles. In the party primaries, the candidate receiving the most votes is designated the party nominee for the general election (or, in the South, two primaries are held; a "first" primary and then a "run-off" primary using the plurality principle). In the general election, the winner is determined by a plurality of the votes.

Throughout much of the world, *proportional representation,* quite a different system, is used: a number of candidates are elected from a single district to the same office—say, five members of the national legislature will be selected from the same district—and parties offer slates containing as many nominees as there are vacancies to fill. The voter then indicates how he wants these five seats divided. There are a great many schemes for dividing the vote. In some proportional representation systems, the voter may vote a straight party ticket, or separate his vote among any five candidates he desires regardless of party. In other systems, he can weight his vote by indicating the *order* in which he prefers any five candidate, voting for his first choice by ranking him "1," for his second choice with a "2," and so forth. After votes are cast, a complex system is used to award the seats being contested. Ideally, the system works so that the number of seats to be filled are divided among the parties in rough proportion to their voting strength in the constituency. This means, among other things, that parties without a plurality of voters in a district may still elect some representatives.[32]

The purpose of proportional representation is to create representative assemblies that are a "miniature replica of the spectrum of opinion in the electorate." Defenders of the system point out that it is considerably more sensitive to the true divisions of opinion in the electorate than the American system which permits minority parties no representation in electoral districts, no matter how large they may be. Also, the argument often proceeds, proportional

---

[30] See Key's theory of dualism in a moving consensus in Key, *op. cit.,* pp. 222–227.

[31] Two representative arguments for the impact of the electoral system may be found in Duverger, *op. cit.,* pp. 203–255; and E. E. Schattschneider, *Party Government* (New York: Holt, Rinehart and Winston, 1942).

[32] A standard reference that details the variety of proportional representation systems is Wolfgang Birke, *European Elections by Direct Suffrage* (Leyden, Netherlands: A. W. Sythoff, 1961).

representation is more democratic since a voter does not necessarily "waste" his vote if he supports a minority candidate; indeed, such a voter may often succeed in electing some representatives.

Most political experts believe that whatever the merits of these systems may be, the American system encourages two-partyism and proportional representation favors multi-partyism. Of the eleven nations with two-party politics, at least six (the United States, Great Britain, Australia, Canada, New Zealand, and the Philippines) use the American system. The American system seems to encourage political interests to combine in coalitions rather than to separate, fragment, and multiply; since only pluralities ordinarily succeed at the polls, the American system favors the formation of broadly-based, competing "ins" and "outs." Since this system awards no electoral victories to interests that remain outside very broad coalitions, political wisdom favors compromise and bargaining between interests. The result, of course, will not be elections where parties represent reasonably clear and uncompromised platforms. The coalitions that win elections as a rule will be a mix of interests; the candidates they promote will attempt to appeal to the broadest electoral combinations.

Whatever the reasons for party dualism, the majority of Americans in the past apparently considered two-partyism normal, as the "American way"; and relatively few voters deserted the major parties for third-party candidates.[33]

Decentralization. All observers of American parties will agree that the parties are decentralized; seldom is there a firm and stable distribution of power between party committees, officials, and candidates. Lower levels of the official party often act independently of higher levels with impunity, frequently in direct opposition to instructions from above. There is often no commanding focus of power within the national parties where the sprawling, frequently quarreling array of disparate state and local units can be forged into a coordinated electoral machine with a clear sense of direction and purpose. In 1964, therefore, few observers were surprised when the official Democratic organization in Alabama refused to enter on the ballot a slate of electors pledged to the party's nominee, Lyndon Johnson; rather, the Alabama Democrats put an unpledged slate of electors on the ballot. Thus, there was no way a voter could indicate his preference for Johnson. Nor was it considered unique for New York Republican Senators Javits or Keating to sit on their hands during the 1964 Goldwater campaign, conspicuously refusing to commend the Republican presidential nominee. Such instances of defection within the party ranks are not typical, but they are far from unprecedented.

---

[33] One of the few studies which deals directly with public attitudes toward the American party arrangement may be found in Jack Dennis, "Support for the Party System by the Mass Public," *American Political Science Review* (September 1966), pp. 600–615.

An official party organization exists, at local, state, and national levels. Roughly parallel in both major parties, this organizational scheme follows the hierarchy of American electoral units from the smallest to the largest and imparts a nominal order to party life. However, this scheme results in a hierarchy of party units but not a hierarchy of power. The state organization usually begins with the lowest electoral unit; the precinct committee (if it exists) represents local party members. Above the precinct in large metropolitan areas there may be ward, district, or city committees. The county committee, however, is most often the lynch pin of the state party structure, the strongest organizational unit in the state party. Finally, a state committee nominally governs these lower units.[34]

In almost all states, the powers and duties of the county and state committees are dictated by the state legislatures. As a rule, state legislators have written the laws affecting party organizations so that unwieldy, ineffective, politically punchless organizations have resulted.[35] State legislators have seldom been concerned that the party committees have the powers to create a disciplined party; virtually no state provides the higher-level party committees with the tools to control party nominations or to impose compelling penalties for lower-level insurrections against party discipline. In many states, the party committees are so large that they cannot be cohesive; in New York, for instance, a county committee may include several thousand members; in California, the state committee consists of several hundred. Two thirds of the states forbid party committees from endorsing primary candidates and, moreover, the direct primary takes control of primary nominations out of the hands of the party quite effectively. The direct primary permits rank-and-file party members to select the party's general election candidates at a "primary" election several weeks ahead of the general election. Ordinarily, there is little that party committees can do to control these nominations except possibly to work behind the scenes to influence voting behavior.

In reality, most state legislatures have attempted to reduce the official party bodies to "auxiliary machinery to the state's regulations of nominations and elections."[36] State law charges the party organization with calling a state convention, dispersing such campaign funds as it has, arranging the details of primary elections, and performing a multitude of other housekeeping operations

---

[34] There is very little consistency in the way these committees are selected, and in their composition. For details, see Sorauf, *Party Politics in America,* Chapter 5; or Hugh A. Bone, *American Politics and the Party System* (New York: McGraw-Hill Book Co., 1965), Chapters 6–7.

[35] State legislators often emasculate the party committees deliberately. Most legislators are traditionally elected by their own efforts and electoral organizations; they do not relish the emergence of a strong state committee which effectively controls campaign funds and party officials—one that might eventually control the selection of primary candidates. In Sorauf, *Party Politics in America,* p. 67.

[36] *Ibid.*

connected with elections, few of them designed to give the party organization much power or glory.

Above this welter of state party units is the national organization, in both parties consisting of a national chairman, a national committee, a national headquarters bureaucracy, the party campaign committees in both houses of Congress, and the quadrennial presidential nominating conventions. This national superstructure provides a veneer of organizational integration among the fifty state-party groups and imparts to the party whatever semblance of national status they possess. On most occasions, the national units sit at the apex of the party only on the organizational chart:

> In absolutely no important way does any national party unit limit the autonomy of state and local party organizations; with virtually no exceptions, they pick their own officers, nominate their candidates, take their own stands on issues, raise and spend their own funds. Every four years they come together as a national party to select a presidential candidate and write a platform, careful always to leave none of the trappings or structure of national organization behind when they break up.[37]

The evidence that the national party officials and committees wield little power over their state organizations—or over each other—is amply documented. In principle, the national committees of both parties are elected by the national conventions, but in practice the conventions merely ratify nominations made by the state organizations. Further, all states and territories have approximately equal representation on the national committees, regardless of past loyalties, with little attention to the relative strength or success of the different party organizations.[38] The national committees meet infrequently; the responsibility for representing the national party interests falls, as a rule, on the national chairman who is very likely to be chosen by the party's presidential candidate, not the national committee that nominally selects him.

The national chairman and national committee members are forced to skirmish constantly with party governors, congressional delegations, and local units for money, manpower, ideological supremacy, and rank-and-file loyalties. National committeemen, who often have no official position in the various policy-making units at state and local levels, must be content much of the time with

---

[37] Sorauf, *Party Politics in America,* p. 108. A very thorough and convincing argument for the impotence of the national committees is in Cornelius P. Cotter and Bernard C. Hennessy, *Politics without Power* (New York: Atherton, 1964).

[38] The Republican Convention recently added to their one committeeman from each state a committeewoman from each state and extra representatives from states which had recently elected a Republican governor, had a Republican majority in its Congressional delegation, or gave its electoral votes to the Republican presidential nominee.

exercising moral suasion or resorting to informal influence to make their point with local leaders. The campaign committees of each party in both houses of Congress consider the national committee's job as one of raising money for presidential campaigns, thus relieving the congressional committees to look after the political fortunes of congressional candidates. When it seems expedient, the congressional campaign committees make policy statements without regard to the preferences of the national leaders.

The divisiveness of the national party is especially clear when one of the parties does not control the White House and the legitimate national spokesman for the party becomes an issue. After Senator Barry Goldwater's defeat in 1964, his position as titular head of the party—one of the most politely fictional terms in the American party lexicon—meant little in light of the repudiation he suffered at the polls. Senator Everett Dirksen and Representative Charles Halleck, the Republican leaders in the Senate and House, arranged a weekly press conference (the "Ev and Charley Show") to establish a national forum which was intended to create a new party image. Earlier, presidential liberals in both parties had been unwilling to work with their more conservative national committees between 1952 and 1960, so they set up the Democratic Advisory Committee (1956) and the All-Republican Conference (1960). Neither Democratic nor Republican congressional delegations showed much inclination to defer to the pronouncements of these ad hoc committees.

Party unity is supposed to rise when the party controls the presidency. But even this does not guarantee an easy peace. The presidential election of 1968 is a memorable example. One of the oldest political maxims asserts that an incumbent president eligible for renomination never fails to get it. Ironically, Lyndon Johnson's downfall was precipitated by his own party's bitter internal divisions over the Vietnamese conflict. Senator Eugene McCarthy's forays against Johnson in the early Democratic presidential primaries in New Hampshire demonstrated how divided the party had become and, moreover, how unsteady the President's support was. Faced with the prospect of an angry, divisive primary contest for delegates and the apparently widespread dissatisfaction with his administration within his own party, Johnson announced his retirement from office in a surprising reversal of political tradition. His successor, Republican Richard Nixon, soon faced a revolt of liberals within his own congressional party over his proposed continuation of an income tax surcharge and the Anti-Ballistic Missile System he had strongly advocated. After the usual honeymoon period immediately following his election, a president can expect his own party delegation in Congress to fragment.

Many of the divisions within the national parties can be traced, as we have suggested, to the constitutional system with its emphasis upon maximizing the interplay of competing interests and institutions within the government. The major political parties attempt to fill the majority of 500,000 elective offices in the United States, most of which represent different sectional, economic, and social interests. Besides these social interests, institutional rivalries come into play. It is worth noting that the acrimonious, prolonged debates between Democratic "doves" in the Senate and President Lyndon Johnson involved not only disagreement over the handling of the Vietnamese war, but—as Senators Fulbright, McCarthy, McGovern, and Church took pains to emphasize—over the respective powers the Congress and the president should exercise in formulating foreign policy.[39]

The collisions of interest between the president and his staff on one side and his party representatives in Congress also reflects the different electoral bases of the Congress and presidency. It is true, as Herbert Hoover glumly remarked at the end of his disastrous term, that the presidency "has become increasingly the depository of all national ills, especially if things go wrong," but he is also the single federal official elected on a national basis and, hence, an impressive and commanding symbol of the nation. Presidents consider themselves national spokesmen, standing above the play of purely localistic interests. In response to a question regarding his stand on possible wage increases for steelworkers in April 1963, President John Kennedy made the national sweep of the chief executive's interest plain:

> I know that there are important editorial interests . . . who really don't feel that this [wage problem] is the president's business. They have never really defined what his business is, but it is not this. I take a somewhat different view . . . in that if there is a wage demand, it has a number of effects upon the public interest. . . . I find that when things are going badly, it becomes our business. When the stock market goes down, letters are addressed to the White House. When it goes up, we get comparatively few letters of appreciation. But when you have high unemployment, it is because the president hasn't gotten the country moving again.[40]

Congressmen usually regard themselves as ambassadors from their districts whose first obligation as a matter of political survival is to tend to the folks back home. As one veteran congressman explained,

> My experience is that people don't care how I voted on foreign aid, federal aid to education, and all those big issues, but they are very much interested in

---

[39] The existence of a presidential and a Congressional wing in both major parties has long been recognized and documented. The causes and consequences have been explored by James McGregor Burns, *The Deadlock of Democracy* (Englewood Cliffs, N.J.: Prentice-Hall, 1963).

[40] Quotation by John F. Kennedy at a meeting of newspaper editors, April 1963. From *The American Heritage History of the Presidency,* by Marcus Cunliffe. © Copyright 1968 by American Heritage Publishing Co., Inc.

whether I answer their letter and who is going to be the next rural mailcarrier or the next postmaster. Those are the things that really matter.[41]

So long as constituency interests and the president's program do not conflict, the president and his party cohorts in Congress can usually work with reasonable accord. But if, as often happens, the president or his program prove unpopular in local districts, even his own party representatives from those districts in Congress are likely to be less than cooperative with the administration.[42] In many states, the legislatures have staggered gubernatorial and legislative elections so they do not coincide with presidential election years in an attempt to minimize the influence of the presidential campaigns on local party contests.

Nonideological Politics.   Neither of America's major parties is considered "ideological" by most standards of judgment. In a very strict sense, an "ideology" is a sweeping, integrated, and coherent set of attitudes and values. This is used to place economic, social, and political life into a broadly meaningful order.[43] Measured against this standard, party platforms and candidates seldom achieve such clarity of thought or expression. Measured against such "ideological" groups as the Communist parties of the Soviet Union and mainland China, or to some extent even the British Labor party, which all have a well-developed theoretical framework for interpreting politics, American party programs seem vague and nebulous. Even to the man on the street who is not concerned with such subtleties, the major parties are frequently "Tweedledee and Tweedledum," two accomplished practitioners of "me-tooism." Amid such consensus, it is hardly surprising that one American historian has said that "spread eagle" is the ideological stance of the parties.[44]

The apparent lack of ideology has often been criticized by many who feel this contributes to the impoverishment of American political discourse. Since the

---

[41] Charles L. Clapp, *The Congressman* (New York: The Brookings Institution, 1964), p. 53.

[42] In his recent study of congressmen, Clapp found that most members of the House couldn't define "liberal" or "conservative" in general terms. "Basically, in the House we vote our district and that defines our bloc," reported one representative. *Ibid.,* p. 324.

[43] This definition suggested by Herbert McClosky, "Consensus and Ideology in American Politics," *American Political Science Review* (June 1964), p. 362; and Bone, *op. cit.,* p. 132.

[44] The "spread eagle" style, the writer continues, is "a compound of exaggeration, effrontery, bombast, extravagance, mixed metaphors, platitudes, defiant threats thrown at the world, and irreverent appeals flung to the Supreme Being." Daniel J. Boorstein, *The Genius of American Politics* (Chicago: University of Chicago Press, 1968), p. 149.

parties do not join electoral battle arrayed in different coalitions with distinctively different programs, the argument runs, voters cannot usually distinguish between party programs which, in any case, are so similar that real alternatives are seldom offered to the electorate. As Barry Goldwater said, they offer an echo but no choice. Thus, American party politics is essentially a contest for power in a vacuum of ideological conflict.

As often happens when such judgments are tested, qualification is needed. Although American parties are clearly not "ideological" in some pure sense of the term, they are not so undifferentiated or lacking in political clarity as is frequently assumed. First of all, there are consistent, significant differences between the political elites of the two major parties on a number of political values and attitudes, differences which persist over long periods of time. The elites are "distinct communities of cobelievers who diverge sharply on many important issues."[45] On 23 of 24 issues studied by researchers, the leadership groups in the two parties differed substantially. Democrats, for instance, were more likely than Republicans to favor increased farm support, government regulation of business, public utility control, and anti-monopoly laws; they were less likely than Republicans to favor increased trade union regulation, higher tariffs, or further restrictions on credit. The Republican leaders, in turn, were far more likely to espouse a "balanced budget" (without deficit spending), to favor greater tariff protection for domestic industries, and to approve a tough military posture toward the Soviet Union. In general, as many other studies have found, Democratic leaders could be distinguished from the Republican elite by greater economic liberalism, a commitment to expanded welfare programs, a desire for further business regulation and greater internationalism.[46] Not surprisingly, Democratic leaders agreed with a self-definition of "liberal"; Republicans accepted the "conservative" label.

Studies of congressional and legislative voting during the last twenty years reveal that voting usually follows party lines more often than it follows sectional, urban-rural, or socioeconomic divisions within legislative bodies. One study, for instance, concluded after examining congressional roll calls between 1949 and 1954 that "the average senator of the administration party supported the president on three fourths to four fifths of the votes he cast," while opposition congressmen in both houses supported the president less than half the time.[47] In state legislatures between 1931 and 1964, the party-line vote was more erratic.

---

45 This is from a careful study comparing political attitudes among the leaders and rank-and-file members of the two major parties made in the late 1950s, in Herbert McClosky, Paul J. Hoffman, and Rosemary O'Hara, "Issue Conflict and Consensus among Party Leaders and Followers," *American Political Science Review* (June 1960), p. 410.

46 *Ibid.*, p. 412.

47 Malcolm E. Jewell and Samuel C. Patterson, *The Legislative Process in the United States* (New York: Random House, 1966), p. 419.

The political party appeared to be a much more significant reference group in the Northeast than in the West; in the South where most state legislatures were entirely Democratic, party affiliation and voting were unrelated. The authors concluded that in states where a vigorous two-party system existed, there was a greater incentive to party-mindedness among legislators.

One can also discover party differences in the issues which cause party-line votes. The issues which cause the parties to organize into relatively clear opposition are strikingly similar in Congress and state legislatures. Usually, these issues involve the political prestige of the administration, welfare, business, labor, or procedural votes which will determine the relative strength of the parties in the legislature—for instance, votes on the leadership of the legislative chambers. Congressional Republicans tend to unite in favor of greater governmental assistance to business, greater labor regulation, less governmental involvement in agriculture, lower support levels for welfare. When the program of an incumbent administration is at issue, members of the administration party are likely to unite in its support.

The evidence, therefore, suggests that the American parties do sometimes behave as disciplined units and frequently are consistently divided on major issues. In the last decade, party cohesion in Congress has been variable; in some congressional sessions, party-line votes occurred on as few as 40 percent of the votes; at other sessions, the figure was 60 percent.[48] Measures of party cohesion usually make the relatively undemanding requirement that a majority of one party vote together for a party vote to occur; if the standard were raised to 75 percent agreement, for instance, the number of party votes in Congress and the states would drastically decline. While a party which votes together more than half the time may seem cohesive by American standards, by British standards it would seem intolerably disorganized. Though American parties are far from the disunited, unpredictable coalitions which they are sometimes supposed to be, by world-wide standards they are still far from disciplined. Obviously, party cohesion and discipline are relative terms.

The ideological fuzziness and confusion often observed within our major parties is the price parties pay for operating within an electoral system that encourages them to blur ideological distinctions and to aim at creating broad majorities through compromise and bargaining. In the United States, party success is inescapably tied to majorities and to the strategies which create majorities, whatever the cost to ideological clarity in party competition. In contrast, proportional representation, the electoral procedure used in many western nations, is far more likely to reflect accurately the divisions of opinion among the electorate in the platforms of parties. But this advantage is counterbalanced by the fact that proportional representation often produces so many

---

48 Sorauf, *Party Politics in America,* p. 342.

parties that a government capable of action may be difficult, if not impossible, to create. Proportional representation, furthermore, seems to encourage parties to harden and intensify their differences, while our plurality system appears to moderate and compromise them. Thus is appears that our electoral arrangements encourage moderate major parties and less party divisions at the cost of perhaps greater insensitivity and less attention to the finer shadings of opinion within the electorate.

If party leaders and spokesmen often fail to be ideologists, party styles do seem admirably suited to the capacities and interests of most voters. The majority of American voters simply do not think in ideological terms and show little inclination to change their ways. In a careful attempt to determine how voters make their partisan choices, the University of Michigan's Survey Research Center arranged a national sample of Americans during the presidential elections of 1952 and 1956 according to how they evaluated party, candidates, and issues. The Michigan group developed four broad categories of voters. Those with an "ideology" or "near ideology" could explain their voting choices by relating ideas or values in a fairly coherent, reasonably consistent manner. Next, there were individuals who apparently voted on the basis of group benefits, determining their choice by deciding which groups would benefit from which candidate (labor, business, or poor people, for instance). Third, many Americans seemed to vote according to the nature of the times. If times were good—whatever this may have meant to the voter—they favored the presidential incumbent or the incumbent party; if times were bad they preferred the opposition. Finally, there were citizens whose decision could not be related to ideology, groups, or the times—individuals who apparently made their decision without considering any issues. The distribution of the sample among these four categories is presented in Table 6.2.

Table 6.2. How Americans Evaluated the Candidates, 1956

Orientation	Percent of Total Sample (Includes Nonvoters)	Percent of Voters
Ideology or near-ideology	11.5	15.5
Group benefits	42.0	45.0
Nature of the times	24.0	22.0
No issue content	22.5	17.5

Source: Reprinted with permission from Angus Campbell, *et al., The American Voter* (New York: John Wiley, 1960), p. 144.

The number of individuals in the Group Benefits and Nature of the Times categories together with the more than one in five with no discernible issue orientation clearly indicates an electorate where party loyalties do not seem tied to ideological thinking. In such an electorate, one would expect to find many instances of inconsistent and contradictory political attitudes.

There is considerable evidence that this is the condition of the American electorate. Party identification and issue positions often do not correspond. One 1967 study revealed that party preference and positions regarding the Vietnamese conflict were not strongly associated;[49] in the study of party elites and rank-and-file party members cited earlier, the Republican rank-and-file disagreed more with its own leadership on specific issues than it disagreed with the opposition leaders.[50] Candidates, leaving no matter unattended that might produce a victory, usually discuss issues but many do not know how important the finer philosophical points may be to the voter; some are convinced that issues matter little.[51]

Candidates who address the American voter in highly philosophical terms seldom succeed. The 1964 Goldwater campaign seems to confirm this judgment. Goldwater pitched his campaign at a theoretical level uncommon in American politics. Crossing the nation expounding the tenets of his conservatism, Goldwater thought of himself as an educator as much as a politician, a man who would give the public "a choice, not an echo" by etching on public consciousness the philosophical differences between a conservative and the liberal incumbent president, Lyndon Johnson. Goldwater failed to demonstrate the existence of a latent conservative majority that needed only a true leader. He also failed to carry large segments of his own party.[52] His opponent—the archetype of the seasoned professional politician—stuck to a meat-and-potatoes campaign, reminded his audiences that they never had it so good (and would have it better if he were returned to the White House) and steered clear of philosophical

---

[49] Sidney Verba *et al.*, "Public Opinion and the War in Vietnam," *American Political Science Review* (June 1967), pp. 317–333.

[50] McClosky *et al., op. cit.*, p. 410.

[51] A recent study of elected and defeated candidates for a variety of federal and state offices in Wisconsin indicates that both winners and losers believed that voters were more concerned with party labels and candidate personalities than with the issues: see John W. Kingdom, "Politicians' Beliefs about Voting," *American Political Science Review* (March 1967), pp. 137–145. Asked "What would you say is the most important reason" they voted for the congressional candidate of their choice in 1962, the largest proportion of a national voting sample (36 percent) mentioned party identification, the next largest group (20 percent) mentioned the candidate's record. University of Michigan, Survey Research Center, Political Behavior Program *1962 Election Study* (Ann Arbor: Inter-University Consortium on Political Research, 1969), pp. 21–22.

[52] The empirical evidence for the lack of a latent conservative majority and one explanation for Goldwater's nomination in spite of widespread opposition in his own party is explored by Philip E. Converse, Aage R. Clausen, and Warren E. Miller, "Electoral Myth and Reality: The 1964 Election," *American Political Science Review* (June 1965), pp. 321–336. The ideological component in the Goldwater campaign and its use are discussed in greater detail in John H. Kessell, *The Goldwater Coalition* (Indianapolis: Bobbs-Merrill, 1968), pp. 177–297; and Karl A. Lamb and Paul A. Smith, *Campaign Decision-Making* (Belmont, Calif.: Wadsworth, 1968), especially Chapter 6.

subtleties. Such a contrast in campaign styles and philosophies was rare in American political history. Though Johnson's election by the largest plurality in American history—61.1 percent of the popular vote—was produced by many factors, it seemed apparent that Goldwater's style was a handicap.

The Goldwater disaster is a pointed illustration that the American political system is loaded structurally and culturally against the development of ideological major parties. Yet in such a system where ideological conflicts seldom materialize between the major parties and both parties strive to accommodate the widest range of interests without exactly fitting many of them, numerous Americans have chosen—or have been forced—to find alternative ways of bringing major issues before the public, sharpening them, and clarifying the alternatives. Third parties and street politics represent two such alternatives. In different ways, both techniques of political action are attempts to introduce a more direct and sharper dialogue over major policy issues than the major parties often attempt.

Third Parties: Ideological Protest at the Polls.   Third parties, those quadrennials of American political life, represent attempts to promote candidates and platforms, usually at the presidential level, altogether outside the major party structure. Quite often, the foundation of third parties lies with individuals deeply committed to distinctly defined programs or principles to which the major parties cannot, or will not, give recognition either in their platforms or through their presidential nominations, dismissing them as interesting but insignificant sideshows in the American political arena. In fact, major policy issues and alternatives have often been defined through third parties, and Americans dissatisfied with the customary ideological vagueness of the major parties have been given a voice.

It is true that most third parties in the past attracted only a miniscule portion of the American electorate and proposed programs so narrow or eccentric that their relevance to current public issues seemed almost nonexistent. The thirteen minor parties on the presidential ballot in 1960 were able to attract only about 216,000 votes altogether; the six appearing in 1964 drew little more than 125,000 ballots. Moreover, parties expounding the virtues of theocracy, prohibition, vegetarianism, tax cut, and other less than consuming national issues could not be expected to excite popular enthusiasm.[53] However, besides these narrow and eccentric third parties, two other types—Marxist and splinter parties—have made an impact upon American politics.

[53] The most comprehensive treatment of third parties in the United States may be found in William B. Hesseltine, *Third Party Movements in the United States* (Princeton: Van Nostrand, 1962).

The Marxist parties in the United States, though they have seldom made an impressive electoral showing, have often introduced an element of ideological dialogue lacking in major party platforms and, in the case of some socialist parties, have proven to be prophetic in some of the programs they have espoused in the past.[54] The Communist party, additionally, has by its presence and program generated major constitutional issues and political conflicts within the mainstream of American political life. The Socialist Labor party and Socialist Worker's party continue to promote presidential candidates but received fewer than 75,000 votes in 1968. The Socialist party, considerably bigger and more ably led, did better. Under Norman Thomas, who died at 81 in 1968, the party usually polled at least 100,000 votes and came close to the million mark on three occasions prior to 1948. Though the party virtually disbanded after receiving fewer than a thousand votes in 1956, it did have an influence on American politics; Thomas had advocated such measures as social security, government medical insurance, extensive federal regulation of business and industry, and consumer protection, long before the major parties embraced them.

The American Communist party which of all the doctrinal parties has had the greatest impact on American politics, has excited the greatest attention and, in general, by its presence in the United States has raised issues which vastly transcend the party itself. The party has never been large; at its zenith during the Depression decade of the 1930s, it probably numbered slightly more than 100,000; by 1964, its strength had dwindled to an estimated 10,000. It is, however, the only political party specifically prevented by law from participating in elections.[55] After World War II, party members were successful in infiltrating a few major labor unions. In the early 1950s, communism became a major national issue. Wisconsin's Senator Joseph McCarthy, playing upon public anxiety over the Cold War, the loss of mainland China, the looming power of the Soviet Union, and the apparent impotence of the United States government to roll back communist advances in Europe, seized upon the communist issue and initiated a temporary but vicious attack not only on communism but on liberal philosophies and individuals in all walks of life. Before it subsided, McCarthyism left in its wake loyalty oaths, loyalty hearings, bitter accusations against liberals and communists alike, and smoldering political controversies which reached from Washington to universities and colleges and to the mass media. Communism was transformed into a demonology by America's radical right, and "fighting communism" became an orthodoxy for any candidate who expected to succeed in major elections.

---

[54] David A. Shannon, *The Socialist Party of America* (New York: Macmillan Co., 1955), contains a detailed study of the American Socialist party, perhaps the most prophetic of these Marxist parties.

[55] Following congressional legislation, the Supreme Court held that the party, with its Marxist gospel, was a dedicated revolutionary organization intent on overthrowing the United States government.

Much more significant at the polls and in the thinking of major party leaders have been the movements splintering from the major parties to promote their own national programs and presidential candidates in this century. These movements have often explored the strength of new issues and stimulated new segments of public support for them; sometimes, such movements have rallied dissident elements within the parties balking against too much innovation. In either case, these movements have often demonstrated that sizeable segments of the electorate may be loosening their loyalties to one or the other major parties and are, consequently, "up for grabs." When such movements do make a significant showing at the polls, therefore, they may force the major party leaders to accept a new strategy or a rethinking of past programs; there is always the possibility, moreover, that such a splinter movement may deny one party a presidential victory.

The most impressive third party showing in this century was produced by Teddy Roosevelt's Bullmoose party of 1912, a superheated group of liberal Republicans in full revolt against the conservative leadership of the national Republican party. The Bullmoosers captured 35 percent of the popular vote and 88 electoral college votes, thus denying the White House to the Republican incumbent William H. Taft and bestowing it upon Democrat Woodrow Wilson. In 1924, the Progressive party of Robert LaFollette drew support from the liberal wings of both major parties in protesting the dominant conservative coalitions in each; the Progressives, capturing almost 5 million popular votes and 13 electoral college votes, did not win a major electoral triumph yet their strength did persuade the Democratic party's leadership to make a more determined appeal to liberal electoral elements who seemed ready to desert the party.

Beginning with the Dixiecrats in 1948, a succession of third parties rooted initially in Southern resistance to racial integration have attempted to draw Southern support away from the Democratic party's presidential candidates and to force one or both parties to take a more conservative stance on racial integration and other matters. This third-party revolt was represented by George Wallace's American Independent Party of 1968. The Alabama governor's heavy emphasis upon the evils of "forced integration" appealed especially to many Southerners but extended outside the South and encompassed a wide variety of other issues. Wallace dwelt upon the need for law and order, took a rather hawkish stance on the Vietnamese War, attacked the liberal bias of the news media, lashed out at many college professors and other intellectuals who were allegedly betraying traditional American principles, and in general voiced a lexicon of complaints against what he called liberal and radical elements in the United States. Opinion polls showed that the Wallace movement drew considerable sympathy not only from the South, but from many lower-middle-class voters, blue-collar workers, urban ethnic minorities and some rural Americans.

Wallace's hope that he could win enough electoral college votes to deny an electoral college majority to either major party candidate, thus throwing the election into the House of Representatives, failed. Yet he did amass over 9 million popular votes, about 13.4 percent of the total national presidential vote. Wallace's performance in 1968—and his intention to run again in 1972—was apparently a major factor in the development of Richard Nixon's "Southern strategy" for 1968 and 1972. Essentially, this "Southern strategy" amounted to cutting back federal pressure for immediate and complete school integration, more attention to civil rights abuses outside the South, a tough stand on law and order and other measures that would appeal to conservative Southern voters. This strategy allegedly had several purposes. It was aimed immediately at wooing Southern Democrats away from traditional Democratic loyalties and to the Republicans, a move that, if successful, would make the Republican party truly national and could conceivably aid in creating a new Republican majority in the United States. Moreover, the many non-Southern groups who were also involved seemed increasingly restive and disenchanted with the Democratic party's national leadership for whom they had traditionally voted.[56] And, of course, this strategy sought to deflate the Wallace boom that seemed to draw support away from the Republicans. In short, the American Independent party was no passing irrelevancy. It was attempting to move one or both major parties toward a more conservative position by demonstrating considerable support for Wallace's policies.

Street Politics: Ideological Protest by Demonstration.   The protesters who opened this chapter are an example of the street politics that rose to major political significance in the 1960s and early 1970s. Despite numerous programs, sponsors, and forms, street politics retained one common element: it was direct, organized, mass political demonstration for major political programs promoted outside the party structures.

Essentially, the various forms of street politics were attempts to create and mobilize public opinion behind major political objectives which seemingly could not be effectively promoted through the major political parties. One inspiration was the philosophy of Martin Luther King, Jr., whose "direct action"—described in Chapter 5—advocated peaceful civil disobedience to segregation as a means for dramatizing its evils. By the late 1960s, however, the techniques of street politics and the programs it espoused had diversified enormously.

There were peaceful demonstrations in the form of anti-war moratoriums,

---

[56] The Nixon administration claimed it had no such "Southern strategy" but there seemed little doubt that it was attempting to forge a new coalition based on appeals to Southerners, Northern ethnic groups who previously had been Democratic and the traditional hard-core Republican vote. See, for instance, James Boyd, "Nixon's Southern Strategy: It's All in the Charts," *The New York Times Magazine* (May 24, 1970), p. 25 ff.

protest marches and rallies, hunger strikes, teach-ins, and marathon political camp meetings that mixed politics with folk music and the symbols of youth's counterculture. Other public demonstrations, whether intentionally or not, were provocative and frequently incited violence. Mass blockades of draft head-quarters, induction centers, and trains carrying troops, munitions or chemical-warfare product manufacturers often resulted in arrests and clashes with law-enforcement officials. On the campus, demonstrators sometimes seized or destroyed campus buildings, struck classes, and attempted to obstruct the work of campus recruiters for the armed services and corporations with defense-re-lated contracts. The topics for street demonstrations read like a melancholy inventory of America's major social problems—racial prejudice, the Vietna-mese war, student rights, the draft, environment contamination, police brutality, and others.

By implication, the traditional activities of the major parties were involved in street politics as well as these specific issues. In many instances, organizers of street politics demonstrated a profound suspicion of major party leaders, the decision-making structures of the major parties, and the traditional methods of party platform-building. The party structures, so the argument ran, were biased against major social change, and the leadership was too insulated from rank-and-file opinions to appreciate the strength for such demands; moreover, major political leaders often blurred and compromised their positions in order to please majorities rather than presenting issues to the public and debating them. The social composition of the parties was alleged to be heavily biased toward middle- and upper-class members with the result that the lower social classes and the young had little influence. In many respects, indeed, street demonstrations seemed an especially fruitful way to attract and mobilize the lower classes in ways that normal party procedures could not. The majority of blacks, the poor, many lower-class groups, and minority groups have been largely politically unorganized in the past; street politics dealt with concrete issues, stimulated direct action, often drew leaders from these unorganized social groups, and cost virtually nothing except the will to participate. In addition, white middle-class young people—who constituted a major segment of support for street politics—were often provided a means of political expression they otherwise lacked since many were not old enough to vote.

Street politics was undoubtedly encouraged, as well, by knowledge that these demonstrations, if truly massive and relevant to major social problems, would draw considerable mass media attention and thus greatly magnify the scope and impact of the performance. This, indeed, had special appeal to those political activists who were strongly issue-oriented. Frustrated by the seeming lack of ideological clarity and dialogue between the major parties, street politics seemed a means for reintroducing issue politics in a way that would command a national audience. Therefore, for a variety of reasons growing out of the issues and the structure of our major parties, street politics appealed to a great many Americans—though not a majority. The long-range impact of these demonstrations, however, was far from clear; in the early 1970s, some organizers were becoming discouraged and others uncertain about the value of such demonstrations.

Though third parties and street politics both demonstrate dissatisfaction with the structure and strategies of both major parties, these two parties have shown considerable durability and continuity in the face of such challenges now as well as in the past. Many other forces encourage the stability and endurance of the two-party system and these, too, deserve mention.

The Incentives for Cooperation.   Looking at the decentralization, ideological fuzziness, and separatism within both major parties, one may wonder why they endure at all. Yet there must be strong forces that counterbalance fragmentation and disunity since the two parties command the loyalty of more than 70 percent of the electorate and since they are—together with the president and Congress—the most salient symbols of the political system. And, they have demonstrated a remarkable ability to rise from the ashes of apparent collapse.

Until the 1950s, the promise of patronage in return for party loyalty was a powerful stimulant to party solidarity; this played upon plain materialism for its effect. Beginning with the Jackson Administration in 1828, federal officeholders became hostages to political fate; their jobs were usually given or taken away with changes in administration for the next fifty years. Jackson's own use of the federal bureaucracy for patronage was modest by later standards. He removed between 10 and 20 percent of the 10,000 federal officeholders and replaced them with Jacksonian Democrats; his Postmaster General was more successful, turning more than 13,000 postal positions over to the party faithfuls and creating the practice of using postmasterships as patronage positions. By 1840, the inauguration of a president—William Henry Harrison—was the signal for a massive onslaught of job seekers on the White House. The result, notes one historian, was that

> after Harrison's inauguration, the White House was surrounded and invaded by a frantic crowd of office seekers. The President, trying to hold a cabinet meeting, could not find a vacant room. He could not persuade the throng to leave him alone; they insisted that he receive their mass of papers on the spot and made him promise to receive them. In desperation, he agreed.[57]

[57] From *The American Heritage History of the Presidency,* by Marcus Cunliffe. © Copyright 1968 by American Heritage Publishing Co., Inc. Reprinted by permission.

The high tide of federal patronage was reached in the middle of the last century. The gradual recession of patronage jobs within the federal government had many explanations, among them the desire of presidents themselves to be rid of most patronage decisions. The long, squabbling lines of office-seekers were irritating and distracting; the bickering and jockeying for patronage among party leaders badly strained party unity and, like other politicians, the president usually made ten enemies but only one friend for each position he filled. Furthermore, administrative reformers were recognizing that wholesale patronage diminished administrative morale and efficiency; political hacks were more likely to make mistakes than trained professionals, especially when governmental administration was becoming more technically demanding. Then, too, federal patronage positions gradually became less important to many of the party faithful who preferred more lucrative jobs which were becoming increasingly available in an affluent society. By 1900, civil service reforms had placed the great majority of federal jobs on a merit system that substituted competitive job examinations and security of tenure for the job auctioning of the patronage system.

As succeeding administrations have incorporated progressively more federal jobs under the merit system, the patronage positions available to an incoming administration have continually shrunk. After twenty years in the political wilderness, the Republicans, upon taking control of the White House, could find only 20,000 patronage jobs for the Eisenhower Administration by the most diligent searching. Today, probably less than one percent of federal positions are still available for patronage; these are positions like federal judge and attorney, U.S. marshal, internal revenue collector, customs official, and postmaster.

State and local party organizations have considerably more patronage to dispense. The governor of Pennsylvania may have 50,000 jobs to award; there are about 75,000 municipal patronage jobs in Manhattan. Studies indicate that in St. Louis in the early 1960s about 40 percent of Democratic officials held patronage positions; in the late 1950s, almost three quarters of the Democratic committeemen in Pittsburgh held such positions. Thus, patronage cannot be dismissed as an unimportant incentive to party unity, especially at the state and local level.

At the national level, patronage is no longer the spur to partisanship it once was, so one must look for less tangible incentives. Undoubtedly, there is a very general sense of orientation that unites a great many party leaders, despite the absence of an ideological consensus. In the past, voters and party activists alike tended to consider the Democratic party as oriented toward the liberal position, the Republicans toward the conservative position. A certain amount of self-selection occurs when a man chooses a party affiliation, especially if he is a political activist. People who think of themselves in a vague, but personally meaningful way as liberal or conservative are likely to cluster to the party with "their" label. Often, of course, party leaders are also united by a shared sense of identification with key reference groups which, in turn, they associate with the parties. Thus, Americans identify the Democratic party nationally with labor, minorities, the "little guy," intellectuals, and liberals.[58] Republicans are perceived as the party of the grey flannel suit; it represents business, most of the professions, the relatively better-off part of the population, the party of sound money and economic conservatism. To the extent that one associates his own group allegiances with these values, he is likely to gravitate toward the same party as others with a similar identification. And, as noted earlier, many Americans have been socialized by family tradition or education to identify with one or the other party.

Beyond these psychological forces, many activists join and remain within parties because of the values of the party label, irrespective of its vagueness. As we shall see in Chapter 7, the party label is an important cue to voters, evoking a set of emotions and ideas which are a sort of standing judgment about candidates, in many cases without reference to the particular candidate. Simply to carry the party label, therefore, is a political asset, since it may immediately summon voter support and identification for the candidate in its own right. Thus, in an interesting way, the two-party system encourages its own survival by making third-party labels and programs an electoral disadvantage, thus encouraging candidates (unless moved by strong ideological compulsions) to adopt the label of a major party—though not necessarily the outlook of others bearing the same label.

Party Politics and Foreign Policy.   The existence of two major parties, third parties, street politics, and other examples of issue conflict and debate illustrate the extent to which the American political system encourages organized political division. Indeed, in a nation committed to the ideal of making the government responsive to the public, the idea of party conflict seems particularly important. An "out" party is supposed to have a major place in government: it criticizes and opposes the party controlling the government. This, presumably, is a way of holding the administration responsible for its actions, to present alternative programs to the electorate and to educate the public on major political issues; the "out" party stands ready with candidates to replace members of the "in" party if the electorate so desires.

Interestingly enough, this defense of party conflict often seems limited to domestic matters and is not usually applied to foreign affairs. Quite the contrary. Party conflict and competition are thought to have many undesirable results in

---

[58] Until recently, the South was an exception. There, to be a Democrat was to affirm a belief in the racial *status quo* above all else, to be in favor of segregation and the political arrangements that made it possible. On national images of the parties in the past, see Angus Campbell, *et al., The American Voter* (New York: John Wiley, 1960), Chapters 3 and 7.

foreign policy. A division between a president of one party and a Congress controlled by the opposition might threaten national stability in international affairs; party divisions on foreign policy might undermine continuity in handling international matters; when one party surrenders control of the administration to another, an abrupt change of policy may result. Further, if broad support for the administration's foreign policy is not dependable, those who presume to speak for the nation in international matters may be vulnerable to extremist attacks from the left or the right, and the nation's credibility in dealing with allies and enemies may be undermined. Given these possibilities, it is often considered desirable that party divisions should be replaced with bipartisanship in foreign affairs—both major parties should agree to remove foreign policy questions from their competition for power so that neither major party "plays politics" with issues of peace and war.[59]

Bipartisanship, so the argument runs, would make American foreign policy dependable, allow the country to make long-range foreign commitments, and supply the broad support needed for such commitments while presenting other nations with a united front at home. In brief, bipartisanship is thought necessary to overcome the handicaps of our constitutional separation of powers and decentralized two-party system. If successful, it would confer upon the United States some of the advantages frequently attributed to the totalitarian states: continuity of purpose, a capacity for rapid commitments, adjustments to change, and the appearance of a single will. American presidents have used many strategies to win support of members of the opposition party. Members of the opposition party may be included in the Cabinet or lower administrative positions, or new policies might be adopted only after consultation and frank discussion with opposition leaders within and outside Congress. Members of the opposition party might be used as observers or negotiators at international conferences. Whatever the method, the objective has been to remove foreign policy from the arena of party conflict.

In large part, post-war American presidents have been able to attract such support for their foreign policies from the loyal opposition. One major reason for this has been that executive officials responsible for the formulation of foreign policy and congressmen have often shared the same premises about the nature of our opponents and our role in the world. One reason they think alike, according to Laurence Radway, is that they live in Washington—sometimes in the same neighborhoods, read the same newspapers, attend the same parties and churches.[60]

---

[59] Two historical analyses of World War II and post-war bipartisanship are Daniel S. Cheever and H. Field Haviland, *American Foreign Policy and the Separation of Powers* (Cambridge: Harvard University Press, 1952); and Bradford H. Westerfield, *Foreign Policy and Party Politics* (New Haven: Yale University Press, 1955). The latter author, in fact, prefers the term "extrapartisanship."

[60] Laurence I. Radway, *Foreign Policy and National Defense* (Atlanta: Scott, Foresman and Company, 1969), pp. 117–118.

Circumstances have also played a crucial part. When a major crisis situation in international affairs was perceived, both administration and opposition felt compelled to rally round the flag and demonstrate solidarity behind the president; and when in addition, a president's policy was conspicuously successful, the opposition was left with little to criticize. But bipartisanship did not survive certain situations. In the case of some international crises, such as the outbreak of the Korean and Vietnamese Wars, opposition support for the president's policies was less the result of common political convictions and shared foreign policy outlooks than the result of a situation that temporarily convinces the parties to strike a truce. Furthermore, when a policy was unsuccessful, the support of the opposition party tended to evaporate; the "out" party in such circumstances could not resist the temptation to exploit the situation in order to enhance its congressional representation and, more important, to capture the White House.

Clearly, the record of bipartisanship is a mixed one—generally good on European policy, poor on the Far East where the United States has suffered the major setbacks and frustrations (the collapse of Nationalist China and two limited wars). Despite appeals to "stop politics at the water's edge," or to abandon Democratic and Republican foreign policies for an "American foreign policy," neither major party has consistently adopted the higher loyalty and foregone the partisan wrangling over foreign affairs. This may, in fact, be fortunate. If differences of views and alert criticism of governmental policy are as crucial domestically as is often argued, then surely they are even *more* crucial in foreign affairs.[61] Not only is national survival at stake in a nuclear era, but the diversion of resources from domestic affairs to foreign matters is a major factor in intensifying problems within the country. Thus, foreign policy is a significant issue in itself but, in addition, it cannot be neatly separated from domestic affairs. Moreover, what is best for the national interest is seldom so obvious that policy debate is unnecessary. It may perhaps be "revealed" after an attack upon this country: who could doubt that the defeat of Germany and Japan was in the American national interest during World War II? In peacetime, however, no matter how tense the international situation is, what is best for the national interest is not clearly definable. It is understandable, therefore, that the major parties should be divided on some important issues. Partisan controversy over foreign policy, as over domestic policy, is the offspring of a democratic government and open politics. It is contradictory to argue that an alert party opposition is necessary for a healthy democracy, but that sharp criticism of foreign policies, especially unsuccessful ones, is-inimical to the national interest.

---

[61] Cecil V. Crabb, *Bipartisanship and Foreign Policy: Myth or Reality* (White Plains, N.Y.: Row, Peterson & Co., 1957). Crabb expands on this theme in what is probably the most balanced analysis of the problems inherent in bipartisanship.

Interest Groups

Since at least 1768, when a group of disgruntled North Carolinians formed an association to protest being "continually squez'd and oppressed by our Publick Officers with regard to their Fees as also in the Laying on of Taxes," voluntary associations of all types flourished in the United States. Unlike this group, many of these early associations began for nonpolitical purposes. By the 1740s, the young nation had nine library associations, and "knots of men rightly sorted" were forming social groups for all purposes, including raillery. Alexis de Tocqueville was only one of many early foreign observers to note the American "propensity to form associations." The United States is distinguished by the number and variety of its voluntary associations but such associations are certainly not restricted to the United States.

The Scope of
Voluntary Associations

Voluntary associations are a part of western culture to an extent not duplicated elsewhere. One recent study indicates that voluntary groups are found in 80 percent of western nations, but in only 4 percent of nonwestern societies.[62]

Equally important, the western nations with vigorous voluntary associations customarily permit these groups considerable freedom for political activities. The multiplication of voluntary associations throughout the West is attributable to many factors. Cultural pluralism and industrialization have been mentioned already. Democracy, with its encouragement to freedom of expression and its emphasis upon mass political participation, also proved congenial to these voluntary groups. Even within that group of western nations where voluntary associations exist, however, the United States has developed a particularly vigorous and varied group life that distinguishes it from other western nations.

Excluding political parties, a very conservative estimate would place the number of voluntary associations in the United States at 100,000. These groups, which are essentially nationally organized associations which further some mutual interest of the members, have steadily increased for a century. Within this aggregation, the range of organizational strength and importance runs all the way from almost anonymous, small, exotic groups (like the American Seal Breeders Association) to mammoth organizations such as the one and one-half million member Teamster's Union. There are at least 6,000 trade associations in

[62] Arthur S. Banks and Robert B. Textor, *A Cross-Polity Survey* (Cambridge: Massachusetts Institute of Technology Press, 1963), p. 89, Variable 33.

the United States—one estimate suggests there may be as many as 14,000—which collectively purport to speak for almost all major American economic interests.[63] These voluntary associations spend billions of dollars annually, enlist millions of Americans in their work, and are composed of most levels of American social life.

To some extent, the existence of so many groups marks an American cultural trait; Americans seem particularly impressed with the value of group action and organizational devices for realizing personal and political goals. In a 1960 study, two political scientists confronted citizens of five nations with a question concerning how they would try to influence local government and found that more than half the American sample (56 percent) would attempt to organize informal groups or utilize some other form of collective action; among British, German, Italian, and Mexican citizens, the comparable figure was much lower.[64] Though many Americans belong to some voluntary associations, they seem much more likely than most other people to prefer outgoing activities that require group cooperation. This is apparent in Table 6.3, also taken from the 1960 study.

Table 6.3

". . . aside from your work and your family, what are the activities that interest you most, that you spend your free time on?"

Percentage Interested in	U.S.	U.K.	Germany	Italy	Mexico
Civic-political activities	2	2	3	1	0
Economic interest groups	0	0	1	0	0
Other interest groups	3	0	0	0	0
Charitable and welfare activities	8	5	2	2	1
Religious activities	20	7	4	2	4
"Social" activities	18	18	8	3	6
Total percentage choosing outgoing activity*	40	30	16	7	11

* Percentage in this row less than the sum of those above since some respondents chose more than one outgoing activity.

Source: *The Civic Culture: Political Attitudes and Democracy in Five Nations* by Gabriel A. Almond and Sidney Verba. Copyright © 1963 by Princeton University Press; Little, Brown and Company, 1965. Table 4 on p. 304 of Princeton University Press edition. Reprinted by permission of Princeton University Press.

Undoubtedly, the American penchant for group activity also reflects the availability of so many voluntary associations which encourage this form of interest expression.

[63] Estimates from Bone, *op. cit.*, p. 558; R. Joseph Monsen, Jr., and Mark W. Cannon, *The Makers of Public Policy* (New York: McGraw-Hill Book Co., 1965), p. 7.

[64] Gabriel Almond and Sidney Verba, *The Civic Culture* (Boston: Little, Brown and Co., 1965), p. 148. The responses for other nations on this matter were: Great Britain, 34 percent; Germany, 13 percent; Italy, 7 percent; and Mexico, 26 percent.

Only a small proportion of all voluntary associations are, however, persistently engaged in political affairs. Even among those in the political arena, this activity is usually secondary to other organizational purposes. For clarity, when voluntary associations make political claims or engage in political action we shall call them pressure groups, or interest groups, as most political analysts do.[65] The most important pressure groups are those representing the most substantial American economic interests—business, labor, the professions—and major ethnic, racial, and religious groups. The U.S. Bureau of Commerce estimates that there are at least 5,000 trade associations involved in politics; if one adds to this group religious, ethnic, and racial organizations, as well as the ad hoc national organizations inspired by a brief, consuming matter like the Poor People's March on Washington, the number of pressure groups active in politics at any one time approaches 10,000.

Although voluntary associations attract public attention most often when they are embroiled in national political issues, many of these groups are also "private governments" with considerable formal or informal control over matters directly affecting their members such as working conditions. Among professional associations, for example, the American Medical Association has been continually active in setting standards for medical education and improving the educational and professional status of physicians. The American Pharmaceutical Manufacturers' Association, a trade group representing the majority of prescription drug manufacturers in the United States, was found by the Kefauver Committee in the late 1950s to regulate the price at which allegedly competitive drug manufacturers sold their products to druggists and physicians —an example of informal (and illegal) price controls which aroused considerable indignation when it was revealed. Thus, political action is likely to be only one activity among the major pressure groups.

The Politics of Pressure Groups

Most of the major national pressure groups were formed in response to economic and social problems which seemed beyond the ability of individuals or small local groups to handle. Formation of agricultural groups was stimulated by depressions which forced farm prices downward to disastrous levels and threatened to wipe out the independent farmer. Labor groups were forged, in part, as a counterforce to the organization of business into national associations. Such associations form in "waves." Depressions, wars, social crises, and other nationwide emergencies encourage the formation of nationwide organizations to deal with them. Inevitably, almost all large voluntary associations gravitate

---

[65] This definition is suggested by Truman, *op. cit.*, p. 33.

toward government whether by design or circumstances. Thus, recourse to government becomes a necessity for the farmer anxious to stabilize farm prices, the doctor interested in enforcing minimal educational standards for physicians, or the manufacturer who wants tariff protection from foreign competition. Although national pressure groups may seek different objectives, a common set of tactics prevails.

Lobbyists and Lobbying.   The lobbyist is the key intermediary between pressure groups and government, the point where private and public matters join. In 1968, 656 lobbyists were registered with the federal government; they reported collective expenditures of $5.1 million.[66] Both figures drastically understate the scope and cost of lobbying. For instance, the AFL-CIO alone has more than 100 lobbyists in the Washington area, appropriately specialized for a technological era: there are "testifiers-experts," "contact men," and "campaign organizers."[67] The Federal Regulation of Lobbying Act of 1946 is the only general lobbying registration act Congress has passed and it leaves many loopholes which permit most lobbyists to remain unregistered and their expenditures unreported. Further, one lobbyist may represent many interests; one prominent midwestern ex-Senator, employed as a lobbyist in 1963, registered as a representative for 34 groups, ranging from the Trailer Coach Manufacturer's Association to the United States Cane Sugar Refiners' Association.[68] Thus, the actual scale of Washington lobbying vastly exceeds that which reported lobbying expenditures could possibly support. Congress seems disinclined to enforce stricter reporting provisions. The money actually spent on lobbying may run to millions and the true number of lobbyists probably exceeds several thousand.

The public, stimulated by bad fiction and inherited prejudice, is likely to conceive of lobbying in sinister terms; the lobbyist, an irresistible scapegoat of cartoonists, is often relegated to a twilight respectability. The lobbyist actually performs at least three functions critically important to legislators and executives: (1) he communicates information; (2) he defends the interest of his employers; and (3) he defines the political implications of legislative matters.[69] Most legislators regard these as desirable, even indispensable activities. Congressmen are expected to examine and vote upon a staggering number of bills; in

---

[66] The number of registrants reported in *Congressional Quarterly Weekly Report* (January 16, 1970), p. 183; expenditures reported in *ibid.* (July 31, 1970), p. 1964.

[67] Monsen and Cannon, *op. cit.,* p. 72.

[68] Congressional Quarterly Service, *Legislators and Lobbyists* (Washington: Congressional Quarterly Service, 1965), p. 19.

[69] Lester W. Milbrath, "Lobbying as a Communications Process," *Public Opinion Quarterly* (1960), p. 35.

the 89th Congress (1966), more than 24,000 measures were introduced, and 1,283 were passed by both houses. Congressmen can give attention to only a fraction of this legislative avalanche; even when attention turns only to those matters which are especially important, a legislator is likely to be informed on only a small proportion of them. At this point, the lobbyist becomes important.

Lobbyists often play the role of technical analyst, informing legislators on the substance of a proposal and providing reliable information about its implications. Equally often, the lobbyist communicates political intelligence, suggesting what important political alignments and repercussions are likely to develop from pending legislation—an extremely important function when a congressman or senator may have little interest in the substance of a bill yet needs to know the political stakes involved. In general, through contact and conversation with lobbyists, the legislator is often able to develop an accurate impression of what political forces and issues will be involved in his decision on a great number of bills.

The lobbyist's techniques, too, have been frequently misunderstood by the public. Political folklore often supposes that lobbying implies deliberate misrepresentation of information, blatant pressuring, continuous wining and dining, perhaps bribery, or other forms of chicanery that violate the ethical standards that ought to govern the legislative process. In fact, as Abraham Holtzman suggests, the ground rules among professional lobbyists give an entirely different picture of their technique. Most lobbyists, Holtzman suggests, believe (1) a lobbyist must be trustworthy, (2) he must avoid threats and other badgering, (3) bribery is largely ineffective, (4) entertaining, while useful, is not alone a successful persuasive device, and (5) it pays most to work on friends or neutrals and to forget about clear enemies.[70] One might be tempted to disbelieve such a code; it seems entirely too polite for practical politics. These norms undoubtedly are violated, but respect for them is quite common, since they are based upon solid political logic. Threats and heavy-handed attempts to intimidate legislators almost always backfire because they are irritating and insulting. Legislators often know, without diagrams, the political potency of groups and how much weight they carry in the home constituency. One congressman, commenting on the difference between business and labor lobbyists in the 1950s, contrasted two lobbying styles:

> When these [business] guys wine and dine you . . . they never see you about anything in particular. It's just to get acquainted. I simply couldn't be- gin to name a list of all the industries that have done this. . . . There, I think labor makes a mistake. God knows, I'm not working for more of it; I'm tired to death of it all; but labor groups ought to do it. They don't. They

---

[70] Abraham Holtzman, *Interest Groups and Lobbying* (New York: Macmillan Co., 1966), pp. 77–83.

have a chip on their shoulder. But what will labor do? Send in a delegation and threaten you so you want to vote against them [to] show them you aren't the man to be intimidated. They're crude as hell.[71]

Since it is in the nature of the legislative process that today's opponents might be tomorrow's allies, it is usually unwise to permanently antagonize a potential ally whose vote might later be crucial. Courtesy, friendliness, respect, and subtle pressure, therefore, are more than social conventions which precede the real transaction of business; they are themselves political tactics dictated by the nature of the legislative process.

The high priority lobbyists give to group collaboration as opposed to going it alone also reflects that fact that all pressure groups, even the largest, are still relative minorities in the United States. No single pressure group can predictably produce legislative majorities especially when there is opposition, which is almost always the case with significant legislation. Collaboration pools the fragmented political strength of individual organizations; group spokesmen and lobbyists are, by instinct, ready to "logroll" on most issues, or trade their vote on one matter for another group's vote on something else. Such is the importance of group collaboration that so-called natural opponents such as business and labor will often cooperate. One recent study indicates that lobbyists rate group collaboration as the most effective of all lobbying tactics.

Reliability in dealing with governmental officials has an equally practical basis:

> The legislative system operates in such a manner that no one individual has absolute power, knowledge, or independence. . . . Legislators are vulnerable to their colleagues, the press, and the voters. All actors must depend to a certain extent upon others. . . . The lobbyist must work, therefore, toward developing such traits as honesty, dependability, sincerity, respect for one's sources, and a willingness to provide information and services when called upon. One major mistake in this respect . . . destroys . . . any future relations with a legislator.[72]

It is worth noting that entertaining in its many forms is absent from the list of lobbying fundamentals. Contrary to public myths, good food, drink, and company are seldom influential; by the time most legislators have been in office awhile, an appeal on this basis alone usually bores them. At best, entertainment provides a situation in which other forms of influence might be exerted.

---

[71] Robert Lane, *Political Life* (New York: The Free Press, 1965), p. 66.

[72] Holtzman, *op. cit.,* p. 77.

Pressure Groups and the Administration. Although legislative lobbying is likely to be most familiar to the public, pressure groups have been equally adroit at bringing pressure to bear upon the executive establishment. The sharp attention which most national pressure groups give to executive activity reflects the instinct of such groups to move into any area of government which will affect them.

All the major executive departments—Commerce, Labor, Agriculture, Health, Education, and Welfare, and others—were established in response to mobilized interests dedicated to bringing governmental power to bear on their problems. Once established, the federal departments and agencies were surrounded by clusters of *client groups*—pressure groups representing the interests affected by the department. Thus, the Department of Agriculture is enmeshed in a complex web of continuing political connections with the Grange, Farm Bureau Federation, Farmer's Union, and the hundreds of other commodity associations which speak for segments of the agricultural community. Similarly, the U.S. Chamber of Commerce, National Association of Manufacturers and several hundred trade associations constantly observe and attempt to affect the conduct of the Commerce Department and the Treasury Department.

The intricate connections between private voluntary associations and public agencies arise from several different sources. First, in the United States, the members of the federal bureaucracy often have great discretion in deciding how laws shall be implemented; Congress and the president often delegate to the executive departments and agencies very broad authority with very general guidelines, leaving administrators free to work out details like who will be affected and how by the law. At this point, pressure groups alert to their stake in such decisions make their presence felt.[73] For instance, in late 1969, the Federal Communications Commission (FCC), one of the many "independent regulatory commissions," was faced with choosing a policy toward radio and television commercials for cigarettes. The choice arose from Congressional reluctance to pass legislation promoted by many public health groups and Congressional allies that would have banned all radio and television advertisements for cigarettes after a stated period. Initially, the battle had been fought in the Congressional arena; on one side were public health groups, many Congressmen, some agencies of the federal government, and other sympathizers; on the other side stood cigarette manufacturers, tobacco growers, and their supporters. When Congress refused to take any affirmative action on the legislation, the FCC

---

[73] For an earlier rehearsal of this battle illustrating many of the same principles suggested above, see A. Lee Fritschler, *Smoking and Politics* (New York: Appleton-Century-Crofts, 1969). This excellent study deals with cigarette labeling legislation.

asserted its prerogative to act in the absence of a Congressional mandate and all the conflicting interests turned their attention and efforts toward influencing the FCC.

The federal government was, moreover, caught serving two different and competing sets of interests. In an example of the right hand working against the left, the FCC and a majority in Congress were demanding that the government warn consumers about the potential danger in cigarette smoking, while tobacco growers—a major clientele group of the Department of Agriculture—were receiving substantial federal assistance in growing their crops. Possibly as a means for preventing Congress from banning all cigarette advertising, spokesmen for the cigarette industry offered a compromise: they would voluntarily phase out all radio and television advertising in return for governmental guarantees that advertising through other media could continue. While this controversy was untypical of most administrative decisions because it became a major public issue, it reflects both the administrator's discretion in making policy and the movement of interest groups toward such pressure points.

In addition to administrative discretion which draws groups toward the executive branch, there is often a community of interest between administrators and client groups that breeds natural alliances. Groups which successfully promote legislation will rise to defend or enhance the position of agencies administering it. Conversely, administrators embroiled in interdepartmental or congressional struggles will often seek the alliance of client groups to alter the terms of the conflict. The collaboration between client groups and administrators may be observed almost anywhere in Washington; the Defense Department is an excellent example. Since it is so large, the range of client groups concerned about Pentagon policies is particularly broad. Each major branch of the Defense Department is supported by a professional private association of lobbyists composed, in most cases, primarily of active or retired military personnel. Thus, the Air Force Association (60,000 members), the Army Association (63,000), and the Navy League (38,000) fight vigorously for appropriations and other advantages to their respective services and—equally often—against the other services when interdepartmental rivalry occurs. The Defense Department is currently the largest employer among government agencies (over one million civilian employees) and the biggest spender (in the 1960s its annual budget equalled 10 percent of the gross national product).

The Pentagon also awarded more than $25 billion in annual defense contracts which indirectly supported the work of some four million civilians in defense-related industries. Defense contractors have formed two large associations—the Aerospace Industries Association (79 member companies) and the National Security Industrial Association. As early as 1958, when defense spending was relatively low and the Vietnamese conflict still in the future, the Aerospace Industries Association reported an income of $1.4 million to promote the manufacture and sale of "aircraft and astronautical vehicles of every nature and description."[74] To the military associations and industrial groups, one should add many other client groups for the Defense Department: the American Legion and other veterans' associations, the National Guard and other reserve groups, plus state and local governments which derive more than $12 billion annually from military installations. There is seldom any agreement among all these groups on most matters; indeed, states often compete for military installations as defense contractors contest for contracts. The intertwining between the Pentagon, pressure groups, and other governmental agencies is, perhaps, the most vivid example of the constant intermingling of private and public groups in the conduct of government.[75]

Pressure Groups and the Public.   Lobbying represents only one aspect of pressure group political activity. Major pressure groups are often involved in continuing and costly campaigns to build a public image not only to enhance the status of the group but to bolster its impact when it attempts to turn public opinion to its side in a political struggle. The Retail Clerk's International Association, for instance, regularly sponsors major network news broadcasts; the union's commercial emphasizes its dedication to improving working conditions and fringe benefits for store employees, providing a secure economic future for its members, and providing college scholarships for deserving members and their children. The American Medical Association's announcements inform radio and television audiences on matters ranging from drug addiction to highway safety. While neither these nor many other kinds of public-relations propaganda are ostensibly political, such advertising is assumed to predispose the public to view the group's political arguments favorably. Finally, many national pressure groups will actively enter the electoral process to promote or defeat candidates for public office.

One pressure group which does all these things, and does them well, is the American Medical Association. The AMA is a Brahman among pressure groups by any measure of status, influence, or political skill. The political behavior of the AMA can be regarded as a primer in the successful use of the public for political purposes by an interest group.

---

[74] Data cited about the Defense Department are taken from Monsen and Cannon, *op. cit.,* pp. 258–305; Congressional Quarterly Service, *op. cit.,* pp. 23–30.

[75] The most complete study of interest groups and government will be found in Truman, *op. cit.,* Chapter 3. A shorter, lucid discussion occurs in Harmon Zeigler, *Interest Groups in American Society* (New York: Prentice-Hall, 1964), Chapters 9–11. For a broad analysis of the intermixture of the private and public economic spheres, see John Kenneth Galbraith, *The New Industrial State* (New York: The New American Library, 1968).

The AMA is effective, ironically, in spite of the generally low regard in which most physicians have held politics.[76] "Trained to expect a clear scientific decision to a problem, they develop a patronizing attitude toward the compromise inherent in the solution of political problems."[77] However, when medical practice and politics do appear to intersect, the AMA is a formidable political force. The Association enjoys many advantages; it represents the most prestigious American profession, includes the wealthiest single occupational group in the United States, speaks for a cohesive, well-educated, and group-conscious membership that seems to possess the special information the public often attributes to highly skilled professionals. Additionally, the AMA seldom faces strong opposition, though it represents only 72 percent of the nation's physicians.

In addition to continually promoting the status, security, and standards of the medical profession, the AMA has generated massive, expensive public campaigns in support of national legislation it considers vital to the medical profession. In general, the AMA has taken a free enterprise attitude toward medical practice; it has tenaciously fought most governmental programs it believed would interfere with the doctor-patient relationship. Its most notable political victories occurred when it opposed federal health insurance and other attempts, as it argues, to "socialize" medicine. When President Truman proposed a government-sponsored national health insurance program in 1949, the AMA defeated it through one of the best-executed publicity campaigns ever devised by an American pressure group. The highly successful California public relations firm, Whitaker and Baxter, was hired to organize the nation-wide campaign. Each doctor was assessed $25; though some refused to pay, a handsome pool of $1,100,000 was made available for the struggle. Over one-half million dollars was allocated for full-page advertisements in 11,000 local papers throughout every state. Many physicians mailed anti-insurance propaganda to patients with their bills. Many waiting rooms were sprinkled with comic books ("The Sad Case of Waiting-Room Willie"), brochures ("You can't socialize the black bag"), and other anti-insurance polemics. Through these and other tactics, the AMA was able to delay a federally sponsored health insurance program for more than a decade.[78]

Beginning in the early 1960s, the AMA established a separate political arm, the Political Action Committee. Like the parent organization, the PAC strenuously fought the King-Anderson bill which also proposed a federal health

[76] On physicians' low regard for politics, see especially William A. Glazer, "Doctors and Politics," *American Journal of Sociology* (November 1960), pp. 230–245.

[77] Zeigler, *op. cit.,* p. 203.

[78] A very complete and readable account of this campaign is Stanley Kelley, Jr., *Professional Public Relations and Political Power* (Baltimore: Johns Hopkins University Press, 1956).

insurance program. In 1962, the PAC distributed $250,000 to various state affiliates to support the congressional campaigns of approved candidates who opposed the King-Anderson measure. The AMA spent an additional $83,000 to influence Congress on the proposal and, later, another $163,000 for other advertising against the bill.

The AMA's entrance into elections came rather late in its development and has been quite recent. In contrast, labor unions have been actively involved in elections for thirty years. National labor leaders have endorsed presidential candidates for at least two decades, and local unions in most states have worked regularly for candidates "sympathetic to labor." In Detroit, where the United Automobile Worker's Union figures importantly in state and local politics, local political committees have sponsored radio and television advertising for candidates, organized district election committees to contact union members and persuade them to vote for endorsed candidates, and arranged political meetings at which candidates presented their programs. Among the major national pressure groups, labor unions have probably been the most consistently and publicly active in political campaigns.

Labor and the American Medical Association illustrate particularly well that national pressure groups can seldom afford to confine their activities to lobbying. By attempting to make private interests into public matters, pressure groups are mobilizing—or attempting to mobilize—citizens for political action and, therefore, to extend the scope of the political system. This confirms the tendency in modern societies for public and private interests to merge.

The Illusion of Undivided Interests. Pressure politics in the United States is often described in starkly simple terms: "business" opposes "labor," the "military-industrial complex" dominates Congress, "agriculture" fights for a farm program. These stereotypes, appealing because they simplify politics, greatly exaggerate the unanimity of opinion within major interest blocs and provide an excellent example of the observer's selective and thus distorted perception.

"Business," for instance, includes the National Association of Manufacturers (NAM) speaking in terms congenial to many very large industrial organizations, while the U.S. Chamber of Commerce is rooted in the small local business and the small-business ideology; the small but vocal Committee for Economic Development, a group of several hundred corporate executives and educators, is far more likely than the other two to advocate business and governmental cooperation for economic planning. The Chamber of Commerce, unlike the NAM, is concerned with governmental aid to business, and is less tolerant of intellectual elements in the business community. In addition to these groups, 130 of the 200 largest American corporations have their own Washington representatives, which reflects that what is good for General Motors is not necessarily good for Chrysler; nor do distillers and lumbermen speak a common political tongue.

"Agriculture" is no less divided. The three largest agricultural associations— the Farmer's Union, the Grange, and the National Farm Bureau Federation— disagree on many matters. The Farm Bureau, the largest and newest of the three, is more conservative economically and politically than the others. Unlike the Grange and the Farmer's Union, the Farm Bureau opposes any significant governmental price supports for the farmer, arguing instead for "free competitive markets." Because of such divisions within agriculture, one commentator concluded that "while almost no one is willing to defend the existing agricultural policies, still it is almost impossible to organize an effective majority to change the *status quo* in any given direction.[79] Even the American Medical Association, which often seems to represent a united profession, has its internal critics. The AMA has been persistently divided on policy matters between medical practitioners and medical school faculties; the academic faction often regards federal health insurance and other liberal programs more sympathetically than the practicing physician.

Ordinarily, in the heat of political conflict, almost all pressure group spokesmen will claim to speak for their membership as if they had a consensus. This is seldom the case. Many internal divisions of opinion exist within major interest groups; however, in most of these groups, only a small proportion of members take any continuing interest in the group's programs so the leadership often operates with considerable freedom from rank-and-file control. Thus, it often happens that the leadership speaks for the leadership and the minority of others in the group who care what the leadership is doing.[80]

The Bias of the Pressure System.   The pressure system has been biased in at least two respects. The great majority of pressure groups in the past have spoken with a strong upper-class accent. Studies of American voluntary group memberships indicate that it is principally the middle and upper classes who have traditionally belonged to such groups and, consequently, most of these

---

[79] Monsen and Cannon, *op. cit.,* p. 131.

[80] The tendency for leadership in large voluntary organizations to enjoy great freedom from rank-and-file control has long been observed. The classic statement is the "iron law of oligarchy" in Roberto Michels, *Political Parties* (New York: Dover Publications, 1959), especially Part 6.

organizations did not directly involve other social groups in political life. Moreover, even among the pressure groups that did enter the political arena, it is clear that they involved a relatively small proportion of the population. America, in short, may be a nation of associations but it is not the nation of joiners it is often imagined to be.

In political life it is very often true that the opinions that matter, the ones that gain an audience and penetrate the governmental apparatus, are those that find organizational expression. It is not surprising, therefore, that middle- and upper-class interests should be especially well represented in Washington. As we saw when examining American political culture (Chapter 4), the majority of organization activists in the past were, indeed, middle- to upper-class individuals. Not only are middle- and upper-class Americans likely to dominate the membership of most pressure groups, but those who belong to such groups are likely to belong to multiple groups: among professional households, for instance, almost half the members belong to three or more voluntary associations. In Table 6.4 the strong association between social status and group membership can be observed; here education, a key measure of social status, is compared to organizational memberships.

Table 6.4. Education and Group Membership
in the United States, 1961

Level of Education	Percentage of Respondents Belonging to Some Group
Primary school or less	46
Some secondary school	55
Some university	80

Source: *The Civic Culture: Political Attitudes and Democracy in Five Nations* by Gabriel A. Almond and Sidney Verba. Copyright © 1963 by Princeton University Press; Little, Brown and Company, 1965. Table 4 on p. 304 of Princeton University Press edition. Reprinted by permission of Princeton University Press.

Although the middle and upper class most often populate pressure groups, far from a majority of these classes are active in this way. Indeed, as studies repeatedly indicate, most pressure groups draw their membership from a relatively thin stratum of the population. The extent to which group membership is unequally distributed among the American population is apparent in Table 6.5 which shows typical responses to questions dealing with the number of groups to which Americans belong.

Table 6.5. Voluntary Group Membership in the United States, 1955, 1958

Number of Associations	Percent of Adults Who Were Members, 1953	Percent of Families with Members Belonging, 1955
0	64	47
1	20	31
2	9	12
3	4	5
3	3	4
4+	3	4
Not ascertained	0	1

Source: Charles R. Wright and Herbert H. Hyman, "Voluntary Association Membership of American Adults: Evidence from National Sample Surveys," *American Sociological Review* (June 1958), pp. 284–294.

Considering that this table does not distinguish between membership in a pressure group and membership in a voluntary association without political purposes, the number of Americans active in an explicitly political association must be even smaller than this table suggests. For instance, as much as half the total population belongs to perhaps no other voluntary association except a church. And a 1956 survey showed, somewhat suprisingly, that 60 percent of the farm households had no members in an agricultural group.

Thus, there is considerable evidence that pressure group politics in the United States has in the recent past occupied a relatively small and socially distinct segment of the population. However, this may well be changing. One of the most significant events of the 1960s was the emergence of new organizations and techniques for mobilizing the previously unorganized, an effort which continues into the 1970s and might transform the nature of the pressure system in important ways.

Organizing the Unorganized. Attempts to mobilize the least politically organized segments of American society have proceeded steadily through the 1960s and early 1970s, progressively widening the range of affected groups. Simultaneously, leaders struggling to capture the imagination and loyalty of the politically unorganized have developed new techniques to stimulate interest and involvement. The result has been a broadening of the base of political activism in the United States.

We have already seen that the most sustained and diverse work in mobilizing the politically unorganized has been done among blacks. Since the early 1960s, the techniques of black leaders have become progressively more militant, more inventive, and more pragmatic in efforts to create meaningful symbols and programs for the poor black. Yet, as our discussion of "street politics" suggests, the sweep of this movement is not confined to blacks. College students—for many years generally regarded as politically apathetic—have been brought into a variety of political movements through street politics and other forms of political activity. American Indians and Mexican-Americans, minorities who have long been almost wholly dependent upon white middle-class groups for political representation, have recently demonstrated the stirrings of political militancy. Young Indians have suggested that Red Power should begin with direct demonstrations for greater equality. For example, they led a seizure of the abandoned federal prison Alcatraz Island in San Francisco Bay and demanded that it be turned into an Indian cultural center. In the later 1960s, a sustained nationwide grape boycott was promoted by leaders of Mexican-American migrant workers in California attempting to unionize field workers over the vigorous opposition of most grape growers. Thus, the reach of this new political mobilization has been extensive indeed.

It seems quite clear that such attempts to mobilize the previously unmobilized has resulted, on the whole, in a greater awareness and participation in the political process by these groups. Moreover, as the variety of leaders and groups competing for the loyalty of these individuals multiplies further, the stimulation to participate will probably increase.

Interest Groups and Foreign Affairs. Given the enormous scope of pressure group activity and its impact in domestic politics, it might be supposed that this impact is equally great on foreign policy and affairs.[81] This is not the case, even though most of these groups are affected by foreign affairs. Two groups—the major economic and ethnic groups—are probably influential in foreign affairs to a limited extent. Business, trade, agricultural, and shipping associations and, to a lesser extent, labor organizations are naturally affected by American foreign affairs. These groups tend to be concerned with trade policies and tariffs, for instance, because foreign trade levels and tariffs determine how much foreign agricultural and business activity will compete with domestic business and farming.[82]

---

[81] For a general evaluation of the influence of interest groups on foreign policy, see especially Lester W. Milbrath "Interest Groups and Foreign Policy," in James N. Rosenau (ed.), *Domestic Sources of Foreign Policy* (New York: The Free Press, 1967), pp. 231–251; and Bernard C. Cohen, "The Influence of Nongovernmental Groups on Foreign Policy-Making," in Andrew M. Scott and Raymond H. Dawson, *Readings in the Making of American Foreign Policy* (New York: Macmillan Co., 1965), pp. 96–116.

[82] See the impact of the West coast fishing industry on the Japanese peace treaty in Bernard C. Cohen, *The Political Process and Foreign Policy: The Making of the Japanese Peace Settlement* (Princeton: Princeton University Press, 1957), pp. 253–77.

Also, in a nation of immigrants, ethnic groups (the "hyphenated Americans") often press for specific policies respecting their mother country. It is hardly surprising, therefore, that the American Irish, Germans, and Italians opposed entrance into wars on the side of Great Britain. In the post-war period, probably the most influential and effective ethnic group in foreign affairs has been the Jewish minority. Domestic Jewish pressure groups were extremely influential in securing President Truman's recognition of the new state of Israel in 1949 and have subsequently lobbied vigorously and effectively for continuing American diplomatic, military, and economic support to the new state. Despite a relatively modest membership of 600,000, these groups raised more than $100 million annually for the new Jewish state in the late 1940s.[83]

Nevertheless, the influence of pressure groups directly involved in foreign affairs is limited. Maritime interests may have been successful in obtaining legislation requiring that one-half of the foreign aid cargoes leaving America must be carried in American ships,[84] but they have had no appreciable influence on the size of the foreign aid budget. Business interests may want protective tariffs or "escape clauses" allowing the President to raise tariffs on certain products, but they have been unable to prevent the enactment of generally liberal trade policies which successive presidents since 1945 have felt were in the national interest. Similarly, ethnic associations, because their numbers are relatively small, have little impact on general foreign policy. We are, of course, no longer fighting Germany alongside Great Britain. Instead, West Germany is now an ally; and German and Irish Catholics—both vehemently anti-communist—have supported the broad outlines of American foreign policy instead of opposing it as they did before our entries into World Wars I and II. Even the Jewish minority has not been able to halt continued American economic aid and military assistance to various Arab countries including Egypt or obtain for Israel all the American arms she has wanted. While the United States had defended Israel's right to exist, the government has often taken a middle position on specific issues; it has sought to advance a compromise settlement between Israel and her Arab neighbors. The evidence seems to suggest that

> It is questionable, in fact, whether we are really entitled to talk about group influence on "foreign policy"; with very rare exceptions, the influence of nongovernmental groups is on particular, discrete, rather highly specialized matters, which, even if they may be deemed to be within the foreign policy field, are very far from constituting or defining that field.[85]

---

[83] Samuel Halperin, "Ideology or Philanthropy? The Politics of Zionist Fund-Raising," *Western Political Quarterly* (1960), p. 950.

[84] Truman, *op. cit.*, p. 364.

[85] Cohen, "The Influence of Nongovernmental Groups on Foreign Policy-Making," p. 116.

Why are pressure groups so effective in domestic affairs, while confined, so it seems, to the periphery of significant foreign policy formulation? The first reason is knowledge. Interest groups possess this in great abundance on domestic matters concerning them; on foreign policy questions they seldom have comparable skill and experience. Instead, this kind of skill and knowledge is provided by foreign policy experts, either those who are familiar with specific countries or issues, or those who belong to such agencies as the RAND Corporation or the Institute for Defense Analysis. Second, interest groups are regularly consulted by their respective executive departments as domestic legislation is drawn up, since these interests are the department's clientele. In foreign policy, however, the departments involved are their own constituencies. In brief—and this is a most significant difference—in foreign policy decisions, it is the *institutional interests within the government* that predominate over *associational interests outside it*. Foreign policies are made by the various government departments such as the State and Defense Departments, as well as other foreign policy-oriented agencies, the president's personal advisors, and members of Congress.[86] Third, while foreign policy decision-making is basically an executive matter, pressure groups are more influential in the Congress where they can effectively exploit the many points along the legislative route where their influence is effective. Finally, as in domestic affairs, specific interests rarely unite behind a common foreign policy issue such as tariffs. In short, in domestic politics there is a stable structure of interest groups. In foreign matters this structure is weak. The conflict between pressure groups on domestic affairs is replaced by conflict within the executive branch on foreign policies.

The Impact of the Pressure System

As another expression of the "spirit of faction," pressure groups have a collective impact upon the political system that may often be ignored when observing any single group. As institutions for political communication and articulation, pressure groups not only close the potential gap between government and society, but in many ways they are more effective institutions for communicating political demands than parties. Elections, at best, are imperfect devices for communicating specific voter policy demands on government. Though voting is widely supposed to communicate some message, it is often difficult to discern what policy preferences the voter is attempting to express when choosing a candidate—especially when voters do not choose the same man for the same reason. Though meanings are often read into elections after they occur, a clear mandate is rarely discovered. Pressure groups, in contrast, customarily press for reasonably clear and relatively narrow domestic programs.

---

[86] See Chapter 9.

In a sense, pressure groups "fine tune" political communications and demands upon government; by doing so, they greatly sharpen the meaning of such demands.

Multiple pressure groups also decrease the tendency within a society toward political *polarization*—the tendency for social groups to divide into two opposite extremes on political questions. When political polarization occurs, there is no significant middle-group of opinion; the sides tend to be intense and extreme. This introduces a dangerous condition into political affairs; crises may follow, as in international politics, from attempts to resolve such a bipolar conflict. Since a great many Americans are multiple-group members, the intensity of identification with any single group is somewhat diminished; on many questions, the typical American is cross-pressured by conflicting group loyalties. For example, the typical union member is a registered Democrat; unions have traditionally encouraged members to identify the interests of labor with the Democratic Party. But a union member may also be a Protestant, a member of the American Legion and the National Rifle Association. What particular position would such an individual take regarding a federal gun control law similar to one proposed by President Johnson in 1967? How would such an individual feel about voting for John Kennedy, a Catholic, in 1960? In both cases, we can easily imagine cross-pressure. In the first instance, our union member may be strongly opposed to gun control legislation in accord with the National Rifle Association, but may also feel the pull of his party loyalties and, perhaps, the admonitions of his church. Or, in the second example, our voter may prefer a Protestant Democrat, yet, perhaps, his party loyalty will overcome his religious preferences—conversely, in 1960, many Democrats voted against Kennedy because he was a Catholic. These examples can be multiplied by simply creating a different mix of group identifications and issues. These conflicting loyalties are powerful inhibitors to intense, uncompromised dedication to one interest at the expense of all others.

Interest group competition also ensures, most of the time, that no single interest or combination of interests will get all they want from government. The basic logic of interest group conflict in the United States is countervailing power. We noted earlier the high priority placed by lobbyists on collaboration with other pressure groups which means bargaining and compromising. Thus, interest groups to some extent internally check each other and inhibit the victory of faction feared by the Founding Fathers.

In several respects, the impact of the pressure system may be changing, however. If, as we observed, street politics and other attempts to mobilize many previously unorganized Americans succeed in creating long-range political interests and commitments, the previous domination of the pressure system by middle- and upper-class Americans may be weakening. And change may be occurring, as well, in the impact of pressure politics on foreign affairs. The great importance that the Vietnamese War and other foreign policy issues have assumed in the street politics of the 1960s and early 1970s may auger a heightened interest and involvement in foreign policy among Americans; this may well result in a movement toward creating more enduring organizational means to express foreign policy preferences and to influence the administration and Congress. Thus, the pressure system in the future may incorporate new groups—previously passive or not sufficiently represented, if at all—into foreign affairs within the scope of its activities.

From Parties and Interest Groups to Elections

Party politics, interest group lobbying, and street politics know no season in the United States; all are continuing forms of political linkage and those institutions and individuals involved are constantly active in the process. Still, with the exception of those relatively few street demonstrations capturing a national audience, most of these activities, especially those of interest groups, customarily remain invisible to the public, virtually unnoticed by those who are affected.

Such is not the case with nominations and elections for public office. Especially when the presidency or another major office is involved, nominations and elections in the United States become visible, interesting, and significant to large portions of the public. Indeed, of all the various ways through which government and society are linked in the United States, it is the nominating and electing process which is probably the most continually familiar to the public. It is this activity which absorbs a great portion of political party effort and interest group attention; and this activity can make and unmake a government. Understandably, it merits attention. We shall examine it in greater detail in the following chapter.

7

Political Linkage: Nominations and Elections

By almost any measure, Americans produce the most extravagant display of electoral activity in the world. No modern nation attempts to organize campaigns and elections for more public offices—about 500,000 national, state, and local positions are filled by ballot. In 1968, the campaigns for these offices cost the candidates one quarter billion dollars, by conservative estimate; actual expenditures may have been double this amount. Certainly no other election in the world surpasses the scale and cost of the quadrennial presidential struggle. In 1968, it cost the Republicans about $29 million to put Richard Nixon into the White House; Nixon himself paid an additional $10 to 12 million to secure the nomination.[1] To entice the electorate, the Republicans used: 20,500,000 campaign buttons, 9 million bumper stickers, 560,000 balloons, 400,000 posters, 20,000 straw hats, 3,500,000 copies of speeches and position papers, 12,000 paper dresses, uncounted jewelry elephants and other exotica.[2]

American politicians and parties have been acknowledged pioneers and innovators in campaign techniques, mostly from necessity. Almost from the nation's inception, parties and candidates were forced to mobilize an electorate

---

[1] Herbert E. Alexander, "Financing Parties and Campaigns in 1968: A Preliminary Report," paper delivered at the American Political Science Association Convention, New York City, September 1969, pp. 1–2, 6.

[2] *Ibid.*, p. 55.

of unprecedented size without prior examples for guidance. As a result, the parties and candidates began experimenting with an unending series of new campaign techniques—beginning with torchlight parades and continuing today with television—that have been carefully observed and often copied elsewhere. Even before the turn of this century, most European political observers recognized that Americans had a special flair for campaigning; they predicted that American techniques were the wave of the future as mass elections spread throughout the world.[3] In the twentieth century, it is no exaggeration to suggest that campaign techniques have been an American cultural export which, like many other American exports, is regarded with varying degrees of admiration and disgust.

Mass elections and campaigns are now almost universal; even totalitarian regimes feel obligated to present an electoral charade from time to time. (The political leadership of the Soviet Union, for instance, can claim to be the world's most popular regime because its elective officials customarily receive more than 99 percent of the votes cast—a suspiciously large sum that nonetheless testifies to the importance mass elections have achieved as prestige symbols among world governments.)

Given their world-wide incidence—and, more particularly the enormous investment of time, money, and energy Americans give to them—one may well ask what elections accomplish and why they seem so important in political systems. Some Americans wonder whether faith in elections is justified by their results. To start answering these questions, let us first consider the several purposes that elections and nominations may serve in political systems before discussing the United States in detail.

What Nominations and Elections Accomplish

Nominations and elections are forms of political linkage: by choosing candidates for public office, campaigning for them and electing them, people link a government to other elements in the political and social system. As the last chapter revealed, linkage has several purposes. Yet when nations are compared, it seems clear that no national nominating and electing procedure serves all these ends to the same degree. Let us examine how well nominations and elections fulfill each of these various purposes of linkage.[4]

---

[3] See, for example, M. Ostrogorski, *Democracy and the Organization of Political Parties: Vol. II: The United States* (New York: Doubleday & Co., 1964), p. 165.

[4] Several studies have influenced our evaluation of elections. For a thoughtful and generally sympathetic view of the ballot, see Gerald M. Pomper, *Elections in America* (New York: Dodd, Mead & Co., 1968), especially Chapters 1, 2, and 10. For a brief but critical appraisal, see Thomas R. Dye and L. Harmon Zeigler, *The Irony of Democracy* (Belmont, Calif.: Wadsworth, 1970), pp. 149–174.

Communicating and Aggregating Political Demands

In the United States and many other political systems, nominating and electing candidates is supposed to "bring governmental policy roughly in line with intense public preferences over a reasonable span of time."[5] In some manner, the outcome of elections communicates to government what the public expects it to do and—equally important—passes a verdict on the government's past performance. In effect, elections involve more than choosing governmental officials; they are also assumed to be a method of opinion polling through which political demands are communicated and aggregated for governmental use.

This expression and organization of opinion through elections is assumed to occur in several ways. First, the success of candidates and the parties they represent depends on their finding those issues and opinions that will rally majorities.[6] "The two political parties . . . act as transmission belts for policy preferences in the general population. . . . They must gain support from a variety of groups . . . by offering inducements to the electorate and to the organized groups which represent its various interests."[7] Moreover, parties and candidates also stimulate the public to form opinions on major issues through the propaganda and controversy of rival candidates. In the end, so this argument concludes, party competition in nominations and elections has the effect of creating political demands, for articulating existing demands, and for organizing both into comprehensive programs espoused by candidates and parties.

Even if, as some critics have charged, a nominating and electing system seldom produces a clear mandate to guide the future course of governmental policy, the system has still been defended on the grounds that it does impose accountability on government for its past performance. By this reasoning, the voter has the opportunity to vote "no confidence" in existing majority parties or incumbent officials; he may select new office holders or aid in creating a new majority party. In various ways, therefore, governmental policy-makers must take account of electoral opinions in some manner, knowing that eventually they must face the electorate.

In the United States and elsewhere, many voters undoubtedly do attempt to provide some policy cues to government when they cast ballots for candidates; to some extent, therefore, preferences for future policies and judgments on past government performance are sometimes part of the electoral calculus. Given the

---

[5] Nelson W. Polsby and Aaron B. Wildavsky, *Presidential Elections,* 2nd ed., (New York: Charles Scribner's, 1968), p. 280; Chapter 6 contains an excellent summary of American expectations for elections.

[6] The "marketplace" nature of elections and its impact upon party policy has recently been explored by Andrew Scott, *Competition in American Politics* (New York: Holt, Rinehart and Winston, 1970), especially Chapters 1–2.

[7] Polsby and Wildavsky, *op. cit.,* p. 273.

enormous weight of expectations upon nominating and electing systems as methods for communicating political demands to government, a judgment about results is clearly important. Any decision regarding the United States, at least, must wait until we have discussed American nominations and elections in greater detail.

Political Mobilization

Whatever else nominations and elections may accomplish, they are viewed in most political systems as an instrument for mobilizing members of a polity and for involving them in the activities of a political system. This may serve several ends.

Participating in the election of public officials is very often a symbolic exercise for the masses that ties them to the established political order. In effect, participation becomes a civic ritual through which individuals affirm their commitment to the political system's rules and officials; tacitly, at least, this is a method for confirming the political system's legitimacy. At election time, for instance, Americans are often implored by the media to "vote for the candidate of your choice, but vote!"—implying that the voting act itself carries important political significance and constitutes an important duty of citizens: following the rules of the game in selecting public officials demonstrates support for the basic procedures of the system.

Elections also provide an opportunity for mobilizing opposition to governmental policies, or in some cases, opposition to the governmental structure itself. In effect, elections may provide a setting in which opposition and dissent can be given some practical expression and individuals stimulated to do something tangible about their political views. Thus, nominations and elections give disaffected groups and individuals a *form* of political activity that stimulates the conversion of attitudes and beliefs into political action.

By mobilizing individuals to political action, in brief, the electoral process joins an individual to his political system, or politicizes him. For a great many citizens in most nations, an election is the place where private and public life intersects most tangibly, where the macrocosm of political affairs temporarily touches the microcosm of the citizen's own private affairs. In the United States, for instance, more than 72 million Americans voted in the 1968 presidential election, a collective political act whose magnitude is unparalleled by any other form of political activity in the nation; for a majority of Americans, voting is probably the only significant political act they will perform.[8]

---

[8] On American voting patterns, see Chapter 4.

Recruiting and
Legitimating a Government

Nominating and electing public officials may be a major form of political linkage because it is one method for recruiting governmental officials. Nominating arrangements, in effect, will often determine who among a potentially vast number of individuals in a society are available to govern; electoral arrangements will designate who will finally govern. Equally important, in many modern political systems it is only by going through this procedure that major governmental leaders are presumed to have the right to their office—public nomination and election legitimizes their authority. Americans have applied this principle with a vengeance. In the United States, the right to govern has been so intimately associated with public election and this has been so closely tied to democracy that Americans insist upon electing not only major public officials but justices of the peace, school superintendents, school boards, sheriffs, tax assessors, and a multitude of lesser luminaries, allegedly including the dogcatcher.

It is true that these procedures sometimes are a sham formality in which the electorate enjoys no significant freedom of choice. In totalitarian societies, for instance, a single dominant party may so completely control nominations and elections that the system serves not to *recruit* officials but only to legitimize choices made by inner-party circles. Also, nominations and elections are seldom the only means for recruiting political leaders; bureaucrats and other administrators are often recruited by examination and appointment from within the government itself. In some cases—rather common in many contemporary Afro-Asian and Latin American nations—governments are frequently overturned by a military *coup d'état* and a new set of rulers forcibly install themselves.

Notwithstanding these important exceptions, in the United States and many other political systems, nominating and electing are still important for recruiting governmental leaders from among competing factions and candidates; thus, it is a major means for creating a government, transferring political power, and legitimizing it.

The Organization of
American National Elections

Elections seem to intrigue Americans primarily when great issues or strong personalities spice the contest, when conflict, uncertainty, or drama attend the outcome. Under these conditions, as election studies consistently show, voting turnout rises, attention to campaigns increases, and concern for the outcome intensifies. For most Americans, the importance of an election seems to depend upon the personalities of the candidates, the offices at stake, and the issues discussed.[9]

In comparison, the various details of our nominating and electing arrangements may seem dull. Indeed, few Americans know or seem to care much about these details—except, perhaps, on the few occasions when a presidential election may end in the House of Representatives, or literacy tests are abolished in the South, or some other event momentarily dramatizes the importance of these rules. Yet what elections accomplish depends in good measure upon how the "nuts and bolts" of electoral law are arranged; operating continually, often unobtrusively with their true importance unrecognized, these arrangements shape the meaning of elections as surely as do the candidates, issues, and offices that command a major part of the electorate's attention and interest.

In many respects, electoral arrangements in the United States are uncommon compared to those of other western democracies. The responsibility for establishing the rules, for instance, is dispersed between the federal government, fifty state governments, and innumerable local governmental units. These rules are often inconsistent or contradictory; the states and federal governments have almost always been embroiled in contention over some of them. In many western nations, no such pluralism of election law exists; a uniform electoral code is set by the national legislature and prevails for all national elections, no matter where held.[10] In addition, Americans, as we have seen, elect a staggering number of officials. This is one reason for the severely high cost of elections in the United States.

Not least important, the United States elects its national officials—the president, vice president and members of Congress—by different systems. The party convention, once used for nominating most members of Congress and state officials, has been abandoned for this purpose but still prevails in presidential nominations. The primary system, now used in almost every state for nomination to Congressional and state offices, is used in a minority of states to select delegates to the party nominating conventions. Insofar as national offices are concerned, there is not one electoral system but many. Despite these differences which we shall shortly examine, both presidential and Congressional elections have at least one common element—registration procedures.

---

[9] On the relationship between types of elections and voter interest, see especially: Walter Dean Burnham, "The Changing Shape of the American Political Universe," *American Political Science Review* (March 1965), pp. 7–28; and V. O. Key, Jr., *Parties, Politics and Pressure Groups,* fifth ed. (New York: Thomas Y. Crowell Co., 1964), pp. 579–585, for long-term statistics on turnout fluctuations.

[10] In most European nations, uniform election laws result because local governmental units are not independent governments as in the United States. Rather, they exercise powers delegated to them by the national legislatures.

Registration

The first and most important question in any election is "who may vote?" This determines whose opinions count at the polls, to what audience the candidates will address their pleas and programs, and to whom, in the long run, members of the government feel accountable. Registration requirements directly affect voting turnout as well. A recent intensive study of seventy-eight major American cities concluded that registration requirements may be more important than any other community characteristic, including class distributions, educational, racial, or economic factors, in determining voter turnout.[11]

The United States places far more responsibility upon its citizens to register than do many other nations. In most European countries, the voting registrars regularly canvass their districts to seek out and enroll electors. In Australia and the Scandinavian countries, nonvoters are fined; in almost all European nations, voting and registration are possible on Sundays which may increase public participation in elections. In comparison, the United States places the initiative to register entirely on the voter and confronts him with a variety of different registration requirements from state to state.

As the framers intended, the United States Constitution permits the states to set voting requirements with considerable independence, subject to several important exceptions. The nineteenth amendment (1919) forbids the exclusion of women from the polls and the twenty-fourth amendment (1964) abolishes the poll tax which, in any case, had ceased to be an important voting deterrent by that time. However, it took almost a century before the fifteenth amendment (1870) affected most of the South. This amendment, which forbids any state to deny or to abridge the right to vote "on account of race, color, or previous condition of servitude," was widely and publicly violated in most Southern states through a variety of ingenious laws, including the poll tax and "grandfather clause" (which limited the eligible electorate to those whose fathers or grandfathers had been eligible to vote before 1866, thus excluding all blacks), that kept most blacks from the polls. The Southern states opened the polls to blacks only in the last few decades, mainly through pressure from the Justice Department, federal voting registrars, and aggressive federal courts.

The last Southern bastion against black voting was the "literacy test." Of all recent state voting requirements, this was the most controversial and the most effective; as late as 1960, about 2 million Southern blacks were disenfranchised by it.[12] In the Deep South there was seldom a pretense that these tests were

---

[11] Stanley Kelley, Jr., Richard E. Ayres, and William G. Bowen, "Registration and Voting: Putting First Things First," *American Political Science Review* (June 1967), pp. 359–379.

[12] Outside the South, about 1.3 million otherwise eligible voters were classified as illiterates in 1960; see William G. Andrews, "American Voting Participation," *Western Political Quarterly* (December 1966), pp. 639–652.

impartially administered. A white citizen whose claim to literacy was little more than optimism could usually vote, while many educated blacks were disqualified, primarily on the basis of minor technical errors, slightly inexact or ambiguous responses—though a great many blacks were in fact quite illiterate, principally because of the miserable education they had received in "separate but equal" facilities. An interesting example of how literacy examinations could be administered to the disadvantage of blacks was Alabama's examination procedure. Alabama's voting registrars were armed with a possible 399 questions from which any four could be selected for any applicant. A prospective voter might, for example, be asked: (a) to name the president; (b) to decide if communism was "a type of government in the United States, Russia, or England"; (c) to describe "one kind of drink referred to as an alcoholic beverage"; or (4) to state what "a person seeking public office is called." Or, the registrar might ask: (1) where presidential electors cast their ballots; (2) what governmental bodies set Congressional districts; (3) from what year the Constitution forbids the importation of slaves; and (4) to name "one board or commission with countywide authority which is appointed instead of elected."[13] Blacks in deep Southern states such as Alabama, Mississippi, Georgia, and Louisiana complained that they almost always got the hard questions.

So long as literacy tests and other means of excluding blacks from the polls in the South prevailed, they were excellent examples illustrating how electoral arrangements can deny a major proportion of a population any significant linkage with government and, in the process, establish the basic terms of political power within states. The federal government's recent vigorous enforcement of the fifteenth amendment in the South means that the law has now been truly nationalized, and by doing so, the federal government has forced a new pattern of political linkage upon many Southern states.

Despite these constitutional restraints, the states still enjoy considerable freedom in setting voting requirements with the result that registration codes are not uniform or consistent. State residence requirements excluded an estimated 5 million otherwise qualified citizens from the polls in 1968. Most states require at least a year's residence before voting—Mississippi and Alabama require two—though three states, at the other extreme, permit citizens to vote in presidential

---

13 See *Code of Alabama,* Title 17, Sections 30, 32, for the statutes creating the examination. Questions are cited in *St. Petersburg Times,* March 25, 1964. Since the literacy test might exclude a great many whites as well, many Southern states followed Mississippi's procedure of requiring a prospective voter either "to read any section of the state constitution; or, to be able to understand the same when read to him, or give a reasonable interpretation thereof." The "reasonable interpretation" clause gave registrars the discretion to register whites and exclude most blacks. Apparently, white interpretations were more generously judged: The U.S. Civil Rights Commission reports that one Mississippi white citizen was declared literate because, in response to a request to interpret the phrase, "The Senate shall consist of members chosen every four years by qualified electors of the several districts," he responded "equible wrights . . ." Cited in Frank J. Sorauf, *Party Politics in America* (Boston: Little, Brown and Co., 1968), p. 178.

elections even if they do not meet residence requirements for other elections. Even though many states have relaxed their residency requirements over the years (in 1960 more than 8 million voters had been excluded by these provisions), most residency requirements have not been adjusted to the nomadic nature of contemporary American society where citizens move much more frequently than in an earlier, more leisurely era.[14] Other voting requirements also exclude a surprising number of Americans from the polls. Perhaps three million Americans eligible to cast absentee ballots fail to do so because of the difficulty, or impossibility, of satisfying state absentee voting laws. In addition, about three million adults in the United States are classified by the states as "aliens" who may not vote.[15]

Even age is not a uniform restriction. Although the majority of states set the minimum age at twenty-one, Kentucky and Georgia permit residents to vote at eighteen, while Alaska grants the privilege at nineteen and Hawaii at twenty. In early 1970, the Congress passed and the president signed a bill extending the voting privilege to eighteen-year-olds uniformly throughout the United States. Although President Nixon favored its purpose, he signed the measure reluctantly. He believed that only a constitutional amendment could accomplish these objectives legally. The legislation was challenged in the federal courts but in late 1970 the Supreme Court upheld its constitutionality; beginning in 1971, eighteen-year-olds will be voting in federal elections with increasing numbers as the decade progresses.

Even disregarding age restrictions, registration requirements of other kinds still limit the electorate appreciably; as many as 10 to 15 percent of the eligible electorate over the age of twenty-one cannot vote because of some state registration restriction. Thus, while turnout for presidential elections is often considered low by worldwide standards (about 60 percent of all Americans over twenty-one), when registration restrictions are considered, the turnout among the *eligible* electorate approaches 85 percent, a more respectable figure.

Congressional Nominations

The selection of nominees for the United States Senate and House of Representatives revolves around the direct primary system in most states. The distinctively American direct primary system is one example of a nation

[14] On the impact of residency requirements on voting, see Gallup Poll *Index* (December 1968), p. 6; Andrews, *op. cit.;* President's Commission on Registration and Voting Participation, *Report* (Washington, D.C.: U.S. Government Printing Office, 1963); and W. Ross Yates, "The Function of Residence Requirements for Voting," *Western Political Quarterly* (March 1962), pp. 469–488.

[15] In addition, about 53,000 "aliens" were excluded from the polls in 1960 simply because they became naturalized Americans after the closing date for registration, Andrews, *op. cit.,* p. 642.

developing its own political formula to solve the problem of selecting political leaders. No other nation uses the direct primary; none seems anxious to experiment with it. Through the direct primary, the United States permits its electorate a much more direct voice in selecting party nominees than the voters of most other nations enjoy. It is difficult to overestimate the impact of the direct primary system on congressional elections, for it defines the political rules which candidates must observe in order to be elected and, hence, sets the terms under which parties must operate.

The Direct Primary.   The direct primary theoretically permits most registered voters to participate directly in the naming of the party candidates for Congress and most other state offices. The primary customarily precedes the general elections by several months; following the winner-take-all election system, the candidate for a particular office from a given party who receives the most votes in his party's primary usually becomes the party's general election nominee, carrying the party label into contest with opposition party nominees. This would seem a strange procedure to the voters of most other western democracies.[16]

In Great Britain, the selection of party candidates is handled almost entirely from within the party apparatus itself. Prospective party candidates for Parliament are screened and placed on a central party list of available candidates; when the party association in local constituencies needs a candidate, it considers, interviews, and selects one from this list. In nations such as France, that use proportional representation and multi-member districts, party committees usually have as much control of who is nominated as British parties do. Party committees in France present voters at the general elections with a list of nominees equal to the number of Parliamentary seats to be filled from that district. The candidate's fortune in a district is tied to his position on the list. Although voters customarily vote for an entire party list, when Parliamentary seats are divided according to party strength in the district, one party will rarely win all the seats; the seats a party does win on the basis of its vote are filled, according to number, from the top of its candidate list down, so that candidates at or near the top always stand the best chance of being elected. Both the British and French systems, like most European nominating procedures, give party

---

[16] The direct primary came to the United States only gradually, after other nominating procedures seemed less desirable. In the earliest days of the nation, the caucus system was used for congressional nominations, later a state party convention, finally the direct primary. Brief and useful studies of earlier nominating systems may be found in William Nisbet Chambers, *Political Parties in a New Nation* (New York: Oxford University Press, 1963), and William Nisbet Chambers and Walter Dean Burnham (eds.), *The American Party Systems* (New York: Oxford University Press, 1967).

committees firm control over their own nominations. In France, the party controls the names on the ballot and their all-important position. In Great Britain, a nominee "standing" in a district without a major party's endorsement is almost certain to lose.

The peculiarly American direct primary system reflects an effort to introduce greater "democracy" into the selection of party nominees and, in the process, to strike a blow against the power of party organizations. Until the turn of this century, party nominations were mostly controlled by party committees. These committees, together with other elements in the national party structure, were attacked with increasing severity by reformers appalled at the blatant corruption that frequently attended the selection of party nominees. Nominations were often, in effect, auctioned to the highest bidder, rank-and-file party members frequently had no significant voice in naming party candidates, and the system often perpetuated control of the parties by a small group of "bosses." The direct primary, reformers urged, could change this. The direct primary would give the rank-and-file party members direct control over their party nominations, would purge from the party many of the hacks and tame nominees who served the bidding of inner-party circles and would alleviate the corruption believed generalized throughout the party apparatus. Moreover, it would probably increase competition for nominations. Thus, the direct primary would make nominations a truly representative process by undercutting the influence of party officials, by restoring control of nominations to "the people," and by encouraging greater competition for office.

While the party apparatus throughout the United States was not as thoroughly tainted with corruption as reformers sometimes alleged, the general wave of anti-partyism and reform enthusiasm sweeping the country at the turn of the century was sufficient to bring the direct primary—or one of several variations of it—into most states.

Variations on a Theme. Wisconsin adopted the first compulsory primary in 1904 and almost all the remaining states enacted similar laws quickly thereafter. Today all fifty states have a compulsory primary system but not the same one.[17] The different primary systems reflect differences in how much freedom of choice state legislatures have felt they should give voters for selecting primary nominees, to whom the parties should be responsible, and how much animosity

---

[17] Current primary systems are usefully catalogued in the *Book of the States* issued biennially by the Council of State Governments. General summaries of primary systems and their impact on the electorate may be found in Key, *op. cit.,* Chapter 14; Sorauf, *op. cit.,* Chapter 9; and Hugh A. Bone, *American Politics and the Party System* (New York: McGraw-Hill Book Co., 1965), Chapter 11.

is felt toward the parties; several of these primary systems were attempts to remove the party organizations from any effective role in selecting their own nominees.

Forty-two states use the *closed* primary in which only party members may vote—an individual may vote only in the primary of the party in which he is registered. In contrast, the *open* primary—used in Alaska, Hawaii, Michigan, Minnesota, North Dakota, Vermont, and Wisconsin—allows the voter to decide on election day in which party primary he will vote.

To the extent that party officials favor any direct primary, they ordinarily prefer the closed primary on the grounds that it permits only registered party members to select party nominees, thereby assuring that the eventual nominees will represent some segment of rank-and-file party loyalists. Since the voter must declare his party affiliation before the particular personalities and issues of the primaries develop, some party officials suggest that the closed primary encourages "party-mindedness" and gives importance to party labels and party affiliations.

The open primary, in comparison, gives the voter more options; he is not forced to make a commitment to a particular party or its candidates before the issues and candidates emerge. Generally, those who favor the open primary place the voter's freedom of choice above party loyalty. Opponents of the open primary argue that this system permits members of one party to "raid" the opposition's primary, often with a guileful intent to produce weak candidates. Further, critics argue that the open primary threatens to make nonsense of any claim that the party primaries represent rank-and-file opinion because there is no guarantee that the party nominations will go to people who are supported by party loyalists. There has been occasional evidence of "raiding" in the open primary states, but it has not been so frequent or serious as is sometimes alleged.

Washington carries the voter's freedom of choice a step further. In Washington's "blanket" or "jungle" primary, the voter is not limited to casting ballots in any single party primary at all; he may cross party lines as he pleases, voting in *any* party primary contest provided only that he does not vote for more than one nominee for any single office. The Washington plan, by allowing the voter to roam all the party primary ballots, absolves the voter from making any commitment to a party and removes any party restrictions on voting.[18]

The peculiarities of one-party politics led eleven Southern states to adopt a two-primary system involving a "first" and a "run-off" primary. Until recently, the Democratic party had no effective opposition in state elections; winners of

---

[18] Until its abolition in 1959, California's cross-filing system was the most complete attempt to reduce party organizations and labels; a candidate could file *simultaneously* for both major party primary nominations; the ballot did not indicate his true party affiliation. Frequently, candidates won both major party primary nominations and thus were elected in the primaries. On the curiosities of the cross-filing system, see Robert J. Pitchell, "The Electoral System and Voting Behavior: The Case of California's Cross-Filing," *Western Political Quarterly* (June 1959), pp. 459–484.

the Democratic primary were, in effect, already elected since no serious challenge occurred at the general elections. Under these circumstances, all serious contenders for office thronged to the Democratic primaries, frequently fragmenting the vote—as many as ten to fifteen candidates might offer themselves for a major office such as governor or U.S. senator. To avoid a situation in which a candidate with a small proportion of the primary vote might win the nominations, and, therefore, the election as well, Southern legislatures have required that the two leading candidates in the "first" major party primaries must engage in a "run-off" contest where the winner, who would have a clear majority of the vote, would represent the party in the general elections.

The Impact of the Primaries.　As usually happens with reforms, the direct primary has produced results somewhere between what the reformists hoped and what its opponents feared.

The direct primary has not always reduced state party organizations to impotence in the nominating process; in some instances the party organizations have shown an ability to reassert effective control over their nominating procedures. Nor has the direct primary always produced the flourishing of candidate competition, voter interest, and participation that might be assumed. In some states, for instance, the parties have been able to reassert some control over their own primaries. Colorado, Connecticut, Massachusetts, Rhode Island, New Mexico, and Utah permit the parties to hold a "pre-primary convention" where candidates for the party primary are either endorsed or nominated; these pre-primary conventions have proven reasonably effective in promoting candidates favored by the party organization successfully. Even in California, where the legislature went to exaggerated lengths to render party organizations totally impotent in the primaries, the parties have reasserted limited strength. Through the "club movement," dedicated Republicans and Democrats have formed extra-legal statewide "clubs" which, unlike the official party committees, may endorse candidates. Through the use of pre-primary conventions and endorsements, these clubs in both parties have been able to successfully promote the fortunes of particular primary nominees.

In some states, party leaders—who seldom savor a primary fight that splits the party and leaves scars—arrange quietly for the withdrawal of competitors to the favored nominee, sometimes with a promise that others will have their turn at the nomination if they avoid a primary battle. In any case, it frequently happens that the majority of those who do vote in the party primaries are strong party loyalists, reasonably familiar with the political intricacies of the nomination and the candidates; in this way party organizations sometimes control nominations by manipulating the turnout. (In New York City, for example, both major parties deliberately set their primaries in early September when many people are away on vacation; turnout tends to be low, confined to those "cued" to the candidates and issues.[19]

The direct primary has indisputably increased the number of individuals who have a voice in selecting party nominees for Congress, but outside the South, primary turnout has customarily been low. Excluding the South, one careful estimate indicates that between 1920 and 1952 probably not more than 35 percent of the eligible electorate participated in one or the other major party primaries in two thirds of all the primaries held;[20] a total primary turnout of barely one in four voting-age adults is not uncommon in non-Southern primaries, especially in nonpresidential election years when voter interest languishes. In Congressional elections, at least, the direct primary has not produced sustained high levels of voter participation.[21] Part of the explanation for this low turnout lies in the fact that the great majority of incumbent Senators and Congressmen seeking reelection have no primary opposition and voter interest wanes. Additionally, in a great many electoral districts one party has so little chance of winning a major office that its primary contests, far from heated, are often filled with a few reluctant nominees engaged in a listless campaign for a foredoomed nomination.

The direct primary has greatly increased the cost of Congressional elections, however, and thereby places rather substantial limitations on access to office, a situation which would have greatly disturbed many reformers who promoted the direct primary system. Candidates for Congress with any significant opposition must appeal to a large electorate and must wage two campaigns, one for the primary nomination and another at the general elections. By reasonable estimate, the cost of a contested House seat runs between $100,000 and $250,000, but a Senate campaign may set candidates back as much as $1,000,000 apiece in the populous states.[22]

In many states, the direct primary has weakened or sometimes eliminated entirely the party organization's control over its own nominations, as the proponents of the direct primary often intended. Among other things, this means that the party organization is deprived of the power to impose tests of loyalty, belief, or commitment upon candidates for the party's nominations, a condition which undoubtedly contributes to the considerable difference in political values and programs found among legislators ostensibly representing the same party. Also, the direct primary means that the party organization often cannot guarantee a place on the ballot as a real or potential reward to party workers and contributors. Party officials intermittently complain that the direct primary too

---

[19] Donald C. Blaisdell, "The Riverside Democrats," in Paul Tillet (ed.), *Cases on Party Organization* (New York: McGraw-Hill Book Co., 1963), pp. 64–92.

[20] Key, *op. cit.*, p. 378.

[21] For the long-range impact of these voting fluctuations, see Burnham, *op. cit.*

[22] Committee for Economic Development, *Financing a Better Election System* (New York: Committee for Economic Development, 1968), pp. 34–35.

often saddles the party with sure losers or "hostile" candidates and, sometimes, thrusts incompetents into the reluctant arms of the party. In 1962, for instance, a Cleveland realtor and handyman, Richard D. Kennedy, won the Democratic nomination to oppose Republican Robert Taft, Jr., for Ohio's at-large Congressional seats. Kennedy had won an eleven-way primary contest, apparently on the basis of his name; he was openly repudiated by Democratic Governor DiSalle and other party leaders.[23] Such miscarriages of the primary system are not frequent, but state parties have often ended up with primary nominees who have no strong support in the party organization itself.

To summarize: while the direct primary has not wholly removed the influence of party organizations in Congressional nominations, it has appreciably weakened it. Despite evidence that in some states, some of the time, the parties have managed to recapture control of Congressional nominations, the majority of state parties have not.

Presidential Nominations

The nomination and election of the president involves a contest for enormous power and prestige. If any American civic ritual can be said to approach drama or spectacle that commands national and international attention, it is the presidential election. The man who would be president must win the nomination through a physically punishing, tortuously long and formidable nominating campaign, representing two centuries of American political tradition. He must deal with an enormously large electorate in an extremely large nation. He must be prepared to spend money at a profligate rate. Americans, it would seem, have conspired to create a presidential nominating system as imposing in its complexity and demands on the candidates as the presidential office is imposing in power.

The Presidential Primaries.   Since Wisconsin enacted the first presidential primary law in 1905, the primaries have gradually come to occupy a position often as important as the convention vote in determining presidential nominations, this in spite of the primary's failure to become what it was intended to be.

The presidential primary was another reform promoted by Progressives at the turn of the century which, along with the direct primary, would produce greater rank-and-file control in party affairs. The purpose of the primary was to

---

[23] Stimson Bullitt, *To Be a Politician* (New York: Doubleday & Co., 1959), p. 83.

give party members a means of expressing their preferences concerning whom the presidential nominating conventions should select. The presidential primary seemed an effective means to attack the corruption which had infected the national presidential nominating conventions much as it had the state nominating conventions.[24] By 1916, twenty-six states had adopted some form of presidential primary; by 1968, the number had diminished to sixteen, partly from opposition by the state parties and partly from legislative disappointment with the presidential primary's results. While the remaining primaries, now firmly established, have altered presidential campaigning materially, they have failed to achieve the purpose of their promoters, largely because of the way they have been organized.

The states using the presidential primary usually tie the expression of rank-and-file party preferences to the selection of convention delegates, yet this is often done in a way that makes any clear reading of voter opinion extraordinarily difficult. In six states, including politically important Illinois, New York, and Pennsylvania, state law permits competing slates of convention delegates to run in a party's primary but prohibits the ballot from indicating to which candidate the various slates might be pledged, if to anyone.[25] Unless the voter knows the delegate's commitments, he can make no indication of which candidate he prefers by selecting the appropriate slate; since voters cannot obtain such information on the ballot, voting is often a gamble with different delegate slates and the voting results often indicate little of the voters' real candidate preferences. In three additional states—South Dakota, Massachusetts, and New Jersey—the ballot *may* show delegate preferences *if* candidates consent to permit their names to be used. Often, candidates do not permit their names to be used for a "pledged" slate on the ballot; thus voters frequently have no opportunity to express preferences among all the contenders.[26] In New Hampshire and Florida, generally considered the best-arranged presidential primaries, the ballot may show a delegate's candidate preference without the candidate's consent; there is a greater likelihood that most of the major contenders will be represented by delegates on the ballot in this situation. Finally, California, Ohio, and Wisconsin require all delegates and delegate slates to be pledged—except

---

[24] Though not typical of all convention delegations, the composition of the Cook County (Chicago), Illinois delegation to the 1896 Democratic convention suggests the low estate to which convention delegations sometimes fell: "Seventeen had been tried for homicide, 46 had served terms in the penitentiary for homicide or other felonies, 84 were identified by detectives as having criminal records. Considerably over a third were saloon keepers; two kept houses of ill-fame; several kept gambling resorts." Cited in James W. Davis, *Presidential Primaries* (New York: Thomas Y. Crowell Co., 1967), p. 24.

[25] This typology follows that developed in Paul T. David, Ralph M. Goldman, and Richard C. Bain, *The Politics of National Party Conventions,* 2nd ed. (New York: Vintage Books, 1964), Chapter 10.

[26] Candidates usually refuse to permit a "pledged" slate for two reasons: they do not want to risk an almost certain defeat or they do not want to antagonize the state party organization which prefers not to have a primary fight among competing slates.

that a candidate must consent before a slate pledged to him can appear on the ballot. Additional problems of interpreting the meaning of presidential primaries arise because five of the states that permit pledged slates also permit "no preference" slates even when, as often happens, the slates really do have a preference.

These different primary systems seem calculated to obscure, rather than to clarify, the rank-and-file presidential preference of party members. In 1964, for instance, Florida Republicans were given a ballot at their presidential primary on which they could vote for a delegate slate pledged to Barry Goldwater or for an apparently "unpledged" slate that also supported Goldwater. The competing slates represented factional conflicts within the Florida Republican party, not different candidate preferences; a voter casting his ballot for the "unpledged" slate on the assumption he was not voting for Goldwater was deceived. In the same year, 100,000 Indiana Republicans voted for Harold Stassen—a politically insignificant, perennial "also-ran"—as the only alternative to a Goldwater vote in their presidential primary. In California, public opinion polls suggested that 40 percent of Republicans there favored neither Goldwater nor Rockefeller, but, since write-ins were prohibited, they had to choose either candidate or none.[27]

Some states have a "presidential preference poll" apart from the selection of convention delegates by direct election. In eight states—Illinois, Massachusetts, Nebraska, New Hampshire, New Jersey, Oregon, Pennsylvania, and West Virginia—party voters were given a chance to express their preference among the party's major presidential contenders on a pure popularity vote. This vote, however, is almost never binding upon the delegates selected in the same primary—it is purely "advisory." Not infrequently, a slate of convention delegates who favor one candidate may be selected while the preference poll indicates party opinion leans in another direction. In the 1960 West Virginia Democratic primary, John Kennedy won a convincing victory in the party preference poll, yet only fifteen of the state's twenty-five Democratic convention delegates voted for him. Critics of the primaries cite such curious and inconsistent results to justify a major redrafting of the presidential primary system.

The primaries have also prolonged an already lengthy presidential campaign and further inflated the cost of presidential elections. Beginning with the January New Hampshire campaign, the primaries stretch until early June, adding six months of campaigning for most serious presidential contenders. And the costs continue to rise. A candidate unable to obtain at least several million dollars for a primary campaign can almost never hope to make a serious bid for the presidency today.[28]

Since these primaries occur in less than one third of the states, seldom permit an unfettered expression of voter opinion, often produce meaningless

[27] Bone, *op. cit.,* p. 311.
[28] See Table 7.2, p. 289, for figures on the cost of recent presidential primary campaigns.

"victories" or contradictory results—to say nothing of their cost—why do they remain? For one reason, they give candidates "exposure" through the invaluable free coverage and attention lavished on the primaries by the media, especially television. The media treat the primaries as "political Olympics"; in 1964, New England Telephone and Telegraph brought one-half million dollars in equipment to New Hampshire to cover the nation's first primary. The New Hampshire and California primaries in 1968 were treated as major elections; national television networks coopted prime time.

The primaries appeal to a variety of candidates. For political unknowns, mavericks, and underdogs, the primaries offer the chance to build an image, to gain voter familiarity, and to prove their appeal to the public; for any contender whose ability to pull votes is questionable, the primaries are almost mandatory. In 1960, John Kennedy—a Catholic, youthful, and relatively unknown at the outset of the campaign—used the primaries to demonstrate that his youth and religion were assets; in the West Virginia primary, he convincingly demolished the assumption that a Catholic nominee would not strongly appeal to Protestant voters. In 1964, Barry Goldwater used the primaries in an attempt to convince skeptical, if not wholly hostile, eastern Republicans that he could draw rank-and-file enthusiasm; his victory over Nelson Rockefeller in the fiercely fought California primary consolidated his strength and seemed to demonstrate his ability to win over the eastern "establishment."

In 1968, both Eugene McCarthy and Richard Nixon used the primaries to their advantage. For Nixon, the primaries were an opportunity to shake the "loser" image that had haunted him ever since the 1960 presidential elections; the "new" Nixon that emerged from the primaries, unlike the "old" Nixon, seemed confident and effective before the public. Eugene McCarthy's early primary victories in 1968 over incumbent President Johnson demonstrated the President's shaky standing among many rank-and-file Democrats and the existence of deep divisions within the Democratic party over the President's handling of the Vietnamese War—although, as public opinion polls indicated, the issues were more complex than the Vietnamese War alone. McCarthy's early primary performance eventually contributed to Johnson's decision to withdraw from the elections and cast doubt on the old political saw that an incumbent presidential eligible for reelection is impossible to defeat in his own party.

Not least important, the primaries are a testing ground for candidates where strengths and weaknesses are often revealed. George Romney's withdrawal from the 1968 Republican presidential campaign, for instance, resulted from several early primaries in which his inexperience and ineptness in handling foreign affairs were starkly revealed when he was forced, as all primary contenders are, to deal with them before a public audience. Such instances of candidate drop-out following poor primary performances suggests that the primaries are often a pruning device for the major parties to eliminate the least suitable contenders.

The Other Delegates. It surprises most Americans to learn that the majority of convention delegates are not selected by the presidential primary. While the noisy, spectacular primaries customarily monopolize media attention and public interest preceding the nominating conventions, the majority of states select a majority of their convention delegates quite differently. Thirty-four states select about 55 percent of both convention delegates without a presidential primary.[29] This proceeds for the most part quietly, within the apparatus of the different state parties, without great public scrutiny. To presidential contenders, locked though they may be in a presidential primary struggle, their stakes in these "other" procedures are often as great as their investment in the presidential primaries.

The majority of the states select their convention delegates through special party committees or conventions whose membership is elected at party primaries or, in some cases, by local precinct organizations.[30] This process, continuing for months preceding the national nominating conventions, often stimulates rivalry and maneuvering by leading presidential contenders as they attempt to influence these delegates in advance of the convention. Often, therefore, while the public sees the leading contenders publicly battling for delegates in the relatively few presidential primaries, the candidates are also fighting on a second front, in the state party conventions and committees where the majority of delegates will be designated. If a candidate labors diligently and successfully, he may enter the convention backed by a solid phalanx of pledged delegates that almost assure his nomination—this, often, to the bafflement of some observers who witnessed the candidate fight in the presidential primaries to an inconclusive finish and cannot understand where such massive delegate support arose.

Both Barry Goldwater in 1964 and Hubert Humphrey in 1968 used this kind of delegate support to great advantage. Goldwater entered the 1964 Republican nominating convention with about 650 pledged delegates, a majority from states where they had been selected entirely within the state party apparatus.[31] Indeed, the Goldwater workers had been working diligently ever since 1960 to win control of a great many state party organizations; by early 1964 they had so effectively dominated many of them that Goldwater's delegate support almost assured his nomination many months before the actual nominat-

---

[29] A convenient summary of state delegate selection procedures may be found in Polsby and Wildavsky, *op. cit.,* pp. 111–114.

[30] There is very little uniformity in how the conventions that select delegates are themselves chosen, nor for that matter on what party unit will "instruct" the delegates. See, for example, David, Goldman, and Bain, *op. cit.,* Chapter 11, for a detailed discussion.

[31] Indeed, Goldwater had almost enough delegates pledged to him from nonprimary states to win the nomination without additional support, but the Arizona Senator felt compelled to demonstrate his popular support in the primaries. See Karl A. Lamb and Paul A. Smith, *Campaign Decision-Making* (Belmont, Calif.: Wadsworth, 1968), p. 71.

ing convention. In a similar way, Humphrey's 1968 Democratic convention nomination rested heavily on the support of delegates drawn from nonpresidential-primary states; almost all his pre-convention delegates came from this source.[32] In fact, it was Humphrey's heavy dependence upon delegates selected without a presidential primary that led critics to charge that his nomination was "unrepresentative" of rank-and-file party preferences.

Often, no candidate will win a preponderance of delegates selected by the state parties; in fact, considerable confusion may arise concerning which candidates the members of a state delegation are pledged to support. This confusion arises because delegates to the national convention may run for their position with an understanding that they favor one candidate or another, yet when the full state delegation is finally appointed, a state party committee or convention may instruct the delegation for whom to vote. The result, not surprisingly, is often argument within the state delegation that spills onto the convention floor during the national nominating struggle. The "polls of the delegation," bickering between delegation leaders and members, and other evidence of internal dissent within the state delegations often arise from this confusing practice of choosing state delegates by one method while instructing them by another.

However they are selected, once state delegations have been chosen, the center of national attention and candidate strategy focuses upon the national nominating conventions, another unique American contribution to the political arts.

The Nominating Conventions.   "No American institution so fascinates and so appalls the citizenry of the republic," wrote one journalist, "as do those vulgar, those quarrelsome, those unspeakably chaotic rites by which the U.S. political parties choose candidates for the presidency."[33] Now more than a century old, the nominating conventions are a curious spectacle, a collision of opposites that seems to demand explanation if not justification. The convention combines solemn purpose with carnival antics, infuses the struggle for presidential power with moments of low comedy, banality, transparent posturing, and hackneyed oratory. All this is displayed before a huge audience. Undoubtedly, the conventions have become the most thoroughly exposed party institutions to both foreign and domestic audiences. In 1964, representatives of the media outnumbered delegates to the Republican National Convention; ordinarily, almost 90 percent of Americans will have viewed some of these proceedings.[34]

---

[32] Humphrey announced his candidacy too late to file for entrance into most of the presidential primary contests.

[33] Paul O'Neil, "Conventions: Nominations by Rain Dance," *Life* (July 5, 1968), p. 21.

[34] John P. Robinson, Jerrold G. Rusk, and Kendra B. Head, *Measures of Political Attitude* (Ann Arbor: Institute for Social Research, 1968), p. 598.

At the very least, to many people the conventions appear an unseemly, coarse, and disorganized way for the world's most powerful nation and leading democracy to choose its chief executive. More important, in recent years the basic convention structure has been vigorously attacked for a wide range of alleged evils. In 1968, the ugly, vicious encounters between police, youthful demonstrators, and media representatives at the Democratic Convention in Chicago—a spectacle witnessed by millions of television viewers—stimulated a torrent of criticism led by many young people, intellectuals, journalists, minority spokesmen, and others. They charged that the conventions were too large to permit full discussion of issues and careful deliberation, too unresponsive to important minorities, too biased, too manipulated by bosses against the interest of party members—in general, that the conventions were "undemocratic" because the true preferences of party members, and minority groups particularly, were given little consideration. Before evaluating these criticisms, we must establish the purpose of the conventions.

The nominating conventions have had two sweeping purposes. First, they have been a device for creating the political coalition necessary to elect a president. The convention represents a solution to a formidable problem posed to American parties by the Constitution: how can the parties, decentralized and state-based, effectively organize to nominate and elect a president who must be chosen on a national basis? The convention has persisted because it seems a workable, reasonably effective solution to this electoral problem. Through the national convention, the disparate state parties (1) can be mobilized behind a single presidential candidate; (2) the various policy demands of party factions and associated interests can be aggregated into a platform comprehensive enough to unite many groups into a national electoral coalition; and (3) a candidate capable of uniting the various interests can be recruited.[35]

In addition, the nominating conventions create a national organizing center for the state party units—indeed, the only one. The national convention creates a semblance of national party identity and purpose by electing national officers and committees, by bringing various state and Congressional leaders together for a variety of purposes, and by developing whatever sense of national objectives and unity there may be within the major parties. Moreover, by their proceedings, the national conventions stimulate voter interest and loyalty to the major party symbols and spokesmen, thus investing the national party with psychological impact and reality to the electorate. Without these activities, a truly national party would hardly exist. In a very important sense, therefore, the national conventions preserve the identity and role of organized parties in nominating the president and give the party organizations a major voice in these procedures.

The larger ends of the convention, of course, are realized in day-to-day flow of convention activity: the progression of the official convention agenda; the

---

[35] The electoral objectives of the conventions are ably reviewed and defended in Polsby and Wildavsky, *op. cit.,* pp. 228–242.

overblown public rituals and rhetoric; the endless private delegate discussions; the huddles between presidential contenders, their organizers, and potential allies; and a multitude of other events transpiring on and off the convention floor. Much of the real bargaining occurs privately, invisible to the public and the media. Much of the public convention business is purely ceremonial or largely exhortatory. The demonstrations following the nomination of presidential candidates are no more spontaneous than a stage play; many of the speeches intend to kindle only tribal loyalties and spark enthusiasm from tired delegates. However, there are several strategic points in the convention agenda where major decisions—and power struggles—are likely to occur with important consequences.

Two important events in convention procedure usually occur before the convention is officially convened: the meeting of the credentials and platform committees. Often, crucial decisions affecting the strength and balance of convention factions are made in the credentials committee; these determine which delegations are entitled to be seated at the convention. In cases where two different state delegations claim the right to be seated as the official state representative, the credentials committee's decision may influence the balance of strength between the leading contenders for the presidential nomination or it may affect the fortune of various issues debated at the convention. Often, major candidates or partisans become deeply involved in these credentials fights, for they look upon the outcome—either materially or symbolically—as a victory or defeat. In 1964 and 1968, for example, the Democratic credentials committee was faced with competing delegations from several Southern states; the "regular" state delegates were challenged by Freedom Democratic party delegates who charged that they were excluded from the selection of state delegates because they were black. After an acrimonious debate, the credentials committee in both years divided several state blocs between the contesting delegations, thus giving a symbolic victory to the liberal challengers of the official Democratic organizations and, in the process, demonstrating that liberal elements could and would control the convention business.

Like the credentials committee, the platform committee customarily meets before the formal convention opening and often becomes an arena for a power struggle between competing candidates and issue partisans. While the party platforms have often been criticized for their excessive length, customary vagueness, and ideological fuzziness, the business of platform-making is still a highly important one. The platform has great symbolic importance to interests inside and outside the party, for what is said or omitted may be a cue as to which groups and interests will be dominant in the convention or will receive the most attention in the campaign. For instance, the first in a series of Deep South exits from the Democratic National Convention started in 1948 when President Truman succeeded in nailing a strong civil-rights "plank" onto the platform over vehement Southern objections. In 1964, the first major test of strength between the Goldwater forces and their opposition occurred during the Republican platform committee hearing preceding the convention. The committee's failure to give a sympathetic hearing to proposals by New York Governor Nelson Rockefeller and other liberals was a Goldwater triumph. In this initial encounter, Goldwater demonstrated his influence among the party professionals, revealed the weakness of the liberal opposition, and molded the platform into a form he could accept; to many wavering delegates, this victory demonstrated Goldwater's almost certain convention victory and undoubtedly hastened the movement toward him on the convention floor.

To most convention observers, however, it is the actual floor voting for the presidential nomination that most dramatizes the convention and climaxes it. It is, in short, the most important decision the convention makes. While voting for a presidential candidate is the most crucial of all convention decisions, it seems in the process of becoming not the climax but anti-climax of the convention; what the observer witnesses is likely to be only the formal ratification of a decision basically settled before the voting begins. Since 1928, for example, 9 of 11 Democratic and Republican presidential nominations have been secured on the first ballot; since 1956, no convention struggle has gone to a second ballot. It appears that the modern function of the convention is less to decide on a nominee than to validate a victory already won and to generate excitement and enthusiasm for the candidate and his party.

Several reasons have been suggested for the apparently declining role of the convention as a truly deliberative body. Increasingly, suggests one analyst, "the crucial bargaining and trading of support, the committing of some and the weeding out of the others, takes place . . . at the preconvention stages."[36] The major candidates have better, faster, more efficient facilities for gathering information about delegates, for moving across the country to strike bargains and win over doubters; moreover, the availability of elaborate public and private opinion polls, radio and television resources, and other communications media keep candidates better informed on delegate activity before the conventions and lessen the need to use the convention as a primary negotiating arena. In addition, the major contenders are now national personages with a truly national audience, due largely to television. The expectations and preferences of the public now figure more importantly in convention decisions than the wishes of a multitude of state local party leaders; they now feel compelled to defer to popular opinion. Therefore, convention delegates and leaders feel less independent in making candidate decisions, and the candidates themselves, using all the available devices of modern technology, can create convention majorities without depending upon the convention itself.

Though the function of the conventions may be changing, the convention procedure still remains the sole method by which the parties choose their

---

[36] Sorauf, *op. cit.*, p. 290.

presidential nominees. It is this procedure, with all the steps that precede it, that has come under periodic criticism. Are the critics correct when alleging that conventions are too large, undemocratic, unresponsive to important minorities, biased, and bossed? With some knowledge of the presidential nominating system, we can evaluate a few of these criticisms.

Should the Conventions Be Reformed?   An almost universal criticism of the convention system relates to the elephantine size of the conventions; the two conventions exceed the proportions of any other nominating body and most deliberative bodies of any type anywhere. Most experts believe the conventions should be greatly reduced in membership, thereby encouraging a more deliberative atmosphere and diminishing the apparent disarray of the proceedings. However, the parties believe that convention size represents an effort to accomplish two important objectives: to permit wide representation of party opinion and to reward the faithful—the "fat cat" contributors and effective state organizations—with convention seats. The conventions were originally intended to be no larger than Congress; with the nation's growth, they continually expanded to accommodate new party organizations. In 1964, the Republicans, always the smaller convention, seated 1,308 delegates and 1,300 alternates; in 1968, the Democrats seated 6,511.[37] Considering their size, the conventions have managed to complete their business with reasonable dispatch; almost two thirds of the two major party conventions between 1832 and 1964 nominated candidates with less than four ballots, though critics argue that this was achieved only at a loss of careful, deliberate attention to all the important candidates and a lack of open airing of important issues.[38]

A more fundamental criticism of the conventions relates to the personnel and the fairness of the proceedings. Many Americans, particularly articulate journalists and intellectuals, perceive the conventions to be the ultimate smoke-filled room populated principally by political hacks, narrow partisans, or selfish zealots who are dubiously qualified to select the president; others believe the conventions are bossed or otherwise manipulated so that the eventual nominees do not represent genuine rank-and-file party opinions.

By the standards of education, social status, political information, ex-

---

[37] Both major party conventions have also increased seating to reward productive state organizations with "bonus" seats. In 1964, for instance, the Democrats awarded bonus seating to state parties that had carried their states for the party in the 1960 presidential election or had won a number of other important state offices for the party between 1960 and 1964.

[38] Figures on the length of conventions may be found in Congressional Quarterly Service, *Politics in America, 1945–1964* (Washington, D.C.: Congressional Quarterly Service, 1965), p. 33.

perience, and interest, the majority of convention delegates are far superior to the average American; the delegates are the activists we described earlier in Chapter 4. To the extent that education, social status, and political expertise are considered important in those nominating the president, such qualities are represented by convention delegates. At least one third of the delegates to both party conventions customarily have a post-graduate education, another fifth a college degree, and at least 75 percent have some college experience. The greatest number are public officials, lawyers, and judges; a second large group represents business and the professions. Very few blue-collar occupations, skilled and unskilled workers, or minority groups—particularly blacks—have been represented in the past.[39] Recently, both parties have made an attempt to remedy the absence of substantial black representation.

Because the conventions are populated with middle- and upper-class delegates with the orientation of the "activists," they are predisposed toward nominating political moderates or conservative innovators and avoiding extremists or radicals, although Barry Goldwater's 1964 nomination proves the rule is not unbroken. This tendency toward centerism in the selection of presidential nominees, together with the unrepresentative social composition of convention delegates compared to the social structure of American society generally, have been two key indictments from critics who want to see the direction or speed of political change drastically quickened and the voices of America's lower classes directly expressed in the nominating system.

The conventions are also frequently criticized because they do not speak for rank-and-file majorities, or because conventions are managed, thus preventing an honest, open vote. In cases where a candidate clearly establishes a commanding lead in opinion polls, as Eisenhower did in 1952, conventions almost always nominate them. Convention delegates seem, generally, to be alert and responsive to public opinion polls and primary votes, yet the "cues" may be difficult to discern or to follow. No candidate may enjoy a convincing advantage in the preconvention trial heats in opinion polls; primary results may be ambiguous. Moreover, the delegates may be faced with one candidate who shows well among the party faithful, while another potential nominee will perform better in trial heats with opposing party candidates. This is an especially difficult situation. In 1964, Barry Goldwater seemed reasonably popular among Republicans, but he often ran poorly in the polls matching potential Republican candidates against President Johnson, the certain Democratic nominee. In such instances, delegates are confronted with the dilemma of choosing between a strong *party* favorite and a candidate who is potentially stronger with the general public; there are plausible arguments for either choice. Often, convention delegates have no clear mandate from either their state's voters or the party organization.[40]

---

[39] Figures cited in David, Goldman, and Bain, *op. cit.,* pp. 229–247.

[40] By the time the conventions are held, presidential primary results may no longer be relevant to delegates. Early primary winners might withdraw before the convention or run

Arguments about the degree of bossism in conventions also require qualification. Those who charge "bossism" assert that entire conventions, individual state delegations, or both are controlled by a small clique of individuals or perhaps only one; as a result, the argument runs, most procedures in the convention and the state delegations are tightly controlled by the leaders, most dissent is suppressed, and nominees are thrust upon delegates without proper respect for the wishes of the party rank-and-file. Party leaders, it is true, are more concerned with attaining a majority for some candidate as quickly and convincingly as possible than with calling attention to the divisions within the party. Generally, the longer a convention takes to nominate a candidate, the less likely he is to win the subsequent election, for long ballots testify to disunity and leave divisions which are slow to heal. Therefore, when an incumbent president is eligible for reelection, the dominant coalition usually succeeds in creating an image of a harmonious convention, and the opposition seldom gains any important voice in the proceedings. A classic example of a managed convention was the 1964 Democratic gathering in Atlantic City, a location chosen because the president and his staff would be close to the proceedings and able to manage the effects, especially to forestall any appearance of disunity between the Johnson and Kennedy forces. Whenever a confident majority clearly controls a convention, whatever the circumstances, minorities are likely to receive short treatment, as happened when the Nixon forces seized firm control of the 1968 Republican convention.

There is another side to the matter. Many conventions begin without a controlling coalition; many state delegations are not bossed. In 1960, for instance, the California delegation to the Los Angeles Democratic Convention entered the convention ostensibly pledged to its "favorite son," Governor Edmund G. "Pat" Brown, who was also the official delegation leader. Brown made no pretense of being a serious presidential candidate, but he had persuaded the delegation to unite behind him temporarily to maximize his ability to bargain with the leading presidential contenders for the state's support. This strategy soon failed, for Brown could not keep his restive delegates in line. The delegates, anxious to give their support to the candidates they actually favored and increasingly indifferent to Brown's appeal for solidarity behind him, finally forced a meeting at which the majority agreed to abandon the facade of unity and to divide the delegation's vote according to its true candidate preferences.[41] Instances of insurrection within state delegations and of fragmented and divided convention leadership may be found in many conventions, and the ability of

---

hopelessly behind as the convention begins. A more complicated circumstance arose in 1968 when Robert Kennedy's tragic death left state delegations pledged to him without a clear alternate choice.

[41] The story of the California delegation is told in John H. Bunzel and Eugene C. Lee, *The California Democratic Delegation of 1960* (University: University of Alabama Press, 1962).

controlling coalitions to impose their will upon dissenters is often exaggerated. In 1948, 1952, and 1956, segments of many Southern Democratic delegations walked out of the party convention rather than support liberal civil rights candidates; in 1964 and 1968, Democratic leaders in Georgia, Alabama, Mississippi, and Louisiana actively worked for opposition parties: for Goldwater in 1964, Wallace in 1968. The Republicans have also had their delegate revolts. Following Goldwater's failure to extend the usual conciliatory hand toward defeated Republican liberals at the 1964 convention, many eastern Republican leaders took a vacation from the campaign, pointedly refusing to endorse the Senator. As these examples suggest, there are many occasions when neither the convention as a whole nor many of its state delegations are "bossed," as critics allege they are consistently.

Defenders of the conventions, therefore, point out that many accusations leveled against the conventions are exaggerated and that, if the adequacy of the convention is to be judged by the quality of candidates it produces, it has done a respectable job. Most presidential candidates, so the argument runs, have been competent and some in this century, like the two Roosevelts and Woodrow Wilson, have been exceptional. Almost all have been experienced, tested leaders, committed to the values considered important in the political system. Beyond this, some would add that the conventions have made a very important contribution to political stability by nominating moderates, thus assuring that American party politics at the presidential level is conducted in the broad "middle zone" of political debate.[42]

The most important proposal offered by critics of the convention system has been a direct, nation-wide presidential primary which would eliminate the need for a party nominating convention. Such a proposal usually suggests that on a given day, presidential primaries should be held simultaneously in all the states with the winners representing their respective parties at the November elections. Advocates of this idea assert it has several advantages. First, it permits a direct, open expression of rank-and-file party preferences without the distortion that delegations, conventions, or other intermediaries between the voter and the candidates can cause. Second, it would remove control over presidential elections from a small elite of the party; this argument is especially popular among those who are most suspicious of professional politicians and party organizers. Finally, a national primary, so the advocates contend, would force candidates to expose themselves and their programs to a whole nation, attract greater national attention, and generally increase voter information and participation in the nominating system.

Adopting a national primary would also materially increase the already astronomical cost of presidential campaigns, in all likelihood reducing further

---

[42] Many points raised about the conventions here are suggested by Herbert McClosky, "Are Political Conventions Undemocratic?," *The New York Times Magazine* (August 4, 1968), p. 10 ff.

the number of candidates who could enter these contests. Many observers believe that a national primary would probably eliminate any important role the major parties might play in presidential selection, virtually destroying the shaky national party organization, perhaps making it easier for political radicals to achieve election. Finally, some critics believe that a national presidential primary, by undercutting the national party organizations, would make the candidates less responsible or predictable in their behavior, since they would have no organizational commitments to honor.

Presidential Campaigns:
The "New" Politics

America's presidential election is the longest, most expensive, most exhausting political campaign on earth. "It is terribly expensive," remarked a tired Adlai Stevenson in 1956, "it's exhausting physically; you burn up yourself, you burn up your ammunition, and burn up your means."[43] National elections in most democracies last less than a month—a mere seventeen days in Great Britain. In comparison, major party nominees in the United States usually campaign for eight to ten weeks after their nomination but, in fact, they have been campaigning unremittingly since the early primaries; the actual campaign stretches across ten months. This campaign must be conducted across a large nation and must reach most of the 75 million voters at some time. Notwithstanding the problems of organizing a campaign on this scale, the successful candidate must somehow become sensitive to the electorate's interests and preoccupations, able to read the public mood with sufficient discernment to respond in a way conducive to winning. And the contest is expensive. In 1968, the postconvention struggle cost Hubert Humphrey $19 million, and he lost.[44]

The history of presidential campaigns is a story of continual experimentation; unquestionably, the presidential campaigns have been the genesis of many campaign innovations—the nominating convention, the torchlight parade, the use of radio and television for political purposes, public opinion polling to determine the campaign's effect, and many more. Yet presidential campaigns have changed so significantly in the last three decades that many writers speak of

---

[43] David, Goldman, and Bain, *op. cit.*, p. 21. Before jet transportation, things were no better. Harry Truman reports in 1948 that he delivered 356 speeches in 35 days—10 a day on the average, 16 on one day. Harry Truman, *Years of Trial and Hope* (New York: Doubleday & Co., 1956), p. 219.

[44] *Congressional Quarterly* (April 11, 1969), pp. 513–516. This does not include expenditures of state and local party organizations.

the "new" and "old" politics to accentuate the difference. The presidential campaign of "new" policies is characterized by (1) increasing reliance on television as the principal medium through which candidates reach the voter with a corresponding decrease in the importance of the local party units to mobilize the electorate; (2) new forms of political communication—the "Madison Avenue style"—tailored to the mass media; and (3) increasing reliance on public opinion polls and pollsters to shape the campaign format and to assess the campaign's progress. Though Americans unfamiliar with campaigns before the 1950s will find nothing exceptional in these circumstances, these three aspects mark a departure from older campaign styles.

The Impact of Television. Throughout most of the 19th century and well into the 1930s, presidential candidates relied on local party organizations with their ward "heelers," precinct captains, and other regulars to rally the electorate, communicate political information, implement campaign strategy, and otherwise make an impact on the citizenry; during these years, the newspaper was the only mass medium of political significance. Party leaders depended upon face-to-face contact between workers and electorate to "translate" the candidates and issues into meaningful terms for the voter.[45] Beyond contact with the local party organization, the voter's only other source of partisan information was likely to be the press or, less often, a noisy, gaudily resplendent rally where the candidates appeared.

First radio and then television conclusively altered the manner in which the candidate, the issues, and the parties were presented to the voters. Radio and television enabled the candidate to present himself simultaneously to millions of voters under carefully controlled conditions where advisors and staff had the maximum advantage in engineering the proper effects. Moreover, radio and television appealed to presidential nominees because it appeared to reduce the unit cost of getting a vote even while it increased total campaign expenses. The more candidates came to rely on the media, especially television, the less important and active the local party activists became in the elections. "The media have done to the campaign system what the invention of gunpowder did to the feudal kingdom—destroyed the barons and shifted power to the masses and the prince. A candidate now pays less attention to district leaders than to opinion polls."[46]

The exit of the local party chiefs came slowly. Radio was first used as a

---

[45] Ostrogorski, *op. cit.,* pp. 167–168, contains an excellent description of the style of those party workers.

[46] Bullitt, *op. cit.,* pp. 83–84. Literature on the political impact of television is enormous. Among useful studies used in this discussion see: Bernard Rubin, *Political Television* (Belmont, Calif.: Wadsworth, 1965); Stanley Kelley, Jr., *Political Campaigning* (Washing-

major campaign device in 1928 (to the disadvantage of Democratic candidate
Al Smith whose gravelly voice and lush Bronx accent startled many Americans).
In 1932, for the first time in history, both major parties spent more for radio
than for printed handbills and other campaign literature; radio became the principal media expenditure for both parties until 1952.[47] Television became a
major political medium in 1952 when the Republicans gave television equal
priority with radio in the Eisenhower campaign. In 1956, both parties' television
expenditures more than doubled those of the previous election; after 1956,
"electronic campaigning" through television alone accounted for 20 to 25 percent of total campaign expenditures in both parties.[48]

Television's importance arises from its wide distribution in American homes.
In 1952, the year television was first used as a major campaign medium, about 47
percent of American households had a television set; in 1968, more than 98
percent did.[49] According to opinion surveys, the public's most used source of
political information in 1950 was still the newspapers, by a margin of 57 to 51
percent over television; in 1967, television led 64 percent to 55 percent. More
significantly, the public seems far more likely to find television a reliable news
source than any other; according to one 1967 survey, the public found television
the most "believable" news medium by a vote of 41 percent compared to 24
percent for newspapers, the next-most-trusted medium.[50] Television's ability to
command vast audiences has been amply demonstrated. In 1960, 101 million
Americans—the largest audience in American television history—watched at
least one of the Nixon-Kennedy "Great Debates": after these encounters, John
Kennedy's Gallup poll preference vote increased 3 percent, Nixon's dropped a
percentage point.[51]

The decline in local party activism and effectiveness in presidential campaigns has been gradual over the last thirty years and cannot be wholly
attributed to television; television, however, has undoubtedly hastened the
withering of local campaign organizations by making them relatively unnecessary. A 1962 survey suggests that more than one fifth of the party committee
positions in Kansas, South Dakota, North Dakota, and Iowa were unfilled for

---

ton: Brookings Institution, 1960); Stanley Kelley, Jr., *Professional Public Relations and
Political Power* (Baltimore: Johns Hopkins University Press, 1959); Robert McNeil, *The
People Machine* (New York: Harper & Row, Publishers, 1968).

[47] A brief, interesting study of the "displacement" principle through which one medium
successively replaces another over American political history may be found in Alexander
Heard, *The Costs of Democracy* (Garden City, N.Y.: Doubleday & Co., 1962), pp.
351–357.

[48] Congressional Quarterly Service, *op. cit.,* p. 83.

[49] Figures cited from *U.S. Book of Facts, Statistics and Information* (New York: U.S.
Department of Commerce, 1967), p. 729.

[50] Elmo Roper and Associates, *The Public's View of Television and Other Media: 1959–
1964* (Report to the Television Information Office, 1964); News Release, Roper Research
Associates, April 7, 1967.

[51] Bone, *op. cit.,* pp. 396–397.

lack of candidates; in St. Louis, more than 27 percent of the party activists in a recent survey did not perform any significant electoral work, while in Massachusetts and North Carolina, perhaps no more than 25 percent of all party workers performed any critical electoral task.[52] Especially noteworthy is evidence of decline in the Eastern urban party organizations, traditionally the strongest and most cohesive local party units. In Detroit as early as the late 1950s, one investigator found in both parties that "[at] the top was an executive nucleus which performed certain responsibilities irregularly and ineffectively, if at all. The top nucleus seemed confused about which tasks could and should be performed, who could perform them, and who was and should be involved. . . ."[53] Things were little improved at the bottom; during the 1956 presidential election in Detroit, 54 percent of Democratic precinct teams and 68 percent of Republican teams had done *no* house-to-house canvassing.[54]

Diminishing party activism at the local level is reflected in recent voter surveys. In November 1968, at the end of a fiercely contested presidential election, the Gallup Poll reported that only 12 percent of Republicans and 8 percent of the Democrats surveyed had been personally contacted or telephoned by their party's workers. In 1960, 1964, and 1968, less than 15 percent of the electorate received a direct financial appeal from either party.[55] The precinct leaders, ward bosses, and party middlemen who hustled for votes and campaign money at the local level are gradually vanishing, their services largely displaced by television.

Television has also offered to presidential aspirants an opportunity to develop an electoral following in the pre-convention campaigns by appealing over the head of the party organizations and leaders to the electorate itself. Through this strategy, for instance, Eugene McCarthy's 1968 protest campaign against President Johnson was possible; McCarthy relied primarily on television and a dedicated army of enthusiastic youthful followers to give him an image and political force. The success of the McCarthy effort might be a prophecy. Television may prove not only an effective replacement for the local party organization but, in the end, may offer the means by which candidates can by-pass the party organization entirely in building a campaign following.

Among the many changes accompanying the advent of television as a major campaign medium, another is the new idiom which television has introduced in political campaigns, a langue adapted to the problems and opportunities of television communication. Sometimes called "Madison Avenue politics," this new technique was adapted from procedures common in commercial advertising

---

[52] Sorauf, *op. cit.,* pp. 70, 97.

[53] Samuel Eldersveld, *Political Parties* (Chicago: Rand, McNally & Co., 1964), pp. 355–356.

[54] *Ibid.,* pp. 350–351.

[55] Gallup Poll *Index* (November 1968); Robinson, Rusk, and Head, *op. cit.,* p. 603.

and altered to the needs of candidates for public office. More than any other group, professional public relations men were the technicians and creators of this approach to political communication.

"Madison Avenue Politics."   The impact of professional public relations men and their thinking on political campaigns approaches a revolution in political communication: "Just as the big-city boss symbolized the political techniques of the nineteenth century, so the public relations man is a character-istic figure in today's campaign." Unlike the boss whose aim was to build a bloc of voters loyal to him despite candidates and issues, "the public relations man fights his battles in the mind of the voter; he specializes in building attitudes and standardizing opinions on controversial issues."[56] The ethos of professional public relations men was first introduced in the 1952 presidential campaigns when the Republicans hired several New York firms to create a plan through which television, for the first time a major medium, could benefit Dwight Eisenhower. This recourse to professional advertising men was understandable: they were trained in using television to influence mass thinking and preferences, they knew the technical problems associated with this medium, and they could readily adapt their skills to politics. Applying commercial logic to presidential politics, one leader of a firm advising the Republicans in 1952 felt his job was "merchandizing Eisenhower's frankness, honesty, and integrity, his sincere and wholesome approach."[57]

In one sense, of course, presidential campaigns have always involved "merchandizing" the candidate and advertising his merits. Yet television was a unique medium for such a job: it provided instantaneous, direct, person-to-person contact between the candidate and millions of viewers. Furthermore, television came to prominence at the same time that mass opinion polls, developing since the 1930s, had become increasingly sophisticated and reliable, providing campaign managers with detailed, accurate information about public political opinions and preferences, about the impact of their candidate on the public's political perceptions. Thus, the possibilities of television for political campaigning were enhanced.

Basically, modern television political campaigning, as it evolved in the 1950s, developed a number of characteristic approaches to audiences: (1) attention-getting devices and gimmicks became common as a means of winning an audience; (2) viewers were presented with relatively short, cogent presentations; and (3) extremely careful control over almost all aspects of the staging

---

[56] Stanley Kelley, Jr., "P. R. Man: Political Mastermind," *The New York Times Magazine* (September 2, 1956), p. 54.

[57] Kelley, *op. cit., Professional Public Relations and Political Power,* p. 156.

and presentation of the candidate became mandatory. The emphasis on attention-getting devices and the brevity of the presentation itself indicate a realistic calculation that most Americans will seldom watch purely political presentations for long. Gimmicks, of course, have long been common fare in political campaigns. According to one historian, George Washington found it necessary to provide "an appetizing outlay of rum, punch, wine, cider-royal, and beer to please the varied tastes and win the vote of electors of his district" early in his political career.[58] Nineteenth-century presidential rallies were usually made as spectacular as possible with bands, fireworks, mass torchlight marches, entertainers, and, in earlier days, a generous supply of spirits to arouse enthusiasm.

In the television era, campaigning begins with an arresting image, an intriguing voice, or curious situation. In 1964, for example, the Democrats introduced one television spot with an outline of the United States east coast; as the viewer watched, a saw slowly and noisily severed the coast from the continent. As the detached coast receded into the Atlantic Ocean, an offstage voice reminded the audience that Barry Goldwater had once observed that it might be better if "the East coast fell into the Atlantic" and wondered, pointedly, if a man of such convictions was sound presidential timber.[59] In 1968, capitalizing on public debate over the conduct of the Vietnamese War, Republicans at one point televised a film strip of still shots taken from combat, reflecting the grimness and pathos of the war, while reminding viewers that the Democrats had instigated the war's escalation.[60]

Once attention is captured, it is directed toward a short, pointed message. Today the campaign spot rather than the campaign speech receives greatest attention. As early as 1952, the Republicans spent a relatively lavish $1.5 million on such spots; this was considered modest by later standards. After consulting with George Gallup, the Republicans chose three themes: corruption, high prices and taxes, and the Korean War. Each spot began with an announcer proclaiming "Eisenhower Answers the Nation," and then:

Voice: Mr. Eisenhower, can you bring taxes down?
Eisenhower: Yes. We will work to cut billions in Washington spending and bring your taxes down.

or

---

[58] Cited from Chambers, *op. cit.,* p. 4.

[59] Though the Democratic television spots were regarded as more effective, the Republicans spent more on television time, one indication that money does not necessarily "buy" elections. See Alexander, *op. cit.,* p. 52.

[60] Cited in Joe McGinniss, "The Selling of the President, 1968," *Harper's* (August 1969), pp. 46–60.

Voice: It was extra rough paying my income taxes when I read about the internal revenue tax collectors being fired for dishonesty.

Eisenhower: Well—how many tax payers were shaken down, I don't know. How many crooks escaped, I don't know. But I'll find out after next January.[61]

The Republicans introduced one of their 1968 spots with the scene of a youthful mob taunting the police, while flames engulfed an apartment house; the scene then dissolved to a patrolman guarding a deserted street in the aftermath. "It is time for some honest talk about the problems of order in the United States," began Richard Nixon. The scene next shifted to a montage of perplexed middle-aged faces. "There is no cause that justifies resort to violence. . . . There is no cause that justifies rule by mob instead of reason," added the candidate.[62] These spots customarily last 30 seconds to one minute; in 1964, 60 percent of the campaign money spent by candidates for television time went to such presentations. In 1966, an "off" election year when voter interest and turnout usually falls below presidential election levels, one survey reported 3,397,783 such political spots appeared on radio and television.[63]

Filmed and edited television presentations give campaign managers optimal control over the message's effect on viewers; virtually every element—lighting, clothes, make-up, voice, set arrangements, and the sequence of events—can be manipulated until the desired effect is achieved and the proper qualities are projected to the audience. While some candidates like Dwight Eisenhower and John Kennedy performed well in spontaneous situations and were often presented in this manner to television audiences, most campaign managers favored pre-arranged and structured settings, or at the very least carefully edited versions of candidates in informal, unrehearsed situations.

Behind the effort to control as many facets as possible of the candidate's appearance to the audience is an acute sensitivity on the part of advisors to image and television's ability to create, powerfully and subtly, good and bad images. Image is not the candidate as he is, but as the public perceives him in all dimensions—personality, capabilities, record, behavior—after exposure through the media. Like other public attitudes, beliefs about candidates are malleable, especially if the media are skillfully used. At the outset of the 1968 presidential campaign, Richard Nixon's television advisors evaluated the negative aspects of the Nixon image:

---

[61] Kelley, *Professional Public Relations*, p. 189.

[62] "The Political Pitch," *Newsweek* (October 14, 1968), p. 74. The Wallace advisors tried an interesting version of the same scene. After showing a burning building, the announcer observes "Look, America. Take a good look. This was done by anarchists, revolutionaries— the Molotov cocktail set." *The New York Times,* November 3, 1968, p. 56.

[63] Alexander, *op. cit.,* p. 54; Committee for Economic Development, *op. cit.,* p. 41.

Let's face it, a lot of people think Nixon is dull. . . . They look at him as the kind of kid who always carried a book bag. Who was forty-two years old the day he was born. . . . He'd always have his homework done and he'd never let you copy. Now you put him on television, you've got a problem right away. He's a funny looking guy. He looks like somebody hung him in a closet overnight and he jumps out in the morning with his suit all bunched up and starts running around saying, "I want to be President." That's why these shows are important. To make them forget all that.[64]

The advisers' strategy included specific objectives: (1) the candidate would be shown "as a person larger than life, the stuff of legend"; (2) correction of his apparent humorlessness; and (3) great opportunity for the candidate to demonstrate his "emotional involvement in the issues."[65] Such calculated image manipulation was not, of course, peculiar to the 1968 Nixon campaign. In 1960, John Kennedy's campaign advisors were quick to exploit the youthful, attractive Kennedy clan, including particularly the President's wife, to achieve an aura of youth and vigor about the President; in 1964, Goldwater advisors played upon his western heritage to emphasize his rugged individualism and knowledge of the country. Most of this conjuring with the candidate's image is inevitable and occurred long before television; television gave it new impact and techniques.

Polls and Pollsters. Public opinion polls have brought presidential candidates closer to the public mind than probably any other device for translating public opinion into terms useful to candidates. Public opinion polls and pollsters have become indispensable to modern presidential candidates for many reasons: (1) they give the voting preferences of key socioeconomic groups such as labor, agriculture, blacks, and other electoral blocs with great precision and detail; (2) they define what people know and think about the parties, candidates, and issues; and (3) they identify the "switchers" and others who may be particularly important in determining the electoral outcome.[66] The polls discover the terms of the campaigns and are becoming increasingly important.[67]

Presidential candidates normally scrutinize all the major syndicated polls like the Crosley, Roper, and Gallup surveys, during their campaigns, but major

[64] McGinniss, *op. cit.,* p. 55.

[65] *Ibid.,* pp. 46–48.

[66] These key objectives suggested by Louis Harris, "Polls and Politics in the United States," *Public Opinion Quarterly* (Spring 1963), pp. 3–8.

[67] By 1962, in addition to the pollsters employed by all the major presidential candidates two years earlier, two thirds of all Senate candidates, three quarters of the gubernatorial candidates and perhaps one tenth of the Congressional nominees running for office that year used some kind of poll.

contenders ordinarily commission their personal pollsters to produce intelligence on the progress of the campaign.[68] In 1960, John Kennedy not only relied extensively on pollster Louis Harris to direct his campaign strategy, but he also employed an organization called Simulmantics, Inc., to conduct computer simulation of the voting for him; in 1964, Nelson Rockefeller commissioned the Crosley organization; Barry Goldwater depended upon Thomas W. Benham of the Gallup staff to provide special-purpose surveys. John Kennedy decided to attack the issue of his Catholicism squarely and repeatedly after early Harris polls revealed this was a major public concern; in 1964, the Goldwater strategists chose to concentrate their campaign almost exclusively outside the East after private polls revealed that Goldwater stood little chance of carrying any important eastern state. In 1968, Hubert Humphrey's explicit break with the Johnson Administration over the advisability of a bombing pause in North Vietnam was made after polls indicated that the Vice President's failure to support a bombing halt was losing him considerable rank-and-file Democratic support.

Polling introduces yet another costly adjunct to the presidential campaigns. In 1960, presidential candidates spent between $1 and $1.5 million on public opinion surveys; by 1964 this figure had risen to $5 million.[69] One reason for this soaring cost is that many types of polling must be continual over the whole course of a campaign. In 1964, the Goldwater organization commissioned repeated interviews with a panel of voters, another study of a national cross-section of the electorate at several different times, "trial heat" surveys early in the pre-convention campaign, measurements of public reaction after Goldwater trips through Southern cities, measurements of the Midwest campaign impact, and studies of audience reaction to television advertising by both parties.[70]

The Cost of Elections

Since 1952, each succeeding presidential contest has cost the major parties between 15 and 30 percent more than the previous election. This soaring cost is apparent in Table 7.1, which reports post-convention expenditures by the two major parties since 1952.

---

[68] Harris, *op. cit.*, p. 3. Some of these polls, however, were *extremely* unprofessional. In one survey of the San Francisco area congressional races recently, an investigator found that many Congressmen purchased "quick and dirty" polls which were haphazard and careless. Only one pollster used trained interviewers, many were based only on postcard inquiries, many did not report the questions asked and only one poll was able to describe the issues important to the voters. David A. Leuthold, *Electioneering in a Democracy* (New York: John Wiley, 1968), pp. 52–53.

[69] Davis, *op. cit.*, p. 238.

[70] Thomas W. Benham, "Polling for a Presidential Candidate," *Public Opinion Quarterly* (Summer 1965), p. 185.

Table 7.1.   Reported General Election Expenditures by
the Republican and Democratic Parties for
Presidential Elections, 1952–1968

Year	Republicans	Democrats	Cost per Vote
1952	$12,229,239	$ 5,121,698	$.32
1956	13,220,144	6,492,634	.35
1960	12,950,232	11,800,979	.40
1964	19,314,796	14,948,791	.54
1968	29,592,832	19,065,993	.81

Source: *Politics In America* (Washington, D.C.: Congressional
Quarterly Service, 1965); *Congressional Quarterly* (April 11, 1969),
pp. 513–516.

These figures are undoubtedly conservative since they take no account of the
primary costs which may be as much as an additional half of the general election
costs.

Some idea of primary costs to candidates may be gathered from Table 7.2,
which gives estimated expenditures for the contested 1968 Republican and
Democratic primaries.

Table 7.2.   Estimated Presidential Primary Costs:
Leading Contenders, 1968

Republicans		Democrats	
Richard Nixon	$11,000,000	Hubert Humphrey	$4,000,000
Nelson Rockefeller	7,000,000	Robert Kennedy	6,000,000
George Romney	1,500,000	Eugene McCarthy	9,000,000

Source: Herbert Alexander, "Financing Parties and Campaigns in 1968: A Preliminary Report," paper delivered at the American Political Science Association
Convention, New York, September 1969.

Estimates of presidential campaign costs also do not include expenditures by
state and local party organizations (who are not required by federal law to
report campaign spending as candidates are) nor do the estimates take account
of the many loopholes in federal campaign reporting laws which permit numerous expenditures to go unrecorded. Actual costs for presidential campaigns,
including both the primaries and the general elections, may be twice as great as
reported expenditures.

Why this inexorable progression in campaign costs? Inflation is one factor,
but the principal explanation lies in the increasing use of television and opinion
polls by almost all candidates and parties, and the cost of television time
continues to rise. Also, levels of campaign spending are affected by the closeness

of the elections and the degree of contest in the primaries; recent presidential elections have involved spirited primary contests in one or both parties and several close general elections, which have contributed to rising campaign expenditures.

By way of comparison, while American parties and candidates spend, in absolute terms, more money than candidates and parties in any other democracy, the United States is not the leader in the cost per vote among these nations. According to one estimate, in at least five democracies—Israel, the Philippines, Italy, Japan, and India—party general election expenditures exceed those of the United States in the unit cost.[71] Therefore, American parties are not as lavish with the campaign dollar as is sometimes supposed, yet the total amount necessary for campaigns is staggering.

Where does the money come from? Each major party depends on a relatively small and distinguishable group of donors and interests for the bulk of their campaign contributions. Generally, Republican candidates draw contributions from business and professional groups, individuals associated with corporations, and small businessmen. Democratic candidates draw contributions principally from labor, intellectuals, the various ethnic and minority blocs. The total number of contributors to the presidential campaigns of either party probably does not exceed, by the most generous estimate, 15 percent of the electorate. Furthermore, both parties depend more on a relatively few large donors, or "fat cats," than on many small donations; indeed, repeated attempts to encourage widespread, rank-and-file member donations in both major parties have failed dismally.[72]

As in the United States, the major political parties of other democracies such as Great Britain, Australia, the Philippines, Germany, and France also derive the bulk of their income from a relatively limited number of individuals and interests. In one respect, however, the campaign financing in other democracies is somewhat easier. In most of these nations the total cost of political campaigns is somewhat reduced because campaigns are customarily short; moreover, "leftist" socialist and labor parties can expect a modest but dependable income from party subscriptions. Still, as television has become a major campaign medium in other democracies, the cost of campaigns has risen so much that most major parties must solicit contributions from a few affluent donors. Thus, the relatively limited base of campaign contributors in the United States does not seem exceptional.[73]

The constantly rising cost of elections has restricted the number of can-

---

[71] Arnold J. Heidenheimer, "Comparative Party Finance: Notes on Practices and towards a Theory," *Journal of Politics* (November 1963), p. 798.

[72] The most complete study of campaigning contributors may be found in Heard, *op. cit.*, Chapters 4–7. An excellent case study on the problems associated with "grass roots" giving may be found in Bernard Hennessy, "Dollars for Democrats, 1959," in Paul Tillett (ed.), *Cases on Party Organization* (New York: McGraw-Hill Book Co., 1963), pp. 155–182.

[73] On campaign financing, the entire issue of *Journal of Politics* (November 1963), devoted to articles on campaign funds in other nations; and Leon Epstein, *Political Parties in Western Democracies* (London: Pall Mall Press, 1967).

didates who can mount an effective campaign. Many observers of our present election system have pointed out that if presidential politics is not yet a rich man's game, it is certainly a contest in which a candidate must have access to wealth, either his own or that of others. For almost a month after the Democratic convention, the Democratic National Committee was unable to secure funds for a single advertising spot on national television or radio for Hubert Humphrey, while the Republicans spent almost a million dollars in the same period. To a great many observers, the failure of the Democrats to mount an effective media campaign in this critical time created an almost unbeatable advantage for Richard Nixon.[74]

Although a candidate's failure to appeal to potent economic interests almost always guarantees failure, it does not follow that the more money a candidate has available the better his electoral chances. During the Eisenhower years it was true that the Republicans, who spent the most on presidential campaigns, did win the elections of 1952 and 1956; but in 1960 and 1964 the winning party spent less than the losing party. In fact, it is not clear that a party spending the most money and capturing the White House has won *because* of its expenditure; rather, it may be that "the flow of funds to a candidate might simply reflect his prior popular appeal rather than create it."[75]

The "New" and "Old" Politics in Retrospect. Presidential campaigns today are certainly not conducted in the style and with the resources of a few decades ago. Modern presidential campaigns are not fought along the skirmish lines of precinct organizations, with contesting party workers engaged in door-to-door voter mobilization and local campaign organization logistics. The struggle for voter loyalty and electoral following has shifted to the mass media, to the polls, the pollsters, and the public relations men who influence the style and strategy of the modern presidential contest. Modern technology created television and radio and thereby left its indelible impression on politics, as on almost everything else. It is an open question whether party organizations themselves may not be the ultimate casualty of technological innovation.

Voting

Probably no other political act in the United States has been more often studied than voting. In the last thirty years, largely due to the development of sophisticated survey research and new interviewing techniques, we have a far

---

[74] Theodore White, *The Making of the President, 1968* (New York: Atheneum, 1968), p. 353.

[75] Heard, *op. cit.,* p. 17. Chapter 2 contains an excellent analysis of how much money influences electoral success.

more detailed and accurate understanding of the forces shaping the vote than ever before, although information is still incomplete and in some ways unsatisfactory. As more information accumulates, however, it becomes apparent that the ostensively simple act of voting represents a complex decision-making process in which a great many factors play a part, some only dimly perceived by the voter, some not at all.

The Role of Parties

One of the most impressive facts about American voting patterns is the extent to which the two major parties dominate the partisan loyalties of the electorate. More than 75 percent of the electorate in 1964 and 1968 identified to some degree with one of these parties; the two parties, consequently, have become the most salient, continuous symbols around which most people orient themselves toward political life and elections.

The Strength and Stability of Partisanship.   The Republican and Democratic parties not only dominate partisan loyalties in the United States, but hold these electoral sympathies with remarkable consistency. In Table 7.4, this stability is apparent in the strength of party identification in the United States from 1952 to 1968.

Table 7.3.   The Distribution of Party Identification in the United States, 1952–1968

	1952	1954	1956	1958	1960	1962	1964	1966	1968
Democrat									
Strong	22%	22%	21%	23%	21%	23%	26%	18%	20%
Weak	25	25	23	24	25	23	25	27	25
Independent									
Lean Demo.	10	9	7	7	8	8	9	9	10
Independent	5	7	9	8	8	8	8	12	10
Lean Rep.	7	6	8	4	7	6	6	7	9
Republican									
Weak	14	14	14	16	13	16	13	15	14
Strong	13	13	15	13	14	12	11	10	10
Apolitical									
Don't Know	4	4	3	5	4	4	2	2	2
	100	100	100	100	100	100	100	100	100
N =	1614	1139	1772	1269	3021	1289	1571	1291	1557

Source: John P. Robinson, Jerrold G. Rusk, and Kendra B. Head. *Measures of Political Attitudes* (Ann Arbor, Mich.: Survey Research Center, Institute for Social Research, 1968), p. 496; Survey Research Center. *1968 Election Study*, Variable 119. Copyright 1968. Reprinted by permission.

Despite the relatively short-term fluctuations in the intensity of party loyalties across these eighteen years, party identifications seem highly resistant to significant long-term change. Several reasons have been suggested for this. Some observers point to early political socialization in the home which tends to perpetuate partisan loyalties across generations and to the absence of other institutions during early socialization that might interfere with this family-based partisanship.· Another explanation suggests that most individuals tend to spend their adult lives in social environments in which political pressures tend to move in the same partisan direction, thus reinforcing and stabilizing party loyalties.[76] Whatever the reasons, once they are established, party identifications tend to be stable.

Besides nonpoliticals, the one segment of the electorate whose party loyalties are least developed is the youngest voters. A November 1968 Gallup survey indicated that a full 40 percent of voters between ages 21 and 29 considered themselves "independent," a much higher proportion than is usually found among older voters.[77] Some commentators, linking this to the apparent upsurge in student radicalism in the late 1960s, have proposed that this high nonpartisanship represents alienation from and rejection of the major parties. While this is not inconceivable, the evidence is quite unclear. Young voters generally show the highest incidence of "independents" in almost all national opinion surveys, a fact which might indicate less a feeling of hostility toward the parties than the absence of well-developed political orientations and loyalties which mature with time; some support for this conclusion arises from the fact that voters between ages 21 and 30 traditionally have the lowest rate of voter turnout and political participation compared with older citizens. What the high proportion of "independents" among the young does strongly suggest is that the young voter is more open and flexible in determining his party preferences than older voters.

The Social Basis of Partisanship. Across the range of American social groups, there are pockets of support for one or the other of the major parties; these enclaves of partisans distributed throughout the social structure constitute the core of the party, the dependable base from which the party operates and to which party leaders are customarily oriented. American political parties are not as tightly class-based as in Europe, where it is not uncommon to find parties whose support lies almost entirely within a well-defined social or occupational stratum, such as labor or religious groupings. American parties do draw their loyalists from significantly different social groupings, as one would expect given

---

[76] An excellent statement of the role of social "living spaces" on partisanship is contained in Robert Lane, *Political Life* (New York: The Free Press, 1965), Chapter 13.

[77] Gallup Poll *Index* (November 1968), p. 3.

the different social base for campaign contributions to the major parties. Generally, Republicans appeal most to older, more affluent, better educated Americans, to the business and professional groups, to the WASPs (White Anglo-Saxon Protestants); Democrats draw their greatest support from minorities, labor, Catholics, the middle- and lower-classes. Two facts about this social map of the parties deserve particular mention. First, each party enjoys at least significant minority support in almost all social groups; quite often, the partisan divisions within social groups are quite close. This has inhibited the tendency of the two parties to appeal exclusively to the narrow interest of limited social and occupational groups. Second, the strength of support for each party, even within a social group where party identification seems quite one-sided, can vary extensively over time. Among any group of party identifiers will be found some weak identifiers who are tenuously attached to a party and who may be wooed away to the opposition; sometimes, even strong party identifiers may desert their party's candidates if the attraction of an opposition candidate is unusually strong (or if their own candidate is particularly offensive to them). Thus, party *identification* does not always guarantee that a man will vote for his party's candidate without fail. In 1964, an estimated 20 percent of Republican identifiers voted for Democrat Lyndon Johnson and 13 percent of Democratic identifiers voted for Republican Barry Goldwater.[78] Such "cross-over" voting encourages both parties to broaden the base of their support which, again, works against narrow class or occupational appeals.[79]

How the Voter Decides

To vote is to choose: between parties, between candidates, and often between competing voter needs and demands. What elements enter into the voting calculus, impelling the voter to choose one presidential candidate rather than another? Though many factors affect the voter's choice of presidential candidates, three seem to be particularly influential: parties, candidates, and issues.

The Impact of Party.   The presidential candidates confront the electorate bearing a party label; they are *party* leaders and spokesmen. Nominating conven-

---

[78] Congressional Quarterly Service, *op. cit.,* p. 97.

[79] The evidence suggests, moreover, that class has little subjective reality or political influence on many American voters. A short, comprehensive discussion of the relationship between social status and political behavior may be found in Don R. Bowen, *Political Behavior of the American Public* (Columbus: Charles E. Merrill, 1968), Chapters 3 and 4.

tions are celebrations of party spirit and the subsequent campaigns abound in party imagery. Since party identifications are very widespread in the electorate, the candidate's party label has great relevance to the vote he gets; however, a few qualifications must be mentioned.

To a great many voters, the party label is the most compelling signal and cue that orients them toward the campaign and sets the course of their voting choice; many voters are disposed, or entirely decided, on their candidate choices once they know what party labels the nominees will bear. Probably, two thirds of the American electorate consistently identifies with one or the other major party; most of these voters will seldom vote for an opposition candidate.[80] Party labels are especially compelling signals to that one third of the electorate who identifies *strongly* with one party. These strong party identifiers almost always vote for their party's nominees; intense party identification represents virtually a standing decision to select one presidential contender over the other even before the campaigns are underway and, in this respect, strong party identification simplifies the voting choice for millions of Americans and assures each major party a minimum, guaranteed quadrennial vote. This strong influence of the party label on intense identifiers is one reason why candidates value the label so much: it means they can count on a core of support at the outset of their campaign. Conversely, third-party candidates work at a disadvantage in presidential elections because they must overcome the tug of other party symbols and loyalties on the electorate.[81]

To millions of Americans, party labels are meaningful voting cues because each major party is assumed to represent a different set of interests—the "group image" of each party dominates evaluations of parties and candidates for such voters. The University of Michigan's Survey Research Center has estimated that about half the electorate makes its choice this way; for these voters, the "group benefits" they assume will follow from having one party or the other in the White House is the decisive voting factor.[82] Although "group benefits" do not influence all voters to the same degree, in the past most of the electorate has at least believed that the two major parties stood for different interests. To most Americans, the Republicans are the more "conservative" party, favoring business, the professions, the better-off economic groups; a "sound economy," and

---

[80] Angus Campbell *et al., The American Voter* (New York: John Wiley, 1960), p. 87. An excellent brief summary of the impact of party identification on voting may be found in William H. Flanigan, *Political Behavior of the American Electorate* (Boston: Allyn and Bacon, 1968), pp. 33–40.

[81] What seems to draw voters to third parties is, most often, an overriding preoccupation with an issue, or issues, that undercuts customary party allegiance. On this matter, see especially the 1968 "Wallace voter" as described in Philip E. Converse *et al.,* "Continuity and Change in American Politics: Parties and Issues in the 1968 Election," Paper delivered at the American Political Science Association Convention, September 1969.

[82] In 1956, the Survey Research Center estimates that at least 45 percent of the voters made up their mind on the basis of which groups would be benefited by the candidates. This, in turn, was closely tied to group images of the parties. Campbell et al., *op. cit.,* p. 144.

tight money. The following comments regarding the Republican party from voter interviews in 1956 are fairly typical:

> Well, I think they're more middle-of-the-road, more conservative. They are not so subject to radical change.

> Oh, they're more for a moneyed group.

> My husband's job is better. . . . Well, his investments in stock are up. They go up when the Republicans are in. My husband is a furrier and when people get money they buy furs.[83]

In comparison, the Democrats represent the working man, small businessman, farmer, minority group; they are the party of the unbalanced budget, liberal spending, expanding government, and welfare:

> They're more inclined to help the working class of people, and that is the majority of the country. . . . They're too much for federal control of utilities.

> They put out more liberal legislation for all the people.

> I think they have always helped the farmers.

> I know nothing about politics but I like the Democratic party because I know that they are more for the poorer people.[84]

These group-related images are, not surprisingly, most influential in the case of voters with strong group identifications and greatly simplifies their choice in the voting decision.

One interesting aspect of American party imagery is the extent to which public perceptions of the parties are projections from the past—from the Great Depression and the crucial 1932 presidential elections—although the parties altered considerably since that time. The long shadow which political history casts over contemporary party imagery was especially striking to one analyst

---

[83] *Ibid.,* pp. 129–138.

[84] *Ibid.* Interestingly, little had changed even among Southern whites in 1960 who were often intensely hostile to the national Democratic civil rights program. See Donald R. Matthews and James W. Prothro, "The Concept of Party Image and Its Importance for the Southern Electorate," in M. Kent Jennings and L. Harmon Ziegler (eds.), *The Electoral Process* (Englewood Cliffs, N.J.: Prentice-Hall, 1966), especially pp. 151–159.

who studied public evaluations of the parties' domestic programs between 1952 and 1964. "To an unusual degree, these elements of the party image have roots in the past, extending back at least to the Roosevelt New Deal," he writes. "Indeed, the benefit to the Democrats from their party's sponsorship of the disadvantaged elements of American society is an antique theme in our party politics."[85] This lag is partially the responsibility of parties themselves: once a party has established public favor and wins the White House often, it will continue to hammer on whatever imagery has been successful. This is but one indication that voting decisions are often judgments on the past, related as much to what the parties and candidates have done as to what they will do.

Though the party label strongly influences many voters, it is not a decisive factor for many others. The number of voters identifying with one party who nonetheless vote for an opposition candidate—a cross-vote whose intensity varies among presidential elections—suggests that factors besides party label sway the voting decision. Among these other factors, feelings about the candidates themselves is major, often overcoming the pull of party identification and party loyalty.

The Candidates. Studies of the 1968 elections reveal some startling conclusions: one in five Goldwater voters in 1964 chose Hubert Humphrey or George Wallace in 1968; 3 in 10 white Johnson voters of 1964 went to Nixon or Wallace in 1968; and 40 percent of the Nixon vote came from Johnson supporters four years earlier. The number of voters casting ballots for the same party's candidates in 1964 and 1968, they concluded, was lower than at any other time in recent American history.[86] This heavy cross-party movement in 1968 underscores rather dramatically that Americans often cross party lines from election to election, though the flow varies from one election to another. Most voting analysts believe that this happens when the candidate seems more important than his party.[87]

The impact of candidates rather than parties on presidential elections can be well observed in the 1952 through 1968 elections. Between 1952 and 1960, surveys indicated that party identifications and public estimates of the parties' performance shifted only moderately in favor of the Republicans. During these years, however, public approval of Dwight Eisenhower compared to his opponent in 1952 and 1956, Adlai Stevenson, shifted strongly toward the General;

---

[85] Donald E. Stokes, "Some Dynamic Elements of Contests for the Presidency," *American Political Science Review* (March 1966), p. 20.

[86] Converse et al., *op. cit.*, p. 3.

[87] For detailed analysis of candidate images and impact on voting decisions, see Campbell et al., *op. cit.*, Chapter 2; James C. Davis, "Charisma in the 1952 Campaign," *American Political Science Review* (December 1954), pp. 1083–1102; Stokes, *op. cit.*

this, it appears in retrospect, accounts for the great swell of voter support for the Republican party. In 1964, survey data suggested again that, while party identifications and assessments of the parties remained reasonably stable since the elections of 1960, a great many Republican identifiers said that they thought Barry Goldwater was an "amalgam of doubts—a wild and erratic campaigner, muddled and unclear, unstable, poorly educated, and so on," with the result that perhaps 7 million Republicans voted for Goldwater's opponent.[88] Because candidate personalities and performances do impress the public deeply, voting analysts usually explain short-range changes in party control of the White House in terms of a strong shift in voter attitudes regarding the candidates rather than in major realignments of party identification. The 1968 election is a good example. In 1964, Lyndon Johnson was elected to office by the largest plurality in American history, an overwhelming 61.4 percent of the vote; in 1968, not only did President Johnson feel compelled to withdraw from the election himself, but his Vice-President and successor as candidate of the Democratic party attracted only 42.9 percent of the total vote. During this four-year period, no significant shift in party identification had occurred but, instead, public opinion surveys indicate that the Johnson image had become strongly identified with the war in Vietnam and a generally unsatisfactory record for himself and his party in managing foreign affairs.[89]

Even though candidates figure so importantly in the presidential choices of most voters, candidate images are still tied in many instances to party identifications or—to a lesser degree—to policy matters, underscoring that the various elements influencing the voting decision are interdependent. Party identifications, for instance, often influence voter estimates of the candidates through selective perception: the more favorably one feels toward a party, the more likely one is to be disposed favorably to the party's candidate. If some single policy issue preoccupies a great many voters, as the Vietnamese conflict did among young voters in 1968 and John Kennedy's religion did in 1960, this will color many voters' attitudes about candidates. Party identification or issues do play a role in shaping the presidential preferences of most voters most of the time.

The Issues. Presidential elections are supposed to be more than contests between personalities and parties; candidates are expected to discuss issues upon which the electorate can express a preference through voting. How meaningful and important are issues to voters?

A former congressional candidate said, "People want to know what a can-

---

[88] Stokes, *op. cit.,* p. 22.

[89] On the "Johnson image" and its influence on the 1968 campaign, see especially, Converse *et al., op. cit.,* pp. 1085–1090.

didate proposes to do about pending specific problems."[90] Most candidates would agree. To the extent that policy questions do interest voters and influence their presidential preferences, the questions are likely to be either "bread and butter" issues of immediate economic relevance to the voter or other tangible, concrete matters: taxes, wages, school integration, and the like. Conversely, broad, philosophical issues (such as the difference between "liberal" and "conservative" approaches to government) or abstract problems (such as our Asian policy) do not seem to influence or interest most voters.

A great many voters seem indifferent or confused concerning where the major parties and candidates stand on important policy questions. A 1956 study of the Detroit electorate indicated that during that presidential election year, over half of those voters calling themselves liberals were not clear where each party stood on the most important campaign issues. Moreover, a sizable minority of those who identified with each party felt the opposition party was closer to their own policy positions.[91] In 1968, many of those who voted for Senator McCarthy in the New Hampshire primary did not know his position on the Vietnamese war (although his support was widely assumed to come from "doves" who protested the conflict). At least some of those voting for the Senator were admonishing the president for not pushing the conflict vigorously enough.[92]

This evidence does not mean that voters customarily have no policy criteria for casting a vote. Ordinarily, most voters are motivated by their own determination of self-interest to select the candidate which in their subjective judgment is closest to their preferences. To probably a majority of the electorate, this boils down to voting on the basis of group interests—voting for the candidate who the voter perceives will benefit the groups most important to the voter.[93] This kind of subjective decision-making means that those who end up supporting the same candidate often do not share a great many policy preferences. For instance, a 1964 survey indicated that while most of those preferring Lyndon Johnson were generally satisfied with his handling of the Vietnamese conflict at that point, there was no strong relationship between preference for the President and beliefs about how the war should be managed in the future.

The fact that a great many voters are confused about the policy positions of the candidates and parties is not the fault of the voter alone; it is often difficult

---

[90] Bullitt, *op. cit.,* p. 96.

[91] Eldersveld, *op. cit.,* p. 539. In another study, Herbert McClosky found in the early 1960s that Republican rank-and-file voters seemed closer to opposition leaders than to their own party leadership on major policy questions. See Herbert McClosky, "Issue Conflict and Consensus among Party Leaders and Followers," *American Political Science Review* (June 1960), p. 426.

[92] Converse, *et al., op. cit.,* p. 1092.

[93] On the influence of groups on political preferences, see Herbert McClosky, "Primary Group Influence on Party Loyalty," *American Political Science Review* (September 1959), pp. 757–776; Campbell *et al., op. cit.*

or almost impossible to get a clear, accurate, unambiguous explanation of the candidates' policy positions—especially from the candidates. American political discourse, as many observers have pointed out, involves a certain calculated ambiguity that leaves the candidate room for maneuvering later:

> Even when he is taking a forthright position on a serious issue, an effective politician learns he cannot use extreme language. . . . It often means nothing more than the unwillingness of a politician to offend his opponents on an issue since he may need them as allies on another issue.[94]

So, in the place of clear prose, jargon and generality are often substituted —certainly not the stuff from which orderly understandings of candidate differences can be constructed. Thus, in some respects the electorate merely reflects our techniques of political communication.

Some segments of the public, often called "issue publics," do possess a high degree of policy interest and information. These "issue publics" are constituted mostly from the activists in American civic life. Occasionally, a presidential contender may emerge with a following drawn from individuals almost unanimously united on one or a few policy matters: George Wallace's followers were united in this way in the 1968 presidential elections. This is the characteristic origin of American third parties.

The Impact of the Campaigns.   It seems clear from voting surveys that at least one third to perhaps one half of all American voters have a clear candidate preference before the campaign begins; for the strong party identifier, the "straight-ticket man," and those very strongly attracted to one candidate or another, the preference is established once candidates are known. Even though such individuals possess a strong candidate preference, campaign managers are not indifferent to them. Campaign managers customarily seek to assure their party loyalists that the candidate is firmly grounded in party principles so that this core vote will go for the candidate. Furthermore, although many voters have a strong candidate preference, campaign managers must insure that these voters are sufficiently motivated to cast their ballot for the candidate. So, the candidate who wins a party nomination, especially if he is not the favorite of strong party identifiers, will usually make his peace with the rank-and-file. After Dwight Eisenhower won the 1952 Republican nomination over the rank-and-file fa-

---

[94] Arnold M. Rose, *The Power Structure* (New York: Oxford University Press, 1967), p. 81.

vorite, "Mr. Republican" Robert Taft, Eisenhower held a well-publicized conference with the Ohio Senator and the two demonstrated their accord on
important campaign matters. Barry Goldwater's deliberate failure to offer a
conciliatory gesture toward the Eastern, liberal wing of the Republican party
following his 1964 convention victory cost him substantial support from this
normally dependable group. One purpose of the campaign, therefore, is usually
to reinforce the commitment of party loyalists.

Many Americans, however, are not firmly committed to a party or a
particular candidate at the outset of a presidential campaign; this group is an
important target for campaign managers. By the best estimate, between 35 and
40 percent of Americans eligible to vote are "weak identifiers," whose loyalty to
one party might be undercut by an effective opposition campaign. An additional
25 to 30 percent of the eligible electorate only "leans" toward one major party
or is "independent." Many individuals in these groups do not ordinarily vote; but
many others do—or can be persuaded to vote by a sufficiently strong campaign.
The polls used by candidates usually identify among what social groups these
voters may be found and intensive campaigns are often launched to win them
over and to get them to the polls. Since 1960, Southern Democrats have become
a "target population" for Republican candidates seeking to capitalize on
Southern disenchantment with the Democratic party's national leadership regarding civil rights. In 1960, John Kennedy's organization made a special effort to
convince Protestant Democrats that Kennedy's Catholicism would in no way
compromise his loyalty to the Constitution or his performance in office. The
social composition of the target populations will shift from one election to
another, yet campaigns almost always pay special attention to these individuals.

How much the electorate learns from a presidential campaign about the
important issues and alternatives facing the nation is a much debated question.
Perhaps a minority of the electorate learns what national problems and priorities
are at stake during the election. To some voters, undoubtedly, elections clarify
their own position on the spectrum of parties and issues. But to a great many
other voters an election is usually a repetitious affair, a civic ritual through which
they simply reaffirm prior loyalties to parties and candidates.

The Electoral College

Strictly speaking, presidential election day is not the first Tuesday in
November of a presidential election year but sometime thereafter when members
of the electoral college meet in their respective states and, as the Constitution
prescribes, "vote by ballot for President and Vice-President." Americans, in
fact, do not vote for the president but for *electors* customarily pledged to
presidential candidates. Thus does the archaic electoral college force a tech-

nically indirect election of the chief executive and introduce an element in our electoral system as incongruous as a modern president in a powdered wig.

Shortly after Congress convened in early 1969, President Nixon sent it a proposal, strongly endorsed by the Administration, that the electoral college be abolished and presidential elections be determined wholly by popular vote. For the seventh time since 1948, a major bill to alter or abolish this antique institution lay before Congress. The 1969 proposal seemed urgent to many members of Congress and the Administration. It is always possible that a three-way presidential race could end with no candidate receiving an electoral college majority but in 1968, third-party candidate George Wallace was actively seeking such an event, and it is likely he will do so again in 1972. Few Americans apparently wanted this; polls indicate that most Americans would prefer to see the electoral college disappear entirely.[95]

Today, the electoral college is a cumbersome arrangement; to its critics it is dangerous, unnecessary, and undemocratic. While it is not without defenders, to the great majority of Americans the electoral college seems peculiar and unnecessary. Yet when it was created almost two centuries ago, it was viewed in a very different light and served quite different ends than it does today.

Like most aspects of the Constitution, the electoral college was a compromise. The Constitutional Convention was faced with proposals that the president be elected by Congress, by state legislatures, or directly by the people. The Convention rejected Congressional and state legislature selection on the grounds that it would make the chief executive too dependent on legislative bodies and weaken the independence of the office; direct popular election found few supporters since it seemed to invite demagoguery and rule by untutored mobs. The electoral college seemed an admirable compromise among these conflicting demands that could draw enough support to win Convention approval.

The electoral college was originally conceived to be a truly deliberative body, composed of men from each state who would represent sound judgment, political expertise, and responsibility. Ideally, from their collective deliberations would emerge presidents of quality and stature. By granting each state an electoral college vote equal to its Congressional delegation, even a small state was assured at least three votes (two for its Senators, at least one for the minimum Congressman guaranteed each state); this arrangement gave the small states individually some voice in the presidential selection and the opportunity to combine and collaborate for greater influence. The Constitutional Convention assumed that members of the electoral college would be chosen by their respective state legislatures, yet the legislatures were left free to determine how electors

---

[95] According to a December 1968 Gallup poll, which asked a sample of Americans if they approved a constitutional amendment abolishing the electoral college and basing the presidential election solely on the popular vote; 81 percent approved, 12 percent disapproved, 7 percent had no opinion. Gallup Poll *Index* (December 1968), p. 11.

were chosen, allowing popular selection of presidential electors if the legislatures so decided. In many ways the electoral college struck a balance among competing Convention plans: it achieved presidential independence from legislative institutions, yet assured that the president would be selected by qualified electors; it gave large and small states a voice in his selection and permitted the states great latitude in determining how electors would be chosen.

The new Constitution had hardly been adopted before the electoral college's role began to change. In 1800, emerging party spirit led state electors to run on slates pledged to announced candidates; soon an increasing number of state legislatures permitted direct popular voting on electoral college members. By 1830, almost all the states adopted the rule, familiar to modern Americans, that a state's entire electoral college vote went to the candidate whose slate of electors received a plurality of the state's general election vote. By Abraham Lincoln's election in 1860, the electoral college had assumed its familiar modern role: no longer a deliberative body, its members met long enough to cast their electoral votes to the winners of the state general elections and then disbanded.[96]

Even though the electoral college is now a formality in the sense that it usually follows the formula of ratifying the states' popular votes, it is far from unimportant. Its existence has shaped many aspects of presidential campaigns. First, it has generally encouraged candidates to concentrate their campaigns in states such as New York, California, and Illinois that deliver very large blocs of electoral college votes, often minimizing the importance of electors in the smaller states. Moreover, it favors the selection of presidential candidates who appeal to the electorate of urban areas and who lean to the moderate or liberal end of the political spectrum, for the larger states are the most urbanized and usually the most politically liberal. Also, the electoral college works against the success of third parties, splinter groups, and other minorities that attempt to promote presidential contenders; such groups can attain no electoral college vote unless they win a plurality of popular votes in some states—an unlikely event most of the time. As a result of this bias, there is usually little incentive for such groups to organize a presidential campaign; even if they gain significant minority following in many states, it counts for nothing under the "winner-take-all" scheme for allocating state electoral ballots.

The electoral college has had many critics and many indictments. One charge is that the electoral college permits a presidential candidate to win the

---

[96] The electoral college, in fact, no longer meets as a unit. The state delegations meet in their respective states after the presidential elections, cast their ballots, and forward them to the President of the Senate in Washington. There is also a curious inconsistency in present electoral college practices. All states legally require that the entire state vote be given to the winner of the state presidential election—splitting the vote in proportion to the actual candidate votes among the electorate is not permitted—yet few states legally require individuals on an electoral college slate to vote for the man they have ostensibly pledged to support. Occasionally, a few state electors bolt their own slate and cast a ballot for another candidate, although this has not been a serious problem in recent years.

White House even if he represents only a plurality rather than an absolute majority of the popular votes; such critics prefer an electoral system in which a president is backed by a clear majority (50 percent plus one, at least) of the popular vote. To support this argument, they point out that since 1824 the United States has had fifteen Presidents who received less than 50 percent of the popular vote, yet won an electoral college majority.[97]

Critics, again emphasizing how the electoral college can distort the popular vote, point out that under certain conditions it is possible for a minority candidate—one who does not receive even a plurality of the popular vote—to become president. This has happened only twice in our history: when Samuel J. Tilden (1876) and Grover Cleveland (1888) each won a plurality of the popular vote but lost in the electoral college. And such an event is not inconceivable again, but it would be likely only if one candidate won the electoral votes of some states by razor-thin margins while losing other states by enormous ones.

Finally, some critics emphasize that under the present electoral college rules a presidential election can be thrown into the House of Representatives for resolution, when no candidate receives a majority of the electoral college vote. Such an event, the argument runs, would have doleful consequences. It would undermine the political effectiveness of the eventual winner (who could not claim an electoral victory), would open the door to Congressional intrigues and "bargains," and would generally cloud public confidence in the President and his administration.

Defenders of the electoral college argue that many of these objections are hypothetical and that the electoral college has generally performed well. They point out that most presidents chosen under the system have been competent or better, that only once—in 1876—did a candidate with an absolute majority of the popular vote fail to win the White House, and that the likelihood of a presidential election being thrown into the House of Representatives is actually remote.

As the debate has continued over many decades, a number of reform proposals have been made. The least radical proposal has been to divide a state's electoral college vote among presidential candidates in as close proportion to the popular vote as possible. Under this plan, for instance, if the two major party candidates divided the state popular vote 57 to 43 percent, then the state's electoral college vote would be divided as close to these proportions as possible. This would mean, in substance, that votes for minority candidates would not be "wasted" and that candidates would be encouraged to campaign even in states where they do not expect to win a plurality in the hope of combining various minority votes into an important voting bloc. A more radical proposal would be to assign one elector to each Congressional district in a state, with the candidate winning a plurality of the Congressional district vote gaining the electoral vote;

---

[97] The most recent is Richard Nixon, who received 43.6 percent of the popular vote in 1968. For the others, see Congressional Quarterly Service, *op. cit.,* p. 67.

usually some extra electoral votes would be given to the candidate who wins the state-wide contest. Finally, the most radical proposal has been to abolish the electoral college entirely, turning the United States into one gigantic electoral district where the candidate with a plurality of the general election vote wins office. According to another variation, if no candidate receives a majority of the popular vote, then a run-off should be held between the two leading contenders.

There is a certain familiarity about these current debates. Proposals for a district plan of presidential electors have been made since the first Congress. Ideas about dividing state electoral votes proportionally to the popular vote and bills to abolish the electoral college entirely have appeared almost without interruption in Congress since 1932. The electoral college, like most other Constitutional arrangements, has a peculiar, and not entirely explicable tenacity. Change may come. Yet this political dinosaur has amazing perseverance. Americans, in spite of their love for change and progress, seem reluctant to part with this institution when the actual decision must be made.

The Impact of the System

Any nominating and electing system is bound to be biased. It will favor some candidates over others, give advantage to some political groups at others' expense, encourage campaign styles conducive to winning under the electoral rules while inhibiting campaign techniques that prove unproductive. So it is with nominations and elections in the United States.

It seems clear that the American system usually gives an electoral advantage to candidates who reject rigid ideologies, who have the instinct for compromise and bargaining that builds a broad electoral following, who move toward the moderate, middle-range political opinions among their constituents. Conversely, the way is hard for the ideological candidate, for the candidate unprepared to barter and compromise, for the candidate espousing extreme political opinions. The result of this bias, particularly in presidential elections but also in most Congressional contests, is that ideological differences between the major party candidates are blurred and the alternative policies they propose are seldom sharply differentiated. Rather, the nominees ordinarily seek to embrace such a wide range of voting groups and political opinions that they are usually pulled toward moderate center positions on most political issues and discouraged from drawing their platforms too precisely and unequivocally.

The American nominating and electing system is also effective in creating electoral majorities for candidates but seldom produces a clear "mandate" for the winners. Although a winning candidate is usually backed by at least a plurality (and ordinarily an absolute majority) in his constituency, it is often extremely difficult or impossible to decipher what policy preferences—if any— this majority is attempting to communicate to the winner. Candidates often take ambiguous positions on major policy questions while declaring themselves on a wide range of issues; therefore, it is difficult to ascertain which issues or what positions were most significant to voters. Moreover, Americans often vote for the same candidate for quite different reasons. They may select a candidate because they are emotionally attached to the party label, because they favor the man, because they believe he takes a particular position on policy, because they presume specific group benefits will flow from one man's selection over another, or for no reason more substantial than "the nature of the times"—and there can be many combinations of these motivations. Though there are exceptions, especially when candidate choices represent sharply different policy positions, most of the time in American politics the nominating and electing system serves far better for designating what individual or party the electorate wants in office rather than *what* it expects the winner to do.

The campaigns for nomination and election to major political office are also becoming so expensive that it is increasingly difficult for candidates with modest resources to make an effective bid for election. In any democracy, some initial advantage will lie with the candidate who has more of whatever resource a successful campaign requires—money, status, influential associates, media support, or whatever. But as campaign expenses continue to soar, propelled by the cost of television advertising, the extreme length of many electoral contests, and the inflationary spiral, the number of individuals who have the resources to make effective bids for office may diminish to the relatively few who are truly affluent—or who have wealthy collaborators. This problem is especially acute in the presidential contest where the prohibitive cost of mounting a serious drive for the White House seems destined to reduce access to the presidency to a handful of candidates. This trend is not inevitable—the government could take steps that might alleviate the cost to candidates of presidential campaigns—but it is a major direction of current political campaigns.

Finally, American nomination and election arrangements seem most likely to produce major parties and political leaders that favor incrementalism and moderate political change over radical innovation and sharp discontinuities in policy. These arrangements seem designed to inhibit the "polarization" of the major parties into extremely divergent bands of leaders and followers, each band pledged to distinctly different and possibly irreconcilable policy positions. Most elections in the United States, as a result, do not become "crisis" contests, in which the policy outcomes of one candidate's victory over the other are so different that a large group of people feels threatened. Not suprisingly, therefore, those who favor moderate political change and fear too great a policy rift between the major parties are likely to defend existing electoral arrangements or to call only for modest reforms that do not undercut the bias of the system. But those who feel that major new directions in public policy are imperative, who are impatient with the pace of existing change, and who decry the lack of policy conflict among the major parties are likely to find many aspects of the electoral system unsatisfactory.

8

Policy Making in the Federal Government: A Comparative Overview

Dominating all state and local governments in the United States, the federal government stands at the epicenter of policy-making decisions: how to maintain order, how to facilitate social change, and how a society's resources will be allocated. It is this policy making that concerns us here and in the following three chapters. First, in this chapter, we will compare the American policy-making process to those of other nations. Second, we shall offer some very generalized descriptions of the total policy-making pattern within Washington, which, because they are generalized, allow us to see an overall design. Then, in succeeding chapters, we shall turn to the three familiar branches of the federal government and consider in greater detail how policy develops within them and what place they occupy in the broader pattern of federal policy making.

Why the Rules Matter

In all but the most primitive societies, many different policy-making procedures exist, each with its different rules. In the United States, for example, formal rules determine how a bill will be passed through Congress, how the courts must hear cases, and how the president must go through the cumbersome process of preparing a budget. Moreover, besides these formal rules, informal or unofficial procedures also exist. These are necessary if governments are to function effectively, for each new decision cannot be a "happening" with an entirely new and unpredictable set of participants and procedures.

The Rules Apportion
Advantages in Policy Making

In any political system, some interests are so powerful that they must be given a voice in governmental policy making. But governmental policy-making arrangements almost never give equal advantages to all participants in policy making. Rather, some interests gain more advantages from the arrangements than others, and hence the rules work to their benefit. Policy-making rules almost invariably create these inequalities of advantage among those participating; to alter the rules usually means redistributing inequalities rather than eliminating them. Nothing about governmental policy making is more significant than the fact that the rules are almost always "loaded" to the advantage of some interests over others.[1]

Because disparities of advantage do result from the policy-making rules, the rules become crucial and often contentious to those involved. Those who believe the rules work to their disadvantage will ordinarily attack and change them if possible; those who feel benefited by the arrangements will defend them. And the abolition of some established rule—or the possibility of alteration—will often set off a conflict among those affected as they attempt to arrange procedures to their differing advantages. Thus, arguments about what policy-making rules should be or how they should be changed are power struggles between interests sure to gain or lose advantage by the outcome.

The following two brief examples suggest how these special advantages are created. The informal "seniority rule" used in both houses of Congress gives Southern Senators and Congressmen a distinct advantage in becoming committee chairmen; since committee chairmen wield enormous power in the legislative process, Southern interests benefit accordingly.[2] The advantage arises because

---

[1] Social analysts have long recognized that governmental structures are instruments for apportioning power and for doing so inequitably, consequently the literature on this topic is voluminous. A useful summary and exploration of the impact of structural arrangements on political power and influence can be found in Joyce M. Mitchell and William C. Mitchell, *Political Analysis and Public Policy* (Chicago: Rand, McNally & Co., 1969), particularly Chapters 8–11 and their extensive bibliographies.

[2] The implications of the seniority system are explored in Donald R. Matthews, *U.S. Senators and Their World* (New York: Vintage Books, 1960), Chapters 5–7; and Nicholas A. Masters, "Committee Assignments," *American Political Science Review* (June 1961), pp. 345–357.

the Democrats have normally controlled both houses of Congress in recent years and because of the peculiarities of one-party politics in the South. The "seniority rule" awards the committee chairmanship to the committee member from the majority party who has the longest record of continuous service in that chamber. In the past, most Southern legislators have been Democrats. Coming from "safe" one-party districts where they have seldom faced a serious Republican challenge, many Southern legislators have served for a long time and, as members of the majority party, have often risen to committee chairmanships faster than legislators from other areas. Small wonder, therefore, that legislators anxious to reduce Southern influence in Congress have attacked the seniority system and that Southern interests have stoutly defended it.

Those wishing to restrict the president's ability to make major military and diplomatic commitments without congressional scrutiny, debate, and approval have been frustrated by the president's power to make "executive agreements." Unlike formal treaties, which the president is required by the Constitution to submit to the Senate for its "advice and consent," these executive agreements need no formal congressional approval, even though such agreements may have the status and substance of a treaty. Since President Jefferson, acting without any congressional approval, authorized American negotiators to purchase all of the Louisiana Territory (doubling the size of the new United States) in 1803, executive agreements have been intermittently attacked whenever the policies they furthered incurred the ire of congressional opponents. Particularly since World War II, congressional opponents of expansive presidential power in diplomatic and military matters have repeatedly attacked executive agreements. These attacks came closest to victory in February 1954 when the Bricker Amendment, which would have prevented the president from signing executive agreements without prior congressional approval, failed passage in the Senate by a single vote. No legislation since the Bricker Amendment has threatened the president's powers to make executive agreements so gravely, but growing congressional dissatisfaction in recent years with presidential management of the Vietnamese conflict has resulted in renewed demands that presidential initiative in making military and diplomatic agreements be restricted. Still, presidential power to make executive agreements remains intact and the president consequently continues to enjoy this major means of sidestepping congressional approval on major foreign policy matters.

The Rules Shape the Outcome

The rules determine or powerfully influence what policies can be made. In this perspective, every policy-making arrangement makes some results more likely than others, some kinds of decisions easier to reach than others. One can see how the policy-making process is "loaded" in favor of some decisions over others by observing the presidency.[3] We shall later note that there are actually two presidencies: the military-diplomatic role and the legislative-administrative role.[4] Because the Constitution gives the president great initiative and independence in conducting military and foreign policy, in these areas he can be much more assured that policy will represent his views and interests. In domestic affairs, however, the Constitution forces the president to share his powers much more extensively with Congress; he must often bargain and compromise with many interest groups and congressional factions; therefore, his domestic policy will represent a consensus between himself and Congress; it will be much more compromised than might be the case in military or foreign affairs. Indeed, if one examines the way in which all governmental policy-making is prescribed by the Constitution, it seems clear that the framers wanted to maximize bargaining and compromise and that they favored the creation of policies representing a common denominator between conflicting interests; the result is a system that produces moderate, middle-of-the-road policy much of the time.[5]

Though they may never use the term "structural bias"—many preferring more pungent and passionate language—many young Americans have transferred this issue into a national debate. They find this bias offensive. These young people see the system as stacked against the poor, the black, the unorganized minorities, the underprivileged, and the young. To them, it looks like a system unable or unwilling to accommodate the need for rapid, massive alteration in the basic social and economic structure of American society which they argue is now imperative. They view the system as one which promotes old men and conservatives to power in Congress through seniority, caters only to established interest groups who all have a stake in the *status quo,* and, at a time of a senseless war and need for social change at home, places the presidency in the hands of a middle-aged, largely unperceptive, white middle America as well as the white South. Many of these young people, therefore, see a system which will not deal with those who demand radical change, oppose the "military-industrial complex," and espouse rapid innovation.[6] Some even argue that if they cannot be heard through the established rules of the game, then civil disobedience, street protests, even riots must be used until the system responds; the

---

[3] The theoretical relationship of a decision-making structure to the possible policy consequences is explored in Herbert A. Simon, *Administrative Behavior,* 2nd ed. (New York: The Free Press, 1965), particularly pp. 61–78. An interesting examination of how structural bias affects conflict resolution in the United States may be found in E. E. Schattschneider, *The Semi-Sovereign People* (New York: Holt, Rinehart and Winston, 1960), Chapter 2.

[4] Aaron Wildavsky, "The Two Presidencies," *Trans*-action (December 1966), pp. 7–14.

[5] This pluralist bias in the American governmental structure is most fully explored in Robert A. Dahl, *A Preface to Democratic Theory* (Chicago: University of Chicago Press, 1956).

[6] A thorough, carefully reasoned critique of existing American pluralism is made by Theodore Lowi, *The End of Liberalism* (New York: W. W. Norton & Co., 1969).

street becomes a forum, the protest march a symbol, the rhetoric of revolution the idiom. Perhaps one can see most vividly the importance of the rules of the game when they are presented in such a dramatic way.

The Rules Express Values

There is another, frequently overlooked but crucial way in which the rules of the game are not neutral: every design for decision-making expresses in some way ideas about what is good and desirable in political life. Often, value judgments about what government should or should not do are assumed to enter into decision-making only when a particular policy choice must be made. When one must decide, for instance, whether it is better to expend scarce resources on fighting environmental pollution or acquiring a technologically new set of arms, one is clearly faced with a value problem: which program is more important? Yet *how* decisions are to be made is also a function of similar value judgments.

Totalitarian political systems—such as that of the Soviet Union or, earlier, of Germany during the Hitler era—usually develop major governmental policy within a closed system that confines participation and information to high-ranking members of the single national political party, representatives of the administrative apparatus, and a select group of others. The mass public first hears of policy decisions only after they are completed. This indicates a judgment that the conduct of political affairs should be confined to a small group of men who have the right to rule because, as the vanguard of the proletariat, they will promote the proletarian revolution and build the proletarian state on behalf of the working class, or because as the guardians of the superior Aryan race they will preserve its purity and expand its rule over inferior races. This elitist, anti-democratic attitude views the public as something to be manipulated, without any legitimate role in the fashioning of policy. In contrast, the procedural rules in American politics were created to reflect the commitment to democratic values: broad suffrage (albeit limited at first by property and religious requirements, later by racial discrimination in the South), a competitive two-party system, regular elections, interest group representation, and such freedoms as the right of assembly and free speech.

Moreover, the greatest good was thought to lie in a pluralistic power struggle within the social and political system. American politics was organized so that a broad range of different social groups, interests, and political institutions would compete for power; governmental policies would result from this pluralistic power struggle. Interests would organize to influence policy, parties would compete for power; both would try to win new votes by satisfying the demands of many different social and economic groups. In the end, this would create widespread satisfaction with the system and an ability to change with circumstances.

Many modern critics of this system question that a significant degree of democracy has actually been achieved by these arrangements. Some argue that even if the United States has democratic procedures—trial by jury, popular elections, and the freedoms guaranteed by the Bill of Rights—it has failed to produce a government that serves "the people." The nation, they argue, has yet to provide all men with equal opportunities for personal fulfillment, a decent living standard, and a wholesome environment—which should be the basic living conditions in any democracy. Some critics even argue that procedural democracy in the United States is largely a sham; they point to the "bosses" who, they claim, control parties and nominating conventions, and to the apparent inability of the system's opponents to obtain a fair trial, as support for their contentions.

Other critics, taking a different line, argue that permitting the widest latitude for pluralism to govern political life does not produce the greatest good for the greatest number. Fundamentally, critics of American pluralism often assert that while there may be a pluralistic competition in American politics, it is competition among those already committed to the system, principally middle- and upper-class Americans. By this reasoning, many important minorities are not represented in the pluralistic struggle, or if they are represented, they are not sufficiently organized to gain significant access or influence with policy-makers. Who, then, is represented? Essentially, the corporate interests, the labor unions, the more affluent farmers, the professional people, and others in the higher social strata; the underprivileged, the black, the poor, consumers, or citizens worried about environmental pollution are not represented well, if at all. In this light, two political scientists suggest that the political system often makes "nondecisions" through which demands to change the existing distribution of benefits and privileges are squashed and the existing inequalities of influence and representation in the pluralistic struggle are perpetuated.[7] In brief, these arguments suggest that "all forms of political organization have a bias in favor of the exploration of some kinds of conflict and the suppression of others because *organization is the mobilization of bias.*"[8] In the United States, so the argument concludes, the bias of pluralism is clearly toward the most privileged and socially conservative Americans.

In different ways, both critics and defenders of American pluralism acknowledge that any set of political rules will express ideas concerning what is good or bad in political life and, in the end, will realize some values at the cost of excluding others; the argument hinges on what is achieved or thwarted by the existing pluralistic struggle. But in a larger perspective, to argue for some particular rule of the game is always to make a value judgment about what ought to be. It is realistic, therefore, to be concerned not only with values in government when a particular policy is discussed, but also with the way

---

[7] Peter Bacharach and Morton S. Baratz, *Power and Poverty* (New York: Oxford University Press, 1970), pp. 44–45.

[8] Schattschneider, *op. cit.*, p. 71.

decisions are made. One must examine which values are—intentionally or not —embodied in the process, since no decision-making system is, or can be, unbiased.

The Characteristics of Federal Policy Making

Though decision making in Washington is extremely varied and complex, certain characteristics consistently recur and, as we would expect, end in creating a particular distribution of advantages, a certain policy-bias, the affirmation of certain values in day-to-day decision-making. Of these, the following ones seem most important and, hence, merit special consideration.

Decentralized Power

Behind the constitutional design of the national government lies what Robert Dahl has called a "fundamental axiom" that powerfully shapes the whole policy-making process. "Instead of a single center of sovereign power, there must be multiple centers of power, none of which is or can be wholly sovereign."[9]

Many considerations inclined the Constitution's writers to favor a national government that dispersed, fragmented, and divided power and authority within it, a situation that would result in setting "power against power." First, their view was that men are not angels; countervailing power was the best assurance against abuse of power by any single institution or individual.[10] This sensitivity to overpowerful government was reinforced by their experience with the English Crown before the Revolution. Second, they suspected that governments, like machines, should be "checked and balanced" internally for maximum effectiveness.

Also, there were practical political calculations. To secure ratification, the Constitution would have to draw the approval of at least 11 state legislatures who differed on many sectional, economic, racial, and religious interests. One constant strategy used by the Convention to marshal support for the new document was to divide and disperse power among a great many governmental institutions and officials in such a way that most major interests felt themselves

---

[9] Robert A. Dahl, *Pluralist Democracy in the United States* (Chicago: Rand, McNally & Co., 1967), p. 24.

[10] This view, currently called "Madisonian politics," is most fully examined in Dahl, *A Preface to Democratic Theory*. A useful examination and critique of this view may be found in George D. Beam, *Usual Politics* (New York: Holt, Rinehart and Winston, 1970), especially Chapters 1, 3, 5, 6, and 7.

protected in some way by the arrangements. Many state and sectional interests, for example, were brought to favor the Constitution by its division of Congress into two houses to be apportioned and elected differently, in a manner that gave significant representation to small and large states, Northern and Southern ones, great sectional interests, the states themselves, and local electorates. But the two master strategies for dividing and decentralizing power were—and in many respects still are—the separation of powers and federalism.[11]

"Separation of powers" is often called the "horizontal" division of power in the federal government because it apportions power across the federal level between different institutions. Most often this horizontal division of power is described as a trinity—there are three separate branches of government called executive, legislative, and judicial; more familiarly, they are called the presidency, Congress, and the courts. This is far too simple a description; the way power is divided across the federal government is actually more complex and merits brief explanation so its true intricacy can be appreciated. Perhaps the most significant division of power in comparative terms is the separation of the executive and legislative branches into two different institutions, each separate in the sense that neither depends upon the other for its existence, and each possesses a different electoral base and powers guaranteed to it by the Constitution itself. For instance, Congress alone is granted the constitutional authority to apportion money, to tax, and to legislate, while the president is the nation's military commander-in-chief with all the powers associated with this position.

This description of our federal government's separate branches gives too little attention, however, to the fact that in our government, these separate institutions must *share* power.[12] For example, the president can veto legislation and propose it, thus sharing in the legislative process; Congress, through its ability to appropriate funds for the executive branch, can and often does limit what programs the president can achieve within his own departments or through them. And, of course, the federal judiciary has the ability to declare acts of the president or Congress unconstitutional. Or—as happened with respect to school desegregation many times since 1954—the judiciary can prod Congress and the president to act more swiftly or resolutely in implementing a policy. In mid-1969, for instance, the Supreme Court, in a series of rulings, ordered immediate, full-speed integration of school districts at a time when the president reportedly favored lessening the pressure for immediate integration. In these and other ways power is dispersed, yet it overlaps the three ostensibly separate branches of the government. This means that many institutions and individuals ordinarily participate in federal policy-making, and policy-making on great national issues and

---

[11] A useful general account of the Constitution's creation and the ideas that inspired it is in Charles Warren, *The Making of the Constitution* (Boston: Little, Brown and Co., 1928); on federalism see Kenneth C. Wheare, *Federal Government* (London: Oxford University Press, 1953).

[12] Richard E. Neustadt, *Presidential Power* (New York: John Wiley, 1960), p. 33 ff.

programs can proceed effectively only when these various institutions are brought into some reasonably workable coalition.

When the Constitution was written, this creation of separate executive and legislative branches, especially the creation of something called the "presidency," was unprecedented. Today,· according to several estimates, there are 34 nations with a significant division of powers between an executive and a legislative branch; among western nations, about 17 of 51 have such a division.[13] Interestingly, where such divisions of executive and legislative authority occur, a presidency of some kind is usually created; some of them resemble the American presidency in powers and authority, though most are less powerful.[14]

Throughout much of the world, no such formal separation of the legislative and executive authority exists. At least 33 nations have a "parliamentary" system (20 in the west) in which the Prime Minister is elected by a majority of the legislature (usually a parliament); he then selects his cabinet. Formally, all these members of the cabinet are members of the parliament itself.[15] When parliamentary systems function effectively, as in Great Britain, this fusion of executive and legislative branches means that the prime minister and his cabinet has a dependable party majority in the parliament. It can therefore usually plan and implement a program with the assurance of legislative support and not encounter the rivalry and conflict that frequently emerges when the executive and legislative branches are independent of each other for their existence and much of their power. By apportioning power between a separate executive and legislative institution, therefore, the American Constitution encourages institutional rivalry and conflict between the executive and legislative branches of the government—in fact, it almost guarantees it.

Political power is also decentralized and dispersed in the United States because our system is based on federalism—the "vertical" division of power within the government. This means power is apportioned between the various levels of government—national, state, and local. Basically, political power is arranged "vertically" in the United States in such a way that there are fifty state governments whose existence does not depend upon the federal government and who exercise many powers independent of the federal government.[16] Furthermore, in a great many matters affecting citizens of the country—commerce, taxing, justice, welfare, health, and transportation, for example—both federal and state governments exercise powers; in this respect, American federalism has become a governmental system with "a strong national government coupled with

---

[13] This estimate by Arthur S. Banks and Robert B. Textor, *A Cross-Polity Survey* (Cambridge: Massachusetts Institute of Technology Press, 1963).

[14] A brief but useful survey of these other presidencies is contained in Austin Ranney, *The Governing of Men* (New York: Holt, Rinehart and Winston, 1966), p. 447 ff.

[15] Banks and Textor, *op. cit.*

[16] An excellent survey of federalism's role in national political organization is Kenneth C. Wheare, "Federalism and the Making of Nations," in Arthur W. MacMahon (ed.), *Federalism, Mature and Emergent* (New York: Russell and Russell, Inc., 1962).

strong state governments in which authority and power are shared, constitutionally and practically."[17]

The existence of federalism, of course, increases the number of places in American society where political power can be gathered and exercised to some extent independently of the federal government. The resulting conflict between the states and federal government has undoubtedly been exaggerated; and "cooperative federalism," in which state and national governments work in considerable harmony, has not received the same attention in the media. Nevertheless, the existence of a federal system multiplies and disperses political power in the nation, vastly increases the range of interests and governments that must be brought into federal policy-making, and creates numerous places where opposition to federal policies can be organized and expressed.

Unlike the United States, very few of the world's nations use any form of federalism. Among those that do, the United States is singular for the size of its federal structure. By the best current estimate, only eight nations in the world have any significant divisions of powers between a national government and local governments that give to local governments any important measure of political independence or autonomy; they are Australia, Brazil, Cameroon, Canada, West Germany, Switzerland, Uganda, and the United States.[18] Among them, the United States has easily the most complex federal structure in the number of governmental units involved, the size of the polity, and the number of individuals affected.

The Soviet Union provides an interesting contrast to the constitutionally imposed fragmentation of power within the United States. While the Soviet Union is formally a federal republic, national political power is in fact concentrated within a relatively small and well defined cadre of individuals, most of whom represent the great institutional powers in Soviet politics—the party, the governmental bureaucracy, and the army. Indeed, following the assumption that this top echelon does control most of Soviet political life, one favorite way of analyzing and interpreting Soviet politics has been "Kremlinology," which attempts to discern the shape of Soviet policy by studying the divisions between hawks and doves, Stalinists and anti-Stalinists, and the various strengths, weaknesses, and idiosyncrasies of those within this circle.[19] Even if this inner circle falls short of the absolute control over Soviet society implied by the term "totalitarian," Kremlinologists assume that its powers are sufficiently great that no major decision in any sphere of Soviet life can be taken without its knowledge and approval.

---

[17] Daniel J. Elazar, *American Federalism: A View from the States* (New York: Thomas Y. Crowell Co., 1966), pp. 3–4.

[18] Estimate by Banks and Textor, *op. cit.* The number of polities which have a formal (as distinguished from effective) federal system is about seventeen, including the Soviet Union.

[19] Two excellent examples of Kremlinology may be found in Robert Conquest, *Power and Policy in the U.S.S.R.* (New York: St. Martin's Press, 1961); and Michael Tatu, *Power in the Kremlin: From Khrushchev to Kosygin* (New York: The Viking Press, 1969).

In the Soviet system, political power pyramids to the top; the most important struggles over policy and position in national politics occur within this top echelon. This struggle may become more overt and clearer to us when a succession crisis erupts following the death or removal of the leader, but it continues even when the leadership seems settled. One normally rises by eliminating one's opponents—physically in the old Stalinist days, bureaucratically now. Stalin murdered most of his former associates and rivals, Khrushchev purged from power many of those who had helped him attain it, and Brezhnev and Kosygin first deposed and then denounced their former mentor, Nikita Khrushchev. The requisites for getting ahead in the Soviet system seem to be an enormous appetite for power and a total dedication to achieve it (risking the unpleasant consequences of losing), a single-minded ruthlessness that permits one to survive and gain promotion by denouncing colleagues, as well as an intense suspicion of others.[20]

In Great Britain, too, power is highly centralized in the hands of the Prime Minister, his cabinet, and the administrative bureaucracy. Unlike in the United States, individual members of the legislature (Parliament) are relatively unimportant in national politics. Half of the Parliament—the House of Lords, or upper chamber—is composed of members sitting by virtue of titles who today have little influence in the conduct of government. In the lower chamber, the House of Commons, the candidates who stand for election do so as loyal members of a disciplined party and the British electorate is conscious that in voting for individual candidates they are actually choosing the government because the leader of the majority party in the House will become the Prime Minister and his leading party colleagues the cabinet.

British parliamentary elections are really contests between party leaders; the voter expresses his preference for a government by voting for candidates to the House of Commons. It is the party leaders who establish the programs and issues upon which the election will be decided (and upon which, therefore, the fate of the party's candidates will depend). While the Prime Minister is normally backed by a dependable and cohesive majority party in the House, this does not mean—as we shall see below—that he is inattentive to the dissenting opinions of his parliamentary party colleagues upon whom he depends for office. Yet the practice of voting with the party and deference to the executive leadership is so deeply entrenched that it is extraordinarily rare for members of the majority party to deviate from the leadership on crucial votes.[21]

Even though political power is fragmented and decentralized in the United States while it is centralized—albeit in different ways—in Great Britain and the Soviet Union, the conduct of political life in these three systems has become

---

[20] For comments that suggest how the personal experiences of Soviet leaders affect their attitude toward one another as well as the outside world, see Henry Kissinger's article "Domestic Structure and Foreign Policy," reprinted in his book, *American Foreign Policy* (New York: W. W. Norton & Co., 1969), pp. 36–37.

[21] On the tradition of party regularity, see R. T. McKenzie, *British Political Parties* (New York: St. Martin's Press, 1955), Chapters 3 and 7.

fairly routine, the rules are generally settled and a political formula has developed. In many of the new nations of Afro-Asia, the rules have yet to crystallize; they are still fluid and unpredictable. In a sense, these economically underdeveloped nations are *politically* underdeveloped also.

In these nations, modernization leads to greater political consciousness and participation in public affairs by the various ethnic, linguistic, racial, and religious groups. Consequently, demands on the political system multiply. But most of the ex-colonial states do not possess any effective institutional framework to conciliate and mediate the conflict that results; charismatic personal leaders, normally supported by a single party or military rule then substitute for the absent or ineffective institutions of government. Conflicting groups often use whatever means seem most immediately effective in achieving their demands: "The wealthy bribe; students riot; workers strike; mobs demonstrate; and the military 'coup.' "[22] In the absence of accepted and legitimate procedures, therefore, direct action becomes normal; instability and violence become commonplace.

The Pluralistic Power Struggle

Another feature of Washington policy-making is that it is also institutionally a pluralistic power struggle, because at any level within a branch of the federal government, or in the relationship between the various branches, there are many actors, interests, and values involved in policy-making. A multitude of competing institutional interests is normal and conflict between them therefore permeates the government. In this respect, decision-making on the Potomac follows a common pattern, for this is true in almost all modern governments, however much it may be concealed.

The true extent of pluralism and conflict within governmental institutions is often obscured by the language of political discourse, by misconception, and by the deliberate effort of political leaders to camouflage it. As literary fiction, it is convenient to talk of governments as if they were persons with a single will—"The Soviet Union turned down a proposal . . . ," "Washington agreed that . . ."—but, of course, such personification is not realistic.

Perhaps only the very naive and uninformed fall into this error, yet others may uncritically accept a more subtle version: they recognize that governments incorporate many individuals and institutions yet assume that when policy is declared, the government can arrive at a collective consensus and purpose—that a monolithic "we" has spoken. Most governmental leaders often seek to create this illusion of agreement within government or within particular agencies to minimize or obscure internal dissent. Totalitarian nations have probably gone

---

[22] Samuel P. Huntington, *Political Order in Changing Societies* (New Haven: Yale University Press, 1969), p. 196.

farthest in concealing from public view the true nature of their governmental internal decision-making with the inevitable clash of interests; they are armed with a controlled press, a carefully supervised (and often intimidated) bureaucracy, a disciplined party apparatus, and political police. Policy is announced and the monolithic "we" seems to have spoken.

What are the major interests and actors involved in the pluralistic struggle within the federal government? First, there are three major branches of the federal structure—the executive, legislative, and the judiciary. Each branch has elected and appointed members who usually nourish ideas about where their branch of government should fit into the over-all decision-making process and what interests it should protect and pursue.[23] Also, *within* the various branches of the federal government, an enormous number of institutions, units, and individuals compete with each other and pursue conflicting interests. The executive branch, for example, contains twelve major departments whose leadership and personnel are usually committed to their various departmental programs and perspectives; even a single department includes several hundred smaller units— bureaus and agencies—who may have different objectives.[24] The Department of Defense, perhaps the most extreme example of interdepartmental division, is itself a conglomerate of three other departments—the Army, Navy, and Air Force—any one of which exceeds many other departments of the federal executive branch in budget and personnel.[25] Furthermore, the president, his advisors, special administrative assistants, and staff form the "Executive Office of the President" with its own political objectives, interests, and goals to pursue within the larger executive structure; between the president's men on one side and the permanent departments and bureaucracy on the other, there are often divisions, conflict, and disagreement.[26] Though Congress is a much smaller institution than the executive branch, it too, is pluralistic; there are divisions of interest between various committees in both houses, between party groups, between the houses of Congress, between constituencies.

To these divisions between major branches and within them must be added

---

[23] The crosscutting loyalties of individuals to different governmental institutions and the results are explored in James McGregor Burns, *The Deadlock of Democracy* (Englewood Cliffs, N.J.: Prentice-Hall, 1963).

[24] Bureaucratic units customarily develop a vested interest in their own institutional survival and an institutionally-related value system as they mature. The development and consequences of this "bureaucratic ideology" is nicely summarized in Anthony Downs, *Inside Bureaucracy* (Boston: Little, Brown and Co., 1967), pp. 237–246.

[25] And the Defense Department is an organizational arena in which the three separate services compete constantly on every dimension of bureaucratic politics. Among many studies that focus on this matter, two useful ones are Samuel P. Huntington, *The Common Defense* (New York: Columbia University Press, 1961); and Jack Raymond, *Power at the Pentagon* (New York: Harper & Row, Publishers, 1964).

[26] The conflicts between the presidential advisors and the bureaucracy have been amply documented. A good, brief account is Peter Woll, *American Bureaucracy* (New York: W. W. Norton & Co., 1963), Chapter 5. Many aspects of this matter are also touched on in the collection of essays by Thomas E. Cronin and Sanford D. Greenberg, *The Presidential Advisory System* (New York: Harper and Row, Publishers, 1969).

the pluralism that results from many "subgovernments" that link various individuals across institutional lines in various alliances. Within the federal government, many such coalitions between Congressional committees, agencies within the bureaucracy, and interest groups collectively exercise major control over special policy areas.[27] Moreover, several thousand organized pressure groups seek to influence governmental policy-making; very often these become the clientele groups of the major federal departments and agencies, aggressively seeking a voice within the administrative units concerned with their special interests.

Why this institutional pluralistic power struggle? Answers lie in the nature of western societies and government mentioned earlier. American society, like almost all other societies, is pluralistic; political interests, economic groups, life styles, and other signs of social differentiation continue to multiply. Equally important, as government "penetrates" societies, almost all important social problems become political ones. In the United States, therefore, the larger pluralistic conflicts in the society are often projected through the government.

Important as cultural pluralism and governmental "penetration" may be in explaining the clash of interests within the federal government, the nature of government itself should not be underestimated as a cause. Fragmentation of power has occurred in the federal branch because our government, like other western governments, has become bureaucratized to the point where the federal administrative apparatus is the largest, most expensive, most complex of all the governmental branches. Creating bureaucracy means creating and multiplying institutions that, like organizations everywhere, develop a vested interest in their own survival. These institutions within the government—departments, agencies, bureaus, and the rest—are clusters of individuals who usually develop very strong identification with their own organizational units; committed to the organization's survival and prosperity, the personnel within the federal administrative structure become an interest in their own right ready to struggle within the government for their daily bread in the form of personnel, prestige, and (most important) a share of the budget.[28] Thus, conflict in institutions—not only interdepartmental but also intradepartmental—adds yet another significant element to the competition between interests within the federal government.

Coalition Building

The result of this inter-governmental pluralism is that policy must be formed, as a rule, through both conflict and consensus-building. The conflicts are

---

[27] These "subgovernments" are described and analyzed by J. Leiper Freeman, *The Political Process: Executive Bureau-Legislative Committee Relations,* revised edition (New York: Random House, 1965).

[28] This institutional rivalry can be seen with great clarity during the process of presidential budget-making. See, for example, Aaron Wildavsky, *The Politics of the Budgetary Process* (Boston: Little, Brown and Co., 1964), Chapters 2 and 3.

obvious; their reconciliation through accommodation and consensus-building among the various participants will ordinarily produce policy. In short, the American policy process is one of negotiation and bargaining, the constant search for allies, of attempts to widen the base of support for programs through continuing modification of proposed policies as concessions are made to meet specific objections.[29] And coalitions appear, as well, among those intent on defeating programs.

The final "balance of power" between coalitions promoting and opposing policy normally determines who is successful in this domestic version of power politics. Since official policy always represents the victory of one coalition over another, it is quite misleading to speak of *the* government policy, in the United States or elsewhere. Quite the opposite is true: in modern governments, coalition-building is likely to spill over institutional and governmental lines, involving a great many interests and actors. Moreover, those who lose one policy battle will usually live to fight another day when, perhaps, they will be among the victors.

This pattern of policy formation through coalition-building is a common characteristic of the large bureaucratic governments found in highly urbanized, industrialized societies like the United States, but it occurs in other political settings, as well.[30] For example, behind the facade of monolithic Kremlin unity, a multiplicity of interest exists. These are not interest groups or associational interests as in the United States, for Soviet citizens are not free to create their own voluntary associations. Instead, these interests are the typical institutional interests within the government—for example the party, army, police, and industrial and agricultural interests with managers and spokesmen to represent their demands to the government. Unlike the United States, these spokesmen and the groups they represent do not have an autonomous existence. They operate instead within a system where the Communist party controls all appointments and promotions within them.[31] Furthermore, these groups do not enjoy the ability to mobilize the public directly in their support and, if necessary, against the governmental or party leadership.

Increasingly, however, these groups play an important role in Soviet policy-making, particularly in a succession crisis that follows the death or deposing of a Soviet leader. For example, after Stalin's death, each of the remaining rivals attempted to gain Stalin's previous position by appeals to various institutional interests within the government. Malenkov, the new premier, based his strategy on appeals to the governmental bureaucracy and the industrial managers plus the promise of a higher standard of living for the Soviet population. Khrushchev, the

---

[29] Roger Hilsmann, *To Move a Nation* (New York: Doubleday & Co., 1967).

[30] Zbigniew Brzezinski and Samuel P. Huntington, *Political Power: USA/USSR* (New York: The Viking Press, 1963), pp. 196–197.

[31] For a study of the making of British military policy, see William P. Snyder, *The Politics of British Defense Policy, 1945–1962* (Columbus: Ohio State University Press, 1964), especially pp. 151–177.

new party chief, built a coalition of the party organization and the military by promising to strengthen the Soviet armed forces; he then split the industrial managers by bringing the producers of military hardware to his side.[32] Khrushchev won because he was able to put together a winning coalition, not unlike the way an American presidential candidate tries to build a majority coalition among the electorate.

In a democracy, however, this coalition must be built from the various interests of the general populace—a more difficult task than winning the support of a few top men in key positions. In addition, the losers in power struggles within the Soviet government are liable to be purged, in Stalin's days often losing their lives but now normally losing their former status and spending their remaining years in obscurity. Purges of this kind are rare in western nations, especially in democracies, but peaceful attempts to ease dissidents out of government or to gag them are fairly common. Regardless of how coalitions are created, all the opposition from within can never be eradicated; at best, it can only be silenced.

Incrementalism and Crisis

With the continuous bargaining common in the federal government and the pluralistic struggles that normally ensue, it is hardly surprising that policy changes are the result of a series of minor modifications made in response to concerns of the moment. Indeed, sometimes policy moves forwards, then sideways or even backwards, only to move forward again later.[33]

One important reason for this incrementalism is that once a major policy is created and a coalition cemented behind it, the coalition is more likely to favor modification of the policy rather than another major struggle and bloodletting over a completely new policy. Moreover, forging ahead too quickly with new policies is almost sure to intensify group conflicts and to upset established political coalitions. In a sense, governments are always caught in the cross-pressuring demands that they meet urgent national problems by innovation while at the same time reconciling group conflict; often they can innovate only at the cost of group conflict, or reduce group tensions only by neglecting innovation. Very often, the tendency is to keep group conflicts at a minimum, which means putting brakes on innovation and rapid change.

[32] For an interesting analysis of the role of foreign and defense issues in the struggle between Malenkov and Khrushchev, see Herbert S. Dinerstein, *War and the Soviet Union* (New York: Praeger, 1959).

[33] The tendency toward incrementalism is analyzed and explained in Charles E. Lindblom, "The Science of 'Muddling Through'," *Public Administration Review* (Spring 1959), pp. 79–88; a more elaborate examination of this logic is found in David Braybrooke and Charles E. Lindblom, *A Strategy for Decision* (New York: The Free Press, 1963).

Thus, there is a tendency in Washington for policy-makers to concentrate upon immediate problems. This tendency to neglect long-range policies and innovation is further intensified by a pragmatic outlook among most policy-makers who prefer to deal with actual problems rather than speculative future conditions. American policy-makers often act like switchboard operators: they only answer the phones that ring. A seemingly distant problem will usually be ignored or neglected unless it reaches a crisis stage and begins "ringing."

This step-by-step policy-making, with its need to reconcile the needs of many conflicting groups and institutions, does tend to produce middle-of-the-road policies. In one way, this is highly conducive to stability in a political system. In another way, gradual, moderate policy-making is not effective in dealing with such pressing problems as racial unrest, poverty, and urban decay: civil rights policy is watered down so it does not alienate conservative groups; legislation against air and water pollution is moderated to omit punitive sanctions in deference to corporations that cannot afford to redesign and replace equipment; various policies affecting public welfare, conservation, and education are compromised in order not to disrupt the *status quo* because of the traditional prerogatives of state and local political organizations.

All this assumes that policy does move "forward" and that the bargaining process with its coalition-building does not produce stalemate and policy paralysis. At times, it does. Ironically, policy tends to be most innovative when reacting to such crises; indeed, it may be that both domestically and externally, a crisis is needed to trigger a change in the balance of forces supporting present policy—to shake alliances, to awaken a sense of danger great enough to dampen momentarily the institutional conflicts, to create a sense of urgency, creativity, and common purpose otherwise lacking or only latent among governmental units. It took a Great Depression to produce major changes in the federal government's role in the economy and society. It took a Pearl Harbor to mobilize American power to deal with the Japanese and German threats to American security. Symbolically, Franklin Roosevelt called himself "Dr. New Deal"—the president-physician who was called in to cure the ailing economy; after December 7, 1941, he changed his name to "Dr. Win-the-War." Similarly, after World War II it was the overwhelming Russian threat that allowed Truman to mobilize the country for containment; before the threat became so obvious, Truman had been unable to take such counter-measures as preventing the massive demobilization of American armed forces after World War II. Finally, it took the drama of the Negro and white sit-ins, the brutal unleashing of police dogs on blacks in Birmingham, Alabama, and the assassination of Martin Luther King to produce long overdue civil rights legislation. Just as it took Castro with his virulent anti-Americanism and attempts to stir up anti-American revolutions among other Latin American countries to produce the Alliance for Progress to ameliorate the conditions which breed revolutions, it took the ghetto riots in Detroit and Los Angeles, among other cities, to stimulate federal aid to the ghetto blacks in order to prevent a spread of Negro rioting and burning and to begin to change some of the conditions breeding widespread dissatisfaction. "Progress-through-Crisis" sums up much of the American policy process.[34]

Incrementalism may be a characteristic of all large-scale government. If there are differences, they may be differences of degree rather than of kind. The British parliamentary system, for instance, is not as immune to incrementalism as might be thought from the fact that the two British parties confront one another at election time, leaving one party a winner with a specific mandate that the Prime Minister and his cabinet can presumably transform into legislation, because they can invoke party discipline. Although they can invoke this discipline, they cannot lead their party where it does not want to go. In fact, the prime minister must first resolve differences among his cabinet members who represent different institutional and associational interests.[35] A sensible prime minister avoids policy departures unless he has the support of his cabinet ministers; otherwise, some of them would be glad to replace him.

The prime minister must also enlist the loyalty of the party's rank and file, the "backbenchers," and must therefore be sensitive to their opinions. He not only wishes for maximum support and unity from his party, but from his rivals, as well, since each of them would prefer to see himself as the party's leader. The prime minister, in short, must constantly woo his colleagues.[36] "Seldom will a prime minister try to force a decision widely and genuinely unpopular in his party. The prime minister must preserve the unity of the party, for it is not possible for him to perpetuate his rule by constructing a series of majorities whose composition varies from issue to issue [as in the United States]. He is,

---

[34] If the policy process is frequently slow and conservative, or even stalemated, this does not necessarily imply that the absence of a pluralistic struggle would produce wise and effective policies quickly. The abortive Cuban invasion of 1961 is the most dramatic evidence. The CIA, which drew up the plans, amazingly enough kept its own intelligence research branch in the dark; it was not once asked to evaluate the feasibility of the invasion devised by the Agency's leaders. The very men who proposed the invasion, and who had thereby gained a vested interest in the success of their operation, were the ones who could deny anyone the right to properly evaluate their plan. Since it was a secret operation, the State Department was also kept in the dark. Only the Secretary of State was informed and he simply acquiesced. So apparently did the Joint Chiefs of Staff who reportedly had only a superficial knowledge of the CIA's operational plans. Perhaps if there had been genuine debate among the various agencies involved, we might have avoided the oversimplification of the invasion issue, the exaggeration of the danger to American security stemming from Cuba, and the overselling of the invasion as a means to solve the issue of Castro once and for all.

[35] In this context, it has been remarked that a leader with strong views who likes to take initiative makes a worse prime minister than one who is a good compromiser and arbiter. One reason is that the prime minister is, first of all, the chairman of a committee—his cabinet—and a forceful leader may create division and friction rather than collaboration. See Byrum Carter, *The Office of Prime Minister* (Princeton: Princeton University Press, 1956), pp. 209–210.

[36] See Richard Neustadt, "White House and Whitehall" and George W. Jones, "The Prime Minister's Power" in Richard Rose (ed.), *Policy-Making in Britain* (London: Macmillan Co., 1969).

therefore, constrained to crawl along cautiously, to let situations develop until the necessity of decision blunts inclinations to quarrel about just what the decision should be."[37] The massive continuity produced in both the United States and Great Britain leads to slow adjustment to changing circumstances, policy deadlocks, and evasion of issues until they become crises. Bold new ventures are few and far between.

A more striking contrast to the United States would seem to be the Soviet system which has repeatedly demonstrated a capacity to launch significant policy innovations as well as reversals of policy directions. For example, the following policies have been instituted since 1920: the New Economic Policy (which permitted a high degree of private ownership of property and enterprise in agriculture and light industry); the succeeding five-year industrial plans; agricultural collectivization; the France-Soviet Pact followed within a few years by the Nazi-Soviet Alliance; the sudden reversal after 1945 from collaboration with the West (brought on by Hitler's attack on Russia in 1941) to hostility toward the West; then the de-Stalinization programs and "peaceful coexistence."

Stalin's absolute power for three decades and Khrushchev's relatively firm position after he had won the succession struggle seem to be one important reason for this record; when the governmental reins can be gathered largely in the hands of one man, this kind of comprehensive, deliberate policy management is possible. In future years, however, Soviet policy increasingly may also be the product of coalition and counter-coalition within the small group that constitutes the Soviet policy-making elite; as Soviet society and the economy develop, incremental and more moderate policies plus fewer major departures from established policy seem likely, at least in domestic affairs. But in foreign affairs, the Soviet Union—like the United States and Britain—will continue to be confronted by sudden and unexpected events which will create circumstances necessitating innovation and upsetting the continuity and step-by-step policy development more likely in domestic matters.

Slowness

Washington's policy-making process is customarily slow. Proposed policy is usually first discussed within the executive branch. It is circulated in the originating department and then to other interested departments, receiving clearances as it goes along, as well as modifications as it gathers broader support on its way to the president; the continual conferences and bargaining within the executive branch are obviously time consuming. The process takes even longer if it needs further Congressional and public approval.

[37] Kenneth Waltz, *Foreign Policy and Democratic Politics* (Boston: Little, Brown and Co., 1967), pp. 59–62.

If policy emerges from the executive branch, potential opponents occupy many veto points to block legislation within Congress, such as the House Rules Committee, the House and Senate committees hearing particular legislation and, naturally, the floor votes in both chambers. In domestic affairs, in fact, the advantage usually lies with those who oppose legislation because it is difficult to jump all the hurdles along the route to passage.[38] It ordinarily takes months for legislation to pass through committee hearings and committee amendments; after this, it must await scheduling on the agenda for debate and voting on the chamber floor; this obstacle course is then repeated in the second chamber. Some legislation takes years to enact. Harry Truman, for example, first proposed comprehensive medical insurance for older people in the late 1940s; it was not until well over a decade later that Medicare became law.

In foreign policy, no clearly definable veto points can be located, but the path of executive policy-making is no easier, smoother, or quicker. Because decision-making in western nations is fundamentally a matter of negotiation within a pluralistic governmental structure, the policy process is in fact a matter of multiple decisions and approvals over a period of time. Even in Moscow where no leader has held absolute power since Stalin, the presumed ability of a totalitarian system to make rapid decisions has declined as the leader has had to share some of his power with his colleagues in what the Soviets call "collective leadership."

Given this slow process and the immense effort needed to overcome formidable obstacles to pass major policy, old policies—and the old assumptions on which they are based—tend to survive longer than they should. In foreign matters, for instance, policy was based on the assumption that the communist world was monolithic even after the Russian-Chinese conflict had surfaced in the late 1950s; the preoccupation with strategic deterrence continued after the need for a limited war capacity had been painfully demonstrated by Korea. Domestically, it can be argued that urban decay, racial discrimination, environmental pollution, and overpopulation were all problems that went neglected so long that they may now be insoluble—and not only because of any systemic biases.

Noise

The American policy process, permeated by so many different interests and perspectives, is also noisy. In this intensely competitive milieu, the participants, often convinced that their proposals best advance the nation's welfare at home or its security abroad, will not remain quiet; they have ample resources for making their views heard. Only when crisis decisions must be made—when time is limited, decisions must be reached with dispatch, and secrecy is imperative— will silence and secrecy surround decision-making. But most governmental

[38] See Chapter 10 for an examination of these hurdles.

decisions are not crisis decisions. By world standards, the normal policy process in Washington is accompanied by an unusual display of public argument and debate within the government that is continually monitored by the mass media.

Charges and countercharges are made by individuals and institutional spokesmen within the government; reports on daily political affairs replete with inside stories appear in the media; policy-makers constantly proclaim their intentions; divergent views are aired before Congressional committees; street clashes and public debates occur between dissidents and defenders of a policy or institution. On occasion, one can see the public discussion reflected on that peculiarly American forum for debate, the automobile bumper: in 1969, typical slogans on bumper stickers were "No ABM," "ABM: America's Biggest Mistake," or "ABM is an Edsel." The newspaper "leak" is a venerable Washington ritual: if some public official wants to embarrass another or test public sentiment on some matter, he may use the media to make an "unofficial" disclosure.[39]

The rich diversity of information on current policy-making in Washington is revealed, for instance, in a casual survey of a daily newspaper's headlines:

> New U.S.–Saigon Friction Looms
> Air Officials, Controllers To Meet With Mediator
> Burch Doubts FCC Can Curb Commercials
> Congressmen Bar Banking Probe
> Nixon Friends Challenge TV License
> 18-Year-Olds: Should the U.S. Let Them Vote?

While such headlines may excite little reflection from most Americans, the availability of information on the internal procedures and issues current in government, the public airing of conflict by governmental officials themselves— especially when decisions are in the process of being made—would seem quite unseemly to most citizens and public servants of other countries.

Kremlinology would not be necessary if the Soviet policy process were open. Only occasionally will a newspaper headline denounce a particular leader or policy; sometimes only the protocol rank of Soviet leaders at a public function or promotion or demotion of second-rank officials provide clues about the alignment of the Soviet elite on particular issues. Vast purges, as in Russia after 1936 or in Communist China after 1965, are clear indicators of conflict. But a Great Terror or Cultural Revolution is hardly a frequent event. Even in other democracies, the open display of intergovernmental conflict is not common. The British bureaucracy may be riddled with conflict; nonetheless, it remains quiet in public. Infighting rarely becomes news. The civil servants of the Administrative

---

[39] The role of the mass media in national politics is explored in Dan D. Nimmo, *Newsgathering in Washington* (New York: Atherton Press, 1964) and, more journalistically, by Douglas Cater, *The Fourth Branch of Government* (Boston: Houghton Mifflin Co., 1959).

Class, who are the elite corps of the British civil service, and their Foreign Office counterparts simply do not allow their quarrels to become public; they are sworn to secrecy. Furthermore, they work closely with the politically appointed ministers; together the minister and the bureaucratic elites govern England as a virtual duopoly. Hence they share a mutual interest in partnership and self-restraint.[40] In any event, the British party system provides no channels for establishing links with dissatisfied backbenchers in the governing party to fight cabinet-approved policy.

If Washington policy making is noisier than in other western capitals (in underdeveloped countries, the "noise" comes primarily from direct action in the streets or from the rumble of tanks engaged in a coup) one principal reason is the "Fourth Estate"—the press, radio, and television. Independent of government, the media give the affairs of government public shape and substance; they amplify and project the arguments in Washington across the nation and interpret the complexities of government in terms meaningful to various parts of the public. Furthermore the media's business has been to poke and pry within the governmental structure, to expose governmental blunders, to become an investigator, inquisitor, and an almost constant critic of government—often to the dissatisfaction of government officials; losers in a policy struggle are only too glad to help by "leaking" information favorable to their own policy views.

The media, therefore, benefit by exploiting the continuous policy conflicts. They have a strongly vested interest in keeping the governmental noise level high.[41] By contrast, in a system like Britain's where the cabinet is sworn to secrecy and controls the legislature through the majority party, where the bureaucracy does not talk, the media have less to exploit and the policy conflicts within the government do not provide headlines as often as in this country. Headlines come essentially from the House of Commons where the two parties debate national issues once the government has decided its policy.[42]

The Importance of Public Opinion

The extent to which American governmental officials are willing to expose their conflicts and ambitions to the public, the presence of a large and politically

---

[40] Sir Ivor Jennings, *Cabinet Government* (Cambridge: University Press, 1951), pp. 110–123, and Neustadt, "White House and Whitehall," p. 293. A good journalistic description of the civil service is given by Anthony Sampson, *The Anatomy of Britain Today* (New York: Harper & Row, Publishers, 1965), pp. 249–285.

[41] For the role of the press in foreign policy issues, see Bernard C. Cohen, *The Press and Foreign Policy* (Princeton: Princeton University Press, 1963).

[42] Sampson, *op. cit.,* pp. 155–157. One merely needs to compare what Americans know about a Cuban Missile Crisis—about which journalist Elie Abel wrote the best available book, *The Missile Crisis* (New York: Bantam Books, 1968)—and how little is still known in Britain about the Suez War of 1956.

influential Fourth Estate, and much of the diffuse noise in Washington testify to the importance of public opinion—or, more exactly, to the importance of the opinions of various parts of the public—in policy making.

Although public opinion plays an important role in any democracy, this term requires careful explanation. In the heat of political battle, it is quite common to hear the public discussed as if it shares a common attitude, a common will, or a common interest: "the public wants . . . ," "public opinion will not toler-ate . . . ," or "the public will rise up and. . . ." Such monolithic public opinion does not exist any more than a monolithic will exists in government.[43] Rather, one must distinguish between different parts of the public involved in different matters.[44]

One part of the public includes those who participate in elections. In addition, there are the multitude of interest groups that follow particular policy matters closely. Also, many Americans who do not necessarily belong to an interest group may be drawn into a number of issues. Thus, if the Defense Department cancels draft deferments for fathers or college students, these men and their families will join the public most immediately concerned with this issue. Usually, the public involved in any major policy issue is a mix of various interest group members and leaders, government officials and departments, and others concerned with the outcome. The public involved in a particular interest will rarely constitute a majority of Americans. Further, the mix of individuals and interests involved with one issue will usually vary from those concerned with another. Those who agree on draft reform will usually not agree on changes in Medicare. While the nature of publics differs on differing issues, the cumulative impact of this complicated tangle of publics on the conduct of federal policy-making is extremely important.

One way in which public opinion is reflected in governmental policy-making is obviously through the electoral process. Federal elections in the United States are frequent, regular, and affect the composition of the representative institutions of the federal government over relatively short periods: the president is elected every four years, the entire House of Representatives and one third of the Senate are elected every two years. In England, the fact that the prime minister can dissolve Parliament at any moment and call for a general election—and is likely to do so when he thinks political conditions favor his party's fortunes—means that Britain is in virtually a constant state of elections.

Even though elections are imperfect devices for reading the will of the voters, candidates and incumbents do try to read it, and such interpretations

---

[43] That a monolithic public is an illusion has long been recognized. A very comprehensive examination of the myths concerning the public is contained in Floyd H. Allport, "Toward a Science of Public Opinion," *Public Opinion Quarterly,*

[44] The causes and consequences of different "publics" is briefly and comprehensively explored in David B. Truman, *The Governmental Process* (New York: Alfred A. Knopf, 1960), Chapter 8.

often govern the conduct of elected officials.[45] Not all nations use elections in this way. In the Soviet Union, they serve quite different functions: to reaffirm loyalty to the party, to impress both the Soviet citizen and the foreign observer with the strength of the regime and its unity with its people, and to create an illusion of participation in governmental affairs. But the regime remains uncriticized; its leaders continue to believe that they are the best guardians of the people's interests, and they, not the people, define these interests.[46] In many of the new nations, elections serve primarily to instill a national consciousness through participation in a national election for a national government among people whose loyalties are still essentially local and parochial.

In any event, the impact of general elections in democracies is only one way of influencing government. The opinion of the various interest groups that are integral parts of the federal policy-making procedures form another constant input into Washington or London politics. In addition, the constant dialogue between legislative representatives and their various constituents may provide Congressmen or Members of Parliament and political leaders with a sounding of public feelings that have yet to emerge in some form of electoral expression or interest group activity. There is also another increasingly popular technique of influence. Groups that feel they do not have enough power to gain sufficient redress of their grievances may abandon nonviolent protest and threaten or use violence. Finally, there is the continuous flow of information from the interpretative media that attempts both to express significant opinions and to influence the many publics' opinions.

Even though these various publics play an undeniably important part in federal policy-making, their impacts upon policy-making will vary in several ways. Perhaps most important, the various publics are organized and oriented toward foreign and domestic affairs in significantly different ways. The domestic affairs publics include many thousands of associational interests with well defined, continuing programs; these associations give continuity and expression to the interests they represent, are continually alert, mobilize their members for important political action, and frequently initiate programs or powerfully influence their shape within the government. Moreover, many citizens have a personal and tangible interest in domestic affairs and, therefore, develop well defined attitudes and preferences about various domestic programs. The major economic interests such as labor, business, or the professions have many associa-

---

[45] These interpretations may be no more than opinions of analysts, based on no conclusive evidence. Electoral returns, however, are only *one* source of influence upon policy-makers, albeit an important one. Useful collections of articles dealing with the role of elections and other factors in shaping governmental policy may be found in Edward C. Dreyer and Walter A. Rosenbaum, *Political Opinion and Behavior,* 2nd ed. (Belmont, Calif.: Wadsworth, 1970); and Norman R. Luttbeg, *Public Opinion and Public Policy* (Homewood, Ill.: Dorsey Press, 1968).

[46] Alfred G. Meyer, *The Soviet Political System* (New York: Random House, 1965), pp. 272–274.

tional groups with lobbyists representing them in the capital, but individuals within different social groups also develop specific preferences and concrete ideas about how to handle labor policy, regulation of medical practice, or taxes on industrial profits.

In foreign affairs, however, the various publics involved or interested are seldom well organized, and there is seldom a continuity of organizations over long periods. Also, the vast majority of Americans is for the most part poorly informed and uninterested in foreign policy. It sometimes happens, nonetheless, that a foreign policy issue becomes dramatically relevant and personally meaningful to many individuals. When the abstract issues assume concretely relevant meaning to the average American—when a Vietnamese War means drafting sons and fathers (and, perhaps, eventually killing or maiming them), when the media project the realities of the conflict with harsh detail into living rooms nightly, when young people march in the streets to protest the war—then there may indeed be extensive public involvement and sharpened policy preferences. But these issues are relatively infrequent, especially given the range of military and foreign matters with which the government customarily deals.

Most of the time, the president or prime minister takes the initiative in foreign and military affairs and most Americans remain generally supportive; frequently, of course, a leader must act before any firm public opinion has cohered. There may be at times a rather diffuse and general mood which governmental policy-makers sense and may, accordingly, use in a very general way to guide their decisions on foreign affairs; in this sense, the "mood" may set broad limits on what policy-makers think they may do, but very seldom does the public give a president, a prime minister, or other major decision-makers any specific, operational cues about foreign policy. In short, the opinions of most Americans on foreign policy, unlike domestic matters, are unstructured and unorganized.

The impact of opinions among various publics will also depend on other considerations. How important a public's opinions may be in government may depend upon a particular public's relevance to particular decision-makers; constituency opinions in one congressional district or state may be a matter of indifference to legislators in other areas.[47] The opinions of social groups lacking political organization, articulate spokesmen, or weight at the polls—the situation of the poor and the black until recently—may have a less profound and immediate impact upon policy-makers than the opinions of organized, articulate, and politically influential groups. Long-range, enduring opinion shifts—such as the slow movement toward increasing dissatisfaction with the Vietnamese War between 1964 and 1968—are usually more important than flash surges of opinion that may soon dissipate. There are, therefore, a number of circumstances that determine how intensely the opinions of various groups in the

---

[47] A thorough and readable study of constituency influences on Congress is Lewis A. Froman, Jr., *Congressmen and Their Constituencies* (Chicago: Rand McNally & Co., 1963).

population will be felt by government decision-makers and how much weight these opinions will carry in government decisions.

Choices Are Limited.   Public officials are often judged by unrealistic standards. The average man is likely to overestimate the freedom of choice of political leaders, even that of the most powerful ones; this often leads to inflated expectations concerning what leaders can, and should, accomplish. A popular assumption seems to be that the leaders of the major governments create most of their own policy alternatives, that their course and success is determined largely by will, ability, and intelligence. Presidents are often plagued not only by their political opposition, but by such public myths, as well.

What constraints are there on governmental policy-makers?[48] We have already noted a significant one: *The rules and characteristics of the decision-making process.* For example, a president of the United States must give more weight to legislative opinion than the premier of the Soviet Union or Communist China does because the rules of the respective governments differ. Or, incremental decisions, each one made to meet an immediate problem but giving momentum to a particular line of policy, tend to mean that long-range policy becomes the prisoner of short-range decisions.

A society's *resources,* human and material, impose limits on its governmental policy. Most Afro-Asian nations, for instance, cannot hope to launch ambitious diplomatic and military policies in the international sphere that will propel them even to modest status among world powers because, unlike western nations, they lack an industrial base, scientific technology, manpower, and the productive economy necessary for the task. Even among western nations, as Great Britain discovered after World War II, it may not be possible to produce enough of both guns and butter. England's slow and agonizing slide from a major world power to an admittedly second-class power is an ample illustration that governments, shackled with limited resources, are not free to be, or to do, all they may wish. Domestically, our federal government, in spite of its vast resources and budget, is now faced by the fact that it cannot marshal sufficient resources for meeting many of our domestic ills without cutting back foreign policy and especially military expenditures.

Choices are also limited by the *values and attitudes of decision-makers themselves.* The men who make public policy come to the job fully freighted with the human allotment of prejudice, bias, value preferences, subjective priorities about what is to be done and how, and other attitudes and orientations that influence the final decisions and their enactment. During the tense, ten-day

---

[48] This discussion is suggested by Neustadt, *Presidential Power.*

period in October 1962, when John Kennedy and his small, informal "executive committee" were planning the U.S. strategy to force the Soviet Union to withdraw its offensive missiles from Cuba, one plan that was considered and then dropped by the President was a preemptive surprise air strike at the missile emplacements. The reason for its dismissal is instructive. The President felt that in his and the public's eyes, it would seem "too much like a Pearl Harbor" and that a democracy did not strike without warning.[49] Such value judgment occurs constantly at all levels of government, although not usually as dramatically. Similarly, at the end of World War II when the West held the Soviet Union in high esteem due to its heroic war effort, the Soviet leadership threw away the opportunity for working out a *modus vivendi* by its denunciations of the western powers followed by the attempted thrusts into the eastern Mediterranean area. Its policy choices were undoubtedly limited by an ideology which condemned capitalism and saw the weaknesses of the West at the end of the war as an opportunity for an expansionist policy.

Choice for governmental policy-makers is also narrowed by *time and information.* Crisis decisions are usually made quickly, under tremendous pressure, and usually with even more limited information than at noncritical moments; action and response are demanded immediately and there is neither time for extended deliberation nor lengthy fact-gathering. Crisis decisions in modern governments are often triggered by international military or diplomatic events—wars, invasions, sudden shifts in diplomatic or military alliances in some part of the world—but even in domestic matters, about which decision-making is more leisurely, time may still restrict the decision-makers' choices. For instance, in cases where considerable time seems available for making decisions, more individuals and institutions and a greater number of political interests and values may be included in the decision-making process with the result that policy may evolve too slowly, or it may be so compromised and confused by the need to accommodate so many interests that the eventual product may not be what policy leaders want—rather, it may be what they must accept. The quip that a camel is simply a horse put together by a committee is relevant to government; in governmental policy-making, many voices and interests—given sufficient time—can turn policies that started out to be horses into camels.

Furthermore, governmental decision-makers are always at the mercy of their information. Political folklore cautions that one who would understand the decisions of kings (or premiers, prime ministers, or presidents) had better look for "the gray eminence behind the imperial purple"—to those who advise and inform decision-makers. What policy-makers know and the quality of their information bear heavily upon their eventual choices. In a sense, the installation of the "hot line" between Moscow and Washington testifies to the importance of this fact; it represents an attempt by the world's two superpowers to prevent a

---

[49] The story of this decision is told by Elie Abel, *op. cit.,* p. 51.

possible nuclear attack triggered by a decision made without adequate information about the opponent's intentions and actions.

Priorities Are Limited

In any government, those with the greatest responsibility for deciding what issues must be resolved are never completely free to set the agenda. There are some matters which must be handled whether or not policy-makers wish to do so; their hand is frequently forced. Thus, regardless of who became president of the United States in 1968, he had to find an effective and convincing strategy for resolving the Vietnamese conflict. This was, in the victorious Richard Nixon's opinion, the most compelling problem he faced and it would have been so for any of his opponents. The president might have wished to deal with environmental pollution, inflation, or devote his attention to any number of other matters first. However, his priorities were, in some respects, set; his options were limited.

The problem of limited control over which issues are to be handled is common to governmental decision-makers everywhere. Crisis may erupt in the form of internal violence or economic collapse or, perhaps, a sudden change in foreign or military affairs that quickly sweeps aside other issues. Or, less dramatically (and more normally) previous decisions resulting from the incremental nature of the policy process may limit what can be done in the present. All policy-makers, therefore, work within restraints on what they can do and when. Looking back on the many monumental decisions he made during the Civil War, Abraham Lincoln once wrote, "[I] confess plainly that events have controlled me." This was only a partial truth, since Lincoln had many options in dealing with the problems he confronted, yet it is accurate enough to epitomize a major problem for decision-makers, particularly at the highest levels of government. The leader may enjoy, perhaps, the technical right to set priorities, but *which* priorities and goals he sets may have been powerfully fashioned by events over which he has little or no direct control.

Themes and Institutional Variations: A Transitional Note

In this chapter we have examined what might be called the recurrent themes in American national policy-making. We have spoken of decentralization and the pluralistic power struggles within the government, of the incrementalism, delay, and noise that surround our policy-making together with many other patterns recurrent in our national decision-making. We have spoken, as well, of the limitations on policy-makers and their opportunities. As we observed, many patterns are not unique to the United States.

In the chapters to follow, our focus will shift from a broad overview of policy-making to the major institutions within the federal government where this policy-making occurs; we are interested in discovering how the broad pattern of our policy-making is worked out in detail and the variation within these different institutions. Thus, we are turning from generalizations to examples and from broad patterns to their institutional embodiment. We will begin with the executive branch of the federal government where many of these patterns are most clearly and dramatically revealed.

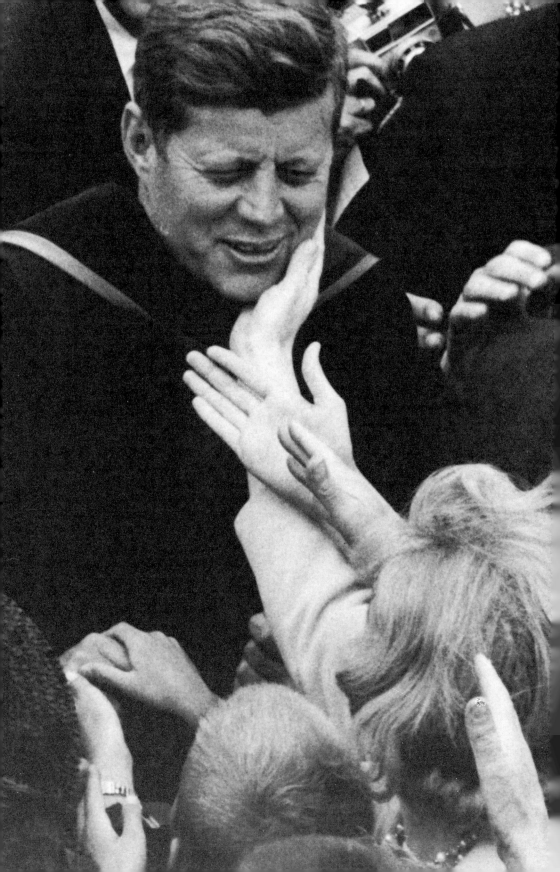

9

Policy Making in the Executive Establishment

Winging over the Atlantic in Air Force One, the President's personal Boeing 707, Richard Nixon is still in charge. As a co-passenger observed, "He telephoned Washington once in that amazing air-to-ground hookup. The special teletype system was kept clacking with new information. That faint sense— always riding with Air Force One—of somehow mastering all that lies below crept into the cabin."[1] Far ahead over the Atlantic, commerical air traffic leaves the President's flight path; military installations in the United States and Europe monitor his progress.

Air Force One is just another airplane. But when the president of the United States is aboard, it becomes the nerve center of the western world and of the world's most powerful military machine. Such, by one measure, is the prestige and power of the American presidency.

For Americans the president personifies the state and speaks in the name of the people. As the paramount symbol of the republic and the repository of its most concentrated power, the presidency is the focus of great expectations and equally intense animosities, of the loyalties and contentions that inevitably flow to the seats of political power. Small wonder, therefore, that a recent study of 2,000 American grammar students reported that all the children expressed "the

---

[1] Hugh Sidey, "The Dutiful Tourist," *Life* (March 7, 1969), pp. 22–23.

highest esteem for the President."[2] This does not last, of course, because children gradually abandon their naive worship of the President. But apparently they do not loose their interest in the President nor the conviction that he is at the center of political events in the United States. Indeed, most adults retain a belief that the President, more than any other political figure in the nation, is the active and accountable agent in the nation's successes and misfortunes. "Hey, hey, LBJ, how many kids did you kill today?" taunted young people at President Johnson during a 1967 protest against the Vietnamese war. Such epithets give a particularly vicious twist to assumptions about the President's power, but such is the nature of the office. The other side of the coin of Presidential power is responsibility, and with it the unremitting weight of public passion and expectations resting on the President's shoulders when the nation finds itself in trouble.

The extent to which the American people identify with the President and develop strong emotional attachments, either positive or negative, to the man who occupies the White House illustrates how government penetrates society through the political culture. Though tragic, it is in the death of Presidents that the emotional attachment of the American people to the Presidency can be most vividly recognized. One can glimpse how intimately the American people relate to the Presidency, for example, in the days that followed the assassination of John Kennedy in Dallas, Texas, on November 23, 1963. The initial public response was shock and confusion. Most people compared the President's death to the passing of a friend, parent, or close relative.[3] A college student reported:

> I didn't believe it at first . . . then I thought, well, by God, it can't happen here and it can't happen now. . . . Then I got very angry, physically and emotionally sick, you know. . . . Well, my legs were shaking. First, I smacked the wall and then I just kind of shook and then I sat down. . . . I was just emotionally blah, just exhausted.[4]

President Kennedy's death was especially poignant for young Americans, for he had a special appeal to them; but his death cut deeply into the consciousness of most Americans regardless of age, class, or political affiliations. During the four days of public mourning that followed the assassination, 95 percent of the people spent some time keeping up with events either on television or radio.[5] Kennedy's death was also a world event of first magnitude. Nothing better

---

[2] David Easton and Robert D. Hess, *Children in the Political System* (New York: McGraw-Hill Book Co., 1969), p. 177.

[3] Robert B. Sheatsley and Jacob J. Feldman, "A National Survey On Public Reactions and Behavior," in Bradley S. Greenberg and Edwin B. Parker (eds.), *The Kennedy Assassination and the American Public* (Palo Alto, Calif.: Stanford University Press, 1965), p. 158.

[4] Fred I. Greenstein, "College Students' Reactions to the Assassination," in Greenberg and Parker, *op. cit.*, p. 225.

[5] Greenberg and Parker, *op. cit.*, p. 24.

symbolized the dimensions of his power and responsibilities than the cortege that followed John Kennedy's coffin down Pennsylvania Avenue to Arlington Cemetery. It included political leaders and representatives of most nations of the world.

Along with the increased power, responsibilities, and exposure of the presidency in the twentieth century has come a tendency to popularize and dramatize the man who fills the office. Nothing, apparently, is too trivial to merit mention if it concerns the Chief Executive; his clothes, his family, his dogs, his interest in sports, what he eats, what he drinks, his manners and morals. Presidents discover, often to their annoyance, that their private life is tasty fare for the general public and that private matters have definite political consequences. President Johnson, for example, acutely sensitive to public opinion and intensely anxious to bask in popular approval, was infuriated to discover soon after his succession to the presidency that a high-speed romp over his Texas ranch with reporters was reported in the press as something quite different. Johnson's harmless diversion was revealed by one major magazine as a beer-drinking reckless dash across the Texas prairie that endangered life and limb.[6] Though the media occasionally carry this preoccupation to the point of tastelessness, the president is inevitably a public personage whose life is critically scrutinized by several hundred million people.

Whether one measures the presidency by its power and prestige, its emotional impact on public sentiment, or its visibility and interest, it remains the dominant political office in the United States. Indeed, in almost all modern nations during the twentieth century, political power has gravitated to the executive.

The presidency is a forge where some men have been hammered into greatness and even immortality. Neither Abraham Lincoln, a gangling backwoods politician, nor Franklin D. Roosevelt, a genial aristocrat, was initially considered a man destined for fame. And Harry Truman, a little-known senator and vice president, became one of the great men of American history because of his record in the White House.

The presidency is also a crucible in which some men have been tried beyond their strength. As president, a dying Woodrow Wilson saw his greatest moment and a dream of a better world slip away when the Senate rejected the Treaty of Versailles and American entrance into the League of Nations. His successor, Warren G. Harding, came into office totally unprepared for the job but buoyed by an adoring public; shortly after his death three years later his name became synonymous with incompetence and scandal, his reputation fouled by the Teapot Dome scandals.

In the American political system, the White House is the scene of the greatest moments—a place of drama, passion, and conflict where decisions of

---

[6] The story of the President's trip, the press reports, and the President's ire is told in Rowland Evans and Robert Novak, *Lyndon B. Johnson: The Exercise of Power* (New York: New American Library, 1966), pp. 407–409.

world-wide significance are made. The presidency is, as John Adams observed, a "splendid misery" but it remains the grand prize of American politics.

In this chapter we shall examine why power in the American political system has converged upon the presidency, how this power has been created, and how it is exercised. And in discussing the presidency, we must discuss the men who have served in the White House, because no other political office in the United States bears so clearly the stamp of the men who have occupied it.

We shall also speak of the sharp differences between the "imaginary" presidency, created by public misconceptions of the office, and the actual presidency as we understand it. The American people have often seen the office and its occupants much larger than life, with qualities and powers that far exceed reality. A comparison of myth and reality may bring surprise, enlightenment, and sometimes disappointment.

The Preeminence of the Presidency

When George Washington took the first presidential oath of office on the snowy portico of New York's Federal Hall in 1787, the power of the president and his role in the government were vague and undetermined. Since that day, the power and role of the president have expanded beyond anything Washington could have foreseen. The president's power is not uniformly great, nor is it unlimited. But only a few other political offices in the world today approach the stature of the U.S. presidency.

The enlargement of executive power in the United States is a part of a world-wide trend. The twentieth century has seen executives in modern governments move to the center of the political stage. Legislative institutions have either assumed different functions in the policy-making process or have become subservient to other governmental officials. Although flagrant and brutal examples of excessive executive power have occurred in this century, the executive has customarily dominated the legislature in western democracies, particularly in European parliamentary systems. But the evolution which once shifted power from kings to elective assemblies has now come full circle, and power again flows away from assemblies and toward executives—presidents, premiers, and prime ministers.

There are many reasons for executive ascendency in modern political systems. Rapid technological advances, which flowered first and most fully in the West, created scientific, industrialized, and pluralistic societies which required of governments the skills possessed by executive and bureaucratic institutions. Wars and other national emergencies demanding strong, immediate, effective governmental action have encouraged nations to turn to executives for leadership rather than to representative assemblies.

In England, the prime minister and his cabinet dominate the Parliament. In France, the adoption of the Constitution of the Fifth Republic in 1958 gave the president control of the government. The English trend toward cabinet government gradually increased the power of the executive in response to the changing realities of government and politics in a society experiencing social and economic transformation. In France, the shift to executive power was more abrupt, growing from a constitutional crisis brought on by continuous periods of instability under assembly government and the inability of French governments to decide what to do about their colony, Algeria. The trend in the United States is similar although, as we shall see, while the legislative functions of Congress have changed, Congress has not become as subservient to the president as it has in Britain and France.

In the United States today, the power and authority of the presidency stems from several sources. The most important of these is the Constitution. This Constitution invests the office with potentially enormous power through specific grants of authority, such as that of commander-in-chief; these specific grants were left sufficiently nebulous to be open to interpretation and expansion. The Constitution further grants the president what it vaguely calls "the executive power"—a truly great, undefined source of additional authority whose exact nature and limits are not precisely stated.[7] Many of the Constitution's "great silences" leave the President free to experiment and to test the powers of his office, molding its power and authority according to his perceptions of the nation's needs. Moreover, the president is not dependent on Congress. He enjoys a fixed term; his continuation in office does not depend on his standing with Congress or on shifting congressional party strength. Here again, he enjoys great independence of power and action.[8]

A second source of the president's power derives from his position as the only truly national political leader in the United States. He is the only public official with a national constituency who is chosen by a national electorate. As such, he enjoys a singular vantage point in American government, one which expands the opportunities for the exercise of power. For example, he is the head of state; he can summon to himself the strong patriotic emotions with which most Americans invest symbols of the Republic. A particular president "borrows" public loyalties which surround the presidential office when he attains it; he becomes something more than simply a partisan leader or the official head of government. In many other nations, the head of government is not the head of state. In Great Britain, for example, the monarchy symbolizes the state and stands above politics and quarrels over public policy. It is the symbol of national

---

[7] The implications of this vagueness and some of the legal problems it creates are explored in Edwin S. Corwin, *The President: Office and Powers* (New York: New York University Press, 1957), Chapter 1.

[8] Indeed, the president's independence of Congress was deemed critical for the development of a strong national executive and, consequently, a major issue between those members of the convention who favored a strong or weak national government. The view of the strong presidency's proponents may be found in *The Federalist, Nos. 67–74.*

unity and represents the historic continuity of English government. The prime minister is head of government. As the true executive he participates actively in politics and policy-making. In England, it is easy for citizens to separate their partisan feelings from their respect for the government. In the United States, however, these two elements are combined and, therefore, Americans often exhibit love/hate attitudes toward the presidency.

As a unique national official and as head of state, the president faces almost continuous visibility and attention. More than 1,200 accredited White House correspondents follow his activities, and all major television and radio networks daily report his actions.[9] Given this great accessibility to the nation's communication system, the president has an "open line" to the people. He can turn his office into what Theodore Roosevelt once called "a bully pulpit." He can preempt the news whenever he chooses and force the discussion of public issues along whatever lines he prefers, speaking in behalf of his programs and policies and defining the interests and goals of the nation. In 1970, when the nation was at odds over President Nixon's decision to send American troops into Cambodia, Senator J. William Fulbright, an opponent of Nixon's policies, decried the fact that the President had open access to nation-wide television and that Congress did not enjoy the same privilege. His point was well taken.

A third source of the president's power and authority is his role as leader of his political party. The presidency is a legal office that draws its basic powers from the Constitution, but it is a political office as well. The president is a partisan, nominated by his party and elected to office through its efforts. As party leader, he can tap the resources of partisan organizations to strengthen his control over the government and increase his influence in the policy-making process. Though American political parties are loosely knit, decentralized organizations based primarily in states and local communities, party loyalty plays a significant role in politics. The president can capitalize on this fact.

Finally, the president's power and authority have been enhanced by the continued expansion of his role in military and diplomatic affairs. The Constitution makes the president commander-in-chief of the Armed Forces and gives him broad authority in the making of foreign policy. The initiative and energy he expends in these areas tend to spill over into domestic affairs. In war or other national emergencies the people instinctively turn to the president to lead them; undoubtedly, war and other severe national crises magnify presidential authority somewhat; yet the preeminence of the presidential office in public consciousness remains almost constant.

Yet the president's power and authority is by no means unlimited. It is circumscribed by Constitutional limitations, political restraints, and the limita-

---

[9] A relatively short but illuminating discussion of the opportunities for influence inherent in this great media exposure can be found in Richard E. Neustadt, *Presidential Power* (New York: John Wiley, 1960), particularly Chapters 3, 4, and 5. For a more extended analysis of presidential influence on public opinion, see Elmer E. Cornwell, Jr., *Presidential Leadership of Public Opinion* (Bloomington, Ind.: University of Indiana Press, 1965).

tions of the men who fill the office. Also, when one speaks of presidential power, one must distinguish between power in international policy-making and power in domestic policy-making. In the latter role, wrestling with Congress and managing the giant bureaucracy, the president's prerogatives are not so clear and so unchallengeable as they are in diplomatic and military affairs.

Furthermore, the stature of the presidency depends upon who occupies the office. An aggressive and imaginative president, drawing upon the deep reservoir of Constitutional powers and political opportunities inherent in the office, can elevate the presidency to preeminence. A weak or passive president, lacking the will or imagination to grasp the possibilities of office, can dissipate its vigor and let it lapse into little more than a clerkship.

The Dual Presidential Tradition

Throughout most of our history, the presidency has alternated between vigorous presidents and weak ones. This has been partially due to differences in temperament, but at the heart of the matter is a profound and significant difference in the interpretation of "executive power." The result has been conflicting precedents for the modern chief executive. Though presidents may differ regarding the details of their power, they generally gravitate toward one or the other of the following positions.[10]

The Weak Presidency.   Weak presidents have, as a rule, assumed that the president should take little initiative and assert no authority unless the power to take such action is clearly specified by the Constitution, Congress, or the Courts. Executive power is narrowly interpreted and is limited to what is specifically described in the Constitution. The motto of the weak president has been, "that which is not expressly granted to me I cannot—and should not—do." Such presidents have regarded the presidency as merely one of three coequal branches of the government. They have executed the formal and official duties of the office, presided over and respected the proper balance between the three branches of the government. They have seen that laws are faithfully executed but have not become active and forceful participants in the policy-making process. Their stance toward Congress has been passive, preferring to let Congress

---

[10] An interesting study of the opposing concepts of office in this century is Edwin C. Hargrove, *Presidential Leadership* (New York: Macmillan Co., 1966); a useful collection of documents illustrating both concepts of office and drawing upon presidential writings themselves is John P. Roche and Leonard W. Levy (eds.), *The Presidency* (New York: Harcourt Brace Jovanovich, 1964), pp. 7–34.

promote legislation and define national problems. Weak presidents have radiated a certain distaste for power; they distrust the opportunities for positive leadership inherent in the presidency. And they have rarely attempted to anticipate national problems or to sway public opinion. "If you see ten troubles coming down the road," remarked that model of presidential passiveness, Calvin Coolidge, "you can be sure that nine will run into the ditch before they reach you and you have to battle with only one of them."[11]

William Howard Taft, Warren G. Harding, Calvin Coolidge, Herbert Hoover, and Dwight Eisenhower were adherents of this tradition. They regarded their role in the legislative process as negative rather than positive. They wanted to prevent harmful legislation rather than sponsor laws designed to change the status quo. They wanted to restore "balanced government" by restraining the power of the presidency rather than use their office as an agent of reform. They were sympathetic to slowing the pace of change and innovation rather than hurrying it along. President Eisenhower exhibited these traits: he never felt comfortable exercising the strong powers of the presidency. He once observed:

> A president does not lead by hitting people over the head. Any damn fool can do that, but it's usually called "assault"—not "leadership." . . . I'll tell you what leadership is. It's *persuasion*—and *conciliation*—and *education*—and *patience*. That's the only kind of leadership I know—or believe in—or will practice.[12]

The Strong Presidency.   Strong presidents have regarded their office as a large reservoir of undefined political powers. Their motto has been, "that which the Constitution, Courts, or Congress do not expressly forbid me to do, I may do—or at least attempt to do—when my responsibilities require it." Strong presidents have imaginatively and forcefully asserted many new powers that have enlarged the scope of presidential prerogatives in relation to Congress and to the nation. Strong presidents typically have relished power and its exercise; they have been ambitious for office and anxious for the opportunities office provides. Franklin D. Roosevelt, it is said, had "a love affair with power." And Abraham Lincoln—whose legendary humility, understanding, and wisdom often obscure a use of power that bordered on arrogance—was said by his law partner to be a man whose "ambition was a little engine that knew no rest."[13]

---

[11] Quoted in Michael Harwood, "Calvin Coolidge," in *American Heritage History of the Presidents of the United States,* Vol. II (New York: Simon and Schuster, 1968), p. 746.

[12] Quoted in Emmet John Hughes, *The Ordeal of Power* (New York: Atheneum, 1963), p. 124.

[13] Quoted in Richard Hofstadter, *The American Political Tradition* (New York: Vintage Books, 1957), p. 93.

The strong president's view of his role as chief executive often goads him to test the limits of his power. Usually, such presidents feel they have a singular and inescapable responsibility to guide the government and the nation in a given direction. A strong president may try to exert more authority than public opinion, Congress, and the Courts are willing to tolerate. For example, in 1951, President Truman relieved General Douglas MacArthur, a national hero, from command of American forces in Korea because MacArthur had challenged Truman's powers as commander-in-chief of the Armed Forces.[14] In 1952, Truman seized the nation's steel mills in order to preclude a nationwide strike that he believed would endanger the war effort in Korea.[15] John Kennedy, already in trouble with Congress and the public after the 1962 Bay of Pigs fiasco and the failure of his legislative program, nonetheless threatened to tame the steel industry if it did not rescind its price increases.[16] In 1970, President Nixon sent American troops into Cambodia to disrupt North Vietnamese staging and supply areas, even though he knew the opposition in Congress and in the country at large would be staggering. In all three cases, strong American presidents placed their power and prestige on the line against formidable opponents.

Theodore Roosevelt, Woodrow Wilson, Franklin D. Roosevelt, Harry Truman, John Kennedy, Lyndon Johnson, and Richard Nixon have demonstrated the great possibilities of their office. Such a presidency becomes a model for later aggressive presidents. In a sense, these presidents have protected the office from the eclipse and impotency it undergoes with a weak president. Indeed, throughout most of our history, a strong president was usually followed by a weak one—Grant after Lincoln, Harding after Wilson, and Eisenhower succeeding Truman. In these cases, strong presidents asserted the inherent powers of the office and thus assured its continued vitality.

Strong presidents have asserted their powers most vigorously in military and diplomatic affairs. Perhaps this is because almost all strong presidents—Washington, Lincoln, Wilson, Franklin Roosevelt, Truman, Kennedy, Johnson, Nixon —held office during wars or other national emergencies. In such times, American presidents have consistently tried to exercise great authority and to assert the fullest powers of their office. On those rare occasions when either Congress or the Courts have opposed presidential decisions—Congressional opposition to President Nixon's Cambodia venture in 1970, for instance—such action has come long after the president had already attained his goals. This combination of presidential initiative and legislative-judicial support has made the president's military and diplomatic powers the most imposing aspect of this office.

---

[14] A careful exploration of Truman's decision and the circumstances surrounding it is contained in John W. Spanier, *The Truman-MacArthur Controversy and the Korean War,* rev. ed. (New York: W. W. Norton & Co., 1965).

[15] See Grant McConnell, *The Steel Seizure of 1952* (University, Ala.: University of Alabama Press, 1960). Published for the Inter-University Case Program.

[16] This struggle is discussed in Grant McConnell, *Steel and the Presidency* (New York: W. W. Norton & Co., 1963).

Prior to 1932, the American presidency alternated between the weak and strong traditions. Theodore Roosevelt, our first twentieth-century president, was a strong and active chief executive. He was followed in office by William Howard Taft, a genial representative of the weak tradition. Taft's strong successor, Wilson, was followed by Harding, Coolidge, and Hoover, all weak or passive presidents.

It is doubtful, despite the dual presidential tradition, whether modern presidents can again revert to the weak interpretation of office that suited Calvin Coolidge or Herbert Hoover. The modern presidency is and must be a strong one. Since 1932, the United States has become so thoroughly urbanized and industrialized, so deeply affected by wars, depressions, and other national emergencies that strong executive leadership is not only required but expected. Every American president since Franklin Roosevelt—who, significantly, came to office in the midst of the nation's most terrible depression—has been forced, sometimes in spite of his predispositions, to exercise executive power with some vigor. Even Dwight Eisenhower could not always avoid doing so. He did, for example, display considerable aggressiveness during the Little Rock integration crisis. Time and circumstance have combined to thrust the mantle of leadership upon even a reluctant president.

The Two Modern Presidencies

Despite the preeminence of the modern presidency and the vigorous performance of recent presidents, the president still must turn to the differing responsibilities of his office with unequal powers and opportunities for leadership. The Constitution, political history, and circumstance have conferred upon the president differing measures of power in dealing with domestic and foreign affairs. Thus, the enlargement of the Presidency has not proceeded uniformly in all directions of presidential responsibilities. Rather, when looking at the president's powers in domestic and foreign matters, it is well to speak of the "two presidencies" to underscore the differing aspects of power they present.[17]

Measured by the president's freedom of action and his ability to determine policy, the domestic presidency is by far the weaker of the two presidencies. Domestically, the president is expected to manage the government's huge, sprawling bureaucracy and to see that "the law be faithfully executed" through the executive branch of government. Moreover, the president is expected to initiate legislation, secure its passage through Congress and rally his congressional party to support it. But the federal bureaucracy seldom yields easily to presidential direction, almost never without a struggle and often not at all. The Congress, with whom the president shares legislative powers, often frustrates the

---

[17] This distinction is suggested by Aaron Wildavsky, "The Two Presidencies," *Trans*-action (December 1966), p. 93

president's legislative intentions while his own congressional party frequently fails to provide cohesive support at crucial stages of the legislative struggle. Whether dealing with Congress or the bureaucracy, in addition, the president must contend with a broad assortment of energetic, disputing interest groups that often become his antagonists and competitors in the struggle for policy leadership in domestic affairs. Domestically, as David Truman has observed, the task of presidential leadership is not so much a job as an ordeal.[18]

Far more impressive are the president's capacities to deal with foreign affairs. The president, as the constitutionally appointed commander-in-chief of the armed forces, is expected to defend the nation's security, direct its military efforts and manage its military establishment. As the nation's diplomatic leader, he is expected to create foreign policy and guide the nation safely through the maze of international politics. To both these tasks the president may summon the enormous power which the Constitution vests in him as a military and diplomatic leader and the additional prerogatives which the chief of state uniquely enjoys in these tasks. Indeed, it is in dealing with foreign affairs that the presidency most clearly epitomizes the enormous power which the public often uncritically assumes attends all the president's responsibilities.

These two aspects of presidential power, this discrepancy between the president's resources in dealing with domestic and foreign affairs, are a reminder that the scope of modern presidential power, for all its undeniable growth in this century, should not be exaggerated. As we examine the details of executive decision making, we shall often observe this power disparity between the "two presidencies" and, in the process, lay to rest the myth of presidential omnipotence.

The Pluralistic Executive

Harry Truman liked to speak colorfully and bluntly, a talent that endeared him to many Americans and appalled others. Once, reflecting on his job over a bourbon and water, he reportedly growled: "They talk about the power of the president, how I can just push a button and get things done. Why, I spend most of my time kissing somebody's ass."[19] As a man who liked to act with independence and authority, the problems of presidential leadership were often bound to annoy him. Especially when attempting to exercise leadership within the executive branch—ostensively "his" own branch—Truman was frequently frustrated and defeated, his will often constrained by the pluralistic conflicts within it. Like other presidents, Truman had constantly to struggle for leadership of the executive departments.

---

[18] The "ordeal of the executive" is fully discussed in David B. Truman, *The Governmental Process* (New York: Alfred A. Knopf, 1960), Chapters 13, 14.

[19] Quoted in *Time,* January 5, 1968.

As Truman discovered, the executive branch of the federal government is not a monolithic organization acting with a single will under the firm control and direction of the president. It is, rather, a pluralistic organization composed of a host of different actors, each with strong policy convictions that are likely to differ from those of his associates as well as those of the president. For example, the Department of Transportation and the Department of the Interior do not agree on the proposal to build a jetport in the Florida Everglades. Top officials in the Department of Justice and the Department of Health, Education, and Welfare disagree over the proper pace of school desegregation in the South. The Department of State and the Department of Defense do not always see eye to eye on the question of arms control; and the Treasury Department may oppose efforts of the Defense Department to develop a particular weapons system if it costs too much.

Different views also exist within the same department or agency. In 1968, over half of the civil rights lawyers in the Justice Department met to protest the policies of Attorney General John Mitchell on school desegregation. In 1970, employees of the Department of Health, Education, and Welfare called a mass meeting to question their Secretary about his policy objectives. During the same year, employees in the State Department, including some foreign officers, publicly announced their opposition to the nation's policies in Southeast Asia, which were sponsored by the President and their own superiors. Agencies within an executive department are frequently as splintered as the entire executive branch. Very rarely are they of one mind on major policy questions. And even when a department head has taken a public position on a policy question, dissidents remain who feel that the announced policy is wrong.

Conflict must be moderated and consensus built throughout the executive branch if decisions are to be made and supported. Officials and agencies within one department seek support in other departments or from the president or his advisors. The president's success as a policy leader is very largely determined by his skills in consensus building. Where conflict exists among his advisors or between departments, he must make the final decision as well as build support for it.

Retaining the support of the losers is almost as important as making the correct policy decision. Although he is the key decision-maker in the executive establishment, "the president does not control government in either making or administering policy."[20] In 1970, for example, President Nixon made the decision to send American troops into Cambodia. The decision was difficult, but persuading other officials either to support it or at least go along with it was equally difficult. And Nixon was not entirely successful. Executive decision-making is not merely a matter of rationally determining the best policy. It often means reconciling conflicting ideas of what policy is best, and then trying to build a consensus in support of a compromise.

---

[20] Grant McConnell, *The Modern Presidency* (New York: St. Martin's Press, 1969), p. 94.

The president is the one individual who can provide leadership, unity, and coordination in the policy-making functions of the executive branch. To the extent that he is successful, he becomes the *nexus,* the connecting link, of the policy-making process. An influential cabinet member or agency head may carry great weight in the making of particular decisions—Secretary of State John Foster Dulles under President Eisenhower, Attorney General Robert Kennedy under President Kennedy, and Attorney General John Mitchell under President Nixon are good examples—but such officials lack the constitutional and political powers necessary for continuing leadership. Thus, while the president does not have a free hand in policy-making, because many other powerful officials and agencies work with him—and often against him—in the executive branch of the government, he is clearly the dominant figure.

Three Decision-Making Circles

One way to look at the policy-making process in the executive branch is to see it as comprising three concentric circles.[21] The innermost circle includes the president, his most intimate advisors, and members of the Cabinet who have immediate responsibilities in the policy area where a decision must be made. The president himself is the key figure in this circle; he may include anyone—either government officials or private citizens—if he needs their knowledge or advice. Decision making in times of crisis, particularly in the foreign or military policy, tends to be confined to this first circle. Here, decisions must be made and carried out in a matter of hours or days. There is no time to include agencies of the bureaucracy, members of Congress, or interest groups that in non-crisis situations could expect to be consulted.[22]

The second circle may include other Cabinet members, presidential advisers, and heads of government agencies and commissions. Their decisions do not concern immediate crises and do not require immediate implementation. The more time available for a policy decision, the greater the likelihood that it will be made in this wider second circle.[23]

Only the third circle of decision making extends outside the executive establishment. It includes other governmental institutions, interest groups, the press, and those citizens who are attentive to public affairs. Most important executive decisions in domestic policy and those foreign policy decisions that do

---

[21] The three circles are suggested by Roger Hilsmann, *To Move a Nation* (Garden City, N.Y.: Doubleday & Co., 1967), pp. 542–544.

[22] An excellent case study of crisis decision-making by one who participated in such a decision is Robert F. Kennedy, *Thirteen Days: A Memoir of the Cuban Missile Crisis* (New York: W. W. Norton & Co., 1969).

[23] See Thomas E. Cronin and Sanford D. Greenberg, *The Presidential Advisory System* (New York: Harper & Row, Publishers, 1969); a very thorough and readable account of the cabinet's role in policy-making is found in Richard F. Fenno, *The President's Cabinet* (New York: Vintage Books, 1959).

not require immediate action are ultimately debated in this circle. For example, the decision of the Nixon administration in 1969 to build the ABM system was made within the two inner circles, but before this weapons system could be funded the debate spilled over into the third circle. Congress, interest groups, the press, and the country at large participated fully in this debate and ultimately played an important role in its outcome.

The fact that this third circle is public—including congressmen, the media, and private citizens—does not lessen its importance. Executive decisions made in the inner or second circle may be subsequently reversed because of the reactions of the third circle. Vietnam is the most dramatic example of such a reaction. . . . The third circle may also become involved in decision making when members of the inner circle, fearing that they are losing, deliberately leak information, hoping that publicity will perhaps bring support for their point of view.

Decisions can be made and implemented within the two inner circles, but major policy decisions ultimately must be supported in all three circles. President Kennedy's decision to blockade Cuba was made after consultation with only a very few officials, but it received support throughout the executive establishment, in Congress, and in the nation at large. President Nixon's decision to invade Cambodia was made very much the same way, but major support in the two outer circles did not materialize. After the decision had been made and implemented, strong pressures in Congress, in the nation, and within the executive establishment itself forced the President to reconsider and to pledge publicly that the troops would be withdrawn after achieving only limited objectives. Had the decision been debated in the two outer circles, it probably would never have been made; had strong support followed the decision, the President would not have felt obliged to reiterate his limited objectives and pledge a quick withdrawal.

In crisis situations, the president must act on the advice of the first circle, but then he must work diligently within all three circles to muster support for what he has done. In all other major decision-making situations he must bargain, negotiate, and compromise before the final decisions are made. The pluralistic nature of the executive establishment, the power of other officials and agencies within the government, and the limitations on presidential power make this necessary. We will now examine the policy-making process in the executive establishment in terms of the president's relationship with his advisers, the bureaucracy, and Congress.

The President and His Advisers

Presidential leadership is vitally affected by the kind of information and advice the president receives. Quite obviously, no one man can even begin to acquire personal knowledge of the endless issues that come to the president for action. His decisions must be made on the basis of intelligence received from others. How this intelligence is gathered, processed, interpreted, and evaluated shapes the "picture of reality" that the president has before him when he makes decisions.

Every president is free to establish the kind of advisory system he prefers, and to use it or not at his discretion. Franklin D. Roosevelt brought experts in large numbers from the universities and from industry to Washington to help design and implement governmental programs during the Depression and World War II. President Roosevelt took a highly personalized approach to his staff, and followed no clearly defined institutional guidelines in using his advisers.[24] President Eisenhower, accustomed to the order and formality of the Army, attempted to institutionalize the presidential advisory system.[25] He selected Governor Sherman Adams of New Hampshire as his "executive officer," and all information and intelligence had to be channeled through Adams' office to reach the President. President Kennedy reverted to the Roosevelt approach and involved himself personally in the advisory system. He tended to ignore institutional lines of authority, developing contacts and resources throughout the presidency and the wider bureaucracy. President Johnson blended the two approaches, exercising his personal prerogatives as president, but placing "greater reliance upon the [executive] departments than Kennedy or Roosevelt did."[26] President Nixon uses an institutionalized advisory system like Eisenhower's.

The presidential advisory system expanded under Kennedy and Johnson. Kennedy, attempting to exploit the resources of the nation planning long-range programs, created many "task forces" to advise him on public policy problems. Johnson continued this practice; by the summer of 1968, he "was reported to have created about one hundred special task forces to assist in the development of his legislative programs."[27] There are now over one hundred seventy White House–level advisory commissions and boards, to which the president appoints some twenty-five hundred members.[28]

The present presidential advisory system consists of "channels" through which information and advice are routed to the chief executive. There are four

[24] Roosevelt's highly informal and unpredictable approach to policy-making has been reported by many of his advisors and cabinet members. Especially interesting is Robert E. Sherwood, *Roosevelt and Hopkins: An Intimate History* (New York: Harper & Row, Publishers, 1948) and Harold L. Ickes, *The Secret Diary of Harold L. Ickes: The First 1000 Days* (New York: Simon and Schuster, 1953).

[25] On Eisenhower's decision-making approach, see Richard E. Neustadt, "Presidency and Legislation: Planning the President's Program," *American Political Science Review* (December 1955), pp. 980–1021; and "The Presidency and Legislation: The Growth of Central Clearance," *American Political Science Review* (September 1954), pp. 641–671.

[26] Louis W. Koenig, *The Chief Executive*, rev. ed. (New York: Harcourt Brace Jovanovich, 1968), p. 176.

[27] Cronin and Greenberg, *op. cit.*, p. xvi.

[28] *Ibid.*, p. xvii.

such channels: (1) The president's Cabinet and sub-Cabinet committees; (2) The White House personal staff, composed of policy and program advisers, legislative liaison staffs, political and appointment advisers, press secretaries, speech-writing staffs, and special counsels and consultants; (3) An inside network of support staffs, composed of the Office of Management and Budget, Council of Economic Advisers, National Security Council, Central Intelligence Agency, and other agencies that are part of the Executive Office of the Presidency; and (4) An outside network of support staffs, composed of personal friends and allies, advisory commissions and boards, White House conferences, task forces and study commissions, private foundations, and interagency committees.[29]

The advisory system can be either an indispensable asset or a crucial limitation on the president's power because it screens the intelligence he uses to make important policy decisions. Consider, for example, President Kennedy's handling of the Bay of Pigs fiasco and his subsequent resolution of the Cuban Missile Crisis. Both decisions were made on the strength of information that came to the President through his advisory system. In the first crisis, the CIA (part of the inside network of support staffs) did not give the President all the information he needed to make a wise decision. The inadequacy of the advisory system limited the President's view of the situation at the Bay of Pigs and led to a blunder that seriously shook the confidence of the young President. But Kennedy learned his lesson well. Faced with the presence of Russian offensive missiles in Cuba the following year, and fully aware of the pressures of time and the need for quick action, he nonetheless refused to act until he had the most accurate appraisal of the situation that could be obtained from advisers both inside and outside the government.[30] His decision to establish a blockade of Cuba, his call for the removal of all offensive missiles, his mobilization of massive military forces, and his threat to take even more drastic action proved effective. The Russian missiles were removed. Both decisions—one right, one wrong—stemmed in part from the way the President used his advisory system.

In summary, the president's power and effectiveness in policy making is largely determined by the quality of his advisory staff. Regardless of the institutional arrangement the president uses, the men who surround him in office play crucial roles in either the success or failure of presidential administrations. Presidents know this; they recognize that their ability to attract and retain well qualified advisers is an important measure of their capacity to handle the duties and responsibilities of the presidency.

---

[29] *Ibid.,* pp. xvii–xviii.

[30] On Kennedy's handling of the Cuban missile crisis, see in addition to Robert F. Kennedy, *op. cit.,* Elie Abel, *The Missile Crisis* (New York: Bantam Books, 1966), and Theodore C. Sorensen, *Kennedy* (New York: Harper & Row, Publishers, 1965), Chapter 24.

The President and the Bureaucracy

The growth of bureaucracies is a form of specialization in government characteristic of western political systems. Of course, bureaucracies are not peculiar to modern western political systems; they existed in the earliest and crudest forms of government. But modern bureaucracies are distinguished by their enormous size and their influence in the policy-making process. The American bureaucracy is a fourth branch of government within the executive establishment. The president is its official head, but his control over the bureaucracy is so nebulous, the capacity of executive departments and agencies to oppose and frustrate his policies so great, that he is its head in name only. As one political scientist has observed:

> power is not concentrated by the structure of government or politics in the hands of a leadership with a capacity to budget it among a diverse set of administrative activities. A picture of the presidency as a reservoir of authority from which the lower echelons of administration draw life and vigor is an idealized distortion of reality.[31]

Before identifying some of the president's problems in this area, it may be helpful to discuss the basic functions of the bureaucracy.

The official function of the American bureaucracy is *administrative*. The laws of Congress, for example, the decisions of the federal courts, and the executive decisions of the president must each be administered by some department or agency. After Congress passes broad and general laws, bureaucrats fill in the details, deciding precisely how and to whom the laws apply. This gives the bureaucracy much influence in determining what the ultimate meaning of a law shall be and which interests shall be promoted by it.[32] Thus, Supreme Court decisions and Congressional legislation set national goals for ending racial segregation in the United States; they rarely prescribe detailed procedures for achieving these objectives in specific cases. The details are worked out in the bureaucracy and issued in the form of guidelines binding on state and local authorities. The furor in Congress—particularly among the Southern states— over these guidelines stems from many people's belief that they go far beyond the intent of Congress and exceed the authority of the bureaucracy. The fact that

[31] Norton E. Long, "Power and Administration," in Francis E. Rourke (ed.), *Bureaucratic Power in National Politics* (Boston: Little, Brown, and Co., 1965), p. 15.

[32] This is usually called the "quasi-judicial" function of the bureaucracy. The adjudicatory role of bureaucracy is nicely summarized in Peter Woll, *American Bureaucracy* (New York: W. W. Norton & Co., 1963), pp. 61–109.

the bureaucracy must use discretion in interpreting and implementing national policies suggests how potentially powerful it is.

Bureaucratic agencies are frequently accused of becoming "tools" or "protectors" of their clienteles. For example, independent regulatory agencies like the Interstate Commerce Commission often seem to protect certain industries rather than defend the public interest.[33] Does the Federal Communication Commission regulate the television industry in the interest of the public, or does it protect the networks from regulations that would prevent them from turning handsome profits? In 1961, Newton Minow, Chairman of the FCC, charged that American television was a "wasteland," and that public criticism of violence on television had led to few restraints except those that the networks chose to accept. It is true that regulation in the public interest and protection of the industry are not necessarily conflicting functions. But in many instances, the two functions do not complement each other. What the FCC does about violence on television may well depend upon the training, experience, and personal preferences of the members of the commission and their relationships to the networks rather than on the intent of Congress or the desires of the president. The same is true of other agencies.

The bureaucracy also performs a *legislative* function. Since most important legislation is initiated by the executive establishment, the bureaucracy helps determine what programs the president will send to Congress. And when these programs are introduced in Congress, bureaucrats often testify in committees on the merits of these proposals. This testimony is important in shaping the decisions that ultimately determine whether or not the legislation will be enacted into law.[34]

The bureaucracy performs a *judicial* function. Where a government penetrates deeply into society and regulates people's lives, many disputes as to the meaning of rules and regulations will arise. When it created administrative agencies, Congress in many cases also provided that the agencies themselves should settle such disputes. The Veterans' Administration is performing a judicial function when it settles disputes over benefits; the National Labor Relations Board when it settles disputes between labor and industry; the Internal Revenue Service when it resolves a tax controversy with an individual or corporation. Millions of such disputes arise each year in the United States over the meaning and application of administrative rules. Adjudication by the agencies themselves is the only way such disputes could possibly be settled. The

---

[33] Indeed, the "life cycle" of most independent regulatory commissions like the Interstate Commerce Commission eventually brings them to identify with the interests of the regulated. This process is discussed in Marver Bernstein, *Regulating Business by Independent Commission* (Princeton, N.J.: Princeton University Press, 1955).

[34] This participation continues notwithstanding federal laws which would seem to prohibit it. How this is accomplished and why is briefly but clearly explained by J. Leiper Freeman, "The Bureaucracy in Pressure Politics," *Annals of the American Academy of Political and Social Science* (September 1958), pp. 11–19.

nature of the disputes and the volume of the work involved precludes efficient handling by the federal courts. Furthermore, as Peter Woll has shown, most of these controversies are resolved without recourse to formal adjudicative procedures. This serves the best interests of all parties because it avoids the publicity which surrounds the use of such procedures.[35]

The bureaucracy's importance in reconciling conflict cannot be overemphasized. Its use of judicial power illustrates this importance in two ways. First, the exercise of judicial power by administrative agencies is formally prescribed by Congress. But the agencies enjoy much discretion in performing this function. Woll points out that "regardless of legal provisions governing administrative procedures and judicial review, the environment of decision making gives the agencies virtually complete discretion."[36] Second, the administrative agencies settle far more disputes than the federal courts. "It is quite common for one agency, like the Internal Revenue Service, Veterans' Administration, or the Social Security Administration to handle more cases in a year than the entire federal court system combined. The figure for the federal courts is under two hundred thousand cases a year; the Internal Revenue Service handles close to a million; the Veterans' Administration around two million."[37]

Finally, the bureaucracy performs a *representative* function. In some quarters, the greatest fear of big government stems from a belief that bureaucracies are autonomous, unrepresentative, and therefore irresponsible; they are not elected by the people, and most of their members are protected by civil service laws and fixed tenure. Furthermore, bureaucracies tend to be status quo institutions that resist change. They are highly susceptible to the debilitating effects of red tape and rigid procedures. Nevertheless, bureaucracies are consistent with the principles of representative government and perhaps are essential to it. Several aspects of the American bureaucracy support this point of view.

First, the administrative branch tends to be more responsive to the needs and demands of well-organized interests than any other branch of government. As Samuel P. Huntington expressed it, "the American system of government is moving toward a three-way system of representation. Particular territorial interests are represented in Congress; particular functional interests are represented in the administration; and the national interest is represented territorially and functionally in the presidency."[38] Administrative agencies cannot exist very long in isolation or without the support of their constituency. They must adjust themselves to the needs and demands of those groups in society to which they are closely related and upon whose support they depend. The Interstate Com-

---

[35] Woll, *op. cit.,* pp. 62–69.

[36] *Ibid.*

[37] *Ibid.*

[38] Samuel P. Huntington, "Congressional Responses to the Twentieth Century," in David B. Truman (ed.), *The Congress and America's Future* (Englewood Cliffs, N.J.: Prentice-Hall, 1965), p. 17.

merce Commission, the Veterans' Administration, the Office of Education, and the agencies within the Department of Agriculture for instance must attune themselves to the concerns of industry, veterans, educators, and farmers if they are to function effectively—if indeed they are to survive—as ongoing agencies within the government. The bureaucracy represents such groups in the policy-making process; it promotes and protects them and regulates their interests. The provision of this kind of functional representation for organized interests in society serves the purposes of representative government.

Secondly, after a presidential election in which the "out" party gains control of the White House, there is mass influx of newly-appointed political officials into the government. (This influx, however, occurs primarily in the top administrative jobs, and must not be confused with career positions in the bureaucracy.) Hundreds of positions are filled, as a rule, by men who are in sympathy with the policy preferences of the new president and the majorities who elected him to office. When this occurs, existing governmental programs are reviewed; pending programs not yet funded are delayed and reexamined; and judicial and executive appointments not yet approved in the Senate are frequently aborted. In comparing the representative nature of Congress with that of the bureaucracy, Huntington concludes:

> Every four years, the American people choose a president, but they elect an administration. In this century, the administration has acquired many of the traditional characteristics of a representative body that Congress has tended to lose. . . . Administrative officials, unlike congressmen, are more frequently mobile amateurs in government than career professionals in politics. The patterns of power in Congress are rigid. The patterns of power in the administration are flexible. The administration is thus a far more sensitive register of changing currents of opinion than is Congress. . . . Here truly is representative government along classic lines and of a sort which Congress has not known for decades.[39]

Though this argument can be carried too far, it does suggest the representative nature of that segment of the bureaucracy that is staffed by political appointments.

After the election of Richard Nixon to the presidency, the ideas and values of the political forces that brought the Republicans to power gradually came to bear on governmental politics with the selection of a new Cabinet and the appointment of new administrative officials in the bureaucracy. With no major changes in laws previously passed by Democratic administrations, governmental programs such as the War on Poverty, desegregation of public schools, federal

---

[39] *Ibid.,* p. 17.

aid to education, and the like were reviewed and adjustments were made to reflect the values or the influence of the coalitions in society that supported the President in the election. In this sense, the bureaucracy reflects to some extent the changing values of society; in doing so it performs a representative function.

Presidential Control of the Bureaucracy. Administrative agencies and executive departments are quite capable of resisting presidential leadership, and they frequently do. For example, President Roosevelt once recounted to a top aide some of his frustrations with the bureaucracy:

> The Treasury is so large and . . . ingrained in its practices that it is almost impossible to get the action and results I want. . . . But the Treasury is as nothing compared with the State Department. You should go through the experience of trying to get any changes in the thinking . . . of the career diplomats and then you'd know what a real problem was. But the Treasury and State Departments put together are nothing compared to the Na-a-vy. . . . To change anything in the Na-a-vy is like punching a feather bed. You punch it . . . until you are finally exhausted, and then you find the damn bed just as it was before you started punching.[40]

Variations on this complaint have been voiced by most modern presidents.

There are several reasons why presidents fail to control the bureaucracy as often as they succeed. First, the enormous size of the bureaucracy almost precludes successful management. Prior to 1932, the growth of the bureaucracy was gradual and episodic. With the election of Franklin Roosevelt and the nation's acceptance of the welfare state with its commitment to planning and regulation, the bureaucracy began to expand dramatically. Between 1930 and 1940, the number of federal civilian employees increased 100 percent; it has continued to grow ever since. The bureaucracy now employs 7 percent of the nation's work force; three fourths of all present federal positions have been created since 1932. The federal bureaucracy today consists of 12 executive departments, 8 independent regulatory agencies, and an almost endless number of other governmental corporations, commissions, bureaus, and agencies.

The growth of the administrative process in American government represents a normal stage in the development of the political system. As in other western political systems, the vast administrative apparatus designed to regulate the social, economic, and industrial growth of the country developed in response

---

[40] Marriner S. Eccles in Sidney Hyman (ed.), *Beckoning Frontiers* (New York: Alfred A. Knopf, 1951), p. 336. Quoted in Woll, *op. cit.,* p. 193.

to the changing demands of a modernizing society. As Peter Woll has written about the growth of independent regulatory commissions, "in virtually every case these additional regulatory agencies were established as a result of political pressure for some form of national control, arising directly from economic problems associated with the industries concerned."[41]

Moreover, Congress may interfere with the president's efforts to control the bureaucracy. Since 1949, the president has had the authority to reorganize the bureaucracy as he chooses, unless Congress formally rejects the changes.

Every president after Franklin Roosevelt has tried to reorganize the bureaucracy, hoping to strengthen his control over its activities, to reduce duplication, to make the vast administrative structure more manageable. These efforts have failed more often than they have succeeded. For example, at least 50 percent of President Kennedy's reorganization plans were rejected by Congress;[42] Congress created the bureaucracy and tends to protect it, regarding it as a check on the president. Presidential efforts to expand control over the bureaucracy are thus usually suspect in Congress. This is especially true when such efforts affect administrative agencies that have carefully cultivated friends on congressional committees.

A third problem, suggested by President Roosevelt's remark about the Navy, is that the federal bureaucracy—like any large bureaucratic organization—is sluggish, conservative, and prone to maintain the status quo. Recognizing this, presidents Roosevelt and Kennedy—both more than ordinarily alert to administrative complexities—preferred to create new agencies to administer new programs, thereby bypassing the "old line" departments in favor of more flexible and imaginative new organizations.[43] The result of this approach, however, was to further increase the number of executive bodies.

A fourth problem springs from the differences in outlook between the president, his political advisers, and the professional bureaucrats who staff the federal agencies. The daily concerns and often the long-range goals of the president and the bureaucracy are not the same. The president and his advisers are, in a sense, administrative amateurs whose expertise lies in politics and whose responsibilities are primarily political; they are often transients in Washington whose terms of office customarily end after eight years or less. The career civil service, on the other hand, is mainly composed of professional, permanent administrators and experts. Careers officials, Harry Truman once complained, "regard themselves as the men who really make policy and run the government. They look upon the elected officials as just temporary occupants."[44] Such an

---

[41] Woll, *op. cit.*

[42] Woll, *op. cit.*, Chapter 4.

[43] On Roosevelt's distrust of "old line" agencies see Arthur M. Schlesinger, Jr., "Roosevelt as Chief Administrator," in Rourke (ed.), *op. cit.*, pp. 89–101.

[44] Quoted in Marcus Cunliffe, *The American Heritage History of the Presidency* (New York: Simon and Schuster, 1968), p. 300.

accusation ignores the goodwill and faithful cooperation that the career bureaucrat usually renders to the president, but it does emphasize why cleavages and tensions often arise between civil service and presidential administrators.

Finally, many of the president's most serious administrative problems arise from the political struggles within the bureaucracy. Established bureaucratic agencies develop a strong vested interest in their own survival and in their continued participation in policy-making. They will oppose any measures or any other agencies that appear to threaten their status or their control over funds or programs. Often, therefore, the federal bureaucracy is riddled with interagency and interdepartmental competition for funds, personnel, and favors. Sometimes the president becomes the focus of this competition and congressional committees and interest groups are usually drawn into the conflict on various sides. One frequent result of this rivalry is that particular departments or agencies, in search of political alliances to bolster their strength, develop strong ties with influential congressmen, specific congressional committees, and influential interests in the country that are affected by the agencies' work. All federal departments, for example, have congressional lobbyists; the successful agencies often achieve such status in Congress and such intense support among their constituents that they become virtually immune from serious presidential direction. This has been the case with the Federal Bureau of Investigation and its director, the venerable J. Edgar Hoover; so firmly rooted in Congress and the nation is the FBI that presidents have chosen to avoid any serious struggle with it.

Conflicts within the bureaucracy often force the president to spend much of his time acting as a referee between competing claims over programs and personnel. Too often, compromises are sought. The result is that control and management of governmental programs and policies remain divided among several agencies or departments, and duplication, with the expense and confusion it entails, persists in the bureaucracy. For example, the Central Intelligence Agency was supposed to become the principal intelligence arm of the federal government following the National Security Act of 1947. But all the armed services, the FBI, the State Department, and even the Atomic Energy Commission have continued their own intelligence activities. This pluralistic power struggle within the bureaucracy, which involves Congress and interest groups as well as the president, also means that the president must often compete for control of the administrative apparatus.

In the end, many of the president's problems could be solved if he possessed enough authority to administer the executive branch adequately. Considering his immense responsibilities as the chief executive, his actual authority over his own branch of government is extremely limited. He can appoint, but not dismiss, many officers; he can create but not enact a budget; he cannot make major reorganizations in any department if Congress vetoes the change; many of his administrative subordinates exercise independent authority delegated directly to them by Congress—and so forth. It is doubtful, however, whether the president's administrative powers will be significantly expanded as his diplomatic and military powers have been. Attempts to do so have not proven very effective.

The President and Congress

Less than a year before he became president, Senator John Kennedy spoke optimistically about the powers of the chief executive. The president, he said, must be the "chief executive in every sense of the word," prepared to exercise "the fullest powers of the office." Quoting Woodrow Wilson approvingly, Kennedy concluded: "The president is at liberty, both in law and in conscience, to be as big a man as he can. . . . His capacity will set the limit." Three years later President Kennedy spoke of his office in different terms:

> The president . . . is rightly described as a man of extraordinary powers.
> . . . Yet it is also true that he must wield these powers under extraordinary
> limitation. . . . Lincoln, Franklin Roosevelt once remarked, "was a sad man
> because he couldn't get it all at once." And nobody can. Every president must
> endure the gap between what he would like and what is possible.[45]

Like other presidents nourishing energetic concepts of the chief executive, John Kennedy had come to terms with the difference between the president's great diplomatic and military authority in international matters and his much more constricted domestic powers in dealing with Congress and the bureaucracy. His authority is less predictable, his influence more variable, the constraints upon him more consistent in this area. In the right hands and under the proper circumstances, the president is capable of truly dazzling legislative performance; his legislative influence may then seem as compelling as any of his other powers. During the first hundred days of Franklin Roosevelt's administration, in an unparalleled demonstration of executive leadership, the President sent an avalanche of revolutionary legislation to Congress. This legislation was passed by Congress almost as fast as the president and his bleary-eyed advisers could write it.[46] Within his first year, Lyndon Johnson moved the long-delayed Civil Rights Bill, the War on Poverty Program, tax reform bills, and other major legislation through Congress so swiftly that his reputation as a superlative political practitioner seemed vindicated. Yet these performances are memorable because they are exceptional. Neither Roosevelt nor Johnson continued to enjoy such success

---

[45] Quoted by Tom Wicker, *JFK and LBJ* (New York: William Morrow & Co., 1968), pp. 27–28.

[46] The early, hectic days of the New Deal are well recounted in Arthur Schlesinger, Jr., *The Coming of the New Deal* (Boston: Houghton Mifflin Co., 1958).

with Congress, and most presidents' legislative programs have met much resistance and delay. Most of the time, the president's legislative power is the capacity to propose, rather than the power to dispose, legislative programs.

The Constitution itself granted the president a positive and a negative role in the legislative process. In his positive role, the chief executive is to "give Congress information on the state of the union, and to recommend to their consideration such measures as he shall judge necessary and expedient . . ." This is the basis for presidential initiative and influence. In his negative role, he can veto any measure sent to him by Congress—although Congress can override his veto by a two-thirds vote in both chambers. However, the veto has never been a principal instrument used by presidents with major legislative programs.

Strong presidents have constantly expanded their legislative role until today the president is considered the "chief legislator." This imposing title badly misstates the president's true legislative powers—he can, after all, legislate nothing; he only proposes legislation and campaigns for it—but it admirably reflects the responsibilities he is expected to assume. "We look to him because he has unlimited powers to make proposals for action. He can, if he chooses, espouse any cause, from simplified spelling to the soil bank, and whatever he says will be heard and noticed."[47] To be heard and noticed, of course, is not necessarily to be followed. Nevertheless, a president's record, the compendium of defeats and victories that he eventually submits to public judgment, is fashioned on the legislative battlefield as much as anywhere else.

The American federal government is a set of separate institutions sharing powers.[48] This is especially the case in legislative affairs. Either house of Congress may bury proposed legislation in committees, defeat it on floor votes, or sidetrack it at innumerable other points in the legislative process. What is almost as effective, Congress may drastically rewrite or emasculate presidential legislation until it no longer resembles its original form. Indeed, because the legislative process is essentially conservative, the initial advantage usually lies with those opposing legislation.

The party system, ostensively a device through which presidents may rally dependable partisan support for their programs, often works to their disadvantage. If the White House and Congress are controlled by different parties, impasse and legislative stalemate may result, especially in domestic policy. In the last two years of Harry Truman's first term, while urgent post-war problems awaited solution, the congressional Republican majority—fully expecting a thumping Republican victory in 1948—did nothing to enhance Truman's legislative record. Republican inaction prompted the peppery chief executive to make "that no-good, do-nothing 80th Congress" a major (and effective) campaign issue. Presidents enjoying nominal congressional majorities seldom find them dependable. John Kennedy reportedly considered a majority of 89 Democrats

[47] Koenig, *op. cit.*, p. 6.
[48] Neustadt, *Presidential Power*, p. 33.

in the House and 28 in the Senate insufficient because many of these Democrats were conservative Southerners; his judgment was prophetic. The Administration's farm bill, Medicare, the proposed Department of Urban Affairs, and other major proposals divided Democrats in both chambers and remained stalemated in Congress throughout Kennedy's term. Congressional reactions to Nixon's legislative programs proved that party infidelity is bipartisan. Nixon had promised Southern delegates at the Republican nominating convention that he would extend provisions of the 1965 Voting Rights Act to the nation, and thereby take the heat of federal voting supervision off the South alone. His initial proposal was defeated in the House Judiciary Committee when 12 of 15 Republican members voted to extend the life of the 1965 Act instead. "I don't like fighting the White House," remarked the senior Republican on the House Judiciary Committee, "but maybe after this they'll listen to some of us."[49]

Congressional control over taxes and appropriations poses another formidable challenge to the president. In government, budgeting is policy-making; the power to apportion money is the power to say what shall be done. Congress may assert its budgetary powers over the chief executive in many ways. Appropriation committees often reward or punish various agencies, administrators, or programs according to their standing with influential members of the committee; appropriations may be increased handsomely or decreased to the point of killing an agency or program. Furthermore, Congressional committees may write allocations for programs opposed by the administration but favored by the committee chairman into an appropriation bill. This control of funds, of course, gives Congress an important potential role in diplomatic and military affairs. In recent years, Congress has continually reduced foreign aid appropriations below levels acceptable to the Johnson and Nixon administrations. And it was the threat to cut off funds for further American military operations in Cambodia in 1970 which the Senate used to reassert its demand that it be consulted on foreign policy matters, especially those involving the commitment of American forces.

Both houses of Congress may also harass incumbent administrations, and perhaps cost them votes at the polls by formally investigating them. Such investigations are more likely to occur when congressional committees rest in control of the "out" party; the temptation to launch expeditions in search of administration blunders is especially strong. Senate Democrats, using President Eisenhower's vaunted integrity as a foil, relentlessly exposed the indiscretions of the President's most trusted adviser, Sherman Adams, through investigations of the House Committee on Legislative Oversight. They thereby caused Adams' resignation from office, acutely embarrassing the President himself and tarnishing his image.[50] Yet Eisenhower had suffered earlier at the hands of his own party's congressional investigators. Beginning in 1953, Senator Joseph McCarthy, a

---

[49] Representative William M. McCulloch of Ohio, quoted by the Associated Press, September 5, 1969.

[50] See Hughes, *op. cit.*, pp. 266–272, for an assessment of the Adams affair by the President and his advisers.

Republican from Wisconsin, waged an inflammatory and reckless search for "subversion" in the federal government. McCarthy's tactics bitterly divided the Republican party and the nation, demoralized the federal bureaucracy, and ended with accusations of disloyalty against the President, ex-Secretary of State George Marshall, and other major military and political figures.

In any discussion of congressional checks upon the president, however, the Senate deserves· special consideration. The Constitution bestows many singular powers upon this body that vitally affect the president's conduct, especially in diplomatic and military affairs. It obliges the president to ask the Senate's "advice and consent" on treaties and to submit all ambassadorial appointments to this body as well. It establishes the Senate's prerogative to approve "all other officers of the United States," unless Congress chooses by law to exempt certain federal offices from this requirement. Though civil service laws now place the great majority of federal positions on a merit basis that excludes Senatorial approval, the most important policy-making positions still lie in the realm of Senatorial consent: ambassadors, cabinet officials, heads of independent regulatory commissions, members of the Supreme Court, and lesser federal courts, the postmaster, and others.

Senate leaders, especially members of the Senate Foreign Relations Committee, are customarily consulted and briefed on diplomatic and military affairs and often participate personally in major diplomatic events.[51] Moreover, the Senate's opinions and problems of whatever nature affect this body's attitude toward diplomatic affairs; presidents, accordingly, have become sensitized to the influence that even ostensively domestic political problems may have on foreign affairs. According to one report, when President Johnson met West German Premier Erhard on the LBJ Texas ranch about a month after John Kennedy's assassination, the discussion turned to Cuba, NATO, Russia, and chickens. "No easy agreement on the touchy question of Germany's semi-embargo on American chickens"[52] was reached. President Johnson wanted the embargo stopped. The ban hurt Arkansas, a major poultry-producing state and home of J. William Fulbright, Chairman of the Senate Foreign Relations Committee. Fulbright, the President reminded the Premier, might retaliate in some unspecified manner. However incongruous, the intrusion of the chicken problem on discussions of high diplomacy testifies to the role that the Senate's politics play in the president's conduct of foreign affairs.

Superficially, the Senate's role in confirming presidential nominees to high office seems relatively cooperative and deferential, for the Senate rarely rejects such nominations. However, this cooperation is achieved through understandings between president and Senate that indicate the Senate has considerable influence

---

[51] The major work on Congressional participation in foreign policy is still Robert A. Dahl, *Congress and Foreign Policy* (New York: Harcourt Brace Jovanovich, 1950). The particular role of the House of Representatives is discussed in Holbert N. Carroll, *The House of Representatives and Foreign Affairs,* rev. ed. (Boston: Little, Brown and Co., 1966).

[52] Senator Fulbright's chickens are discussed in Evans and Novak, *op. cit.,* p. 389.

in the nominating process; moreover, notwithstanding these accommodations, the Senate has sometimes risen to defeat major presidential nominees, a continuing reminder of the chamber's capacity for independence. Wisely, the Senate customarily leaves the president great liberty to select his cabinet officials and other close advisers. Through the informal practice of "senatorial courtesy," however, presidents are expected to nominate individuals to federal positions in the states (such as lower-court judges and postmasters) only after consultation with the ranking Senator of the president's party in the states affected. In any case, presidents normally take senatorial opinion into account before making any nominations; men unlikely to receive senatorial approval are rarely nominated. Still, these strategies for minimizing conflict between president and Senate may fail to prevent a direct senatorial challenge to presidential nominees: the Senate's refusal to confirm the appointment of Clement Haynsworth and G. Harrold Carswell to the Supreme Court during President Nixon's first administration is an excellent case in point.

The result of the Constitution's check-and-balance system seems clear: Congress and president are usually uneasy and fitful collaborators. Periods of sustained deadlock have been infrequent, but so have periods of dependable and unobstructive collaboration. Congress most often seems to be a rival rather than an ally of the president. Yet this is not inevitable. In times of crisis, war, depression, and national disaster, Congress feels persuaded to yield—albeit temporarily—to executive leadership. Broad and indeterminate grants of legislative power are delegated to the president, as occurred during World Wars I and II and the Great Depression, and Congress usually cooperates in supporting presidential programs, though partisan rivalries do not disappear. Ordinarily, however, there is conflict, because congressional constituencies are states and parts of states and their interests are local rather than national. "A labor union, a Chamber of Commerce, or a citizen's group normally has greater impact upon a senator's or representative's future than all the will and might of the president of the United States."[53] Explaining why he voted to reject Clement Haynsworth, one Senate Republican said candidly that Nixon's Attorney General, then strenuously campaigning for Haynsworth, carried no weight at home. "It doesn't do me a bit of harm at home to have John Mitchell mad as hell at me," he observed.

Conversely, presidents are prone to think in terms of national interests, national problems, the flow of the nation-wide vote. These different constituencies, with their often different perspectives on national politics and problems, almost guarantee that congressmen and presidents, under the best of circumstances, will usually entertain different ideas of the public interest and of their political interests.

To summarize: in his administrative and legislative capacities, the President is seldom the all-powerful executive the public imagines him to be. The gap between the real and the imaginary presidency is wide. A president who wants to

---

[53] Koenig, *op. cit.*, p. 135.

be a strong chief executive must find a formula that maximizes his power and influence and reduces as much as possible the obstacles to effective executive leadership. To do so, he must persuade governmental institutions to cooperate by overcoming the pluralism and divisions within and among them. He must master the complexities of the governmental process if he is to give concerted purpose and direction to the nation's public policy.

No president succeeds entirely at this task. However, as we suggested earlier, there is more scope for success in diplomatic and military than in domestic affairs. We turn now to an examination of the reasons for the president's preeminence in these areas.

Presidential Preeminence in Foreign Affairs

As the nation's diplomatic chief and military leader, the president usually enjoys fuller initiative, greater powers and prerogatives, and more constantly imposing stature than in any of his other roles.

The Nature of the State System

In most lands, the chief executive has long been recognized as at the center of foreign policy decisions. The ruler of the state, whether he was an eighteenth-century king who had inherited the Crown or a twentieth-century prime minister who had been elected to his office, was considered the "guardian of the national interests." An essentially anarchical international system demanded a single source of decision-making so that a state could act with dispatch, continuity of purpose, secrecy, flexibility, and authority. Legislatures were not considered able to act in this manner. Even after they came to be accepted as bodies representing the "will of the people," they were confined to dealing with domestic affairs. As institutions representing the *vox populi,* they were generally thought to be unstable in foreign policy. By the very nature of their function, they debated proposed policies at length, and thus they could not make rapid decisions wisely; because they reflected the popular passions of the moment, they would be too flexible at some times, too rigid at others.

Thus, the primacy of the executive in foreign policy was a response to the primitive nature of the state system[54] and is symbolized by the fact that almost

---

[54] See, for instance, John Locke who distinguished between the executive and federative powers. The former, dealing with domestic policy, was subject to legislative restraint; the latter, concerned with foreign policy, was "much less capable to be directed by antecedent, standing, positive laws than the executive; and so must necessarily be left to the prudence

every major American foreign policy is stamped with a president's name: Washington's Farewell Address (in which he advised his countrymen to pursue a policy of nonentanglement), Jefferson's Embargo, the Monroe Doctrine, Theodore Roosevelt's "Big Stick" policy, Wilson's Fourteen Points, Franklin Roosevelt's Good Neighbor policy, the Truman Doctrine, and the Nixon Doctrine on American overseas commitments, especially in Asia. Indeed, in 1970 President Nixon issued a lengthy report to the Congress entitled "United States Foreign Policy for the 1970s: A New Strategy for Peace."[55] Every president who has been rated a strong leader owes this rating partly to his authority in international politics.

From Eisenhower on, knowledge and experience in international affairs has been a prime qualification for presidential candidates. Every post-war president—except Eisenhower, who had already gained his experience in international politics by a lifetime of service in the Army—was from the Senate where presumably he had gained some knowledge of foreign policy on committees or in debates. Foreign affairs are so much a part of the twentieth-century president's fundamental responsibilities that many of our presidents have also tended to act as their own secretaries of state. At the outset of American intervention in World War I, President Wilson announced his famous Fourteen Points in an effort to define not only American objectives but also the aims he expected the whole allied war effort to accomplish. Franklin Roosevelt almost disregarded his secretary of state, particularly during World War II, when he attended conferences with Prime Minister Churchill and Premier Stalin but left an uninformed Secretary Hull at home.[56] Kennedy selected Dean Rusk, a former Assistant Secretary of State for Far Eastern Affairs during the Truman period, because he was unassertive and would let the President play the primary role.[57] Nixon chose a friend and complete novice to foreign policy, Secretary William Rogers. Since Kennedy, presidents have selected very able Special Assistants for National Security Affairs; these Assistants, carrying more influence with the president than the Secretary of State, have provided the expert advice that has helped the President be his own Secretary of State. Since 1945, only Presidents Truman and Eisenhower relied primarily upon their Secretaries of State, Dean Acheson and John Foster Dulles, respectively.[58]

---

and wisdom of those whose hands it is in . . ." Quoted by Paul Seabury, *Power, Freedom, and Diplomacy* (New York: Vintage Books, 1967), pp. 189–90.

[55] *The New York Times,* February 19, 1970.

[56] See, for example, Herbert Feis, *Churchill, Roosevelt, Stalin* (Princeton, N.J.: Princeton University Press, 1957).

[57] Hilsmann, *op. cit.,* brings this out very clearly, particularly in pp. 41–43; so does Arthur Schlesinger, Jr., *A Thousand Days* (New York: Fawcett, 1967), pp. 401–405.

[58] On this point, see Acheson's memoirs, *Present at the Creation* (New York: W. W. Norton & Co., 1969); and Louis L. Gerson, *John Foster Dulles* (New York: Cooper Square Publishers, 1967).

All postwar presidents have immersed themselves deeply in foreign policy problems. Even when they wished to devote themselves primarily to domestic programs, foreign affairs have taken most of their time and resources. Indeed, so great have been these responsibilities that a failure in foreign policy is unlikely to be redeemed even by a superior performance in domestic affairs. Lyndon Johnson, who always looked upon himself as an old New Dealer with roots in domestic reform reaching back to the great programs of the early Roosevelt Administration, is generally conceded to have accomplished a dramatic and lavishly liberal domestic legislative program. However, Johnson inherited a deteriorating Vietnamese situation which he could not resolve. His massive involvement of American forces in that conflict and his continuing inability to end it—by either military or diplomatic means—eventually fragmented his party and alienated large segments of the electorate.

The American president is judged by his "foreign constituents" as well as by the domestic electorate. He is, in a sense, president of the West, or more specifically, of NATO; he must earn the confidence and support of other western countries as well as that of his own. An American president cannot tell his allies what to do or command their armies; he can only persuade them, so he must first earn their confidence. When Kennedy visited West Berlin and shouted to the thousands of Berliners watching him that he was a Berliner too, he aptly summed up the fact that the president has a multiplicity of foreign constituents who depend on his wisdom and on the strength of the United States for their security.

The nature of the state system, especially during World War II and the succeeding Cold War period of extensive and intensive bipolarity, has thus propelled the president into a preeminent position of foreign policy making. The role of Congress in the field of foreign policy from 1945 until Vietnam has been strictly subordinate, if not peripheral—which can hardly be said of its role in the domestic sphere. There are several reasons for this. The president has the capacity to commit the nation; he has at his disposal more information about other nations than anyone else; he is the chief interpreter of the world to the nation; Congress and the public generally defer to him on foreign policy; and the principal executive agencies involved in policy formulation either are not tied to domestic constituencies (State Department) or else they are divided within and are therefore controllable by the president (Pentagon).

The Capacity to Commit the Nation

The capacity to commit the nation derives from the president's authority as the nation's chief diplomat and commander-in-chief. Because he appoints ambassadors, the president has the power to extend or withhold recognition of other states. He can recognize a state within a few hours of its creation, as Harry Truman recognized Israel, or withhold recognition indefinitely, as Truman and all his successors have done in the case of Communist China. Since the Senate defeated President Wilson and the Versailles Peace Treaty at the end of World War I, it has usually been consulted before any treaty is put into final draft.[59] On the other hand, the Senate can hardly afford not to back the president unless it wishes to undermine his credibility as the nation's spokesman in world affairs and humiliate both him and the United States. Whether on treaties or on broad policy commitments not requiring treaty approval, the president can take the initiative. When Truman declared that "it must be the policy of the United States to support free peoples who are resisting subjection by armed minorities or outside pressure," Congress had no alternative but to approve the Truman Doctrine, which constituted the beginning of a whole series of Cold War measures which Congress felt compelled to approve in the national interest. When Kennedy advocated a limited test ban agreement with Russia, the opposition might have been vocal and skeptical, but in the end the Senate approved.

If he wishes the president can always avoid making treaties. Executive agreements, which have virtually the same standing, need no congressional approval (although such agreements can also be made after Congress has given general authorization to the president to negotiate with another country a particular area). As the Nazi threat to American security increased after the fall of France, President Roosevelt felt it was in the nation's vital interest to prevent Britain, the guardian of the Atlantic approaches to the United States, from being invaded and defeated.[60] He thus made the famous "destroyer deal" which sent fifty older destroyers to help the English guard the Channel in return for the British bases in the Caribbean. In fact, presidents today rarely resort to treaties except on fundamental policy where it is important to clarify to the world the nation's new commitment, as in the formation of NATO or the Nuclear Anti-Proliferation Treaty. But, on the whole, executive agreements vastly outnumber treaties.

Undoubtedly, the greatest source of the president's authority in foreign policy is his role as commander-in-chief. Using this power, Wilson armed American merchant ships prior to our entry into World War I. Franklin Roosevelt, after securing congressional support for a lend-lease program under which the United States would become "the arsenal for democracy," saw little point in sending weapons to Britain unless they got there. With the British navy

---

[59] Bipartisanship emerged after World War I partly as a result of the Versailles Peace Treaty. Presidents were also reminded of their need to consult with the Senate, not spurn its advice as Wilson had done with Republican Senator Lodge, by such eminent historians as Thomas A. Bailey, in *Woodrow Wilson and the Last Peace* (New York: Macmillan Co., 1944) and in *Woodrow Wilson and the Great Betrayal* (New York: Macmillan Co., 1945)—especially in the latter.

[60] The Roosevelt administration's foreign policy is painstakingly reconstructed in William L. Langer and S. Everett Gleason, *The Challenge to Isolation* (New York: Harper & Row, Publishers, 1952) and in *The Undeclared War* (New York: Harper & Row, Publishers, 1953).

stretched thin guarding the Channel and convoying supplies across the Atlantic from this country, he decided to have American warships help convoy the merchant ships to Iceland, where the British navy took over. He also had American ships report German submarines to the British and, after a U-boat finally shot back at a pursuing American destroyer, ordered American ships to reply when fired upon. In short, he engaged Germany in a limited and undeclared naval war in the Atlantic. Since then, presidential initiative has become commonplace. President Truman initiated the Berlin Airlift; Presidents Eisenhower and Kennedy made commitments to South Vietnam in 1954 and 1961, also without formal reference to Congress. Kennedy further launched the abortive Bay of Pigs invasion of Cuba in 1961 and blockaded Cuba during the Missile Crisis a year later. His successor, President Johnson intervened in the Dominican Republic in 1965.

Sometimes, to be sure, the president intervened after Congress had authorized him to use American armed forces. But there is little difference between the president acting on his own and acting after receiving legislative assent through a congressional resolution. Congress could hardly repudiate him after he had publicly requested such authority on the implicit understanding that he already possessed it anyway, but sought bipartisan approval because it would strengthen his diplomatic hand and, hopefully, ward off later domestic criticisms of those actions. Thus, Eisenhower sent forces into Lebanon and committed them to the defense of Formosa, Quemoy, and Matsu; President Johnson—after Kennedy's initial commitment of 16,500 military "advisers"—sent over one-half million men into South Vietnam under the Gulf of Tonkin resolution. Indeed "Truman's war" in Korea and "Johnson's war" in Vietnam clearly demonstrate the nature of the president's authority to define the nation's interests and employ troops to support them. Both were undeclared wars. President Truman, surprised by the North Korean invasion of South Korea, almost immediately committed American forces to the latter's defense. While he called in congressional leaders to inform them of the gravity of the situation, he did not ask for their approval; he assumed the United States had to act, and Congress agreed. Indeed, he *never* asked for nor received formal congressional approval. He felt he already had the authority to commit American forces.[61] Congress did not turn on Truman until the war seemed interminable, the casualty lists had become too long, the economic costs too high, the congressmen had received too many complaints from constituents, and they themselves had begun to feel that the United States should never have involved itself in an Asian land war. In these circumstances, it did not matter whether the President had congressional approval or not. While things went well in Korea and Vietnam, support was forthcoming; when things went badly, no congressional resolution could have shielded the president from the spears of his opposition. The Senate's repudia-

---

[61] Spanier, *op. cit.,* pp. 32–40.

tion of the Gulf of Tonkin Resolution in 1970 was thus largely symbolic; it put the President on notice that in the post-Vietnam period the President should consult that body before launching new military ventures.

Once involved in war, of course, presidents decide military strategy, which has vast political implications. For example, Roosevelt decided, first, that Germany should be defeated before Japan. Next, he chose to invade across the English Channel rather than (as the British wanted) to drive into the Balkans via Northern Italy and Yugoslavia, heading the Russians off in eastern Europe. As a result, the western and Soviet armies met in the center of Germany, leaving Russia in control of eastern Europe. In Korea, Truman—who had already made the unprecedented decision to hasten the end of World War II by dropping two atomic bombs on Japan—decided not only to repel the North Korean invasion but to extend the war effort into North Korea after defeating the communists in South Korea. This decision prompted the Communist Chinese to send thousands of "volunteer" troops into North Korea to counterattack American forces moving north toward their frontier. Determined to avoid a major war with China, President Truman then forbade American forces to extend the war beyond the Yalu river frontier or to attack positions in China itself. This brought a dramatic showdown with one of the nation's great war heroes, Douglas MacArthur. When MacArthur insisted that there was "no substitute for victory" and refused to stop his public criticism of the President's limited war strategy, he was dismissed from his post as commander of American forces in Korea and the Pacific.[62]

No decisions which Lyndon Johnson made in office more deeply affected public consciousness, his party's fortunes, America's image in the world, or the politics of the late 1960s than those he made as commander-in-chief of American forces in Vietnam. None of these decisions was more important than the one made in 1965 to escalate our military commitments. This decision made Vietnam the third most costly war in American history and our largest, most expensive, and bloodiest undeclared war.

Conducting wars is only one of the president's military powers, and not necessarily the most sweeping one. The American presence itself in these conflicts suggests a wider presidential authority. As commander-in-chief and chief diplomat, the president is responsible for assuring the nation's military security and preparedness at all times, a burden that also confers upon him a potentially vast range of powers without precise limits. At a minimum, he is responsible for deploying American forces as he sees fit; for organizing and equipping the military establishment (in cooperation with Congress, which must authorize the appropriations); and—perhaps the most open-ended part of his authority—for defining the nation's military and security interests. Although presidents do not act alone in discharging any of these responsibilities, the presidency has increasingly become the real focus of these powers.

---

[62] *Ibid.,* pp. 187–207.

The Power of Knowledge

Another reason for presidential predominance in foreign policy is the "power of knowledge" possessed by the president. The president, drawing upon the vast capabilities of the executive departments and agencies, far surpasses any other individual within the government in his command of information about international matters. The principal departments concerned with foreign policy, the State and Defense Departments, the Central Intelligence Agency, as well as such second-rank organizations as the Arms Control and Disarmament Agency and departments such as Commerce who are concerned with specific areas of foreign affairs, all collect and interpret data on other countries. The prodigious amount of data digested by the State Department alone can perhaps best be noted by the following statistic: in 1930, the telegraphic traffic for the entire year totaled only two million words; by the 1960s, traffic for every two months was greater than for the whole of 1930.[63]

Congress clearly does not collect such a volume of data. It does not even have enough time to read the information already available, whether it comes from the executive agencies or from special congressional committees appointed to look into specific foreign situations. For example, as the United States was about to launch the Marshall Plan, one of the most dramatic of the early postwar moves, the following exchange took place between the Staff Director of the Republican Senate Policy Committee and Republican Senator Ferguson:

Mr. Smith: Now, Senators, for your amusement as well as to bear out my point on the impossible work load put upon members of Congress, I have gathered here a group of the books and reports, limited solely to an official character, which you should be reading right now on the Marshall plan.

(Mr. Smith here presented a stack of material 18 inches high.)

You are going to take the most momentous step in the history of this country when you pass upon the Marshall plan. . . . [This stack] is what you ought to be studying. It contains the Krug report, the Harriman report, the State Department report, the reports of the Herter committee, the Foreign Relations Committee digest; it includes part of the hearings just completed by the Foreign Relations Committee. It does not include hearings yet to be held by the Appropriations Committees. This is one work load you have now on a single problem out of the many problems you have to decide.

Senator Ferguson: How long would it take in your opinion . . . for a person to read it?

Mr. Smith: Well, Senator, I have been reading for the last 35 years, nearly all my life, in the field of research; and if I could do an intelligent job on that

---

[63] Schlesinger, *A Thousand Days*, p. 380.

in 2 months of solid reading, excluding myself from everything else . . . I would credit myself with great efficiency.

Senator Ferguson: A normal person would probably take 4 to 5 months.[64]

If this situation is multiplied by the many situations which are constantly developing, Congress' dependence upon the executive branch becomes obvious.

But the information by itself is less significant than its interpretation. What do the facts mean? What do they say about another nation's capabilities and intentions, or the meaning of a new country's nationalism, or the domestic evolution of the Soviet Union, or the Sino-Soviet dispute? Here again, since the end of World War II, the Congress and the public have depended on the executive. For instance, prior to the anouncement of the Truman Doctrine, President Truman, Secretary of State Marshall, and Under-Secretary Acheson met with congressional leaders. The congressmen were given Marshall's description of Britain's withdrawal from Greece and Turkey. They were briefed on the situation this would create, and on these countries' vulnerability to Soviet domination. American aid was recommended. Congress was skeptical. The impression the legislative leaders gained from Secretary Marshall's presentation was that aid should be extended for humanitarian reasons and to bolster Britain's middle-eastern position. The congressmen were in no mood to "pull British chestnuts out of the fire"; at the time, their primary concern was domestic. But Acheson rescued the situation by clearly relating help for Greece and Turkey to American security interests. He described at length the persistent Soviet pressures on the two countries as attempts to penetrate and seek control of the Middle East as well as Greece. Because England could no longer support Greece and Turkey, the United States must assume the burden in order to contain Russian expansion. It was not a question of pulling British chestnuts out of the fire, but of protecting American security. When they realized this, the congressmen withdrew their opposition.[65]

Since then, the executive has often interpreted the state of the world to the leaders of Congress. Congress has usually accepted these interpretations as well as administration policies. Congress may be allowed to modify presidential policies so that it—especially the Senate—will feel it is participating in the policy process. But rarely do such modifications touch the essence of executive policy; only on a few issues, such as the recognition of Communist China and the foreign aid program, has Congress asserted its views—by opposing recognition and drastically cutting foreign aid. On the whole, however, the principal function of Congress has been to support and legitimate presidential policy.

Congress is currently taking a more critical attitude toward the role of the United States in world affairs. This attitude reflects a strong feeling that Con-

---

[64] Quoted in Dahl, *op. cit.,* pp. 129–30.

[65] Acheson, *op. cit.,* p. 219. The more detailed and better version may be found in Joseph Jones, *The Fifteen Weeks* (New York: Viking Press, 1955), pp. 138–141.

gress must scrutinize more carefully the president's proposals, and the interpretations of the intentions and capabilities of other nations on which they are based. Congress wishes to avoid more Vietnams, another arms cycle, and perhaps above all, further neglecting urgent domestic problems. This reaction amply testifies to the importance of the way in which the executive interprets the facts; Congress seems determined therefore to scrutinize Presidential policy more carefully in the future, and, if necessary, contest these interpretations.

The post-war record of foreign policy measures advocated by the president and legitimated by the Congress is indeed outstanding. It stands in bright contrast to the presidential record on domestic policies. Aaron Wildavsky has aptly commented that:

> The president's normal problem with domestic policy is to get congressional support for the program he prefers. In foreign affairs, in contrast, he can almost always get support for policies he believes will protect the nation—but his problem is to find a viable policy. . . .
>
> In the realm of foreign policy, there has not been a single major issue on which presidents, when they were serous and determined, have failed. The list of their victories is impressive; entry into the United Nations, the Marshall Plan, NATO, the Truman Doctrine, the decision to stay out of Indochina in 1954 and to intervene in Vietnam in the 1960s, aid to Poland and Yugoslavia, the test-ban treaty, and many more. Serious setbacks to the president in controlling foreign policy are extraordinary and unusual.[66]

If refugee and immigration issues—which Congress regards as domestic—are excluded, the record from 1948 to 1964 shows that presidents prevailed 70

Table 9.1. Congressional Action on Presidential Proposals, 1948–1964

Policy Area	Congressional Action		Number of Proposals
	% Pass	% Fail	
Domestic policy (natural resources, labor, agriculture, taxes, etc.)	40.2	59.8	2499
Defense policy (defense, disarmament, manpower, misc.)	73.3	26.7	90
Foreign policy	58.5	41.5	655
Immigration, refugees	13.2	86.0	129
Treaties, general foreign relations, State Department, foreign aid	70.8	29.2	445

Source: Congressional Quarterly Service, *Congress and the Nation, 1945–1964* (Washington, 1965).

[66] Wildavsky, *op. cit.,* p. 93.

percent of the time on foreign and defense issues, in contrast to 40 percent on domestic issues. President Kennedy's case is an example of this; although his popularity rose after his monumental blunder at the Bay of Pigs, domestically, he had trouble mustering enough support in Congress to pass his policies on civil rights and education into law.

Public Deference to Presidential Policies

If there are two words that sum up the role of public opinion in foreign policy, they are "supportive" and "permissive." Public opinion in the post-war period has mostly allowed the president to determine external policies; only within very broad limits has it established the outer boundaries for government action. It might, of course, be objected that one cannot talk of "public opinion" as if it were a single attitude characterized by a common sense of identification and a common response to general stimuli. Since the "public" is actually a variety of interests and groups that are differently affected by, and therefore react differently to, general and specific policies, it might seem more accurate to discuss the opinions of various publics. Gabriel Almond, for example, has divided the public into three groups: the policy and opinion elites (the political, administrative, interest, and communications elites who really determine policy); the attentive public (the informed, educated, and interested section of the public which constitutes the audience for foreign policy debates); and the mass public (poorly informed and uninterested in foreign policy and in general reacting passively, except in crises, when it reacts in terms of "moods.")[67] Alternatively, one may consider the influence of the many interest groups which make up the public. Obviously, business, labor, and agricultural groups mobilize when their economic interests are at stake, just as veteran groups become aroused by defense issues, and ethnic groups by the plight of compatriots.

Nevertheless, we speak of "public opinion" rather than the opinions of various "publics" because on foreign policy issues the vast majority of citizens are simply ignorant. Even if they were not, these issues are usually so far removed from their own frame of reference that, given the necessary information, they still would not know how to resolve them. As businessmen and farmers, they have experience, competence and opinions which they express domestically. In foreign policy, however, the president can and must exercise far greater initiative.[68]

[67] Gabriel Almond, *The American People and Foreign Policy* (New York: Harcourt Brace Jovanovich, 1950), p. 136 ff. This distinction between elite and mass perception has been questioned, at least on Vietnam, by Sidney Verba, Richard Brody, et al., "Public Opinion and the War in Vietnam," *American Political Science Review* (June 1967), pp. 331–332.

[68] James N. Rosenau (ed.), "Foreign Policy as an Issue Area" in Rosenau's *Domestic Sources of Foreign Policy* (New York: The Free Press, 1967), pp. 24–36.

In addition, the president frequently has to act *before* any firm public opinion has been formed. Even if he wished to follow popular sentiment, he could not. During the late 1950s, as the Second Vietnam War began, and in the early 1960s, as the Kennedy Administration increasingly committed the United States to South Vietnam, opinion on the expanding involvement was not widespread. Only President Johnson's vast commitment of over 500,000 men developed this concern. Even then, opinion swayed between the desire for victory and approval of escalation (Johnson's popularity rose with each escalation in 1965 and 1966[69]), and disillusionment and the desire to end the war with "honor."

Since the Truman Doctrine in 1947, public opinion has been flexible and responsive to presidential leadership. It has supported with equal enthusiasm Cold War policies and moves toward a detente with the Soviet Union. If a President was tough toward Moscow, as Harry Truman was, he received acclaim; if, like Eisenhower occasionally and Kennedy consistently, he sought to relax tensions and negotiate with the Kremlin, he also gained popular support. In a crisis, the public almost unanimously rallies around the president; indeed, he will probably receive the most sympathy and support if he "goofs," as Eisenhower did with the U-2 affair in 1959, or as Kennedy did in the disastrous Bay of Pigs invasion of Cuba in 1961.[70]

This public deference stems from the generally high regard most citizens have for the president, who is their principal source of information and interpretation. This means that the administration in power can usually mold opinion to support the direction it feels the United States should take. In Gabriel Almond's words:

> The general public looks for *cues* for *mood responses* in public discussion of foreign policy. It does not listen to the content of discussion but to its tone. A presidential statement that a crisis exists will ordinarily be registered in the form of apprehension. A reassuring statement will be received with complacency reactions. In both cases, the reaction has no depth and no structure.[71]

Yet public support of the president is not unlimited. If his policies are not successful, do not attain their objectives in a reasonable amount of time and at a bearable cost, the public reserves the right to punish the president and his party at election time.[72] Thus, a Marshall Plan for the economic recovery of western

[69] See Verba and Brody, *op. cit.*, p. 333.

[70] See John E. Mueller, "Presidential Popularity from Truman to Johnson," *American Political Science Review,* March 1970, pp. 18–34, particularly his analysis of "rallying around the flag."

[71] Almond, *op. cit.*, p. 232.

[72] Francis E. Rourke, "The Domestic Scene," in Robert E. Osgood *et al., America and the World* (Baltimore: The Johns Hopkins Press, 1970).

Europe was supported. Its time span was four years, the cost to the taxpayer was not burdensome, and the successful rebuilding of Europe was clearly visible to all. By contrast, foreign aid to underdeveloped countries has become unpopular. Results in the form of rapid modernization or goodwill toward the United States are hardly visible. The program seems to be unending, and almost all forecasts predict an ever-growing gap between the rich western and poor nonwestern nations, suggesting that a closing of the gap would require a long-term and far higher commitment of resources.

Similarly, American military interventions usually receive popular acclaim at first. When a president goes on radio and TV to announce that he has decided to send troops into Korea or Lebanon or the Dominican Republic or Vietnam, public opinion—as well as Congress—takes its cues from him. Some foreign policy experts, including congressmen, may criticize the president's action, but if the intervention is rapidly brought to a successful conclusion, there will be no adverse public reaction at the polls later. But neither the Korean nor the Vietnamese War achieved this goal. Both wars dragged on into stalemate. Victory became increasingly elusive and, to a nation that had never lost a war and harbored an illusion of omnipotence, this was frustrating. Moreover, draft calls rose, the casualty lists mounted, domestic prices and war costs grew inflated, and, in the case of Vietnam, when a tax surcharge resulted, support for the policy ebbed.[73] Congressmen first reflected this growing dissatisfaction and congressional resolution or not, the criticism began: "We should never have become involved"; "We should have bombed the hell out of 'em instead of handcuffing the military politically." To Congress' already well developed sense of institutional impotency was added the constituents' increasing opposition. And a legislative-executive battle was all but inevitable.

As the administration ran into trouble, other sources of information and interpretation gained esteem. During the Korean War, General MacArthur and the conservative wing of the Republican party provided the chief source of opposition to the Truman Administration. The massive Vietnamese intervention of 1965 transformed liberal Democrat senators, especially members of the Senate Foreign Relations Committee under Senator Fulbright's chairmanship, into competing credible interpreters of the war.[74] The news media, too—particularly television—consistently contradicted the optimistic official forecasts by illustrating the devastation and civilian suffering due to the war. The result was that Vietnam, like Korea, caused the retirement of a Democratic president and the victory of a Republican candidate.

By exacting retribution when the shoe pinches badly, the public does set the outer boundaries for presidential policies. Harry Truman did not oppose our

---

[73] In "Trends in Popular Support for the Wars in Korea and Vietnam" (unpublished), Mueller finds a mathematical relationship between drops in popular support and the rise of American casualties.

[74] J. William Fulbright, ed., *The Vietnam Hearings* (New York: Vintage Books, 1966).

rapid military demobilization after World War II, even though Russia was unfriendly. In fact, Secretary of War James Forrestal urged him to go before the public and state his case for remaining strong to enhance his bargaining power with Moscow. Truman refused; the public wanted to relax, "to bring the boys home," and to end the sacrifice. Not until a year and a half later, when the Soviet threat became clearer, could Truman persuade Congress and the public to support his strategy of containment.[75] Truman, in fact, supported the age-old policy of the balance of power, but given traditional American attitudes toward power politics, he needed a better cause to excite the nation's moral zeal. Anti-communism, fitting well into the New World/Old World dichotomy, was the answer. Since then, all presidents have employed it constantly to enlist support and to demand at least some shoe-pinching. Yet the erosion of anti-communist feeling after the sacrifices of Vietnam has raised a fundamental question: what kind of foreign policy will public opinion support in the post-Vietnam world?

Control of Foreign Policy Executives

Finally, the president has more freedom in the conduct of foreign affairs because he can exert more control over the principal departments and agencies which formulate foreign policy. These departments do not represent the same kind of special interests and constituents as do those whose main responsibility is domestic affairs. For example, when the State or Defense Department urges certain policies on the president, it is not speaking for associational interests, as the Department of Commerce does when it speaks for the National Association of Manufacturers. Instead, it is speaking for its own departmental policy views, which it believes to be in the best interests of the United States. Because these departments are not tied to external political groups, they are weaker than domestically-oriented departments.[76] Unable to promise tangible group benefits to their supporters, they have few friends to support them. Henry Adams once wisely observed that the Secretary of State existed only to recognize the existence of a world which Congress would rather ignore. The consequent lack of congressional and popular support weakens the State Department's bargaining power against the president.

The contrast with the alleged position of the Defense Department could not be more startling. The term "military-industrial complex" is intended to suggest that profit-minded industrial executives, job-seeking union leaders, and the desire of various services for ever more and newer arms gives them a vested interest in continuing the Cold War and giving American foreign policy its militaristic

---

[75] For American policy in this interregnum period, see John W. Spanier, *American Foreign Policy Since World War II,* 4th ed. (New York: Praeger, 1971), pp. 31–42.

[76] Samuel P. Huntington, *The Common Defense* (New York: Columbia University Press, 1961), pp. 131–132, 146 ff.

flavor. These groups, moreover, have many friends in Congress who represent areas in which military installations and defense plants are located. The Pentagon is therefore assumed to have great bargaining strength within the executive branch—if it does not, in fact, dominate it.

It is of course true that many industries, unions, and communities have a vested interest in defense spending. But this does not mean that they have increased military budgets significantly, if at all.[77] Since 1945, they have intensified interservice competition for available funds and strategic missions; but military budgets have been determined by the levels of international tension, by a rapidly changing technology, and by the political and economic beliefs of the civilian leadership.[78] And the fierce interservice rivalries within the Pentagon have enabled presidents to control the so-called "military-industrial complex" through divide-and-rule tactics. Presidential views, not those of the professional soldiers, have prevailed in the decisions involving military strategy, weapons systems, force levels, and the division of the military budgets among the services. The irony of the belief in the power of the "military-industrial complex" is surely that the "outstanding feature of the military's participation in making defense policy is their amazing weakness."[79]

If the military has nonetheless played perhaps a major role in foreign policy and if this policy is frequently inclined to force, this has been due essentially to the extensive and intensive bipolar confrontation which has drawn "frontier lines" between the eastern and western blocs. Both sides have relied on military strength to preserve these frontiers and their respective spheres of influence. In addition, American attitudes toward foreign policy include a belief in quick solutions to problems, the illusion of omnipotence, and the feeling that problems can be resolved once and for all by eliminating the trouble-maker (the "cowboy approach" to international problems, as we called this attitude earlier).

A Democracy's
Foreign Policy Dilemma

Once, referring to the red phone which accompanies the president wherever he goes, Lyndon Johnson commented, "If [the commander-in-chief] mashes that button"—and here he stabbed at an imaginary button—"that is it."[80] A president lives in the shadow of a nuclear Armageddon. He commands a thermonuclear capability which can obliterate most of the human race. As

[77] For a post-war analysis emphasizing the strength of the military-industrial complex, see Sidney Lens, *The Military-Industrial Complex* (Philadelphia: Pilgrim Press, 1970).

[78] Huntington, *The Common Defense.*

[79] Wildavsky, *op. cit.,* p. 99.

[80] Quoted by Theodore F. White, *The Making of the President, 1964* (New York: Atheneum, 1965), p. 374.

commander-in-chief of one of the two most powerful countries in the world at a time of great pressures and continual crises, he has become the custodian of the "war power." Congress' role in declaring wars and deciding the strength of the armed forces has, in spite of recent attempts to reassert its authority, been gravely weakened. The fantastic power any president now commands is the result, not of his wanting and therefore usurping it, but of an increasingly competitive state system which is seen as a threat to American security.

The president enjoys vast additional powers in times of war or other national emergency. First, Congress tends during wartime or emergency to delegate great domestic power to the president to be exercised at his discretion. Second, in times of military emergency the president has often felt entitled, as commander-in-chief, to act without direct congressional sanction. How much control over domestic life Congress itself grants the president in a major war is shown by the case of President Roosevelt in World War II. To cite but a few instances, the president was authorized to "place an order with any individual, firm . . . , or organized manufacturing industry for such products or materials as may be required" for the war effort. Failure to comply with such an order was a felony that might authorize governmental seizure of the business. He could determine when the government's needs took priority over the domestic consumer market and for how long. He could control price and wage levels throughout the United States, and prices on the sale and rental of homes. He could institute a national draft and determine its administration. And he could seize foreign bank deposits in the U.S., together with other foreign property, and dispose of them as he saw fit.

Roosevelt added to these authorizations on his own.[81] For example, in 1942, he removed 112,000 Japanese-Americans from their homes and held them in "relocation centers" for the duration. In addition, basing his action on his authority to regulate production in the U.S., he authorized the War Manpower Commission to issue a "work or fight" order to all workers not draft exempt. They would have to move wherever the Board deemed it necessary for national production needs or face induction.[82] During World War I equal power was wielded by Woodrow Wilson—indeed, the Wilson Administration nationalized the railroads and ran them under governmental control. There is no reason to doubt that during another war or extreme national emergency, a president will be granted—or will assert—similar powers and perhaps expand them further. These powers are not only important in themselves, they become precedents which justify such action in future conflicts.

The president's powers as commander-in-chief are remarkable not only for their breadth and variety, but also for the extent to which they may be exercised without effective judicial interference. From the beginning of the Republic, the

---

[81] The extent of Roosevelt's wartime powers is detailed in Corwin, *op. cit.*, pp. 239–262.
[82] *Ibid.*, p. 247.

Supreme Court has been very reluctant to challenge the president's discretion in this area, even when the powers he asserts have been wholly unprecedented. For instance, when Congress delegates very general authority to the president—as when it authorizes him to establish a military draft—the president's authority to write in the details as he deems fit has almost never been successfully curtailed.

Even when presidents have used their military powers without any specific constitutional or congressional authorization, the courts have usually approved. Abraham Lincoln, especially, demonstrated how far the president may go in this respect. He called out the federal army, raised volunteers, transferred money for purposes of mobilization and exercised belligerent rights against the Confederacy—not only without congressional authorization, but in spite of the Constitution's provision that only Congress could declare war, raise an army, and appropriate money for it. The Supreme Court upheld this unprecedented action on the grounds that Congress subsequently approved these measures; thus they avoided having to determine the constitutionality of the actions themselves.[83] In general, the Court's attitude toward Lincoln's continual assertion of novel "war powers"—a term found nowhere in the Constitution itself—was that presidential military decisions during national emergency were based on the president's right to decide what was needed to protect the nation's security. This has been, with few exceptions, the Court's attitude toward the president's military powers ever since.[84]

Even when the Supreme Court has declared a presidential military act unconstitutional, it has come "face to face with the brute fact that [it] cannot coerce the president."[85] Both presidents Lincoln and Franklin Roosevelt, for instance, suspended the writ of *habeas corpus,* held American citizens in military custody, and declared martial law over American territories. Lincoln went so far as to try and sentence American citizens in military courts when civil courts were also available. In both instances, the Supreme Court held the president's acts unconstitutional, but only years after the events occurred and his purposes had been achieved. Further, if the president so chose, he could legally remove almost all his military acts from review by civil courts. In any case, the Supreme Court has no means of compelling presidential acquiescence. "The civil courts have no power to interfere with or control the actions of the commander-in-chief if he wills otherwise."[86]

In this century, no president has asserted his right to act as independently as Lincoln did in military affairs. (Congress today usually provides sufficient powers.) Nor have modern presidents sought to remove such decisions from

---

[83] *Ibid.,* p. 231.

[84] For a summary of the Court's many decisions favoring great Presidential discretion in such security matters, see Glendon Schubert, Jr., *The Presidency in the Courts* (Minneapolis: University of Minnesota Press, 1957), pp. 173–273.

[85] *Ibid.,* p. 270.

[86] *Ibid.,* p. 185.

judicial review. Indeed, given the potential they enjoy for truly unprecedented exercise of military powers, modern presidents, even during wartime, have been reasonably restrained, acting on the whole within the context of congressional legislation, earlier precedents, and American political tradition. Yet the past is still a key to the future. The president's military authority, therefore, seems likely to keep on growing.

It is no wonder, then, that a debate has arisen over the extent of presidential power (and the purported threat of the military-industrial complex). A democracy—certainly American democracy with its tradition of underwriting the fragmentation of power—is suspicious of too vast a concentration of power, be it in the economic sphere or in government. The conduct of external affairs, therefore, poses a genuine dilemma: how to preserve a constitutional domestic order and yet provide the government with sufficient authority to conduct the nation's foreign policy. The protection of the "national interests" in an anarchical external environment, moderated only to some extent by the balance of power, requires virtually plenary authority to act effectively in the international arena. And this authority must be concentrated in a single person who can act with dispatch, flexibility and, if necessary, secrecy—in short, the president.

But in a democratic state like America, the exercise of governmental power has long been identified with the abuse of power. The best government was a weak government—which in practice meant the restraint of executive power by the legislature, the guardian of the people's liberties and "natural rights." The paradox, therefore, is clear: if the executive is granted almost authoritarian power for the conduct of foreign policy, it may threaten the restraints built into the constitutional domestic system. If the executive is enfeebled, however, he may be unable to safeguard the nation from foreign threat. "What in a domestic context was virtue was in an international context a vice. Democracy, incapable of the purposefulness of authoritarian states, could be destroyed . . . by engaging in the necessary acts in which it was by nature least skillful."[87] This dilemma was at the heart of the debate over the president's war-making authority in 1969 and 1970; it is a dilemma which has never been resolved, nor is it likely to be.

---

[87] Seabury, *op. cit.,* thoughtfully discusses this sensitive key issue, p. 185 ff.

10

Policy Making in Congress

In 1960, John F. Kennedy was elected president of the United States. His election was regarded as a great victory by those who looked upon American society as stale and complacent and who wanted to "get the country moving again." Kennedy was attractive, ambitious, articulate, and progressive; he wanted to be president because political power and the opportunities for national leadership were supposedly in the White House. Kennedy made many promises and, by implication at least, suggested that at last the government, now in the hands of a "new generation," would begin solving the nation's long-neglected problems in the areas of civil rights, education, and social welfare. Popular expectations were high.

But Senator Kennedy won the election by the narrow margin of 112,000 votes, out of a total vote of almost 69 million. He received 49.7 percent of the total vote to Richard Nixon's 49.6 percent. And his victory was only in the executive branch, not in the United States Congress. By 1963, it was clear that the coalitions in Congress which supported the President's policy objectives were not strong enough to muster majority support for his legislative programs. Congress rejected virtually every piece of important legislation coming from the White House. The vast powers of the presidency were not sufficient to "get the country moving again." President Kennedy's efforts did, of course, generate enthusiasm. They caused some segments of the nation to dream about the "politics of hope"; but the absence of congressional support meant that the President's legislative program, much of it well-conceived and badly needed, could not be translated into official governmental policy. The reaction of progressive forces in the nation who supported the President was one of exasperation and near despair. Columnist Walter Lippmann pretty well summed up the attitude of congressional critics in his question, "What kind of legislative body is it that will not or cannot legislate?"[1]

Congress' refusal to endorse President Kennedy's legislative program should not have surprised anyone. The presidency and the Congress are different kinds of institutions; conflict is inherent in their relationship. The presidency is an office resting on a national constituency whose elections tend to be decided in large urban states; Congress, however, is a "representative assembly" whose members are elected from local and provincial constituencies where local concerns are strong. It was perfectly natural that many members of Congress would not share the President's concerns and would object to his proposals. But the differences between the two institutions does not mean that under the right circumstances they cannot work together sufficiently well to produce public policy. This in fact occurred in 1964, the first year of President Lyndon Johnson's administration, when the same Congress that rejected Kennedy's efforts proceeded to enact into law virtually the same legislative package. The point is that in a political system, major policy decisions cannot be made unless supporting coalitions are developed across institutional lines; these coalitions ultimately determine what the law of the land shall be. In this sense, all roads lead to Congress because sooner or later, major policies must be supported and financed by the people's elected representatives.

Congress thus holds the high trumps in the policy-making process of the federal government. But the manner in which it participates in policy-making, makes this a very complicated and drawn-out process: Congress is concerned not only with making decisions on public policy but also with the representation of the varied interests and values of a pluralistic society. Congress is a legislative institution making policy, but it is also a representative assembly performing other functions in the political system not directly related to making laws. These nonlegislative or representative functions are an important aspect of congressional work, but they complicate congressional decision-making on public policies; this, in turn, complicates the policy-making processes of the federal government at large. Thus, while our principal concern is its legislative function, we shall first discuss these nonlegislative, representative functions of Congress.

---

[1] Quoted in Samuel P. Huntington, "Congressional Responses to the Twentieth Century," in David B. Truman (ed.), *The Congress and America's Future* (Englewood Cliffs, N.J.: Prentice-Hall, 1965), p. 5.

Congress as a
Representative Assembly

There are two systems of representation in the American political system: Congress and the presidency. Both are based on the principle of majority rule and both serve as vehicles through which the opinions, interests, and values of the American people are expressed and, brought to bear on the political processes. The most fundamental difference between them concerns the kinds of majorities whose opinions each registers. The presidency is headed by one man, the president. He is elected by a national constituency and therefore the majority that he represents must speak "through the authority of one man."[2] The Congress, however, is a pluralistic body, composed of 535 members who are elected from 435 different congressional districts and 50 separate states. "This means that Congress is in fact many Congresses and that it often speaks in several, sometimes contradictory, voices."[3]

No system of representation is unbiased. Both the presidential and congressional systems favor the values of some segments of society over others. Since the president has a national constituency and presidential elections are determined more and more by the outcome of the vote in large urban areas composed of ethnic and racial minorities, it is frequently argued that presidential representation is, on the whole, liberal. Congressional representation, on the other hand, is said to be conservative because members of Congress are "locals" who are tied closely to the interests and values of local constituencies. According to this point of view, the president is the national leader who is supported by liberal majorities in the urban areas. Congress, however, is pulled in many different directions by its ties with a great variety of constituencies; being slow to change, it impedes the more liberal efforts of the president.

Because of the nature of congressional elections, senators and congressmen must pay attention to the needs and values of their local constituents. As Douglas Price has written: "Specific local pressures may only infrequently be decisive, but they constitute the pervasive milieu within which congressmen and senators operate."[4]

First, though there are some exceptions, members of Congress begin their political lives at the local level. "The congressman is part of a local consensus of local politicians, local businessmen, local bankers, local trade union leaders, and local newspaper editors who constitute the opinion-making elite of their dis-

---

[2] John S. Saloma III, *Congress and the New Politics* (Boston: Little, Brown and Co., 1969), p. 62. Our discussion of the dual system of representation is drawn from this source.

[3] *Ibid.*

[4] H. Douglas Price, "The Electoral Arena," in Truman, *op. cit.*, p. 32.

tricts."[5] Senators tend to be less local than congressmen because states, more than congressional districts, include large urban areas where diverse interests create problems that resemble those in the nation at large. Thus, the congressional system of representation includes a wide variety of interests from the subunits of the nation and from the nation as a whole. Consequently, the linkage between Congress and the people living in the subunits of the nation differs from that of the presidency. But it is a mistake to overemphasize the localism and provincialism of Congress. There are other equally important features. John Saloma has suggested that other aspects of Congress as a representative assembly must be recognized if a balanced view of the dual system of representation in the American political system is to be achieved.[6] First, Congress is not simply a "local institution"; *it is a forum for deliberation and decision on national policy.* Congressmen do not merely represent the interests of their local constituencies, but are members of the national elite who, by the very nature of their position, must deal with the broad-gauged issues of national policy. The specialized work of their committees and debates on the floor expose members of Congress "to an education in public policy that few members of the Executive branch ever experience."[7]

Second, though members of Congress are representatives from specific geographical districts and states, *they enjoy considerable independence from their constituencies on most policy matters.* With the exception of such issues as civil rights, members of Congress are not subject to continuing pressures to vote a certain way on legislation. Over 50 percent of the American people do not even know the name of their congressman; less than 20 percent can say how their representative voted on any important public policy issue. Few voters know precisely what they want from their congressmen and the work of Congress is so complicated that the voting records of congressmen remain a great mystery to most of their constituents. Any controls exerted by constituents on congressmen stem mainly from the congressman's perception of the attitudes of his constituents, usually those of the influential elites, rather than from any overt action taken by the folks back home.[8]

Third, rather than being a local politician working for a time in Washington, *congressmen have become professional national politicians removed from the image of the "instructed delegate" from the local district.* There are four ideal types, or models, which provide clues to how members of Congress perceive their roles as members of a representative assembly; trustee, delegate, partisan, and politico. The congressman who assumes the role of *trustee* feels free to use his

---

[5] Huntington, "Congressional Responses," in Truman, *op. cit.,* p. 15.

[6] Saloma, *op. cit.,* pp. 65–70. See also Roger Davidson, "Congress and the Executive: The Race for Representation," in Alfred de Grazia (ed.), *Congress: The First Branch of Government* (Washington, D.C.: American Enterprise Institute, 1966).

[7] *Ibid.,* p. 65.

[8] See Charles F. Cnudde and Donald J. McCrone, "The Linkages between Constituency Attitudes and Congressional Voting Behavior: A Causal Model," *American Political Science Review* (March 1966), pp. 66–72.

own judgment about how he should vote. He votes according to what he determines to be in the best interest of the nation and feels no compelling pressure to merely reflect the judgment of his constituents. The congressman who plays the role of *delegate* tries to adhere to what he perceives to be the will of the voters back home. He sees his purpose as voting as his constituents would vote if they were sitting in Congress, regardless of his personal judgment about the issue under consideration. The *partisan,* by contrast, tries to follow the dictates of his political party as reflected in the party platform on which he was supposedly elected or in the instructions received from his party leaders. Party loyalty takes precedence over personal judgment or constituency preferences. Finally, the *politico* assumes a role combining the other three. He votes his own mind on some issues or votes according to constituency interests as he perceives them in other issues (usually civil rights); he attempts to support his political party when he can. He is a compromiser, a balancer, a career politician who tries to reconcile his voting behavior with all the pressures which come to bear on him.

Which one of these roles do most congressmen assume? One survey of "116 members of the House of Representatives . . . found that about 20 percent of the sample described themselves as 'delegates' bound by instructions, either actual or implied, from their constituencies. Almost 30 percent viewed themselves as 'trustees' acting independently on the basis of their knowledge and convictions. Half of the sample, referred to as 'politicos' alternated these roles on a rather sophisticated basis." In response to questions about the relative weight they assigned to local versus national interests, "roughly 16 percent were concerned with their district only; another 19 percent, with their district first and the nation second; *over* 60 percent gave equal or stronger weighting to national concerns."[9]

Thus, members of Congress have become career politicans. Their orientation has become more national than local. They are remaining in office longer,[10] and the growing size of their constituencies and the increased complexity of national issues forces them to think and act in broader terms. Jet transportation, modern communications systems, and the nationalizing trend in American politics is gradually reducing the local orientation of members of Congress.

Fourth, *dual representation offers both Congress and the president the positions of initiative and opposition.* Though the popular view today is that Congress is a conservative, somewhat recalcitrant institution mainly obstructing and opposing legislative programs initiated by the president, a more balanced view suggests that initiation and opposition are not the sole prerogatives of either. The dual system of representation makes it possible for the American people, interest groups, and political parties to express their support or opposition through either the presidency or Congress. In the early 1960s it was Congress that opposed President Kennedy's civil rights, education, and welfare policies. But from 1896

---

[9] Saloma, *op. cit.,* p. 67. Statistics are from Roger H. Davidson, *The Role of the Congressman* (New York: Pegasus, 1969), p. 122.

[10] See Huntington, "Congressional Responses," in Truman, *op. cit.*

to 1932, the Republican party "worked through the *presidency* to minimize the role of the national government in the economy."[11] During the 1950s, Congress frequently took the initiative; President Eisenhower vetoed much of its legislation. In 1970, Congress appropriated more money for federal aid to education and other welfare programs than President Nixon wanted and he vetoed the legislation.

Though the twentieth century has seen a shift of legislative initiative away from Congress to the presidency, "historically, the Congress has been more often the advocate of social change than the president."[12] The point is that neither the Congress nor the presidency are restricted by the nature of the system to positions of either initiative or opposition. The dual system of representation enables them to do both. Because the president is the only public official in the government who is elected by a national constituency, he comes into office with something of a mandate to take action. In the face of this presidential initiative, Congress—as a representative assembly, whose members are not all elected at one time but who also reflect the varied interests of the nation—is more likely to express itself by asking questions, demanding explanations, slowing down and often defeating the policies proposed by the president. Saloma has suggested that the existence of Congress as a representative assembly "helps to open up the system and provide greater opportunities for access and for accommodation among interests."[13]

Indeed, the growth of representative assemblies. in modern times has been closely associated with human freedom and democratic government. The men who wrote the United States Constitution recognized this association because the first institution they created was the Congress. This was not an accident.

> Congress is first because, living in the long shadow of the Glorious Revolution of 1688 and of its great philosophical defender John Locke, our Founding Fathers fully understood that, although you could have government without a representative assembly, you could not have free government without a representative assembly.[14]

The development of Congress as a representative assembly is rooted historically in the idea that the governed should influence governmental action and that the governors should be both responsive and responsible to those in whose name they make policy. There is much disagreement about whether Congress has been successful in measuring up to these criteria. As a representative as-

---

[11] Saloma, *op. cit.,* p. 69.

[12] Arthur M. Schlesinger, Jr., and Alfred de Grazia, *Congress and the Presidency: Their Role in Modern Times* (Washington, D.C.: American Enterprise Institute, 1967), pp. 79–81. Quoted in Saloma, *op. cit.,* p. 69.

[13] Saloma, *op. cit.,* p. 70.

[14] Stephen K. Bailey, "Is Congress the Old Frontier?" in Marian D. Irish (ed.), *Continuing Crises in American Politics* (Englewood Cliffs, N.J.: Prentice-Hall, 1963), p. 69.

sembly, does Congress represent the needs and feelings of the American people? Does it enhance or decrease the capacity of the government to take effective action in solving the problems of the nation? Is it responsive to the masses of the people, or does it take its cues from the elites?[15] Is Congress an effective instrument of control and thereby keep government accountable to the people for its actions?

The Non-Legislative Functions of Congress

As an elective assembly of men and women who represent separate constituencies, Congress performs several functions that are closely related to law-making but are not the same as law-making. Though the distinction is somewhat arbitrary, these functions are defined as non-legislative because they involve service to constituents, education of the people about policy issues, and the supervision of other governmental institutions. These functions are integral parts of the policy-making process in Congress but they are not the same as formal law-making. They are the "errand boy" or service function, the educative function, and control of the executive.

The "Errand Boy" or Service Function

Modern governments are highly bureaucratic. The lives of the people are perhaps more directly affected by decisions made in the bureaucracy than by any other branch of government. The average man's contact with government is primarily with administrative officials; when he wants something from government he can in most cases get it only from some administrative official. He must deal with an official of the Internal Revenue Service, a lawyer in the Justice Department, a field representative of the Office of Education, or a staff member of the Office of Equal Opportunity. The mystery, size, delay, and red tape of the bureaucracy tends to overwhelm the average citizen.

If a citizen has difficulties in his contacts with government, he is likely to ask his congressman for help or write him merely to voice an objection. He thus turns to his elected representative as an intermediary and asks him to intercede in his behalf. There is a certain amount of relief, comfort, and reassurance in being able to contact one's own congressman and know that he (or, more likely, a member of his staff) will listen to the request or complaint, investigate it, and

---

[15] For an elitist interpretation of Congress, see Thomas R. Dye and L. Harmon Zeigler, *The Irony of Democracy: An Uncommon Introduction to American Politics* (Belmont, Calif.: Wadsworth, 1970), Chapter 10.

provide some assistance—or at least write a letter explaining why nothing can be done. In performing this kind of service function, members of Congress have become key figures in the relationships between people and government. They are "go-betweens" who serve as important linkages between the average citizen and the bureaucracy. Members of Congress serve as "errand boys" for the people who elect them to office. The use of the term "errand boy" is not meant to detract from the importance of this kind of work; on the contrary, this form of service is an important feature of the representative functions of Congress.

Most members of Congress recognize the importance of this form of service to their constituents and, quite obviously, they are sensitive to the political benefits that accrue to them from performing it. Some, however, decry the amount of time and energy that it takes; they claim that it takes them away from their primary task of making laws. The frustrations involved in serving constituents are revealed in the following statement of a member of the House:

> A Congressman has become an expanded messenger boy, an employment agency, getter-out of the Navy, Army, and Marines, a wardheeler, a wound healer, troubleshooter, law explainer, bill finder, issue translator, resolution interpreter, controversy-oil pourer, glad hand extender, business promoter, veterans' affairs adjuster, ex-serviceman's champion, watchdog for the underdog, sympathizer for the upper dog, kisser of babies, recoverer of lost baggage, soberer of delegates, adjuster for traffic violations and voters straying into the toils of the law, binder up of broken hearts, financial wet nurse, good samaritan, contributor to good causes, cornerstone layer, public building and bridge dedicator, and ship christener.[16]

Perhaps the amount of time spent serving constituents has been exaggerated. A recent study of 150 members of Congress shows that only 27.6 percent of a congressman's work week is devoted to constituents while 64.6 percent of his time is devoted to legislative matters. The same study shows that staff members spend over 60 percent of their time answering mail and providing constituency services (see Table 10.1).

These figures suggest that the "errand boy" function of congressmen does not represent a heavy or unreasonable burden on their time; it does not detract from their legislative function, since staff members, not congressmen themselves, bear most of the burden. In addition, the access to government it provides for the average citizen encourages support for the government and tends to strengthen a citizen's identification with the political system. Constituency service makes the inevitable frustrations that are associated with huge governments more bearable by the people.

Quite obviously, however, congressmen do not provide fair and equal

---

[16] Quoted in Saloma, *op. cit.*, p. 190.

Table 10.1. Congressman's Average Work Week Summarized by Function

Function	Hours per Week (average)	Percentage of Time
Legislative	38.0	64.6
Committee work	(11.1)	(18.9)
General	(26.9)	(45.7)
Constituency service	16.3	27.6
Education/Publicity	4.6	7.0

Staff's Average Work Week Summarized by Function

Function	Hours per Week (average)	Percentage of Time
Legislative support	30.8	14.3
Constituency service	53.5	24.7
Correspondence (mixed constituency service, education)	88.6	40.8
Education and Publicity	22.4	10.3
Other	21.4	9.9

Source: John S. Saloma III, *Congress and the New Politics* (Boston: Little, Brown and Co., 1969), pp. 184–185. See also Roger H. Davidson, David M. Kovenock, and Michael K. O'Leary, *Congress in Crisis: Politics and Congressional Reform* (Belmont, Calif.: Wadsworth, 1966).

services to all their constituents. They are naturally more responsive to those groups and individuals in their states or districts who are most influential in helping them be reelected. Thomas R. Dye and Harmon Zeigler have suggested that members of Congress are responsive to the "active, interested, and resourceful elites" of their home districts rather than to the general population.[17] A member of Congress is going to listen more carefully to the president of the local chamber of commerce, or the leading bankers or politicians of his district than he is to janitors, brick masons, or assistant professors of philosophy in the local college.

A better example of the selectivity of congressmen in providing constituency services is the plight of Negroes in the South. When Negroes could not or did not vote, few Southern congressmen ran any errands for them. The result was that this relationship tended to increase Negroes' alienation from the system. This is still the case in many Southern districts although the increase in Negro voter registration in recent years is changing this relationship in those districts where the Negro vote can mean the difference between defeat or success at the polls.

In summary, the service function of Congress is an important part of its

[17] Dye and Zeigler, *op. cit.,* p. 238.

work as a representative assembly. It keeps congressmen in touch with the problems of their constituents and increases their sensitivity to the effect of bureaucratic regulations on the people. By remaining alert to what the administration is doing and interceding on behalf of constituents, Congress exerts a certain degree of control over the bureaucracy. Correcting a problem for a constituent does not, of course, mean that the policy that led to the problem will necessarily change, but it does provide a political check on the bureaucracy that is important in retaining the representativeness and responsiveness of the government. In this sense, in performing these functions, Congress contributes to the maintenance of the political system.[18]

The Educative Function

Try to imagine what the effect on the nation would be if suddenly a great hush descended on the United States Congress. No congressional investigations would be held, no more public committee sessions would be scheduled, no senators or congressmen would appear on *Meet the Press* or *Face the Nation,* no articles would be written by congressmen for *The New York Times Magazine* or *The Atlantic,* no newsletters and questionnaires would be mailed out to constituents, no more five-minute radio reports to the folks back home, no more public speeches at crossroads barbecues and college commencements, and the news media would cease reporting on the daily activities of the Senate and House of Representatives. Some Americans would surely say, "Thank God! Maybe now we can have a little peace." Things would indeed become quieter, but citizens would no longer be in touch with this vital source of information about the government.

The war in Vietnam during the 1960s is an excellent example of Congress as a source of information. So long as Congress was relatively quiet on this issue, the executive branch released information that mainly indicated that the war was going well. The people believed that the war was being won and that the troops "would be home for Christmas." It was not until Congress became an open forum of debate on the war that the public gained access to the growing body of information that dissented from the administration viewpoint. The televised hearings of the Senate Foreign Relations Committee and the numerous interviews with its chairman, J. William Fulbright, and other members of the Committee, stimulated a national debate on the war. When President Nixon sent American troops into Cambodia in May 1970, Congress, especially the Senate, challenged the President's decision and attempted to restrict his authority in the handling of the war. Congress provided different viewpoints to the executive's

---

[18] For an excellent discussion of the justifications for the service functions of Congress, see Saloma, *op. cit.,* pp. 99, 178–195.

regarding the political issues underlying the war, the constitutional powers of the president as commander-in-chief of the Armed Forces, and the constitutional role of Congress in foreign and military affairs. The same was true about the government's decision in 1969 to build an anti-ballistic missile network. Congressional debates on this issue provided much information about the effectiveness of this weapon and, above all, about the impact it would have on the American-Soviet strategic balance, a new arms race in defensive and offensive arms, and on preserving the stable balance then existing through an arms control agreement with Moscow.

In the domestic field, too, congressional consideration of such important issues as civil rights, social welfare programs, tax policies, and environmental pollution raises the question of what level of understanding the nation should have about issues that virtually affect its existence. "Congress is more than an object of public opinion. Its relation to the electorate is reciprocal. Influenced by the voters, it is also constantly engaged in stimulating public interest in current issues and in influencing public thinking."[19]

Congress communicates to the American people in two ways: "through its collective activities and component parts, especially its committees . . . and through the activities of its individual members."[20] Congress as an institution is not a particularly effective educator because it speaks in so many different voices. Also, it has no central office or agency to disseminate its views. It speaks mainly through its committees, sub-committees, and special investigation committees, which often have limited objectives such as confirming predetermined conclusions or using the publicity associated with their work to reap political rewards for their members.

The same is true with individual members of Congress.[21] Congressmen's motives for disseminating information distinguish them into five types: the *persuader, the promoter, the educator, the reticent,* and the *promoter-persuader.* The persuader tries to change the attitudes or values of his constituents or to reinforce the attitudes or values they already hold. The promoter tries simply to build up his own image among the voters to further his political career. The educator tries to instruct his constituents on the issues of the day. He provides information because he feels that congressmen have this responsibility toward their constituents. The reticent keeps as quiet as he can, dissassociating himself from the information he provides and making no effort to build an image, change opinions, or raise the level of understanding among his constituents. The

---

[19] John Bibby and Roger Davidson, *On Capitol Hill: Studies in the Legislative Process* (New York: Holt, Rinehart and Winston, 1967), p. 13.

[20] Saloma, *op. cit.,* p. 172. Our discussion of the effectiveness of Congress in educating the American people is drawn from Saloma's summary of the research in this area.

[21] *Ibid.,* pp. 176–177. These typologies and findings are taken from William C. Love, Jr., "The Congressman as Educator: A Study in Legislator Constituent Relationships," M.S. thesis (Cambridge, Mass.: Massachusetts Institute of Technology, August 1966).

promoter-persuader attempts to change the opinions of his constituents, as well as to promote his own career in the process. Table 10.2 shows how few congressmen and senators fit the role of educator.

Table 10.2. Distribution of Communication Roles in the House Sample Analyzed

Communication Role Category	Number in Category	Percent of Total
Promoter	56	38
Persuader	33	22
Promoter-persuader	25	17
Reticent	22	15
Educator	13	9
	149	101

Distribution of Communication Roles in the Senate Sample Analyzed

Communication Role Category	Number in Category	Percent of Total
Promoter	14	44
Persuader	9	28
Promoter-persuader	6	19
Reticent	2	6
Educator	1	3
	32	100

Source: Saloma, *op. cit.,* pp. 176–177.

These findings show why information disseminated by congressmen—newsletters, questionnaires, speeches—is often biased. Fewer than 10 percent of senators and congressmen see themselves as educators in providing information to their constituents. The most frequent role is that of promoter, suggesting that members of Congress provide information not to educate the public but to further their own careers. It also seems that the longer a congressman stays in office, the more reticent he becomes. Freshmen congressmen actively promote themselves; as they gain seniority, they tend to play the role of the persuader, and when they become firmly established in their positions, they tend to become reticent, especially if their districts are safe and their reelection is assured.

In summary, Congress is an important source of information about politics and public policy. But Congress speaks with many voices. And the members of Congress frequently put more emphasis on the promotion of their political careers than on educating the American public about the vital issues of the day.

The accuracy of the information they provide their constituents is thus compromised by their motives. Yet, this information is an important means of keeping the public informed about current issues and of maintaining government responsibility to the people.

Control of the Executive

Keeping government responsible to the people is a continuing concern in democratic societies. As governments have increased in size and become more and more "executive-centered," the need for controls over the bureaucracy has become increasingly apparent; this is now recognized as one of Congress's most important functions. George Galloway, a highly respected student of Congress, has even suggested that "not legislation but control of administration is becoming the primary function of the modern Congress."[22] In addition, this may be the function that Congress is best equipped to perform in the twentieth century; its highly specialized standing committees are better equipped to deal with the specific problems resulting from administration of policy than with the formulation of broad general policies.[23]

Though most students of government concede the need for congressional controls over the executive establishment, they differ about when and how these controls should be exerted. Those who vehemently opposed the policies of the Johnson and Nixon administrations on the Vietnamese War in the late 1960s and early 1970s called for greater congressional control of the executive and decried the fact that these controls were not as effective as they wanted them to be. On the other hand, those who wanted President Kennedy's domestic legislative program enacted in the early 1960s were unhappy because Congress was able to prevent it. These examples oversimplify a complex question, of course, but they demonstrate the fact that differences of opinion about congressional control of the executive frequently stem from different policy preferences rather than opposing views of the Constitution or administrative theory.

Congress exerts numerous controls over the executive because American government is composed of separate institutions that must share power. The Constitution gives Congress a role in the administrative process and this role has expanded in the twentieth century with the development of the welfare state and the growth of the bureaucracy. Congress's *right,* based on both the Constitution and legislation, to participate in the administrative process acts as a restraining influence on the executive and administrative agencies, even though specific controls are not always applied very effectively; the possibility that Congress will

---

[22] George B. Galloway, *The Legislative Process in Congress* (New York: Thomas Y. Crowell Co., 1955), pp. 56–57.

[23] See Huntington, "Congressional Responses," in Truman, *op. cit.,* pp. 22–25.

use this power may be far more important in keeping government responsible than its actual exercise.[24] Congress has the authority and the methods to control the executive. Whether it does so in specific cases depends on the *will* of members of Congress to devote time and energy necessary to what is viewed as a somewhat thankless and unrewarding job.

Congress has a variety of methods for overseeing and controlling the affairs of the executive establishment. The most important of these fall in three categories; *control of personnel, formal investigations,* and *congressional oversight of administration.* There is considerable overlap among these oversimplified categories; nevertheless, they help us to identify the general nature of congressional controls over the executive.

Congressional Control of Executive Personnel. Congress performs what is sometimes called a "watchdog" function by virtue of its control over high-level executive and judicial appointments and its authority to remove these officials from office through the impeachment process. The Constitution provides that presidential nominees for positions on the cabinet, the independent regulatory commissions, assistant secretaries in the executive departments, diplomats, military officers, and federal judgeships must be approved by the Senate. The Senate rarely objects to these nominations but it sometimes examines them with great care. Of the "more than 700,000 nominations made by Presidents Truman, Eisenhower, and Kennedy, only 12 were rejected outright by the Senate, and only 1700 were withdrawn by the president after an appraisal of possible congressional flak."[25] The Senate may reject a presidential appointee for reasons of policy, lack of qualifications, ideological considerations, political differences, or a variety of other reasons.

The classic case of a presidential nominee being rejected because of a political vendetta was the 1832 rejection of Martin Van Buren as Minister to England. Van Buren, who was Secretary of State at the time, was a political associate and protégé of President Andrew Jackson and was regarded as the heir apparent to the presidency. Jackson named him to the post in England in 1831, too late for the Senate to act upon the nomination. After Van Buren had already assumed his duties in London a year later, the Senate rejected the nomination. The situation in the Senate was rigged against Van Buren so that the vote would be a tie. This gave Vice President John C. Calhoun, Jackson's bitter enemy, the right to cast the decisive vote. The whole idea was to kill Van Buren politically. After the vote, Calhoun is reputed to have said in glee, "It will kill him, sir, kill him dead. He will never kick, sir, never kick." This attack on Jackson and Van

---

24 Stephen K. Bailey, *The New Congress* (New York: St. Martin's Press, 1966), p. 90.
25 *Ibid.,* p. 91.

Buren did not, of course, have its desired effect. Jackson was reelected as president and Van Buren succeeded him in 1836.[26]

In the twentieth century, particularly since the 1950s, Senate delay or rejection of presidential nominees has been based on ethical, ideological, or policy grounds. In the 1950s, during the McCarthy era, the Senate was sensitive to any charge, no matter how spurious, that a presidential nominee was sympathetic toward communism. The delay in confirming the appointment of Charles Bohlen as Ambassador to Russia and Phillip Jessup and Paul Hoffman to other high executive posts are cases in point. The refusal of the Senate to elevate Associate Justice Abe Fortas to the position of Chief Justice of the Supreme Court in 1968, and its outright rejection of the nomination of Clement Haynsworth and G. Harrold Carswell to the Supreme Court in the first year of the Nixon administration, had both ethical and policy overtones.[27]

By holding public hearings on nominations, by examining in detail the qualifications of nominees, by asking pointed questions about policy views and professional ethics, and by debating the fitness of the nominees, the Senate informs the president that Congress and the public have a vital interest in what executive and judicial officials do and that this interest must be respected. The Senate's close examination of Governor Walter Hickel of Alaska, President Nixon's nominee for Secretary of the Interior in 1969, served notice on the nominee and on the President that Congress was going to watch the administration's conservation policies. The same was true in its close scrutiny of Judges Haynsworth and Carswell on civil rights.

The Constitution further provides that certain executive officers, including the president himself, and the judges of the federal courts may be removed from office by congressional action. The House draws up the impeachment proceedings (the indictment), and the Senate conducts the trial. Impeachment proceedings, mainly used against members of the judiciary during the early days of the republic, represent the ultimate weapon that Congress can use to control the actions of the executive. Impeachment proceedings have not been used by Congress since the Civil War period when the President Andrew Johnson was impeached and tried.[28] The Senate refused by the slender margin of one vote to remove the president from office. In modern times, impeachment has mainly served as a veiled threat through which Congress indicates its displeasure with

---

[26] See Glyndon G. Van Deusen, *The Jacksonian Era* (New York: Harper & Row, Publishers, 1959), pp. 57–58.

[27] The Senate rejection of Haynsworth and Carswell will be discussed in some detail in Chapter 11.

[28] The impeachment of Andrew Johnson was only one phase of a general congressional effort to establish legislative supremacy over the whole government in the Reconstruction era. Congress, under the control of the Radical Republicans, attempted to establish its control over the presidency, the cabinet, the electoral college, the amending process, its own sessions, and the army. See J. G. Randall, *The Civil War and Reconstruction* (New York: D. C. Heath & Co., 1953), Chapter 24.

the service of presidential appointees. In 1969, there were threats to impeach Justices Abe Fortas and William O. Douglas. Though these threats grew out of congressional displeasure with the financial affairs of both justices, they were not unrelated to the dissatisfaction of many congressmen with the judicial policies furthered by the decisions of Fortas and Douglas. These pressures from Congress led to Fortas' resignation from the Court, and in 1970 they led to a formal investigation of Douglas to determine if impeachment proceedings against him should be drawn up.

A second form of congressional control of executive personnel is the supervision of personnel services within the executive departments. Personnel management in the executive establishment is not centered under the president. Congress has authority to make laws governing the civil, military and foreign services, and the appropriate committees in Congress, such as the Post Office and Civil Service Committees, have jealously guarded their prerogatives in these matters. Congress has created the bureaucracy by law and it does not regard the bureaucracy as the exclusive domain of the president. Though Congress has given the president the authority to reorganize the bureaucracy, it has reserved the power to veto these plans of reorganization and has frequently done so. The power of Congress to create new agencies and disestablish existing ones, plus its control of personnel services in the bureaucracy, keeps personnel in the executive establishment sensitive to the will of Congress.

Formal Investigations.   Congress must have information in order to legislate, and it conducts investigations to get this information. Though investigatory committees have been used to explore many areas of American life, some of which have little or nothing to do with legislation proposed in Congress, this device has been a frequently used method of supervising and controlling the activities of the executive branch of the government.[29] The first congressional investigation of the executive was an inquiry into a badly handled expedition in 1792 against Indians on the frontier in what is now Ohio. There have been many investigations since, ranging from the 1945–1946 inquiry into the Pearl Harbor fiasco to the infamous McCarthy hearings. Many investigations of the executive branch have been "concerned with the effectiveness of the government in waging war. Formal investigations of federal activities during peacetime have usually been stimulated by some disclosure of incompetence, corruption, or alleged disloyalty."[30]

---

[29] See *Watkins* v. *United States,* 354 U.S. 178 (1957) for the Supreme Court's interpretation of constitutional restraints on the investigative powers of Congress.

[30] Bailey, *The New Congress,* p. 86. In the post-World War II period, congressional investigations of the executive branch "have dealt with such issues as federal officials speculating in grains; communists in government agencies; mismanagement in the Atomic

As the size and influence of the bureaucracy have increased, the use of formal investigations as a means of controlling the bureaucracy has also increased. The Congressional Reorganization Act of 1946 directed the Congress to "exercise continuous watchfulness" over the administration of laws. Since the passage of this legislation, "congressional investigations of the bureaucracy have multiplied: each Congress during the period between 1950 and 1962 conducted more investigations than were conducted by *all* the Congresses during the nineteenth century."[31] And the amount of money Congress has appropriated for investigations has increased tremendously; "funds authorized for congressional investigations almost doubled from $8.2 million in the 83rd Congress (1953–1954) to $15.5 million in the 86th Congress (1959–1960)."[32]

Though the use of formal investigations as a means of congressional control of the bureaucracy has increased, this device is by no means a perfect method of keeping government responsible. Its major limitations are inherent in the nature of Congress as an institution. Investigations cannot be conducted by Congress itself; they must be conducted by standing committees, subcommittees, or special committees set up to look into specific problems. This means that the quality of the investigations is determined by the members of the investigation committee, primarily the chairman. Although most congressmen are fair-minded individuals who respect the rights of witnesses and do not use investigations to serve their own purposes, there have been some awful exceptions, notably Joe McCarthy. While both the Senate and House have taken action to try to improve the conduct of congressional investigations, the equality and effectiveness of this form of congressional control must remain dependent upon the committee chairmen and members.

On balance, the formal investigation is an important method of congressional control because it means that the activities of the bureaucracy can be brought into the spotlight. Neither the president nor the executive departments are immune to congressional investigations; this power of Congress acts as a restraining influence on executive policy making. The investigation does not even have to occur; the mere possibility that Congress might decide to conduct a formal investigation of any government bureau or agency is enough in itself to establish a certain degree of congressional control over the executive establishment. The increased use of investigations since 1946 testifies to the watchfulness

---

Energy Commission; the leading policies of the Reconstruction Finance Corporation; fraud and irregularities in the Internal Revenue Service; "windfall profits" under F.H.A. mortgage practices; favoritism in the Dixon-Yates power contract; questionable information practices in government agencies; inefficiencies in the Civil Aeronautics Administration; the U.S. lag in missile development; improper conduct in the Federal Communications Commission; waste in government stockpiling; security processes in the Department of State; and the use of lie detectors by federal agents." *Ibid.*, p. 87.

[31] Huntington, "Congressional Responses," in Truman, *op. cit.*, p. 25.

[32] Saloma, *op. cit.*, p. 138.

of Congress. It is one way in which Congress helps keep the government accountable and responsible to the people for its actions.

Congressional Oversight of the Executive.

American government, like all contemporary governments in Western political systems, has become executive-centered. The president is today the key figure in policy making. He is "chief legislator"; he is the person who initiates most of the important legislative programs. Though Congress remains an important participant in the policy-making process, its role in legislation has become more and more a matter of reacting to legislation proposed by the president. In reacting to presidential proposals, it examines, criticizes, amends, and sometimes rejects the policies proposed by the president. In this sense, it can control the executive because it has the final say about whether a proposed policy is enacted into formal law.

The term "oversight" is thereby used to refer to these congressional processes which limit and restrain executive policy making. This function is performed by the standing committees which, since the Reorganization Act of 1946, have been reorganized roughly parallel to the executive departments. They function in two ways: through standing committee consideration of executive proposals; committee review of their administration if they are enacted into law; and more important, through the congressional appropriation process in which committees make funds available to carry out approved programs.

It is generally agreed that the most effective form of congressional control over the executive and the bureaucracy is the right of Congress to appropriate money. Increasingly since World War II, the trend in Congress has been toward annual authorization for the expenditure of funds for government programs. Money cannot be appropriated for these programs by the appropriation committees in the Senate and House unless it has been formally authorized by standing committees. Funding programs is thus a two-stage process; money must be authorized by the legislative committees and then appropriated by the appropriation committees. Annual authorization means that the executive gets only enough money to implement a program for one year. Agencies must go to Congress and through the entire process every year. This means they must deal with four committees, two authorizing committees and two appropriation committees, all of which are concerned with their programs. In the process, members of Congress have ample opportunity, if they choose to take advantage of it, to review the work of the agency. Critics of Congress disagree over the wisdom of annual authorizations. Some argue that annual authorization gives congressmen access to executive policy-making and makes it possible for them to perform the important function of administrative control. Others argue that the process is exceedingly cumbersome and makes it difficult, if not impossible, for the executive to deal with the nation's problems on a long-range basis.

Another form of congressional control, used increasingly in recent years, is the "committee veto" under which the administrative agency charged with carrying out a certain policy is required to "come into agreement" with the congressional committee concerned with such matters before it takes action.[33] The committee veto is a technique used by Congress to involve its committees in the administration of policy. A bill passed by Congress may include a provision requiring the agency charged with implementing the bill to return to the committee for review and consultation before it takes any formal action. Clearly the committee veto injects a strong element of congressional control into the administrative process and enables committee members to oversee what the administrative agencies are doing. This technique has been bitterly criticized by executive officials, particularly President Johnson, as an unconstitutional violation of the principle of separation of powers and as an unnecessary complication of the administrative process. It is defended as a method whereby Congress can control the bureaucracy and assure that the intent of Congress is not distorted by the way bureaucrats do their jobs. The constitutional question is debatable; the other arguments, however, are both valid. The committee veto does enhance congressional oversight of administration but it also interferes with the administrative agencies who implement government programs.

Controlling the executive is an important function of representative assemblies in modern political systems where bureaucracies are large and influential. Congress—when compared to legislative institutions in parliamentary systems—is well equipped to perform this function. The British Parliament, for example, has very little power to control the executive or to investigate the activities of bureaucracy. Yet, most students of American government would agree that legislative oversight is a continuing problem in the relationship between Congress and the executive. One reason is that Congress frequently tends to be protective of the agencies it has created. Congress often resists, as strongly as the agencies themselves, any effort on the part of the president or public groups to restrict or control the activities of the agencies. Administrative agencies know the importance of congressional support, and they carefully cultivate friendships in Congress, especially with the committees that supervise their functions and control their funds.

Linkages among administrative agencies, congressional committees, and the groups in society whose interests are affected by the work of these agencies represent a system of subgovernments that wield much influence in the policy-making process. For example, the ties between the Department of Defense, the Armed Services Committees of Congress, and the defense industries are strong and viable. The same is true of the Department of Agriculture, the Agricultural Committees, and farm organizations across the nation. Close relationships between agencies, committees, and interest groups can make presidential efforts

---

[33] For a good summary of the arguments for and against annual authorizations and the committee veto, see *ibid.*, pp. 139–158.

to control the bureaucracy very difficult. These relationships tend to insulate administrative agencies from controls rather than making them responsible and accountable to the people. Since congressional oversight of the bureaucracy is exercised not by the whole Congress but by only a segment of it—the legislative and appropriation committees—the values, attitudes, and goals of the individual members who sit on these committees determine to a great extent the kinds of congressional controls that are brought to bear on the bureaucracy.

In summary, the service, educational, and control functions of Congress represent important features of the work of a representative assembly in an executive-centered government. Though the record of Congress in performing these nonlegislative functions is by no means perfect, the fact that it attempts to perform them increases the degree to which the government remains popularly responsive and responsible. Quite clearly, Congress does not respond impartially to all the interests in society; some are favored over others. Nevertheless, Congress does reflect a broad cross-section of the interests and opinions of the American people. As a representative assembly, it serves as a vehicle through which the pluralism of American life is projected into the policy-making processes of the government.

It is clear that Congress as a representative assembly is also a powerful participant in the policy-making processes of the government. More than any other legislature in western political systems, it has retained its power to initiate major legislation and to obstruct, delay, and reject the policies of the executive. Congress has not become subservient to executive power; its functions have changed, however, and more time is spent reacting to policy proposals conceived by the executive and overseeing the administrative process than initiating major legislation. But its legislative functions are still of major importance because, in the end, Congress—not the president—determines which laws shall be passed. The way Congress participates in this policy-making process makes decision making in the federal government very complicated and protracted. This is true because of the characteristics of the legislative process in Congress.

Congress as a Policy-Making Institution

Edmund Burke once observed that "all government . . . is founded on compromise and barter."[34] Governmental decisions are produced by a process that rests upon the idea of reciprocity. Interests and demands are balanced and accommodated in order to generate support for decisions that provide some

---

[34] R. Joseph Monsen, Jr., and Mark W. Cannon, *The Makers of Public Policy* (New York: McGraw-Hill Book Co., 1965), p. 4.

advantages for everyone concerned. The policy-making process in Congress, in brief, is a political process in which individuals and groups within Congress and organized interests and other governmental agencies outside Congress compete openly and freely in the hope of achieving their policy objectives. The only way major legislation can be passed is to build and maintain a continuous series of coalitions that provide majority support for legislation.

Supportive coalitions are developed and maintained through the mechanism of bargaining and negotiation.[35] Members of Congress—working both formally and informally with each other, with the president, administrative agencies, and organized interests outside the government—work out agreements on legislation in order to develop the necessary support for passage. These agreements may involve substantive changes in the legislation, promises to support or oppose subsequent legislation, or any of the great variety of understandings that people reach in trying to accommodate each other. Negotiation may involve personal charm and influence, political deals, manipulative skills, strategic or tactical acumen, or outright political pressure. Whatever form it may take, bargaining represents the essence of the policy-making process in Congress.

Table 10.3. Points at Which Delay or Defeat May Occur in the House

Delay	Defeat
Committee inaction in referring to a sub-committee	Committee inaction
Sub-committee inaction (prolonged hearings, refusal to report)	Negative vote in committee
Committee inaction (prolonged hearings, refusal to report)	Sub-committee inaction
Rules Committee inaction (refusal to schedule hearings; prolonged hearings; refusal to report)	Negative vote in sub-committee
Slowness in scheduling the bill	Rules Committee inaction
Floor action (demanding full requirements of the rules)	Negative vote in Rules Committee
reading of the journal	Defeat of rule on floor
repeating quorum calls	Motion to strike enacting clause
refusing unanimous consent to dispense	Motion to recommit
with further proceedings under the call of the roll	Final passage
prolonged debate	
various points of order	

Source: Lewis A. Froman, Jr., *The Congressional Process: Strategies, Rules, and Procedures* (Boston: Little, Brown and Co., 1967), p. 18.

[35] See Lewis A. Froman, Jr., *The Congressional Process: Strategies, Rules, and Procedures* (Boston: Little, Brown and Co., 1967), p. 2, for a discussion of the various forms of bargaining.

Without compromise, coalitions to support major legislation cannot be built. The route of a major piece of legislation through Congress is long, slow, and tortuous. Successful passage requires the existence of majorities and favorable decisions at numerous key points along the route. Congress is a highly decentralized institution with many semi-autonomous "power centers" which function with a high degree of independence because no single person or unit is equipped to provide leadership or direction. A negative vote or absence of majority support at any one point along the legislative route usually means defeat for the bill. Indeed, the political process is complex and heavily weighted in favor of delay and defeat rather than successful passage. The difficulty of getting a bill through just one of the houses of Congress, the House of Representatives, is illustrated in Table 10.3.

Policy-making in Congress is such a highly fragmented process and power is so decentralized basically because the structural organization of Congress provides for a bicameral arrangement with two separate legislative chambers and a system of standing committees and subcommittees within each chamber that must act on all legislation.

---

*The Decentralized
Structure of Congress*

The Bicameral Structure of Congress.   Congress is a bicameral body composed of the Senate and House of Representatives. These two chambers were created by the Constitution as independent and equal partners in the legislative process. A bill can become law only if it has the approval of both, and neither chamber can usurp or undermine the authority of the other. Both houses exercise the same powers in the legislative process; however, the Senate alone may ratify treaties and presidential appointments, and the House has exclusive authority to originate revenue bills. The Senate and House are alike in two important ways: "First, both are relatively decentralized political institutions with a high degree of division of labor through the committee system. Second, both are equal in power.[36] But the similarities pretty much end at that point. The Senate and House are separate and independent political institutions and are organized quite differently. Because this is true, the legislative process operates differently in each chamber.

Lewis Froman has suggested that "probably the two most important differences between the House and the Senate, and the two from which most of the

---

[36] *Ibid.,* p. 7.

others are derived, are that the House is more than four times as large as the Senate, and that senators represent sovereign states in a federal system whereas most congressmen represent smaller and sometimes shifting parts of states."[37] The Senate is a relatively small assembly composed of only 100 members representing the 50 states of the federal union. Since there are only two senators from each state, a senator is usually a well-known political figure who enjoys a certain amount of prestige in his home state as well as in Washington. He is elected for a term of six years and thus enjoys relatively long tenure in the Senate whether or not he is reelected. Because the Senate is small, it operates in a casual and informal manner; each senator has his own desk, the rules are usually suspended and debate is unlimited. Far more than is the case in the House, the Senate is an assembly of equals which goes about its business in a friendly and informal manner. Since every member represents an entire state, less attention is given to rank and hierarchy. Junior senators are able to move into positions of leadership rather early in their careers. For instance, Lyndon Johnson, generally recognized as the most effective majority leader in the history of the Senate, assumed that position during his first term in office, and Senator Edward Kennedy won the position of majority whip during his first term. Such a rapid rise to positions of leadership would be impossible in the House of Representatives.

The House of Representatives with its 435 members is such a large body that it could not possibly conduct its business if it tried to operate as the Senate does. The organization of the House is formal, rigid, and hierarchical. Power is more centrally concentrated in the hands of the leaders and new congressmen must serve a long apprenticeship before they begin to exert much influence in the law-making process. It is not uncommon for a congressman to serve as long as ten years before he obtains a position in the committee structure that enables him to influence the work of the House. Speaker McCormack, who retired in 1970, was in his thirty-third year as a member of the House before he assumed the office of Speaker and his successor, Carl Albert, was serving his fourteenth year before becoming majority leader.[38] Since congressmen represent small districts within states and advancement to positions of leadership is slow, they enjoy less prestige than do their colleagues in the other chamber. They serve on a smaller number of committees, have restricted opportunities to speak on the floor of the House, and, because of their two-year terms, are continuously faced with defeat at the polls. These differences between the House and Senate may be summarized as in Table 10.4.

Congress thus is two quite different institutions in terms of organization, constituencies, tenure, and career patterns. The Senate and House are separate and independent of each other; yet they share power and must cooperate with

---

[37] *Ibid.*

[38] *Ibid.*, p. 12.

Table 10.4.   Differences between House and Senate

House	Senate
Larger (435 members)	Smaller (100 members)
More formal	Less formal
More hierarchically organized	Less hierarchically organized
Acts more quickly	Acts more slowly
Rules more rigid	Rules more flexible
Power less evenly distributed	Power more evenly distributed
Longer apprentice period	Shorter apprentice period
More impersonal	More personal
Less "important" constituencies	More "important" constituencies
Less prestige	More prestige
More "conservative"	More liberal

Source: Froman, *op. cit.,* p. 7.

each other because the legislative process comes to a halt unless both chambers are able to negotiate their differences and reach some compromise on legislation.

The Committee System.   It has often been noted that "congressional politics is committee politics."[39] The bargaining and negotiating that ultimately result in congressional decisions occur in the committee rooms rather than on the floors of Congress. By the time an important piece of legislation reaches the floor of the Senate or House, most of the work has already been accomplished. When the final vote occurs, it amounts essentially to a ratification of decisions made earlier in the committee system. There may be debates, stirring appeals to conscience, or dire speculations about the nation's future if a bill is passed or defeated, but the outcome is rarely in doubt. Though there are exceptions, few battles are won or lost on the floor; the debates and the votes are an anti-climax to what has already been decided in committees.

There are several different kinds of congressional committees. First are the *standing committees:* the Senate has sixteen and the House has twenty. Standing committees in both the Senate and House are set up according to specialized areas of competence or jurisdiction. For example, the House has standing committees on Foreign Affairs, Armed Services, Education and Labor, Veterans Affairs, Appropriations, Agriculture, and Banking and Currency, to name only a few. A similar pattern is followed in the Senate, though there are some differences. These standing committees are the "working-units" of Congress; it is here that the bulk of congressional activity related to the passage of bills occurs.

[39] James A. Robinson, *The House Rules Committee* (New York: Bobbs-Merrill Co., 1963), p. 1.

For this reason, committee assignments of senators and congressmen represent vital factors in the success of their congressional careers. Some committees are more prestigious than others because their jurisdictions lie in areas where the vital issues of national security must be resolved. A senator serving on the committees on Foreign Relations, Armed Services, or the Judiciary gets more exposure than those on such committees as District of Columbia or Public Works. Also, a senator or congressman who sits on a committee concerned with issues important to his home district is able to strengthen his position in Congress because he is dealing with issues that are important to the people who actually vote for him.

Second, each chamber also has *ad hoc* or select committees which are formed for a specific purpose and exist only on a temporary basis. A third type of committee is composed of members from both the Senate and the House; there are seven of these; the Joint Committee on Atomic Energy is one example. A fourth type is the *conference committee*. This is a single committee which meets to iron out differences between the two chambers on specific pieces of legislation. It has no permanent membership. Members from each chamber are appointed each time the Senate and House pass the same bill but in different forms.

Congress could accomplish very little if it did not use the committee system. The work load of Congress is so large that it must by necessity delegate this work to smaller units.[40] They enable Congress to specialize and develop expertise in the areas in which it must legislate. By sending legislative proposals to specialized committees that concentrate their efforts in limited areas of jurisdiction, Congress is able to counterbalance to some degree the authority of specialists and experts in the executive establishment.[41] Thus, the use of standing committees has two effects: it decentralizes power in Congress and, therefore, complicates the problem of centralized leadership because the committees are not easily controlled by the parent body; second, it also allows members of Congress to specialize to some degree and thus enables Congress to deal more effectively with complex legislative proposals than would otherwise be the case.

The Committee Chairmen. The committees are the dominant factors in decision making because most floor decisions are mainly ratifications of what has been decided in committees.[42] Standing committees often become the personal tools of the chairmen because of the immense power that rests in the hands of these senior members. Technically, the chairman of a standing committee is

---

[40] Bibby and Davidson, *op. cit.,* p. 24.
[41] Ralph K. Huitt, "The Internal Distribution of Influence: The Senate," in Truman, *op. cit.,* p. 89.
[42] Bibby and Davidson, *op. cit.,* p. 170.

subject to the control of the committee. But in reality, it usually works the other way around; the committee is controlled by the chairman and its output reflects his interests and preferences.

The power of the chairman is enormous: he calls committee meetings; sets the agenda; controls the committee staff; allocates the budget; controls the subcommittee system by determining the jurisdiction of subcommittees, appointing their members, choosing their chairmen, and referring bills; represents the committee before the Rules Committee (only in the House); and channels the flow of legislation from his committee to the floor. The chairman either speaks for his committee on the floor or decides who does, and usually sits on the conference committee when bills from his committee are under consideration.

A committee chairman is free to use these vast powers as he likes.[43] He may push favored legislation through his committee or, more important, he may doom legislation that he doesn't favor. He can assign such legislation to a hostile subcommittee, create an *ad hoc* subcommittee and refer the bill there, keep it in the full committee where he can control the proceedings, refuse to hold hearings, deny funds for investigations, and use his position in a variety of ways to prevent a favorable report. Of course, a chairman can only do what his committee will tolerate. The majority in a committee can overrule him and report out a bill over his objections. But it is rare that a committee will revolt against its chairman. The members are too dependent upon him for money, staff, subcommittee assignments and subcommittee chairmanships. And all of these are vitally important to successfully developing one's congressional career.

A congressman becomes a chairman by seniority. If he manages to get reelected continually, he will probably make it, whether he is a moron or a genius, a party stalwart or a renegade. Among Democrats, for example, committee chairmen have in the past often been from single-party districts in the South. Two arguments supporting seniority are always cited: the experience and knowledge gained during many years of service is the main requirement for a chairman; and bloodshed among committee members is avoided if everyone knows in advance who will be chairman. The principal argument against the rule has been the issue of party loyalty; obviously a chairman elected and reelected from a safe district can defy both his president and his congressional party leadership. The seniority rule therefore makes Southern Democrats, urban Democrats supported by strong organizations, and midwestern Republicans, who have usually been conservative, the chairmen of many important and powerful congressional committees. Nevertheless, change is unlikely. Senior congressmen benefit by the seniority system, and junior members tolerate it in the hope that they, too, will someday enjoy the power and privileges of being chairman. The few who wish to appoint party loyalists to the chairmanships, thereby strengthening party discipline in order to pass presidential programs (assuming the president is of the same party), will continue to be frustrated.

---

[43] The different styles of leadership are discussed in *ibid.,* pp. 170–196.

The Subcommittee System

Most standing committees use a system of subcommittees; and practically all legislation is referred to them for consideration. Subcommittees in both the Senate and House "are very much the creature of the (standing) committee and its chairman."[44] Some standing committees—House committees on Rules, Un-American Activities, and Ways and Means and Senate committees on Aeronautical and Space Science, and Finance—do not normally use subcommittees, preferring to conduct their business in full committee. Since standing committee chairmen have almost complete freedom in establishing subcommittees, determining their membership, selecting their chairmen, and assigning bills, there is no consistent pattern in the operation of these subunits. In some committees, the subcommittees are established with clear areas of specialization and bills are assigned accordingly; in others, this is not the case. Some standing committees tend to accept a bill as reported by a subcommittee without change. Others will reopen the question in full committee and vote on additional amendments. When this occurs, it is possible for amendments voted down in subcommittee to be written into the bill in full committee.

When a major piece of legislation is referred to a subcommittee, the process of consideration usually occurs in two stages. First, hearings are scheduled, and interested parties are given an opportunity to testify. Usually, witnesses from the executive branch are given the opportunity to appear first in order to get the Administration's position into the record. The subcommittee chairman can manipulate these hearings with wide discretion either to pass or defeat the bill under consideration, but as a rule they conduct them fairly.[45] Second, after the conclusion of hearings, the subcommittee meets in executive session to "mark up" the bill; that is, they review the bill in detail, rewrite portions of it, and agree on amendments. This is a crucial stage in the legislative process because if the subcommittee chairman is hostile to the bill or the members of the majority party are divided on its provisions, the chances of a favorable report to the full committee are poor. If all members of the subcommittee feel that legislation is needed on the particular subject in question, and if the members of the majority party stand together on the version of the bill that finally comes out of the "mark up," its chances of support in the full committee are good. If, however, a majority of the subcommittee disagree, the bill may never again see the light of day.[46]

---

[44] Nelson W. Polsby, *Congress and the Presidency* (Englewood Cliffs, N.J.: Prentice-Hall, 1964), p. 67.

[45] *Ibid.,* p. 68.

[46] For a personal account of the "mark up" session, see Clem Miller in John V. Baker (ed.), *Member of the House* (New York: Charles Scribner's, 1962), pp. 13–15.

The Subcommittee Chairmen.   Subcommittee chairmanships are important leadership positions for two reasons: they represent stepping stones to higher positions, and, in committees where the chairman does not dominate, subcommittee chairmen are able to exert a great deal of influence on the legislation that comes before their subcommittees. In standing committees where the jurisdiction of subcommittees is clearly defined and a free hand given to the subcommittee, the subcommittee chairmen become key figures in the investigation of administrative agencies, the study of pending legislation, and the sponsorship of new legislation. This is the case in the Senate Judiciary Committee and the Appropriations Committees in both Senate and House. In other committees where the subcommittees are merely numbered and given no specific jurisdiction or the standing committee chairman appoints himself chairman of the important subcommittees, this position is of little importance. For instance, Emanuel Celler, chairman of the House Judiciary Committee, assigns most important bills to a subcommittee of which he is chairman or keeps the legislation in full committee.[47] Or, subcommittee chairmanships can be handed out as rewards or denied as punishment for members to suit the purposes of the chairman.

The late L. Mendel Rivers of South Carolina, chairman of the House Armed Services Committee, was a good example of a strong-minded chairman who maintained firm control of subcommittees. This committee, dominated by conservatives and Southerners, who tend to vote more money for the military than requested by the Defense Department, is highly protective of the armed forces. Only three members of the committee usually opposed chairman Rivers on military expenditures: Otis Pike of New York, Lucien Nedzi of Michigan, and Robert Leggett of California. In 1969 "when Pike, who has been sharply critical of soaring defense contract cost, came in line to head the standing investigations subcommittee . . . he didn't get the chairmanship. Rivers took the post himself."[48] As might be expected, Rivers' district in South Carolina has many military installations. He was a friend of the military and his friendship reaped its rewards.

An excellent example of a standing committee where subcommittee chairmen play key roles in the legislative process is the House Committee on Appropriations.

The Committee on Appropriations . . . divides its tasks among thirteen largely autonomous subcommittees, whose chairmen have as large a share in

---

[47] William L. Morrow, *Congressional Committees* (New York: Charles Scribner's, 1969), pp. 39–40.

[48] Greensboro *Record*, November 27, 1969.

House decision making as all but a few full committee chairmen. Thus the chairman of the Appropriations Subcommittee on Foreign Aid exercises more influence over that program than does the chairman of the Foreign Affairs Committee. And the equivalent statement can be made about a half-dozen other Appropriations subcommittee chairmen.[49]

By carefully selecting the chairmen of these Appropriations subcommittees, the chairman of the full committee can ensure that certain policy goals will be achieved. When Clarence Cannon—who opposed foreign aid—was chairman of the full committee, he gave the chairmanship of the Subcommittee on Foreign Operations to Otto Passman of Lousiana, who was equally opposed to foreign aid. So long as Passman was chairman of the subcommittee, the President's foreign aid bills were cut substantially. When George Mahon replaced Cannon as chairman of the full committee, Passman's power as subcommittee chairman was reduced. In 1964 when President Johnson's foreign aid bill came up for consideration, Mahon—a fellow Texan—decided to support the President. He not only decided to oppose Passman's efforts to cut the bill, but exercised his prerogatives as chairman to assume the chairmanship of Passman's subcommittee. Passman temporarily stepped down as chairman of the subcommittee and attempted to fight the bill on the floor of the House. In the end, Mahon won.[50]

In summary, the legislative process in Congress is cumbersome and difficult because the two legislative chambers share power, the controls over the legislative process are exerted by semi-autonomous committees and subcommittees, and the local ties of many congressmen predispose them to favor or oppose certain policies. Thus, the decentralized structure of the institution favors those forces in Congress that want to delay and defeat legislation. It creates definite disadvantages for those seeking to bring about policy changes. The decentralized structure of Congress very nearly precludes the passage of major legislation unless a prolonged process of bargaining and negotiation produces acceptable compromises. But formal structure is only part of the reason; the rules and informal norms governing the work of Congress and presidential leadership complicate the policy-making process even further. The effect of structure, rules and norms, and presidential leadership on the legislative function of Congress may be illustrated by examining the congressional struggle over federal aid to education.

---

[49] Richard F. Fenno, Jr., "The Internal Distribution of Influence: The House," in Truman, *op. cit.,* pp. 55–56.

[50] Froman, *op. cit.,* p. 40.

The Legislative
Function of Congress

Government institutions, like all human institutions, are merely established patterns of human relationships, interactions that are uniform, formalized, and relatively stable. The behavior of members of Congress becomes habitual and somewhat consistent through adherence to formal rules and procedures, informal norms and conventions, and through the perception by each member of the role he should be performing. The acceptance of formal rules and informal under-standings by members enables Congress to conduct its business.

These rules and understandings are important for three reasons: (1) they create power by establishing an organizational scheme that gives some members of Congress much greater influence in the legislative process than others; (2) they shape the outcome of the legislative process because in many instances, the rules rather than the merit of a proposal determine whether it is enacted into law; and (3) the rules of the game express the political values of Congress and of American society at large. The rules of the game in Congress, in other words, are not neutral; they favor some political values over others and provide definite advantages to certain segments of American society. It is important to note that the rules and norms of Congress are not established just to facilitate policy making but also to maintain the stability of the institution and to protect the traditional prerogatives of the members of Congress. In fact, Congress will often adhere to its rules and conventions in the interest of preserving its traditional prerogatives even though this may mean that important legislation will be delayed or defeated. Sometimes, however, Congress will depart from its rules and conventions in order to pass legislation.

Federal Aid to
Education: A Case Study
in the Legislative Process

In April 1965, President Lyndon B. Johnson made a trip to Stonewall, Texas. In front of the small one-room schoolhouse where he had begun his education, he signed into law a historic piece of legislation, the Elementary and Secondary Education Act of 1965. This bill represents the first legislation passed by Congress in the twentieth century that provides federal funds for public education. Congress has been the scene of many bitter legislative struggles but none have a history quite so tortuous as federal aid to education.[51]

---

[51] Saloma, *op. cit.,* pp. 117–118.

For almost twenty years, progressive forces in the nation believed that federal aid was a crucial factor in maintaining the quality of public education in the United States; they had tried to push legislation promoting this through Congress. But they always lost, even though many times it was obvious that a majority of the members of both the Senate and House were in favor of federal aid to education in some form. Finally in 1965, after many frustrating defeats, both houses of Congress passed HR2362 by substantial majorities. Why did it take twenty years to pass this legislation? The answer must come from an understanding of the legislative function of Congress and the extent to which the legislative process is affected by the decentralized nature of the institution, the rules and norms that govern the behavior of its members, the political climate in the country, and the role of the president in legislative struggles. A review of the history of this legislation from 1945 until 1965 shows how these four factors shape the legislative function of Congress. The struggle over federal aid was mainly in the House of Representatives, because almost from the beginning the Senate acted favorably on this legislation.

The First Decade, 1945–1955

During this period of years the House Committee on Education and Labor conducted hearings on federal aid on seven occasions, with the most crucial decisions coming in 1949 and 1950.[52] The Senate passed a federal aid bill in 1948 and then passed another bill in 1949 by the healthy margin of 58 to 15. The 1949 bill (S. 246) provided money for teachers' salaries and general operating expenses. And it also provided money for nonpublic schools to use for transportation and books. Soon thereafter, hearings were scheduled before the Special Subcommittee on Federal Aid to Education of the House Committee on Education and Labor. The chairman of the standing committee, John Lesinski (D.-Mich.), a Catholic, appointed Representative Graham Barden of North Carolina as chairman of the special subcommittee. Though Barden publicly expressed his total support for federal aid to education, it was well known that he was a fervent enemy of federal aid. He carried out a carefully laid plan to see that the Senate bill was defeated.

Barden's first technique was a much used device; he proposed a substitute bill for discussion and refused "to entertain seriously testimony on S. 246." He

---

[52] Richard F. Fenno, Jr, "The House of Representatives and Federal Aid to Education," in Robert L. Peabody and Nelson W. Polsby (eds.), *New Perspectives on the House of Representatives,* 2nd ed. (Chicago: Rand McNally & Co., 1969), p. 300. Our discussion of the legislative history of federal aid to education prior to 1965 and the role of the House Committee on Education and Labor in determining the outcome of this legislation is a summation of this article. All quotes are from this source unless otherwise cited. For a more detailed treatment of federal aid to education, see Frank J. Munger and Richard F. Fenno, Jr., *National Politics in Federal Aid to Education,* Economics and Politics and Public Education Series, No. 3 (Syracuse, N.Y.: Syracuse University Press, 1962).

stated simply that, "There are some features in the Senate bill so objectionable to me that I could not find myself going over to it. I am not going to accept it, that's all." Several provisions of the Senate bill were distasteful to Barden, but the aspect of the bill that bothered him most was the provision that allowed federal funds to go to private schools. Barden's substitute bill made no mention of, such aid, and this issue was systematically avoided in the subcommittee hearings. When a committee member or a witness attempted to discuss it, Barden indicated that he was firm in his resolve against federal aid to private schools and that it was useless to discuss it.

As chairman of the subcommittee, Barden "dominated the hearings to a degree unequalled by any representative or senator in any federal aid hearings before or since." Barden's second technique involved the handling of the fifty-eight witnesses who testified before the committee; over 900 pages of testimony was taken. At least one third of all the time devoted to questions and answers was taken up by exchanges between Barden and the witnesses. This practice of scheduling many witnesses and engaging each of them in prolonged conversations is an effective way to delay serious considerations of a particular bill or the broader issues that underly controversial legislation. By refusing to allow the committee to consider the Senate bill, by substituting his own bill that did not include aid to private schools, and by burdening the committee with an excessive number of witnesses, Barden laid the groundwork for its certain defeat in the standing committee.

Barden's bill calling for federal aid to public schools but none for private schools was reported back to the whole committee with a favorable vote of ten to three. It immediately precipitated a national controversy over federal aid to Catholic schools. Lesinski, chairman of the full committee, condemned Barden's bill as anti-Catholic and bigoted. Lesinski further charged that Barden "drew it up that way purposely because he didn't want any aid to education and wanted to kill it." The chairman predicted that Barden's bill would "never be reported out of the Labor Committee." And indeed it was not. But the Senate bill was not reported out of committee either. The national controversy over federal aid to private schools, generated by the open conflict in the committee on this issue, so divided the members of the committee that no compromises on the issue could be obtained.

In August 1949, the full committee refused to report out the Senate bill by a vote of fourteen to eleven. In February of the next year, the full committee met again at the urging of President Truman to reconsider its vote on the Senate bill. The committee again refused to report out the bill by a vote of thirteen to twelve. The question of federal aid to education was dead for that session of Congress. The issue of federal aid to private and parochial schools so divided the committee that a favorable report could not be obtained. There was no room for compromise; some members of the committee wanted no federal aid to any schools, others would approve of aid to public schools but not to private or parochial schools, and the Catholic members of the committee would not approve of aid to public schools unless private and parochial schools were included.

In 1951, by virtue of the seniority rule, Barden became chairman of the full committee; Barden was now in a strategic position to sabotage federal aid to education legislation both in the committee and on the floor of the House. During 1951 and 1952, "Barden did not allow the full committee to meet at all on federal aid questions." When the question came up again in 1955, Barden decided that the full committee would conduct the hearings rather than a subcommittee. As chairman of the full committee, this move gave him complete control of the hearings. Barden's tactic in this instance was to delay the hearings so long that the Rules Committee and the House would not have time to act on a bill even if his committee reported a bill favorably. The hearings lasted two months; Barden refused to place any restrictions on questions, fifty-two witnesses were paraded before the committee, and over 1,000 pages of testimony taken for the record. To confuse matters even further, the committee gave consideration to eleven different bills dealing with federal aid to education.

Finally, fifteen Democratic members of the committee put pressure on Barden to get on with the business at hand. On July 28, these fifteen Democrats joined with seven Republicans and reported one of the eleven bills to the floor. The vote was twenty-two to eight. But Barden's strategy had worked; by then it was too late in the session for the Rules Committee to take action and provide a rule to govern floor action on the bill. The bill languished in the Rules Committee for over a year and was not sent to the floor until June 1956, and then only because of threats to bypass the committee. Thus a majority for federal aid had developed on the Education and Labor Committee but it was apparent that no majority existed on the important Rules Committee.

Before discussing the next critical stage of the history of federal aid to education in the House, the nature of the House Committee of Education and Labor and the quality of its leadership should be discussed. The jurisdiction, membership, procedures, and leadership of this committee were crucial factors in the long struggle in Congress over federal aid to education.

The Committee and Its Leadership. There is more conflict and dissention in the House Committee on Education and Labor than in any other committee in the Congress. "Most of the committee's internal problems are consequences of the fact that within its jurisdiction falls a high proportion of the most controversial, the most partisan, and the most publicized issues of American domestic politics." The issues that come before the committee—federal aid to education is a good example—are frequently issues on which congressmen have had to take firm stands in elections. For this reason, many members of the committee tend to be inflexible and unwilling to compromise their views. As one former member of the committee has observed:

> Some of us were unalterably opposed to federal aid, and some on the other side were just as unalterably in favor of it. . . . There weren't many minds changed by discussion. Everybody had a fixed position when he came there, and nobody changed that opinion that I know of.

The members of the committee also tend to feel strongly about issues and be committed to an ideological position. Most Republicans have stood firm against any form of federal aid to education but the Democrats have been sharply divided among themselves. While the Republicans and Southern Democrats found it easy to get together in opposition to federal aid, other Democrats because of their varied backgrounds, points of view, and political styles had great difficulty agreeing on the form they want federal aid to education to take. As one Republican member who opposed federal aid remarked:

> We work by trying to split the Democrats on the committee, and actually we don't have to work very hard. They'll split off by themselves . . . not on the big issues on the final votes, but on amendments and in the committee. They'll shout at each other, stand up and bang their fists on the table and stomp out.

The jurisdiction and membership of the committee thus encourages conflict and inflexibility rather than bargaining, negotiation, and compromise. The procedures of the committee merely make matters worse. The operating style of the committee is not one of flexibility and accommodation. Rather, it is one of fierce competition, rigid adherence to one's position, and decision making by showdown votes. The committee follows its formal rules closely and there is little reliance on private committee traditions, informal understandings, or committee loyalty. "Sentiments of mutual regard and group solidarity are few. Group morale is not high. The committee's decision-making procedures do nothing to lower tension or to increase cohesion inside the group."

Young members of the committee play a full role in committee work without serving an apprenticeship as is generally the case in Congress. Also, the principle of seniority is not respected, except in the selection of the chairman of the full committee. Senior members are frequently passed over when chairmen of the subcommittees are named. Barden refused to give Adam Clayton Powell a key subcommittee chairmanship even though Powell's seniority warranted the post; when Powell assumed the chairmanship of the full committee in 1960, he did the same to Phil Landrum of Georgia. Contrary to the general practice in Congress, specialization is not highly respected and the full committee rarely ratifies the work done by its subcommittees. Though the committee has few experts in the field of education, those who have gained some experience because of their work in the area do not speak with any more authority than those who know little about the subject. In short, the informal norms of congressional behavior that tend to be followed in Congress generally are not followed in the House Committee on Education and Labor.

The work of the committee is further handicapped by its failure to recruit a "staff of experts on education whose independent judgment has carried any weight at all with the members." As one member of the committee's staff observed about his colleagues:

> This committee has the most incompetent, inept staff of any on the Hill. Barden wanted it that way. He could manipulate a dumb staff easier than a smart one. . . . We haven't had a chief clerk or counsel on this committee for years that knew enough to come in out of the rain.

For these reasons, the committee is not a highly respected committee, either by its own members or by the House. Contrary to the case with most other committees, its decisions do not carry much weight on the floor. It is regarded as a committee whose members cannot agree on much of anything; consequently, its decisions are frequently changed on the floor rather than being accepted as is the general practice in Congress.

Finally, the quality of this committee's leadership over the years has not been strong. The one exception was Graham Barden who was an ardent foe of federal aid to education. As a subcommittee chairman and then as chairman of the full committee, he skillfully used the tactics of "delay, divide, and conquer" in order to sabotage federal aid to education. Barden's tactics included:

1. Refusing to institute committee rules specifying regular committee procedure;

2. Scheduling committee meetings irregularly, sometimes with gaps of two months between sessions;

3. Terminating a committee meeting by declaring the absence of a quorum, even when a quorum of the committee was present;

4. Not recognizing committee members with whom he disagreed;

5. Keeping the committee staff small and inactive;

6. Holding extensive desultory hearings without any coordinated legislative focus;

7. Arbitrarily limiting the range of subjects to be considered in committee hearings (i.e., to legislation on public schools only);

8. Calling a "quickie" vote of the committee to kill legislation when an anti-education majority was present;

9. Giving disproportionate time to opponents of aid-to-education while serving as floor manager of an education bill;

10. Resigning as floor manager of a bill during a critical period of floor consideration.[53]

The Second Decade, 1956–1965

The 1949 Senate bill on federal aid to education died in committee, a victim of the conflict over federal funds for private and parochial schools. The 1955 bill was reported favorably by the committee but lay buried in the Rules Committee for over a year until a threat to bypass the Rules Committee forced a favorable vote and brought the bill to the floor in 1956. The success in getting a bill to the floor of the House in 1956 stemmed from decisions to avoid the parochial school issue. Both the 1956 bill and the 1957 bill provided federal funds for public schools only. The strength of the political parties in the House was about even, although the Democrats held a slight edge. Thus, any aid-to-education bill had to have bipartisan support. The bipartisan support in the House Committee on Education and Labor and in the Rules Committee was sufficient to get both bills to the floor of the House, but that is as far as they got. The 1956 bill was sent back to the committee which effectively killed it for that session of Congress, the 1957 bill was defeated on the floor.

Both bills reached the floor because the issue of aid to parochial schools had been successfully avoided. But both bills "represented the most fragile of compromises between the preferences of President Eisenhower and the preferences of a majority of committee Democrats." Since federal aid had not lacked positive support in the Senate since 1945, House passage of either of these bills meant victory for the proponents of federal aid. But a combination of two factors—the lack of presidential leadership and the issue of racial segregation in the schools—was enough to undermine this bipartisan support.

[53] Saloma, *op. cit.,* p. 120.

President Eisenhower "was never more than a lukewarm advocate of federal aid." And when the issue was being debated in 1956 and 1957, there was only silence from the White House. There was much confusion among House Republicans about whether these bills were actually the President's bills; in the absence of any statement of support from the President, each Republican was free to make up his own mind on the issue. The silence of the President was "disastrous for aid proponents." As one of them remarked after the defeat of the 1957 bill:

> It was what the administration did—or didn't do—that killed the legisla-
> tion. The truth of the matter was that Eisenhower never wanted federal aid.
> I think some of his friends on the golf course must have told him that it was
> creeping socialism. I really do. In 1957, the bill lost in the House by five votes.
> He could have had a bill. A few phone calls to members of Congress, "This
> is the President of the United States calling Congressman So and So"—and
> he'd have gotten the votes. If he had called up Charlie Halleck and Joe Mar-
> tin and said "I want the votes," he could have gotten them. The struggle
> would never have been as close as it was. He just didn't want a bill. He did
> nothing. And in that situation, inaction meant "No."

Segregation began to cloud the issue of federal aid to education immediately after the Supreme Court's decision in 1954. "It nearly paralyzed the House committee" during its discussions of federal aid bills in 1955. An amendment to the 1956 bill sponsored by Adam Clayton Powell of New York prohibiting any federal aid to segregated schools was only narrowly defeated in the Committee. Powell's amendment was attached to the bill on the floor, however, and this, reduced the bill's support among Southern and border-state congressmen who might otherwise have voted for passage. The issue of segregated schools complicated the question of federal aid to public schools just as the issue of parochial schools had done in 1949. The bipartisan majorities sustaining the 1956 and 1957 bills were unstable, and any divisive issue—be it religion or race—was enough to defeat a highly controversial piece of legislation that had no support from the President. With the defeat of the 1957 bill, the entire issue was returned to the committee and the welcoming hands of chairman Barden.

The next crucial stage in the effort to get federal aid to education came during 1959, 1960, and 1961. The situation in the House committee and in the House itself changed to the advantage of federal aid because of the Democrats' success in the 1958 elections. The number of Democrats in the House increased from 234 to 283, and the new ratios on the House Committee on Education and Labor gave the proponents of federal aid firm control. Furthermore, Chairman Barden retired from Congress in 1960 and was replaced by the next senior Democrat on the committee, Adam Clayton Powell of New York, who was a strong advocate of federal aid so long as no funds went to segregated schools. Things looked brighter for federal aid in the committee and in the House chamber. But danger loomed in the Rules Committee.

The House Committee on Rules.   The formal rules and informal under-standings that govern the functions of the Rules Committee in the House of Representatives is an excellent example of how the rules of the game in Congress shape policy-making. The House uses an elaborate set of procedures to control the flow of legislation from the standing committees to the floor. One set of procedures—the Private Calendar, the Consent Calendar, and motions to sus-pend the rules—is used to channel private or noncontroversial bills through the House. Once this kind of legislation is approved in a standing committee, it moves through the legislative process easily and is usually approved by the House without debate or objection. A large percentage of the legislation approved by the House is of this nature. Such bills do not concern the vital issues of public policy that face the nation; therefore the procedures used to assure passage need not concern us here. Major legislation such as federal aid to education takes a different route to the floor of the House. It must go to the Rules Committee and a rule must be assigned to govern further consideration before it can be debated on the floor.

In one sense, the Rules Committee functions the same as the other 20 standing committees; it has jurisdiction over all bills or resolutions that concern the rules and organization of the House and such bills are referred to it when they are introduced. But it performs a second peculiar function: an important piece of legislation cannot be brought from a standing committee to the floor for debate until the Rules Committee provides a "rule" that sets the terms of debate. This sets it apart from other standing committees and involves it in an ongoing controversy about the effect of congressional organization on the legislative process. For instance, after the House Committee on Education and Labor has acted favorably on a bill, the chairman will send it to the Rules Committee with the request that a rule be assigned. On the surface of things, this seems a reasonable procedure because the work load of the House is so great that some subunit, by necessity, must establish certain restrictions on floor action. But problems do arise: the Rules Committee does not have to grant the rule unless it chooses to do so; if no rule is granted, a bill reported favorably by a standing committee cannot be acted upon by the House.

Quite obviously, then, the Rules Committee is in a position to exert considerable influence on the legislative process. What are the powers of the Rules Committee? James A. Robinson in his excellent study of the Rules

Committee has summarized the various ways in which the committee can control the agenda of the House:[54]

Refuse to grant a hearing. This usually means no rule will be assigned.

Grant a hearing, but refuse to grant a rule or simply take no action.

Make a deal with the committee that requested the rule. In essence the Rules Committee says, "change the substance of your bill to suit us, and we will grant a rule so the House can take action."

Grant a rule that allows the House to take action. The rule may be "open" which allows amendments and points of order, or it may be "closed" and forbid any amendments on the floor. Rules also set time limits on debate, usually one or two hours.

When both Senate and House have passed the same bill in different forms it must go to the conference committee. If any member of the House objects to sending the bill to conference, the Rules Committee must then grant a rule before the bill can go to conference. The committee can then refuse to grant the rule.

Report a bill directly to the floor even though it has never been reported out of the standing committee. Though rarely done, the threat to do so can dislodge a bill that has been bottled up in a committee for a long period of time.

Under normal circumstances, the Rules Committee functions smoothly and assigns rules to most of the bills that are sent to it. It functions much like a traffic cop at a busy intersection, assigning precedence to some bills over others, and prescribing the terms under which a bill is to be debated and voted on in the House. But sometimes it functions as a road block, and refuses to allow legislation to proceed any further. The chairman acting alone cannot block legislation permanently. But if he is supported by a majority of his committee members, the obstacles become almost insurmountable. The committee is bitterly criticized when this occurs: first, some criticism is based on the belief that no committee should be able to effectively kill legislation that has been favorably reported by the standing committee that has actually studied the bill; second, most of the criticism of the Rules Committee stems from the belief that it obstructs legislation it dislikes and waves through the bills it approves.

The record of the committee from 1954 until 1966 suggests very strongly that this is indeed what happens. During this period of years, the chairman of the Rules Committee was Congressman Howard W. Smith of Fauquier County, Virginia. Judge Smith, as he was affectionately known, was a crafty, talented,

---

[54] We have paraphrased points made by Robinson, *op. cit.*, pp. 11–12.

and skilled Southern conservative who sought to preserve the rural, traditional political values of his constituency. The majority of the members of his committee were either Southern Democrats or conservative Republicans who shared Smith's views on public policy. During Smith's tenure as chairman, the Rules Committee regularly blocked progressive legislation when it was able to do so. The standing committee that suffered most by the refusal of the Rules Committee to grant rules was the House Committee on Education and Labor, because this committee has been concerned with legislation that calls for greater governmental involvement in social welfare, education, labor affairs, and civil rights.

The Rules Committee and Federal Aid, 1959–1961.   After the electoral victory of 1958, the Democrats were in firm control of the House committee and were able to report out federal aid bills with little difficulty. The Democratic majority on the committee was sufficiently large that Republican support was not needed, thus the committee became more and more partisan in its approach to federal aid. The Democratic partisanship worked well in the committee, but it created a Republican reaction at other key points in the legislative process, particularly in the Rules Committee.

The House Committee on Education and Labor sent four separate federal aid bills to the Rules Committee. The 1959 bill simply died in the Rules Committee because a combination of Southern Democrats and Conservative Republicans prevented a vote. The 1960 bill received a favorable vote of 7 to 5 and was sent to the floor of the House for decision. In terms of its content and the kind of federal aid provided, the 1960 bill had been designed to attract maximum support on the floor. The Powell Amendment barring federal aid to segregated schools was attached on the floor but despite this, the House voted 206 to 189 in favor of the bill. The 1960 bill represents the first time in this century that the House of Representatives passed federal aid to education legislation. The key to its success was the newly elected Democrats who had won their seats in the House in the 1958 elections.

But the Rules Committee was not yet through with the matter. Since the Senate had already passed a federal aid bill, the House bill had to go to the conference committee where the differences between the two bills would be worked out. The rules of the House require that unless all members of the House agree to send the bill to the conference committee, the Rules Committee must grant a special rule before the bill can go on to the conference committee. One member of the House objected, and the 1960 bill had to go back to the Rules Committee for a special rule. It stayed there, because the Rules Committee refused to grant the rule. Two members of the Committee that had voted earlier to send the bill to the floor of the House changed their positions and refused to vote for a rule sending the bill to the conference committee. Though federal aid had finally won a majority on the floor of the House, the bill died because the rules of Congress allow seven members of the Rules Committee to prevent a conference committee to consider the bill.

In 1961, the chances for passage of federal aid to education seemed brighter than at any time since 1949. President Kennedy, who supported federal aid, was in the White House and Graham Barden had been replaced by Adam Clayton Powell. Powell, who by this time recognized that his amendment forbidding aid to segregated schools was a crucial factor in the defeat of all federal aid, had agreed to oppose efforts to add such amendments. Furthermore, the chances of federal aid were improved by the decision of the House to increase the size of the Rules Committee from 12 to 15. Repeated efforts to reduce the power of the Rules Committee or change its composition had failed until 1961. But finally the power and prestige of House Speaker Sam Rayburn, together with the strong support of the White House persuaded the House to "pack the committee."[55] Three new members, who were thought to be less conservative than Judge Smith and his Republican and Southern colleagues, were added to the committee. But it didn't work; the old issue of federal aid to parochial schools that wrecked federal aid in 1949 came up again and divided the Rules Committee along different lines.

In 1961, this issue of federal aid to parochial schools broke up the Democratic majority in the House committee. The Republicans on the committee stood firm against any federal aid, and the Democrats engaged in bitter quarrels over the issue of aid to private and parochial schools. Finally, the committee sent three different bills to the Rules Committee. All three bills were tabled by a vote of 8 to 7. This effectively killed any hope of getting federal aid legislation during that session of Congress. The crucial vote against the bills was cast by one of the newly appointed Democrats who was dissatisfied with the status of aid to parochial schools. Soon after the Rules Committee tabled the bills, the House Committee sent a hastily written bill directly to the floor of the House on Calendar Wednesday (any bill can be brought to the floor on Calendar Wednesday without going through the Rules Committee) but the House defeated it by a large majority. Thus the decision of the Rules Committee proved to be decisive.

Success in 1965: A Partisan Victory

For a period of almost twenty years federal aid to education had failed in Congress because it lacked sustaining majorities at all the key points in the

---

[55] For a good popular account of this struggle, see Tom Wicker, *JFK and LBJ* (Baltimore: Penguin Books, 1969), Part I.

legislative process. The Senate repeatedly acted favorably on federal aid, but success never came in the House because the legislative process in the lower chamber is more formal, rigid, and hierarchical, and the members of the House are more vulnerable to effects of political changes in the country because of their shorter terms in office. More specifically, the absence of continuous majorities in the House Committee on Education and Labor, the Rules Committee, and the House chamber meant that federal aid would be rejected at some point, even though it had been approved at other points.

The 89th Congress, heavily Democratic, was strong enough to sustain federal aid legislation in both houses of Congress. "The result was passage of the first federal aid-for-education legislation in history—one of the legislative landmarks of the post-World War II period."[56] The key to the legislative victory was strong executive leadership and partisan loyalty. The 1965 bill was planned and designed in the executive branch and was written to provide "aid for children," not for schools, thus avoiding the question of federal aid to parochial schools. The strategy of the Johnson Administration and the Democratic leadership in Congress was, first, to introduce a bill that stood the best chance of passage and, second, to assure Senate passage of the same version of the bill as the House so it would not have to go through the conference committee. Thus, it was crucial that Senate passage be obtained without amendment. And it was also important that both houses act as quickly as possible because earlier struggles over federal aid clearly proved that the longer the proceedings lasted, the greater the chances of confusion and ultimate defeat.

The 1965 bill was a high priority item for both the President and the Democratic leadership in Congress. The House Committee on Education and Labor, firmly in Democratic hands, was given some but not much leeway for amendments to the administration's bill. Senators were told to submit their amendments to the House committee if they had any. Not surprisingly, the committee immediately split over the bill. But the Democratic majority held together and the bill was reported to the Rules Committee where it received a favorable vote of 8 to 7 after only four days of hearings. The bill had been introduced into the House in January, and by March 24th it had cleared both the House committee and the Rules Committee and was on the floor for debate. The Democratic leadership in the House allowed only three days for consideration of the bill. Debate, though caustic and highly partisan was tightly controlled; repeated efforts on the part of the Republicans to amend the legislation were beaten down. It was a clear-cut partisan issue, and the Democrats carried the day. Denying repeated efforts on the part of the Republicans to prolong the debate, the Democratic leadership brought the bill to a vote and it passed by a

---

[56] Saloma, *op. cit.*, p. 122. Our discussion of the 1965 federal aid to education bill is drawn from this source. For a more detailed account, see Philip Meranto, *The Politics of Federal Aid to Education in 1965: A Study in Political Innovation*, Education in Large Cities Series (Syracuse, N.Y.: Syracuse University Press, 1967).

majority of 263 to 153. Once the House passed the bill, after bottling up similar legislation for twenty years, it was clear that the struggle was over because the Senate had been supporting such legislation for two decades. The key point was that the Senate pass the bill without amendment in order to avoid the conference committee. Though "none of the arbitrary limitations that had been placed on debate in the House characterized either the committee or floor stage in the Senate, it soon became clear that the majority would permit no amendments by the Senate." On April 6 the bill was reported out of committee. The Senate approved it on April 9 by a vote of 73 to 18. Two days later, on April 11 President Johnson signed the Elementary and Secondary Education Act of 1965 into law.

Characteristics of the Congressional Policy-Making Process (Domestic)

We suggested earlier that decision making in Washington, though extremely varied and complex, has certain characteristics: *decentralized power, pluralistic power struggle, incrementalism, slowness, noise, importance of public opinion,* and *executive dominance*. The case study of federal aid to education legislation demonstrates that the decision-making patterns that recur throughout the whole government also apply in the legislative process in Congress. Quite clearly, power in Congress is highly decentralized; it is divided between the two houses of Congress and then is further decentralized among the committees and subcommittees. The result is that the policy-making process in Congress is highly fragmented. The Senate repeatedly passes federal aid to education bills but the House does not; the House Committee on Education and Labor reports a bill favorably, but the Rules Committee refuses to allow the bill to go to floor for decision. When the Rules Committee allows a bill to come to the floor of the House, it is voted down. Finally, when the House passes a bill, the Rules Committee refuses to allow it to go to the conference committee.

The policy process in Congress is also a pluralistic power struggle between many different groups, parties, committees, and individuals. The incessant conflict within the House Education Committee among its Democratic members, between Democrats and Republicans, between Chairman Barden and Adam Clayton Powell, and between the Catholics and non-Catholics over the many aspects of federal aid to education, was a struggle for power with the intent of increasing their influence over the legislation before them. The power struggle between liberal Democrats, Speaker Rayburn, President Kennedy, and Judge Smith and his conservative supporters on the Rules Committee is another example. The congressional process involves a great variety of actors engaged in continuous maneuvers designed to better their chances of shaping the outcome of the legislative process.

Federal aid to education points up in bold relief the incrementalism that characterizes the policy process in Congress. Under normal circumstances, a bill moves slowly to committee, to subcommittee, back to committee, to the Rules Committee, to the floor, then over to the other chamber, then to the conference committee, and usually back to the floor of both chambers for final passage. The legislative process thus proceeds in increments and it is very time-consuming. Congress can of course act with dispatch, but under most circumstances, it does not. When success is not achieved in one session, the process must start all over again in the next session; this can go on as long as 20 years, as federal-aid-to-education proponents discovered.

The struggle over federal aid to education also demonstrates how much noise is associated with the legislative process. Barden's 1949 refusal to discuss the Senate bill providing aid to parochial schools in subcommittee and his substitution of a public school bill caused a furor in the nation. Cardinal Spellman and Eleanor Roosevelt carried on a highly publicized spat over the issue, and religious spokesmen of all faiths commented on the matter. When major legislation is under consideration, congressmen and concerned interest groups usually have a lot to say, and the news media report these opinions.

The openness of the legislative process assures that the public is a participant in the activities of Congress. Public opinion affects in a significant way what Congress does and when it does it. Congress is rarely ahead of the country, usually moving slightly behind the sentiment of the people. It is not likely to pass controversial legislation when the mood of the nation is clearly against it. However, when the nation seems to be favorably disposed toward legislation in a certain area, the chances that Congress will take action are improved.

The values of the American public are injected into the legislative process through the activity of interest groups lobbying in Congress, through the news media, and through the electoral system. Congress is not just a policy-making institution; it is also a representative assembly reflecting a cross-section of the varied interests of the nation. There is an inherent tension between the legislative function and the representative functions of Congress. In representing the varied interests and values of a pluralistic society, Congress frequently impedes rather than enhances the capacity of the government to act. In preventing passage of federal aid to education for twenty years, the House was representing the values of a segment of the American public. Though members of Congress have greater freedom of movement in voting than is generally believed, on some issues they are clearly restrained by what they perceive to be the desires of their constituents. Thus, on issues which need swift action, "we are faced with the conclusion that the House, if anything, may be *too* representative of the American people."[57]

Most important, the defeat of federal aid to education in the 1950s and early 1960s and its ultimate success in 1965 demonstrates the vital importance of presidential leadership in the legislative process. Truman, Eisenhower, Kennedy, and Johnson all sponsored federal aid legislation but Johnson was the only one to throw the full weight of his office and his personal and political influence into the struggle. And he was the only president who carried Congress with him on this issue. Eisenhower was lukewarm on the issue at best and had no stomach for the rough and tumble atmosphere of legislative leadership. President Kennedy's legislative package in 1961 included several federal aid bills, but Kennedy did not assume personal command of his legislative programs in the sense that Johnson did, and he never faced up to the severity of the parochial school question that ultimately killed the 1961 bill. Johnson's leadership was a key ingredient; he was a "fighter" when it came to getting his programs through Congress. He exerted tremendous energy and used every method at his command to muster support at crucial points in the legislative process. Determination and strategic skill were very important. But the political circumstances that prevailed in the country and in Congress at the time were equally important. The nation was more favorably disposed toward federal aid to education in 1965 than in previous years and, most important, the Democrats enjoyed an overwhelming majority in both houses of Congress. While flimsy and unstable bipartisan majorities supported federal aid during the Eisenhower and Kennedy years, a cohesive partisan majority was present in Congress in 1965 to sustain Johnson's federal aid bill. This made the real difference between defeat and victory. Johnson, of course, had helped create the majority by his remarkable victory over Goldwater in 1964 (or perhaps Goldwater created the majority by frightening so many voters, including many Republicans). Johnson succeeded in winning "more legislative innovations on the home front than any other President in any other single session of Congress in the twentieth century." The record of the Johnson Administration is, in fact, little short of remarkable when compared to the success of presidential programs in Congress between 1936 and 1963. From the second administration of Franklin Roosevelt to the end of the Kennedy Administration Congress passed only two bills of major significance that had been sponsored by the White House; the Fair Labor Standards Act of 1938 and the Taft-Hartley Act of 1947.[58]

Finally, the struggle over federal aid to education demonstrates the importance of the rules and informal norms of Congress in shaping the legislative process. The effect of seniority is clearly demonstrated by the influence on

---

[57] *Ibid.*, p. 119.

[58] Louis W. Koenig, *The Chief Executive,* rev. ed. (New York: Harcourt Brace Jovanovich, 1968), p. 127.

federal aid to education exerted by Barden in the Committee on Education and Labor and Judge Smith in the Rules Committee. The rules that give the Rules Committee such an important role in controlling the flow of legislation from the standing committees to the floor of the House enables a majority on that committee to delay and frequently defeat legislation that might be approved on the floor.

The informal norm of "reciprocity" that discourages either the by-passing of a committee or the discharging of a bill from a committee allows these committees to delay legislation for long periods of time; many members of Congress are themselves sitting on bills that they do not want to report out of committee. The conduct of the House Committee on Education and Labor during the 1950s is a good example of how the disregard of the congressional norms of "specialization," "apprenticeship," and "courtesy" complicate the congressional process. These norms "grease the wheels" of Congress and encourage the bargaining and negotiation that lead to the compromises that make the passage of major legislation possible.[59] The House Committee did not defer to those few members who had a special competence in the area of education, did not follow the lead of its subcommittees, and did not encourage courtesy among its members. Its deliberations tended to be inflexible and doctrinaire rather than flexible, practical, and compromising. Consensus was rarely reached and the conflict in the committee frequently spilled out on the floor of the House in the form of amendments proposed by minority committee members who had not succeeded in influencing the committee. The dissention and conflict in the committee damaged its image in the House generally, and the House did not ratify the committee's decisions as it usually does with most other standing committees. This kind of confusion complicated federal aid to education on more than one occasion.

Though a case study of a single piece of legislation cannot demonstrate clearly all the important characteristics of the legislative process, it does illustrate what is most important about the legislative function of Congress: major legislation of a controversial nature can be passed only through a process of building majority coalitions at key points in the legislative process in both houses of Congress. These majorities may be bipartisan or partisan but, as the success of the federal aid bill of 1965 illustrates, overwhelming partisan majorities succeed where bipartisan majorities easily fall apart. Though political parties organize the Congress, they do not control the votes of the members on issues like civil rights where constituent interests are strongly to the contrary. These majorities are difficult to build because of the representative nature of Congress and because of the rules of Congress. This is true of the Senate as well as of the House. Rule XXII in the Senate, which makes it difficult to shut off a filibuster, is a good example of the ability for *intense* minorities to prevent a majority from taking action.

---

[59] See Donald R. Matthews, *U.S. Senators and Their World* (Chapel Hill, N.C.: University of North Carolina Press, 1960), Chapter 5.

The problem is not that a majority of representatives have not wanted a federal aid measure or could not be persuaded to want one. The problem is that an overall majority—or a federal aid consensus—cannot be obtained at any one point in time for any one legislative proposal. To put it another way, any federal aid majority must be compounded of many submajorities. Different submajorities will be needed to resolve essentially different conflicts—that is to say, conflicts on different issues, in different decision-making units, at different points in time, and in different sets of society-wide circumstances. Furthermore, each submajority must be flexible and cohesive—flexible enough to permit agreement with other submajorities and cohesive enough to make that agreement an asset in legislative maneuver.[60]

The success of the federal aid bill of 1965 was mainly due to presidential leadership and the support of strong Democratic majorities in the Senate and the House. Thus, passage of the bill was based more on party discipline and firm resolve rather than bargaining, negotiation, and compromise. But the circumstances that existed in Congress and in the country at large in 1965 were unusual. Under normal circumstances such as those that existed before 1965, major legislation cannot be passed unless the legislative process is one of bargaining, negotiation, flexibility, and compromise.

Characteristics of the Congressional Policy-Making Process (Foreign)

Congress has vast formal powers in the foreign policy field. The Senate possesses the power to approve treaties, confirm executive cabinet, military, and diplomatic appointments. Both the Senate and the House become involved when legislation is required to implement a particular international move. Both also participate when, as is frequently the case, money has to be appropriated. Committees of either house can, in addition, launch investigations into executive policies and administration regarding foreign affairs. Finally, resolutions may be passed by either or both houses in support of presidential actions, to suggest new commitments to him or to deter him from commitments the Congress will not like.

Nevertheless, the axiom that "the president proposes, and the Congress disposes" by accepting, modifying, or rejecting the executive-initiated and -devised policies is particularly true in the field of foreign policy. Indeed, the Congress rarely rejects; primarily, it legitimates policies devised by the executive,

[60] Fenno, "The House of Representatives and Federal Aid to Education," in Peabody and Polsby, *op. cit.,* pp. 322–323.

either in the original or some amended form. The record of American foreign policy since 1945 shows clearly that all major presidential initiatives, from the Truman Doctrine and Marshall Plan to the Alliance for Progress and the nuclear anti-proliferation treaty, have been accepted and supported by the Congress. Table 10.5, covering primarily the Cold War years until just before the American-Soviet détente after the 1962 Cuban Missile Crisis, also indicates one other highly significant feature besides the rarity of congressional foreign policy initiatives: the virtual absence of congressional participation in the most important decisions, those involving the potential or actual use of violence—thereby suggesting that on the fundamental issue of peace and war, the Congress has not even disposed for most of the post-war period.[61]

In the post-1945 period, the Indochina crisis of 1954 represents the single occasion in which Congress participated decisively in making a foreign policy decision that involved the use of force. The influential role of Congress was made possible by President Eisenhower's indecisiveness about intervening in Vietnam after France's defeat at the battle of Dien Bien Phu. In a meeting with congressional leaders, Secretary of State Dulles indicated that he had not consulted with any major European allies about joint intervention. The Chairman of the Joint Chiefs of Staff, who was also at the meeting, admitted that his military colleagues were opposed to unilateral intervention or to an atomic strike against the Vietminh because such action could not possibly save the French from disaster. Under these circumstances, congressional leaders were reluctant to approve intervention and laid down certain conditions which the administration would have to meet before Congress would sanction such a move. President Eisenhower decided against intervention.[62] The President was aware of the reluctance in Congress to fight "another Korea." Furthermore, Eisenhower, who had been elected to end the war in Korea, had grave reservations about authorizing an air strike that might lead to American involvement in another Asian land war. But suppose President Eisenhower had firmly believed intervention was the right course of action and had been willing to fight another limited war in Asia. Would he have sought the counsel of congressional leaders before making his decision? Probably not. In all likelihood, he would have done what President Truman did when South Korea was invaded from the North in 1950. He would have made his decision and then called in congressional leaders to inform them about what the United States was going to do. Indeed, this is what happened in 1955 when Eisenhower declared that the islands of Quemoy and Matsu would be defended against Communist China and then asked Congress for a resolution supporting this decision. Eisenhower wanted to clearly indicate American intentions to Peking and, if possible, to avoid partisan attacks in

[61] James A. Robinson, *Congress and Foreign Policy*, rev. ed. (Homewood, Ill.: Dorsey Press, 1967), p. 65.

[62] Melvin Gurtov, *The First Vietnam Crisis* (New York: Columbia University Press, 1967).

Table 10.5. Congressional Involvement and Decision Characteristics

	Congressional Involvement (High, Low, None)	Initiator (Congress or Executive)	Predominant Influence (Congress or Executive)	Legislation or Resolution (Yes or No)	Violence at Stake (Yes or No)	Decision Time (Long or Short)
Neutrality Legislation, the 1930s	high	exec	cong	yes	no	long
Lend-Lease, 1941	high	exec	exec	yes	yes	long
Aid to Russia, 1941	low	exec	exec	no	no	long
Repeal of Chinese Exclusion, 1943	high	cong	cong	yes	no	long
Fulbright Resolution, 1943	high	cong	cong	yes	no	long
Building the Atomic Bomb, 1944	low	exec	exec	yes	yes	long
Foreign Service Act of 1946	high	exec	exec	yes	no	long
Truman Doctrine, 1947	high	exec	exec	yes	no	long
Marshall Plan, 1947–48	high	exec	exec	yes	no	long
Berlin Airlift, 1948	none	exec	exec	no	yes	long
Vandenberg Resolution, 1948	high	exec	cong	yes	no	long
North Atlantic Treaty, 1948–49	high	exec	exec	yes	no	long
Korean Decision, 1950	none	exec	exec	no	yes	short
Japanese Peace Treaty, 1952	high	exec	exec	yes	no	long
Bohlen Nomination, 1953	high	exec	exec	yes	no	long
Indo-China, 1954	high	exec	cong	no	yes	short
Formosan Resolution, 1955	high	exec	exec	yes	yes	long
International Finance Corp., 1956	low	exec	exec	yes	no	long
Foreign Aid, 1957	high	exec	exec	yes	no	long
Reciprocal Trade Agreements Act, 1958	high	exec	exec	yes	no	long
Monroney Resolution, 1958	high	cong	cong	yes	no	long
Cuban Decision, 1961	low	exec	exec	no	yes	long

Source: Compiled with permission from James A. Robinson, *Congress and Foreign Policy*, rev. ed. (Homewood, Ill.: Dorsey Press, 1967), p. 65. The assignment of each case to different categories represents a judgement on the part of the author.

Congress later if the policy backfired. This had happened to President Truman when a stalemate developed in the Korean war. The Formosa Resolution, in short, represented action taken by Congress to legitimate a decision the President had already made.

Presidential actions in other post-war situations also illustrate the peripheral role of Congress in policy decisions involving the potential use of force: President Kennedy's moves to defend West Berlin in 1961, his threat to intervene in Laos, his move against the Soviets to force the withdrawal of missiles from Cuba in 1962, and President Johnson's intervention in the Dominican Republic in 1965—none of these actions had the support of a congressional resolution. On the other hand, Johnson sought such a resolution to legitimate air strikes on North Vietnam in retaliation for alleged attacks by North Vietnamese gun boats on American destroyers operating in international waters in the Gulf of Tonkin. The resolution, passed almost unanimously by Congress, authorized the President "to take all necessary measures to repel an armed attack against the forces of the United States and to prevent further aggression" in Southeast Asia. This resolution was used by President Johnson to justify the rapid expansion of the war and the introduction of over 500,000 ground troops into the Vietnamese war. The Tonkin resolution merely supported a course of action already under way by virtue of decisions made in the executive branch. Subsequent congressional criticism that the President had wrongly interpreted the intent of Congress and that he should have come back for another resolution if he wished to intervene massively in Vietnam did not undermine the President's belief that he already had the authority to do what he did.

The implications of these decisions dramatically illustrate the secondary role of Congress in foreign policy making and the limited degree to which it can control the making of national commitments. Technically speaking, Congress has the Constitutional authority to declare war and raise and maintain the armed forces. But as a practical matter, the decisions to use or not use military force in international affairs are made by the president. This issue of congressional versus executive control over foreign and military policy has existed since the beginning of the republic because the boundaries between presidential and congressional power are not clearly fixed. The Constitution provides that the two branches of government share authority over the military establishment. As commanders-in-chief, presidents have repeatedly sent American forces on missions without advance congressional approval. As chief diplomats, presidents can also take actions to which other nations' responses might leave the Congress with little choice but to declare war. Thus, in 1917 Wilson armed American merchantmen to protect themselves against German submarines; and in 1941 Franklin Roosevelt engaged in a limited undeclared naval war with Germany in the Atlantic. Congress' intermittent attempts to check the presidents' power to commit this nation to war in the late 1930s, late 1960s, and early 1970s are eloquent testimony of Congress' feelings of impotence on the fundamental issue of deciding peace or war in an era when the United States was increasingly involved internationally to preserve the balance of power, first against Germany and later against the Soviet Union and other Communist states.

No instance in recent history has demonstrated this more vividly than the Gulf of Tonkin resolution. Testifying before a critical Senate Foreign Relations Committee in 1967, Under Secretary of State Nicholas Katzenbach argued that the congressional power to declare war was outmoded in the modern age when wars had to be fought for limited objectives. Katzenbach, speaking for the Johnson Administration, claimed that the Tonkin resolution together with the SEATO treaty "fully fulfills the obligation of the executive in a situation of this kind to participate with the Congress, to give the Congress full and effective voice, the functional equivalent of the constitutional obligation expressed in the provision of the Constitution with respect to declaring war.[63]

Indeed, the real question was whether the Tonkin resolution had been necessary at all. All postwar presidents have claimed the authority to commit American forces without prior approval by Congress. They have requested congressional resolutions in support of these actions to strengthen themselves politically, both to impress hostile states with American unity and determination, and to allay later domestic criticism. No president has ever submitted a resolution that he thought would be defeated or seriously amended; he has always held prior consultations with congressional leaders of both parties and has known that he would receive bipartisan support.

What accounts for this decline of congressional influence in foreign affairs? First, as we have already seen, is the Constitutional fact of presidential primacy as the nation's chief diplomat and commander-in-chief, symbolized by the frequent identification of major international moves and/or declarations in American foreign policy with presidential names. Chosen in a national election, he has the legal power, the expert help, a vast collection of information, and the capacity to act with the authority, dispatch, and on occasions—especially during war—with the required secrecy. By contrast, Congress represents local interests and, in the case of the House, is so large as to be almost unwieldy. Generally, it is capable only of acting slowly; indeed, as a deliberative body, it is supposed to take its time. However, it usually lacks sufficient sources for its own information and it is to a large extent, therefore, dependent on the executive for identifying the problems confronting the nation and for suggesting alternative policies to resolve them. Finally, the elaborate committee system virtually precludes effective and efficient consideration of foreign policy decisions. One need but note some of the committees that must become involved in one way or another when Congress is considering a foreign policy question: Foreign Relations, Armed Services, Appropriations, Government Operations, Commerce, to name but a few. Each committee can obtain only a partial view of a complex foreign policy

---

[63] See "The Legislative-Executive Foreign Policy Relationship in the 90th Congress," *Congressional Digest* (October 1968), for the pros and cons of this issue.

problem. There is simply no point at which the conflicting interests and views of nonmilitary foreign programs versus military ones, domestic versus foreign policy claims can be balanced and compromised. There is only one such point in the whole government: the presidency.[64] The Congress' awareness of the executive's superior status in these matters is visible in the legislature's expectation of presidential initiative in foreign policy—indeed, in all policies but especially in foreign policy—and in its resigning itself primarily to accepting, modifying, or negating executive-conceived proposals.

A second reason for congressional approval of presidential foreign policies has been the bipartisan support which succeeding administrations have built up across party lines. Indeed, the major thrust of American foreign policy came in the years immediately following World War II, a period looked upon as "the heyday of conspicuous congressional influence upon postwar foreign affairs" because the major policies of the period all needed legislative enactment.[65] But bipartisanship in foreign policy making is one thing; the degree of congressional influence on foreign policy decisions is something else again. It would be fairer to say that Congress went along with the president, primarily because for twenty years after 1945 it agreed with the broad outlines of the containment policy. But it also had little choice in the face of continued crises during the most intensive days of bipolarity. Thus, when a president states that the nation confronts a serious threat to its security, he can usually mobilize the necessary congressional approval for his policies. During the Senate debates on the Truman Doctrine, Senator Vandenberg, the Republican spokesman in foreign policy, remarked in a letter to a constituent that

> the trouble is that these "crises" never reach Congress until they have developed to a point where congressional discretion is pathetically restricted. When things finally reach a point where a president asks us to "declare war" there usually is nothing left except to "declare war." Thus, if we turned the president down—after his speech to the joint Congressional session—we might as well either resign ourselves to a complete Communist encirclement and infiltration or else get ready for World War III.

During this period, the United States confronted an either-or situation in which it acted to protect itself or lost its security. The president's address to a joint

---

[64] Samuel P. Huntington, *The Common Defense* (New York: Columbia University Press, 1961), pp. 130–131.

[65] H. Bradford Westerfield, "Congress and Closed Politics in National Security Affairs," *Orbis* (Fall 1966), p. 747. Also, see Westerfield's *Foreign Policy and Party Politics* (New Haven: Yale University Press, 1955) for a thorough analysis of bipartisanship from Pearl Harbor to Korea. Further, Westerfield suggests that the term "bipartisanship" ought to be replaced by "extrapartisanship."

session of Congress *committed* the nation. Congress could no more fail to support him by approving his programs than it could refuse to provide him with tanks and guns if he had requested a declaration of war. The point is that in "a critical moment, the president's hands must be upheld. Any other course would be dangerously misunderstood."[66] The congressional response in such a circumstance has traditionally been to back up the president.

This either-or feeling, together with the necessity for action, is felt even more keenly in such dramatic moments as the Berlin Blockade, the communist invasion of South Korea, or missiles in Cuba, which take the nation by surprise and demand *immediate* decisions. In such circumstances there is no time at all for congressional debates. Congressional support is usually forthcoming, whether the president asks for it or not. This support will be bipartisan, resulting from a temporary truce due to a common perception of external danger, not a feeling of political unity among the two parties. Thus its basis is tenuous and will erode if the policy does not attain its aims within a reasonable amount of time. Then it becomes fair game for criticism and electoral strategy.

Bipartisan support and the attendant lack of criticism of administration foreign policy is also due to another circumstance. When different parties control the presidency and Congress, the party controlling the legislative branch is left with relatively little choice but to cooperate with the president. To the degree that bipartisanship becomes a symbol of patriotism—of "placing country ahead of party"—vigorous criticism tends to appear as virtually unpatriotic and done only for "political" reasons. The "out" party must give the impression of being "responsible." Thus, from 1946 to 1948 many congressional Republicans led by Senator Vandenberg, expecting Dewey to win in 1948, conveyed this impression by their bipartisan support of Truman. The same was true when the Democrats controlled Congress from 1954 to 1960 during the Eisenhower years. Only after 1948 did the conservative and nationalist wing of the Republicans turn more to partisan opposition. Frustrated by eighteen years out of office, tired of the "me-too-ism" on domestic and foreign policies of Republican liberals and internationalists, the conservatives attacked with relish. They could easily exploit Nationalist China's collapse and the Korean War; also, Senator Vandenberg had died. However, when the "out" party controls both ends of Pennsylvania Avenue, it seems that the restraints resulting from its desire to win the next presidential election are removed.[67] Eisenhower was criticized by the conservatives of his own party during his first two years in office because Eisenhower's policy was felt to be merely a continuation of his predecessor's containment strategy. During the Johnson years, when the Democrats controlled Congress, criticism of Johnson's interventions in the Dominican Republic and especially in

---

[66] Arthur H. Vandenberg, Jr. (ed.), *The Private Papers of Senator Vandenberg* (Boston: Houghton Mifflin Company, 1952), pp. 342–344.

[67] Francis E. Rourke, "The Domestic Scene," in Robert E. Osgood (ed.), *America and the World* (Baltimore: The Johns Hopkins Press, 1970), pp. 168–169.

Vietnam was intense and widespread, particularly in the Senate. The Nixon Administration was vigorously attacked by both moderate Republicans and liberal Democrats because of its ABM and MIRV build-up as well as the continuing war in Vietnam. After Nixon's extension of the war to Cambodia in 1970, as "Johnson's War" became increasingly "Nixon's War," more Democrats joined in the attack. Bipartisanship may now be replaced by a more critical attitude in Congress, especially by the opposition party. The result may well be a greater flexibility in foreign policy and adaptability to changing circumstances.

Thus, presidents from Truman to Nixon have formulated foreign policies and the Congress has gone along—until they turned out badly. Its main function has been to legitimate executive policies by affixing them with the "Great Seal of National Unity"; it may in this process modify these policies and presidents have been willing to accept such modification if the essential substance of their policies remains unaltered. Congress, in short, has acted as a lobby, attempting to influence the executive formulation of foreign policy. The activities of members of Congress critical of the Vietnamese war during the late 1960s and early 1970s, in introducing bills, holding committee hearings, and giving public speeches, were efforts to influence presidents Johnson and Nixon to change their policies. Congress can also play a negative role by saying "no" to certain policy proposals. This establishes boundaries beyond which presidential foreign policy may not go.

As an institution, Congress may be most potent when it acts as a deterrent.[68] If it cannot create foreign policy, it can at least prevent policies it does not like from being made or obstruct their implementation. This is a role the Congress—especially the House, which is more conservative in its attitudes toward international politics than either the Senate or the presidency—has played quite well. The Congress has consistently opposed expensive foreign aid programs, especially to nations that openly criticize the United States. Congress has annually cut foreign aid appropriations which, while they have stayed reasonably steady as an absolute figure, have declined as a percentage figure of the expanding gross national product. Congress has also been reluctant to extend aid to any nation that called itself a socialist state. On the whole, Congress has been more "anti-communist" than any other American governmental institution. For more than two decades, it has insisted that the United States not extend diplomatic recognition to Communist China, and no postwar American president has attempted to do so. Similarly, opposition in Congress has impeded presidents in their attempts to build bridges to Eastern Europe and move toward a détente with the Soviet Union. Finally, Congress has tended to emphasize rather heavily the military component of foreign policy. While it has cut foreign aid with one hand, it has for twenty years approved gigantic military budgets with the other after only the most cursory examinations. On a number of occasions, despite its

---

[68] This analogy is from Roger Hilsman, *To Move a Nation* (Garden City: Doubleday and Company, 1967), p. 559.

constant proclamations about the need for economy, Congress has appropriated greater sums than the administration requested. Until the great ABM debates of 1969, Congress has made it more difficult, rather than less difficult, to slow down the arms race. In limited wars—particularly during the Korean War and also in the Vietnamese war until the disenchantment began in 1967—it was Congress that exercised the most pressure on the president to escalate these conflicts. Only when these wars became stalemated, casualties mounted, and political pressures against the war built up in the country at large, did a chorus of voices in Congress call for de-escalation and peace. At that point, Congress' essential frustration with its subordinate institutional role was reinforced by constituency pressures, and a legislative-executive confrontation became difficult to avoid.

The president therefore cannot ignore Congress on foreign policy because it retains the power of the purse, the right to investigate the executive establishment, the right to "advise and consent" to treaties and nominations, and the right to declare war. After the Vietnamese and Cambodian experiences, it is less likely that a president will—or can—ignore Congress. Congress has passed a number of resolutions since 1969 which are symbolic of its more assertive mood: the National Commitments Resolution, stating that American commitments need executive *and* legislative approval; an amendment to a defense appropriations bill to prohibit the use of American ground forces in Laos and Thailand; and, after President Nixon's move into the Cambodian sanctuaries without consulting Congress or obtaining its approval, an amendment precluding the use of any appropriations for retaining ground forces in Cambodia, or providing air combat support, military advisers, or mercenaries to the Cambodian government after June 30 (the date the president had set for the end of his limited extension of the war), and a more sweeping amendment—labelled "The Amendment to End the War"—was introduced calling for the additional total withdrawal of all United States forces from Vietnam by June 30, 1971, unless Congress declared war. Clearly, congressional critics were willing to use the power of the purse to circumscribe the war-making powers of the president to avoid future combat commitments without assurance that the Congress will support him.

Vietnam has caused many members of Congress to view foreign policy formulation less as a matter of information and expertise and more as a matter of political judgment and the application of values to policy decisions. And it is in this area of political judgment that politicians, not experts, presumably are the most competent. Senator Fulbright has expressed the belief that the Senate should not interfere excessively in the *conduct* of foreign policy but should concern itself with long-range, basic issues.[69] Or as John Finney, a journalist, wrote, "Because it tends to talk with 100 voices, the Senate's advice is still

[69] J. William Fulbright, *The Arrogance of Power* (New York: Vintage Books, 1967), p. 46.

incoherent in terms of specific policies. But it is becoming increasingly apparent that what is developing in the Senate—and to a lesser extent in the House—is a long-range examination of the foreign policy which has guided the United States since the end of World War II."[70]

The Irony of Democracy

In the twentieth century, the power of executive institutions has expanded in most democratic political systems, usually at the expense of representative institutions. In totalitarian systems, they have either been destroyed or rendered ineffective. "If anything is clear in this fretful age, it is that legislative institutions which gave freedom its birth and meaning have been eroded and denigrated in reputation the world around—eroded and denigrated, that is, where they have not been totally destroyed."[71]

This observation is much less true of the United States Congress than it is of other representative assemblies, particularly the parliaments of western Europe.[72] Congress has not lost its power, but its functions have changed. Though Congress has clearly surrendered its function of initiating most major legislation to the president, that power has not been taken away. "Among the major legislatures of the Western world, it alone is still capable of initiating major legislation."[73] And most major legislation, though initiated outside Congress, is influenced by what happens in Congress during the process of becoming law. It remains the most powerful legislative institution in the world.

Congress continues to be a vital institution in an executive-centered system because ultimately it is in Congress that the laws are made. Public policy is of course more than law, but law is and must remain the foundation and framework of public policy in a democratic society. Therefore, in the American political system Congress must place the stamp of legitimacy on policy decisions which are meant to have a lasting effect. Decisions made in other governmental institutions that are vigorously and continuously opposed by Congress cannot be implemented effectively on a lasting basis. In this sense, in contrast to legislatures in other western democratic systems, Congress stands astride the policy-making process and sooner or later every major public policy must have its support. The shift of policy initiation from Congress to executive institutions therefore represents a change in function rather than a loss of power. As Ralph

---

[70] *The New York Times,* February 26, 1967.

[71] Stephen K. Bailey, "Is Congress the Old Frontier?" in Irish, *op. cit.,* p. 69.

[72] For a suggestive comparative study of two democratic states and their conduct of foreign policies, see Kenneth N. Waltz, *Foreign Policy and Democratic Politics* (Boston: Little, Brown and Co., 1967).

[73] Bibby and Davidson, *op. cit.,* p. 3.

K. Huitt has stated in his study of the role of Congress in economic policy: "Whoever tries to weave a . . . web of American economic policy will find soon enough that all threads lead ultimately to Congress."[74] It would be difficult to find any major policy area, including foreign policy, in which Congress has played a distinctly secondary role, where this is not true.

The irony of Congress today is that as a representative assembly, its health and vigor is deemed necessary for the continuation of free government; yet, as an institution that wields much power in the policy-making process, it complicates and delays the capacity of the government to take action. Policy making in a highly industrialized and technological world is dependent upon massive amounts of information, techniques of analyzing and using this information, teams of advisors and assistants trained in specialized fields, a national rather than a local perspective, a national power base, and the capacity for immediate responses to changing circumstances. These tend to be qualifications characteristic of executive institutions rather than representative assemblies. Congress has fallen behind the presidency in its capacity to govern in the modern world.

In performing its legislative functions in a manner that seems to be called for in modern times, Congress is handicapped by its decentralized structure, its lack of centralized leadership, and its traditional ties to local constituencies—although in regard to the localism of Congress it must be added that a gradual move away from local concerns and toward a more national orientation on the part of members of Congress is perceptible. But the trend is slow, and on such issues as civil rights, constituency pressures are compelling. The nature of the electoral system is such that members of Congress, particularly of the House, still maintain strong ties with the traditional segments and concerns of American society. Furthermore, the rules and traditions of Congress tend to favor the *status quo* rather than change; intense minorities who want to *prevent* change profit more from congressional organization and procedures than do intense minorities who are dissatisfied with the *status quo*. For this reason, Congress tends to be insulated from the new social forces, urban groups, angry minorities, and college students, who increasingly are becoming potent factors in American politics. But the organization, rules, and procedures of Congress can be changed if the members of Congress, particularly the members of the majority political party in Congress, want to change them. Thus the problem, as Lewis Froman has pointed out, is not the nature and content of the rules. The real question is who controls the rules.[75] The problem of the contemporary Congress is not one of adaptation as such; Congress has adapted and continues to adapt to

---

[74] Ralph K. Huitt, "Congressional Organization and Operations in the Field of Money and Credit," in Commission on Money and Credit, *Fiscal and Debt Management Policies* (Englewood Cliffs, N.J.: Prentice-Hall, 1963), p. 408. Quoted in Bibby and Davidson, *op. cit.* p. 4.

[75] See Froman, *op. cit.,* pp. 212–217.

changes in American society. The fundamental question has to do with the pace and the direction of its adaptation to the conditions of modern society.

An evaluation of the role of Congress in the political system cannot be based solely on its shortcomings as a law making institution. As the nature of the legislative functions of Congress have changed, its nonlegislative functions have increased in importance. The dilemma of Congress in the twentieth century is the problem of maintaining a proper balance between its representative and legislative functions. In an executive-centered political system, the functions of Congress in overseeing and restraining the president and the bureaucracy cannot be overemphasized. This has become dramatically illustrated in the wake of Vietnam by the struggle over the war-making powers. Yet the resultant dilemma remains: on the one hand, congressional restraint upon the executive is desirable as a means of checking his power and preventing its abuse; on the other hand, the democratic suspicion of unrestrained concentrations of power may be carried to the point where government loses its capacity to take effective actions in response to the domestic and international needs of the nation. Indeed, the question which the growth of the bureaucratic welfare state and the accompanying greater and greater concentrations of power in the presidency has simply but starkly posed is this: are popular accountability and governmental effectiveness in fact compatible?

11

*Policy Making
in the Federal Courts*

When the Nixon administration assumed office in January 1969, the nation waited for signs that would indicate what kinds of policies the new leadership would be likely to sponsor. Foreign policy—particularly American involvement in the Vietnamese war—was of course the dominant concern. But interest in President Nixon's domestic policies in such vital areas as public education, urban affairs, poverty, race relations, and criminal justice was also high. Presidential appointments provide early clues to future policies because of the influence on public policy exerted by members of the cabinet, the independent regulatory agencies, and other high-level positions in the executive establishment. Both the Congress and the nation at large generally concede wide latitude to the president in selecting his cabinet, chief assistants, and advisers. Objections may be raised but rarely are these appointments ever effectively challenged.

Though presidential appointments in the executive establishment have important policy consequences, they are terminal because these officials usually hold their positions only while the president retains his office. Furthermore, executive officials, though influential participants in the policy-making process, are in the final analysis subservient to the president. The president has the power, if he has the will, to assure that executive officials sponsor and implement programs that adhere closely to his policy objectives. Presidential appointments to the federal judiciary are far more significant: federal judges serve for life and their influence on the public policies of the nation extend far beyond the life of the presidential administration that places them in office. President Nixon's judicial appointments, particularly his Supreme Court nominees, were thus seen as more crucial than his executive appointments.

If President Nixon were to serve more than one term in office, he could probably appoint at least four new members of the Supreme Court. Chief Justice Earl Warren, who led the Court during its most innovative and controversial era, attempted to retire during the Johnson administration. He remained on the Court only because Congress refused to confirm Associate Justice Abe Fortas as his successor. Associate Justice Hugo Black is over eighty years of age and Associate Justices William O. Douglas and John Marshall Harlan are over seventy and in poor health. Four new Nixon appointees, together with present Associate Justices Potter Stewart and Byron White, would be likely to give the Court a conservative cast that would be in marked contrast to the Warren Court if President Nixon were to appoint justices who tended to support his views on public policy.

Nixon's choice to succeed Chief Justice Warren was Warren Burger, Chief Judge of the Circuit Court of Appeals for the District of Columbia. Burger was a highly respected federal judge whose judicial career suggested that he would be more conservative in his decisions than the majority of the Warren Court. He was regarded as "Nixon's kind of judge" and his appointment to the Chief Justiceship suggested that the Supreme Court would probably retreat from some of its libertarian positions during the Warren era. His appointment was confirmed by the Senate with little opposition. During the summer of 1969, Justice Abe Fortas resigned from the Court under pressure because of widespread criticism of his financial affairs. Fortas, appointed by President Johnson in 1965, had previously been named to succeed Chief Justice Warren, but opposition in Congress was so strong that the nomination had been withdrawn. His departure from the Court gave President Nixon an opportunity to appoint another justice, his second in the first year of his administration.

Nixon's choice for the vacant seat was Clement Haynsworth, Chief Judge of the Fourth Circuit Court of Appeals. Haynsworth was not well known and his appointment was in trouble in the Senate from the moment it was announced. Critics claimed that Haynsworth's appointment was a political payoff to Senator Strom Thurmond of South Carolina for his support during the presidential election of 1968. Labor organizations and civil rights groups soon joined the opposition claiming that Haynsworth's decisions as an appellate court judge were hostile to the interests of labor and also obstructed the implementation of the Supreme Court's ruling in *Brown* v. *The Board of Education*. When the Senate Judiciary Committee began hearings on the appointment, it was discovered that Judge Haynsworth had been actively engaged in purchasing stock in companies involved in cases before his court. This alleged conflict of interest cast a shadow of doubt on his fitness to serve on the nation's highest judicial tribunal and was enough to undermine his support in the Senate. The appointment was rejected by a vote of 55 to 45. Many Republicans, including Hugh Scott, the leader of the President's own party in the Senate, voted against confirmation.

Why was Haynsworth rejected? Was it because he was a Southerner from South Carolina? Were charges that he was a segregationist at heart actually true? As a wealthy man, did he lack sympathy for the laborer? Had he used his official position as a federal judge to increase his private income? None of these charges were proved to be true, yet they were enough to create an emotionalism that permeated the controversy and strengthened the opposition. Underlying the struggle, however, was the strong belief, if not the firm knowledge, that Haynsworth would strengthen the conservative tendencies of the Supreme Court. Thus, a vote against Haynsworth would be a vote to continue the policies of the Warren Court. In short, the interests of the nation would be well served if the vacancy on the Court were filled by a different kind of judge.

In a second effort to fill the Supreme Court vacancy, President Nixon nominated Judge G. Harrold Carswell, a member of the United States Court of Appeals for the Fifth Circuit. Carswell was even more obscure than Haynsworth. His selection was immediately regarded as another effort on the part of the President to placate the South. Within a week after the appointment, it was learned that Carswell, while seeking a local political office in Georgia in 1948, had pledged eternal loyalty to the principles of racial segregation. Though the Senate was not disposed to reject the President's nominee a second time, this hint of racial bias was enough to endanger the appointment. Subsequent examination of Judge Carswell's record revealed that he had been involved in the incorporation of a segregated golf club in Tallahassee and had connections with land sales involving restricted convenants that discriminated against Negroes. Though Carswell repudiated his campaign pledge of 1948 and denied any prejudice against Negroes, the damage had been done.

Charges of racial prejudice alone were probably not enough to preclude Senate ratification of the appointment but, as the controversy intensified, attention shifted from the racial question to the quality of Carswell's judicial record and to his competence as a judge. He was charged with being a mediocre jurist and a man of only ordinary talents whose judicial decisions and opinions demonstrated a level of competence below that required of Supreme Court justices. To justify this charge, Carswell's opponents pointed out that his decisions as a circuit court judge had been overruled by the Supreme Court much more frequently than was the case with other Southern judges. In civil cases, for example, the Supreme Court had approved only 34 percent of Carswell's decisions while approving 72 percent of the decisions of other members of the Fifth Circuit Court. These percentages were very much the same in other areas of the law.

Thus, Carswell's judicial record suggested that he was not only mediocre but that his view of the law and of the Constitution was not in tune with that of the Supreme Court. The charge of mediocrity was damaging in the extreme because it simply could not be answered; on the other hand, his judicial record could not be called distinguished by any standards. His supporters in the Senate, Senator Roman Hruska of Nebraska in particular, argued that there are a lot of mediocre judges, people, and lawyers who should be represented as well. But it was a lost cause. The Senate rejected his nomination 51 to 45.

The decisive factor in the rejection of Clement Haynsworth was judicial ethics. The decisive factor in Carswell's defeat was judicial competence. Underlying both struggles, however, was the question of policy orientation. Both judges were regarded as strict constructionists who would strengthen the conservative forces on the Supreme Court. They were regarded as men selected by President Nixon to restore balance on the Court and to counter the libertarian trends established during Chief Justice Earl Warren's tenure. This fact alone would have generated strong opposition in the Senate but had the questions of ethics and competence not been raised, either nominee probably would have been approved. Indeed, this is what happened when President Nixon submitted his third nominee to the Senate. Judge Harry A. Blackmun, a member of the United States Court of Appeals for the Eighth Circuit, was approved by the Senate without a dissenting vote. Blackmun, a resident of Rochester, Minnesota, was a conservative and a strict constructionist. But his views on public policy and the likelihood that he would strengthen the conservative tendencies of the Supreme Court did not become an issue because none of the charges that were made against Haynsworth and Carswell could be made against him. More important, the Senate was in no mood to reject a third nominee. A seat on the Court had been vacant for over a year, the reputation of the Court had suffered because of the prolonged wrangling over the President's nominees, and the Senate was anxious to get the matter settled.

Thus, policy concerns affect Senate consideration of judicial appointments, even though these concerns are usually muted. A nominee to the Supreme Court will not usually be rejected for reasons of policy unless other more personal objections such as racial bias, unethical behavior, or judicial incompetence, can be lodged against him.[1] But policy concerns are always present. This is true because the Supreme Court and, to a lesser extent, the lower federal courts, is not just a court of law; it is also a policy-making institution that plays a vital role in determining the kind of public policies produced by the government.

In the minds of most Americans, a court of law is a place where criminals are tried, convicted, and sentenced to prison. It is a place where guilt is determined and legal remedies applied. Courts are thus viewed as legal institu-

---

[1] Judge John J. Parker of the Fourth Circuit Court of Appeals, the only nominee to the Supreme Court rejected in the twentieth century before the defeat of Haynsworth and Carswell, was rejected for policy reasons though ostensibly because of alleged racial prejudice and anti-labor views. See Richard L. Watson, Jr., "The Defeat of Judge Parker: A Study in Pressure Groups and Politics," *Mississippi Valley Historical Review* (September 1963), pp. 213–234; and William C. Burris, "The Senate Rejects a Judge: A Study of the John J. Parker Case," *Political Studies Program—Research Report No. 3* (Chapel Hill: Department of Political Science, University of North Carolina, 1962).

tions that reconcile human conflict through the *application* of law rather than political institutions that actually participate in the making of public policy. The workings of state or federal district courts have shaped the people's understanding of the Supreme Court of the United States so the Supreme Court is generally viewed as a judicial institution—a court of law that stands above and apart from politics and policy making. Its function is to judge, not to legislate or make policy. But the Supreme Court is more than a law court. Since the beginning of the republic, the decisions of the Supreme Court have shaped the nature and direction of public policy. The major decisions of the Marshall Court from 1801 to 1835 were instrumental in determining the relationships between the nation and the states and between the institutions of the national government. In subsequent periods of American history, the Supreme Court has played a vital role in establishing national policy in such important areas as economic regulations, national-state relations, industrial development, and civil rights.

When a particular decision of the Supreme Court—*Brown* v. *Board of Education* for example—has such a dramatic impact on American life that its policy implications cannot be denied, the Court is bitterly criticized for violating its trust and attempting to become a third branch of Congress. Much of the scorn and criticism heaped on the Warren Court after 1954 stemmed from the belief held by many people that the Court was behaving like a legislative institution rather than a law court. It was making policy, which it supposedly had no right to do, rather than performing its assigned function of applying constitutional law. One of the great ironies of American political history is that public support of the Supreme Court is linked to a misunderstanding of its functions. The view that the Supreme Court is a legal or judicial institution that is not involved in politics and policy making is a myth. Yet it is a myth that contributes to the reverence, respect, and public trust that sustains the legitimacy of the institution.

Policy making by the federal courts represents an important feature of the American political system. Our purpose in this chapter is to introduce the policy-making functions of the federal courts, with special reference to the Supreme Court, so that the role of the judiciary in the political system may be viewed in its true perspective.

The Federal Judiciary: An Overview

There are two judicial systems in the United States. The national government has its own system of courts, generally called federal courts, and each of the fifty states operates its own court system. The state court systems are completely separate from each other and only interlock with the federal court system when cases involving federal laws or rights protected under the United States Constitution are appealed from state supreme courts to the Supreme

Court of the United States. State courts operate according to their own procedures and are not subject to the authority of the federal courts except in the sense that the United States Constitution is the supreme law of the land and takes precedence over all laws and constitutions of the states. The two court systems are not linked to each other within a hierarchical relationship. The federal courts cannot impose their own values or procedures on state courts. Even in situations where state courts are ordered by the Supreme Court to conduct new trials in cases involving federal law or constitutional principle, state courts can and frequently do evade the legal or constitutional principle that the Supreme Court has said should govern their decisions.[2]

One example of the refusal of a state court to adhere to a directive of the Supreme Court is the case of *Williams* v. *Georgia.*[3] A Negro, Aubrey Williams, had been convicted of murder and sentenced to death by a Georgia court. Before the sentence was carried out, the Supreme Court held in another case that equal protection of the law is denied when a person is convicted by a jury from which members of his race had been systematically excluded. This decision cast doubt on the constitutionality of Williams' conviction and the Supreme Court accepted the case for review. The Court ruled that Williams had been denied equal protection of the laws because Negroes had been excluded from the jury that convicted him. It remanded the case to the Georgia Supreme Court for reconsideration in the light of this finding. The Georgia Supreme Court, refusing to "supinely surrender sovereign powers of this State," rejected the reasoning of the Supreme Court and ruled that the conviction must stand. A second petition for review by the Supreme Court was denied and Williams, convicted unconstitutionally according to Justice Frankfurter, who had written the opinion, went to his death in the electric chair.[4] Thus, the existence of two separate judicial structures affected the quality of justice in the nation.

The Structure of the Federal Courts

The formal structure of a governmental institution affects the way the institution functions in the political system. The functions of the federal courts are

---

[2] See Charles Warren, "Federal and State Court Interference," *Harvard Law Review* (February 1930), pp. 345–378; Note "Evasion of Supreme Court Mandates in Cases to State Courts Since 1951," *Harvard Law Review* (May 1954), pp. 1251–1259; Note "Final Disposition of State Court Decisions Reversed and Remanded by the Supreme Court, October Term 1931 to October Term 1940," *Harvard Law Review* (June 1942), pp. 1357–1365.

[3] 349 U.S. 375 (1955).

[4] See Walter F. Murphy and C. Herman Pritchett (eds.), *Courts, Judges, and Politics* (New York: Random House, 1961), pp. 602–606.

affected by formal organization, internal operating procedures, and their relationships with each other and other governmental institutions. Some knowledge
of the structure of the federal courts is necessary if their functions, particularly
their policy-making functions, are to be understood. The federal judiciary,
composed of courts that operate at three different levels, is a highly decentralized
institution. *District courts* are the trial courts of the federal judiciary and are
located at the bottom of the system. Each of the fifty states has at least one
district court; there are eighty-seven in the entire country. A district court may
have one or more judges, depending on the size of the district and the quantity of
cases to be heard. These trial courts are the only federal courts that use juries
and it is here that most of the work of the federal judiciary is done. Their work,
which mainly involves the enforcement of federal law, closely resembles the
work of state courts. District judges, who are appointed by the president and
approved by the Senate, usually serve in the district and state in which they live.
Thus, district judges more than other federal judges reflect the cultural, legal,
and political values of local communities.[5]

The second tier of the federal judiciary consists of the *intermediate courts of
appeal,* sometimes called circuit courts of appeal. These appellate courts were
established in 1891 to reduce the burden of appeals going to the Supreme Court.
There are ten judicial circuits in the country with an eleventh court sitting in the
District of Columbia. Judicial circuits are composed of several states, the ninth
circuit being the largest with nine states. Thus, appellate judges are representative of wide geographical areas rather than local communities as district judges
tend to be. Only a very small percentage of the cases tried in the district courts
are appealed to these courts. Juries are not used and the cases are heard and
decided by at least three judges. The number of judges assigned to a particular
court varies from three in the smaller circuits to nine in those circuits where the
case load is heavy. Each circuit court has a Chief Judge who presides over its
proceedings and supervises and coordinates the work of his court and of all the
district courts in the circuit.

The work of the circuit courts is quite different from that of the district
courts. Appellate courts hold hearings in which three judges apply federal law or
constitutional provisions in cases before them rather than attempting to determine the guilt or innocence of the parties involved. It is at this level that federal
court decisions begin to have policy implications. Cases brought to the appellate
courts from the lower courts or from administrative agencies frequently involve
public policy issues. Appellate judges are also involved in any case that arises at
the district level where a party claims his rights under the Constitution have been
abridged. When this occurs, a three-judge district court is convened; one member
of the court must be an appellate judge. Appeals from three-judge district courts

---

[5] See Kenneth W. Vines, "Federal District Judges and Race Relations in the South," *The
Journal of Politics* (May 1964), pp. 337–357.

go directly to the Supreme Court rather than to the circuit courts. The appellate courts resemble the Supreme Court in that some of their decisions are policy decisions and their opinions are written and published in order to explain the grounds upon which these decisions rest. Appellate courts differ from the Supreme Court in that they do not have control of their dockets. They must accept every appeal that comes to them, whereas the Supreme Court has almost complete discretion as to what cases it will hear.

The Supreme Court of the United States represents the apex of the federal judiciary. As a court of last resort, it is the highest and most authoritative judicial tribunal in the nation. Its nine justices are the nation's highest judicial officials as well as important figures in the policy-making process of the government. Though the Supreme Court has original jurisdiction (in cases affecting ambassadors, other public ministers and consuls, and those cases in which a state is a party, the Supreme Court, rather than the district or appellate courts conduct the trial), it is primarily a court of appeals because most of its work consists of hearing cases that come to it from the circuit courts and from three-judge district courts. Of the hundreds of cases brought to it each year, the Supreme Court accepts only a very small number for review. It usually restricts its attention to those important cases that involve questions of public policy with broad implications for the nation, or to those cases where the meaning of federal law or the Constitution needs to be clarified because of conflicting decisions among the circuit courts. The Supreme Court disposes of approximately 1,000 cases each year. Only about 100 cases each year are decided in which written opinions are prepared to explain why the Court reached the decisions it did.[6] The others are discussed in conference and the Court's decisions are announced through *per curiam* opinions, short statements indicating that the Court's decision rests on previously established precedents.

The decentralized structure of the federal judiciary fragments the decision-making process within the judicial system. Though the Supreme Court stands at the apex of the system and is the ultimate authority on questions of law and constitutional interpretation, much of the work of the federal judiciary is accomplished in the district and appellate courts. And the nature of the decisions made by inferior court judges often determines whether a case goes on to the Supreme Court and also shapes the decisions that are made there. The briefs, arguments, and decisions of the lower courts are important inputs into the decision-making process of the Supreme Court. When the Supreme Court reviews a case from the lower courts, it may remand the case to these courts to be resolved according to the legal or constitutional interpretations it has established. The lower courts are then expected to implement the policies of the Supreme Court. The role of lower court judges in implementing Supreme Court policy is an important feature of

---

[6] Rocco J. Tresolini, *American Constitutional Law,* 2nd ed. (New York: Macmillan Co., 1965), p. 31.

judicial policy making because these judges interpret the meaning of Supreme Court directives and their manner of implementation, and this is just as important as the decision itself. As channels through which cases reach the Supreme Court and as instruments for the implementation of Supreme Court policy, the judges of the inferior federal courts are influential participants in the policy-making functions of the federal judiciary. Thus, the decentralization of power that is characteristic of the policy-making process of the whole government is also present in the federal judiciary.

Most cases heard by a federal court at either of the three levels involve a variety of people, interests, and values. A federal court case is an adversary proceeding, a struggle between the conflicting interests of a pluralistic society. Decision making in the judiciary, as is the case with other governmental institutions, is a process of resolving conflict. The procedures and language differ from those used in elective institutions but the process itself and the objectives sought are not greatly different. Cases in law are initiated by individuals and groups not just to gain a redress of grievances but to obtain changes in public policy. In this sense, a case filed in a federal court and a bill introduced into Congress may be seeking the same end, a change in national policy. Just as pressures are brought to bear on Congress or the president to achieve certain policies, so too are pressures exerted against the federal courts in order to influence the outcome of cases. The methods are different, but the objectives are the same. Important federal cases, in the area of civil rights for example, represent struggles between opposing interests in society. They are not merely disputes in which one party is seeking damages from another, or the government is trying to convict someone for violation of law. Such cases are often resolved through compromise rather than the proclamation of the right principles, although the language of the courts suggests that the contrary is the case. Thus, policy making in the federal judiciary is a pluralistic power struggle just as it is in other governmental institutions.

The judicial process is also slow. It often takes years before a case can move through the system from the district courts to the Supreme Court for final resolution. Once a decision is made and the case is remanded to the lower courts for implementation, a great deal of time passes before the Court's ruling is actually brought to bear on the parties involved in the case. If the Supreme Court's decision was not unanimous or if there is a strong feeling in the country that the case was wrongly decided, the matter usually remains unsettled. It is likely to be brought before the courts again in another case and the entire process will begin again. Important policy questions such as voting rights for Negroes, racial segregation in public schools, and the reapportionment of state legislative districts were before the federal courts for decades before they were finally resolved. Thus, policy making in the federal judiciary is not unlike the policy-making process of the whole government.

The Supreme Court as
a Governmental Institution

The Supreme Court is a court of law, a judicial institution. Its style and procedures are those of law courts and its language is the language of the law, not of politics. Cases are heard in the Supreme Court Building, a large, marble "palace" where the quiet, dignified atmosphere creates reverence and awe. The Court is in session usually from October until June. Cases are scheduled for oral argument during the first two weeks of a month and the Court then recesses for two weeks to review the cases in conference and write opinions. Conferences are held each Friday to discuss the cases and to handle routine administrative duties. Decisions are announced in open court, and opinions are published in the *United States Reports*. The Supreme Court Building, the quiet dignity and seriousness of the Court's proceedings, the black robes of the justices, and the formal announcements of the Court's decisions are all designed to accentuate the judiciousness of the Court's functions. The effect is to strengthen the view that the Supreme Court is the "temple of justice" where the law of the land, the rights of man, and the eternal principles of the Constitution are preserved and protected.

But the Supreme Court is also a governmental institution. It is a coequal branch of the national government and has from its earliest days participated in the policy-making processes by which the nation is governed. Even the most casual review of American political history will reveal that this is so. As a coordinate branch of the national government, its decisions have had tremendous influence on the development of the political system and on the kinds of public policies produced by both national and state governments. In the areas of governmental regulation of the economy, national-state relations, national security, and civil rights, Supreme Court decisions have proved to be crucial factors in the determination of public policy. The period between 1890 and 1937, for example, stands out as an era in which the Court was actively engaged in shaping the government's economic policies. And the period of the Warren Court from 1953 to 1969 was a time in which the Court was equally active in the area of civil rights. A brief review of several decisions handed down by the Supreme Court during these periods illustrates how the Court has participated in the governing of the nation.

After the Civil War, industrial development in the United States increased at a rapid pace, and the power and influence of business interests expanded accordingly. The ill effects of industrialization on the lives of the people soon generated a reaction, particularly on the part of the American farmer. This reaction took the form of demands for state regulation. In 1877, the Supreme Court—still controlled by a majority of justices who represented the political values and governmental principles of the Jacksonian era—held in *Munn* v. *Illinois*[7] that a state could regulate rates charged by railroads for the shipment of grain if this served the public interest. In essence, the Court held that political institutions could regulate private property without violating the due-process-of-law clause of the Constitution. By 1890, the composition of the Court had changed and the majority of the justices were men who shared the values of the new industrialism. The businessman's view of life and government prevailed in the country and the economic theory of laissez-faire, with its emphasis on private initiative and its disdain for governmental regulation, was becoming a dominant factor in the national mentality.

Beginning in 1890 with the Minnesota Commission case[8] and continuing through a series of similar cases,[9] the Court struck down as unconstitutional efforts of both Congress and state legislatures to control through regulation the ill effects of industrialization. While standards of reasonableness had been a matter for legislative determination, the Supreme Court now claimed this authority for itself. Between 1900 and 1934 the Supreme Court approved some regulations but denied others. The important point is that governmental policy toward the regulation of the economy became a matter for judicial determination. In 1935 and 1936, when the most important New Deal legislation came before the Supreme Court for review, the Court invalidated almost all of it as being beyond the constitutional authority of the national government.[10] Thus, public policy determined by the judicial branch of the government took precedence over policies passed by the elective institutions.

What had been fair, reasonable, and constitutional in one era according to the decision in *Munn* v. *Illinois* became a denial of due process of law or a violation of the tenth amendment in another era. In essence, what the Supreme Court did was to write the economic theory of laissez-faire into the Constitution. In a series of cases, "the Supreme Court revolutionized the historic interpretation of due process of law and thus established the fourteenth amendment as the specific constitutional authorization for the doctrine of vested rights."[11] Due process of law became the standard by which efforts of both Congress and state legislatures to respond to industrialization were to be judged; and judges, not elected officials, were to make the final decisions. Thus, between 1890 and 1937

---

[7] 94 U.S. 113 (1877).

[8] *Chicago, Milwaukee, and St. Paul Ry. Co.* v. *Minnesota* 134 U.S. 418 (1890).

[9] See *Smyth* v. *Ames* 169 U.S. 466 (1898); *Allgeyer* v. *Louisiana* 165 U.S. 578 (1897); *Lockner* v. *New York* 198 U.S. 45 (1905); *Pollock* v. *Farmers' Loan and Trust Co.* 158 U.S. 601 (1895); and *United States* v. *Knight (E.C.) Co.* 156 U.S. 1 (1895).

[10] See *Panama Refining Co.* v. *Ryan* 293 U.S. 388 (1935); *Retirement Board* v. *Alton Railroad Co.* 295 U.S. 330 (1935); *Schechter Poultry Corp.* v. *United States* 295 U.S. 495 (1935); *Louisville Bank* v. *Radford* 295 U.S. 555 (1935); *United States* v. *Butler* 297 U.S. 1 (1936); and *Carter* v. *Carter Coal Co.* 298 U.S. 238 (1936).

[11] Alfred H. Kelly and Winfred A. Harbison, *The American Constitution: Its Origins and Development* 3rd. ed. (New York: W. W. Norton & Co., 1963), p. 498.

the Supreme Court held the reins of the policy-making power in the country, and only those governmental policies that met the judicial test of reasonableness were allowed to go into effect. Governmental policies concerning freight rates, agricultural problems, industrial regulation, conditions of labor, and the activities of labor unions, were determined by the Supreme Court rather than by the elective institutions of government. In the words of Justice Robert Jackson, it was a period of "judicial supremacy" when the substance of public policy "depended . . . on the outcome of litigation." It was a period in which American government was "government by lawsuit."[12]

Two decisions handed down by the Warren Court in recent years further illustrates the role of the Supreme Court as a governmental institution. In the 1954 case of *Brown* v. *Board of Education,*[13] the Court ruled that racial segregation in public schools was unconstitutional because it denied Negro Americans equal protection of the laws. The legality of racial segregation in the South and border states prior to 1954 rested upon the doctrine established in 1898 in the case of *Plessy* v. *Ferguson*[14] that "separate but equal" facilities were constitutional. For over a half century, public policies—which, passed by state legislatures in the South, effectively isolated Negroes from meaningful participation in the social, cultural, economic, and political affairs of their communities—were based squarely on the racial policies of the Supreme Court. *Plessy* v. *Ferguson,* subsequent decisions in the intervening years, and finally *Brown* v. *Board of Education* in 1954 were crucial factors in determining how the American people were governed during the first half of the twentieth century.

In the 1962 case of *Baker* v. *Carr,*[15] the Supreme Court ruled that disputes over the way state legislatures were apportioned could be resolved in the federal courts. Prior to 1962, the Court had refused to deal with such conflicts on grounds that the questions involved were political and therefore not appropriate for resolution in a court of law.[16] As the United States changed from a rural, agricultural society to an urban, industrialized one, millions of people moved from farms to cities. Though most state constitutions provided for periodic reapportionment to reflect these population shifts, many state legislatures refused to change the number of legislative seats assigned to each legislative district. To do so meant that legislators from rural districts would lose their seats and state government would gradually come under the control of urban areas. As a result, in many areas of the country, state legislatures were controlled by members who represented farm land and cow pastures rather than people. The problem could not be solved as provided by state constitutions because those charged with the

---

[12] Robert H. Jackson, *The Struggle for Judicial Supremacy* (New York: Vintage Books, 1941), p. 287.
[13] 347 U.S. 483 (1954).
[14] 163 U.S. 537 (1896).
[15] 369 U.S. 186 (1962).
[16] See *Colegrove* v. *Green* 328 U.S. 549 (1946).

responsibility for reapportionment were the ones who would lose power by doing so. For years, the conflicts remained unresolved because the federal courts, the only governmental institutions that could deal with the question without any effect on its own membership, refused to "meddle in politics."

The decision in *Baker* v. *Carr* that these questions were justifiable, that is, resolvable by court action, directly affected the policy-making process in state legislatures because it allowed judicial institutions to change the composition of these elective bodies. The decisive case which soon followed was *Reynolds* v. *Sims*[17] in which the Court ruled that both houses of state legislatures must be based on population. In some states where legislatures refused to reapportion in line with these guidelines or drew up plans that clearly circumvented the standard of "one person, one vote," the lower federal courts themselves drew up reapportionment plans and ordered state authorities to carry them out. In breaking the grip of rural areas on state legislatures, the Supreme Court contributed to the ability of state governments to deal with the increasingly complex problems of an urban society. In this sense, the decisions of the Supreme Court will have a significant impact on the kinds of policies produced by state governments.

As a governmental institution involved in policy making, the Supreme Court is an integral part of the political system; it does not stand above and apart from politics. Its relationships to other institutions are determined by the fact that it is a law court; its methods, language, style, procedures, and limitations are not the same as those of other governmental institutions. The policies it produces also have certain characteristics that are peculiar to judicial institutions. Federal judges are not elected, the Supreme Court does not pass laws, make treaties, or design elaborate policy programs in response to national programs. Supreme Court Justices do not take tours of the country, hold press conferences, and appear on television in efforts to generate support for specific policies. But the role of the Supreme Court in shaping the public policies of the nation is as important as that of any other governmental institution.

The Policy-Making Functions of the Supreme Court

Federal courts deal with policy in two ways, they either apply policy to the cases before them or they say what policy is. When the meaning of a statute or a provision of the Constitution is clear, the judges do not make policy, they merely apply it to the case at hand. But when such meanings are not clear, the judges must determine what the policy is before they can apply it. In this sense they make public policy. Only a small percentage of federal court cases require the

[17] 84 S. Ct. 1362 (1964).

judges to make policy. Most cases concern what Professor Herbert Jacob calls "enforcement of community norms;"[18] that is, the courts enforce federal laws and settle disputes arising under these laws. The work of the district courts is almost entirely of this nature and so are most of the cases of the intermediate courts of appeal. But some cases heard in these inferior courts—and these are the cases that usually are appealed to the Supreme Court—involve issues of public policy that have broad implications for the nation and require the judges to determine what public policy shall be.

Since the Supreme Court can hear only a small number of cases each year, it usually restricts its attention to those cases whose implications extend beyond the parties to the case. In deciding cases in such areas as economic regulations, race relations, apportionment, criminal justice, freedom of speech and religion, and national security, the Court is interested not merely in enforcing existing law and assuring that justice is done for the parties in conflict; it is also interested in reexamining public policy in these areas to determine whether new policy norms should be established. For instance, when the Supreme Court held in *Baker* v. *Carr* that the question of reapportionment in state legislature was justiciable, it was not merely interested in the people living in urban areas of Tennessee. It was declaring that the national policy of leaving such matters to local political institutions was to be reconsidered. In subsequent cases, it declared that such policies were to be changed. In declaring that racial segregation in public schools was unconstitutional in *Brown* v. *Board of Education,* the Court was not merely concerned about the problems of the Negro children in Kansas, South Carolina, and other states. It was declaring a new policy in the area of race and public education which was to apply generally throughout the nation.

Policy making in the national government is a complex process involving the institutions within the executive branch, the Congress, and the judiciary. Each institution uses its own peculiar methods in shaping national policy: the president uses his control over the planning of the budget, his authority in foreign and military matters, his potential for leadership in the legislative process, and his position as a national leader to shape governmental policies; the bureaucracy shapes policy through its influence on planning and implementing governmental programs; and Congress participates by virtue of its control of the purse strings, its authority to investigate other governmental institutions, and its ultimate power to determine what bills are passed into law. How does the Supreme Court participate in policy making? Its basic tool is the power of judicial review.

Judicial Review: The Basic Tool of Policy Making

Judicial review is the power of any court of law to review policies made by other governmental institutions and to declare these policies null and void if they

---

[18] Herbert Jacob, *Justice in America* (Boston: Little, Brown and Co., 1965), p. 4.

are found to be in conflict with the Constitution. Without this power, the role of the Supreme Court as a governmental institution would be minimal, particularly in regard to its defense of the Constitution and the supremacy of the national government against policies produced by state governments. Judicial review is one of the vital cornerstones of the American political system. Its exercise by the federal courts, or the possibility that it would be exercised, has been an important factor in the development of American politics.

The Constitution does not explicitly grant the power of judicial review to the Supreme Court. For this reason, critics of judicial review have called it the "usurped power," arguing that it is an unwarranted and illegal one. This argument is academic now because judicial review has become an established practice and the operation of the political system is geared to it. It is likely that the men who wrote the Constitution intended this power to reside with the Supreme Court and did not mention it explicitly because they believed it to be inherent in the functions of the judiciary.[19]

The power of judicial review was first exercised in 1803 in the famous case of *Marbury* v. *Madison*.[20] William Marbury had been appointed as a justice of the peace for the District of Columbia by President John Adams. Before the commission was delivered, however, the Federalist administration had left office. The new president, Thomas Jefferson, ordered his Secretary of State, James Madison, to withhold the appointment. Marbury brought suit in the Supreme Court on grounds that a provision of the Judiciary Act of 1789 gave the Court jurisdiction in the case and authorized the Court to provide relief. He asked the Court to issue a writ forcing Madison to deliver his commission. A careful reading of the statute on which Marbury based his suit suggests strongly that the Court did not have jurisdiction in such cases. The Court could have avoided hearing the case, yet it chose to hear it. Chief Justice John Marshall, writing for the Court, ruled that the statute was unconstitutional because it enlarged the original jurisdiction of the Supreme Court beyond that prescribed in the Constitution. He pointed out that the Constitution, not Congress, determines the original jurisdiction of the Supreme Court.

Marshall went to great pains to explain why a law in conflict with the Constitution could not stand. But he did not speak to the real question at issue: what person or institution has the authority to determine when laws of Congress or acts of courts or other governmental institutions are in conflict with the Constitution? Marshall simply exercised this power; he made no effort to justify its use or explain why it belonged to the Supreme Court. He ruled that Marbury had a right to his commission but that the Court was powerless to assist him in obtaining it because the statute which supposedly gave the Court such power was unconstitutional. Marshall's decision was a bold effort to strengthen the judiciary in its relationship to Congress and the presidency. This was a master stroke. By

---

[19] See Charles A. Beard, *The Supreme Court and the Constitution* (Englewood Cliffs, N.J.: Prentice-Hall, 1962).

[20] 1 Cr. 137 (1803).

claiming for the Court the right to nullify laws of Congress on grounds of unconstitutionality, he "took a court of law and 'made it into an organ of government.' "[21] And he wisely avoided a direct confrontation with the President by refusing to take on the impossible task of forcing the administration to deliver the commission.

In refusing to order the executive to issue the commission to Marbury, the Court lost a minor skirmish, but in claiming for itself the power of judicial review, it won a great battle. President Jefferson strongly objected to the idea that the Supreme Court was to be the final arbiter of constitutional questions. The essence of his argument is revealed in a letter written years later in 1820:

> You seem . . . to consider the judges as the ultimate arbiters of all constitutional questions; a very dangerous doctrine indeed, and one which would place us under the despotism of an oligarchy. Our judges are as honest as other men, and not more so. They have, with others, the same passions for party, for power, and the privileges of their corps . . . and their power is the more dangerous as they are in office for life, and not responsible, as the other functionaries are, to the elective control. The Constitution has erected no such tribunal, knowing that to whatever hands confided, with the corruptions of time and party, its members would become despots. It has more wisely, made all the departments coequal and cosovereign within themselves.[22]

After *Marbury* v. *Madison,* the Supreme Court did not nullify another law of Congress for a half century.[23] It thus protected its claim of judicial review by being very restrained in its exercise during the period before the Civil War. After the Civil War, however, the Supreme Court began to involve itself actively in the nation's policy-making processes. A series of cases decided between 1865 and 1936 show the significance of its new functions. In this period, the Court struck down acts of Congress as unconstitutional in seventy-four cases. Also, it invalidated the public policies of state governments in even greater numbers. The most dramatic period of judicial activism came during the first administration of President Franklin D. Roosevelt "when the Hughes Court struck down New Deal statutes in twelve different cases within a four-year span, and three different presidential acts within a period of less than six months."[24]

Is judicial review essential to the operations of the American political system? Justice Holmes once observed that operations of the national govern-

---

[21] Tresolini, *op. cit.,* p. 67.

[22] Thomas Jefferson to William C. Jarvis, September 28, 1820, in A. A. Lipscomb (ed.), *The Writings of Thomas Jefferson* (Washington: Thomas Jefferson Memorial Association, 1903), pp. 276–279. Reprinted in Murphy and Pritchett, *op. cit.,* p. 557.

[23] *Dred Scott* v. *Sandford,* 19 How. 393 (1857).

[24] Glendon Schubert, *Constitutional Politics* (New York: Holt, Rinehart and Winston, 1960), p. 189.

ment might not be greatly different without judicial review, but that the federal system was dependent upon it. It is essential that some national governmental institution have the authority to nullify state action that violates the Constitution. Some national authority must be able to preserve the supremacy of the Constitution and the laws of the national government. The nature of the political system is such that the Supreme Court is the most suitable institution to perform this function. As a court of law, it is able to settle policy disputes in terms of constitutional principles. In doing so, it clearly makes policy. But its resolution of political conflict occurs at the constitutional level rather than at the level of ordinary law or policy. Its decisions carry greater moral authority, and its resolution of conflict in constitutional terms contributes to the stability of the system by supporting ordinary law with constitutional legitimacy.

The right of the federal courts to exercise judicial review is no longer seriously questioned. What remains controversial is in what areas this power is to be exercised and what the impact of its use will be on the policy goals of the various groups, parties, individuals, and institutions in the country. The wide discretion of the Court in its use of judicial review is recognized by those whose vital interests are affected by public policy. It is recognized that the Court determines for itself whether it wants to involve itself in certain policy areas. Whether the Court is active or restrained depends to a significant degree on the values, policy views, and predispositions of the justices themselves. Thus, the significance of judicial review as a basic tool of policy making is dependent upon *how* and *when* it is used by the justices.

Methods of Judicial Policy-Making

Working within the framework of lawsuits, the Supreme Court uses two methods of policy making, *constitutional interpretation* and *statutory construction*. As a general rule, the Court avoids constitutional issues and decides cases on other grounds unless the case can only be resolved by reference to the fundamental law. In many cases, it can accomplish the same end by merely construing the statute before it without going to the constitutional issue. The Court's policy-making functions hinge on its authority to interpret the Constitution and its practice of determining the meaning of vague or ambiguous statutes.

Constitutional Interpretation. Before appointment to the Supreme Court, Charles Evans Hughes once said, "We are under a Constitution, but the Constitution is what the judges say it is. . . ."[25] Though Thomas Jefferson and others

---

[25] Quoted in Jackson, *op. cit.,* p. 3.

have vigorously argued to the contrary, claiming that each branch of the government has the right to interpret the Constitution, it is a settled practice that the Supreme Court is the final arbiter of constitutional questions. The Constitution of the United States is not a charter. It is a body of political principles that, as Chief Justice Marshall said in *McCulloch* v. *Maryland* "was intended to endure for ages to come and consequently to be adapted to the various crises of human affairs."[26] Human conflicts in the form of legal disputes come before the Court for decision. Where these disputes involve claims under the Constitution, and the constitutional issue cannot be avoided, the Court must interpret the Constitution to resolve the conflict. For example, if a litigant claims that he has been denied equal protection of the laws under the fourteenth amendment through some governmental action, the justices must first determine the meaning of equal protection of the laws. The fourteenth amendment states that no state shall "deny to any person within its jurisdiction the equal protection of the laws." Quite clearly, the provision has no fixed substantive meaning except that which history and the previous interpretations of the justices themselves have assigned to it. In 1898 in *Plessy* v. *Ferguson,* the Supreme Court ruled that segregated public facilities for Negroes, so long as they were equal, did not amount to a denial of equal protection of the laws. Justice Harlan, the grandfather of the present Justice Harlan, wrote a vigorous dissenting opinion to this interpretation of equal protection of the laws. He said in part:

> But in view of the Constitution, in the eye of the law, there is in this country no superior, dominant, ruling class of citizens. There is no caste here. Our Constitution is color-blind, and neither knows nor tolerates classes among citizens. In respect of civil rights, all citizens are equal before the law.[27]

But equal protection of the laws means what a majority of the justices thinks it means, not what one lone dissenter would like it to mean. For over a half-century, the *Plessy* doctrine—a judge-made doctrine—prevailed in the United States and the social and political life of the South and border states developed on this interpretation of the Constitution. In 1954 in *Brown* v. *Board of Education,* the Court in a unanimous decision ruled that segregation in public education was a denial of equal protection of the laws. Though the *Plessy* case dealt with transportation and the *Brown* case with public schools, in terms of its general effect, the Court had completely reversed its interpretation of equal protection of the laws. The wording of the fourteenth amendment had not changed. But American culture, the demands of the Negro minority, and the composition of the Supreme Court had changed. And, quite clearly, the meaning of the fourteenth amendment had changed.

---

[26] 4 Wheat. 316 (1819).
[27] *Plessy* v. *Ferguson.*

How does the Supreme Court determine the meaning of the Constitution? Does it simply discover its meaning, or does it create a meaning for such phrases as due process of law, equal protection of the laws, unreasonable search and seizure, cruel and unusual punishment, commerce, and the right to bear arms? Two theories of jurisprudence have been used to explain how the justices reach decisions concerning the meaning of the Constitution. Prior to the twentieth century, the so-called "mechanical theory" was dominant in the United States. According to this theory, the meaning of the Constitution was fixed and unchanging. The function of the judges was to discover this meaning and simply apply it to the cases before them. Constitutional interpretation and conflict resolution was something of a "matching game," in which the Constitution was compared with the statute in question; if inconsistencies were present, they would be obvious and clear. The oft-quoted statement of Justice Owen Roberts in *United States* v. *Butler* represents this approach:

> The Constitution is the supreme law of the land ordained and established by the people. All legislation must conform to the principles it lays down. When an act of Congress is appropriately challenged in the Courts as not conforming to the constitutional mandate, the judiciary branch of the government has only one duty—to lay the Article of the Constitution which is invoked beside the statute which is challenged and to decide whether the latter squares with the former. All that the Court does, or can do, is to announce its considered judgment upon the question.[28]

According to this view, the values and policy preferences of the justices are not involved to any significant degree in the process of constitutional interpretation. The human element in this process is denied and judges are seen as brokers or objective intermediaries between constitutional principles and the legal issues raised before them. Once the constitutional principle is discovered, it is matched with the issue in the case and the decision follows mechanically. The judges are mere instruments of the law; they do not make law. A judge's legal training, political party affiliation, political experiences, background, and policy preferences are not important factors in constitutional interpretation. The "mechanical theory," even though it is a myth, remains part of the court's mystique.

Though this theory still has many supporters, it has given way in the twentieth century to what is called the theory of "free legal decision." This theory recognizes the element of human creativity in constitutional interpretation. It admits that values, biases, fears, hopes, and policy preferences enter into a judge's interpretation of the Constitution. They are not introduced into the process deliberately or capriciously. But they cannot be isolated because judicial decisions are human decisions and judges cannot cease being themselves when

---

[28] 297 U.S. 1 (1936).

they accept appointments to the bench. The values and policy preferences of judges are thus recognized as important factors in the development of the Constitution. The theory of "free legal decision" points up the policy-making functions of the justices of the Supreme Court. This theory explains split decisions, dissenting views, and overrulings. Justices Brown and Harlan were reading the same Constitution in *Plessy* v. *Ferguson,* yet their conclusions were entirely different.

The theory of "free legal decision" is the better explanation of how justices reach decisions about the meaning of the Constitution. Chief Justice Marshall's decisions in such cases as *Marbury* v. *Madison, McCulloch* v. *Maryland,* and *Gibbons* v. *Ogden* were "written on a clean slate." He had no precedents to follow; these decisions reflect his policy views on the relationship of the Court to other institutions and of the national government to the states. Just as Marshall was influenced in his decisions by his political values and experiences, so were his successors. Chief Justice Taney and Chief Justice Waite, for example, were products of the Jacksonian period of American history and their tendency to defer to the elective institutions of government, a characteristic of both Jeffersonian and Jacksonian democracy, was reflected in their decisions. Associate Justice Field and the men who joined him on the Court after 1880 had had different experiences. Their views of the Constitution reflected a different idea about government and the role of government in the lives of the people. Justice Miller, who served on the Court from 1862 until 1890 during the period when the meaning of due process of law was changed by the Court to protect industry from state regulation, once commented about the effect of background experiences on the decisions of his fellow justices:

> it is vain to contend with judges who have been at the bar the advocates for forty years of railroad companies and all the forms of associated capital when they are called upon to decide cases where such interests are in contest. All their training, all their feelings are from the start in favor of those who need no such influence.[29]

Constitutional interpretation is thus a method of judicial policy making. When a state attempts to forbid the employment of children in industry and the Court nullifies such legislation on grounds that it is unconstitutional, the Court's authority as the final arbiter of constitutional questions is exerted to alter the public policy of a state. When a state legally segregates its people in public facilities on the basis of race and the Court nullifies such action as a denial of

---

[29] Quoted in Wallace Mendelsohn, *Capitalism, Democracy, and the Supreme Court* (New York: Appleton-Century-Crofts, 1960), p. 63.

equal protection of the laws, the Court, rather than the state, has determined policy. When the Court tells the president of the United States that he cannot constitutionally seize the nation's steel mills, it has used its authority to interpret the Constitution as a method of policy making.

Statutory Construction. Statutory construction is a second method used by the Supreme Court in making judicial policies. Almost every case that comes before the Supreme Court rests on a statute. The meaning of these laws must be established before the Court can render a decision. Where the meaning of a statute is clear, the Court does not engage in statutory construction. It is not free to change clearly stated policies of Congress if it disagrees with or disapproves of them. But in those cases where meaning is uncertain, the Court must choose between alternate interpretations. The late Justice Frankfurter once said, "Anything that is written may present a problem of meaning, and that is the essence of the business of judges in construing legislation."[30] Frankfurter, a strong advocate of judicial restraint who frequently criticized his colleagues for interjecting their own policy views into their decisions, believed that "statutory construction implied the exercise of choice, but precluded the notion of capricious choice as much as choice based on private notions of policy."[31] But the line between *construing* a statute and assigning new meaning to a statute through *construction* is very thin. What distinguishes the legitimate exercise of choice on the part of a judge from capricious choice or choice based on policy preferences? Little agreement can be reached on this question.

> The difficult problem—and it is one that is crucial to an understanding of the continuing controversy that has embroiled the judiciary in general and the Supreme Court in particular—is where to draw the line between "judging" and "legislating," especially since there is no agreement on these definitions! In a sense, all judging is "legislating" and all legislating is "judging."[32]

The interpretation of statutes is a highly complex process. "Statutes are not archaeological documents to be studied in a library. They are written to guide the actions of men."[33] In modern times, Congress has passed laws that are couched in broad general language. They are often subject to different interpreta-

---

[30] Alan F. Westin, *The Supreme Court: Views from the Inside* (New York: W. W. Norton & Co., 1961), p. 75.

[31] *Ibid.*, p. 79.

[32] Henry J. Abraham, *The Judiciary* (Boston: Allyn and Bacon, 1965), p. 104.

[33] Westin, *op. cit.,* p. 83.

tions and, when challenged in the courts, their meaning must be established. As a rule, judges attempt to adhere to the policy embodied in the statute. But where alternative meanings present themselves with equal force or where the facts in the case before them are not clearly covered by the law, the Court itself must determine what the law means, or construct its meaning. In doing so, they are making policy. If the Court's construction differs radically from the intentions of Congress, then Congress may clarify its meaning by passing another law covering the same subject. This is rarely done, however, and judicial interpretation usually represents the final authority as to the meaning of legislation.

Two examples illustrate how the Court has used statutory construction to make policy. In *Marbury* v. *Madison,* the Court struck down as unconstitutional the Judiciary Act of 1789 because it supposedly enlarged the original jurisdiction of the Supreme Court. The original jurisdiction of the Supreme Court is established by the Constitution and is not subject to change by congressional action. Section 13 of this statute stated that the Supreme Court could issue writs of *mandamus* in "cases warranted by the principles and usages of law, to any courts appointed, or personnel holding office, under the authority of the United States." The consensus today is that this statute did not enlarge the Court's original jurisdiction. Marshall read this meaning into the statute in order to strike it down as unconstitutional and thereby establish the principle of judicial review. He thus used the method of statutory construction in order to achieve a policy objective.

A more recent example occurred in the Court's interpretation of the Alien Registration Act of 1940 (the Smith Act) in the case of *Yates* v. *United States*[34] decided in 1957. This statue made it a crime for any person "to knowingly or willingly advocate, abet, advise, or teach the duty, necessity, desirability, or propriety of overthrowing or destroying any government in the United States by force or violence, or by the assassination of any officer of any such government." In 1951 in *Dennis* v. *United States,*[35] with Chief Justice Vinson speaking for the majority, the Court upheld the constitutionality of the Smith Act and approved the decision of a lower federal court that had convicted eleven leaders of the Communist party charged with violating the statute.

Several years later, fourteen other leaders and organizers of the Communist party were convicted by a lower federal court for violation of the statute. In the *Yates* decision, the Supreme Court reversed these convictions, not by overruling the *Dennis* decision or reinterpreting the Constitution, but by assigning a meaning to the statute different from that assigned by Chief Justice Vinson in the *Dennis* case. Though both cases are highly complex and other issues were involved, in the *Yates* decision the Court essentially said that the statute did not prevent the *theoretical* advocacy of the doctrine of violent overthrow of the

---

[34] 354 U.S. 298 (1957).
[35] 341 U.S. 494 (1951).

government. Thus, the word *advocate* in the statute as passed by Congress became *theoretical advocacy* in the eyes of the Court. "The Court had in effect amended the Smith Act and rendered convictions under it by the government far more difficult."[36] Congressman Howard Smith, who had sponsored the statute in the House of Representatives, objected to this statutory construction on the part of the Court on grounds that the intent of Congress had been nullified. "Yet with the exception of a relatively minor amendment involving the meaning and extent of the verb 'to organize,' Congress failed to do anything to alter the Court's ruling."[37] Thus, through statutory construction, the Supreme Court changed the nation's policy toward the prosecution of those who teach or advocate unorthodox political doctrines.

Limitations on Judicial Policy Making

The Supreme Court has been described as "the least dangerous branch" of government because the extent to which it can participate in the determination of governmental policies is limited. Alexander Hamilton once wrote:

Whoever attentively considers the different departments of power must perceive, that, in a government in which they are separated from each other, the judiciary, from the nature of its functions, will always be the least dangerous to the political rights of the Constitution; because it will be least in a capacity to annoy or injure them.[38]

As a law court that is also an organ of government participating in the making of public policy, the Supreme Court is an institution peculiar to the American political system. Though its role in the government of the nation is significant, it functions quite differently from other governmental institutions. It does not make policy in the same sense that Congress and the executive branch make laws and issue decrees. Its relationship with other institutions and its policy-making functions have *constitutional, procedural,* and *political* limitations. Many of these limitations, however, are self-imposed. This is true because Constitutional limitations are not always explicit and the Court controls its own procedures to a great degree. And it can ignore political limitations if it is willing to take the risk of antagonizing Congress and other political forces in the system.

[36] Abraham, *op. cit.,* p. 109.

[37] *Ibid.*

[38] Alexander Hamilton, "The Judges as Guardians of the Constitution," *The Federalist,* No. 78. Quoted in Alexander M. Bickel, *The Least Dangerous Branch: The Supreme Court at the Bar of Politics* (New York: Bobbs-Merrill Co., 1962), p. ix.

Constitutional Limitations. The Supreme Court and all other federal courts are empowered to act only when cases or controversies are properly set before them. They cannot initiate suits and do not issue advisory opinions.

As one of three major institutions in a government of separate institutions that share power, the work of the Court is limited by its constitutional relationships with the other institutions of the national government. Congress may either reduce or increase the number of seats on the Supreme Court, bring impeachment proceedings against any of its members, change its appellate jurisdiction and thereby control the kinds of problems that are brought before it, reduce its appropriations, or, in the case of the Senate, refuse to approve those nominated by the president to serve on the Court. In the past, Congress has used several of these constitutional techniques as a means of curbing or controlling the Supreme Court. On many more occasions, it has threatened to use any or all of them because of its objections to the Court's decisions.

The relationship of the executive branch of the government to the Court embodies limitations that are equally impressive. Supreme Court justices and all federal judges are appointed by the president and approved by the Senate. The selection of a Supreme Court justice is a political process and policy considerations are of much importance in determining who is appointed. In this sense, the president controls the composition of the Court and can directly affect judicial policies by appointing men with definite policy preferences. President Nixon's selection of Judge Warren Burger of the Court of Appeals of the District of Columbia to succeed Chief Justice Warren was no accident. Judge Burger was known as a highly capable judge whose views on public policy, particularly in the area of criminal prosecutions, were somewhat more conservative than those of the majority of the Warren Court. He was selected in the belief that his leadership would alter the policies of the Court in certain sensitive areas in which the Court's influence is fundamental. Policy considerations have always been important factors in judicial selection in the United States. American presidents have long been aware of the policy-making functions of the Supreme Court, and no president would appoint a Supreme Court justice whom he does not believe is sympathetic with his political objectives.

The Supreme Court has no power to enforce its decisions. Though most of its decisions are obeyed voluntarily, it is completely dependent upon the executive branch to enforce its decisions when voluntary compliance breaks down. If a president refuses to enforce a decision, then judicial policies have little or no effect. The best known example of this was the case of *Worcester* v. *Georgia*[39] which concerned the applicability of Georgia state law to the Cherokee Indians living in that state. Chief Justice Marshall's decision that the laws of the state did

[39] 6 Peters 515 (1832).

not apply was not enforced by the president. President Andrew Jackson "is reputed to have reacted to the decision by saying, 'John Marshall has made his decision, now let him enforce it.' "[40] This kind of outright refusal on the part of a president to enforce judicial policies rarely occurs. The authority of judicial decisions can be reduced, however, by presidential criticism, delay or evasion. President Eisenhower's lack of enthusiasm for the Court's decision in *Brown* v. *Board of Education* was never a secret, and his lack of full and vocal support of this highly controversial ruling may have contributed to the prolonged evasion that has resulted. Eisenhower was ultimately forced to support the decision by sending federal troops to Little Rock, Arkansas, when a dramatic refusal to comply on the part of local officials, including the governor, left him no alternative. In 1969 the Nixon administration's "go slow" policy in school integration was rejected by the Supreme Court and immediate integration was ordered in some 30 Georgia school districts. President Nixon announced on nationwide television that he would enforce the law. But he equivocated in practice and the opponents of this decision intensified their efforts to evade the Court's directive.

The work of the Court is also limited by its relationship with the executive branch, because the government is a party in many of the cases that come to the Court for decision. The power of the Justice Department to initiate cases and its discretion in either appealing or not appealing cases from the lower courts is an important limiting factor in the work of the Court. "All criminal cases must be initiated by the prosecuting attorney, a quasi-executive official; many important civil actions also depend on executive initiative. Without executive initiation of such cases, the courts would often be restricted to quite routine matters, which have little bearing on the course of public policy."[41] By initiating a case iñ a particular area and planning it carefully in order to carry it to the Supreme Court, the executive can present a problem which, when resolved, will bring about policy change. By declining to appeal another case, the executive can avoid a possible policy change through judicial action. In this sense, the Supreme Court can be used as an instrument of executive policy making, "a weapon in the political arsenal of a president."[42]

While the constitutional principle of separation of powers places the Court in a limited relationship with institutions of the national government, the principle of federalism limits the work of the Court by preserving the judicial and political separateness of the states. Within their own jurisdictions, state courts are not subservient to national judicial policies and may render judgments and follow procedures that establish standards of justice different from those that prevail in the federal courts. Even though national standards of justice are being

---

[40] Jacob, *op. cit.*, p. 191.

[41] *Ibid.*, p. 192.

[42] *Ibid.*, p. 73. See pp. 190–195 for discussion of executive limitations on the Supreme Court.

extended to the states through the due process clause of the fourteenth amendment, much latitude remains with state courts, and evasion of national standards of justice continues. The number of cases tried in state courts is so large, procedural requirements for appeal to the Supreme Court so difficult and expensive, and the opportunities for evasion so wide, that the penetration of national judicial policies into state judicial systems is dependent to a significant degree on voluntary compliance. State court compliance with national judicial policies in such areas as race relations, criminal justice, and freedom of expression still leaves much to be desired.

The constitutional position of the states in the federal union and their power in American politics also represent a limitation on the policy-making functions of the Supreme Court. Despite the power, size, and constitutional supremacy of the national government, the states are still influential partners in the policy-making process. Political parties are highly decentralized institutions and their organizational strength rests in the states and local communities. Members of the Senate are elected from states, and congressmen are dependent upon and loyal to their home constituencies. The electoral system is based on the states, and state political leaders have much influence in the nomination and election of the president. Opposition in state governments to judicial policies represents a significant limitation on the policy-making functions of the Supreme Court.

For example, the Court's decision in *Baker* v. *Carr* threatened state control of reapportionment and its decision in *Reynolds* v. *Sims* established a judicial policy of "one person, one vote" for state legislatures. These decisions were vehemently opposed by the officials of many state governments. In an effort to rescind this decision, many states have exercised their constitutional prerogative of petitioning Congress to call a constitutional convention for the purpose of nullifying the Court's decision by constitutional amendment. This effort was only one state short of the necessary two-thirds of the states required to direct Congress to call such a convention before its momentum was lost and several states rescinded their petitions. This effort on the part of the states may have been unwise, but it was entirely within their rights under the Constitution and illustrates the limiting effect of federalism on the decisions of the Supreme Court.

Procedural Limitations. Several limiting procedures on the policy-making of the Supreme Court are of special significance and must be identified. First, no federal court will render a decision unless a case is properly before it. That is, the case must meet certain specifications. It must be a genuine case or controversy in which the parties involved have valid claims that are enforceable under federal law or the Constitution. The parties in the case must have *standing to sue;* they must be able to show injury resulting from the statute or governmental action in question. The federal or constitutional issue involved must also be substantial. The Court will not hear cases that involve only trivial issues.

The Supreme Court accepts for consideration only a small percentage of the cases that are filed with it with request for review. The procedures it uses in selecting these few cases and the judicial principles it follows in reaching decisions further narrow the scope of its work. Though there are four different ways in which cases reach the Supreme Court, most cases come to the Court under *writs of certiorari*. Requests for *certiorari* come to the Chief Justice who eliminates many of them without any discussion with the other justices unless discussion is specifically requested by one of his colleagues. The others are discussed in conference and at least four justices must agree to grant the writ, otherwise it is rejected. The Chief Justice is thus in a key position to exert great influence on the docket. A strong Chief Justice such as Charles Evans Hughes who is highly respected by his colleagues is able to specify which cases will be heard.

Of approximately 1,000 cases accepted each year for review, only about 100 are scheduled for oral argument. The others are discussed in conference and the Court's decisions announced through *per curiam* opinions, or short statements indicating that the Court's decision rests on existing precedents. In such cases and also in many cases heard in court and followed by written opinions, the Court is adhering to the principle of *stare decisis*.

Stare decisis, or "let the decision stand," is a procedural rule that limits the Court's policy making in a significant way. Deciding cases on the basis of established precedents contributes to stability and continuity in the law and allows for a certain degree of predictability in the judicial processes. Slavish adherence to precedent, however, contributes to stagnation and does not allow for the growth and development of law in response to changing conditions. Adherence to precedents is a tendency in the Supreme Court, but it has never been a hard-and-fast rule. The Supreme Court has frequently refused to be bound by *stare decisis* and has, on numerous occasions, overruled its earlier decisions. Between 1810 and 1956, the Court overruled earlier decisions on ninety separate occasions; forty-nine of these overrulings occurred between 1930 and 1957. Of these forty-nine, twenty-one occurred in the five-year period between 1941 and 1946 during the tenure of Chief Justice Stone.[43]

One of the clearest examples of the Court changing its mind within a short time concerns the constitutionality of coerced flag salutes in public schools. In 1940 in *Minersville School District* v. *Gobitis*[44] the Court held that a state could require public school children to salute the flag even though their parents

---

[43] See Albert P. Blaustine and Andrew H. Field, "Overruling Opinion in the Supreme Court," *Michigan Law Review* (December 1958), pp. 151–194. Reprinted in Robert Sciglaino, *The Courts: A Reader in the Judicial Process* (Boston: Little, Brown and Co., 1962), pp. 393–408.

[44] 310 U.S. 586 (1940).

objected for religious reasons. The Gobitis children, members of the Jehovah's Witnesses sect, were expelled from public school. Three years later in the case of *West Virginia Board of Education* v. *Barnette,*[45] the Court completely reversed itself and ruled that public school pupils could not be expelled for refusing to salute the flag on religious grounds. To do so would be to violate their rights of freedom of religion under the first amendment made applicable to the states through the fourteenth amendment. Why did the Court overrule its earlier decision? The Gobitis ruling was very unpopular, frequently evaded, and widely believed to be an incorrect interpretation of the first amendment. But the immediate reason was that two new justices had been appointed to the Court and three of the remaining justices had simply changed their minds.[46]

Several additional procedures are followed by the Supreme Court that limit its policy-making functions. The Court will not accept cases for review until all remedies available in state courts, lower federal courts, or administrative agencies have been exhausted. The Supreme Court is a court of last resort. More important from the standpoint of policy making, the Supreme Court will not normally decide a case on constitutional grounds if any other grounds can be found on which to resolve the dispute. In short, the Court tries to avoid a constitutional issue. It will resolve a case through statutory interpretation or procedural technicalities if it can accomplish its desired end by doing so. When the constitutional issue cannot be avoided, the Court operates on the assumption that the challenged statute of governmental act is constitutional. Its tendency is to defer to the political institutions of government. It will avoid striking down a congressional statute or an act of the president if it can possibly do so. But there are exceptions; an activist Court may grasp the constitutional issue rather than trying to avoid it. Between 1890 and 1937, the Court superimposed its own policy views over those of the elective institutions and attempted to maintain a position of judicial supremacy in the government. During this period, an activist Court composed of a majority of justices imbued with the economic theory of laissez-faire showed little deference to Congress or state legislatures. The period from 1953 until 1969 was also a period of judicial activism in which the Warren Court vigorously defended the civil rights of individuals against governmental action.

The route of a legal case to the Supreme Court, even if it involves an important policy issue, is long, expensive, difficult, and uncertain. The procedures of the lower courts and in the Supreme Court drastically reduce the number of cases that ultimately reach the Supreme Court for decision. And the judicial principles that govern decision making in the Supreme Court further reduce the range in which judicial policies may be made and applied. Thus the

---

[45] 319 U.S. 624 (1943).

[46] For a detailed discussion of the flag salute cases, see David R. Manwaring, *Render unto Caesar: The Flag-Salute Controversy* (Chicago: The University of Chicago Press, 1962).

procedures and principles that are inherent in the work of judicial institutions limit judicial policy making and distinguish it from the policy-making processes that operate in other governmental institutions.

Political Limitations. Justice Holmes once observed, "We are quiet here . . . but it is the quiet of a storm centre, as we all know."[47] Holmes' remark refers to the political context in which the Court functions. The Court is an integral part of the political system and it is not immune to the political restraints that limit the behavior of all governmental institutions. These restraints are not brought to bear on the Court in the same way that they touch other institutions, but they are very real nevertheless. Chief Justice Earl Warren on retiring from the Court in June 1969 stated that the Supreme Court "has no constituency of its own." The implication in his remarks was that the Supreme Court is not tied to a specific constituency and is therefore free to serve the national interest without catering to special groups. In one sense this is true. The Court is not an elective institution, it does not have to account directly to the people at the polls. But the Court has a national constituency similar to that of the president and it is *indirectly* restrained by the patterns of political life in the nation. The political climate in the country, the relative strength of political forces, and the political demands and supports that come to bear on political parties, interest groups, and the elective institutions of government all have a bearing on the decisions made by the Supreme Court.

Political limitations on the Court become apparent when other governmental institutions, particularly Congress and the president, respond to public criticism of the Court's decisions. The Court itself usually ignores criticism and does not respond publicly to attacks made upon it. But it is neither ignorant of nor immune to criticism. It cannot defend itself, yet many justices recognize that criticism is inevitable and sometimes healthy. Justice Stone, for instance, once said, "Where the Courts deal, as ours do, with great public questions, the only protection against unwise decisions, and even judicial usurpation, is careful scrutiny of their action and fearless comment on it."[48] Ostensibly, the power of the Court is legal, but its authority is moral. It cannot long sustain a position that is widely unpopular or bitterly resented in the country unless it is supported by the elective institutions. Where powerful opposition is channeled through the elective institutions, particularly Congress, the independence of the Court is jeopardized by restraints that are essentially political in nature.

---

[47] Quoted in Walter F. Murphy, *Congress and the Court* (Chicago: The University of Chicago Press, 1962), p. 2.

[48] Quoted in Arthur A. North, *The Supreme Court: Judicial Process and Judicial Politics* (New York: Appleton-Century-Crofts, 1966), p. 154.

The Court cannot and does not ignore the potential threat to its independence posed by political criticism. Though frequently couched in terms of principle, public criticism of the Court historically has come from those segments of the national community who do not like its decisions because of their effect on vested interests. The Court is praised by those who approve of its policies and damned by those who do not. Between 1934 and 1937 when the Hughes Court was striking major portions of Franklin Roosevelt's New Deal, it was praised and defended as a "bastion of liberty" by those who opposed governmental regulation of the economy. To others, who favored such governmental programs and believed the power and financial resources of the national government should be used to overcome the effects of the Depression, the Court was bitterly criticized. It was viewed as nine old men who stood in the path of reform and flaunted the will of the political majorities in the country. When the Court reversed itself in 1937 and began upholding the constitutionality of reform legislation, the supporters and the critics switched sides.

From 1941 until 1946, during the tenure of Chief Justice Stone, the Court handed down numerous decisions protecting the liberty of individual citizens against governmental action. These decisions were well-received by liberal and progressive elements in the country and the Court received their full support. But under Chief Justice Vinson during the period between 1946 and 1953, the Court backed away from its earlier sensitivity to individual rights and upheld several governmental actions that were restrictive of individual liberty. The supporters of the Stone Court became the opponents of the Vinson Court because a different set of interests in the country were being served. The *Dennis* decision, discussed earlier, came during this period and it was regarded by those who favored the directions taken by the Stone Court as a great setback to the cause of civil liberty.

Though the Supreme Court has always been criticized because of its policy decisions, the severe and prolonged criticism of the Warren Court after 1954 represents the most sustained attack on the judiciary in American history. Its decisions in race relations, criminal justice, freedom of expression, reapportionment, freedom of religion, and national security, have had a pronounced effect on public policy in sensitive and controversial areas of American life. These decisions threatened many vested interests in the country. And the Court, Chief Justice Warren in particular, was subjected to the worst forms of abuse and criticism. But public criticism in itself did not constitute a political limitation on the Court except in the sense that it alerted the Court to the degree of opposition facing its policies. The decisions of the Warren Court represented its response to demands from certain segments in the population that had little influence in elective politics. Southern Negroes, prison inmates, atheists and agnostics, political dissenters, and semi-literate youths in the hands of the police do not have much influence in Congress. But the Supreme Court is a different kind of institution. If it chooses to do so, it can respond to demands from these people.

The Warren Court did and antagonized strong political forces in the country and these forces struck back through Congress and the state legislatures. And this opposition, channeled through institutions that have the constitutional authority to curb the Court, created a situation that cramped the Court's work. These limitations were political in nature.

Soon after the Court's decision in the *Brown* case in 1954, a storm of protest erupted in the country. In the Eighty-Fourth Congress alone, more than seventy anti-Court bills were introduced, sponsored primarily by segregationist forces in Congress. Between 1954 and 1957, the Court handed down decisions in a series of cases in the areas of national security, race relations, and criminal justice that offended its critics even more.[49]

The demands of Senator Strom Thurmond on the floor of the Senate are representative of the epithets hurled at the Court during this period: "Mr. President, the Supreme Court—which has recently handed down decisions to give greater protection to communists and criminals—has now issued an edict which will give greater protection to such heinous criminals as rapists and murderers . . . ! The choice we face in this country today is judicial limitations or judicial tyranny. Congress must take action to limit the power of the Court."[50]

The case of *Jencks* v. *United States,* decided in 1957, became the focal point of congressional efforts to curb the Court. In the *Jencks* decision, the Court had ruled that a defendant in a national security case (a labor leader convicted of perjury for falsely taking the non-Communist oath prescribed by the Taft-Hartley law) must be allowed to inspect the information in FBI files that had been used to convict him. If the government chose not to surrender the files, then the case would have to be dismissed.[51] The *Jencks* decision was followed closely by several similar cases in the national security area that protected the individual against government action. The opposition to the Court became intense in Congress and efforts to pass legislation reversing its decisions or restricting its appellate jurisdiction increased. The House of Representatives actually passed five anti-Court bills during this period, but only one of these was ultimately approved by the Senate. This bill, however, proved to be no significant restriction on the Court. It was supported by liberals who were defending the Court and represented only a clarification of the circumstances and procedures under which information in the FBI files would be made available to defendants. The real test came in the Senate when a House-passed bill that represented a serious

---

[49] See *Brown* v. *Board of Education* 349 U.S. 294 (1955); *Communist Party* v. *Subversive Activities Control Board* 351 U.S. 115 (1956); *Pennsylvania* v. *Nelson* 350 U.S. 497 (1956); *Jencks* v. *United States* 353 U.S. 657 (1957); *Watkins* v. *United States* 354 U.S. 178 (1957); *Yates* v. *United States* 355 U.S. 66 (1957); *Sweezy* v. *New Hampshire* 354 U.S. 234 (1957); *Gayle* v. *Browder* 352 U.S. 903 (1956); and *Mallory* v. *United States* 354 U.S. 499 (1957).

[50] Quoted in Murphy, *op. cit.,* p. 115.

[51] *Ibid.,* pp. 99–100.

effort to restrict the appellate jurisdiction of the Court was defeated by the narrow margin of 41 to 40.

This prolonged and bitter congressional attack on the Court was a symbol "of congressional repudiation of the moral authority of the Warren Court to lead the nation. And, lacking either means of physical coercion or control of money, the Court's power teeters on its moral authority far more precariously than that of either Congress or the president."[52] The congressional attacks partially achieved their objectives. After the fight in Congress, "there were visible changes in the Courts' outlook. . . . During the 1956 term, the year of *Jencks, Yates,* and *Watkins,* the Court rejected civil liberties claims in only 26 percent of all cases decided by full opinion; during the next term, the Court rejected civil liberties claims in 41 percent of such cases. The figure rose to 48.8 percent during the 1958 term."[53] The Court thus seemed to be backing away from positions it had taken prior to the showdown in Congress.

It cannot, of course, be said with certainty that the Supreme Court backed away from earlier positions because of the congressional attacks. But the odds are heavy that this was the reason. "The course of the Warren Court's conflict with Congress followed a well-worn pattern."[54] From the time of the Marshall Court down to the present day, the Supreme Court has responded to severe criticism from the country and from Congress by negotiating a "tactical withdrawal" from advanced positions taken on matters of public policy. "First came decisions on important aspects of public policy," followed by severe criticism from other governmental institutions, and the "third step has usually been a judicial retreat."[55]

In summary, the policy-making functions of the Supreme Court are performed within limitations that are constitutional, procedural, and political in nature. As an organ of government created by the Constitution, the Supreme Court is limited by its relationships with other governmental institutions at the national and state levels; as a court of law, it must use procedures appropriate for judicial institutions and the established traditions of the law; as an institution that constitutes an integral part of a political system, the Supreme Court is restrained by the dynamism of political life.

Characteristics of Judicial Policies

As a court of last resort in a constitutional system where public policy must adhere to fundamental law, the Supreme Court is called upon to resolve policy

[52] *Ibid.,* p. 183.
[53] *Ibid.,* p. 246.
[54] *Ibid.,* p. 247.
[55] *Ibid.,* p. 247.

conflicts between other governmental institutions and between private citizens and their government. Policy conflicts that cannot be resolved in other institutions become legal or constitutional conflicts and are then brought to the judiciary for settlement. Here they are resolved in *constitutional terms,* but the resolution of these conflicts has clear policy consequences. In effect, one policy alternative is chosen over another. In this fashion, the Supreme Court ultimately determines what national policy is going to be in many vital areas of American life. This is judicial policy-making. But judicial policies differ significantly from policies produced by other governmental institutions.

Herbert Jacob has identified three characteristics of judicial policies that distinguish them from policies made in Congress and the executive institution.[56] First, policies made by the Supreme Court are more restricted in their application, and usually they apply only to domestic affairs. Only rarely do policy conflicts in the area of foreign relations come before the Court in cases at law. When this does occur, the Court has traditionally deferred to the president on grounds that the conduct of foreign policy is primarily a function of the executive and not subject to same kind of restrictions that apply in the domestic area. Foreign affairs is an area in which "the president alone has the power to speak or listen as a representative of the nation."[57] And in domestic affairs, the Court has traditionally been very restrained in certain areas. "The appropriation of funds and the levying of taxes are almost never successfully challenged in court. . . . Such issues remain the almost exclusive domain of legislative and executive decision making." These, of course, are two vital areas of public policy which involve questions vital to the health and security of the nation. Though the Supreme Court is a governmental institution that responds to the nation's problems, it is clear that it does not normally respond to certain kinds of problems.

Second, policies made in the federal courts are primarily "concerned with the regulatory activities of government," and are "usually directed at other government agencies rather than at private individuals." Judicial policies result from cases in which governmental regulations made by national, state, and local institutions are challenged as being unconstitutional. When the Supreme Court told the state of West Virginia that it could not expel public school children who refused to salute the flag for religious reasons, it was declaring a national policy. When it told a state court in Florida that it could not send people to prison without benefit of counsel, it was declaring a national policy.[58] When the Court told President Truman during the Korean War that he had no constitutional authority to seize the nation's steel mills, it was establishing a policy to be

---

[56] Jacob, *op. cit.* See pp. 50–52. Our discussion and all quotations are drawn from this source unless otherwise cited.

[57] *United States* v. *Curtiss-Wright Export Corp.* 299 U.S. 304 (1936).

[58] *Gideon* v. *Wainwright* 372 U.S. 335 (1963).

followed by all presidents.[59] These decisions and most other Supreme Court decisions which have policy implications are aimed at the government, not at private persons.

Third, judicial policies are usually ambiguous. Judicial policy-making is "government by lawsuit" and lawsuits deal with "the facts of the instant case." Technically, a judicial decision binds only the parties to the case even though the widespread implications of the decision are immediately recognized. The extent of a judicial policy cannot usually be determined until subsequent cases are heard both in the lower courts and in the Supreme Court and until the original ruling is amplified and applied. "The judges who write the opinion may intend their decision to apply to many similar situations, but that intention is usually not clear until other cases have been litigated and the new doctrine has been extended to them. In the meantime, there can be much uncertainty about the policy's extent because its phraseology has been necessarily ambiguous." The case of *Baker* v. *Carr* is a case in point. Ruling that the question of reapportionment in state legislatures was justiciable was only the beginning of a new policy. The Court provided no guidelines for lower courts to follow in deciding the avalanche of cases that immediately descended on them. It was not until some of these cases reached the Supreme Court that the meaning of the new policy became clear. The same is true in the area of racial segregation in the public schools. *Brown* v. *Board of Education* was only the beginning. There is still some ambiguity concerning the Court's policies in these areas and the Court's clarification of its policies can occur only as other cases come before it for resolution.

Judicial policies are thus different in that they are normally restricted to domestic affairs, aimed primarily at governmental agencies, and are ambiguous as to their meaning and application. They are made by men appointed to their positions for life and not directly responsible to the people. They are derived from lawsuits, and the extent of their application is based more on implication and voluntary compliance than upon direct enforcement. They are couched in the language of the Constitution and are announced as statements of Constitutional principle rather than as clear-cut statements of public policy.

Judicial Values and Judicial Policies

The Constitution means what it does today because of the values of the justices who have interpreted it over the years. Supreme Court Justices do not make decisions in a vacuum, free and independent of the forces that shape the decisions of men who control the other governmental institutions. The president and members of Congress are influenced by their social and political back-

---

[59] *Youngstown Sheet & Tube Co.* v. *Sawyer* 343 U.S. 579 (1952).

grounds, legal training, professional experiences, and their personal, political, and philosophical values. So, too, are Supreme Court Justices. These values represent the molds in which their constitutional interpretations are fashioned. Judicial traditions, constitutional precedents, and the "cult of the robe," important and influential as they are, do not transform men into value-free judges.[60]

As a rule, the justices of the Supreme Court reflect the political values of their times. Though there are some historic exceptions, the decisions of the Court have tended to sustain the policy preferences of the nation's political majorities. In this sense, the Court has functioned as a legitimating institution, supporting and sustaining as constitutional the policy decisions made by other national governmental institutions.[61] The Court's decisions between 1890 and 1937, especially its interpretation of the meaning of due process of law, accurately reflected the nation's commitment to business interests and the rights of private property. Justice Miller's already quoted lament about the effect of previous experience on a judge's view of the Constitution points up the significant impact of values on judicial policies. Today we look back at the Court's ruling in *Plessy* v. *Ferguson* and wonder how the nation's highest judicial tribunal could render such a verdict. But this decision was in tune with the climate of the times. Actually, the only surprise in this case was Justice Harlan's dissenting opinion, a dim beacon light indicating the future direction of the Court's decisions in the area of race relations. Harlan was an "eccentric exception"[62] in a period when the Court was dominated by justices whose policy views and personal values differed radically from his own.

Supreme Court Justices do not consciously and deliberately read their own values and policy preferences into the Constitution. It just happens; it is an inevitable part of the process of judging. Such staunch advocates of "judicial restraint" as Holmes and Frankfurter, both of whom repeatedly cautioned their fellow justices about reading their own views into the Constitution, recognized the inevitable creative aspect of their work. And Justice Stone's remark that self-restraint was the only real restraint on the Court was to remind his colleagues that the Court, through its power of judicial review, should not simply superimpose its own policy views over those of other governmental institutions.

Perhaps the close relationship between personal and political values of the men who sit on the Court and the judicial policies produced by the institution is best illustrated by the importance assigned to a president's judicial nominations.

---

[60] Some of the better studies of judicial values and judicial decision making are collected in Glendon Schubert (ed.), *Judicial Behavior: A Reader in Theory and Research* (Chicago: Rand McNally & Co., 1964). See also Thomas P. Jahnige and Sheldon Goldman, *The Federal Judicial System: Readings in Process and Behavior* (New York: Holt, Rinehart and Winston, 1968).

[61] See Robert A. Dahl, "Decision-Making in a Democracy: The Supreme Court as a National Policy-Maker," *The Journal of Public Law* (1957), pp. 279–295.

[62] Justice Frankfurter referred to Harlan as an "eccentric exception" in a concurring opinion in *Adamson* v. *California* 332 U.S. 46 (1947).

The intense interest shown in these nominations by interest groups, party leaders, executive agencies, political forces in Congress, and the country at large is linked to the growing awareness of the Supreme Court as a policy-making institution. The Constitution places no restrictions on the president in selecting Supreme Court justices, except that his nominees must be confirmed by the Senate. Policy considerations have become the most important factors governing this process. Presidents are aware of the policy-making role of the Court, and quite naturally, they select candidates who are believed to share their political convictions. As Robert Dahl has observed, "presidents are not famous for appointing Justices hostile to their own views on public policy; nor could they expect to secure confirmation of a man whose stance on key questions was flagrantly at odds with that of the dominant majority in the Senate."[63]

Since judges are appointed for life and usually remain in office far longer than the president who appoints them, it is clear that selection of Supreme Court Justices is one of the most important functions performed by the president. Dahl has calculated that "over the whole history of the Court, one new Justice has been appointed on the average of every twenty-three months. Thus, a president can expect to appoint two new Justices during one term of office; and if this were not enough to tip the balance on a normally divided Court, he would be almost certain to succeed in two terms."[64] President Hoover appointed three Justices; Franklin D. Roosevelt, in office longer than any other president, appointed nine; Truman made four appointments; Eisenhower, five; Kennedy, two; and Johnson, two.[65] President Johnson attempted to appoint two others but was forced to withdraw these nominations because of opposition in the Senate.

No president can control a justice's decision once he is seated on the Supreme Court; the case of President Eisenhower and Chief Justice Warren is an excellent example. Had Eisenhower dreamed that Warren would have led the Supreme Court in the direction he did, it is unlikely that he would have appointed him. But a careful examination of a candidate's public career and political leanings provides clues that guide a cautious president in making his decision. President Nixon, an astute and experienced politician, fully understands the role of the Supreme Court in the policy-making process. During the first year of his administration, he was able to name two men to the Supreme Court. His selection of Warren Burger as Chief Justice, his unsuccessful efforts with Clement Haynsworth and G. Harrold Carswell, and his selection of Harry Blackmun were deliberate efforts to change the policy directions of the Supreme Court's decisions. All four nominees were appellate court judges, all were known to be more conservative than the majority of the justices on the Warren Court, and all were regarded as "strict constructionists" who were likely to be cautious

---

[63] Robert A. Dahl, *Pluralist Democracy in the United States: Conflict and Consent* (Chicago: Rand McNally & Co., 1967), p. 156.

[64] *Ibid.*

[65] *Ibid.*

about changing the Constitution through free interpretation. In short, they were men who President Nixon believed would share his general policy beliefs and would interpret the Constitution accordingly.

The obvious fact that policy orientation is the key factor in judicial selection does not, however, reflect adversely on the judicial ability of the candidate selected. Nor does the fact that party lines are normally followed suggest that men of mediocre qualifications are given precedence over more able candidates. It is only natural that a president would select members of his own political party for these important positions. Judicial appointments are the prize plums in the patronage system; political debts can be repaid, interest groups satisfied, minority groups encouraged, geographical interests appeased, and political fences mended through judicial appointments. This can be and is done without violating the high standards of the federal judiciary. The quality of American judges has been remarkably high and the partisan and policy standards that govern the selection process have not diluted the quality of justice in America to any significant degree. The process of judicial selection in the United States is highly political because the institutions to be staffed are vital to the making of public policy. By being an integral part of American politics, the process of judicial selection assures that the federal courts are subject to democratic controls.

The Supreme Court and the Development of the Political System

The policy-making process in the American political system does not end after Congress and the executive establishment have taken action. Individuals and groups that suffer defeats in these areas frequently turn to the federal courts and attempt through constitutional arguments to turn their defeats into victories. De Tocqueville's remark that policy disputes in the United States ultimately become legal or constitutional disputes which must be resolved by the Supreme Court was a very perceptive observation. American governmental institutions are separate from each other but they must, by constitutional prescription, share power in the policy-making process. This sharing of power has three clear consequences; it makes the policy uncertain because a decision made in one or even two institutions rarely settles anything; it makes the process fragmented because policy disputes must be debated in several different areas; and, third, this sharing of power means that judicial institutions play a significant role in determining public policy.[66]

---

[66] For a discussion of the consequences of judicial policy making, see Jacob, *op. cit.*, pp. 32–33.

The Supreme Court of the United States has played a major role in the development of the American political system. As Chief Justice William Howard Taft once observed, the Court has been "a stormy petrel in the politics of the country." Through constitutional interpretation and statutory construction, the Court has participated in most of the major policy disputes during the course of the nation's history. Its decisions have had a significant impact on the development of a strong central government, an industrialized economy, a welfare state, and a democratic way of life.

The Development of a National Government

From 1789 to 1865, America was undergoing a period of political unification; one nation was evolving from a confederation of separate and semi-independent states. Adoption of a Constitution that created a national government was the greatest single step toward a centralized system. But constitutions do not make nations. Much more was involved in the development of a strong centralized government than the formal acceptance of this fundamental and binding law.

Under the leadership of Chief Justice John Marshall from 1803 to 1835, the Supreme Court contributed to the growing power of the central government in a significant way. "Excepting *Marbury* v. *Madison,* all of the classic decisions of Marshall's Court were thrust against states-rights localism."[67] Where *Marbury* v. *Madison* established the right of the Supreme Court to overrule policy decisions made by other institutions of the national government, Marshall's other decisions were designed to establish the supremacy of the national government over the states. In *McCulloch* v. *Maryland,* the Court designed the doctrine of *implied powers* which broadened the powers of the national government over the states and also ruled that a state could not use its taxing power against the national government. In *Brown* v. *Maryland*[68] the Court protected a national tariff against the police powers of the states; in *Fletcher* v. *Peck*[69] and *Dartmouth College* v. *Woodward*[70] the Marshall Court struck down efforts of state legislatures to control contracts and vested interest within their own borders. Finally, in *Gibbons* v. *Ogden,*[71] the Court struck a strong blow for nationalism by upholding national prerogatives in the regulation of interstate commerce.

[67] Mendelsohn, *op. cit.,* p. 21. For a discussion of the nationalistic decisions of the Supreme Court, see pp. 19–29.

[68] 12 Wheat. 419 (1827).

[69] 6 Cr. 87 (1810).

[70] 4 Wheat. 518 (1819).

[71] 9 Wheat. 1 (1824).

The general effect of these decisions was to uphold the supremacy of the national government over the authority of state governments. As Marshall said in *McCulloch* v. *Maryland,* "this great principle is that the Constitution and the laws made in pursuance thereof are supreme; that they control the Constitutions and laws of the respective states and cannot be controlled by them." Thus, the Supreme Court was one of the most effective instruments of nationalization during the early days of the new nation.

The Development of
an Industrialized Economy

Between 1840 and 1860, the growth of manufacturing and the expansion of railroads developed to the point that the industrialization of the American economy was well underway. Between 1860 and 1910, the United States became an industrial nation; by the 1920s, the nation was beginning to enter a period of mass consumption.[72] During this period of industrial development, American politics shaped and in turn was shaped by the process of economic modernization.

Industrialization in the United States was accomplished primarily by private initiative; the great corporations, small businesses, transportation systems, and sprawling cities were built by private citizens with few restraints from government. After 1860, the doctrine of the businessman prevailed in the United States and both national and state governments were largely controlled or heavily influenced by businessmen. The economic doctrine of laissez-faire and the belief that private initiative was the most suitable instrument of national growth held sway in the country. Government-aided industrialization followed a "hands-off" policy, thus allowing the business community to expand. "Private initiative created the savings, invested them in capital goods, modernized production and distribution, and created the wealth that eventually"[73] formed the foundations of an industrialized economy.

By remaining essentially neutral and adhering to a doctrine of freedom of contract and property rights, the government allowed middle-class business interests to exploit the natural and human resources of the nation in order to build an industrialized state. During this period, few governmental restrictions were placed on wages and hours, working conditions, child labor, or monopolies. The result was that these conditions were determined by the industrialists themselves. Sporadic efforts in Congress and state legislatures to regulate the ill effects of industrialization were ineffective because of the prevailing sentiment in

---

[72] See W. W. Rostow, *The Stages of Economic Growth: A Noncommunist Manifesto* (Cambridge: The Cambridge University Press, 1960), pp. 38–76.

[73] A. F. K. Organski, *The Stages of Political Development* (New York: Alfred A. Knopf, 1965), p. 58.

the country and in the government that contracts and property were sacrosanct. The role played by the Supreme Court in protecting the right of the business community to do as it pleased was crucial.

The Supreme Court, as we have suggested earlier, tends to legitimate the decisions of the political majorities. Though the Court may perpetuate values of an earlier era due to the long tenure of the justices, it eventually reflects the political values of the nation. From 1865 until 1890, the Supreme Court—still controlled by justices who shared the political values of the Jacksonian period of American politics—held out against the political doctrines of the business community that were gaining ascendency in the country. By 1890, however, the doctrine of *Munn* v. *Illinois* (1877) that allowed state regulation of private property in the interest of the public had been undermined, and the Court came under the control of justices who shared the values of the new post-war industrialism.[74]

In case after case between 1890 and 1937, the Supreme Court protected the interests of the business community by striking down legislation designed to control the ill effects of industrialization. The most effective instrument used by the Court to accomplish this end was the due-process-of-law clauses of the fifth and fourteenth amendments. Though in some instances regulatory legislation was upheld as constitutional, the general pattern of decisions held that governmental regulation was denial of due process of law. But the point is that these were judicial rather than legislative decisions; the Supreme Court rather than Congress or state legislatures determined what the nation's policies toward regulation of the economy were going to be. The Supreme Court's role in protecting industry during this crucial period of development was of vital importance. And the Court protected these industrial interests at the cost of fair wages, living and working conditions, public health, and political participation. The middle classes, particularly the business community, were allowed to govern the country and to govern it in their own interest. The masses were not included and the Supreme Court did little to help them or to ease their plight. Furthermore, it did a great deal to *exclude* them. As one political scientist has observed:[75]

> The importance of this exclusion cannot be overstressed. It was as crucial an aspect of bourgeois politics as the placing of the bourgeoisie in control of the national government, for the function of the middle classes to create capital for industrialization could not have been carried out under existing conditions if the working classes had been given governmental protection against economic expansion at its expense.

---

[74] A brief but excellent account of the Court's decisions during this period is Mendelsohn, *op. cit.* For a more detailed account see Kelly and Harbison, *op. cit.*

[75] Organski, *op. cit.*, p. 65.

The Development of a
Welfare State

"The term 'welfare state' . . . is generally used to denote a situation in which the government provides all its citizens with certain guaranteed minimum aspects of the good life such as formal education, medical care, economic security in old age, housing, and protection against loss of jobs or business."[76] The United States today is a welfare state; its governments, both national and, to a lesser degree, state, are formally committed to providing the basic essentials of life to all citizens. Government in a welfare state is big, it provides many services, and, by necessity, penetrates deeply into the economic and social lives of its people. American governments have been increasing in size and services since the early days of the republic. But the greatest expansion dates from the early 1930s, the era of Franklin D. Roosevelt, and the New Deal. And though some earlier decisions of the Supreme Court sustained welfare legislation, the Court's role as a positive force in "welfare politics" also dates from the days of the New Deal.

President Roosevelt came into office in 1932 pledged to provide a New Deal for the American people. This New Deal was primarily a series of trial-and-error legislative programs that called for the use of vast governmental resources to cope with the Depression and to initiate certain reforms in the economic system. Roosevelt's programs were extremely controversial and it was inevitable that they would be challenged in the courts as unconstitutional. By 1934, welfare legislation passed by several states was on the Supreme Court's docket; by 1935, national legislation was before the Court for review. The Supreme Court was thus called upon to resolve the most historic policy dispute in American politics. The fundamental issue was the constitutionality of the government's efforts to use its vast powers and resources to combat the ills of the nation and protect its citizens against the deprivations of an industrialized society.

The Supreme Court was faced with a choice between the old and the new, between laissez-faire and welfare politics. It was not clear how the Court would react to the New Deal legislation. Several justices were known to favor broad powers for the national government but a majority of the justices viewed welfare legislation with suspicion. The Court was, as Robert H. Jackson (who was subsequently appointed to the Court) has expressed it, "poised between two worlds."[77] The outcome was uncertain because no settled constitutional principles or judicial precedents existed to govern the Court's decisions on legislation of this nature. During the previous 35 years, the Court had resolved cases involving governmental regulations by applying its own standards of reasonable-

---

[76] Austin Ranney, *The Governing of Men* (New York: Holt, Rinehart and Winston, 1958), p. 48.

[77] Jackson, *op. cit.,* p. 85.

ness rather than "any specific constitutional provision or absolute principle of law." Public policy that seemed plausible, sensible, and reasonable to the justices themselves was upheld. Those that did not meet the judicial test of reasonableness were struck down as "unreasonable, arbitrary, and a violation of due process of law."[78]

What is reasonable to an elected politician may not be reasonable to a judge. What is reasonable to one judge may be arbitrary and capricious to his colleague in the next chair. Since the constitutionality of national or state legislation hinged on what the judges deemed to be reasonable, a strong element of inconsistency existed in the constitutional law that related to welfare legislation. During the 1890s, the Court consistently struck down welfare legislation. But after 1900, especially during the administrations of Theodore Roosevelt and Woodrow Wilson when the mood of the country was more progressive, the Court on occasion upheld legislation that clearly would have been nullified a decade earlier. After the election of Warren G. Harding to the presidency in 1920 and continuing through the next decade, the Court reverted to its conservative positions of the 1890s. Laissez-faire again became the guiding doctrine of the justices and the Court consistently struck down efforts of Congress and state legislatures to regulate the economy.

Thus in 1935, when the New Deal legislation appeared on its docket, the Court had accumulated a dual line of judicial precedents governing economic regulation, the conservative decisions of the 1890s and 1920s together with a smaller number of more liberal or progressive decisions during the intervening years. Which line of precedents would it follow? In fact, the Court could and would do as it pleased. It had been deciding cases dealing with welfare legislation on the basis of its own economic and political philosophy for nearly one-half century and it was very likely to review the New Deal the same way. In short, the New Deal would be nullified or sustained on the basis of the policy preferences of the justices rather than any settled principles of constitutional law. And the odds were high that the Court would view this legislation with grave suspicion because only two or three justices were known to be in sympathy with the concepts of government upon which the New Deal legislation were based.

And that is exactly what happened. In 1935 and 1936, the Court struck down as unconstitutional the efforts of the President and Congress to use the power of the national government to bring economic relief to the people and to reform the economic system. It reaffirmed its commitment to laissez-faire economics and in doing so, set itself squarely against the mood of the country and the policy goals of the President and Congress. In a series of cases, the Court struck down both national and state legislation designed to restore the health of the petroleum industry, to provide pensions for railroad workers, to provide relief for farmers who faced the loss of their land through heavy

---

[78] Kelly and Harbison, *op. cit.*, p. 523.

mortgages, to restore the health of industry, to improve working conditions of laboring people, to improve the conditions of agriculture, to regulate the coal industry, to reduce the ill effects of bankruptcy, and to regulate the wages and working conditions of women.[79] The Supreme Court did not merely strike down specific pieces of legislation; it strongly implied, and in some instances clearly stated, that the government had no authority under the Constitution to do any of the things it was trying to do. In Robert Jackson's words,

> in striking at New Deal laws, the Court allowed its language to run riot. It attempted to engraft its own nineteenth-century laissez-faire philosophy upon a Constitution intended by it founders to endure for ages. In overthrowing the [Agricultural Adjustment Act], the Court cast doubt upon all federal aid to agriculture; in laying low the [National Recovery Act], the Court struck at all national efforts to maintain fair labor standards; and in outlawing the New York Minimum Wage Law which had been carefully drawn to overcome the objections raised by the Court in the first minimum-wage case, the Court deliberately attempted to outlaw any form of state legislation to protect minimum-wage standards. The Court not merely challenged the policies of the New Deal but erected judicial barriers to the reasonable exercise of legislative powers, both state and national, to meet the urgent needs of a twentieth-century community.[80]

But the Supreme Court cannot independently sustain public policy that is clearly in conflict with the policy preferences of the elective institutions and the mood of the country at large. The Court's nullification of the New Deal in 1935 and 1936 rested upon an economic and governmental philosophy that had been dissipated by the ravages of the Depression. Its actions represented a clear case of the majority of justices attempting to restrain government from solving the nation's problems because the methods selected were in conflict with their own interpretation of the proper functions of government. Though the Hughes Court wrecked the New Deal, this defeat of the government proved to be only temporary. In 1937, the Supreme Court—with the same nine justices still sitting—reversed itself in a series of decisions and upheld the constitutionality of important welfare legislation passed by the Congress.[81] Most of its nullifying

---

[79] See *Panama Refining Co.* v. *Ryan* 293 U.S. 388 (1935); *Retirement Board* v. *Alton Ry. Co.* 295 U.S. 330 (1935); *Louisville Bank* v. *Radford* 295 U.S. 555 (1935); *Schechter* v. *United States* 295 U.S. 495 (1935); *United States* v. *Butler* 297 U.S. 1 (1936); *Carter* v. *Carter Coal Company* 298 U.S. 238 (1936); *Ashton* v. *Cameron County District* 298 U.S. 513 (1936); and *Morehead* v. *Tipaldo* 298 U.S. 587 (1936).

[80] Jackson, *op. cit.,* p. 175.

[81] The reversal of the Court's position is well illustrated by *West Coast Hotel Co.* v. *Parrish* 300 U.S. 379 (1937); *Sonzinsky* v. *United States* 300 U.S. 506 (1937); *Virginia Ry.* v. *Federation* 300 U.S. 515 (1937); *Wright* v. *Vinton Bank* 300 U.S. 440 (1937); *National*

decisions during the previous two years had been split decisions; the change of one or two votes were enough to make the difference.

Thus, the Court shifted its position and adjusted itself to the policies of the political majorities in the country. By sustaining the constitutionality of legislation that regulated industry and private property in the interest of public safety and welfare, the Court legitimated the welfare state. By rewriting the constitutional law of the nation, the Supreme Court established the firm and now unchallenged principle that American government, both state and national, could regulate the economy and private property in the interest of public welfare. The Court's work in 1937 proved to be one of the great watersheds of American constitutional law because its decisions sustaining the legislation of the Roosevelt administration provided the constitutional foundations for the development of the welfare state.

The Development of a
Democratic Way of Life

By 1941, the constitutional authority of the national government to regulate industry and private property in the public interest had been firmly established; the New Deal had been sustained, laissez-faire was dead, and the tenth amendment (used by the Court in earlier periods to prevent national regulation of industry) was effectively nullified as a constitutional restriction on the regulatory policies of the national government.[82] Thus, one-half century of judicial policy making in the area of economic regulation came to an end. For all practical purposes, the Court withdrew from the field and left these matters to the elective institutions of government.

But the Supreme Court did not abandon its policy-making functions; it merely shifted its attention to a more vital area of concern, the personal and political liberties of the people. This period, since 1941, has been called the period of the "New Constitutional Law" because the Court has rewritten the Constitution to protect the rights and liberties of the people against encroachment by government. During the late 1920s and early 1930s, the Court had shown some concern regarding civil liberties; this was certainly true of Justices Holmes, Brandeis, Cardozo, and Stone. But with the appointment of Justices Black in 1937 and Douglas in 1939, and then Murphy and Rutledge a few years later, "the liberal position on civil liberties became dominant on the Court."[83] By 1941, Roosevelt had appointed seven new justices to the Supreme Court. The

---

Labor Relations Board v. *Jones and Laughlin Steel Corporation* 301 U.S. (1937); *Carmichael* v. *Southern Coal Co.* 301 U.S. 495 (1937); *Steward Machine Co.* v. *Davis* 301 U.S. 548 (1937); and *Helvering* v. *Davis* 301 U.S. 619 (1937).

[82] See *United States* v. *Darby* 312 U.S. 100 (1941).

[83] Kelly and Harbison, *op. cit.,* p. 797.

concern of the Roosevelt Court with the relationships between individuals and governmental authority set the tone and direction of the Court's decisions for the next thirty years. As Kelly and Harbison have written:[84]

> It is apparent upon analysis that the decisions of the Roosevelt Court in the field of civil liberties worked a revolution in the relation of the Court to the states and of government in general to the individual hardly less important than the revolution in federalism consummated at about the same time. To put it differently, if the Court lost one "sovereign prerogative of choice" in the field of congressional versus state legislative power, it gained another such area of discretion and power in its capacity to weigh and determine the respective constitutional and social values of federal and state regulation of private rights as against its concern for the preservation of the integrity of individual liberty itself. This latter-day range of sovereign choice gave the Court an immense new power; in the post-war era, it was to endow the Justices with a significance in the American constitutional order which for a time after 1938 they appeared to have lost.

The decisions of the Stone Court (1941–1946), the Vinson Court (1946–1953) to a somewhat lesser extent, and the Warren Court (1953–1969) revolutionized the constitutional relationships between governmental authority and the rights of private citizens. The protections of the Bill of Rights of the United States Constitution were made applicable to the states through the fourteenth amendment, resulting in much greater freedom from state action in the areas of religion, speech, and all forms of expression. The rights of due process of law were made more specific resulting in much greater protection in state courts for citizens accused of criminal acts. The rights of Negro Americans in voting, public education, employment, and the use of all community facilities were established through a reinterpretation of the equal-protection-of-the-laws clause of the fourteenth amendment. And the rights of political minority groups that sponsor unpopular, unorthodox, or even subversive political views and programs were protected against overzealous governmental action.

Many of these decisions were highly controversial because they protected groups and individuals who were regarded with suspicion by the general public. Small religious sects, criminals, Negroes, communists, and pornographers lived on the periphery of middle-class society and had little voice in elective politics. And government institutions geared to elections paid little heed to their rights and privileges under the Constitution. But their appeals were heard by the Supreme Court, and its decisions in their behalf have generated fundamental changes in the nature of American society. By purging the Constitution of racism, by taking a stand against governmental sponsorship of one religion over

[84] *Ibid.*, pp. 815–816.

another, by expanding the borders of free expression, by protecting the rights of citizens accused of crime, and by assuring that the government obeys its own laws in the prosecution of suspected subversives, the Supreme Court played and continues to play a major role in the development of a democratic way of life in the United States.

The Court
and Policy Change

The Supreme Court of the United States is a governmental institution that is actively engaged in making public policy. As a court of law, its methods, language, style, and relationships with the people differ significantly from those of the elective institutions. The Court is a *reactive* institution; it cannot initiate action but must wait until cases and controversies are brought before it according to accepted procedures of law. Judicial policies are the byproduct of legal decisions in adversary proceedings, and thus their form is quite different from that of policies made by other government institutions. They are ambiguous, aimed primarily at other government institutions, and restricted mainly to domestic affairs. But they are in no sense less significant than the policies produced by decisions made in the executive establishment or in Congress.

Though the Court is a nonelective institution whose members enjoy life tenure, it is not immune to the political life of the nation. On the contrary, it is an integral part of the political system and its decisions over time reflect the political culture of the nation. The Court has functioned mainly as a legitimating institution, eventually sustaining as constitutional the methods and policy goals of the political majorities. In this sense, the Court usually follows rather than leads the nation. But under some circumstances, the Court moves ahead of the nation and generates policy changes that the elective institutions are unable or unwilling to make. This was clearly the case with the Warren Court in the area of race relations and criminal justice. At mid-century, the elective institutions of American government were not doing very much to combat the evils of racial segregation. The climate in the nation was not favorable to changes in this area; political forces—in the nation and in the government, particularly in Congress—were opposed to change and were strong enough to prevent much effective action. In this area and in other sensitive areas, the Supreme Court did take the lead and generated major changes in public policy.

Part Three

12

Political Unification

The Army officers, colonels mostly, took over the country on April 21, 1967, saying as they did that they were the instruments of a National Resurrection and a National Purification. . . . In fact, there was corruption and mismanagement, which there still is, and in the twenty-three years before the [present] officeholders came to power, forty-one governments had risen and fallen. . . .[1]

The country is Greece, but by changing the details, it could be Libya, Brazil, or Tanzania in 1969, Ghana in 1966, the Congo in 1963, or Cuba in 1958. The coup might be peaceful or bloody, might or might not produce a counter-revolution; in rare instances, political order might follow. The revolution might be in the name of communism or anti-communism, against colonialism, imperialism, or the West; in the interest of family, church, party, bread, peace, or honor. Whatever the rationale, military coups, palace revolutions, assassinations, mass uprisings against political authority, and other signs of serious political instability are quite familiar today.

---

[1] John Corry, "Greece: The Death of Liberty," *Harper's* (October 1969), p. 72.

This has been a century of political revolution and governmental instability. Attempts to build nations and to govern them have frequently been frustrated; for many reasons, the survival of governments has been severely tested. To one observer, it seems that "the most important distinction among countries concerns not their form of government, but their degree of government."[2] Looking at the world since 1945, successful coups have occurred in at least 17 of 20 Latin American countries, in six nations of Central Africa, of the Middle East, in West Africa and Central America. According to a Defense Department estimate, the number of incidents of political violence against government has steadily mounted since 1958. In that year, there were 34 recorded incidents of political insurrection ranging from "irregular or guerilla insurgency" to "overt, militarily conventional wars"; by 1962, the number of insurrections had risen to 42, by 1965 to 57.[3] If acts of political violence narrowly averted or revolutions still in the making were added to this list, the evidence of world-wide political instability would be even greater. Even so-called "stable" governments such as that of the United States have endured major political violence and disorder. One need recall only the urban ghetto violence of the latter 1960s or the frequent club-swinging, tear gas–clouded clashes between police and various protestors against the draft, the Vietnamese War, and other policies during the last decade to recognize the universality of political violence.

The political violence so common throughout the modern world has many causes, but much of it flows directly or indirectly from the tensions involved in creating and maintaining national governments, a process which we call "political unification" and which concerns us in this chapter. In this century, political unification—the establishment of effective national governments—has been an acute problem. The societies that seem especially vulnerable to governmental collapse, impotence, recurring cycles of revolution and counter-revolution, and other symptoms of real or potential political disintegration may seem to have little in common with the United States or, perhaps, to have little relevance to it. However, all governments in greater or lesser degree face the same disruptive forces that can, if improperly handled, undercut effective national government. We are concerned in this chapter and the next with the problems of political unification in the United States and elsewhere and with the forces that may erode it. In this chapter we shall discuss briefly what political unification means generally, again using a "model" that suggests some of the common elements found in politically unified societies such as the United States.

---

[2] Samuel P. Huntington, *Political Order in Changing Societies* (New Haven: Yale University Press, 1968), p. 1.

[3] *Ibid.*, pp. 3–4.

The Meaning of
Political Unification

The world is a community of haves and have-nots. The United States and a handful of other societies are the haves, the Joneses of the international community whose patterns set standards other nations seek to imitate. Often, for example, the United States is considered the best example of a modernized society, the leader among a group including most nations of Europe and Anglo-America that together with the Soviet Union and Japan are heavily industrialized, technologically advanced, extraordinarily prosperous by world standards and economically productive.[4] The United States, in a different perspective, is sometimes called a post-industrial society where the problems and dislocations associated with industrializing are over, and a mass-consumption, affluent, welfare state has emerged over the industrial foundation.[5] These and other economic, social, and cultural comparisons emphasize that Americans share with a comparatively few other nations a quality of life that remains for most of the world a compelling, if often thwarted, ambition.

International comparisons also suggest that the United States is one of the world's *politically unified* nations. In one way, this seems again to divide the world into haves and have-nots. However, the problem of political unification in the world is more complicated. For many nations, especially in Afro-Asia, the problem is *to achieve* political unification. For other nations, *to remain* politically unified is the problem. The world's societies have had varied success in coping with the problems of political unification; the United States has been one of the most successful. To see why this is so, let us briefly examine the meaning of political unification.

The Governmental Dimension

Almost any American child knows that the United States is a nation—"one nation . . . indivisible," the Pledge of Allegiance asserts. Here, probably un-

---

[4] A cogent, readable interpretation of modernization may be found in C. E. Black, *The Dynamics of Modernization* (New York: Harper Torchbooks, 1967). Often, the terms "modernization" and "development" are used interchangeably yet the meanings are not fixed and considerable semantic confusion results. On various interpretations of "development" and its relationship to "modernization" see Lucien W. Pye, *Aspects of Political Development* (Boston: Little, Brown and Co., 1966), Chapter 2.

[5] On the social and political meaning of a "post-industrial society" see A. F. K. Organski, *Stages of Political Development* (New York: Alfred A. Knopf, 1965). For a recent, journalistic examination of America's development into a "post-industrial" society see J. J. Servan-Schreiber, *The American Challenge* (New York: Atheneum House, 1968).

wittingly, a great many Americans are discussing political unification in the United States. In the loose, uncritical way political terms are often used, any modern society is indiscriminately called a nation but, to extend the discussion in Chapter 1, this is another example of a political vocabulary that stretches to confusion. Societies become nations when, among other things, they become politically unified. Clearly, many so-called "nations" are in fact nations divisible—into competing governments, each claiming to represent the polity; into rival armies, each dedicated to its own political faction; into breakaway provinces; into fragmented language groups; into ethnic, religious, or cultural groups that have little sense of community or common political loyalties. The difference between a politically unified society and one that is not can be observed in the organization and operation of governments.

The national governments of politically unified societies have several common characteristics.[6] First, in a politically unified society—a nation—*there is a single, sovereign national government;* such a government is considered legitimate throughout the polity. We noted earlier that a government is legitimate when its various institutions are "valued for themselves and considered right and proper" by most of the people governed.[7] Such a government is more than "legal" in the sense that it follows procedures outlined by a constitution or other formal codes; it inspires affirmation, trust, and support from most of its citizens and subjects. Such support, moreover, attaches the "rules of the game." to the basic institutional framework of the government, even though people may disagree vigorously over particular policies or leaders. Legitimacy is "the most powerful ally of government" because it produces "voluntary submission" to governmental officials and decisions most of the time.[8] A government begins to lose legitimacy when individuals cease to identify with its basic rituals, procedures, and offices; if there is enough dissent, widely and intensely held, the government's primary structure may be threatened. And when governments do topple in the face of revolution, the fall usually begins long before the first overt act of rebellion; the fall begins when a significant proportion of governmental subjects fail to believe in the system's worth. "The images of kings topple before their thrones do."[9]

---

[6] The definition of political unification suggested here is synthesized from several sources (where it is sometimes called "political integration"). See especially Claude Ake, *A Theory of Political Integration* (Homewood, Ill.: Dorsey Press, 1967); Pye, *op. cit.,* Chapters 1 and 2; Edward Shils, *Political Development in the New States* (The Hague: Mouton and Co., 1966), Chapters 1 and 2, and especially pp. 9–11, 32–36; and David E. Apter, *The Politics of Modernization* (Chicago: University of Chicago Press, 1965), Chapter 7.

[7] Seymour M. Lipset, *The First New Nation* (New York: Basic Books, 1963), p. 46.

[8] Dennis Brogan, *Politics in America* (Garden City: Doubleday Anchor Books, 1960), p. 12; Mary Shepardson, "The Traditional Authority Pattern of the Navajo," in Ronald Cohen and John Middleton, *Comparative Political Systems* (Garden City: Natural History Press, 1967), pp. 143–144.

[9] Peter Berger, *Invitation to Sociology* (New York: Doubleday Anchor Books, 1963), p. 130.

In many Afro-Asian nations, the legitimacy of the national governments has never been established. Following World War II, a great many Afro-Asians used tactics such as peaceful civil disobedience (India) or guerrilla war (Algeria) to expel the European colonial governments. However, the temporary political unity forged from opposition to a common foreign regime dissipated when the problem of constituting a new government for the independent states arose. The new states, in fact, were often a conglomerate of heterogeneous religious, cultural, tribal, and regional groups who were frequently distrustful of one another and without unifying forces. Often, they collapsed from internal pressures; many states, such as Nigeria and the Congo, were torn asunder by breakaway provinces claiming the right to their own national self-determination. Throughout much of the world, therefore, the new states are politically unified only on a map; others stand dangerously close to civil war.

Politically unified nations not only have a single, legitimate, sovereign national government, but *their government has the authority and resources to meet the most important demands upon it.* One of these resources is customarily a large administrative structure—a bureaucracy of trained professionals to administer and apply law, to extend the scope and effectiveness of governmental policy, and to provide the pool of talent required in a modern government's operation.[10] A second significant resource is the ability to mobilize the masses for various types of political action, especially to support the government when necessary.[11] Political parties are especially important in this respect, and interest groups are, too. Such articulating institutions are an important resource customarily found in politically unified nations. Third, national governments in politically unified societies must be able to deal with a variety of social, economic, and political problems. Last, national governments need the authority to act as sovereign states in international affairs, able to negotiate and commit themselves to agreements. A government in politically unified states, in short, is able to "penetrate" the polity effectively.

Looking at the problem of resources and authority in politically unified nations differently, governments who have the means to function effectively and

---

[10] A large, professionally-trained bureaucracy is not always associated with governments in politically unified nations, but the relationship is quite strong. Among western nations, which have been as a group politically unified longer than most other nations, 86 percent (19 of 22) have bureaucracies of this kind, compared to only 4 percent (2 of 52) among non-Western nations. Arthur S. Banks and Robert B. Textor, *A Cross-Polity Survey* (Cambridge: MIT Press, 1963). Many anthropologists regard large, technically trained bureaucracies as a western export, first developed in the process of western nation-building and then adopted in Africa and Asia through colonialism or cultural assimilation. For an argument of this kind, see John J. Honigman, *Understanding Culture* (New York: Harper and Row, 1963), p. 116.

[11] An excellent comparative examination of the role of political parties in the process of political unification may be found in Joseph Lapolombara and Myron Wiener, eds., *Political Parties and Political Development* (Princeton: Princeton University Press, 1966); a more analytical discussion is contained in Gabriel Almond and G. Bingham Powell, Jr., *Comparative Politics: A Developmental Approach* (Boston: Little, Brown and Co., 1966).

meet demands upon them produce the payoff that persuades politically important groups to work within the existing governmental structure and to accept the rules of the game through which they benefit. These payoffs include domestic peace and order and political or social privileges (voting rights, legal concessions, and provisions for recruitment and representation in government); but economic rewards are almost always important. In the United States, for example, governmental payoffs are everywhere apparent: social security benefits and Medicare for older citizens; governmental fellowships and loans for students; a variety of federal highway and school subsidies for the states; many tax concessions, tariffs, and government contracts for businessmen; minimum wage and hour laws for labor. The federal government's legitimacy over the years has undoubtedly been strengthened by its ability to produce a succession of handsome economic payoffs when important groups demand them. The pattern of American politics has been to deal in an unending line of new interest groups as their demands upon the government for economic favors had to be considered. Such generosity has been possible because the American economy is enormously productive and provides the government with sufficiently ample resources to give almost all major interests that clamor for governmental concessions some important payoff; given such a situation, it has become virtually a tradition that "those who ask powerfully for what they want will get at least some of it."[12] Especially in the last forty years, the procedure has been to constantly expand the size of the federal budget so that all major interests will get some of it. Thus, Congress and the president seldom have been faced with the dilemma of granting concessions to one group only at the expense of preventing other groups any hope of economic favor; rather, Congress and the president must usually decide *how much* of the budget will be apportioned to major interests. Few nations enjoy the remarkable option of waging a multi-billion dollar War on Poverty while simultaneously spending several billions on foreign aid, as the United States federal government did in 1968.[13] Indeed, it may be a peculiarly American failure to overestimate what the government can do through economic means.[14]

Obviously, there are limitations in any political system to the type of governmental payoffs possible, for resources are always limited in some respect and not all groups can be fully satisfied. Ultimately, however, the failure to produce truly important payoffs affects a government's legitimacy. Inability to control or distribute important resources in response to group demands may make a government seem poor and undesirable. Conversely, a government blessed with the ability to deal in important political groups when they must be satisfied argues powerfully for its own preservation. Not accidentally, most of the world's

---

12 Mark Roelofs, *The Language of Modern Politics* (Homewood, Ill.: Dorsey Press, 1967), p. 265.

13 In 1968, the federal budget allocated $2,403 million for foreign aid and about $4,896 million on public assistance and economic opportunity programs.

14 For an interesting historical analysis of America's "psychology of abundance" see David M. Potter, *People of Plenty* (Chicago: University of Chicago Press, 1965).

politically unified societies have had sufficient human and material resources to produce important payoffs. This, as we shall see, has been a crucial handicap among many of the newer nations.

Finally, in a politically unified society, *there is a widely distributed feeling of citizenship and national political loyalty in the political culture.* To think of oneself as a citizen, rather than thinking of the term as a purely legal title, is to feel part of a common political unit with others, to apply to oneself certain political rights and obligations originating in the national government, to feel and express in various forms identification with the national political structure, its officials, and symbols. Moreover, in politically unified societies, a priority of political loyalties exists for most individuals in which the national political structure usually commands first place; primary political loyalty does not extend first to the relatively narrow, parochial interests of family, religion, geographic, or economic groups to the degree that national political obligations are continually subordinated. In many of the newer nations of Afro-Asia and to a lesser extent in Latin America, masses of individuals within a nation share no sense of citizenship in their polity; political loyalties are often confused or varied across the population; quite frequently, the national government is psychologically remote, its operation and officials unfamiliar and unappealing. Instead of a national political loyalty, many people in such societies feel bound to tribal, racial, geographical, or religious groups with an intensity that diminishes competing claims of national governments.[15]

Many nations of Afro-Asia and Latin America provide perhaps the most extreme, graphic examples of political instability and collapsible national governments, thereby most forcefully illustrating the alternatives to political unification. But political unification is still a relative term; no modern state necessarily occupies a fixed position in the division of the world's politically unified and disunited societies. It is true that most of the characteristics we have associated with politically unified societies—legitimate national governments, large bureaucracies, the authority and resources to meet the most important demands upon it—are those of western political systems. (In addition to the Anglo-American and European states, the Soviet Union and Japan are usually included in the "unified" category.) Yet even among these relatively stable national governments, the United States and Great Britain are unique because of their long periods of political unification. Many European nations, though politically unified today, have passed through major political crises in the recent past. Many nations that might have been called politically unified a few decades ago have disappeared or have been drastically altered; other nations unified at present have appeared only recently.

---

[15] The divisive effect of parochial loyalties on attempts to create a national political culture are discussed with particular clarity in Gabriel A. Almond and James S. Coleman, *The Politics of Developing Areas* (Princeton: Princeton University Press, 1960); several case studies may be found in Immanuel Wallerstein, *Africa: The Politics of Independence* (New York: Vintage Books, 1961).

The twentieth century has been a long requiem for the old order. The European colonial empires that once provided a visible if fragile order throughout much of the world have all but disappeared, leaving ex-colonial subjects to attempt their own political unification against formidable odds. In Europe itself, the monarchies, which once were the most visible, impressive symbols of European national order, have been relegated to history or—as in Great Britain—to symbolic and largely impotent imitations of their former vigor and authority. Wars of "national liberation" supported by revolutionary ideologies such as communism have frequently overturned national governments since 1945: Europe contains a divided Germany and its eastern states have become Soviet satellites; in Cuba, there is a new communist government; and Vietnam is in the throes of a civil war in which the United States, the Soviet Union, mainland China, and a host of allies and satellites are involved.

In the long perspective of history, the old order—the national "establishment"—changed relatively slowly; politically unified nations did not appear and disappear rapidly, as they have in this century when national boundaries and governments have simply been altered. The world political map has changed so radically in the last half century that its appearance in 1900 would be unfamiliar to a modern American. Since 1900, the Austro-Hungarian Empire, a landmark in Europe throughout most of the last century, disappeared along with Imperial Germany, Tsarist Russia, and the English, French, and Belgian colonies. Other nations were created in this century: Finland, Poland, Austria, Hungary, Czechoslovakia, and Yugoslavia, to mention a few. In short, this is an era of rapidly shifting national boundaries, of changing political structures within them, and of the death of old orders. Standing at his window of the Foreign Office in London a day before World War I began, the British Foreign Secretary sensed that almost a century of European political stability was collapsing. Observing the lamplighters below in St. James Park, his foreboding found imagery: "The lamps are going out all over Europe; we shall not see them lit again in our lifetime."

Against this background, it is clear why even a few decades of national political unification are fairly uncommon. Still, the nations now considered politically unified have enjoyed longer and more effective periods of governmental order and national integration than have most nations of Afro-Asia, the Middle East, and Latin America.

Crises of Unification

Political unification is not only a condition; it is a *process*. Nations that today can be called unified have become so over time. They continue to confront problems that might, if not adequately managed, undermine national political order. These include at least three kinds of crises—a crisis of authority, of participation, and of legitimacy. Further, once unification is achieved, such crises may erupt again; these crises vary in time and severity, yet the ability to resolve them seems to be the price of national political unification.[16]

A *crisis of authority* involves a dispute over what the proper powers of government are. It is usually triggered by a major social problem of such magnitude that important political groups demand that the government assume powers to deal with it. Other politically significant groups resist. The struggle crystallizes into a dispute—peaceful or violent—which involves: (1) granting powers to government of a kind or scale not previously granted; (2) large numbers of groups and individuals, among them politically powerful members; (3) a problem that is immediate, widely recognized, and threatening to the stability of the nation. In other words, a crisis of authority is political conflict elevated to the magnitude of a sweeping social issue, a dispute in which the powers of the government to act or not to act in the matter have significant consequences for large numbers of citizens in all aspects of social life. Disputes occur constantly over governmental authority in almost all the developed nations because almost all laws have proponents and opponents; however, disputes so severe that they become crises of authority are relatively infrequent.

Crises of authority have involved many different issues. In the United States, for example, one such crisis grew from the economic dislocations produced by the great Depression, which brought the nation to the brink of economic collapse; virtually every sector of the society demanded that the government assume powers to manage the economy and control the social disorder that resulted. This required the United States government to assume powers it had never previously exercised, powers that had been contrary to the prevailing political ideology of leaders of both major parties and most economic leaders in the years preceding the Depression. The New Deal that Franklin Roosevelt inaugurated in 1932 was a revolution in governmental power; it resulted in the enactment of hundreds of major bills from the Social Security Act to the first farm subsidy bill, making government the principal regulator and most important agent in determining the character of the whole economic system. The great Depression was the birthplace of big government and represents one of the most important crises of authority in our history.

The Civil War was in many respects the final culmination of a crisis of authority over the federal government's right to regulate slavery in the new states. This crisis had been developing for several decades before the actual start of the conflict. So important is this crisis in our political history and so useful in explaining how a crisis of authority develops that we will examine it in greater detail in the following chapter. However, it serves here as a reminder that our own national history is characterized by such crises, and that we suffered a disastrous civil war from failure to resolve this particular crisis peacefully.

---

[16] This typology of crisis closely follows Pye, *op. cit.*

The Soviet leadership has also faced a crisis of authority following Khrushchev's de-Stalinization program of 1956. This had both internal and external origins. Domestically, the Communist party is no longer the sole commanding force in Soviet political life; behind the once monolithic facade of Soviet totalitarianism has grown a pluralistic power structure: the industrial managers and chief engineers, the governmental officials of the central bureaucracy and those of the separate republics' bureaucracies, the marshals and admirals of the armed forces, and the intelligentsia (leading scientists, writers, and artists). Although the communist leaders preserve power over these elites through party and police controls as well as social benefits and material incentives, the leadership has increasingly had to accommodate the varied and conflicting interests of these newer groups who find the official party ideology largely irrelevant to their work. These groups have sought greater freedom from party restrictions on their work; the intelligentsia has been especially critical of the lack of feeedom to expose the drabness, inefficiency, and arbitrariness of much of Soviet life. Expelled from the Soviet Writer's Union for allegedly "throwing mud on the motherland," Soviet writer Alexander Solzhenitsyn, whose works have been acclaimed in the West, reportedly sent an angry letter to the Union's Moscow headquarters in which he expressed the rising discontent apparently common among many of Russia's younger writers:

> Wipe the dust off your watches. They are running centuries behind time. Throw open your beloved heavy curtains. You do not even suspect that the dawn has risen outside.[17]

Just as the Tsars in the nineteenth century felt very uneasy about the criticism stemming from Russian writers, the contemporary Soviet leadership feels compelled again and again to censor some authors with increasing severity as examples.

Externally, as the suppression of the Dubcek regime in Czechoslovakia during 1968 dramatically demonstrated, Soviet leaders seem threatened by movements away from communist orthodoxy in the neighboring satellite states of eastern Europe. The Dubcek policies—which might have led to a responsible Parliament, free elections, a free press, and a vigorous opposition—were apparently seen in Moscow as undermining the Communist party's monopoly of power in Prague. If this were permitted, not only might other regimes in eastern Europe follow the Czech example, but the reforms might threaten the very foundation of the Soviet communist system. In short, efforts of eastern European communist governments to proceed with their own definition of communism are seen by Moscow as an external threat to Soviet authority, just as the rising discontent of the intelligentsia is viewed as a domestic threat.

---

[17] "Courageous Defender," *Time* (November 21, 1969), p. 34.

The Soviet leadership's armed and wary attention to its own intelligentsia and its eastern European satellites bespeaks a fear that a crisis of authority may broaden into a crisis of legitimacy—as, indeed, it might. This reemphasizes that the three crises we have mentioned are not insulated from one another to the point that they cannot combine.

In addition to crises of authority, political unification has also been threatened by *crises of participation,* which involve the question of who may participate in political life and under what terms. Such dissent reaches crisis proportions when large masses and powerful interests become implicated in the dispute, when a significant (or apparently significant) shift in group political strength is at stake, and a threat to political order evolves.

Several conditions can precipitate a crisis of participation. One is the inability of minorities to gain a full measure of participation in the civic life of a polity. Quite often, the right to vote is the key issue.

At the heart of voting struggles lies democratic ideology. This has always insisted that no political regime is legitimate unless it rests on public consent ("governments derive their just powers from the governed," in the words of the Declaration of Independence), that voting privileges should not rest on accidents of birth, title, wealth, or economic status, that governments are accountable to their citizens and should be managed by freely elected representatives. When the democratic ideology first gained momentum in the eighteenth century, few regimes were hospitable to this new philosophy. Kings and aristocrats were loath to surrender voting rights to new classes and groups because they correctly perceived that a shift in political power toward the emerging middle classes would follow. After the middle class won its voting privilege (and gradually expanded its political participation to the point where it dominated most national governments), it, too, resisted further extension of the franchise to lower classes, as a rule.

Voting struggles leading to crises of participation have ended in various ways. At one extreme was the bloody French Revolution of 1789 that belongs with the Russian Revolution of 1917–1918 as the most violent political convulsion in recent history. Both revolutions had complex origins, but one common feature was the failure of the aristocracy to yield voting rights to the middle and lower classes. For example, the King and aristocracy that dominated French society in the eighteenth century at first dangerously underestimated the strength of dissent among the masses, particularly among the middle class that demanded the right to vote and participate in national government through elective assemblies sharing power with the throne. When the true dimensions of the crisis became apparent, the King and aristocracy were unable and unwilling to make the concessions that might have placated the opposition and forestalled a revolution against the whole monarchical system. To the dissidents, the only solution seemed to be a radical recasting of the whole political system along democratic lines. The resulting revolutionary conflagration created violence, confusion, political anarchy, and class hatred on a massive scale. This revolution was, in turn, carried to such an excess of political murder and vengeance that a counter-revolution followed, led by more conservative elements. So deeply did the issues and animosities of this revolution scar French political life that its pattern of political hostilities and issues continues to divide Frenchmen well into this century; and a broad, national consensus on the basic governmental form for France could not be established.

In contrast, beginning in the 1830s and continuing until the end of World War I, the middle and lower classes of Great Britain achieved their voting rights much more peacefully; by 1860, the British government, once considered the most stable and representative of European national monarchies, had become essentially a parliamentary democracy with power shifted to an elective legislature and the Prime Minister and his Cabinet, albeit not without resistance. During the latter half of the nineteenth century, the middle classes, then firmly controlling the British government, gradually abolished voting restrictions on the lower classes. The peculiar British genius for accommodation and "muddling through" prevented a potentially dangerous crisis of participation.

In the United States, as we shall more fully explore in the next chapter, the most sustained, bitter, and dangerous crisis over voting has involved black Americans. This represents only one aspect of the blacks' larger struggle for equal political and social opportunity. Indeed, in some respects, black Americans can be said to have won the voting struggle; in the last several decades they have gained access to the ballot in increasing numbers. Today, there are few formal impediments. Yet a great many blacks, particularly the young, still feel that white racism denies them many other meaningful forms of social and political participation in American society.

Another potent cause of crises of participation is the refusal of governments to permit open public criticism or other manifestations of opposition. Quite commonly, when governments determine to suppress opposition, they attempt to quash not only opposition propaganda but also the opposition press, opposition parties, and whatever institutions support an articulate opposition. The attempt to participate in political life by criticising the government is often regarded as illegal if not traitorous; this shows that the idea of legitimate and healthy opposition to a regime has not developed.

The problem of dealing with the political opposition is often acute in newly independent nations where the legitimacy of the government and the terms of the political formula do not seem well grounded in public sentiment. Often, therefore, whatever group controls the government and defends the new political arrangements is likely to regard its opposition—justly or not—as potential destroyers of the national government and too dangerously divisive to be permitted to exist; the result often is persecution of the opposition in the name of national security. This, in fact, almost occurred in the United States when organized party opposition to the Federalists developed soon after the Constitution was adopted. As we shall see in the following chapter, our own national history is an excellent example of how slowly and painfully the idea of a legitimate political opposition may develop in a political culture and how a crisis of participation can develop from this problem.

Finally, a *crisis of legitimacy,* the most sweeping and fundamental of these crises, represents a conflict within a society over its basic political organization; the conflict so rends the political culture and pervades the society that the existence of the national government is threatened or the government is actually overturned.

Sometimes the result is a wholly new or drastically altered governmental structure followed by yet other governments. This has been the pattern in many Afro-Asian nations since 1945. The European colonial governments, once ousted, were first succeeded in most cases by new, independent governments elaborately outfitted with constitutions, elective assemblies and executives, political parties, and other trappings of democracy. Many of these newly minted governments had no standing among the freshly liberated masses; quite commonly, political hostilities within the societies were so intense that the capture of governmental control by one political faction was the signal for violent revolt against the government by the "outs." Often, governments were overturned and replaced by constitutional dictatorships or a succession of military *juntas* ruling by decree; less frequently, the challenges to governmental legitimacy were met by keeping some forms of constitutional democracy, while conducting the government more or less dictatorially.

Crises of legitimacy need not result in violence or a complete restructuring of the governmental framework. Sometimes a peaceful revolution may occur in which no overt change in governmental structures occurs, but great changes in their relative powers emerge. Such a situation developed, for instance, in Great Britain between 1800 and 1900 when strong challenges to the monarchy resulted in a displacement of power from the king to the elective national Parliament; the monarchy persists, and the king reigns but does not rule.

The British experience reflects the fact that numerous crises of legitimacy in the history of nations now considered politically unified have commonly involved the power of kings and aristocracies. Usually, the crisis has ended with the emasculation of monarchical powers and a shift of political power to representative, elective assemblies, and to the middle and lower classes. The American Revolution of 1776 is the earliest example of a successful revolt against king and court, resulting not only in political independence for the new nation but creating a new form of national government as well. The latest revolution of this type occurred in 1917 when the Russian Revolution consumed the last of the great absolute monarchies. With the remains of the old order mixed in blood and winter snow in St. Petersburg, the struggle of the world's major nations to end the reign of kings was practically concluded; it had taken more than 140 years.

The passing of kings has by no means ended crises of legitimacy in politically developed nations, however. Within this century, France has had five different national constitutions; Germany has had a monarchy, a democratic republic, a totalitarian dictatorship, an occupation government, and now a divided government—the western side following a parliamentary democratic pattern, the eastern portion a communist order. There is no reason to assume that further crises of legitimacy will not erupt.

The United States has witnessed several periods of intense attack on the legitimacy of its basic political structures. One of these was during the founding of the republic, including the days of the Constitution's writing and the subsequent campaign for its adoption. To many observers, we are now in another period during which the legitimacy of our basic political structures is sharply debated.

13

Crises of
Political Unification
in the United States

The United States has experienced drastic territorial expansion, several separatist movements, a bloody civil war, a large influx of immigrants from alien cultures, rapid industrialization, two world wars, several severe economic depressions, and intense racial strife. The political system has coped successfully with the problems of unification arising from these experiences; until Vietnam and the reaction against the war, the system was generally considered highly stable when compared to those of most other nations—especially developed nations. But this success was not preordained, nor was it achieved without cost. The system frequently underwent severe stress. Nor were the American experiences unique: the problems that were overcome in achieving and maintaining unification were similar in several ways to the problems that confront many new nations.

Most Americans seem to accept the successful unification of the nation as something that was bound to occur. Aside from the Civil War, they know very little about the political ills that have threatened unification in the past; the United States has been accepted uncritically as a unique and successful experiment in self-government, and its governmental institutions and political processes have been viewed as the best ever designed. Military coups, tribal wars, and prolonged periods of confusion and instability seemed unrelated to anything that could happen in this country.

Nevertheless, political unification in the United States has been, and continues to be, a highly complex and uncertain process. Crises of unification which result from the political struggles inherent in a nation's development cannot be neatly categorized and clearly distinguished from each other. However, it is instructive for analytical purposes to distinguish between crises of authority, participation, and legitimacy. The first two do not seriously threaten political unification unless they escalate into crises of legitimacy, at which point the right of the political system to exist becomes the crucial issue. In other words, problems related to what powers the government should have, or who should participate in public life, can be managed unless those involved reject the legitimacy of the political system and attempt to subvert it. In this chapter, we shall discuss certain historical events in the context of these three kinds of crises.

Crises of Authority

A crisis of authority involves a dispute over what powers the government should have or how they should be used.[1] Most often, such a crisis is triggered by strong disagreements between important factions in society over how the government should deal with major social problems. The dispute may be resolved peaceably or forcibly. The disintegration of the Union in 1860 and the ensuing war constitute the only crisis of authority in American history that brought on a severe crisis of unification. The South was unwilling to accept the authority of the national government to control the extension of slavery into the territories. This crisis of authority became a crisis of legitimacy which disrupted the Union.

Fortuitous circumstances during the first half-century of its history allowed the United States to avoid some of the more disruptive forces that often complicate contemporary attempts to build nations. It did not have to overcome a deeply rooted sense of inferiority due to the more advanced culture of its previous colonial rulers. Nor did it possess a feudal land-owning class which, because of a vested interest in preserving the status quo, would oppose modernizers.[2] Its new political parties were sufficiently loyal to the political order that they did not attempt to subvert it. There was no standing army whose first loyalty was to its generals rather than to the civilian government. The security of the nation was not seriously threatened by foreign powers or international

---

[1] For an interesting discussion of the decline of authority in the West see Glen Tinder, *The Crisis of Political Imagination* (New York: Charles Scribner's Sons, 1964), Chapter 9. See also Carl Joachim Friedrich, *Man and His Government: An Empirical Theory of Politics* (New York: McGraw-Hill Book Co., 1963), Chapter 12.

[2] See Louis Hartz, *The Founding of New Societies* (New York: Harcourt Brace Jovanovich, 1964), Chapter 4.

political movements. On the contrary, the United States enjoyed a common political heritage, a common language, a sound and relatively well-developed economy, a population with some experience in civil affairs, a society that had not been torn asunder by the upheavals of a full-blown social revolution, a well-designed constitution that was venerated by the people, and political leaders whose skills, education, and experience were remarkable for the times.[3]

Why, then, did the Union nearly founder?[4] The crisis occurred because the South refused to be bound by certain national policies, and because political activists increasingly disagreed on what rules should govern the conduct of politics and the making of public policy. No political system can survive if minorities of sufficient size and strength within it refuse to accept and obey policies determined by the duly constituted government. This also means that the willing acceptance of the political procedures, regardless of what policies they produce, is crucial to the stability of the system. In 1860, the South rejected both policies and established procedures.

Economic sectionalism had been characteristic of American politics from the beginning, and it underlay much of the political controversy that occurred during the first sixty years of the nation's history. In the 1850s, political controversy intensified, and the interests, fears, and hostilities of North and South converged on the issue of whether the national government should permit the extension of slavery into the western territories. The many other issues that divided the nation did not, of course, disappear, but they were either overshadowed by or subsumed under this highly explosive question. Southern leadership ultimately dealt the final blow to the strained consensus supporting the system; the leadership rejected the rules of the game rather than allowing itself to be bound by policies it feared the new Republican administration would adopt with regard to slavery in the territories.

The extension of slavery into the territories was first recognized as a potentially disruptive issue in 1819 when the territory of Missouri applied for admission as a state into the Union. The fears of many Northerners about the expansion of slavery and the growing defensiveness of Southerners about an institution they considered essential to their economy revealed the danger to national unity of this situation. There were eleven free and eleven slave states in 1819, creating an equal division of power in the Senate. The Missouri situation was explosive because that state's admission, as either a slave or a free state, would upset the balance of power in the arena where public policy governing slavery in the territories was to be made. In 1820, after months of bitter debate and threats of secession from both sides, the Missouri Compromise provided a

---

[3] Richard P. McCormick, "Political Development and the Second Party System," in William Nisbet Chambers and Walter Dean Burnham (eds.), *The American Party Systems: Stages of Political Development* (New York: Oxford University Press, 1967), p. 114.

[4] For an analysis of how historians have interpreted the causes of the Civil War see Thomas Pressly, *Americans Interpret Their Civil War* (Princeton: Princeton University Press, 1954).

settlement. This agreement admitted Missouri as a slave state, but it also admitted Maine as a free state in order to preserve the balance. Most important, however, the Compromise excluded by law the extension of slavery into any of the new lands acquired from France in the Louisiana Purchase above the latitude of 36°30′. The turmoil subsided, and the Southern acceptance of the agreement suggested that the slave states were willing to allow Congress to determine public policy governing slavery in the territories. But many observers, sensitive to the potential danger of this issue, recognized how highly tentative the agreement was. Jefferson, now retired from public life, likened the turmoil and discord to the sound of a "fire bell ringing in the night." Seeing the conflict over Missouri as a portent of things to come, he said, "I considered it at once the knell of the Union. It is hushed, indeed, for the moment. But this is a reprieve only, not a final sentence."[5]

Many historians mark the controversy over the Wilmot Proviso (banning slavery in any territory acquired from Mexico) and its passage by the House of Representatives in 1848 as the beginning of the end for the Union. The apparent acceptance in the North that Congress would henceforth determine whether slavery would be permitted in new territories and the passage of the Wilmot Proviso by the House contributed to a marked increase in the defensive attitudes of the South. Professor J. G. Randall, for example, has suggested that the solidification of Southern attitudes on slavery and the increased awareness of a common culture dates from these events. This consciousness of a Southern nationalism led to new priorities, which insisted that the authority of the national government would be accepted only if certain policies were followed. When the House of Representatives approved a policy that would prevent Southerners from carrying their property into the territories, Southern reaction was immediate and hostile. "To put the matter succinctly, it was becoming evident that the South would secede rather than submit to the Wilmot Proviso."[6]

Every Northern state but one passed resolutions in favor of the objectives of the Wilmot Proviso. The fact that the Senate (where the strength of the slave states equalled that of the free states) blocked passage of the resolution did not mollify Southern political leaders. John C. Calhoun of South Carolina introduced resolutions in Congress denying the right of that body to restrict slavery in the territories and declaring that the Missouri Compromise, to the extent that it had attempted to do so, was unconstitutional. Alabama, Georgia, Florida, and Virginia endorsed a document called the Alabama Platform, which demanded that Congress protect slavery in the territories and called for the Democratic

---

[5] Quoted in Michael Kraus, *The United States to 1865* (Ann Arbor: The University of Michigan Press, 1959), p. 346.

[6] J. G. Randall, *The Civil War and Reconstruction* (New York: D. C. Heath & Co., 1953), p. 117. Our discussion of the events leading to the Civil War is based on Randall's account, unless otherwise cited. See especially Chapters 4 and 5.

party to deny its presidential nomination to any candidate who would not support this principle. A convention met in Nashville to consider the question of secession from the Union. Though some delegates called for secession, the strength of the moderate forces attending this convention prevented it from taking any action.

With tension running high in the country and the sentiment for secession increasing, California further complicated the situation by requesting admission to the Union as a free state. The churches in the country had now split into Northern and Southern wings, citizen societies favoring one side or the other were springing up, exchanges between the leaders of the two sections were becoming caustic and bitter, and the controversy over the principles embodied in the Wilmot Proviso became intense. California's admission as a free state would upset the balance of political power in the Senate to the South's disadvantage, and this would weaken further the bonds of national cohesion.

But again the crisis passed. Through the conciliatory efforts of men such as Stephen A. Douglas, Daniel Webster, and Henry Clay, Congress passed a series of proposals that have come to be known as the Compromise of 1850. California was admitted as a free state; the territories of Utah and New Mexico were, despite the Wilmot Proviso, organized without restrictions on slavery; the slave trade was declared illegal in the District of Columbia; and steps were taken to assure more rigid enforcement of the fugitive slave law. The Compromise did not satisfy the extremists on either side of the issue, but the country welcomed the passing of the crisis with relief.

The Compromise, however, proved to be only a temporary expedient. The division in the country was too deep and the stakes involved in which policies should govern slavery in the territories too high. Congressional action managed to reconcile the conflict over the admission of California, but it did not provide guidelines acceptable to both North and South as to the admission of the next state. Before the tensions from the crisis of 1850 had subsided, Congress was faced with an even more dangerous situation in Kansas, where very few slaves existed and where there was little likelihood that a cotton economy could be established. By this time, attention had shifted away from areas in which slavery was entrenched to areas where it was practically nonexistent. More specifically, the moral and human aspects of slavery were placed aside as the key issue became what policies would govern its extension into the territories and who would determine this policy.[7] Underlying this dispute was "an identical conclusion drawn up by both sides. The power to decide the question of slavery for the territories was the power to determine the future of slavery itself."[8] The

---

[7] For an excellent analysis of the moral effects of slavery on blacks, see Stanley M. Elkins, *Slavery*, second ed. (Chicago: University of Chicago Press, 1968), Chapters 3 and 4.

[8] Arthur Bestor, "The Civil War Crisis," in Bernard E. Brown and John C. Wahlke (eds.), *The American Political System* (Homewood, Ill.: Dorsey Press, 1967), p. 115.

South saw this question as crucial to the preservation of the Southern way of life. Fear and defensiveness were transforming sectionalism into a narrow and uncompromising Southern nationalism. The real issue, then, was not whether the territories should be slave or free, but rather what the official policy of the national government should be, how changes in the power relationship of the free and slave states might someday affect this policy.

Congress adopted the popular sovereignty doctrine of Senator Stephen A. Douglas in 1854 and passed the controversial Kansas-Nebraska Act. Under this legislation, Kansas and Nebraska were organized as territories, and the status of slavery was left to be determined by their inhabitants when they would write their constitutions and apply for admission to the Union. Further, the Act repudiated that part of the Missouri Compromise excluding slavery from areas of the Louisiana Purchase above the latitude of 36°30′ on grounds that Congress had exceeded its authority. Thus the Kansas-Nebraska Act embodied the principle that Congress should not determine whether slavery should be extended to new territories, but rather should let the matter be settled by the local populations.

This last prewar effort of Congress to reconcile the conflict over slavery solved nothing. Northern antislavery forces were enraged that Congress refused to outlaw slavery in the territories, and Southerners were unhappy that Congress did nothing to protect slavery from future restraints that might be applied by territorial governments. Randall has stated that "this legislation had let loose the dogs of war."[9] It certainly helped precipitate the very things that Douglas, the moving force behind the legislation, was trying to prevent. In a country where the climate was growing increasingly hostile and the consensus supporting the authority of the government was under intense stress because of the caustic and bitter exchanges of political extremists on both sides, the Kansas-Nebraska Act merely added fuel to the flames. It intensified sectional strife, widened the split in the Democratic party, and helped to bring into being the Republican party, whose appeal and support was sectional rather than national. The sectional conflict was thus reflected by 1854 in the party system, thereby weakening the bonds of unity that had been forged in the building of national, comprehensive, office-seeking organizations.

The decline and demise of the American party system, the crisis of authority, and the eruption of civil war are so closely related that they cannot be understood as separate events. A national party system functions to moderate conflict and reconcile extremes in a pluralistic society. By managing sectional differences at the party level, it improves the chances of agreement, compromise, and moderation at the governmental level. This helps preserve national unity. When sectional interests cannot be reconciled at the governmental level, and are so uncompromising that they undermine the national support of parties and

---

[9] Randall, *op. cit.,* p. 133.

bring about a polarization or sectionalization of political life, the authority of the system is severely endangered. This is what happened during the 1850s when the slavery issue wrecked the second American party system.

The demise of the Federalist party by the 1820s had marked the death of the first American two-party system. Signs of the revival of competitive party politics were evident in the election of 1824; by 1840—after sixteen years of gradual development—the second party system was clearly established. The Jacksonian Democratic party and the new Whig party, which had risen to fill the void caused by the death of the Federalist party, were nationally based political organizations using modern electioneering devises to capture control of the government. They were more interested in gaining office than in preserving the purity of some political philosophy. They were not, however, able to manage the conflict over the slavery question when the doctrinaires and extremists in their ranks gained positions of influence and succeeded in developing substantial support among the people. After 1848, when controversy over the Wilmot Proviso intensified the slavery conflict, the strains on the party system became increasingly evident. By the early 1850s, the Whig party had disintegrated; by 1856, the new Republican party of the North had been organized and was almost full-grown and able to take its place. Though the birth and rapid growth of the Republicans were due as much to economic interest as to any love for the Negro, Southern leaders saw this growth mainly as the result of a massive political effort to abolish slavery, upon which the economy of the South was dependent. Thus, the Republican party became anathema in the South, and the possibility that it would gain control of the government was unacceptable to Southern leaders.

The reality of this threat and the impact of the slavery issue on the spirit of national unity at the party level was revealed by the outcome of the 1856 elections. The Republicans, who had won sweeping victories in state elections in 1854, called for passage of the Wilmot Proviso and conducted a campaign based mainly on opposition to slavery in the territories. The Democrats, being a national party closely associated with the South, was more conciliatory and conducted a campaign based mainly on the principle of popular sovereignty that had been embodied in the Kansas-Nebraska Act. Both Northern and Southern Democrats read their own views on slavery into the party's position and thus were able to retain sufficient solidarity and support to win. The narrowness of the victory, however, and the increasing dissension within the party due to the Northern resentment toward the Southern domination of the party, together with the mounting strength of the Republicans in the country, proved to be a portent of things to come.

The tragic story of the nation and the increasing weakening of the Democratic party during the four-year administration of President James Buchanan need only be mentioned. The struggle over the admission of Kansas to the Union, the attempt of the Supreme Court in the Dred Scott case to solve the issue of slavery in the territories by treating it as merely a judicial question,[10] the shock of John Brown's raid on Harper's Ferry, the insistence by the South that the Democratic party adopt its position on slavery in the territories, the refusal of Northern Democrats to abandon the doctrine of popular sovereignty, and the ominous threat of the Republicans waiting to gain control of the government—all these factors brought conditions within the Democratic party to fever pitch. When the Democrats met in Charleston, South Carolina, in 1860 to nominate their candidate for the presidency, these dissensions dominated the proceedings of the convention.

The positions of the opposing factions in the party had so hardened by this juncture that compromise was highly improbable. The convention ended in a shambles; the Democratic party as a national political organization binding together both North and South disintegrated under the weight of the seemingly uncontrollable forces of sectionalism. The subsequent nomination and election of the Republican Abraham Lincoln pushed the South, now severely agitated and led by extremists from the deep Southern states, to the point of no return. This section of the Union was unwilling to accept the authority of a government controlled by a political party that favored policies to which it was unalterably opposed. The Southern states therefore left the Union. Thus a crisis of authority, over whose public policy should govern slavery in the territories, escalated into a crisis of unification that led to secession and civil war.

Crises of Participation

Crises of participation arise in political systems when there are basic and continuing disagreements about who may participate in political life. All disagreements over participation do not, of course, lead to crises. The women's suffrage movement and the current debate over extending the suffrage to eighteen-year-olds represent disagreements over political participation which can hardly be called crises. Disagreements over participation can become crises and threaten the legitimacy of the political system if either of the following conditions exist: if the government does not allow citizens to criticize its policies; or if minority groups either refuse or are denied the right to participate fully in the public life of the community.[11] Both the achievement and the maintenance of political unification in the United States have been threatened by crises of participation growing out of these two conditions.

---

[10] For a brief but excellent discussion of the political nature of the Dred Scott case, see Wallace Mendelsohn, *Capitalism, Democracy, and the Supreme Court* (New York: Appleton-Century-Crofts, 1960), pp. 45–51.

[11] Murray Clark Havens, *The Challenges to Democracy* (Austin: The University of Texas Press, 1965). See Chapters 2–3 for his elaboration of these typologies.

1. *Rejection of Criticism*
and Organized Opposition as
Essential Features of Political Life

In the early United States, as in many of the new nations of the last half of the twentieth century, "[legitimacy] involves sentiments about what should be the underlying spirit of government and the primary goals of national effort."[12] This matter of the underlying spirit of government, and the extent to which this spirit allowed for criticism and organized opposition in the newly established political order, was crucial to the development of the system's legitimacy. The status of criticism and opposition during the first three decades of the history of the republic was unclear; thus the terms under which opposition forces could participate in political life remained uncertain.

A democratic political system must grant its minorities the right to criticize and oppose the policies of the majority and to attempt by constitutional methods to gain control of the government. When both the controlling majority and the opposing minority accept the rules of the game and abide by the outcome of free elections, control of government changes hands peacefully. If, however, the winners look upon opposition as treasonous and regard all criticism of their policies as efforts to destroy the system, or if the losers refuse to accept defeat or abide by the policies of the government, the legitimacy of the system is in jeopardy. In many new nations, political leaders struggling to combine stability with social, political, and economic change are prone to view opposition as disruptive of public order and detrimental to the processes of unification. They interpret criticism of policy and organized opposition as efforts to destroy the nation itself. In Seymour Lipset's words,

> To create a stable, representative, decision-making process that provides a legitimate place for opposition, that recognizes the rights of those without power to advocate "error" and the overthrow of those in office, is extremely difficult in any polity. It is particularly problematic in new states which must be concerned also with the sheer problem of the survival of national authority itself.[13]

The threat to political participation posed by the uncertainty surrounding the role of organized opposition can be seen in the birth, development, decline, and

---

[12] Lucian Pye, *Aspects of Political Development* (Boston: Little, Brown and Co., 1966), p. 64.

[13] Seymour M. Lipset, *The First New Nation* (New York: Basic Books, 1963), p. 36.

ultimate demise of this nation's first system of political parties. Positions in the new government were initially filled on the basis of merit and ability without regard to anything resembling party affiliation. The moving force behind the efforts to abandon the Articles of Confederation and to write a new Constitution had been a desire on the part of many political leaders to overcome the divisive features of American public life and build a strong, stable, and unified nation[14] Washington, Hamilton, Madison, Jefferson, and others who assumed high positions in the new government were either leading participants or observers in the writing of the Constitution. These men were suspicious of political parties and factions and did not appreciate the role of an organized opposition in a political system. Such efforts, they thought, threatened the authority of the government and jeopardized the success of the experiment.[15] Even Jefferson, who was later to become a key figure and finally the leader of an effort which established opposition movements as permanent features of American politics, was slow in accepting the role of such movements in a democratic order.

Washington's first administration was a government of national unity. Staffed by the prominent political figures of the day without regard to factions or cliques, the government's principal task was to establish its identity and authority, extend its authority down through the system, and put into operation the formal structures within which the policy-making process would occur. The government also had to cope with the social and economic problems which beset the new nation, unify the divisive forces of a society still experiencing strong loyalties to states and sections, and establish the new nation as a free and independent member of the international system. The question of whether to accept an organized opposition in the nation's public life became entangled in the government's efforts to formulate its domestic economic program and to determine its relationship with the former colonial powers of Europe. Thus, the question of the acceptability of criticism had to be worked out as the system responded to demands from both the internal and external environments.

Alexander Hamilton, as Washington's first Secretary of the Treasury, eventually became the moving force in determining the policy direction of the new government during the first decade of its existence. Supported by the President and sympathetic forces in the Congress, Hamilton advocated a set of proposals which were designed to promote the nation's economic growth and which rested upon the assumption that a strong, stable government must be linked to the natural aristocracy in society represented by the business and commercial

---

[14] For a recent interpretation of the intentions of the Founding Fathers in writing the Constitution see Paul Eidelberg, *The Philosophy of the American Constitution: A Reinterpretation of the Intentions of The Founding Fathers* (New York: The Free Press, 1968); see also David G. Smith, *The Convention and the Constitution* (New York: St. Martin's Press, 1965).

[15] William Nisbet Chambers, *Political Parties in a New Nation* (New York: Oxford University Press, 1963), p. 5. Our discussion of the party system during the Federalist period is based primarily on this account.

interests.[16] His plan called for the assumption of all state debts remaining from the war, funding of the national debt, establishment of a national bank to handle the financial affairs of the government, a protective tariff for infant industries against competition from foreign manufacturers, and a system of excise taxes to pay the government's expenses and cover its debts; in addition, it promoted governmental assistance for industrial and commercial interests in the United States as a necessary move to consolidate the divergent interests in society and establish the authority of the national government over the states. This scheme was clearly designed to assist those interests in society whose support Hamilton considered vital to the process of national unification. At the same time, Hamilton's passionate and dedicated concern for nationalism, centralization, and the development of the business and commercial classes (he distrusted the common people), blinded him somewhat to the adverse effects of his policies on other interests in American society.

Public policies which create benefits for one group usually create disadvantages for others. Hamilton's view that the disadvantages suffered by agrarian interests, especially in the South, should be willingly accepted as the price of "national power and greatness" indicates that he did not fully appreciate the extent to which some groups disagreed with his view as to what was best for the country. In addition to threatening noncommercial interests, Hamilton's proposals "took too little account of such intangibles as sectional pride, jealousy, and long-standing rivalries."[17] When James Madison announced in Congress that he would oppose passage of Hamilton's economic program, the young congressman was responding to the pressures of his constituency in Virginia and representing the agrarian interests of the South. As spokesman for a different set of economic interests, a different geographical section, and a different political philosophy, Madison's speech against the economic and political nationalism of Hamilton raised for the first time the question of the acceptability of organized opposition in the new political system.

With President Washington standing above politics as a symbol of national unity, the task of organizing support for the government's program in Congress fell to Hamilton. The efforts of the young New Yorker to win congressional approval for his proposals set in motion a movement which culminated in the birth of the first modern political party, the Federalist party. The opposition forces, led at first by Madison and later by Jefferson, represented a different philosophy of government; their attempts to obstruct Hamilton's economic program were the beginning of a countermovement, centered mainly in the South, which was to become the Jeffersonian Republican party. The struggle between these opposing forces over Hamilton's economic program, the election

---

[16] John C. Miller, *Alexander Hamilton and the Growth of the New Nation* (New York: Harper & Row, Publishers, 1959), p. 230. See Chapters 16–20 for an excellent account of Hamilton's ideas on government.

[17] *Ibid.,* p. 294.

of 1796, the Jay Treaty with England, and the election of 1800, all involved the vital questions of who would control the government and which political interests and philosophy would give direction to its policies. The reaction of each to the other, and the attitude of those in power to those who were seeking to take it from them, would answer the far more important question about the role of criticism and organized opposition in the political development of the new nation.[18]

"Whoever forms one party necessarily forms two, for he forms an antagonistic party."[19] In a free society, either a faction within the single party or a separate and distinct political group will form this organized opposition. The cleavage between the Federalist and Republican factions by 1792, though still loosely drawn and fluid, was clearly visible in Congress and was beginning to take shape in the country at large. Opposing newspapers were established as party organs, and the exchanges between the opposing forces became increasingly hostile and caustic. With the Hamiltonians in control of the cabinet and Washington supporting their program with his personal prestige and the powers of his office, Jefferson, as Secretary of State, found his position becoming increasingly uncomfortable. When he "left the cabinet at the end of 1793, rupture at the executive as well as the legislative centers of government was complete."[20]

The growing opposition to the Hamiltonian proposals and the Federalist philosophy of government took many forms: debates in Congress, attacks in the press, formation of anti-Federalist societies in many states, passage of critical resolutions in state legislatures, correspondence between Republican leaders, organized efforts to capture congressional seats, and on one occasion in western Pennsylvania, outright insurrection. The reaction of the Federalists to these efforts to oppose and discredit them shows clearly that organized opposition of this sort was not accepted as legitimate.[21] Hamilton viewed the initial efforts to subvert his programs as efforts to destroy the Constitution. He labored long and hard to organize support for his policies, but when his opponents in Virginia did likewise and pushed resolutions through the Virginia legislature condemning his policies as destructive of the rights and interests of the common man and the individual states, the Federalist leader stated: "This is the first symptom of a spirit which must either be killed, or it will kill the Constitution."[22] The anti-Federalist societies were denounced, and President Washington joined in the

---

[18] The most recent examination of this issue is Richard Hofstadter, *The Idea of a Party System: The Rise of Legitimate Opposition in the United States* (Berkeley and Los Angeles: University of California Press, 1970).

[19] Miller, *op. cit.*, p. 320.

[20] Chambers, *op. cit.*, p. 57.

[21] For a discussion of the tendencies of new nations to develop one-party systems and the problem of establishing the legitimacy of organized opposition see Clause Ake, *A Theory of Political Integration* (Homewood, Ill.: Dorsey Press, 1967), Chapter 6.

[22] Chambers, *op. cit.*, p. 61.

effort to brand these groups as disloyal elements in society. Thus, organized opposition was looked upon as a threat to the security of the nation rather than as an accepted form of political participation by those who differed with the government.

During the administration of John Adams, the question of the new nation's relationship with England and France became a matter of intense debate.[23] This intrusion of international politics into the domestic political situation altered the framework within which the problem of the institutionalization of organized opposition as an acceptable feature of political life was being worked out. Feelings in the United States toward the war being fought between European powers were sharply divided. The Federalists, especially Hamilton and a group of his followers, were sympathetic toward England and looked with dismay upon the revolutionary activities in France. This group spearheaded a strong movement in the Federalist party to abandon the nation's policy of independence and noninvolvement and declare war against the French. Diplomatic difficulties with France and the fact that the French navy was interfering with American shipping on the high seas provided some foundation for their hostility and made it difficult for President Adams to resist this pro-British element in his party. The Republicans, led by Jefferson, who was now vice-president, were sympathetic toward France and actively opposed Federalist efforts in Congress to achieve a declaration of war against the nation which had recently helped the United States free itself from British authority. The charges and countercharges, which were caustic, personal, exaggerated, and extreme, did much to poison the relationship between the two parties. This intrusion of international politics into the already heated cauldron of domestic political controversy led to the passage of the Alien, Naturalization, and Sedition Acts of 1798.

The Alien and Naturalization Acts, designed to control the activities of foreigners living in the United States, were never enforced by President Adams. The Sedition Act, however, was enforced with some vengeance. This bill, among other things, authorized fines and prison terms for anyone who published false, scandalous, or malicious statements about the president, Congress, or the government itself. Whatever the motives of the Federalists in passing this legislation may have been, the fact that it was enforced only against Republicans shows clearly that it was used as a weapon by those in power against their political opponents:

All told, Federalist judges jailed and fined 70 men under the Sedition Act. . . . With few exceptions, the trials were travesties of justice dominated by judges who saw treason behind every expression of Republican sentiment. Grand juries for bringing in the indictments and trial juries for rendering the monotonous verdict of guilty were handpicked by Federalist United States

[23] Lipset, *op. cit.*, pp. 39–45.

marshals in defiance of statutes prescribing orderly procedure. The presiding judges often ridiculed the defendants' lawyers and interrupted their presentations so outrageously that many threw up their hands and their cases, leaving the accused at the mercy of the court.[24]

The Republicans, in the minds of many Federalists, were clearly organizing to destroy the Constitution and impose French rule in America. It followed that prosecuting Republican editors, wrecking Republican printing offices, and generally harassing Republican spokesmen critical of the government were all acts in defense of the Constitution and the authority of the government. In any new nation struggling to establish itself and overcome the forces of disunity, criticism quickly becomes suspect. Those who have created the nation do not easily accept the idea that other men may differ radically with their policies but still approve the fundamental character of the polity. As Immanuel Wallenstein has written about the leaders of the contemporary African states, their choice is not between democracy or dictatorship, but between nationhood or disintegration.[25] Similarly, George Washington warned of the "baneful effects of the spirit of party," and in his Farewell Address he condemned party strife.

> The unity of government which constitutes you one people . . . is a main pillar in the edifice of your real independence. . . . [but] factionalism . . . agitates the community with ill-founded jealousies and false alarms; kindles the animosity of one part against another; foments occasionally riot and corruption, which finds a facilitated access to the government itself through the channels of party passion.[26]

Interestingly, the suffering Republicans used these same tactics against the Federalists once their positions were reversed. While out of office, the Republican charges against their opponents were extreme and irresponsible, and suggested that the Federalists were the real enemies of the Constitution. After gaining office by virtue of Jefferson's election to the presidency in 1800, however, the Republicans cracked down on Federalist opinion. On several occasions, Jefferson initiated suits in federal courts against Federalist editors and ministers for making seditious and libelous statements about the president. And Thomas Paine, who had lashed out in an earlier day against oppression by the British, on one occasion "urged that the public authorities judge and punish

---

[24] Richard Hofstadter, William Miller, and Danial Aaron, *The American Republic* (Englewood Cliffs, N.J.: Prentice-Hall, 1959), pp. 331–332. Quoted in footnote by Lipset, *op. cit.,* p. 40.

[25] Immanuel Wallenstein, *Africa: The Politics of Independence* (New York: Vintage Books, 1961), p. 96.

[26] Quoted in J. N. Larned, *The New Larned History* (Springfield, Mass.: C. A. Nichols Publishing Co., 1851), Vol. X, pp. 8677–8679.

'atrocious statements.' "[27] Thus, the behavior of both political parties indicates that the constitutional principle of free speech and the right to criticize one's government did not become firmly established in American political life just because they were included in the fundamental law. The uncertainty of their acceptance by the clashing political forces during the Federalist period represented a crisis of participation which threatened the unification of the political system. This crisis differed from the situation in many contemporary new states, however, in that the leaders of both parties had not only worked together to establish American independence and later the Constitution, but they had known one another personally and trusted each other for a long time. They recognized that they all belonged to the same "ruling club."[28] Hence, both parties permitted more opposition and criticism than many of the new nations of Asia and Africa have.

---

2. Denial of Participation to Minority Groups in Society

A political system must also respond adequately to the demands made upon it if it is to retain its legitimacy. It must have the capacity for change in order to respond adequately to the demands made upon it, whether these come from social groups within the country or from other nations. Suppose, for example, that a system fails to respond to the aspirations of groups who are becoming increasingly politically conscious and who remain dissatisfied with their lot in society, by denying them meaningful political participation; this will create a potentially disruptive element in the system, and will expose its legitimacy to serious question. By its initial outright denial of citizenship to Negroes, and later by its delayed and grudging admission of them into the system, the United States has created an explosive situation of this kind.

Black Americans were released from slavery only by the coercion of the United States government during the Civil War. For all practical purposes, they were abandoned by the government and the nation at the end of the Reconstruction period as the American people turned to the task of economic modernization. In the 1890s, Negroes were again relegated to servitude when the Southern states adopted, and the Supreme Court and the nation approved, legalized segregation. While Southern society in its social, economic, and political dimensions developed on the foundation of white supremacy, Northern and Western states, satisfied with the unexamined and contradictory principle of separate but equal facilities and opportunities for Negroes, continued their quest for eco-

---

27 Quoted in Lipset, *op. cit.*, p. 43.
28 *Ibid.*, p. 44.

nomic prosperity. Therefore, by virtue of habit and tradition in the South, inattention and insensitivity in the North, and a nineteenth-century interpretation of the constitutional principle of federalism that left the Negro at the mercy of local customs and governments, there was no adequate response by the national political system to black demands for full participation in society. In the South, the Negro was denied the right to vote, barred from public facilities, restricted to segregated and inferior schools, relegated to the bottom of the labor market, scorned and ridiculed in the communications media, and effectively prevented from participating in the life of Southern communities except as a servant. In the North, though not oppressed by legal segregation, black people were faced by de facto situations that were almost as difficult. Forced into urban ghettos and deprived of equal employment opportunities by informal and private discriminatory practices, the Negro became the invisible man. His legal access to suffrage did little to enhance his political power, and he was effectively enslaved at the bottom of the social, economic, and political scale.[29]

During the second quarter of the twentieth century, Negroes began to migrate out of the South in increasing numbers. These migrations reached mammoth proportions by 1950 and, a decade later, a majority of black Americans were living in the urban centers of the North and West. By leaving his traditional home in the South and crowding into Northern cities, the Negro set the stage for the events which in the 1960s would challenge the legitimacy of the political system. Negroes escaped from isolation, from the prevailing culture of white supremacy, and from the fear that kept them "in their place" in Southern communities.[30] Though still isolated in one sense, black people also became part of the national community and were better able to compare their living conditions with those of the white middle classes. Thus freed from the oppressive climate of the South and the fear of "Southern justice," the urban Negro began to articulate his demands and insist that the system respond to his needs. His living conditions were not greatly improved by the migration, but his opportunities for making this fact known to the nation were significantly better. By being exposed to the more open society of the North and West, he began to understand the meaning of progress and came to believe that Negroes had a right to share in the benefits of the "American experiment." Furthermore, he learned to translate his personal grievances into group demands that could be expressed in political terms and injected into the political system.

How did the political system respond to these demands? Prior to the passage of the Civil Rights Act of 1957, the Supreme Court was the only official governmental institution at the national level that was working actively with any

---

[29] For a discussion of the relationship between social position and political participation see Lester W. Milbrath, *Political Participation: How and Why Do People Get Involved in Politics?* (Chicago: Rand McNally & Co., 1965), Chapter 5.

[30] The most complete study of the participation of Negroes in Southern politics is Donald R. Matthews and James W. Prothro, *Negroes and the New Southern Politics* (New York: Harcourt Brace Jovanovich, 1966).

success to bring Negroes into the political system.[31] Responding to cases brought before it initially by the National Association for the Advancement of Colored People, the Court in the 1930s began gradually but persistently to declare unconstitutional state laws and political practices which prevented Negroes from participating fully in the public affairs of the communities in which they lived. Though some action had been taken by the executive branch under the leadership of presidents Franklin Roosevelt and Harry Truman, it was the Supreme Court that first succeeded in removing major obstacles to the development of Negro citizenship. By 1954, the Court had swept away state laws supporting the white primary, restricted housing covenants, unequal wage scales for Negro public school teachers and, finally, segregated public schools.[32]

By the mid-1960s the political system, by virtue of the action of the courts, the Congress, the presidency, and the bureaucracy, had swept away *legal* discrimination in the United States. This response to black demands also embodied a reinterpretation of traditional distinctions between private preferences and the public interest, and thereby established a legal base for an attack against racial discrimination in practically every aspect of American life. This massive response of the system to Negro demands and the effort to admit this group of Americans to full membership in society was taken in the face of determined resistance by conservative and traditional elements in society.

The improvements in the legal status of the Negro would suggest that the responsive capability of the system was sufficient to accommodate the demands and manage the conflict inherent in the situation. This was not the case. Great as the response was, it was too little and perhaps too late. Delayed or grudging admission can be more dangerous to the legitimacy of the system than outright denial of membership because groups that are given nothing and have no hope of improving themselves are less dangerous than groups which are led to believe that they will be admitted but then must wait in frustration because of the slow pace of change.[33] Furthermore, protest movements—once launched—may assume their own momentum, their own reason for being; they may never be satisfied no matter how many of their demands are met.

The response of the system did improve the opportunities for educated, middle-class Negroes. But it did not significantly improve the plight of the nation's poor Negroes, who had believed that governmental programs, such as

---

[31] There is a wealth of literature dealing with the role of the Supreme Court in combating racial segregation. For a selection of the leading Supreme Court decisions see Joseph Tussman (ed.), *The Supreme Court on Racial Discrimination* (New York: Oxford University Press, 1963).

[32] See: *Smith* v. *Allwright* 321 U.S. 649 (1944); *Shelley* v. *Kraemer* 334 U.S. 1 (1948); *Alston* v. *School Board of the City of Norfolk* 112F (2d) 992 (1940) (The *Alston* case was decided by the Fourth Circuit Court of Appeals and the Supreme Court approved this decision by refusing a writ of *certiorari*.); *Brown* v. *Board of Education of Topeka* 347 U.S. 483 (1954).

[33] See Pye, *op. cit.,* for a discussion of this point in respect to the frustrations of new nations in the twentieth century beginning the process of modernization.

the War on Poverty, were actually going to benefit them. In 1967, for instance, while this domestic "war" was being waged, blacks constituted 11 percent of the labor force but had only 6 percent of the professional and technical jobs, 3 percent of the managerial ones, and 6 percent of the positions in the skilled trades. Their median income was only 58 percent that of whites in equivalent jobs. In housing, approximately 1.7 million black families—that is, 29 percent of the total—lived in substandard housing; 28 percent were overcrowded. In cities, 15 percent had no hot water and shared bathrooms with other families; 21 percent had neither bathtubs nor showers.[34] All in all, while white America was living well and just beginning to grumble about the war in Vietnam, the black community was living in a depression which, if it had happened to white families, would have been considered a national disgrace demanding immediate attention.

Since the end of World War II, three factors have prevented the massive response called for by the situation: the Cold War, the nature of the political system itself, and the insensitivity of the majority of the American people to the true nature of the problem. The postwar administrations concentrated on foreign policy, which diverted their attention and national resources from domestic problems; anti-communism was a greater passion than the fight against racial segregation. Even after the Supreme Court brought the issue before the conscience of the nation in 1954, foreign policy problems continued to dominate the attention of the government: the change from bombers to missiles, the space race, and after 1965, the expensive Vietnamese war which eventually reached a cost of $20 billion a year. Second, one of the principal characteristics of the American policy-making process is incremental change. Because of the strategic position of the South in Congress, civil rights legislation made little progress until the first confrontations in the late 1950s. Street demonstrations—some of which resulted in violence—were needed to trigger the nation's attention, presidential leadership, and congressional action in the late 1950s and early 1960s.

Yet, the fundamental reason for the political system's inadequate response would seem to be "white racism."[35] The white middle classes, who support the system and, more than any other group, shape its policies, plus the interest groups, which wield the greatest influence in domestic affairs, do not really appreciate the problems plaguing the Negro masses. The frequently heard question, "What else do Negroes want?" reveals this lack of appreciation. The white middle classes, who have always profited from their membership in the system, do not comprehend the depth of the feelings of those who remain outside. They do not appreciate the rejection felt by black people due to the slow pace of reform. The fact that most whites continue to attribute black riots to

---

[34] *Newsweek* (November 20, 1967), pp. 41–42.

[35] See Hugh Davis Graham and Ted Robert Gurr, *Violence in America, Historical and Comparative Perspectives: A Report to the National Commission on the Causes and Prevention of Violence, June 1969* (New York: The New American Library, 1969).

"trouble-makers," instead of seeing them as essentially a protest against economic poverty, slum conditions, and above all the dehumanization of the Negro, testifies to white lack of comprehension, if not hostility. "Why don't they work their way up instead of wanting handouts?" "Why don't they keep their children in their own neighborhood schools instead of sending them where they are not wanted and forcing our children to go to schools they don't want to attend?" Such questions reveal the whites' wish that Negroes would stop being so "pushy" and settle back into their former, more passive status. It also reveals that white America does not seem ready to make either the material commitments or psychological adjustments to launch large-scale programs to end racial injustice.

The hope and promise embodied in the *Brown* decision was one thing; fulfillment of these promises was something else again. Realization in a practical and meaningful sense could only follow drastic changes—indeed, revolutionary changes—in the social and cultural habits of whites. The discriminatory laws held unconstitutional were, after all, only the symptoms of deeply held attitudes and values prejudicial to the full participation of Negroes in public life. As the decade of the fifties, which had begun so hopefully, moved toward its close, the patience of those blacks whose expectations had risen began to wear thinner. Nor was this a matter of disappointed hopes only; for almost 170 years, the United States had failed blacks, even when, as after the Civil War, it had seemed to promise better days. The principal reason for the increasing indignation and outrage was the continuing contrast between black and white life-styles and standards of living in a supposedly "affluent society." With young college students leading the way, the Negro's demand for his fair share of the American dream developed a sense of immediacy and ultimately found its way into the streets.

The adoption of methods of physical persuasion in the form of sit-ins, demonstrations, freedom marches, and civil disobedience increased the tempo of the controversy and raised the stakes of the game. While the national government, many political leaders, and some segments of the white community responded with sympathy and understanding and called for greater haste in righting old wrongs, the attitudes of many whites hardened; some whites resorted to violence in order to prevent meaningful change. In conservative and traditional circles, resistance to change became an article of faith and a sign of patriotism. The inability of additional court decisions and numerous civil rights bills passed by Congress to deal with the roots of the problem, and the continuing resistance of many whites to further concessions, only served to polarize the situation. As the Negro moved closer to some of his goals during the Kennedy and Johnson years, the narrowing gap between the remaining restrictions and the fulfillment of his rights became more and more frustrating. In these circumstances, Negro leaders pledged to nonviolence were not always able to control their followers in the slums. "Thinking black" and "black power" represented the mood of the new younger and angrier Negro leaders such as Malcolm X who increasingly shaped public discussion of what was to be done;

the Kings, Wilkinses, and Youngs now had competition for leadership. Whites pledged to violence to preserve segregation complicated the efforts of public authorities (where those authorities did not condone or actively support such violence) to manage and control the growing unrest.

By the middle 1960s, the hopelessness and frustration of Negroes in the urban slums provided a fertile recruiting ground for the Negro spokesmen who had abandoned hope and were calling for the use of violence and the destruction of the system itself. Thus, the nature of the protest began to shift again. The inability or unwillingness of the system to respond to the true scope of the problem and the unwillingness of the white community to accept fundamental changes—symbolized by the assassination of Martin Luther King, the leading voice of nonviolence—created a situation in which the system itself, rather than the inequities or discriminatory policies produced by the system, came under attack. The seriousness of the racial crisis in America and the decreasing confidence of blacks in the United States were underscored by the urban riots in 1966 and 1967.

> . . . the Los Angeles riot and the others like it stem from the widespread alienation of lower-class Negroes from American society. Rioting seems not to be directed toward any particular civil rights objective; rather it is an unorganized spontaneous lashing out at "the system." The destruction of property and the attacks on police suggest a desire to destroy what ghetto residents cannot control. The burning, demolition, and looting of property is symbolic of the have-not frustration felt by ghetto dwellers, and the violence directed at the police expresses resentment at the symbols of control over their lives. Thus they [the rioters] display their feelings of powerlessness and resentment that their lives are shaped by masters over whom they have no control whatever.[36]

This challenge to the legitimacy of the political system posed by the new, more militant, black leaders must be kept in perspective. The great majority of Negro Americans abide by the law, support the system at least tacitly, and make no efforts to disrupt the orderly processes of society. But they, too, in increasing numbers will question the legitimacy of a system which responds so reluctantly to their request for full participation—particularly as the percentage of blacks in the population rises from 10 to 20 percent and the vast majority of blacks remains at the bottom of American society, beyond the help of government programs and steady, meaningful, well-paying work. The membership of the Black Panther party may be small, but its leaders probably speak for more blacks than is generally believed. In any event, the Panthers have come to overshadow other prominent organizations, such as the Student Nonviolent

---

[36] Duane Lockard, *Toward Equal Opportunity* (New York: Macmillan Co., 1968), p. 141.

Coordinating Committee and the Congress of Racial Equality, which have increasingly turned away from the system.

The ultimate question, therefore, is whether this country has the will to remove the obstacles preventing full black participation in the life of the nation. Unless it has, the alienation that now afflicts a militant minority will spread with dire consequences. If one were black, one might at times wonder if America would ever live up to her professions of virtue, for in a ten-day period in the middle of May, 1970, one could read the following items in the newspapers: in Augusta, Georgia, six blacks were shot in the back; four of the men were bystanders at a riot which followed the death of a Negro youth in jail. In Jackson, Mississippi, two black students were killed and nine wounded when state police, without apparent provocation, shot a volley of 200 shots into a crowd of students in front of a girls' dormitory. And in Chicago, where a Black Panther leader had earlier been killed by the police in what had been officially described as a gun battle with armed Panthers, a grand jury found that only one bullet had been fired at the forces of "law and order."

In a speech some time after his retirement, former Chief Justice Earl Warren summed up the whole issue by speaking, as usual, to the point:

> We are, indeed, in a crisis. We have had many crises in prior years, but none within the memory of living Americans which compares with this one. A number of factors contribute to it—war; inflation; unemployment with resulting poverty; a deterioration of our environment; an atmosphere of repression; and a divisiveness in our society to a degree of intensity that has not been equaled in the past hundred years.
>
> There are many causes of the crisis, but none, I believe, as basic as our neglect in reaching the ideal we fashioned for ourselves in the Declaration of Independence that "All men are created equal; that they are endowed by their Creator with certain inalienable rights; that among these are life, liberty, and the pursuit of happiness."[37]

Crises of Legitimacy

Crises of legitimacy are the most dangerous threat to the unification of a political system because they challenge the right of the system to exist. The legitimacy of a system can be jeopardized in several ways. The Civil War, which reversed the process of political unification for a time, stemmed from a quarrel over the authority of the government to regulate a highly controversial policy area. The legitimacy of the Union was also threatened by the uncertain status of

[37] *The New York Times,* May 16, 1970.

dissent and criticism during the early days of the Republic, and the failure of the system to allow full participation by Negroes in public life well into the mid-twentieth century. But crises of legitimacy need not be generated directly by disputes over authority and participation. In the American experience, crises of legitimacy have been caused by two other forms of disagreement: (1) widespread differences of opinion among the elites or political activists about the nature of governmental institutions and the procedural rules governing the conduct of politics; and (2) political alienation[38] which causes many citizens to believe that their government—the "Establishment"—has nothing to do with them or offer them because the political system is a closed entity, and is designed to prevent any changes in either the goals of society or the procedures used to define and pursue those goals.[39] Quite clearly, questions of authority and participation are involved in such disputes. But these disputes concern the fundamental character of the political system and go well beyond the questions of what the government can do and who can participate.

The first type of dispute is best illustrated by the controversy surrounding the adoption of the Constitution in 1789, when differences of opinion about the fundamental character of the new political order almost prevented its creation. The second type of disagreement leading to political alienation in which citizens reject the system as evil was more severe in the late 1960s and early 1970s than at any other time since the Civil War.[40]

1. Disagreement about the Fundamental Character of the Political Order

By the end of the Revolution, the American people were moving toward nationhood, but there was no consensus about the kind of government that would replace the authority of the British Crown. The ties that bound Americans

---

[38] Robert Lane has defined political alienation this way: political alienation refers to a person's sense of estrangement from politics and government of his society. It may be taken to mean a feeling that these public matters are not "my affairs," that the government is not "my government," that the Constitution is not "my Constitution." In this sense, it is a disidentification. It implies more than disinterest; it implies a rejection. *Political Ideology* (New York: The Free Press, 1962), pp. 161–162.

[39] These two typologies are taken from Havens, *op. cit.,* Chapter 2.

[40] We draw a distinction here between political and cultural alienation. The culturally alienated person simply withdraws from society; he becomes a social dropout and attempts to live his life according to his own private values. This form of rejection does not threaten the legitimacy of the political system because the culturally alienated do not point at the political system as the villain and attempt to change it. The politically alienated person accepts society and wants to remain within it, but he rejects the government because he sees it as the cause of the evils of society. He therefore desires to change the political system. The existence of alienated groups in a society does not threaten the legitimacy of a political system by definition: a crisis of legitimacy exists only when these groups refuse to be bound by the policies of the government or attempt to change the system by using methods inconsistent with the accepted rules of the game.

to their individual states were much stronger than those that bound them to a single nation or to a single government. The quarrel with England did not begin because of great groundswells of sentiment calling for independence and the creation of a new and sovereign nation. It was initially an effort on the part of the colonists to regain and protect what they believed to be their rights as Englishmen. The sentiment that culminated in the writing of the Declaration of Independence only developed after the conflict was well under way. As is frequently the case in military conflicts, the war developed its own reason for being and did not become a War of Independence until the British were on the verge of abandoning their halfhearted effort to restore their authority in America.

Many Americans did not support the war. Others actively assisted the British in their efforts to put down the insurgency. But life in America was developing in its own direction; social, political, and economic institutions, though similar to their counterparts in English society, were becoming distinctly American.[41] Although the colonists who joined the effort against the British had no long-range political objectives, the war gave them a common cause and served to create national unity. Through Committees of Correspondence and through the First and Second Continental Congresses, Americans began working together in crude governmental institutions that encouraged a unified effort against the British. The Second Continental Congress in 1776 approved a set of proposals—the Articles of Confederation—designed to legalize and formalize the governmental structures and procedures that had developed informally during the struggle against England. Though not ratified by all the states until 1781, the Articles of Confederation were designed to provide some semblance of unity and organization in the efforts against the British. The Articles created a legal government in America for the first time; it was separate and distinct from the authority of England. They represent the first Constitution of the new nation that was gradually coming into being.[42]

This government was in essence a "league of friendship" resting upon the individual states. Its authority was not extended directly to the people of the several states. Political power remained in the hands of the political leaders who controlled state governments and, at the end of the war, very few of these men had much sympathy for the creation of a national government. The people remained loyal to their own state governments and tended to be jealous of their newly won independence. Congress, the only institution created by the Articles, was a unicameral legislative body with insufficient powers to govern. It could not levy taxes, enforce its own legislation, or regulate interstate commerce. The

---

[41] See Louis B. Wright, *The Cultural Life of the American Colonies, 1607–1763* (New York: Harper & Row, Publishers, 1957), and Vernon Louis Parrington, *The Colonial Mind, 1620–1800* (New York: Harcourt Brace Jovanovich, 1927).

[42] For an account of the nation during the period of the Articles of Confederation see Merril Jensen, *The New Nation: A History of the United States during the Confederation, 1781–1789* (New York: Alfred A. Knopf, 1950).

Articles did not create either executive or judicial institutions; thus the new government could not deal effectively with many political and economic problems that immediately beset the nation. Congress could not prevent the states' tariff wars with one another, could not negotiate commercial treaties with foreign governments very effectively because it had no power to compel the states to respect such agreements, could not easily borrow money in foreign markets because its inability to tax the people made it a poor financial risk, and could not effectively muster the resources of the nation to protect itself from foreign intervention. Nevertheless, as an initial step toward union of the states, the Articles represent a vital step in the unification of the American political system. The government created by the Articles was not strong or effective, but it was legal. And this government proved to be an important step toward the creation of a truly national government resting on the American people rather than on the American states.

A movement to revise the Articles of Confederation began almost immediately after their ratification in 1781. A constitutional convention finally met in Philadelphia in 1787 to consider revisions of the Articles. This convention did not meet in response to widespread public demands for a greater degree of national unity under a strong, centralized government. It came about because of the continuous demands of a small group of political leaders who felt strongly that the government was too weak to deal with the problems confronting the nation. They wanted a government that could command the loyalty of the people, control commerce among the states, and strengthen the nation in the eyes of the world, both for political and commercial reasons. Numerous efforts had been made after 1781 to have Congress summon a constitutional convention, but these had not been successful. Congress agreed to call the convention only after it became obvious that it would meet regardless of congressional support.

Delegates attending the convention were authorized by the states only to revise the Articles of Confederation. And the Articles could be revised only by the unanimous consent of the states. Rhode Island did not even bother to send delegates. Thus, the convention could not legally change the existing constitution. Among the delegates there was no common agreement about what specific changes should be made, though there was a recognition that those who had called the convention generally wanted a stronger national government. The delegates had no authority to discard the Articles of Confederation and write a completely new constitution. But when the first proposals for change were submitted for discussion it was clear that this was the intention.

These first proposals called for a highly centralized national government resting directly on the people rather than on the states.[43] The Virginia Plan

---

[43] Our discussion of the Constitutional Convention is drawn from Alfred H. Kelly and Winfred A. Harbison, *The American Constitution: Its Origins and Development,* 3rd ed. (New York: W. W. Norton, 1963), Chapters 4 and 5.

proposed a national government composed of a bicameral legislature, a national executive, and a national judiciary. The members of the lower house of Congress were to be elected by the people and the members of the upper chamber were to be chosen by the lower house from a list of nominees submitted by the state legislatures. Congress would select the national executive, define the extent of its authority in respect to the states, and determine in what areas the states could exercise their authority. It could also disallow state legislation and coerce the states if they failed to fulfill their responsibilities under the Constitution. In short, the Virginia Plan proposed a drastic change in the political system. It called for an end to state sovereignty and the creation of a truly national government. It clearly focused the issue which was to dominate the convention, nationalism versus state sovereignty.

The Virginia Plan was discussed at length in the Committee of the Whole, and several changes were made. The idea of allowing members of the lower house of Congress to select members of the upper house was not popular and was abandoned. It was replaced by a provision calling for the election of the upper house by the state legislatures. The crucial aspect of the Virginia Plan was its method of apportioning the two legislative chambers. Delegates from the larger states favored the Virginia Plan because it called for proportionate representation in both houses of Congress, with the people being represented, rather than the states. Delegations from smaller states insisted on an arrangement that preserved the equality of the states. Though there were other important issues at stake in the convention, this issue proved the most divisive. When the discussions in the Committee of the Whole ended, the large states had won the day. The committee report called for proportionate representation in both chambers, with the lower house being elected by the people and the upper house chosen by the state legislatures.

Before the Virginia Plan came to the floor of the convention for discussion and action the delegates from the small states introduced an alternate proposal, the New Jersey Plan. In essence, this plan called for some modifications of the Articles of Confederation. It was an effort to prevent the creation of a highly centralized government which would be supreme over state governments. Its most important provisions called for the preservation of state equality in Congress and the establishment of a national executive subject to state control. When this plan was voted down in committee, the conflict between nationalism and state sovereignty—that is, between a centralized national government resting on the people and a national government of limited power resting on the states—was brought to the floor of the convention.

Clearly, the delegates did not agree on what the fundamental character of the new political order should be. Most delegates favored a stronger government than the one existing under the Articles. But they were in basic disagreement about the structure of the new government and the proper role of the states. Discussions on the floor became bitter; the convention deadlocked and nearly floundered on the issue of nationalism versus state sovereignty. Finally, a special committee was set up to work out a compromise. It recommended that the lower house be elected by the people on the basis of proportionate representation and that each state should select two members to sit in the upper chamber. Though this compromise "was regarded by the nationalists as a distinct setback to their cause,"[44] the recommendation was approved. This removed the major stumbling block before the convention, and the delegates were able to work out additional compromises over other points of disagreement.[45]

The Constitution was finally completed and signed. Not everybody was happy about what had been produced. Some delegates left Philadelphia in the midst of the proceedings, and others refused to sign the finished document. Some of those who had worked most diligently to create a strong central government signed the Constitution in a spirit of resignation in the belief that anything was an improvement over the Articles of Confederation. The delegates were practical politicians trying to produce a Constitution that would be ratified by the states. Though strong views had been expressed, and opinions had polarized for a time around the issue of nationalism and state sovereignty, in the end the spirit of compromise had prevailed. John P. Roche has written that

> The Framers were busy and distinguished men, anxious to get back to their families, their positions, and their constituents, not members of the French Academy devoting a lifetime to a dictionary. They were trying to do an important job, and do it in such a fashion that their handiwork would be acceptable to very diverse constituencies. No one was rhapsodic about the final document, but it was a beginning, a move in the right direction, and one they had reason to believe the people would endorse.[46]

The Framers, in short, had produced a Constitution that was a "mixed bag" with a little in it for everybody.[47] It did not preserve the principle of legislative supremacy embodied in the first version of the Virginia Plan and did not preserve the principle of state sovereignty called for by the New Jersey Plan. Legislative supremacy never would have been accepted by the states, and

---

[44] *Ibid.*, p. 129.

[45] The dispute over the nature of the national executive was resolved through a compromise that provided for the election of the president by an electoral college rather than directly by the people or by Congress. And the dispute over whether or not to count slaves in determining the number of seats each state should have in the House of Representatives was resolved by deciding that three-fifths of the slaves should be counted. This purely arbitrary figure was used only because it could be agreed upon.

[46] John P. Roche, "The Founding Fathers: A Report on a Caucus in Action," *American Political Science Review* (March 1961), p. 813.

[47] For an account of the "mixed" ideas of justice, liberty, and general welfare embodied in the Constitution see: Eidelberg, *op. cit.*, Chapter 11.

preservation of state sovereignty would have condemned the new government to weakness and ineffectiveness. The Constitution spoke about "We the people of the United States"; it implied that the people were being united under one government. More than anything else, the Constitution created a more permanent union of the states, leaving many of the problems of national unification to be worked out later. The Constitution "was a patchwork sewn together under the pressure of both time and events by a group of extremely talented democratic politicians."[48] It did not please many people at the time, and it did not provide a foolproof formula for solving the nation's problems. Nevertheless, it represents the most important step taken by American political leaders toward centralizing the government and unifying the American people. The Constitution provided a legal and philosophical framework within which the process of political unification could occur.

Political unification, however, is a historical process. It does not happen just because political leaders sign a Constitution.[49] The signing of the Constitution was an important step, but a long and tortuous process of negotiation had been required before this could occur. The convention had almost collapsed because of the absence of consensus on the nature of the new government. The delegates had been sensitive to the political interests within their states, and the conflicts within the convention reflected these diverse interests. The signing of the Constitution did not resolve these conflicts, and the degree of disagreement in the country at large about the nature of the proposed government became obvious when the Constitution was sent to the states for ratification. The controversy that broke out in the ratifying conventions in the various states reveals the intensity of these disagreements and indicates how narrow the margin of victory was.

The convention agreed that the Constitution should be ratified by *ad hoc* state conventions and that the Constitution would go into effect after nine states had approved it. Even though this method was clearly illegal, it was adopted because it seemed the best method for getting the Constitution ratified. The Articles of Confederation required (1) that all amendments be submitted to the states by Congress and (2) that the states unanimously approve each amendment. Had the convention used the prescribed methods, ratification would have been significantly less likely. Also, had the Constitution been submitted to state legislatures for ratification rather than special conventions, its chances for approval would have been smaller. The Constitution proposed drastic changes in the political system at the expense of state governments, and state legislatures would have been less favorably disposed toward these changes than special conventions called for the express purpose of approving the document.

The deadlock in the convention was the first stage of this crisis of legitimacy;

---

48 Roche, *op. cit.,* p. 815.

49 For an excellent account of formal law as it relates to justice, equality, and politics see Carl Joachim Friedrich, *The Philosophy of Law in Historical Perspective,* 2nd ed. (Chicago: University of Chicago Press, 1963).

the controversy during the ratification process was the second. The deadlocks in the convention were resolved through secret bargaining; delegates were thus able to reach agreement without being pressured by outside forces or having to defend their decisions in public. The ratification stage was different because the conventions were not secret, and in several states, well-organized forces were determined to defeat the Constitution—not just change some of its provisions.

Eight states ratified the Constitution quickly and with little difficulty: in one of these states, Massachusetts, the vote was close. In New Hampshire, the ninth state to ratify, the debates were intense and ratification succeeded by a narrow margin. The real tests came in New York and Virginia, because their political importance, size, populations, and geographical locations made their membership in the Union a necessity. Even though the necessary nine states had ratified the Constitution, the Union would have been a fiction without these two important states.[50]

In the Virginia convention, Patrick Henry and other opponents of the Constitution made a major effort to prevent ratification. They branded the writers of the Constitution as criminal conspirators, argued that the new government would destroy the liberties of the people and the authority of the state governments, and predicted that the aristocratic features of the Constitution would ultimately lead to monarchy and despotism in America. They objected to the legal details of the structure of the proposed government, to the powers that had been granted to the institutions of national government, and to the political principles upon which many sections of the Constitution rested.[51] The proponents of the Constitution, led by James Madison, defended the Constitution skillfully, and it was ratified by the narrow margin of 89 to 79.

In New York, the outcome was in even greater doubt. Governor George Clinton, an opponent of the new Constitution, delayed calling the convention for months. When he finally called it, delegates known to oppose the Constitution won over two thirds of the convention seats. Virginia was now in the Union, which meant that ten states had ratified the Constitution. Only New York, North Carolina, and Rhode Island remained outside the Union. The Union had become a reality, but the entry of New York was essential if the new nation was to have a viable beginning. Governor Clinton, who was president of the Convention, was one of the leaders of the fight against the Constitution. Alexander Hamilton, who himself had serious reservations about the new government, led the supporters of the Constitution. Just as the skills of Madison had won the day in Virginia, the effective floor management of Hamilton overcame the negative sentiment in the New York convention. The Constitution was finally ratified by the close vote of 30 to 27. The strength of the opposition forces and the intensity of their objections to the character of the new government was so strong, however, that

---

[50] Roche, *op. cit.,* p. 814.

[51] For a good summary of these debates, see Kelly and Harbison, *op. cit.,* pp. 151–166.

the convention felt it necessary to adopt unanimously a resolution calling for a new constitutional convention to reconsider the whole matter.[52]

Two states remained out of the Union. North Carolina did not make its decision until November, 1789, and Rhode Island, the one state which did not help write the Constitution, rejected the document in town meetings when it was first considered. On May 29, 1790, however, in a convention called to reconsider the matter, it reversed itself and became a part of the United States by the narrow margin of 34 to 32.

Nation-building is always a time of crisis. Attitudes and political values are not well developed, and behavioral patterns are not well established. Debates and discussions are focused on the fundamental character of the political system, and opinions easily become polarized around philosophical or ideological positions. During constitution-making, the polarization of opinion threatens the process of negotiation and makes compromise difficult. It can become disruptive if the participants are closely identified with geographic regions or social and economic classes. It can become dangerous if participants are supported by military forces or dedicated mass followings. Each provision of a proposed constitution must be weighed and balanced against the strength of clashing political ideas and interests. Inclusion or exclusion of particular provisions may depend upon their chances of being approved by the people rather than their logic and consistency. This can destroy the system if opposing forces are unable or unwilling to compromise their ideas and objectives to achieve unification.

In the United States, the initial crisis of legitimacy was a "straightforward constitutional problem," as is often true in new states.[53] It was a time of crisis because the outcome of the controversy surrounding the adoption of the new Constitution would determine whether a new government strong enough to deal with the nation's problems would be accepted as legitimate. The opponents of the Constitution attempted to prevent the creation of the new government; they did not offer feasible alternatives for dealing with the political and economic problems besetting the new nation. Thus, the choice was not between two acceptable forms of government; rather it was a choice between adopting a constitution offering a legal and political framework within which a truly national government could unify the nation, or retaining state sovereignty and, therefore, obstructing the processes of political unification.

The Constitution was written, signed, and accepted because American political leaders were able to compromise their ideas and interests. They were able to reach at least a minimal agreement on the basic structure of the new government, the status of the states in the Union, the basis of representation, the means for filling public offices, and the status of minority groups. Ratification did not permanently legitimatize the new government. But it did indicate that the new nation had survived its first crisis of legitimacy.

---

[52] *Ibid.,* p. 159.
[53] Pye, *op. cit.,* p. 63.

2. Disagreement about
the Organization of Society

Legitimacy can also be endangered by widespread questioning of the fundamental political organization of society. The movement generally referred to as the *New Politics* (if it can even be referred to as an organized movement) seems to represent the political manifestation of much of the confusion, disorder, disruption, and alienation present in American society in the 1970s. The New Politics in fact represents more of a mood than an organization. Organizationally it is badly split between moderates and radicals, and the radicals spend as much time disputing among themselves as opposing the system. Yet, the New Politics testifies to the diffuse and dimly visible hopes and aspirations of many American citizens who are dissatisfied with American society and the American political system. They see the needs of racial minorities, the poor, and the unfortunate going unattended; the environment being polluted by industrialization; and the problems of overpopulation being ignored. They are morally revolted by the war in Indochina. They generally see our far-flung global commitments and involvements as a corruption of America's moral mission in the world—to make itself a truly democratic and just society at home which could stand as a moral example to the whole world. In short, they see their government functioning in traditional and outmoded ways which they believe to be incapable of coping with the problems that plague America and the world.

Most of the dissatisfied reformers simply want the political system changed so it can function more in accordance with the purposes they think it ought to pursue at home and abroad. They are uneasy with the Old Politics and call for something new—even though they are often vague about the alternate means they would adopt to attain justice, peace, and brotherhood. They offer little in the way of a program or an ideology. Rather, they articulate a feeling that the system—the "Establishment" or the "power structure"—is hypocritical because of the huge gap between its aspirations and achievements; consequently, the system is condemned as unworthy of their trust and support.

This growing dissatisfaction with the American political system became clearly evident by the mid-1960s. Its main impetus was the civil rights movement. The quest of black Americans for full participation in the system, and the resistance—both within and outside of government—to these efforts to change our traditional way of life, exposed the rigidity of American society and American government at all levels. The demands that political action be taken to eradicate racial injustice expanded into wider demands that the government act with dispatch in dealing with urban blight, poverty, inadequate educational opportunities, unemployment, and the like. The response of the political system to these demands, particularly the national government during the early days of President Johnson's administration, was positive and significant when viewed in historical perspective. But not enough was done; hopes and expectations remained unfulfilled. Mass demonstrations, urban and campus riots, arson in the cities, and mass marches on the seats of government increased. And the climate in the nation was affected by the increased intensity and hostility of political debates concerning these demands on the system and by the wide and rapid dissemination of these debates by television.

Dissent and conflict over domestic issues, particularly civil rights and poverty, grew each year during the 1960s. After 1965, with the Dominican intervention and the escalation of the war in Vietnam, opposition to the government's international policies began to intensify. By 1968, the conflict over domestic and foreign policies, especially the frustrating war of attrition in Vietnam, had broadened into something that resembled a general opposition movement against the government itself. By the time of the Tet offensive of that year and the later presidential primary campaign, opposition to the war had grown to such proportions, particularly among young people in the colleges and universities, that this issue dominated the national scene.

The stalemate on the battlefields of South Vietnam, long lists of casualties, the daily "body counts," and the absence of any signs that the conflict would soon end contributed to a general malaise among the American people. The war seemed to "poison our politics" and brought to the fore all the things that divided us as a people: the bitterness over the war; the disorder in the cities; the attacks upon the government by many liberal intellectuals; the extra strains of the election year; the serious cleavages in the major political parties, especially in the Democratic party; the birth of a third political party whose leader, an out-and-out segregationist, gave voice to the frustrations of many upset by the relative liberalness of government policies; and the development of an active and vocal student protest movement which seemed to provide a catalyst for every form of dissatisfaction existing in the nation—all these things intensified a feeling of political alienation among a sizable minority of the American people.

Although the beginning of the Paris peace talks with the North Vietnamese and the election of Republican Richard Nixon as president quieted things down somewhat for a while, the mood of uneasiness about the political system and its ability to cope with the nation's problems did not go away. Indeed, Nixon's "Vietnamization" program, his apparent "Southern [electoral] strategy" on integration and Supreme Court appointments, and his decision in April 1970, to send American troops into Cambodia to destroy Vietcong and North Vietnamese staging areas only stoked this mood.

Among the disenchanted elements in American society, many of whom are young, are some revolutionaries who are so alienated from the political system that they want to destroy it by whatever means are necessary. They believe that it has not only failed to fulfill the American dream but is incapable of doing so. More important, they regard the political system as the cause of America's problems rather than as a means of solving them. In their view, the system (and not just its current members or policies) is illegitimate; it is wrong and unworthy of support. Consequently, changing those in office or altering the direction of public policy is not the answer; replacing the ancien régime is the only way to create a society in which all men can live in justice, brotherhood, and peace.

The young revolutionaries committed to changing the political system by violence represent only a small fraction of those who are "turned off" by the system and want major changes. But their numbers noticeably increased in the late 1960s and early 1970s. The most militant elements of the Black Panther party and some elements of the Students for a Democratic Society, such as the Weathermen, as well as such other organizations as the Progressive Labor party, fall into this category. The young Negro militants in the Black Panther party have simply given up on the system because they see it as oppressive and impossible to change without violence. Their grievances are those that most black Americans have against the system; their use of violence—or, more correctly, their fervent pledges to use violence against the system—represents action based on despair. Use of violence against the system by the young white radicals in SDS and by those on college and university campuses who hold no formal affiliation with any organization is, however, much more complex because they have benefited and continued to benefit, at least materially, from the way the system operates.

Who are the young radicals?[53] Most student activists are idealists who were raised in upper-middle-class families. Their parents tend to be liberal, concerned with moral values, and active in politics. The discipline of their children was based on reason and persuasion. A great deal of emphasis was placed on the importance of ideas, on the expression of feeling, and on humanitarian values and service to others. Independent thought and action by their children was encouraged. Thus, student activists tend to be idealists who share the value systems of their parents. In short, the student activists, when compared with student populations generally, are elites who are vitally concerned with moral issues.[54] They are not "hooligans" or "bums," even though their hair, dress, and behavior at times suggests to their more conservative elders that this may be the case.

Why do such students revolt against their political institutions and against the system itself? One explanation is that the student revolt is an "Oedipal rebellion" in which students act out their hostilities against their fathers by attacking "authority figures like college presidents, generals, the Establishment, and government policies and leaders."[55] Another theory suggests that student

---

[53] Our discussion of the young radicals is drawn from the major study of Kenneth Keniston, *Young Radicals: Notes on Committed Youth* (New York: Harcourt Brace Jovanovich, 1968).

[54] Kenneth Keniston, "Notes on Young Radicals," *Change* (November-December 1969), p. 30.

[55] *Ibid.,* p. 28.

radicals are "red diaper babies," the children of yesterday's radicals who are merely carrying on where their parents left off. A third theory blames the problem on Dr. Benjamin Spock. Today's radicals allegedly were raised in permissive families where they never learned self-restraint, limitations on their behavior, or respect for authority. In short, they are "brats" who have never learned to respect their elders. A fourth explanation suggests that student revolts are a reaction against "historical irrelevance." Students are in rebellion against the technology of post-industrial society. They see man being replaced by machines and they see no place for themselves in this kind of society. They feel irrelevant, obsolete, and they lash out against society in protest. This explanation views student revolt as a "counter-revolution" that seeks to restore the humanitarian values of an earlier day.[56] But the radicalism of today's youth is a complex phenomenon, and these explanations do not really seem adequate.

Professor Kenneth Keniston has suggested an explanation which seems to provide the best clue to an understanding of the radicalism of contemporary youth.[57] The affluence of the United States and other western societies, he argues, has postponed the time when young people must enter the adult world and become actively involved in social, economic, and political institutions. During the Middle Ages, children were brought into the work force by the age of 8, and no stage of life compared to what we today call adolescence. The adolescent stage of life, in which young people continue in school, developed in the nineteenth and twentieth centuries when the industrial revolution created the wealth to make this possible and created jobs for which advanced education was needed to provide technical skills. In the mid-twentieth century, the success of the industrial revolution in many parts of the world, particularly in the United States, has created, on the one hand, such a high degree of affluence and, on the other, a need for highly trained professional personnel. In some cases, the period of adolescence plus postadolescence extends almost to the age of 30. The postadolescent stage of life may be called the stage of "youth."

Youth is a period in which young people of middle and upper-middle-class families continue their formal education, deferring the day they assume responsible positions in society. During this period they remain uninvolved in adult institutions and do not therefore develop positive attachments to these institutions. More important, this extended period of noninvolvement gives students the opportunity to look long and critically at themselves and society. In Keniston's words,

Attendance at a college or university is a major part of this extension, and there is growing evidence that this is, other things being equal, a good thing

---

[56] Kenneth Keniston, "You Have To Grow Up in Scarsdale To Know How Bad Things Really Are," *The New York Times Magazine* (April 27, 1969), pp. 28, 122.

[57] *Ibid.*, pp. 126–130.

for the student. Put in an oversimplified phrase, it tends to free him—to free him from swallowing unexamined the assumptions of the past, to free him from the superstitions of his childhood, to free him to express his feelings more openly and to free him from irrational bondage to authority.[58]

Thus, by extending the period of noninvolvement and nonresponsibility in adult society, by providing colleges and universities which encourage critical and independent thought, and by providing the affluence which has accomplished these things, industrial societies have created conditions that encourage criticism and independence on the part of their young people. In this sense, the success of these societies has generated the criticism and disruptions that, today at least, jeopardize their legitimacy.

Why has freedom to study, think, and criticize led to disapproval, anger, and rejection of existing institutions? This is, in some form or other, the question most often asked by adults who are repelled by the activities of today's young radicals. "How dare they attempt to destroy a system that has given them greater opportunities and advantages than any other generation in history?" The question is a proper one but is not easy to answer. Youths have been "brought up in family environments where abundance, relative economic security, political freedom, and affluence are simply facts of life, not goals to strive for. To such people the psychological imperatives, social institutions, and cultural values of the industrial ethic seem largely outdated and irrelevant to their own lives."[59] Since they have always enjoyed the blessings of industrial society, they view these things not as goals but as *rights* that should be extended to everyone. And they are enraged that many Americans and millions of people elsewhere still live in poverty and are subject to discrimination. Accepting material comforts and equality as rights rather than goals, they condemn the system because it has not yet successfully distributed the benefits of industrial society to all people. Furthermore, they denounce the system because it does not share their goals which are moral and qualitative rather than material and quantitative. They reject the system as immoral and corrupt.

Any effort to defend existing institutions or to persuade the young to restrain their activities or to consider conforming to traditional modes of behavior is rejected out of hand. They regard such efforts as oppression and denounce them as outrageous and authoritarian. Since they view morality, ethics, and humanitarian values as being all on their side, they tend to be arrogant, self-righteous, and uncompromising in their dealings with traditional institutions and authorities.

Keniston suggests that what is occurring on college campuses in the United States and in other western nations today is a fusion of two revolutions, one old

[58] *Ibid.,* p. 124.
[59] *Ibid.*

and familiar, the other new and only dimly understood. The first is the continuation of the industrial revolution with its goals of economic security, expanded political liberties, and social rights. This revolution, which has been in progress for over two centuries, is "in many respects, a *quantitative* revolution. That is, it concerns itself less with the quality of life than with the amount of political freedom, the quantity and distribution of goods, or the amount and level of injustice."[60] The second is the revolution of post-industrial societies, a revolution concerned with the *quality* of life. It is manifested most clearly in the rhetoric and activities of the young radicals. They may be well fed, well clothed, and well housed; they may enjoy a degree of political freedom unequaled anywhere; yet they sense that society and its institutions lack a moral purpose and a concern for the quality of life. They, more than any other group in America, have reaped the benefits of the industrial revolution; nevertheless, they feel that the "humane world" that they desire has not been achieved. These students are the cutting edge of a wider mood of discontent in American society. They have few positive programs to suggest and no ideology to guide their actions. This explains their negativism; they voice their opposition to the existing system because they can more easily identify its wrongs than articulate goals which they only dimly understand.

What are these goals? First, the youth movement rejects materialism and economic prosperity and focuses on the moral qualities of life. It assigns a great deal of importance to the creative, imaginative, and aesthetic aspects of human existence. Second, it rebels against the "melting pot" view of life with its emphasis on uniformity and standardization. It insists that "individuals be appreciated, not because of their similarities or despite their differences, but because they *are* different, diverse, unique, and noninterchangeable."[61] Third, the movement rejects rigidity and favors a society which encourages openness, motion, and continuing human development. Finally, and most importantly from the point of view of the effect of the movement on the legitimacy of the contemporary political system, the young radicals tend to reject centralized authority, be it in the universities or in the government itself, because existing institutions are perceived as morally corrupt. This places the young radicals, both peaceful and violent, squarely in opposition to the forces that govern American society.

Among the moderate wing of the student movement, this suspicion of centralized authority takes the form of demands for greater involvement in the making of decisions that affect their lives, both in education and in politics. In colleges and universities, for example, they insist that their education is not relevant unless they participate fully in all facets of the educational experience. And this means a degree of participation in the operations of the college or

---

[60] *Ibid.*, p. 126.
[61] *Ibid.*

university. Such participation is deemed essential to the emotional, moral, and intellectual growth of the student members of the academic community.

Such participation is not, however, to be confined to the traditional educational process. Many active students demand that all military-related research should be ended and R.O.T.C. should be abolished. Colleges and universities should not support the "war system." On the contrary, they should become a political base from which to attack the *status quo*. This is necessary, it is asserted, because "higher education" cannot remain neutral in the face of compelling social issues; indeed, to be neutral is to accept "the system," at least tacitly. Whether the traditional ideal of the university as an assembly of scholars, who share and create ideas and who provide a broad intellectual atmosphere in which undergraduates can develop their minds, can survive if such demands become compelling and remain insistent is a question for the future.

Perhaps more serious than the demand for the politicization of the universities is the demand for "participatory democracy." The most radical elements in the student movement shout the slogan "All Power to the People," as they march in the streets and across the campus green, often in the light of burning buildings and to the tune of police sirens. The assumption is that "participatory democracy" is a form of government which would cure alienation, set right the nation's social and economic problems, and in general create a morally worthy society. Implicit in this concept of participatory democracy seems to be a rejection of the representative institutions, as methods of managing conflict and making public policy, which have evolved in the democratic political systems of western industrialized nations. A national regeneration, a new unity of people in a society that has moral authority and significance cannot allegedly be achieved through capitalism and bureaucratic government. This is why many young revolutionaries are contemptuous even of the Soviet Union, which they consider "bourgeois," and find themselves drawn to such political leaders as Castro, Ho Chi Minh, and Mao Tse-tung, who have made revolutions and are first-generation leaders of revolutionary countries. These leaders share a highly moralistic political rhetoric and ideology; all of them articulate visions of the New Jerusalem here on earth which they, as rulers in a "participatory democracy," claim they will realize on behalf of the people.

It is surely somewhat ironic to claim that freedom and justice will result from following the examples of leaders of totalitarian states. There have been many such leaders, convinced that they alone knew how to liberate man and achieve the Good Society. Rather than curing the ills of society and clarifying the moral purposes of a united people, the rule of these advocates degenerated into a monopoly of political control by the single party of "true believers," the violation of the dignity of the individual, and the glorification of the state. In the twentieth century, "participatory democracy" has been the rallying cry of those who have destroyed representative institutions and established totalitarian states.

Claiming exclusive possession of truth and morality, they have silenced all who disagree with them.

Nevertheless, the advocacy by radicals of "participatory democracy" should not be confused with the genuine and deeply felt concerns of the young collegiate protesters for the future of the nation and the world. The nature of American society today, and of institutions of higher learning in particular, encourage young people to examine and criticize traditional wisdom and authority, existing institutions, and acceptable methods of change more than in earlier periods. They have been encouraged to think and act independently, and they have done so. In this sense, American society has spawned the very people who present it with the most serious challenge since the Civil War. Many of the young people vitally concerned about the failures of the political system have already rejected the system instead of trying to correct its problems by working within it. In rejecting the legitimacy of the system, they have nothing to lose by disrupting it. In the words of Carl Oglesby, a former president of the Students for Democratic Society, their fundamental revolutionary motive is not to construct a Paradise but to destroy an Inferno.[62] For them, injustice and society are only different words for the same thing, and therefore they have no stake in the system. Yet many more of the disenchanted may give the system "one more chance," to see if it will respond to their aspirations. In the wake of the Cambodian incursion and the shooting of four Kent State students by the Ohio National Guard in the spring of 1970, the first signs of student political activity since the McCarthy campaign of 1968 reappeared as many began to organize for future elections by raising money and campaigning for "peace candidates." Thus, the fundamental questions for the future remained, on one hand, whether students would work through the system and, on the other hand, whether the system would be responsive. The answer to these questions will be critical for the continued legitimacy of the United States.

Political Unification: The Uncertainty of the Future

Political unification in the United States, as in all political systems, is not a condition that, once achieved, remains forever intact. It is a process shaped continuously by social, economic, and political forces which are at work in both the domestic and international environments. The United States achieved political unification once, and thus far has maintained it by effectively coping with a series of political ills that have threatened its existence as a nation. But the future of the Union hinges on factors that we shall consider in the final chapter.

---

[62] Carl Oglesby and Richard Shaull, *Containment and Changes* (New York: The Macmillan Company, 1967), p. 147.

14

The Meaning of the Seventies

The United States entered the 1970s ill at ease with itself and uncharacteristically uncertain about its future. Not since the depression-ridden 1930s had Americans seemed more inclined to ponder and debate the value of their fundamental political institutions or to anticipate the future with more reservation. This mood was sufficiently pervasive to convince most foreign and domestic observers that a shift in the public temperament had occurred. Gone was the optimism, self-confidence, and relative domestic tranquillity that seemed to epitomize the Eisenhower years; the mood of the early 1970s was sober, self-searching, and anxious.

The reasons for this transformation in the national mood are reasonably clear. The legacy of the 1960s had not been peace but the sword. It had been a bitter, divisive decade that destroyed the mood of the Eisenhower years while leaving its own problems and divisions unresolved in the 1970s. The Vietnamese conflict continued—vicious, inconclusive, terribly costly in life and wealth, intensely controversial. Racial unrest, urban violence, poverty, student dissent and environmental pollution, all major problems of the sixties, were still major problems in the early 1970s. Three successive presidents had promised to "get the country moving again," to "build a great society," and to bring us together again," but the grave social ills they professed to alleviate endured, and sometimes worsened. To a people who often advertised, and sometimes flouted, the virtues of their political and economic order, the severity and duration of such problems were bound to be unsettling.

And there were striking, sometimes cruel paradoxes that seemed to hint at something profoundly amiss in the social order. While millions of Americans lived in the squalor and despair of poverty, the Gross National Product was approaching one trillion dollars. The same society possessing the technological sophistication to place the first humans on the moon nonetheless seemed unable to arrest the accelerating destruction of its natural environment. A nation pledged to democracy—one that historically regarded itself as the world's leading democracy—was plagued by strife created by racial discrimination. And many who should have been most content with American life plainly were not. The sons and daughters of the middle class, children of affluence who seemingly had within their grasp wealth, education, and leisure unknown to any previous American generation, often turned upon this American Dream with indifference or contempt—many professed their intention to reconstruct American society until its major social problems were solved.

Looking upon such problems and paradoxes, some thoughtful Americans concluded that the United States lacked not the human material resources to cure its ills but the right political and economic institutions. Thus began—particularly among segments of the young, intellectuals, and minorities—a sweeping evaluation of the American system; it often dwelt upon the inadequacies of American social institutions and values, their contribution to American social ills, and the need to alter American life radically. The response was predictable. Many Americans at all national levels reacted by bitterly condemning such criticism and truculently defending the status quo. Many others were confused or threatened by this attack upon their basic social values and institutions. Some listened and reflected. In any case, debate and disagreement were in the air.

Such events, among others, contributed to what seems the dominant mood of the early 1970s. Running debate about American political and economic institutions and mulling over of the fundamentals of our social life are facts with great consequence for the 1970s. The crucial issue of the seventies will not be whether this searching reappraisal can somehow be stopped—one could as well sweep back the sea. Rather, the question is whether Americans can find realistic, workable solutions to the fundamental issues raised by this debate. Three of these matters seem particularly significant and will be discussed in the remainder of the chapter.

How Much Can Government Do?

Americans today are deeply divided by a conflict of expectations. They disagree, often profoundly and sometimes violently, over how far and how fast the government can go in solving America's social ills. In many respects, this is a crucial issue of the 1970s, for confidence in our fundamental political structures is at stake.

It is this conflict of expectations that feeds the current controversy over the value of existing governmental institutions; disagreements over how far government can go in meeting social problems become arguments over how well existing government serves the people. Continuing public confidence depends upon how well the public believes these institutions handle their social responsibilities. In short, the value Americans place upon their governmental institutions and their willingness to change such institutions seem to flow from concepts of what government can and should do about social ills.

Certainly nothing stimulates current criticism of our political institutions more than a vast impatience with the scope and speed of governmental attacks on social problems. Critics of American government, divided on much else, commonly unite in condemning the government for doing too little about social maladies—the government is too slow, too irresolute, too unimaginative, too conservative. From this impatience frequently follows the charge that the fault lies in the basic institutions themselves; they perform badly, the argument concludes, because they are designed badly.

Criticism of our existing governmental institutions implies a standard for judgment and a basis for comparison. Usually, a vision—in addition to impatience—is the basis for much of the sweeping condemnation. The standard for judgment and comparison is some ideal government in the mind of the critic that is capable of doing what American government allegedly cannot: such a government could resolve to his satisfaction whatever social problems most trouble him and would command whatever powers are needed to produce the social effects most desired. This ideal government may be imagined vaguely or concretely or it may be modeled after another government's arrangements; but its existence in the mind of the critic intensifies his discontent.

No thoughtful person should deny the enormous gravity of our current political problems, nor the need for government to tackle them incisively and comprehensively. Better policies for remedying America's social ills might well be devised; our governmental structures might indeed be improved by alterations that would enhance their ability to handle our pressing social emergencies. Much of the current criticism therefore seems both appropriate and useful.

Yet some criticism seems unwarranted; in fact, it sometimes impedes the government in doing what its critics demand it do. Such criticism springs from an exaggerated concept of how fast social problems can be solved. When grave social maladies persist or fail to yield to complete solutions quickly, the blame often falls upon the government which has allegedly proven its inadequacy; but the inherent difficulty of many special problems—the fact that their complexity may forbid rapid or complete solution—is frequently ignored. Behind this sometimes inflated concept of the speed with which social problems can be handled lie some common traits of the American temperament.

Americans have seldom had a strong sense of history. They are often insensitive to the historically tangled, complex roots of their social problems, unappreciative of the role of time in creating and solving social ills, unreflective about the subleties of social problems.[1] Further, Americans place great confidence in social engineering—they believe that most social problems can be solved if only the right laws, institutional arrangements, or proper talents are brought to bear on the problems. Supporting this confidence, too, is a sometimes battered optimism flowing from a belief in "progress" and the future's promise. For these reasons, among others, the American's sense of social time is compressed: he often thinks in terms of days, months, or years to the solution of problems instead of reckoning in terms of the decades or even generations that may sometimes be necessary. An attitude of "getting things done now" is a healthy, essential goad to attacking social problems resolutely, but it should not always be taken literally. When it becomes a dogma, it inevitably leads to disappointment when many social problems stubbornly refuse to disappear before the onslaught of American impatience.

More than a simple impatience with the pace of social change leads to unreasonable criticism of government, however. Social problems sometimes persist or worsen because Americans take a superficial approach to their solution; it is not the governmental structure, but American concepts of public policy that are often at fault. The American people generally spurn theory, long-range planning, and comprehensive concepts in treating social ills. Political leaders often prefer to deal with social problems piecemeal, creating ad hoc policies under the pressures of the moment; moreover, these policies often deal with the symptoms rather than the cause of social ills. The fault, to be sure, is often practical politics: political leaders anxious to placate public opinion—and thus stay in office—often propose whatever policies they think expedient to satisfy the short-range preferences or anxieties of the public. But the policy style of public officials is also inspired by the American penchant for seeing social problems in relative isolation; this betrays the lack of any overall concepts of how public policy should develop or how social problems are fundamentally related. Often, therefore, criticism of government itself could be better directed at the characteristic American formulation of public policy.

In another respect, also, American discontent with government can be traced more appropriately to the American people themselves. An enfeebled public spirit often hobbles government attack on social problems.[2] The govern-

---

[1] For a brief but excellent discussion of the need to judge governmental effectiveness in terms of longer time periods than Americans customarily accept, see E. E. Schattschneider, *Two Hundred Million Americans in Search of Government* (New York: Holt, Rinehart and Winston, Inc., 1969), Chapter 5.

[2] This argument is reflectively and forcefully presented in Andrew Hacker, *The End of the American Era* (New York: Atheneum, 1970), Chapter 8. Hacker believes that this decline in the public spirit is a crucial factor in what he believes is the decline of the United States as a nation.

ment of the United States frequently can go no further toward solving social problems, nor command more resources or powers for the task, than the American people are willing to concede it. And much of the time, the American people seem to lack a genuine, deep, dependable desire for government to command the full capacities it might to solve American social problems. One reason seems to be that Americans, with some exceptions, are consumed with private concerns, with their quest for material comforts, and with other preoccupations that relegate great social programs through government to an inferior status. This triumph of privatism means that Americans customarily evaluate the worth of governmental demands upon their time and resources in terms of how much they interfere with private pleasures—their private preferences are massive but their public ones are weak. Moreover, most Americans place such importance upon "individuality"—which often means doing what one pleases with as little interference as possible—that they are an extremely difficult people to lead when government does attempt social reform; we are a "nation of 200 million egos."[3] In short, Americans are too often disposed to condemn their government for failures that lie within themselves.

Finally, without minimizing the imperfections of American government, one can reasonably inquire whether a standard of judgment based upon some idealized government is not an illusion. Often, this ideal government turns out to be wholly hypothetical, when critics of existing government reflect carefully upon what inspires their discontent. Such an imaginary government consists of one that will eliminate all social inequalities, one constantly sensitive to reform, one without any self-serving bureaucrats, without the divisions of party spirit, or one that is super efficient. All such images are fictions, concepts of a government that has never existed nor is ever likely to exist. To judge American institutions against such a standard is unrealistic and, when examined, quite unpersuasive.

However, the ideal government sometimes appears more plausible. Rather than being imaginary, it is some aspect of an actual government somewhere else which is used to evaluate American institutions. Yet such a standard can be suspect also, because it is often romanticized aspect of that other government. Consider, for instance, the argument that a communist government such as that of China, North Vietnam, or Cuba might be more desirable because it would destroy gross inequalities of wealth and privilege that the American system allegedly perpetuates. There are, indeed, millions of poor in the United States and great disparities of wealth; our governmental system may conceivably contribute to this condition. It is questionable, however, whether the communist regimes in the developing areas would eliminate inequalities. Within the highly industrialized and urbanized Soviet Union, by comparison, the privileged economic class exists in the form of Communist Party members while many racial, religious, and linguistic groups endure systematic discrimination that keeps them in inferior social positions.

---

[3] The term is found in Hacker, *op. cit.*

In several ways, therefore, these harsh judgments upon the value of existing governmental arrangements seem unreasonable. The intellectual poverty of these arguments is particularly dangerous when such criticism rationalizes the demand that the whole governmental structure be radically recast, perhaps through violent revolution. However, we should not conclude that such demands for change in governmental policies or structures be ignored. Instead, if one recognizes the bad logic inherent in a demand, arguments for change can be based upon more reasonable expectations concerning what government can do— and this may lead to more realistic goals and possibilities for change. Further, to recognize no virtues in our governmental structures is as arbitrary as to admit no weaknesses. If Americans recognize that there are some commendable aspects to our political arrangements, they can maintain the healthy impulse to protect the good while altering the undesirable.

A New Public Philosophy

Even if one dismisses the most irresponsible criticism of American government, the political debates of the seventies still reveal significant problems that need immediate attention. One such problem is our traditional means for making public policy. Many thoughtful observers believe that America's grave social ills can now be met only if Americans gradually develop a new public philosophy—a new concept of what social needs must come first in governmental policy.[4] Further, this may well require some alterations in the traditional procedures through which policies have been made in the past. Many proposals have been made for initiating this change, but the arguments for moving in this new direction can be summarized briefly.

Traditionally, the American philosophy of governmental policy-making emphasizes the right of privately organized groups to participate vigorously at almost all stages of the decision-making process. Indeed, so completely have organized interests entered into federal policy-making that almost all domestic public policies have been materially shaped, if not entirely created, from this interplay of private interests. In such a situation, the government itself very often assumes the role of a referee or a mediator among conflicting interests; playing such a role, the government often strives to create policies that strike a satisfactory compromise between conflicting private interests and restore a measure of political peace among them.

This customary American attitude toward public policy has several significant consequences. Generally, those interests represented by effective pressure organizations and skilled lobbyists enjoy a great advantage in securing govern-

---

[4] For example, see Theodore J. Lowi, *The End of Liberalism* (New York: W. W. Norton and Co., Inc., 1969).

mental attention and benefits—the agenda for governmental action is extremely dependent upon pressure group politics. This sensitivity to pressure politics means that government efforts are unequally divided between the so-called private and public sectors of society. The most effective pressure groups represent private interests and strongly influence the allocating of governmental resources. Conversely, broad public interests often do not receive the attention they deserve because effective lobbyists and pressure organizations are lacking in these areas.

Among private interests, for example, major corporations and their concerns receive great governmental attention. "In about half the economy—that half characterized by the large corporations or where needs of large corporations are being served—production is efficient, men are well paid; for those who belong there is no poverty. In consequence, our supply of automobiles, gasoline, highways, household appliances, detergents, gargles, space vehicles, and weaponry is excellent."[5] But the public sector languishes from governmental inattention. One example is the quality of urban life. "Housing, surface transportation, hospital and health services, street cleaning, police services and the courts, other municipal services, and education are now provided with increasing relative, and often increasing absolute, inefficiency."[6] One explanation for this relative neglect of the public sector is that this area, unlike the private one, relies on government to take action on its own volition, without the prompting and goading of potent pressure groups. Often, therefore, government response is laggard and conservative.

Another consequence of policy making by pressure group politics is that governmental policy is slower, more incremental, and less coherent than it might be. The reason lies in the bargaining inherent to pressure politics and the ad hoc schemes that often emerge. Governmental policy is usually made through attempting to satisfy the demands of a great many organized interests with a stake in a policy decision—or at least by satisfying a sufficiently powerful segment of these interests. The tendency is to create a patchwork policy whose logic is the something-for-everyone rule. Such a solution often lacks internal consistency and clarity of purpose. Moreover, finding a compromise scheme encourages a conservative impulse: the temptation is to press no further in innovation or change than is necessary to create sufficient group support for the program. And all this bargaining takes time. In the end, therefore, policies that result from pressure-group politics customarily move slowly and ultimately represent improvised solutions to the particular political conflicts of the moment.

Finally, the pervasive influence of pressure groups in formulating governmental policy often results in major pressure groups controlling, or strongly influencing, the agencies that are extensively established to regulate them. This

---

[5] John Kenneth Galbraith, "Who Needs the Democrats?" *Harper's* July 1970, p. 47.
[6] *Ibid.*

is a familiar, and well documented, fact of political life in Washington. Very often, for instance, the independent regulatory agencies of the federal government—the Federal Communications Commission, the Federal Aviation Agency, the Interstate Commerce Commission, and others—speak for the interests they are supposed to supervise. The major radio and television networks often look to the Federal Communications Commission to protect their interests and represent them in government, as do the major transportation groups—the airlines, railroads, and truckers—with the Interstate Commerce Commission. The "capture" of the regulators by the regulated, has often proceeded so far that the independence and impartiality of the regulatory agencies must be questioned.

Few responsible critics of our existing public philosophy argue that private interests should be denied representation in government, or that interest group activities should be drastically curtailed. But they do commonly propose that the great priority currently given to private interests in policy formulation must be materially reduced; this will inevitably require some alterations in our traditional decision-making schemes on public policy.

Essentially, these proponents of change argue that our most urgent national problems now lie principally in the public sector—education, housing, race relations, environmental pollution, urban blight, and unemployment, to cite but a few examples. Because this is so, they contend, our first national objective should be to establish the public sectors as the major policy concern of the future—even at a considerable cost, in the short run, to private interests. If we are to do this, it will require the development of a public philosophy that stresses the urgency of problems, rather than the strength of political pressure or the number of interests advocating a program, as the principal justification for governmental action.

In addition, if the public sector is to receive such attention, government's power to act in this area without depending on collaboration of private interests or their governmental representatives must increase. Needless to say, government would require the power to engage in long-run social planning, would require significantly increased taxes, and might need to extend its regulation of economic life so far as ownership of some major economic enterprises if it is to meet the needs of the public sector adequately; most, if not all, of these measures, are bound to stimulate opposition from the private sector. Yet the problems of the public sector are so imperative, it is difficult to imagine any effective governmental attack on these problems without a reduction in the influence private interests now enjoy in government.

Finally, the success of any effort to reorient our public policy depends upon the public mind. Any change of the magnitude we have considered would necessarily require public willingness to sacrifice many traditional concerns and narrow private interests for a larger view of the public good and a new concept of the government's proper role in society. While it is naive to assume that all our major social problems can be entirely eliminated, there is no doubt that Americans have the material resources to dramatically reduce the scope and severity of these problems and perhaps to eliminate at least some altogether. Whether Americans have the will to do so is less certain. Any meaningful progress toward alleviating our currently grave social ills depends upon our rethinking, and to a significant degree restructuring, traditional public philosophy.

The Dilemma of Power Politics

Internationally, as well as domestically, the United States faces some hard decisions in the 1970s. The most fundamental one, because it bears heavily upon the direction of future American foreign policy, grows from changes in the Cold War and the deep domestic divisions over the Vietnamese conflict. Essentially, the question is whether American political leaders can continue to rally public support for the United States to play an active role in the international system. At the moment, American political leaders appear to be facing a major dilemma. Most, though not all, believe the United States must continue to play the game of power politics for security reasons, yet the traditional arguments that once aroused public support for the conduct of a very extensive American foreign policy are losing acceptance. Thus, what seems necessary— and what is still uncertain—is the development of a new, publicly acceptable logic that will reestablish domestic backing for a foreign policy based on power politics. Let us examine, briefly, how this situation has developed.

Since the onset of the Cold War at the end of World War II, American foreign policy was guided by age-old power maxims. Despite an accompaniment of zealous anti-communist rhetoric, the American post-war containment policy did not aim at destroying the Soviet Union; rather, it aimed toward reestablishing the international balance of power destroyed by World War II. Thus, wherever and whenever the balance of power was threatened by the Soviet Union or its allies, Washington reacted to protect the territorial status quo. Containment eventually became global during the intensive bipolarity after World War II. The United States thus acquired the reputation of a "world policeman" as it sought to preserve a precarious global balance of power. In effect, the Cold War had become a global version of the age-old power struggle between a status quo power (the United States) and a revisonist nation (the Soviet Union).

American policy makers were well aware they were playing the classic game of power politics.[7] But they had to formulate their policies in terms that were not only publicly palatable but would arouse enthusiasm, as well. The solution was to justify their policies in lofty and noble terms, to disguise the steely logic

---

[7] For Secretary of State Dean Acheson's perception of the state system, see his autobiography, *Present at the Creation* (New York: W. W. Norton & Co., 1969) and Ronald J. Stupak, *The Shaping of Foreign Policy* (New York: The Odyssey Press, 1969), pp. 47–64.

of power politics in idealistic sentiment. The reason for this procedure is that, as we have seen earlier, the United States from its inception considered itself a morally superior post-European society that could preserve its virtue by only two means: by abstaining from the corroding influence of power politics through isolationism or—if a resort to power politics were necessary for defense—by justifying this action as a moral crusade. Thus, the United States through most of its history preferred relative noninvolvement in international power politics but when drawn into World Wars I and II, fashioned its participation into a crusade to democratize the world, or to totally defeat an evil enemy, or to defend various endangered moral values.

It is understandable, then, that when American foreign policy makers felt compelled to engage in the power politics of the Cold War they should seek to justify such involvement in moralistic terms. An anti-communist crusade for freedom became a major theme, one that played not only upon moral values but upon the traditional moral dichotomy between the New World and the Old World that appealed to Americans.[8] So long as an extensive and intensive bipolarity prevailed between the United States and its allies on one side and the Soviet Union and its allies on the other, this formula for justifying power politics domestically worked reasonably well.

The problem today is that several events have apparently eroded public support for this strategy while forcing foreign policy makers to reevaluate it. The once pervasive bipolarity of the world is increasingly becoming a polycentrism. Especially within the communist bloc, there is a growing pluralism of power and greater internal divisions over policy, so that a simple anti-communist rhetoric that treats the communist camp as monolithic seems less persuasive to the public. Also, American foreign policy makers themselves can no longer trust a simple strategy for dealing with communist nations. As long as a tight bipolarity prevailed, when the Soviet Union or any of its satellites pushed, the United States felt compelled to push back. Now, however, American foreign policy makers must take into account the differences of interest and policy within the communist bloc; they must decide which nations within the bloc they wish to contain, which they do not, and how they can respond to the often complex cross-pressures within the once cohesive communist world.[9]

Vietnam was an additional blow to post-war American foreign policy. Vietnam forced the United States to realize, finally, that striking a self-satisfying and self-righteous anti-communist pose can extract a terrible, and perhaps intolerable, price. In light of Vietnam, traditional anti-communism and containment no longer excite a widespread enthusiasm—indeed, the Vietnam conflict

---

[8] Paul Seabury, *The Rise and Decline of the Cold War* (New York: Basic Books, 1967), pp. 37–53.

[9] A comprehensive critique of American foreign policy may be found in Hans J. Morgenthau, *A New Foreign Policy for the United States* (New York: Praeger, 1969).

seems to have weakened the American will for extensive foreign policy commitments in general. For Vietnam was a wrenching experience. Television for the first time permitted Americans to watch in living color the violence that the exercise of power caused. The negative reaction that often followed was hardly surprising. Many Americans were outraged by the inhumanity of the struggle; many believed the war contradicted our professed democratic and liberal values and represented an apparent break with our moral traditions. Because Vietnam dramatically portrayed what it meant to be a leading power, especially a military one, many former supporters of containment-through-power repented as if previously they had been unwitting sinners.

Senator William Fulbright, for instance, Chairman of the Senate Foreign Relations Committee and a vigorous long-time supporter of containment, now attacked that policy and accused the United States of an "arrogance of power."[10] Fulbright asserted not merely that Vietnam had been an unwise commitment, but something far more fundamental: he charged that all Great Powers seem impelled to demonstrate that they are bigger, better, and stronger than other nations. It was this "arrogance of power," Fulbright concluded, that now afflicted the United States and ultimately created international conflict. In brief, it was the exercise of power per se, regardless of intentions, that made a nation arrogant. No title for a book could have been more characteristically American. Power had become an evil, its exercise tantamount to the abuse of power; abstention from power politics and providing an example of a just and democratic society to the world—the old American formula—were the alleged cures. Though intellectually denying that he was an isolationist, the Senator's disillusion not only with our Vietnamese policy but with our overall foreign policy with its extensive commitments, reflected the *emotional* yearnings of an old isolationist. Quoting with approval John Quincy Adams' admonition that the United States should be "the well-wisher to the freedom and independence of all" but "the champion and vindicator only of her own," the Senator seemed to be speaking for a growing number of other Americans as well. More specifically, he reflected the mood of a nation which, having committed itself with enthusiasm to the purported task of reforming the world, was now swinging back to a desire to concentrate on its own affairs, for the world clearly was not reformable and probably not worth reforming. All-or-nothing, involvement–withdrawal, optimism–cynicism—all these old emotional dispositions clearly still lay underneath the surface.

Confronted with this discontent, American foreign policy makers face an essential problem. Can the United States continue to shoulder the world responsibilities that are the glory and burden of its enormous power—especially if such responsibility must now be justified by undisguised, unromantic, morally

---

10 J. William Fulbright, *The Arrogance of Power* (New York: Vintage Books, 1967), pp. 1–22, 245–258. Also, Ronald Steel, *Pax Americana* (New York: Viking Compass, 1968).

ambiguous "power politics?"[11] Anti-communism no longer seems able to mobilize public opinion massively behind foreign policy leaders; moral crusades in international politics lack their previously potent appeal. In these circumstances, the key question for the future of American foreign policy becomes whether the United States can continue to play its role in balancing power in the state system based upon the logic of power politics itself. To argue that it can, of course, seems to many Americans a blatant appeal to the very logic they have historically denounced in the Old World and feel has corrupted contemporary America by making it almost a warfare state.

How our political leaders resolve the conflicting demands of the foreign and domestic systems will be a most important test for them. The most frequently offered solution is that we reduce the scope of our foreign policy commitments to include only a few strategic areas of the world. Such a strategy would be based upon the assumption that the United States, for all its wealth and power, cannot have global commitments because it must also attend to vast domestic needs that will drain its resources. Therefore, we should carefully choose our international priorities; usually, Europe and Latin America are suggested as the areas where we should concentrate our power. By this logic, Vietnam should be a chastening experience that warns us against overextending ourselves and convinces us to take a more sober and restrained international role in the future.

However, one need but briefly reflect upon our early post-war policy to realize that this strategy of limited international priorities was attempted, but proved unfeasible. The Truman Administration, despite its missionary statements, did decide upon its priorities and did attempt to keep its commitments limited—first to the eastern Mediterranean and then to western Europe. It did not, for instance, intervene in a major way during the Chinese civil war because Washington wished to avoid a military involvement on mainland Asia. Similarly, to husband its resources and keep a balance between commitments and power, the United States withdrew its troops from South Korea. But relegating continental Asia to a secondary interest proved untenable. Our withdrawal from Korea left the Republic of Korea in a power vacuum. The Soviets and North Koreans apparently presumed that our willingness to abandon Chiang in China and our withdrawal from the Korean peninsula indicated we were writing off South Korea. Consequently, in June 1950, the North Korean army marched southward across the 38th parallel and suddenly we found ourselves engaged in our first limited war.

Why did we fight in South Korea if we seemingly did not consider it a vital interest? The answer is that while South Korea itself might not be so important —she was not an ally to whom we had legal obligations—the political and

---

[11] A discerning comment on this question has been given by J. H. Huizinga, "America's Lost Innocence," *The New York Times Magazine* (January 26, 1969), p. 30H.

psychological consequences of our inaction in the face of such blatant aggression were considered so serious that they would affect the global balance of power in an intensive bipolar system. In Asia, the United States hoped at some time to reestablish an American–Japanese alliance to counterbalance our lost ally in mainland China; an American demonstration of fear or indifference to the fate of Korea would hardly win Japan to an alliance with a nation that would permit a communist power to establish itself in Korea just 100 miles across the water from Japan.

In Europe, too, the United States had just obligated itself through NATO to protect its allies there. Europeans were still conscious of America's withdrawal into isolationism following World War I and were apprehensive that the United States might do so again, leaving them to make whatever peace they could with the looming Soviet power. If the United States remained indifferent to the North Korean aggression, such fears would have been intensified and NATO itself might have collapsed. Thus, though Korea and mainland Asia were ostensively secondary interests, America's world-wide security seemed jeopardized by the Korean events; thus, a commitment which had been deliberately excluded from America's top priorities in terms of the "limited power" logic became a commitment anyway.[12] If earlier the United States had symbolically kept a few thousand soldiers in South Korea and had pledged help in South Korea's defense, the communist invasion might have been deterred and spared us a three years' war. In short, it was not the lack of knowledge that our power was limited, or a failure to appreciate that we had to use power carefully and discriminatingly, that led the United States into global commitments soon after World War II. These commitments were made in spite of the policy makers' knowledge of these correct but difficult-to-apply axioms; they were made because the demands upon the United States during intensive world bipolarity persuaded policy makers that limited commitments were still a wish while extensive involvement was a necessity.

But one need not look backward. Let us concede that the United States must now establish its foreign priorities and that Europe is our most vital interest. Let us admit, further, that the objectives of our policies must be balanced with our great, but still limited, resources. Yet what good are such maxims for policy makers if in the future China should attack India and badly defeat her? Or what should be our response if in the continuing Arab-Israeli conflict, the Soviets increasingly commit themselves to the Arabs? The reason for raising such hypothetical, but not improbable situations, is to emphasize that our international obligations are often determined not by a priori selection, but by contingencies and events at the moment when decisions must be made.

Perhaps, looking at the world somewhat differently, it might be said the

---

12 John W. Spanier, *The Truman-MacArthur Controversy and the Korean War,* rev. ed., (New York: W. W. Norton & Co., 1965), pp. 15–30.

United States has been a "world policeman" because the world needed a certain amount of "policing." Certainly, many countries have come to expect us to play the policeman while at the same time criticizing our performance. Let us consider, in this context, one further possible policy. Suppose that in a post-Vietnam period the United States ceases to act as a policeman, at least in Asia. The President has, in fact, suggested that under the Nixon or Guam Doctrine the United States might send military and economic aid to a beleaguered friendly country, but it would not send troops. Thus, it would seem, the countries of South and Southeast Asia cannot count upon our direct help if threatened and must look elsewhere. The likely result in these circumstances is that the smaller countries will have to make their own peace as China's power grows in the absence of any countervailing power. The larger nations, like India, confront a China armed with nuclear weapons and will probably see little alternative except to conciliate China or to develop nuclear stockpiles and delivery systems of their own. If they develop nuclear delivery systems, they will have to violate the nuclear nonproliferation treaty supported by so many critics of the Vietnamese conflict. It may happen, in effect, that those who oppose American globalism by urging us to "get out of Asia" may encourage the proliferation of nuclear weapons which they also oppose because it will make the world even more combustible than it is already. At least the superpowers generally act with restraint and have moved closer for their joint effort to keep the peace.

Countries like India have publicly stated that if they abandon the development of nuclear arms they must be able to depend upon American and/or Soviet nuclear support in the event of nuclear attack. Thus, to prevent nuclear proliferation throughout the world would seem to require a continuing American globalism—it may even require an extension of American defense commitments to nations such as India with whom this country does not now have a defense treaty. Conversely, if the United States reduces its world-wide commitments by designating Asia as an area of secondary importance, we should expect China's potential opponents—Japan, Indonesia, and India—to acquire their own nuclear arms sooner or later. And this would probably expand nuclear proliferation further because rivals of these major Asian nations (such as Pakistan in the case of India) will also seek nuclear arms to maintain some power parity with their opponents.

Even the bonds of our principal alliances with European nations, where presumably our security interests are most involved, are slackening because Europeans are uncertain that the United States will protect them in future military emergencies. Because of this, first Britain, then France developed their own small nuclear deterrents and West Germany may some day follow the example. This urge for armaments and uncertainty of American protection may intensify after Vietnam, if the United States no longer seems to relish the responsibilities of her great power.

In the end, the price for repudiating the game of power politics may be enormous. Concentrating on making America a showcase for democracy, or an example to the world, is worthy in its own right. But it is no substitute for continuing to play our necessarily large role in preserving the balance of power —the basis for the existence of all states—and avoiding a nuclear conflagration. So the dilemma remains. American foreign policy makers are trapped between the premises of the state system and the vanishing domestic support which allowed them to play this role during the bipolar period when power politics could be disguised as ideological politics in terms of New World democracy against Old World autocracy. It was easy to crusade against communism when the Sino-Soviet bloc was still a cohesive unity. But once that unity fragmented and power politics could no longer be camouflaged, the old guilt feelings about its use returned. Thus, if the United States is to play a major future role in world politics, it may have to find public acceptance of power politics on its own terms, without all the embellishment of moral crusades and righteous rhetoric— of which the public is now apparently tired, anyway. Whether, on the other hand, America can develop such attitudes is less certain. This, among other things, is one issue that makes the 1970s interesting, politically crucial, and dangerous.

A Postscript

In San Francisco, a shop with the improbable name of "Gorilla Records" is worth considering. There, for two dollars plus tax, one can buy a particularly striking poster—or order it and wait, since it is frequently sold out. The poster is an enlargement of *The New York Times'* front page announcing America's first astronaut's landing on the moon, complete with his photograph beside the flag he has just planted. The page is intact except for an added headline: in bold, aggressive type, it asks, "SO WHAT?" This poster sells well, no doubt, because it captures the apparently pervasive discontent of many young people with some fundamental American values: the great victory in the space race, long desired by American political leaders at the cost of so much of America's resources in the 1960s, is dismissed. The political meaning of the poster is significant; the ultimate importance of this decade may well rest in what the poster symbolizes.

Like few other generations of young Americans, this one seems determined to reexamine the basic structure of American social life, to hold its own commitments to traditional American values in abeyance or, in some cases, to place its faith elsewhere. It is these young people who are the future American electorate. Thus, as the young think, so may the nation be in a few decades. It seems almost certain that the young will change America in many respects significantly, that the "SO WHAT?" in the poster only hints at the depth of reappraisal in American life the young have initiated. By asking such questions, the young have moved the country into a dangerous, creative period, as are all periods of great social change. While they are not solely responsible for the great political conflicts of the seventies, they will be the ultimate beneficiaries or victims of whatever solutions are created. One can only wish for them a judgment equal to the tasks they have set for themselves.

Index

  in Constitution, 315–316
Decision making (*see* Policy making)
Decision-making circles, 351–352
Declaration of independence, 34
Defense Department, 87–90, 240–241, 321
Definitions, 16
De Gaulle, Charles, 24, 69, 198
Democracy, 357–358
  elections in, 263, 358
  interest groups in, 60–61, 201–203,
    233, 357–358
  political linkage in, 194, 201–204, 233
  as a political system, 54–61, 488–490
  and social pluralism, 58, 201–202
  in the United States, 20, 55–57, 201–204
Democratic Party:
  and public opinion, 331
  versus Republican Party, 209–210,
    219, 226, 229–230
  in the South, 208, 210, 311
  voting for, 294, 296, 301
Demonstrations (*see* Militancy)
Dennis, Jack, 123
Deterrence, 77, 80
Deutsch, Karl, 22
Dewey, Thomas, 437
Diplomacy, 344
Direct action, 182
Direct primary, 214, 261–267
Discriminatory institutions, 162–163
Dixiecrats, 225–226
Domestic affairs:
  versus foreign affairs, 66–68, 328,
    348–349
  policy making in, 328, 332–333, 345,
    348–349, 365, 427–431
  and public opinion, 21, 332–333
Dominant political culture, 163–164
Douglas, William O., 400, 446, 488
Drake, St. Clair, 174
Dulles, John Foster, 96, 351, 368
Dye, Thomas R., 393

Easton, David, 35, 123
Economic development, 57–59
Economic system, 27, 56–57, 58
Education, 47, 59–60, 145
Effective government, 38
Eisenhower, Dwight D.:
  and Congress, 364, 390, 398, 420, 421,
    429, 432
  in elections, 277, 284, 286, 291, 297,
    300, 301
  and executive, 346, 347, 348, 351, 353,
    364, 368, 371, 377, 398
  in foreign affairs, 66, 79, 91, 93, 94,
    96, 106, 368, 371, 377, 432
  and judiciary, 469, 480
  and political parties, 209, 229
  public confidence in, 121, 125
Eldersveld, Samuel, 143
Election law, 258
Elections, 253–306
  authority from, 257

Elections (continued)
  to Congress, 261–267
  Constitution on, 302–303
  in a democracy, 263, 358
  interest groups in, 251, 293–294, 299
  Negroes in, 259–260
  and policy making, 331–332, 358
  political activism in, 277
  political issues in, 298–300
  political parties in, 255, 264, 279–280,
    282–283
  president in, 267–280, 358
  in the South, 259–260, 264–265, 301
  in the Soviet Union, 254, 332
  voting in, 256, 261, 291–301
Electoral college, 225–226, 301–305
Electoral system, 257–291
  and political campaigns, 280–291
  and political parties, 212, 264,
    279–280, 282–283
England (*see* Great Britain)
"errand boy" function, 391–394
Establishment, 139
Ethnic groups, 164, 248
Europe, 68–69
Executive:
  and Congress, 90–91, 328, 355, 356,
    360, 362–366, 397–404, 440–442
  and the Constitution, 343, 345
  in federal government, 316, 321,
    327–328
  and foreign affairs, 87–91, 328, 348–349,
    367–383
  and interest groups, 239–241, 357–358
  and the judiciary, 357
  and legislation, 440–442
  policy making by, 316, 321, 327–328,
    339–383, 397–404, 440–442
  social pluralism in, 321, 350
  in western democracies, 69, 342–343,
    355
Executive agreements, 311
Executive departments:
  and interest groups, 49, 239–241,
    357–358
  policy making by, 349–362, 379–380
  and the president, 349–362, 379–380
Extensive–intensive bipolarity, 73–83

Family, 146–148
Federal aid to education, 414–427
Federal budget, 35
Federal Communications Commission,
  239–240
Federal courts (*see* Judiciary)
Federal government:
  Congress in, 310–311, 312, 321, 328
  the executive in, 316, 321, 327–328
  the judiciary in, 454–457, 482–483
  policy making in, 309–336, 454–457,
    482–483
  political system of, 49–50, 482–483
  the president in, 311, 312, 321, 333
  and social pluralism, 49, 313, 314,
    320–322